INTERMEDIATE MICROECONOMICS

INTERMEDIATE
MICROECONOMICS

MICHAEL B. ORMISTON
ARIZONA STATE UNIVERSITY

THE DRYDEN PRESS
HARCOURT BRACE JOVANOVICH COLLEGE PUBLISHERS

Fort Worth   Philadelphia   San Diego   New York   Orlando   Austin   San Antonio

Toronto   Montreal   London   Sydney   Tokyo

For My Mother and Father

Acquisitions Editor: *Rick Hammonds*
Developmental Editor: *Sarah Smith*
Production Editor: *Katherine Watson*
Designer: *Linda Harper*
Art Editor: *Louise Sandy-Karkoutli*
Production Managers: *Mary Kay Yearin, Lesley Lenox*

Cover and part opener photography: *David Bishop*

ISBN: 0-15-541386-4

Library of Congress Catalog Number: 91-76022

Printed in the United States of America

PREFACE

■ For students interested in the economic problems facing modern societies, microeconomics is one of the most important courses in the economics curriculum. Microeconomics provides a logical framework for explaining and predicting economic behavior. The principles learned in this course are essential for understanding and evaluating budgeting decisions, business decisions, public policy, and how economic systems function.

In writing Intermediate Microeconomics I had two primary

goals—to give a clear and understandable presentation of the fundamental principles of modern microeconomic theory and to get students involved in using microeconomics to analyze and evaluate economic problems. To accomplish the first goal, I have emphasized the basic concepts and techniques central to microeconomic theory. I believe that students with a thorough understanding of the basics will be able to use microeconomics on their own long after the course has ended. To accomplish the second goal, I have used solved problems within the chapters to develop the economic principles being discussed and to show students how they can apply microeconomics outside the classroom. These solved problems are not the typical "boxed" examples or "case studies" found in many texts. Rather, they are examples designed to get students involved in setting up and analyzing actual economic problems. They present a mix of real-world and hypothetical situations but they always deal with events or phenomena that are pertinent to the real world.

The examples within the chapters are designed to address one basic principle at a time and have two parts. The first part states the economic problem and the second solves it. The solutions are annotated so that students have not only answers but also explanations of how to set up and solve the problems. Over the years I have found that many of my students have not learned a systematic method of solving problems. These students find it difficult to appreciate microeconomic theory because they must learn not only new economic concepts but also a new way of thinking. I endeavor to overcome this obstacle with the solved problems. As the book progresses, the solved problems are used to demonstrate economic theory at work, and economic theory is used to improve the student's problem-solving capabilities.

There are several additional features that set this book apart from other intermediate microeconomics textbooks. First, Chapter 2 demonstrates how to use equations and graphs to set up and analyze equilibrium and optimization problems. This serves a dual purpose. It provides a review of the supply and demand model and exposes the student to marginal analysis. I believe that if students have a good grasp of these techniques at the beginning of the course, later on they will be able to concentrate on learning economics.

Second, in addition to the solved problems in each chapter, I have included three chapters devoted solely to real–world applications: Chapter 5 "Applications Using Consumer Theory"; Chapter 11, "Applications Using the Competitive Model"; and Chapter 13, "Applications Using the Monopoly Model." These applications *illustrate how to apply the concepts and techniques developed in the theory chapters to a variety of important economic issues. For example, in Chapter 11, "Applications Using the Competitive Model," the theory developed in Chapters 3–4 and 6–10 is used to examine the economic effects of excise taxes, income taxes, wage and price controls, cost-saving innovations, and trade restrictions.*

Third, in contrast to most texts, which place the discussion of input markets near the end of the book, I discuss input markets simultaneously with output markets. For example, Chapter 8 discusses both output supply and input demand for a competitive firm, Chapters 9 and 10 discuss competitive output and input markets respectively, and Chapter 11 considers how the policy being analyzed affects both output and input markets. I have found that discussing input and output markets together results in a more efficient presentation of material and helps reinforce the circular flow nature of a market economy.

Fourth, I discuss economic efficiency and market failure in a partial equilibrium framework (Chapter 15) immediately after the discussion of price and output determination in competitive and imperfectly competitive markets. Most other texts place much of this material in the last chapter of the book. However, the ordering here seems preferable since in many of the field courses—public finance, labor economics, industrial organization, and international trade, for example—partial equilibrium analysis is used extensively to analyze the welfare implications of government intervention in competitive markets, the regulation of monopoly, and other forms of market failure.

Fifth, I have designed the last two chapters in the book, Chapters 17, "Investment Decisions and Capital Markets," and 18, "Decision Making and Risk," in such a way that either or both can be assigned right after the discussion of competitive markets. This gives the instructor the option of modifying the course to fit the needs of the students.

Finally, I have provided between 15 and 25 questions and problems at the end of each chapter. These problems range from easy to difficult and are meant to give students ample opportunity for practicing what they have learned in the chapter. The end-of-chapter questions are an essential part of this book and I encourage students to work them all.

I have written this book for undergraduate students who have had one course in principles of microeconomics. The only prerequisites needed are an elementary understanding of algebra and graphs plus a willingness to learn new concepts.

Many economics programs, including the one here at Arizona

State University, require students to take at least one calculus course prior to enrolling in intermediate microeconomics. Although in the main body of this textbook no calculus is used, most chapters have an appendix that contains a calculus treatment of the basic topics covered in that chapter as well as more advanced topics. While these appendixes are not meant to be rigorous mathematical analyses, they do provide a fairly complete introduction to the mathematical tools used by economists and allow the instructor to use calculus when desired.

Intermediate Microeconomics offers instructors enough flexibility to design a course to meet their needs. For a one-quarter or one-semester course emphasizing the core principles and techniques of microeconomics, I would suggest using Chapters 1–4, 6–10, 12, 14–15, and selected applications from Chapters 5, 11, and 13. A more rigorous course would include Chapters 16–18 and most of the appendixes. A course designed primarily for business majors would include Chapters 17 and 18 and all of Chapter 13.

After completing this course, students should be able, on their own, to translate an economic issue into a problem that they can analyze using the tools developed during the course. I firmly believe that the best way for students to achieve this goal is to practice. For this reason, Dr. Catherine Schneider, Boston College, and I have prepared a Workbook that should be used along with the textbook. The Workbook contains additional examples that are carefully designed to aid students in learning how to use their newly acquired tools. Each problem in the workbook begins on a new page and leaves plenty of room for "scratch work." This makes it easy to assign and grade workbook problems.

I have also written an Instructor's Manual to accompany the textbook. This contains three sections. Section I gives solutions to all of the end-of-chapter questions and problems while Section II gives answers to all of the workbook questions and problems. I think having the author's suggested answers makes it easier for the instructor to choose problems to assign as homework or to use on examinations. Finally, Section III contains a test bank of multiple-choice questions for those instructors teaching large sections.

The approach taken in this book is the result of the many discussions I have had over the years with friends and colleagues who have taught microeconomic theory. In particular, Raymond Battalio, Texas A&M University, Timothy Gronberg, Texas A&M University, and Jack Meyer, Michigan State University provided *invaluable insights into teaching economic theory to undergraduates.*

I have had the assistance of many people who reviewed the manuscript at various stages. Their comments and suggestions improved the book substantially and I would like to thank them all: William Carlisle, University of Utah; Yang-Ming Chang, Kansas State University; Eleanor Craig, University of Delaware; Larry DeBrock, University of Illinois at Urbana-Champaign; Carroll B. Foster, University of California, San Diego; Gary Fournier, Florida State University; James P. Gander, University of Utah; Jim Hagermann, Reed College; Simon Hakim, Temple University; George Heitman, Pennsylvania State University; Walter "Dub" Lane, University of New Orleans; Ashley Lyman, University of Indiana; Daniel Orr, University of Illinois; Catherine Schneider, Boston College; Charles T. Strein, University of Northern Iowa; Steven Tomlinson, University of Texas; Nancy Virts, California State University at Eau Claire; Harry Watson, George Washington University; Kathleen West, California State University at Fullerton; Greg Wozniak, University of Tulsa; and Mark Zupan, University of Southern California.

Finally, I extend a special thanks to my graduate assistant, Su Zhou, my first student from the People's Republic of China.

CONTENTS

PART 2

CONSUMER CHOICE AND DEMAND   47

INTERMEDIATE MICROECONOMICS

PRELIMINARIES

■ *Part 1 introduces some of the basic concepts and tools we will use in our study of microeconomics. Chapter 1 discusses the difference between microeconomics and macroeconomics and shows how microeconomics helps us understand public policy and business decisions. The chapter also explains how microeconomics uses theoretical models to explain and predict real-world behavior and briefly reviews the market economy model, which should look familiar from our introductory economics course. This review is especially relevant in light of the recent efforts of many Eastern European countries to shift to a market economy.*

■ *Chapter 2 introduces the two basic types of problems encountered in microeconomics: equilibrium problems and optimization problems. As an example of equilibrium analysis, the chapter reviews the basic principles of supply and demand, which, again, should look familiar from our introductory economics course. This review is important because supply and demand analysis is frequently used to investigate real-world economic problems. It will be developed extensively in the book. The chapter also shows how marginal analysis is used to examine both unconstrained and constrained optimization problems. Marginal analysis is extremely important because it is the primary tool that microeconomics uses to help us understand an individual's budgeting and business decisions.*

INTRODUCTION TO MICROECONOMICS

LEARNING OBJECTIVES

After completing Chapter 1 you should be able to do the following:

■ Explain the basic difference between microeconomics and macroeconomics.

■ Discuss the use of theoretical models in microeconomics.

■ Compare positive economic analysis to normative economic analysis.

■ Describe the circular flow of economic activity in a market economy.

■ Discuss the role prices play in a market economy.

EXAMPLES

■ **1–1** Using Microeconomics to Design and Evaluate Public Policy: U.S. Agricultural Policy

■ **1–2** Using Microeconomics to Understand Business Decisions: General Motors' Saturn Project

Economics is a social science, which means that it deals with the activities of people. Traditionally, it is divided into two broad fields called microeconomics (*micro* meaning small) and macroeconomics (*macro* meaning large).

Microeconomics focuses on the behavior of individual economic units—that is, consumers, workers, owners and managers of business firms, investors, and individual industries. **Macroeconomics,** on the other hand, focuses on the large-scale operation of the entire economy. It is concerned with the behavior of aggregate markets—such as the markets for goods and services, labor, and money—and with the determination of aggregate economic quantities, such as national product, national income, and interest rates.

The study of microeconomics helps us understand how individual economic units make decisions about buying and selling, and how the economic environment influences these decisions. We learn, for example, how individual consumers allocate their limited incomes among all the different commodities that are available and how changes in prices and incomes affect their choices. We learn, too, how individual producers decide how much capital and labor to employ, how much output to produce, and how changes in prices affect *their* decisions.

Microeconomics also analyzes how individual economic units interact in markets to determine the prices and quantities of commodities exchanged. For instance, we learn how producers and consumers, interacting in the market for personal computers, determine their prices and how many are produced each year. The field of microeconomics also analyzes how government policies affect prices and quantities.

Recently the distinction between microeconomics and macroeconomics has become less important. The reason is that in order to understand fully how aggregate markets behave, we must first understand the behavior of the individuals that make up the aggregate markets. In fact, to a large extent, modern macroeconomics is an extension of microeconomics.

1.1 THE ROLE OF THEORETICAL MODELS

■ In economics, as in any social science or other science, we use theories, or *theoretical models*, to help us *explain* and *predict* observed, real-world phenomena. Can we explain why some workers prefer fringe benefits to higher salaries? Can we predict how an increase in income tax rates affects work effort, employment, and wage rates? The real world provides us with a multitude of facts; however, facts alone cannot explain why certain events occur nor predict how events might change in response to changes in the economic environment. Theoretical models organize facts into testable hypotheses, so that we *can* explain and predict human behavior and economic interactions.

Microeconomic analysis usually begins by isolating and defining a real-world problem. It is then up to the economist to choose from a large tool box full of theoretical models one that can be used to analyze the problem. The goals of the analysis are to form testable hypotheses and to explain and predict economic behavior.

A theoretical model does not reconstruct the real-world but simplifies it by abstracting the most important factors of an economic problem. Its usefulness depends on whether or not it succeeds in explaining and predicting what it is designed to explain and predict. It must undergo test after test so that any errors or inconsistencies can emerge. If an old model does not work well, a new one is created which is itself subject to continual testing in all possible ways. If it does not stand up, it must be corrected or abandoned.

When evaluating a theoretical model, however, remember that none ever explains and predicts perfectly. Let's take as an example the wave theory of light, from physics. This theoretical model holds that light travels in waves carrying energy, and that when these waves strike certain objects, energy is released as heat. This theory explains why it gets hot when the sun shines, and predicts that standing in the shade will be cooler than standing in the sun.

How good a theory is the wave theory of light? Actually, it is based on assumptions that no one has ever verified: no one has ever seen a light wave or the energy that it is supposed to carry, and no one has observed light energy changing to heat energy. Moreover, the wave theory of light cannot explain all observed phenomena. For instance, it fails to explain why a light shining on certain metals produces electricity (the photoelectric effect). Does this mean that the wave theory of light is a bad theory? Certainly not. We should not discard a theory just because of its assumptions or because it fails to explain or predict perfectly. Rather, it should be judged on its ability to explain and predict what it is designed to explain or predict. The wave theory passes this test.

The theoretical models developed in this book explain numerous economic phenomena and accurately predict the consequences of changes in economic conditions, but these models do not explain all economic phenomena. Given their limitations, they may be replaced someday by better theories. However, economists generally agree that the theories discussed in this book are the best ones presently available.

1.2 POSITIVE AND NORMATIVE ANALYSIS

■ With the help of theoretical models, microeconomics addresses both *positive* issues (about which an affirmation can be made) and *normative* issues (of, relating to, or prescribing norms). **Positive analysis** has to do with explaining and predicting; **normative analysis** is concerned with what is good or bad. If the government increases the federal gasoline tax, will the price of gasoline rise? If so, by how much? What effect will the tax have on the quantity bought and sold? How will it affect the prices of other goods? Will people purchase smaller cars? Which economic groups will the tax harm and which will it benefit? Answering these questions is within the range of *positive analysis*. This analysis is independent of ethical considerations; it deals with assumptions and hypotheses that can be evaluated with respect to their logical underpinnings and the empirical data at hand.

Positive analysis alone, however, is not sufficient to evaluate the overall desirability of the policy. Making this determination also involves *normative analysis*. Normative analysis deals with what is good and bad and, often, is based on the beliefs and values of the decision maker. If a tax generates revenues that become transfer programs for the poor, some may consider this a desirable redistribution of income while others may not. Microeconomics can help us evaluate and compare economic policies, but when subjective value judgments are involved it cannot alone tell us which policies are desirable. These are ethical judgments society must make.

1.3 THE IMPORTANCE OF MICROECONOMICS: A PREVIEW OF WHAT LIES AHEAD

■ Microeconomic theory does not exist in isolation. It is important because it provides the basics to help us design and evaluate public policies such as taxes, wage and price controls, agricultural policies, and international trade restrictions. It is also important because it helps us understand business decisions such as why companies offer price discounts, when to introduce new product lines, and how much to charge for a particular product. Here are two examples of how the theoretical models discussed in this book can address various economic problems.

EXAMPLE 1–1

USING MICROECONOMICS TO DESIGN AND EVALUATE PUBLIC POLICY: U.S. AGRICULTURAL POLICY

Since the 1930s the U.S. government has played a dominant role in U.S. agriculture. The most recent comprehensive farm law, the

Food and Security Act of 1985, instituted various programs designed to maintain farmers' incomes by artificially keeping prices high. The law targeted producers of commodities such as dairy products, tobacco, wheat, cotton, rice, and corn.

Designing and evaluating a program like the Food and Security Act of 1985 involves a lot of economic analysis. First, since price supports increase the cost of certain goods, we have to evaluate their impact on consumers. This involves an analysis of consumer preferences and demand: Will people spend less on milk and more on other goods? Will they be better off or worse off? (Chapters 3 through 5 will discuss consumer choices and demand.)

Second, we need to evaluate the impact of price supports on producers. Do price supports lead to overproduction? Do they increase the demand for fertilizers and insecticides? Will a higher wheat price increase the cost of producing flour, breads, and other wheat products? If so, are these added costs passed on to consumers in the form of higher prices? (Chapters 6 and 7 will discuss production and cost, Chapter 8 will examine profit maximization, and Chapters 9 through 11 will cover price determination in competitive markets.)

Finally, we need to evaluate the overall effects of the program. Do farmers' incomes actually rise as a result of price supports? If so, does this improvement outweigh the additional costs imposed on consumers and the government? Are there alternative programs that would maintain farmers' standards of living and yet burden consumers less? (Chapters 15 and 16 will discuss these issues.) ∎

EXAMPLE 1–2

USING MICROECONOMICS TO UNDERSTAND BUSINESS DECISIONS: GENERAL MOTORS' SATURN PROJECT

In July 1990, the Chairman of General Motors Corporation, Roger B. Smith, test-drove the first production model of the long-awaited Saturn. Saturn is a new line of GM small cars designed to compete head-on with Japanese small cars like the Honda Civic and Toyota Corolla. According to Smith, the Saturn project is "the key to GM's long-term competitiveness, survival, and success." (*Business Week*, April 9, 1990: 56.) Most experts agree that if it succeeds, the Saturn project—conceived in 1983 and based on Japan's management system—will begin a new era for American industry.

Designing and producing a new product line like Saturn involves a good deal of economic analysis. First, GM had to consider consumer preferences and demand: How important to consumers are factors such as styling, handling, gasoline mileage, and reliability (Chapter 3)? To what extent will the demand for Saturn depend on its price, the price of competing cars, and the incomes of consumers (Chapter 4)? All these issues were important aspects of the Saturn project as it developed.

Second, GM needed to consider the cost of the project. How would costs relate to the number of cars produced, prices of raw materials, and wages paid to workers (Chapters 6 and 7)? How would unions affect wage rates (Chapters 10 and 13)? How many cars should GM produce each year in order to maximize profit (Chapters 8 and 12)? And how much capital and labor would produce the profit-maximizing number of cars (Chapters 8 and 12)?

Third, GM had to consider how its competitors would react to Saturn. If Saturn was priced below the Civic and Corolla, would Honda and Toyota try to undercut GM? How would Chrysler and Ford react to a low-priced Saturn (Chapter 14)?

Finally, since the Saturn project would require a $3 billion investment over several years, GM had to decide whether or not the project was worth undertaking at all. How would the return on investing in Saturn compare to other possible investments (Chapter 17)? How might uncertainties concerning oil prices, costs, and the prices of other small cars affect GM's decisions (Chapter 18)? ■

These are just two examples of the problems that microeconomic theory can address. Later chapters will give many more examples. Now let's outline the general theoretical model underlying our study of microeconomics.

1.4 THE MARKET ECONOMY MODEL

■ Microeconomics analyzes economic decisions made by individuals, how changes in the economic environment affect these decisions, and how buyers and sellers interact through the free exchange of goods and services. In this text, the general theoretical model addressing these issues is the **market economy model,** where resources are privately owned. Decentralized decision making characterizes a market economy. In such an economic environment, prices perform the rationing task; that is, prices act as signals that coordinate economic activity via markets.

The main reason for using the market economy model is that it can explain and predict economic behavior for many of the world's economies. The economies of the United States, Great Britain, Germany, and Japan are examples of economies that can be represented with the market economy model. These economies operate essentially through markets *not* controlled by government. Moreover, the recent efforts of many Eastern European countries— East Germany (now reunified with West Germany), Poland, Czechoslovakia, Romania, and even the Soviet Union—to shift to a market economy highlight the importance of the market economy model.

A **market** is a group of buyers and sellers expressing their desires by exchanging goods and services. Many interesting economic questions and problems concern how markets work. For example, are workers better off with a minimum wage law? Are domestic firms better off if the government limits imports? Do cost-saving innovations necessarily lead to lower prices? Should the government regulate public utilities? Understanding markets and the factors that affect markets is what microeconomics, and this book, are all about.

MARKETS AND PRICES

There are many factors that influence the choices of buyers and sellers but the most important are prices. **Prices** are the very essence of market transactions. They reflect the value of the goods and services that buyers and sellers are exchanging. It is important to realize that in a market economy, market transactions *alone* determine the prices and quantities of goods and services that are bought and sold. There is no central authority stepping in to coordinate economic activity. In a market economy we say the *invisible hand* coordinates economic activity (a term first coined by 18th-century political economist Adam Smith).

Figure 1–1 illustrates the **circular flow of economic activity** in a market economy with no government participation. (We shall consider the intervention of government shortly.) In this figure, the economy divides into two sectors: households and firms. Households consist of individuals consuming goods and services and owning or controlling resources—land, labor, capital, and natural resources—that firms value because they can use them to produce goods and services. Firms are businesses that organize those same resources, also called *factors of production*, to produce goods and services. The consumer makes economic decisions within the household, while the producer makes economic decisions within the firm.

THE CIRCULAR FLOW OF ECONOMIC ACTIVITY

Consumers and producers interact in two types of markets: markets for products (goods and services) and markets for resources. As shown in Figure 1–1, this interaction generates a flow of goods and services from firms to households and a simultaneous flow of resources from households to firms.

FIGURE 1-1   **THE CIRCULAR FLOW OF ECONOMIC ACTIVITY**

Households purchase goods in product markets and sell the services of the resources they own in resource (or factor) markets. Firms sell goods in product markets and purchase the services of the resources they need in resource markets.

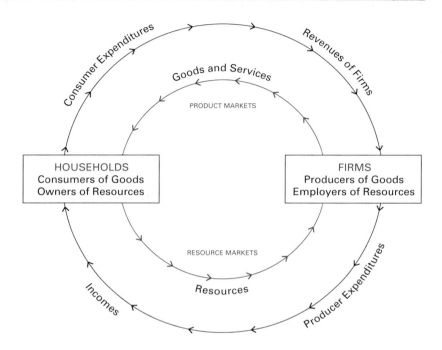

Consumers purchase goods and services to satisfy their consumption needs. Individual consumers indicate their desires by purchasing goods and services in various product markets. Firms, on the other hand, respond to these desires by producing goods and services and delivering them to the appropriate market. The interaction of buyers and sellers in the product markets determines the *market clearing price* (the selling price on the open market) for each good and service.

At the same time, individual consumers supply the resources used in the production process. Firms desire these resources (the factors of production) in order to produce goods and services. They indicate their needs by purchasing factors of production—land, labor, capital, and natural resources—in the various resource markets. Their purchases generate income for consumers. Hence, resources flow from households to firms. The interaction of buyers and sellers in the factor markets determines factor prices.

In the market economy model depicted in Figure 1–1, the circular flow of economic activity indicates just how interdependent households and firms are. One needs the other and both participate in the various markets because both have something to gain.

   The market economy described above and illustrated in Figure 1–1 has only a *private sector*. It does not have a *government sector*. However, as we all know, in most economies government plays an important economic role. Governments purchase resources from households, and goods and services from firms. These purchases generate incomes for households and revenues for firms. To pay for its purchases, a government raises revenues by requiring households and firms to pay taxes. In addition, the government uses tax revenues to make transfer payments, such as social security and unemployment benefits, to individual households.

   Most of this book focuses on the private sector of a market economy; however, there are also many questions and problems that address the way government policies affect economic behavior. Thus, we must remember that government plays an important role in the circular flow of economic activity.

SUMMARY

1. Economics studies how people or groups of people use scarce physical and human resources to satisfy their wants and needs.
2. Microeconomics explains and predicts the economic choices made by individual producers and consumers and examines how the interaction of buyers and sellers determines prices.
3. Theoretical economic models are used to explain and predict human behavior. A theoretical model simplifies real-world economic problems by abstracting the important factors of the economic environment.
4. Positive analysis explains and predicts the economic effects of government and corporate policies. Normative analysis deals with what is good or bad.
5. Microeconomic theory is important because it helps us understand and evaluate public policies as well as business decisions.
6. Households represent individuals who purchase goods and services and own or control productive resources. Firms are businesses that organize the factors of production—land, labor, capital, and natural resources—in order to produce goods and services.
7. The circular flow of economic activity indicates the interdependence of households and firms. Consumers sell the services of their resources for incomes which they spend on goods and services. Producers sell goods and services from which they receive the revenues used to pay for the resources needed in the production process.
8. In a market economy, the interaction of buyers and sellers in every market leads to prices that balance demand and supply. There are two broad types of markets: markets for goods and services and markets for resources.
9. Governments play an important role in a market economy. They use tax revenues collected from households and firms to purchase resources and goods and services. Many of the examples in this book focus on the way government policies affect economic behavior.

KEY TERMS

Microeconomics
Macroeconomics
Positive Analysis
Normative Analysis
The Market Economy Model

Market
Prices
The Circular Flow of
Economic Activity

1. Economists sometimes say that in a market economy prices "ration" goods and services. What do you think this statement means?
2. Compare and contrast positive and normative economics. Why is it important to distinguish between them?
3. "Theoretical models based on assumptions that are unrealistic have no value outside the ivory towers of academia." Comment on this assertion.
4. Suppose you are at a party and you overhear two economists discussing import restrictions on automobiles. Both economists agree that import restrictions reduce the quantity of automobiles available to domestic consumers; however, they cannot agree on whether or not import restrictions are desirable. One economist argues that such restrictions are undesirable because they lead to higher automobile prices while the other argues that such restrictions are desirable because they increase profits of domestic firms. Does this mean that economics is of little use in resolving such debates? Explain.
5. Government sometimes plays an important role in a market economy. Modify Figure 1–1 to include government in the circular flow of economic activity.
6. One of the most important lessons we have learned from the 1970s to the present is that all economies, large and small, are affected to some extent by events occurring outside their borders. Even the U.S. economy, one of the largest in the world during most of the twentieth century, cannot survive in isolation from the rest of the world. The actions of the Organization of Petroleum Exporting Countries (OPEC) have significantly affected economic events in the U.S. ever since the early 1970s. American farmers, automobile workers, and steel workers are keenly aware of the effects of foreign imports on local economies. Modify Figure 1–1 to include a foreign sector in the circular flow of economic activity.

REFERENCES

Baumol, W. J., and A. S. Blinder. 1991. *Economics, Principles and Policy*. 5th ed. San Diego: Harcourt Brace Jovanovich.

Friedman, M. 1971. "The Methodology of Positive Economics." In *Readings in Microeconomics*, ed. William Breit and Harold Hochman. New York: Holt, Rinehart and Winston.

McCloskey, D. 1983. "The Rhetoric of Economics." *Journal of Economic Literature* 21, 2: 481–517.

PROBLEM SOLVING IN MICROECONOMICS

LEARNING OBJECTIVES

After completing Chapter 2 you should be able to do the following:

■ Explain what equilibrium and optimization problems are.

■ Analyze simple equilibrium problems using the supply and demand model.

■ Analyze simple optimization problems.

2

EXAMPLES

■ **2–1** The Market for Athletic Shoes

■ **2–2** How Long Should the Wine Be Aged?

■ **2–3** Investing in Stocks

As students of microeconomics, one of our most difficult tasks is to learn a systematic method of solving economic problems. Solving problems, economic or otherwise, involves finding a way out of some sort of difficulty—that is, finding a way to attain a goal that is not readily attainable. It is an art that we can learn if we develop a solid plan of action and if we practice. At every step in the development of the theoretical models presented in the chapters ahead, we must diligently practice solving the economic problems. These problems will range from determining the effects of an individual's personal budgeting decisions to determining the economic effects of the 1986 Tax Reform Act and of removing international trade restrictions. In this chapter we introduce the two basic types of problems encountered in microeconomics: equilibrium problems and optimization problems.

■ We can classify almost every economic problem as either an equilibrium problem or an optimization problem. An **equilibrium problem** is concerned with how the interaction of buyers and sellers determines the prices and quantities that will prevail in particular markets. These prices and quantities are called *equilibrium* values because there is no tendency for them to change. For example, if we are studying the market for motorcycles, we will want to know the selling price of motorcycles, how many are bought and sold, and how restrictions limiting foreign imports affect these values. Supply and demand analysis is one type of equilibrium analysis that is discussed in Principles of Microeconomics.

An **optimization problem** sets out to choose the best, or optimal, plan of action. For instance, when we study consumer behavior, we will consider this optimization problem: "What amounts of goods and services should an individual choose to purchase if his or her goal is to be as well off as possible?" When we study producers, we will ask: "How much should a firm produce to maximize its profit?" In both of these instances, we will be searching for the best plan of action, given some predetermined objective.

While the notion of solving "equilibrium" and "optimization" problems may sound ominous, it really is not. In fact, in this book the only tools we use to solve these problems are equations and graphs. Quite often, we can analyze and solve complicated economic problems by using equations and graphs to illustrate particular situations.

■ One of the most important equilibrium models of a market economy is the *supply and demand model*. The material presented here will be a review of some of the basic concepts discussed in

2.1 TYPES OF ECONOMIC PROBLEMS

2.2 EQUILIBRIUM PROBLEMS: SUPPLY AND DEMAND

Principles of Microeconomics; however, discussing the supply and demand model now is one of the best ways to see how to use equations and graphs to analyze economic problems. Our primary goals here are to use the supply and demand model to determine the prices and quantities that arise as a result of buyers and sellers interacting and to investigate how these *equilibrium values* change as the economic environment changes.

DEMAND AND SUPPLY CURVES

Demand tells us how much of a particular good or service buyers will purchase at different prices given their incomes, the prices of other goods and services, their economic wants and needs, and their expectations. A *demand curve* is the graphical representation of demand. A demand curve represents the relation between the quantity consumers are willing and able to purchase and the price, when all other factors influencing consumption do not change.

Figure 2–1(a) illustrates a hypothetical demand curve for potato chips. The vertical axis measures the price of potato chips and the horizontal axis measures the number of bags of potato chips purchased per week. The demand curve, labeled *D*, shows the total amount consumers will purchase at each price. Point *A*, for example, shows that at a price of $3.50 per bag, consumers will want to purchase 300 bags of chips each week. If the price falls to $2.00 per bag, then quantity demanded will increase to 600 bags per week, point *B* in the diagram. Notice that we do not say that demand has increased. *Demand* refers to the entire relation between price and quantity while *quantity demanded* refers to a single point on the demand curve. The demand curve slopes downward—it is *negatively sloped*—which means that consumers are willing to purchase more at lower prices.

Supply tells us how much of a particular good or service producers will sell at different prices, given the prevailing cost of resources used in the production process, the technology, and expectations. A *supply curve* is the graphical representation of supply. A supply curve represents the relation between the quantity producers are willing and able to sell and the price, when all other factors influencing production do not change.

Figure 2–1(b) illustrates a hypothetical supply curve for potato chips. The supply curve, labeled *S*, shows the total amount producers will want to sell at each price. Point *C*, for example, shows that at a price of $3.50 per bag, they will produce for sale 700 bags each week. If the price falls to $2.00 per bag then quantity supplied will decrease to 400 bags per week, point *F* in the diagram. Notice that we do not say that supply has fallen. *Supply* refers to the entire relation between price and quantity while

DEMAND, SUPPLY, AND MARKET EQUILIBRIUM   **FIGURE 2-1**

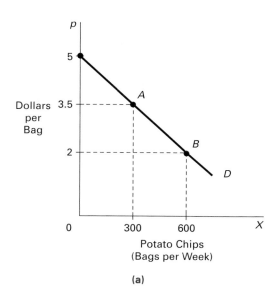

(a)

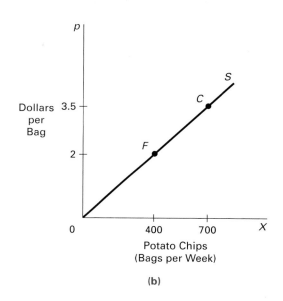

(b)

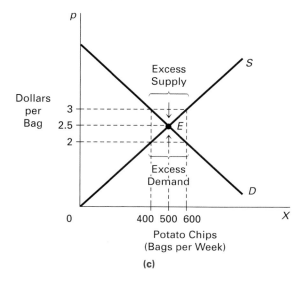

(c)

(a) Demand curve D represents the relation between the number of bags of chips consumers are willing and able to buy per week and price. (b) Supply curve S represents the relation between the number of bags of chips producers are willing and able to sell per week and price. (c) The intersection of the two curves determines the equilibrium price and quantity. At $2.50 per bag, buyers want to buy 500 bags of chips and sellers want to sell 500 bags.

quantity supplied refers to a single point on the supply curve. The supply curve slopes upward—it is *positively sloped*—which means that producers are willing to sell more, the higher the price of the good.

FINDING THE EQUILIBRIUM PRICE AND QUANTITY USING SUPPLY AND DEMAND CURVES

In order to determine the equilibrium price and equilibrium quantity, we must put the demand and supply curves together. We define the equilibrium price and quantity in detail in Chapter 9. For the moment, however, it is enough to say that equilibrium means there is no tendency for price or quantity to change.

Now how can we determine the equilibrium price and quantity by using demand and supply curves? In Figure 2–1(c), we have combined the demand and supply curves for potato chips. The intersection of these curves, point E, represents equilibrium. At this point there is no tendency for price or quantity to change, because consumers want to purchase exactly the quantity producers want to sell. In this instance the **equilibrium price** is $2.50 per bag of potato chips. At this price buyers want to purchase 500 bags of chips and sellers want to sell 500 bags. Therefore, the **equilibrium quantity** is 500 bags of chips per week.

MARKET ECONOMIES AND THE INVISIBLE HAND

So far we have seen how to use supply and demand curves to determine the equilibrium price and quantity graphically, but is there any reason to suppose that these values will actually be attained? In the supply and demand model we usually assume there is an automatic mechanism that gives rise to the equilibrium price and quantity. For example, suppose that the present market price is above the equilibrium price, say $3.00 per bag. At this price producers want to sell 600 bags of chips but consumers want to buy only 400 bags. Not all producers will be able to find consumers to buy their product and inventories will build up to unacceptable levels—potato chips have a limited shelf-life because they tend to go stale. In order to eliminate this *excess supply*, producers will offer to lower the price. This reduction in price will lead to an increase in quantity demanded and a reduction in quantity supplied. Price will continue to fall until there is equilibrium. As indicated in Figure 2–1(c), when there is an excess supply of goods, there is downward pressure on price.

Now suppose that the market price is below the equilibrium price, say $2.00 per bag. At this price producers offer for sale only 400 bags of chips but consumers want to buy 600 bags; that is, there is an *excess demand* for chips because quantity demanded exceeds quantity supplied. Consumers will not be able to buy all the potato chips they want and will be willing to pay more to get more potato chips. Suppliers will realize that consumers want more and are willing to pay a higher price. As a result, the price of potato chips will begin to rise. This increase in price will lead to a reduction in quantity demanded and an increase in quantity supplied. Price will continue to rise until there is equilibrium. As indicated in Figure 2−1(c), when there is an excess demand for goods, there is upward pressure on price.

In the supply and demand model of a market economy, the interaction of buyers and sellers alone causes price and quantity to adjust to their equilibrium levels. As we learned in Chapter 1, Adam Smith termed this adjustment process the *invisible hand* because no central authority steps in to coordinate economic activity.

Obviously, few real-world markets adjust to equilibrium exactly the way they are assumed to adjust in our theoretical supply and demand model. The managers of K-Mart, Walgreens, and Safeway usually do not lower prices just because some individuals are not willing to buy at the posted prices. Rather, the supply and demand model predicts that if prices are above their equilibrium values they will *tend* to fall, and if they are below they will *tend* to rise. Remember, a theoretical model is meant to explain and predict behavior. It is not meant to be a precise representation of reality.

We have seen that graphically the intersection of the supply and demand curves represents the equilibrium price and quantity. We also want to be able to solve this type of equilibrium problem using functions that represent supply and demand.

A *demand function* is an equation representing the relation between quantity purchased, prices, and incomes. Since the price of a good is the most important factor affecting the amount of it consumers wish to purchase, demand functions quite often focus only on the relation between quantity purchased and the price of the good. For example, the equation below represents the hypothetical demand curve for potato chips illustrated in Figure 2−1(a):

$$X = 1,000 - 200p$$

where X is the number of bags of potato chips purchased each week and p is the price of a bag of potato chips. As the diagram showed, this demand function is linear—that is, it is a straight line.

A *supply function* is an equation representing the relation between quantity sold and price. The following equation represents

FINDING THE EQUILIBRIUM PRICE AND QUANTITY USING LINEAR SUPPLY AND DEMAND FUNCTIONS

the hypothetical supply curve for potato chips illustrated in Figure 2−1(b):

$$X = 200p$$

where X is the number of bags of potato chips sold each week and p is the price of a bag of potato chips. As the diagram showed, this supply function is also a straight line.

Now how can we find the equilibrium price and quantity by using the supply and demand functions given above? Since equilibrium occurs when quantity supplied is equal to quantity demanded, we simply equate the supply and demand functions and solve for price. In this instance we have:

$$\text{(demand) } 1{,}000 - 200p = 200p \text{ (supply)}$$

and solving for p gives the equilibrium price; that is, $p^* = \$2.50$ per bag. (We use an $*$ to denote the equilibrium price.) We find the equilibrium quantity by substituting the equilibrium price into either the supply or demand function (remembering they are both equal at the equilibrium point). This gives: $X^* = (200)(2.50) = 500$ bags of potato chips per week.

CHANGES IN DEMAND OR SUPPLY

The intersection of the supply and demand curves determines the equilibrium price and quantity. Now what would happen to these equilibrium values if either demand or supply changed?

Figure 2−2(a) illustrates a situation where demand for vitamin C increases but supply remains unchanged. (In fact, such a situation occurred in the 1970s when nobel laureate Linus Pauling declared that vitamin C could prevent or even cure the common cold.) Prior to the increase in demand, the equilibrium price and quantity are p^* and X^* respectively. When demand increases, the demand curve shifts to the right, and if firms have not fully anticipated the shift in demand, a shortage arises; that is, since at every price consumers want to purchase more vitamin C, at the original equilibrium price quantity demanded exceeds quantity supplied. This, in turn, causes the price of vitamin C to rise until quantity supplied and quantity demanded are once again equal. In Figure 2−2(a), the new equilibrium price and quantity are p_1 and X_1 respectively. Thus, as a result of an increase in demand, both the equilibrium price and the equilibrium quantity rise.

What happens if, instead, supply increases? As Figure 2−2(b) shows, an increase in supply causes the supply curve to shift to the right. This may be caused, for example, by a technical innovation

CHANGES IN DEMAND OR SUPPLY FIGURE 2–2

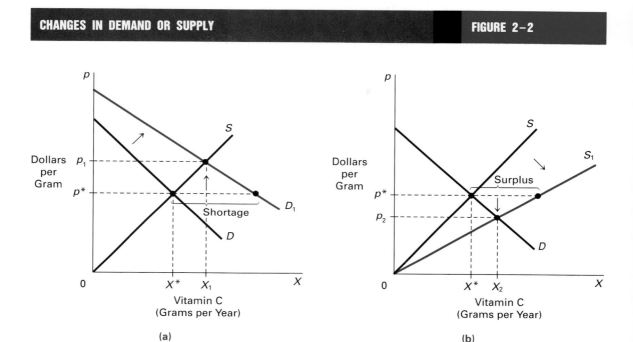

(a)

(b)

(a) When demand for vitamin C increases, the demand curve shifts to the right from D to D_1. As a result, price and quantity both increase. (b) When supply of vitamin C increases, the supply curve shifts to the right causing price to fall and quantity to rise.

that makes it possible to produce vitamin C at a lower cost. At every price producers are now willing to supply more vitamin C and, as a result, a surplus arises. This surplus causes price to fall until quantity demanded is equal to quantity supplied. In the diagram, the new equilibrium price and quantity are p_2 and X_2 respectively. Thus, as a result of an increase in supply, price falls and quantity rises.

EXAMPLE 2–1

THE MARKET FOR ATHLETIC SHOES
Suppose the demand and supply functions for athletic shoes are given by

$$\text{(demand)}\ X = 200{,}000 - 5{,}000p$$

$$\text{(supply)}\ X = 5{,}000p$$

where X is the number of pairs of shoes purchased per year and p is the price per pair. (a) Graph the demand and supply curves and show the equilibrium price and quantity. (b) Determine the equilibrium price and quantity algebraically. (c) Recently, an increase in the general public's health consciousness has lead to an increase in the number of people taking up running. As a result, suppose that the demand for athletic shoes increases and is given by

$$X = 400{,}000 - 5{,}000p.$$

Illustrate this new demand curve and find the new equilibrium price and quantity.

■ **SOLUTION** (a) Figure 2−3 graphs the market for athletic shoes. The horizontal axis measures the number of pairs of shoes bought and sold per year and the vertical axis measures the price per pair. The

---

FIGURE 2 - 3   **THE MARKET FOR ATHLETIC SHOES**

When the demand for shoes increases, the equilibrium price increases from $20 to $40 and the equilibrium quantity increases from 100,000 pairs of shoes per year to 200,000 pairs per year.

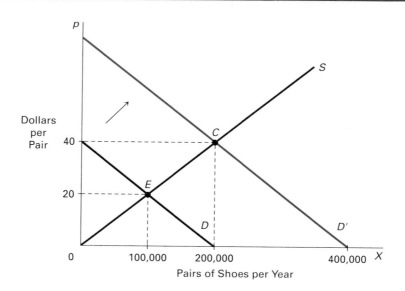

equilibrium price and quantity correspond to the intersection of the supply and demand curves.

(b) Algebraically, we calculate the equilibrium price by equating the demand and supply functions. This gives

$$200,000 - 5,000p = 5,000p$$

or, solving for p, $p^* = \$20$ per pair of shoes. The equilibrium quantity is found by substituting this price into either the demand or supply functions. This gives $X^* = 100,000$ pairs of shoes.

(c) In Figure 2–3, the increase in demand is represented by a shift in the demand curve from D to D'. From the diagram it is clear that the equilibrium price and quantity both rise. Algebraically we can verify this by following exactly the same steps as in (b). Thus, the new equilibrium price will be \$40 per pair of shoes and the new equilibrium quantity will be 200,000 pairs. ∎

At this point we should be comfortable using the supply and demand model to analyze simple equilibrium problems. In Chapters 9 through 11 we will investigate this type of equilibrium problem in much greater detail. However, now we turn to a discussion of optimization problems.

■ In microeconomics, analyzing optimization problems is often referred to as *marginal analysis*. This is because the analysis involves using marginal changes in economic variables to explain the decisions made by producers and consumers. For example, in Chapter 8 we will show that the profit-maximizing level of production for a firm corresponds to the point where the marginal rise in revenue that results from increasing production a small amount is just equal to the marginal cost.

We classify optimization problems as either *maximization* or *minimization* problems. Maximization problems aim to find the plan of action that maximizes some given objective function; by contrast, minimization problems aim to find the plan of action that minimizes some given objective function. We begin by looking at a maximization problem.

Suppose that Jimmy sells TV sets. From past experience, Jimmy knows that revenue depends on the number of sets sold, which in turn depends on how much is spent on advertising. Furthermore, he estimates that the relation between revenue and advertising expenditures is given by: $R = e - .01e^2$, where R denotes revenue per year and e, annual advertising expenditures. If Jimmy's goal is

2.3 OPTIMIZATION PROBLEMS

to maximize revenue, how much should he spend on advertising each year?

Jimmy's goal is to find the value of e that maximizes R. Our goal is to find a general decision rule that, if followed, leads to the quantity-maximizing level of advertising expenditures. Figure 2–4(a) shows graphically the relation between revenue and expenditures. As advertising expenditures increase, revenue increases, reaches a maximum, and then declines. The maximum point occurs when expenditures are e^*.

Notice that in order to formulate a general decision rule for finding e^*, we can describe the shape of the curve in Figure 2–4(a) in terms of *marginal revenue*. In this instance, marginal revenue is the rate of change in revenue with respect to expenditures; that is, marginal revenue is the *slope* of the curve in Figure 2–4(a). Now note that to the left of e^* marginal revenue is positive, to the right of e^* marginal revenue is negative, and at e^* marginal revenue is zero. Figure 2–4(b) shows the relation between marginal revenue and advertising expenditures: as expenditures increase, marginal revenue changes from positive to negative.

FIGURE 2–4   **MAXIMIZATION AND MINIMIZATION PROBLEMS**

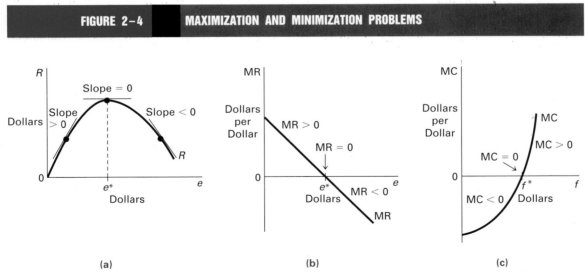

(a)   (b)   (c)

(a) and (b) If marginal revenue changes from plus to minus, then revenue from the sale of TV sets is maximized at e^*, which is where marginal revenue is zero. (c) If marginal per-unit cost changes from minus to plus, then per-unit cost is minimized at f^*, which is where marginal per-unit cost is zero.

This observation gives us a decision-making rule for determining the level of advertising expenditures that maximizes revenue:

If, as advertising expenditures increase, marginal revenue changes from plus to minus, then revenue is maximized when the level of advertising expenditures is such that marginal revenue is equal to zero.

In Figure 2−4(b), marginal revenue is zero when e* is spent on advertising.

To convince ourselves that this decision rule will, indeed, lead to the level of advertising expenditures that maximizes marginal revenue, suppose Jimmy spends less than e* dollars on advertising. At any e less than e*, MR (marginal revenue) is positive. This means that if Jimmy were to increase expenditures, revenue would also increase. Thus, spending anything less than e* does not maximize revenue. If Jimmy spends more than e* dollars on advertising, then MR is negative which means that if he were to decrease expenditures, revenue would increase. Thus, spending more than e* does not maximize revenue either. Only at e* is revenue as large as possible.

Next, consider a minimization problem. Suppose Homer grows corn. From past experience, Homer knows that the cost of growing corn varies with the amount he spends on fertilizer, and he estimates that the relation between marginal cost and fertilizer expenditures is $MC = f^2 - 100$, where MC denotes marginal cost and f, annual fertilizer expenditures. If Homer wants to minimize the cost of growing corn, how much money should he spend on fertilizer?

Figure 2−4(c) graphs the relation between marginal cost and fertilizer expenditures. Note that at any expenditure level less than f^*, marginal cost is negative, which means Homer can lower cost by increasing fertilizer expenditures. Also, at any expenditure level greater than f^*, marginal cost is positive, which means he can lower cost by decreasing fertilizer expenditures. Thus, Homer minimizes cost if he spends f^* on fertilizer.

We can now state the decision-making rule for determining the level of fertilizer expenditures that minimizes cost:

If, as fertilizer expenditures increase, marginal cost changes from minus to plus, then cost is minimized when the level of fertilizer expenditures is such that marginal cost is equal to zero.

EXAMPLE 2–2

HOW LONG SHOULD THE WINE BE AGED?

E. J. Jones owns a winery. From past experience, E. J. knows that how much revenue she generates from the sale of her wine depends on how long the wine is aged. She estimates that the relation between marginal revenue and aging time is: $MR = 8,000 - 2,000t$, where MR denotes marginal revenue and t is the aging time in years. (a) If E. J.'s goal is to maximize revenue, how long should she age her wine? (b) One of E. J.'s managers suggests that the wine be sold immediately. He argues that when $t = 0$ marginal revenue is as large as possible, so revenue is increasing as rapidly as it ever will. Evaluate this argument.

■ **SOLUTION** (a) In order to find the aging time that maximizes revenue, set marginal revenue equal to zero and solve for t. This gives $t^* = 4$ years. To be sure that this is a maximum and not a minimum, we must check marginal revenue for values of t less than 4 and greater than 4. For example, when $t = 3$, $MR = 2,000$ and when $t = 5$, $MR = -2,000$. Since MR changes from plus to minus, $t^* = 4$ is a maximum.

(b) The manager's argument is incorrect if the goal of the firm is to maximize revenue. When $t = 0$, $MR = 8,000$. This means that if the wine is aged a little longer, revenue increases $8,000. Suppose the wine is aged one year. At this point, marginal revenue is only 6,000. Does this mean that we should have sold the wine a year earlier? Certainly not, because even though marginal revenue has fallen, *it is still positive*. This means that if the wine is aged a little longer, revenue still *increases* $6,000. Thus, $t = 0$ cannot be the revenue-maximizing point. ■

Optimization problems like the ones discussed above are called *unconstrained optimization* problems because the decision maker is not constrained in any way. In microeconomics, there are also *constrained optimization problems,* so named because there *are* constraints restricting the choices of decision makers. We will look at one such problem below. We will encounter other constrained optimization problems when we discuss the theory of consumer choice in Chapter 3 and the theory of cost in Chapter 7.

Let us tackle a constrained maximization problem. In this example, we consider the economics of time rather than money, but we apply the same methods to solve our problem.

Amy is studying for her final exams in economics and accounting. She has 10 hours of study time left. According to her best estimates, each additional hour she spends studying will increase her grades as shown in Table 2–1. If Amy's goal is to maximize the sum of her economics and accounting grades, how should she allocate her time?

The entries in column one of Table 2–1 represent the *marginal value of time spent studying economics*, denoted by MV_t^e. MV_t^e is the change in Amy's economics grade per unit change in the time she spends on economics. For example, if MV_t^e is equal to 10 then this means that Amy's grade will increase 10 points per additional hour spent studying economics. Similarly, each additional hour spent studying accounting increases her accounting grade by the *marginal value of time spent studying accounting*, denoted by MV_t^a. MV_t^a represents the change in Amy's accounting grade per unit change in the time she spends on accounting.

In this problem, Amy faces a constraint: she only has 10 hours left to study. Thus, not all combinations of study time are possible. For example, according to Table 2–1 studying 10 hours for economics and 10 hours for accounting maximizes her cumulative grade. But this would require a total of 20 hours of study time, which Amy does not have, given the constraint she faces.

Let's try to develop a general decision rule for allocating Amy's time given the constraint she faces. Each additional hour that Amy spends studying economics increases her economics grade by MV_t^e. Now suppose that Amy is currently planning to study 1 hour

Study Time (Hours)	MV_t^e	MV_t^a
0	—	—
1	18	27
2	16	24
3	14	21
4	12	18
5	10	15
6	8	12
7	6	9
8	4	6
9	2	3
10	0	0

TABLE 2–1

THE MARGINAL VALUE OF STUDY TIME

Amy's grades depend on how long she studies for each subject. The marginal value of time spent on economics decreases from 18 to 0, while the marginal value of time spent accounting decreases from 27 to 0.

for economics and 9 for accounting. Is this the allocation of time that maximizes her cumulative grade? If it is, then she should not be able to reallocate her study effort in such a way that her cumulative grade increases.

From Table 2−1 we see that if Amy spends 1 hour on economics, then the $MV_t^e = 18$, and if she spends 9 hours on accounting, then the $MV_t^a = 3$. If Amy spends 1 less hour on accounting, her accounting grade falls by the MV_t^a, or by 3 points. Her economics grade, on the other hand, increases by 18 points since she now has 1 more hour to spend on economics. The net change is an increase in her cumulative grade of (18 − 3) or 15 points. Therefore, studying 1 hour for economics and 9 for accounting does not maximize the sum of her grades.

How long can we make this type of argument? As long as the marginal value of time is different between the two activities, Amy can always reallocate her study effort in such a way that her cumulative grade increases. Thus, Amy maximizes her cumulative grade by allocating her time so that $MV_t^e = MV_t^a$, provided she spends no more than 10 hours studying.

We can now use Table 2−1 to determine the optimal allocation of study time and solve Amy's problem. There are three allocations that satisfy $MV_t^e = MV_t^a$: 1 hour of economics and 4 hours' accounting; 7 hours' economics and 9 hours' accounting; and 4 hours' economics and 6 hours' accounting. However, only one of these—the last—also satisfies the time constraint. Thus, Amy should study 4 hours for economics and 6 hours for accounting if her objective is to maximize her cumulative grade.

EXAMPLE 2–3

INVESTING IN STOCKS

Karl has $10,000 that he plans to invest in two stocks. According to his best estimates, the marginal return on each of the stocks is given by

$$MR_1 = 20,000 - 2I_1 \text{ and } MR_2 = 30,000 - 3I_2,$$

where I_1 and I_2 are the amounts invested in each of the stocks. If Karl's goal is to maximize the total return on his investment, how much money should he allocate to each stock?

■ **SOLUTION** This is a constrained optimization problem since Karl has only $10,000 to invest; that is, $I_1 + I_2 = \$10,000$. Karl should allocate his money in such a way that the marginal returns are equal across investments, provided he spends only $10,000. Setting MR_1 equal to MR_2 we have

$$20,000 - 2I_1 = 30,000 - 3I_2.$$

Now we must solve for I_1 and I_2, but how can we do this when we have only one equation to work with? The constraint provides another equation. Solving the constraint for I_2 and substituting into the expression given above, we have

$$20,000 - 2I_1 = 30,000 - 3(10,000 - I_1).$$

Solving this equation for I_1 gives: $I_1{}^* = \$4,000$ and substituting this into the constraint gives $I_2{}^* = \$6,000$. ■

Later in the text we will find it useful to interpret the solutions to optimization problems in yet another way. In microeconomics we will always try to explain the decisions of producers and consumers in terms of the additional costs incurred and benefits gained from undertaking a particular plan of action. The additional cost associated with undertaking a particular activity is called **marginal cost** and the additional benefit that accrues is called **marginal benefit.**

Let's see if we can describe Amy's decision-making rule in terms of marginal benefit and marginal cost. Suppose Amy studies one additional hour for economics. As a result, we know that her economics grade will increase by the marginal value of time spent studying economics. This is the *marginal benefit* of an additional hour of study time devoted to economics, and we denote it MB^e.

Does this mean that Amy should study economics until $MB^e = 0$? As we saw above, the answer is no. This is because there is also an *opportunity cost* associated with spending time on economics — the foregone opportunity to increase her accounting grade. For every additional hour Amy spends on economics, she has one less hour to spend on accounting. But if she spends one less hour on accounting, her accounting grade will fall. (Chapter 6 discusses opportunity cost fully.) The reduction in Amy's acounting grade associated with an additional hour devoted to economics represents the marginal cost (MC) of studying for economics. Notice that the MC of studying economics is the negative of the MV_t^a.

Now, as Amy devotes more time to economics, two things happen: her economics grade increases and her accounting grade falls. Since she should allocate her study time in such a way that the marginal value of time is equal across subjects, she should study until the marginal benefit of studying an additional hour for economics is just equal to the marginal cost.

In Table 2–2 we illustrate how to determine the optimal allocation of time by comparing marginal benefit and marginal cost: column 1 lists hours spent studying economics; column 2 lists the marginal benefit of devoting an additional hour to economics; and column 3 lists the marginal cost. We can see that as study time for economics increases from 1 hour to 2, Amy's economics grade increases 16 points and her accounting grade falls 6 points. If Amy spends another hour on economics, her economics grade increases 14 points and her accounting grade falls 9 points. This confirms our earlier conclusion: Amy is doing the best she can when MB = MC or when she studies 4 hours for economics and 6 for accounting.

The marginal cost–marginal benefit interpretation of the solution to an optimization problem is used extensively and is the essence of marginal analysis in microeconomics. We can also illustrate this solution to Amy's optimization problem using a simple graph. In Figure 2–5, we measure the hours Amy spends studying economics on the horizontal axis and the points per hour of study time on the vertical axis. Line AA' plots the marginal benefit of studying for economics (MB) using the data in Table 2–1. Line EE' plots the marginal cost of studying for economics (MC).

TABLE 2–2

THE MARGINAL BENEFIT AND COST OF STUDYING FOR ECONOMICS

The optimal number of hours to study for economics is where marginal benefit equals marginal cost. This occurs when Amy studies 4 hours for economics and 6 for accounting.

Study Time	Marginal Benefit	Marginal Cost
0	—	0
1	18	3
2	16	6
3	14	9
4	12	12
5	10	15
6	8	18
7	6	21
8	4	24
9	2	27
10	0	—

AMY'S MARGINAL BENEFIT AND MARGINAL COST CURVES

FIGURE 2-5

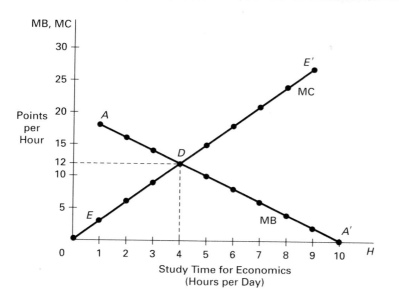

MB measures the increase in Amy's total grade for each additional hour spent studying economics and MC measures the decrease in Amy's total grade for each additional hour spent studying economics. If Amy maximizes her cumulative grade, then she should study up to the point where MB = MC, or 4 hours for economics and 6 hours for accounting.

Amy maximizes her cumulative grade when the marginal benefit of an additional hour spent on economics is just equal to the marginal cost. This occurs at point D in Figure 2–5. Here $t_e^* = 4$ hours and $t_a^* = 6$. Note that if $t_e < 4$, then MB > MC and Amy can increase her cumulative grade by spending more time on economics. If $t_e > 4$, she can increase her cumulative grade by spending less time on economics. Amy is doing the best she can do when MB = MC.

We will see as we progress through our study of microeconomics that the equality between marginal benefit and marginal cost plays a crucial role in interpreting both individual decision making and the interaction of buyers and sellers in a market economy.

SUMMARY

1. An equilibrium problem is concerned with how the interaction of buyers and sellers determines the prices and quantities that will prevail in particular markets.
2. An optimization problem sets out to choose the best, or optimal, plan of action. Maximization problems aim to find the plan of action that maximizes some objective function while minimization problems aim to find the one that minimizes some objective function.
3. Supply and demand analysis is one type of equilibrium problem. Demand tells us how much of a particular good buyers will purchase at different prices, and supply tells us how much producers will sell. Equilibrium occurs when supply is equal to demand.
4. In the market economy model, no central authority is needed to coordinate economic activity. Market forces alone ensure that supply is equal to demand.
5. In general, we solve optimization problems by equating marginal benefit and marginal cost, given any constraints. Basing decisions on marginal benefit and marginal cost is one fundamental principle underlying much of microeconomic theory.

KEY TERMS

Equilibrium Problem	Equilibrium Price
Optimization Problem	Equilibrium Quantity
Demand	Marginal Cost
Supply	Marginal Benefit

QUESTIONS AND PROBLEMS

1. Anna owns Business Software, Inc., a firm that manufactures and sells an accounting software package for personal computers. The price of the software is currently $300 per package.
   a) If the cost of manufacturing software packages is $150 per package regardless of how many packages are produced, determine the relation between profit and the number of software packages sold per year.
   b) Graph this relation.
   c) If the cost of manufacturing software packages is $150 per package for the first 100,000 packages and $200 per package thereafter, determine the relation between profit and the number of software packages sold per year.
   d) Graph this relation.
2. Shawn is considering joining a country club. In order to become a member of the club, Shawn must pay an annual membership

fee of $5,000. This entitles him to play all the golf he wants for the year.

   a) If Shawn joins the club, determine the relation between his annual golf expenditures and the number of rounds of golf he plays.

   b) If the club changes its membership policy and charges an annual fee of $3,000 plus $20 per round of golf, determine Shawn's annual golf expenditures as a function of the number of rounds he plays.

   c) Graph both of these relations.

3. A small manufacturing firm uses labor to produce designer suspenders. The owners of this firm pay workers $150 per day.

   a) If each worker can produce 100 suspenders per day, determine the relation between the firm's labor costs and the number of suspenders produced per day.

   b) Graph this relation.

4. Sue has decided to attend the state fair. Upon arriving at the fair, Sue finds two of her favorite rides: the ferris wheel and the roller coaster. Each ride on the ferris wheel costs $1, while each ride on the roller coaster costs $2. Since the fair has attracted many visitors, Sue must wait in line to ride either the ferris wheel or the roller coaster. Thus, each ride on the roller coaster takes 1 hour of her time, while each ride on the ferris wheel takes 15 minutes.

   a) If Sue wants to spend $20 on rides and stay for 6 hours, how many times should she ride the ferris wheel and the roller coaster?

   b) Illustrate with a graph.

5. Using supply and demand curves, discuss the effect of a reduction in demand for cigarettes on price and quantity.

6. Consider the market for airline services. Using supply and demand curves, explain the effect on the equilibrium price and quantity of:

   a) a prolonged strike by baggage handlers;

   b) increased frequency of hijackings; and

   c) "frequent flier" programs.

7. Oftentimes students find that they must wait in long lines to obtain university-subsidized goods and services such as health care and housing. Explain this phenomenon using supply and demand analysis. (Be sure to discuss what you are measuring on each axis.)

8. One Crafty Lady, owned and operated by Y. J. Denton, is a small firm specializing in manufacturing and selling custom-made rag dolls. Suppose that the number of dolls ordered by

customers per year, Y, is given by: $Y = 200 - 2p$, where p is the price of dolls.

a) If Y. J. makes 40 dolls per year, what price should she charge if she wants to sell all 40 dolls?

b) Illustrate this with a graph where price is measured on the vertical axis and the number of rag dolls on the horizontal axis.

c) If the number of dolls Y. J. makes per year is equal to 3 times the market price of dolls, what price will guarantee that the number of dolls produced is just equal to the number of dolls ordered?

d) Illustrate this with a graph.

9. Suppose you are taking a course and have a mid-term examination coming up. A friend of yours remarks that you should study until the marginal value of your time is zero. Under what circumstances would you agree with this statement? Under what circumstances would you disagree? Explain.

10. Mal Fortune works in an automobile factory. The relation between Mal's weekly take-home pay, I, and the number of hours he works, L, is given by: $I = wL - .001(wL)^2$, where w is the hourly wage rate. The change in income per unit change in hours of work is: $MI = (w - .002w^2L)$.

a) If Mal earns $20 per hour, how many hours should Mal work each week in order to maximize income?

b) Illustrate your calculations.

11. A book publisher commissions a well-known economist to write an intermediate price theory text. The publisher estimates that revenue from the book will be $R = 200Y - .02Y^2$ and marginal revenue will be $MR = 200 - .04Y$, where Y is the number of books sold.

a) How many books should be sold to maximize revenue?

b) Graph the revenue and marginal revenue curves.

12. A manufacturer of software estimates that profit for a new software game will be $\pi = 30x - .01x^2 - 5,000$, and the rate of change of profit will be $M\pi = 30 - .02x$, where x is the number of games sold. This firm can produce at most 1,000 of these games per accounting period.

a) Find the level of production that maximizes profits per period.

b) Illustrate your calculations.

13. Andy Allright, Amy's twin brother, is also studying for final exams. He has only 12 hours of study time left. His objective is to get as high an average grade as possible. Andy, however, is

taking a heavier load than Amy (he is repeating marketing), and he must decide how to allocate his time between accounting, marketing, and economics. According to his best estimates, his grades will depend upon the time he allocates to each course as follows:

Expected Grade per Hour of Study

Hours	Accounting Grade	Marketing Grade	Economics Grade
0	58	85	0
1	58	95	5
2	62	98	23
3	68	100	43
4	78	100	58
5	88	100	70
6	90	100	80
7	92	100	85
8	94	100	88
9	96	100	90
10	98	100	91
11	99	100	92
12	100	100	93

How should Andy allocate his time?

14. Assume that a fox can hunt rabbits in 2 separate patches of grass. The number of rabbits that the fox can capture in any particular patch depends only on how much time he spends in the patch. For any single day the fox's objective is to capture as many rabbits as possible. A biologist estimates that the number of rabbits a fox can capture on each of the 2 patches and the marginal capture rate for each patch are given by

Patch 1: $R_1 = 5t_1 - t_1^2$; and $MR_1 = 5 - 2t_1$;

Patch 2: $R_2 = 10t_2 - 2t_2^2$; and $MR_2 = 10 - 4t_2$.

The biologist also has determined that a fox can hunt at most 6 hours a day. If the travel time between patches is zero, how long does the fox spend in each patch?

15. Ivan has $1,000 that he is going to invest in two stocks. Ivan expects to earn the same return on each stock and he estimates this return to be

$$R = 2I - .001I^2,$$

where R is the return and I the amount invested. Ivan is interested only in maximizing his expected return. He argues that since the expected returns are the same for both stocks, he can put all of his $1,000 in either of the stocks and maximize expected returns. Do you agree with this line of reasoning? Explain.

16. A manufacturer of office furniture has 10 assembly lines, each of which produces 20 desks per hour. The cost of setting up each line for a production run is $1,000. The cost of running n of the lines for one hour is $200 + 10n$.

a) Determine the relation between the total cost of producing 900 desks and the number of assembly lines in operation.

b) Explain how you would go about finding how many lines the manufacturer should run in order to produce 900 desks at the lowest possible cost.

REFERENCES   Baumol, W. J., and A. S. Blinder. 1991. *Economics, Principles and Policy*. 5th ed. San Diego: Harcourt Brace Jovanovich.

Chiang, A. C. 1989. *Fundamental Methods of Mathematical Economics*. New York: McGraw-Hill.

MATHEMATICAL TOOLS

In this appendix we will discuss some of the mathematical concepts used in intermediate microeconomics. We will also show how calculus is used to analyze unconstrained and constrained optimization problems.

A2.1 FUNCTIONS AND GRAPHS

A *function* is a rule that describes the relation between variables. For each value of variable x, a function assigns a unique value for variable y according to some rule. For example, the function given by y = 3x indicates that the value of variable y is equal to 3 times the value of variable x.

Often in microeconomics we know that some variable y, the *dependent variable*, is a function of some other variable x, the *independent variable*, but we do not know the exact algebraic relation between the variables. In this instance, we write y = f(x), which means that the dependent variable y depends on the independent variable x according to the rule f.

One way to represent a function is with a *graph*. The graph of a function illustrates the relation between one variable and another with a picture. Figure A2–1(a) shows the graph of the function y = 3x. In mathematics the horizontal axis usually represents the independent variable and the vertical axis represents the dependent variable. However, in economics we often graph the inde-

---

GRAPHS OF LINEAR FUNCTIONS   **FIGURE A2–1**

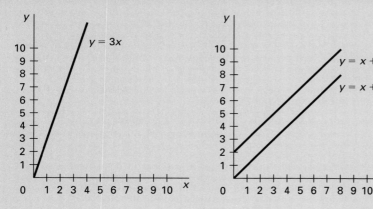

(a) The graph of the function y = 3x is a straight line with a slope equal to 3. (b) The graph of the function y = x + 2z shows the relation between x and y, holding z constant.

pendent variable on the vertical axis and the dependent variable on the horizontal. For example, the demand and supply functions discussed in Chapter 2 are usually depicted with price on the vertical axis and quantity demanded on the horizontal axis.

Sometimes one variable y depends on several independent variables such as x and z. In this instance, we write $y = f(x,z)$, which indicates that both x and z together determine the value of y. When we graph this type of function, only one of the dependent variables is allowed to change. The other is held constant. Figure A2–1(b) shows the graph of the function $y = x + 2z$ when z is held constant at 0 and 1. The dependent variable y is shown on the vertical axis and independent variable x is shown on the horizontal axis. Along each line, the independent variable z is held constant.

A2.2 TYPES OF FUNCTIONS

A *continuous function* is one that can be drawn without lifting a pencil from the paper. There are no "jumps" or "gaps" in a continuous function. A *smooth function* is one that has no "kinks" or "corners." A *monotonic function* is one that always increases or always decreases. For a monotonic function, not only is there a unique value of y associated with each value of x but there is also a unique value of x associated with each value of y. The function $y = 3x$ shown in Figure A2–1 is a monotonically increasing function.

Given the monotonic function $y = f(x)$, we call the function $x = g(y)$ the *inverse function*. The inverse function is calculated by solving for x as a function of y. For example, given the function $y = 3x$, the inverse function is $x = y/3$.

A *linear function* is a function that has the standard form $y = ax + b$, where a and b are constants. The function $y = 3x$ is a linear function. In this instance, $a = 3$ and $b = 0$. In microeconomics, linear functions are often expressed implicitly by forms like $ax + by = c$. We can convert this to the standard form by solving for y as a function of x: $y = (c/b) - (a/b)x$. The graph of a linear function is a straight line.

A2.3 EQUATIONS AND IDENTITIES

An *equation* asks when a function is equal to a particular number. For example, $5x = 10$ asks when the function $y = 5x$ is equal to 10. The equation $f(x) = 0$ asks when the function $y = f(x)$ is equal to zero. The *solution* to an equation is a value for x that satisfies the equation. The equation $5x = 10$ has a solution of $x = 2$. We do not know the explicit solution for the equation $f(x) = 0$ since we do not know what rule f represents; however, we can denote the value of x that satisfies this equation by x*. That is, x* is the value of x such that $f(x^*) = 0$.

An *identity* is a relation between variables that holds for all values of the variables. For example, $5(x + 2) \equiv 5x + 10$ is an identity. The symbol $\equiv$ means that the left hand side is equal to the right hand side for all values of x. An identity is different from an equation because an equation only holds for certain values of the variables while an identity holds for all values of the variables.

A2.4 DERIVATIVES AND SLOPES

Using the greek letter Δ to denote change, we read the expression Δx as "the change in x." For example, if x changes from x_1 to x_2 then the change in x is $\Delta x = (x_2 - x_1)$. If Δx refers to a small change in x, we say Δx represents a *marginal change*.

Given the function $y = f(x)$, the *average rate of change* of y with respect to x is the ratio of the change in y to the change in x. It is denoted by

$$\frac{\Delta y}{\Delta x} = \frac{f(x + \Delta x) - f(x)}{\Delta x}.$$

The average rate of change measures how y changes as x changes.

For a linear function, the average rate of change of y with respect to x is constant. For a nonlinear function, the average rate of change of the function will depend on the value of x and the size of the change.

Graphically, the average rate of change of a linear function is the *slope* of the line. The linear function shown in Figure A2−1(a) has a constant slope equal to 3. The average rate of change of a nonlinear function is the slope of a *chord* connecting two points satisfying the function. Figure A2−2 shows the graph of the function $y = x^2/8$, for positive values of x, and the chord connecting points A and B. The slope of this chord is 4/3 which means that the average rate of change of the function between $x = 4$ and $x = 8$ is 4/3. The *derivative* of a function $y = f(x)$ is defined to be the limit of $\frac{\Delta y}{\Delta x}$ as Δx approaches zero and is denoted by

$$\frac{dy}{dx} = \frac{df(x)}{dx} = \lim_{\Delta x \to 0} \frac{\Delta y}{\Delta x}.$$

The derivative of a function measures the rate of change of y with respect to x for small changes in x.

FIGURE A2–2   THE GRAPH OF A NONLINEAR FUNCTION

The slope of the chord between points A and B measures the average rate of change of y between x = 4 and x = 8. The slope of tangent line tt' is the slope of the function at x = 4.

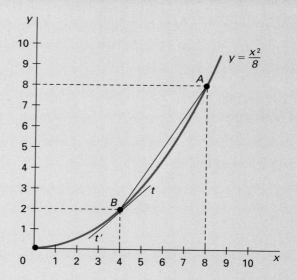

Graphically, the derivative of a function is the *slope* of the function itself. For a linear function, the average rate of change is equal to the derivative of the function. The slope of a nonlinear function at x is defined to be the slope of the *tangent line* at point x. In Figure A2–2, *tt'* is the tangent line associated with the point x = 4. The slope of the function at this point is equal to the slope of *tt'*. In this instance, the slope is positive. This means that as x increases, y increases, or that Δy and Δx have the same sign. If, on the other hand, Δy and Δx have opposite signs, the slope of the function will be negative.

The *second derivative* of a function is the derivative of the derivative of that function. If y = f(x), the second derivative of y with respect to x is written as $d^2f(x)/dx^2$. The second derivative is useful because it measures the curvature of the function—that is, it measures how the slope of the function is changing. A function with a negative second derivative at some point is concave near that point. Its slope is decreasing. A function with a positive second derivative at some point is convex near that point. Its slope is increasing. A function with a zero second derivative at some point is flat near that point.

Given the function y = f(x,z), the *partial derivative* of y with respect to x is defined by

$$\frac{\partial y}{\partial x} = \frac{\partial f(x,z)}{\partial x} = \lim_{\Delta x \to 0} \frac{f(x + \Delta x, z) - f(x,z)}{\Delta x}.$$

The partial derivative of y with respect to x is just the derivative of the function with respect to x, *holding z constant*. Likewise, the partial derivative of y with respect to z is just the derivative of the function with respect to x, *holding x constant*.

A2.5 RULES FOR FINDING DERIVATIVES

The few basic rules for calculating derivatives are listed below. We calculate partial derivatives using exactly these same rules.

If $y = k$, *where k is a constant, then* $dy/dx = 0$.   **Constant Rule**

If $y = kx^n$, *where k and n are constants, then* $dy/dx = nkx^{n-1}$.   **Power Rule**

If $y = f(x) + g(x)$, *then* $dy/dx = df(x)/dx + dg(x)/dx$.   **Addition Rule**

If $y = f(x) \cdot g(x)$, *then* $dy/dx = g(x)[df(x)/dx] + f(x)[dg(x)/dx]$.   **Product Rule**

If $y = f(x)/g(x)$, *then* $dy/dx = \{g(x)[df(x)/dx] - f(x)[dg(x)/dx]\}/[g(x)]^2$.   **Quotient Rule**

If $y = f(z)$ *and* $z = g(x)$, *then* $dy/dx = (dy/dz) \cdot (dz/dx)$.   **Chain Rule**
If $y = f(x,z)$ *and* $x = g(t)$ *and* $z = h(t)$, *then* $dy/dt = (\partial y/\partial x)(dx/dt) + (\partial y/\partial z)(dz/dt)$.

A2.6 UNCONSTRAINED OPTIMIZATION

Often we want to consider the maximum or minimum of some function. The notation we use to represent a maximization problem is the following:

$$\max_x y = f(x).$$

This means we want to find x^* such that $f(x^*) \geq f(x)$ for all possible values of x. The function $f(x)$ is called the *objective function* and the variable x is called the *choice variable*. If $f(x)$ is a smooth function that attains its maximum at x^*, then

$$\frac{df(x^*)}{dx} = 0 \text{ and } \frac{d^2f(x^*)}{dx^2} \leq 0.$$

The first expression is called the *first order condition* while the second is called the *second order condition*. The first order condition indicates that the objective function is flat at the optimal point, x^*, and the second order condition indicates that it is concave near x^*.

Similarly, the notation we use to represent a minimization problem is the following:

$$\min_{x} y = f(x).$$

This means we want to find x^* such that $f(x^*) \leq f(x)$ for all possible values of x. If $f(x)$ is a smooth function that attains its minimum at x^*, then

$$\frac{df(x^*)}{dx} = 0 \ \text{ and } \ \frac{d^2f(x^*)}{dx^2} \geq 0.$$

The first order condition indicates that the function is flat at the optimal point, x^*, and the second order condition indicates that it is convex near x^*.

If there is more than one choice variable, the notation we use to represent a maximization or minimization problem is the following:

$$\max_{x,z} y = f(x,z) \ \text{ or } \ \min_{x,z} y = f(x,z).$$

This means we want to find x^* and z^* such that $f(x^*,z^*) \geq f(x,z)$ for a maximum, $f(x^*,z^*) \leq f(x,z)$ for a minimum. If $y = f(x,z)$ is a smooth function that attains its maximum or minimum at some point (x^*,z^*), then the first order conditions are

$$\frac{\partial f(x^*,z^*)}{\partial x} = 0 \ \text{ and } \ \frac{\partial f(x^*,z^*)}{\partial z} = 0.$$

The second order conditions for this optimization problem are more complicated and must be left until a more advanced stage.

EXAMPLE A2–1

As in Section 2.3, let y denote annual sales of TV sets and E denote advertising expenditures. Suppose the function relating sales to expenditures is given by $y = f(E) = 800E - 100(E/1000)^2$. Find the level of advertising expenditures that maximizes sales of TV sets.

■ **SOLUTION** We can summarize this optimization problem by

$$\max_{E} y = 800E - .01E^2.$$

The first and second order conditions are

$$\frac{dy}{dx} = 800 - .02E^* = 0 \text{ and } \frac{d^2y}{dx^2} = -.02 < 0.$$

Notice that the second order condition is satisfied for any value of E. Solving the first order condition for E^*, we find that $E^* = 800/.02$ = \$40,000 per year. ■

A2.7 CONSTRAINED OPTIMIZATION

We usually write a constrained optimization problem as follows:

$$\max_{x,z} y = f(x,z)$$

$$\text{subject to } g(x,z) = k.$$

This means that we want to find x^* and z^* such that $f(x^*,z^*) \geq f(x,z)$ for all values of x and z that satisfy the equation $g(x,z) = k$. The function $f(x,z)$ is called the *objective function* and the equation $g(x,z) = k$ is called the *constraint*.

There are two ways to solve a constrained optimization problem. The first way is to solve the constraint for one of the choice variables in terms of the other and then substitute it into the objective function. This eliminates the constraint and transforms the constrained optimization problem into an unconstrained optimization problem.

The second way to solve this type of problem is to use *Lagrange multipliers*. In microeconomics this is how we solve most constrained optimization problems. We start by defining an auxiliary function known as the *Lagrangian*:

$$L = f(x,z) + \lambda[k - g(x,z)].$$

The new variable λ is called the *Lagrange multiplier* because it is multiplied by the constraint. Given this auxiliary function, Lagrange's theorem says that optimal values of the choice variables, (x^*,z^*), must satisfy the following first order conditions:

$$\frac{\partial L}{\partial x} = \frac{\partial f(x^*,z^*)}{\partial x} - \lambda \frac{\partial g(x^*,z^*)}{\partial x} = 0,$$

$$\frac{\partial L}{\partial z} = \frac{\partial f(x^*,z^*)}{\partial z} - \lambda\frac{\partial g(x^*,z^*)}{\partial z} = 0,$$

$$\frac{\partial L}{\partial \lambda} = k - g(x^*,z^*) = 0.$$

There are three important things to notice about these first order conditions. First, these equations are simply the partial derivatives of the Lagrangian with respect to x, z, and λ. Second, the partial derivative of the Lagrangian with respect to λ is just the constraint. Third, we now have three equations which are to be used to solve for the three unknowns, x, z, and λ.

There are also second order conditions for constrained optimization problems but, once again, they are more complicated and beyond the scope of this discussion. The interested reader can find a discussion of this technique for solving constrained optimization problems in most calculus books and a proof of Lagrange's theorem in most advanced calculus books. However, in intermediate microeconomics we need only know the statement of the theorem and how to use it.

EXAMPLE A2–2

Suppose that the XYZ company produces and sells two products, and that its total cost is given by

$$C = f(x,z) = 8x^2 + 10z^2 - 2xz,$$

where x is its output per hour of the first product, and z is its output per hour of the second product. Because of commitments to retail stores that sell these two products, XYX must produce a total of 60 units each hour, but any mix of x and z is acceptable. Find the optimal product mix if the firm wants to minimize cost.

■ **SOLUTION** We can write the constraint for this problem as $x + z = 60$. Forming the Lagrangian gives

$$L = 8x^2 + 10z^2 - 2xz + \lambda(60 - x - z).$$

Differentiating the Lagrangian with respect to x, z, and λ gives the first order conditions:

$$\frac{\partial L}{\partial x} = 16x - 2z - \lambda = 0,$$

$$\frac{\partial L}{\partial z} = 20z - 2x - \lambda = 0,$$

$$\frac{\partial L}{\partial \lambda} = 60 - x - z = 0.$$

Solving the first equation for λ and substituting into the second equation gives

$$20z - 2x - 16x + 2z = 0,$$

or $z = 18x/22 = 9x/11$. Substituting this into the third equation and solving for x gives: $x^* = 33$. Thus, the optimal value for z is $z^* = 9x^*/11 = 27$. Notice that $x^* + z^* = 60$ as required. ∎

CONSUMER CHOICE AND DEMAND

■ **CHAPTER 3** The Theory of Consumer Choice

■ **CHAPTER 4** Individual and Market Demand

■ **CHAPTER 5** Applications Using Consumer Theory

■ *Part 2 investigates how microeconomics models consumers'*

demands for the goods and services they buy. Our primary goals in

this part are to derive both individual and market demand curves

for a product and to investigate how a change in the economic

environment affects them. We will see how microeconomics

models the way individuals make their budgeting decisions and

how individual and market demand curves reflect these decisions.

The theory of consumer choice is important because it helps us

understand how both public and corporate policy affect demand

and because it helps us understand budgeting decisions.

■ Microeconomics explains consumer demand by recognizing three factors: consumers have limited incomes to spend on goods and services; they have preferences or tastes for goods; limited incomes and preferences together determine which commodities consumers purchase and how much of each they purchase. For example, an individual may want to buy a boat because he or she likes to sail (preference) but chooses not to because that income can be used to buy many other things (limited income). Part 2 shows how consumers make choices given their limited incomes and preferences and how changes in the economic environment affect these choices.

■ Chapter 3 discusses how microeconomics models a consumer's budgeting decision problem. It begins by defining a budget constraint, the device used to reflect the fact that a consumer has a limited income to allocate among various goods. Next the chapter develops the concept of the indifference curve, used to represent preferences. Finally, it discusses how individuals decide to allocate their incomes to get the greatest level of satisfaction. This is our first example of a constrained optimization problem and of how marginal analysis is used in microeconomics.

■ Chapter 4 examines demand. The first half of the chapter investigates how consumer choices change when prices or income change. Such analysis is pertinent because it can help explain, for example, how a tax on gasoline affects the amount of gasoline an individual buys. Since this analysis tells us how a person reacts to price changes, it can be used to derive demand curves, which is the primary goal of Part 2. The second half of the chapter shows how we can add up individual demand curves to obtain a market demand curve. It discusses elasticities, the concept used to measure how demand responds to changes in income or prices, and consumer surplus, the concept used to measure changes in economic well-being. Both elasticities and consumer surplus are used in many real-world applications of microeconomics.

■ Chapter 5 applies the theory of consumer choice to real-world economic situations. This chapter investigates the effects of corporate policies (such as price discounts and making people wait in line to buy a good) and public policies (such as the elimination of tax deductions and the food stamp program) on the choices consumers make. Chapter 5 also shows how the basic model developed in Chapters 3 and 4 can be extended to explain work effort and saving behavior. The chapter looks at two examples: how income taxes affect work effort; and how lower interest rates affect saving and the demand for goods and services.

THE THEORY OF CONSUMER CHOICE

3

LEARNING OBJECTIVES

After completing Chapter 3 you should be able to do the following:

■ Define market basket, budget constraint, budget set, and indifference curve.

■ Determine the slope of a budget constraint and discuss its economic significance.

■ Explain how a change in economic conditions affects the budget constraint and budget set.

■ Discuss the four basic properties of typical indifference curves.

■ Explain what utility functions are and how they can be used to represent preferences.

■ Show graphically and algebraically how to find the consumer's optimal market basket.

■ Explain intuitively the conditions characterizing the consumer's choice of which market basket to purchase.

EXAMPLES

■ **3-1** Buy One, Get One Free

■ **3-2** Introducing a New Product Line

■ **3-3** Marginal Utilities and the Marginal Rate of Substitution

■ **3-4** Finding the Optimal Market Basket

We begin our study of microeconomics by examining a vital part of the circular flow of economic activity: consumer demand for goods and services (shown in Figure 1–1). In this chapter and the next, we will see how consumers choose to allocate their incomes, how these choices determine the demand for goods and services, and how changes in income and prices affect demand.

The *theory of consumer choice* has several important applications. First, it helps us understand how *public policy* affects the demand for goods and services. For example, in 1990 the U.S. government enacted a Deficit Reduction Bill which provided a five-year plan for reducing the federal deficit. One provision of the bill was a $.05 per-gallon increase in the federal tax on gasoline. Such a tax increase raises important questions: How will the tax increase affect gasoline consumption? How will it affect a consumer's standard of living? If low-income families are hurt by the tax, what can be done to maintain their standard of living? An analysis of consumer behavior can help answer these questions by determining how consumer purchases of gasoline and other goods are affected by changes in prices and income levels.

Second, the theory of consumer choice—or consumer theory—helps explain how *corporate policies* affect demand. For example, suppose the manager of a doughnut shop wants to stimulate sales by offering some type of price discount. In choosing the appropriate pricing strategy the manager of the firm must determine how consumer demand will respond to various types of pricing schemes. In other words, what type of price discount should be offered to bring in the biggest profit? Buy six doughnuts at the regular price and get six more at half price? Two for the price of one? Fifty percent off a dozen doughnuts for the first 100 customers? Again, an analysis of consumer behavior can help answer these types of questions.

In Chapter 5 we will discuss in detail these two applications of consumer theory as well as several others. However, in addition to helping us understand the ways public policy and business decisions affect consumer behavior, the principles of consumer choice apply to many of the budgeting problems that we as individuals face every day. They provide us with a framework for making sound economic decisions.

In this chapter, we develop the basic model for a single consumer. Since an individual's choice of how much of each good to purchase depends on income, the prices of goods, and tastes, the model is best understood in three steps. The first step is to recognize that every consumer faces a budget constraint; that is, because resources are scarce, consumers have only limited incomes to spend on goods and services. Given the prices of different commodities, incomes limit the combinations of goods consumers can purchase. Every dollar spent on one commodity is one less dollar that can be spent on another commodity. Second, we investigate consumer preferences. If we are to explain the choices made by consumers, then we need a way to describe their tastes for different combinations of goods. The third step is to combine budget constraints and preferences to determine the quantities of goods and services consumers ultimately choose to purchase.

■ To understand how incomes and prices limit choice, let's consider a situation in which an individual consumer has a given weekly income of I dollars that can be used to purchase only two goods, x and y. The price of x is p_x dollars per unit and the price of y is p_y dollars per unit. Income and prices are known with certainty. For now, we assume that the consumer spends all income on these two goods; that is, no income is saved.

The **budget constraint**—the restriction that limited income imposes on consumer spending—indicates all the combinations of x and y that a consumer can purchase. Algebraically, the budget constraint (BC_1) is given by

$$BC_1 : I = p_x x + p_y y. \qquad (3.1)$$

Equation (3.1) shows that the amount of money spent on good x, $p_x x$, and the amount spent on good y, $p_y y$, together must be equal to the income available. Notice that the budget constraint requires the consumer to spend all of his or her income on goods x and y.

Figure 3–1 illustrates budget constraint BC_1 given above. On the vertical axis we measure the quantity of good y and on the horizontal axis the quantity of good x. Every point in this diagram represents a particular market basket. A **market basket** is just a collection of one or more commodities. For example, point B represents a market basket consisting of 18 units of good x and 10 units of good y, while point C represents a market basket consisting of 10 units of x and 19 units of y. In this instance, the budget constraint is a straight line. It shows all the different market baskets that the consumer can purchase with his or her income, given the prices of the goods.

The intercepts of the budget constraint show the maximum amount of one good that can be purchased if nothing is spent on the other good. The y-intercept, point A in Figure 3–1, shows the amount of good y the consumer can purchase if nothing is spent on

3.1 THE BUDGET CONSTRAINT

THE INTERCEPTS OF THE BUDGET CONSTRAINT

FIGURE 3-1   **THE BUDGET CONSTRAINT AND THE BUDGET SET**

The budget constraint is the collection of market baskets available to a consumer if all income is spent. The slope of the budget constraint is minus the price ratio. The budget set is the collection of all market baskets that a consumer can purchase with all or part of a given income.

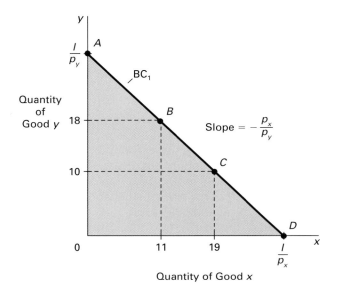

good x. Point A represents the market basket consisting of zero units of x and I/p_y units of y. Similarly, the x-intercept, point D in Figure 3–1, shows the amount of good x the consumer can purchase when nothing is spent on good y. Point D represents the market basket consisting of zero units of y and I/p_y units of x.

The intercepts also have another interpretation that is often useful. We can interpret the y-intercept as the consumer's income measured in units of good y and the x-intercept as the consumer's income measured in units of good x. For example, if bananas are measured on the vertical axis and apples on the horizontal axis, then I/p_y is the number of bananas that I dollars can purchase, or the consumer's income in terms of bananas, and I/p_x is the consumer's income in apples. This is an important point. When measuring income, the units of account are not important. Income can be measured in dollars, bananas, apples, or any other unit of account.

THE SLOPE OF THE BUDGET CONSTRAINT

In microeconomics the *slope* of the budget constraint plays an important role and it will prove essential to our understanding of consumer behavior. The slope of the budget constraint measures the rate at which one good *can* be exchanged for another—that is, how many units of good y the consumer must give up to purchase one more unit of good x. The easiest way to see this is to solve the equation describing the budget constraint for the variable on the vertical axis as a function of the remaining variables. Since in Figure 3–1 we have chosen good y to be on the vertical axis, we solve the budget constraint for y. This gives

$$y = (I/p_y) - (p_x/p_y)x.$$

When the budget constraint is written this way, it is in *slope–intercept* form and the slope is the coefficient of variable x (the variable on the horizontal axis). In this instance, the slope of the budget constraint, $\Delta y/\Delta x$, is equal to the negative of the **price ratio**—the ratio of the prices of the two goods—or $-p_x/p_y$. The price ratio indicates the relative cost of each good. Since the price of good x is the number of dollars needed to purchase a unit of x, and the price of good y is the number of dollars needed to purchase a unit of y, the price ratio indicates the relative cost of each good. Thus, the slope of the budget constraint measures the rate at which one good *can* be exchanged for another.

We can also interpret the slope of the budget constraint as measuring the *opportunity cost* of consuming good x. The opportunity cost of undertaking one plan of action is the foregone benefit associated with adopting an alternative plan of action. In this instance, the opportunity cost of consuming an additional unit of good x is the amount of good y that must be sacrificed. This is also called the economic cost of consuming more of good x.

For example, suppose the two goods under consideration are apples and oranges and that the quantity of oranges is measured on the vertical axis of our graph and the quantity of apples on the horizontal axis. If the price of apples is $20 per bushel and the price of oranges is $10 per bushel then the price ratio is $20 per bushel of oranges divided by $10 per bushel of apples or two bushels of oranges per bushel of apples. Given these prices, apples and oranges can be exchanged at the rate of two bushels of oranges for one bushel of apples. The opportunity cost of consuming one more bushel of apples is the lost opportunity of consuming two bushels of oranges.

To summarize, the budget constraint is the collection of market baskets that can be purchased if all income is spent. The slope of the budget constraint, which is equal to minus the price ratio, measures the rate at which one good can be exchanged for another.

So far we have assumed that only two goods are available to consumers. This allows us to represent budget constraints and preferences with graphs. However, we can extend our use of graphs

USING A COMPOSITE GOOD

to instances in which many goods are available for purchase by using the composite good convention. Suppose that there are many goods available to consumers: food, clothing, automobiles, and compact discs, among others. Further, suppose we are interested in determining how many compact discs a consumer purchases given his or her income and current prices. If we let compact discs be good x then we can continue to use the two-good framework to depict budget constraints if we assume that good y is a **composite good** representing all goods other than compact discs. Usually it is convenient to measure consumption of the composite good by total expenditures on it. This means that the price of the composite good is one and the budget constraint becomes:

$$I = p_x x + C$$

where C denotes expenditures on all goods other than good x. This equation requires that the amount of money spent on good x, $p_x x$, plus total expenditures on all other goods, C, equal I, the amount of income the consumer has to spend. (Notice that the budget constraint given above is, algebraically, exactly the same as the budget constraint we used earlier with $p_y = 1$.)

One caveat should be noted here. The composite good approach to analyzing an economic problem only makes sense if the prices of the goods that make up the composite good do not change. If these prices vary as the analysis proceeds, then a dollar's worth of the composite good no longer has the same meaning.

SHIFTS IN THE BUDGET CONSTRAINT

Income and the prices of goods determine a consumer's budget constraint. However, income and prices often change, causing the budget constraint to shift. Let us see precisely how the budget constraint is affected by changes in income or prices.

A CHANGE IN INCOME

What happens to the budget constraint if income increases? To answer this question, we must determine how such a change in income affects the intercepts and slope of the budget constraint. Let I_1 and I_2 be the two levels of income under consideration. The budget constraints associated with these incomes are given by

$$BC_1: I_1 = p_x x + p_y y \text{ and } BC_2: I_2 = p_x x + p_y y.$$

Since the price ratio, p_x/p_y, does not change when income changes, both budget constraints have the same slope: a change in income causes a parallel shift in the budget constraint. In this instance, we are considering an increase in income, $I_1 < I_2$, and so the budget constraint shifts outward. This is illustrated in Figure 3–2(a).

THE EFFECTS OF CHANGES IN INCOME AND PRICES ON THE BUDGET CONSTRAINT

FIGURE 3–2

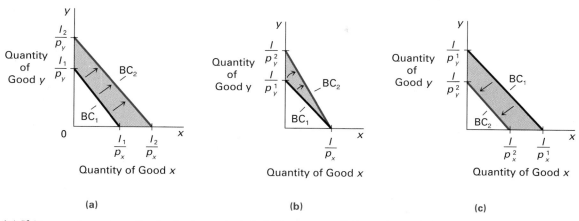

(a)   (b)   (c)

(a) If income increases, the budget constraint shifts out parallel to BC_1 and the budget set increases. (b) If the price of good y falls, the budget constraint swivels out about the x-intercept and the budget set increases. (c) If all prices double, the budget constraint shifts in parallel to BC_1 and the budget set shrinks.

Another important change in economic conditions is a change in the price of one commodity. Let p_y^1 be the initial price of good y and p_y^2 be the price after it falls. The budget constraints before and after the change in the price of good y are

A CHANGE IN THE PRICE OF ONE GOOD

$$BC_1: I = p_x x + p_y^1 y \text{ and } BC_2: I = p_x x + p_y^2 y.$$

Notice that income and the price of good x are the same for both budget constraints. If the price of good y falls, $p_y^1 > p_y^2$, which implies that $p_x/p_y^1 < p_x/p_y^2$. That is, the price ratio is larger because a smaller number in the denominator of a ratio results in a larger ratio. Since the slope of the budget constraint is minus the price ratio, the budget constraint becomes steeper after the price change.

Next consider the intercepts. The x-intercept, I/p_x, remains unchanged. Changes in the price of good y have no impact on the amount of x that a consumer can purchase if all income is spent on x. The y-intercept, I/p_y, becomes larger. A lower price for y means that a consumer can purchase more of that good with the same income if nothing is spent on good x. Thus, as shown in Figure 3–2(b), the budget constraint becomes steeper and pivots about the x-intercept.

In both cases discussed above, only one parameter describing the economic environment changed. Quite often, however, two or more variables change simultaneously. For example, we might want to know what happens to the budget constraint if the price of good x and the price of good y both double.

If both prices change in the same proportion, the slope of the budget constraint does not change. However, each intercept gets smaller since both goods are more expensive. As is shown in Figure 3–2(c), the budget constraint shifts inward parallel to the original budget constraint.

We also might be interested in a situation where the economy experiences a pure inflation or pure deflation. A *pure inflation* occurs when income and all prices *increase* in the same proportion; a *pure deflation* occurs when income and all prices *decrease* in the same proportion. If either of these phenomena occurs, the budget constraint does not change because the slope and intercepts do not change.

THE BUDGET SET   A concept closely related to the budget constraint is the budget set. The **budget set** is the collection of all market baskets that a consumer can purchase with all or part of his or her income. Algebraically, the budget set is given by

$$I \geq p_x x + p_y y.$$

Graphically, the budget set is the area between the budget constraint and the axes (shown in Figure 3–1 as the shaded area). Notice that the budget set contains all market baskets on the budget constraint.

The concept of the budget set is important to understand because if it expands or contracts as income or prices change, then, *with no additional information*, we can determine whether or not the consumer is better off or worse off.

For example, in Figures 3–2(a) and 3–2(b) the budget set gets larger as the result of a change in the economic environment. This means that the collection of market baskets that the consumer can purchase after the change includes everything that was available before *and more*. Thus, after the change the consumer can be no worse off than before since he or she can always purchase the market basket purchased before the change. In these particular instances, we can conclude that an increase in income, holding relative prices constant, or a decrease in relative prices, holding money income constant, leaves the consumer no worse off.

Budget constraints play a central role in determining demand so it is important for us to understand how corporate and public policy affect an individual's budget constraint. The next example shows how to derive the budget constraint associated with a particular economic situation.

EXAMPLE 3–1

BUY ONE, GET ONE FREE

This month Bones Pizza is offering its customers a special deal on pizza—buy one, get one of equal value free. If we consider market baskets consisting of pizza and a composite good that represents all other goods, how will this special affect a typical consumer's budget constraint?

■ **SOLUTION** Assume that the market price of pizza is p_x dollars per pizza and that the consumer has I dollars to spend on pizza and other goods each month. Using the composite good convention, we describe the individual's pre-special budget constraint as

$$BC_1: I = p_x x + C$$

where x is pizza and C is expenditures on all other goods. In Figure 3–3, line AC is identical with the budget constraint BC_1. Area $0AC$ represents the budget set.

Now when the special goes into effect, the first pizza still costs p_x. This means that the first part of the consumer's budget constraint is line segment AB. In addition, however, the consumer receives another pizza free. Effectively, the price of the second pizza is zero. This means that the second part of the consumer's budget constraint is the horizontal line segment BR in Figure 3–3.

Should the individual want another pizza, he or she will have to pay the market price, p_x. Thus, the next part of the consumer's budget constraint is parallel to BC_1, RD in Figure 3–3. Continuing in this manner, we can see that the consumer's new budget constraint will be a series of steps between A and E.

Notice that the "buy one, get one free" special increases the consumer's budget set from $0AC$ to the shaded area in Figure 3–3. Therefore, without any further information we can say that the consumer will be at least as well off as he or she was prior to implementation of the special. ■

FIGURE 3-3   BUY ONE, GET ONE FREE

The pizza special shifts the budget constraint out and increases the budget set from 0AC to the shaded area.

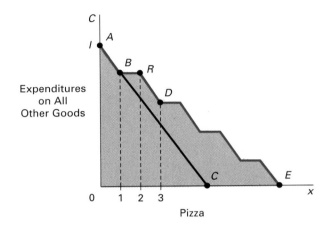

It is important to be able to construct budget constraints from a description of a particular economic situation. Several of the problems at the end of the chapter ask you to do this exercise for a variety of new circumstances. Now that we understand how to represent the collection of market baskets that consumers can afford to purchase, we can move on to discuss their preferences.

3.2 PREFERENCES OF CONSUMERS

■ So far we have learned that budget constraints describe the alternatives available to consumers, given their incomes and market prices. But which particular market basket on the budget constraint do consumers actually purchase? The answer to this question depends on their tastes or preferences for commodities. **Preferences** reflect the wants and needs of consumers; they reflect each individual's tastes for consuming different market baskets.

THE AXIOMS OF PREFERENCE

The fundamental building blocks used by economists to describe the preferences of an individual are the **Axioms of Preference.** An axiom is an assumption that can be regarded as a self-evident truth. The Axioms of Preference are the assumptions upon which the modern theory of consumer behavior rests.

In order to understand the Axioms of Preference, we need to introduce the notions of preference and indifference. Suppose we ask a typical consumer, Ms. Jones, to rank two market baskets, denoted C and D. If Ms. Jones says that she prefers basket C to basket D or considers them equally satisfactory, we say that Ms. Jones considers basket C to be *at least as good as* basket D.

Knowing if one market basket is at least as good as another allows us to define precisely what we mean by preference and indifference. If Ms. Jones says that market basket C is *preferred* to D, then this means that C is at least as good as D but D is not at least as good as C. *Preference* for one market basket over another indicates that a consumer is better off with the preferred basket. If Ms. Jones says that market basket C is *indifferent* to D, then this means that C is at least as good as D and that D is at least as good as C. *Indifference* between market baskets implies that a consumer is equally well off with either basket.

Given these notions of preference and indifference, we can set out the Axioms of Preference. These axioms describe a simplified picture of an individual's preferences and they pave the way for the development of a device that will allow us to describe preferences in a convenient manner.

For any pair of market baskets A and B, an individual's preferences are such that A is preferred to B, B is preferred to A, or the consumer is indifferent between the two baskets. In addition, if A is preferred to B, then B cannot be preferred to A; and if A is indifferent to B, then B is indifferent to A.

Axiom 1— Comparability

For any three market baskets A, B, and C, if A is preferred to B and B is preferred to C, then A is preferred to C. Similarly, if A is indifferent to B and B is indifferent to C, then A is indifferent to C.

Axiom 2— Transitivity

If market basket A contains as many units of every commodity as does basket B and more units of at least one commodity, then A is preferred to B.

Axiom 3—More is Preferred to Less

Axiom 1, sometimes referred to as the axiom of completeness, guarantees that individuals have the ability to rank all market baskets. Axiom 2 guarantees that every individual is consistent in his or her ranking of market baskets. Taken together, Axioms 1 and 2 imply that individuals can rank all market baskets consistently in order of preference.

Axiom 3—more is preferred to less—implies that commodities are "goods" and not "bads." Were they in fact bads, which are commodities that consumers do not like, more would not be preferred to less. Pollution and garbage are examples of bads. By assuming that more is preferred to less, we are not denying that bads exist, but instead are restricting our analysis to those situations where more is preferred to less. Our analysis will focus on the collection of market baskets that are relevant for the types of economic decisions we are making.

USING INDIFFERENCE CURVES TO REPRESENT PREFERENCES

The Axioms of Preference are, in general, a reasonable characterization of preferences. We can, in fact, proceed to the modern theory of consumer behavior using Axioms 1−3. For our purposes it is convenient to describe preferences graphically using indifference curves. An **indifference curve** is the collection of all market baskets yielding the same level of satisfaction. A consumer feels indifferent between any two market baskets on the same indifference curve.

Figure 3−4(a) shows a representative family of typical indifference curves. The consumer whose preferences are represented by the indifference curves in this diagram is indifferent between any two market baskets on the same indifference curve. For example, all market baskets on u_0, the indifference curve that passes through basket A, are considered equivalent to basket A because they all yield the same level of satisfaction.

PROPERTIES OF INDIFFERENCE CURVES

If indifference curves are to be an accurate representation of preferences, then at the very least they must not violate the Axioms of Preference. In fact, each axiom gives us certain information concerning indifference curves.

AN INDIFFERENCE CURVE THROUGH EVERY MARKET BASKET

Axiom 1 implies that we can rank all market baskets in order of preference. What implication does this have for indifference curves? If we can rank any two market baskets, then given any particular basket, we can always find all market baskets that are indifferent to it. This means that there is an indifference curve passing through every market basket.

INDIFFERENCE CURVES CANNOT INTERSECT

The second property of indifference curves is that they cannot intersect. If indifference curves did intersect, then Axiom 2, the axiom of transitivity, would be violated. Consider Figure 3−4(b), in which we have drawn two indifference curves, labeled u_0 and u_1, that intersect. Market basket A is on both indifference curves. From the definition of indifference curve u_0, the consumer is indifferent between basket B and basket A. However, by the definition of u_1, he or she is also indifferent between A and C. Using Axiom 2, this means that basket B should be indifferent to C. Clearly, this cannot

A REPRESENTATIVE FAMILY OF INDIFFERENCE CURVES   FIGURE 3–4

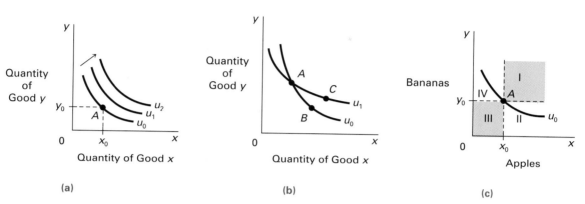

(a) Point A represents the market basket consisting of x_0 units of good x and y_0 units of good y. All market baskets on indifference curve u_0 yield the same level of satisfaction as basket A. (b) Indifference curves cannot intersect. If they did, then Axiom 2 would be violated. The consumer is indifferent between baskets B and A. The consumer is also indifferent between baskets A and C. By Axiom 2, this means that the consumer is indifferent between baskets B and C. But B and C are on two different indifference curves which is a contradiction. (c) Axiom 3 implies that indifference curves are negatively sloped. This means that satisfaction increases for movements in a northeasterly direction.

be because each indifference curve represents a distinct level of satisfaction, and baskets C and B are on different indifference curves.

The third characteristic of indifference curves is that they are negatively sloped. This property follows from Axiom 3. To see why, consider the market basket labeled A in Figure 3–4(c). It consists of x_0 apples and y_0 bananas. Suppose we are asked to determine all the market baskets that are better than A and all the baskets that are worse than A for a typical consumer, Adam, with preferences satisfying Axioms 1 to 3.

From Axioms 1 and 2, all we know is that Adam can rank all market baskets and that his ranking is consistent. However, assuming that more is preferred to less adds a great deal to our knowledge of Adam's preferences. In Figure 3–4(c), all market baskets in the shaded area labeled I are preferred to bundle A because they have at least as many apples and bananas as bundle A.

INDIFFERENCE CURVES ARE NEGATIVELY SLOPED

Similarly, market basket *A* is preferred to all baskets in the shaded area labeled III since bundle *A* contains at least as many apples and bananas as any other bundle in III.

So what does this imply about the slope of the indifference curve that passes through point *A*? Given that this indifference curve cannot pass through any point in region I or region III, it must slope from the northwest (region IV) to the southeast (region II). Thus, if more is preferred to less, indifference curves are negatively sloped. In Figure 3−4(c), u_0 is an indifference curve with this property.

There are two important implications of negatively sloped indifference curves: (i) satisfaction increases with movements in a northeasterly direction and (ii) there is a trade-off between the consumption of one good and another. For example, consider Figure 3−5 which shows a family of indifference curves representing the preferences of Simon Baggins. Simon currently has market basket *A* which consists of 10 bottles of cranberry juice and 5 wedges of Swiss cheese. Suppose we arbitrarily confiscate 3 bottles of Mr. Baggins' juice. He now has market basket *B*; because more is preferred to less, *B* is on a lower indifference curve and Baggins is worse off. Thus, in order to restore Baggins to his original level of satisfaction, while still offering him an *alternative* to market basket

FIGURE 3−5 · **SIMON BAGGINS' INDIFFERENCE CURVES**

Along any indifference curve, the consumer can substitute one good for another in such a way as to leave the consumer with the same level of satisfaction.

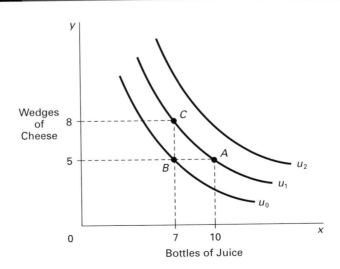

A, we must increase his holdings of cheese. Simon would then have market basket *C* on indifference curve u_1. Thus, there is a trade-off between juice and cheese consumption. One good can be substituted for another in such a way as to leave the consumer with the same level of satisfaction.

The three properties of indifference curves that we have discussed are implied by the Axioms of Preference. The fourth property of indifference curves is that they are convex to the origin (bowed in towards the origin). Note that all the indifference curves we have drawn to this point have been convex.

Convexity of indifference curves is not implied by the Axioms of Preference. Why then do we assume convex indifference curves? Essentially, convexity implies that an individual is less willing to give up relatively scarce goods and more willing to give up relatively plentiful goods—a reasonable assumption to make for most goods.

To understand this more fully, consider the preferences of Joanne, a typical consumer. In Figure 3–6, a representative indifference curve depicts Joanne's preferences for bread and milk. She is indifferent between basket *A*, consisting of x_0 pints of milk and y_0 loaves of bread, and basket *B*, consisting of x_1 pints of milk and y_1 loaves of bread. Suppose Joanne currently has market basket *A*. If she is offered $(x_1 - x_0)$ pints of milk, how many loaves of bread will she be willing to exchange to get the milk?

Since Joanne is indifferent between *A* and *B*, the maximum she will be willing to exchange is exactly the number of loaves that will restore her to her original indifference curve. Then she will be just as happy as she is now with basket *A*. In Figure 3–6 this quantity is $(y_0 - y_1)$ loaves of bread.

Now suppose we take the ratio of $(y_0 - y_1)$ to $(x_1 - x_0)$. This ratio measures the *average* rate at which she is willing to substitute milk for bread, because $(y_0 - y_1)$ is the quantity of bread that Joanne is willing to give up in exchange for $(x_1 - x_0)$ pints of milk. If we let basket *B* approach basket *A* along indifference curve u_0, the ratio $(y_0 - y_1)/(x_1 - x_0)$ approaches the slope of the tangent line, *LL'*, at point *A*. The slope of *LL'*, which is the slope of Joanne's indifference curve at point *A*, measures the *marginal* rate at which she is willing to substitute milk for bread. (See the Appendix to Chapter 2 for a review of average and marginal rates of change.)

We define the **marginal rate of substitution** between *x* and *y*, denoted MRS_{xy}, as the number of units of *y* that must be sacrificed per unit of *x* gained so as to maintain the same level of satisfaction. The marginal rate of substitution measures the rate at which an

The marginal rate of substitution is minus the slope of the indifference curve. It measures the rate at which a consumer is willing to exchange one good for another.

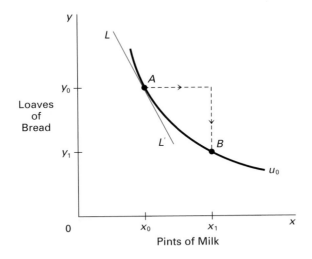

individual is willing to trade one good for another. Historically, economists have defined the MRS_{xy} as a positive number for the sake of convenience. Since typical indifference curves are negatively sloped, the marginal rate of substitution is equal to *minus* the slope of the indifference curve.

Now notice that if indifference curves are convex, then the MRS_{xy} diminishes as we move down along them. This is illustrated in Figure 3–7. At point A, $MRS_{xy} = 2$ which means that the consumer would be willing to give up two units of good y in exchange for one unit of good x. At point A the MRS_{xy} is minus the slope of tangent line TT', or $-(-2)/1$, which equals 2. Compare this to the MRS_{xy} associated with market basket B. Here $MRS_{xy} = 1/2$. The consumer is now willing to give up only half of a unit of y in exchange for one unit of good x. At point B the MRS_{xy} is minus the slope of tangent line RR', or $-(-1)/2$. As good y is exchanged for good x, the tangent line becomes flatter and the MRS_{xy} falls.

The observation that the marginal rate of substitution falls as one good is substituted for the other (resulting in convex indifference curves) is sometimes called the Law of Diminishing Marginal Rate of Substitution. This is not a "law" in the sense of an irrefutable fact but instead a *property* of preferences that economists have found to be typical of nearly all individuals. Essentially, diminishing MRS_{xy} means that as good x becomes relatively plentiful and

DIMINISHING MARGINAL RATE OF SUBSTITUTION

FIGURE 3–7

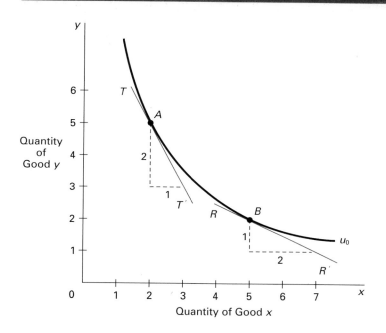

If indifference curves are convex, then the MRS diminishes as we move down along an indifference curve. At point A the MRS is equal to two. At point B the MRS is equal to one half.

good y relatively scarce, individuals are willing to give up fewer and fewer units of good y to obtain more of good x. For example, market basket A in Figure 3–7 consists of a lot more of good y and a lot less of good x than market basket B. When we compare market basket A to market basket B, good y is relatively plentiful and good x is relatively scarce. Given these circumstances, it seems reasonable to suppose that a consumer with market basket A would be willing to exchange a large quantity of good y (the plentiful good) for a small amount of good x (the scarce good); but that a consumer possessing market basket B would be willing to trade in only a small amount of good y (now scarce) for more of good x (now plentiful). We can summarize this argument by saying that the MRS_{xy} at A is greater than at B.

The shapes of indifference curves imply different relative tastes for commodities. For example, the indifference curves in Figure 3–8 represent Janet's and Jim's preferences for pizza and diet cola. Notice that Janet's indifference curves are relatively flatter than Jim's; that is, Janet's marginal rate of substitution between pizza and diet colas is relatively low. This means that Janet has a stronger

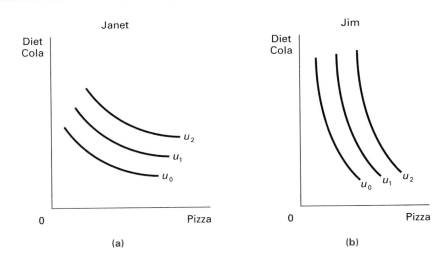

FIGURE 3–8   INDIFFERENCE CURVES FOR DIFFERENT TYPES OF PREFERENCES

Janet's indifference curves are flat compared to Jim's. This means that Janet has a stronger preference for diet colas than Jim.

preference for diet colas than Jim. Janet is willing to give up a very little amount of diet cola to obtain another pizza while Jim is willing to give up quite a lot.

Preferences are not only important for individual decision making but also for owners and managers of firms interested in introducing new products. Consider Example 3–2.

EXAMPLE 3–2

INTRODUCING A NEW PRODUCT LINE

Suppose a cereal company has hired you to develop and introduce a new breakfast cereal. Upon undertaking a marketing survey, you learn that two of the most important attributes of a good breakfast cereal are taste and nutritional content. A better taste and a greater percentage of U.S. recommended daily allowances of vitamins and minerals lead to greater demand. In addition, suppose you learn that 90% of the targeted consumer group—say children—have the preferences shown in Figure 3–9(a), while 10% have those shown in Figure 3–9(b). Knowing that better taste and nutritional value are both costly, how would you decide how much of each attribute to offer?

PREFERENCES FOR BREAKFAST CEREAL ATTRIBUTES   FIGURE 3-9

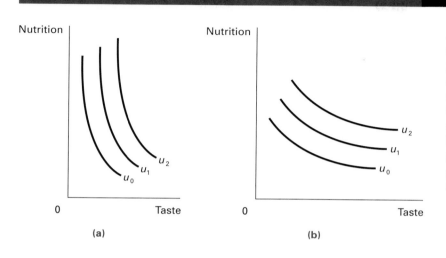

(a)   (b)

If 90% of the targeted consumer group have preferences that can be represented by the indifference curves in (a) while 10% have those shown in (b), then it may be profitable to offer a new cereal that tastes good rather than one that is highly nutritious.

■ **SOLUTION** To reach your decision you would need to assess both the relative costs of improving each attribute and consumer preferences for each attribute. The indifference curves shown in Figure 3–8(a) indicate that 90% of the targeted consumer group have a relatively strong preference for taste. These consumers are willing to sacrifice a lot of nutrition for a little better taste. The indifference curves shown in Figure 3–8(b), by contrast, show that only a small minority prefer nutrition to better taste. They are willing to tolerate a tasteless cereal if it is good for them.

Now combining this information concerning consumer preferences with the information concerning the cost of providing each attribute, you should be able to choose exactly what type of new cereal to introduce in order to maximize its chances of success. If, for example, it costs the same to improve the nutritional value as it does to enhance taste, then you should offer a cereal with a lot of sugar! ■

Actually, the cereal industry began in the 1800s when Dr. John H. Kellogg, his brother Will K. Kellogg, and C. W. Post developed products based on consumer preferences. As director of a health spa, Dr. Kellogg fed his patients oatmeal for breakfast. One of those patients, C. W. Post, decided to go into business for himself. Post added sugar to his cereal to make it taste better and marketed the product as Post Grape-Nuts. The Kelloggs countered by sweetening their cereal, and the breakfast food industry was born. (W. Nickels, J. and F. McHugh, *Understanding Business*, 2d. ed., Urwin, 1990.)

An analysis of consumer preferences is undertaken all the time by firms interested in introducing new products. For example, General Motors' Saturn line of small cars (see Chapter 1) was designed specifically to satisfy the preferences of consumers who currently prefer Japanese autos. Designers focused on such things as an interior that would look and feel like the imports, a four-cylinder engine with good gasoline mileage and good acceleration, and an automatic transmission that could shift smoothly and quietly.

USING UTILITY FUNCTIONS TO REPRESENT PREFERENCES

Indifference curves provide a convenient way to represent preferences *graphically*. Economists discussing the theory of consumer choice often use utility functions to describe preferences algebraically. In this section, we will explain the use of utility functions in microeconomics and how they relate to indifference curves.

Each indifference curve representing the preferences of a consumer corresponds to a particular level of satisfaction. Once the consumer has ranked all market baskets, we can think of assigning each basket a number representing the level of satisfaction associated with it. Baskets that have the same ranking—that are on the same indifference curve—are assigned the same numerical value; baskets with higher rankings are assigned higher values; and baskets with lower rankings are assigned lower values. Economists call the numbers assigned to each market basket the *utility* associated with the basket. A utility index is a convenient way of keeping track of the ordering or relative ranking of different market baskets.

The scheme by which numbers are assigned to different market baskets is usually represented by a **utility function,** denoted by $u = u(x,y)$. This function assigns a number to each basket according to the following rule: given any two market baskets, $A = (x_1,y_1)$ and $B = (x_2,y_2)$, then $u(x_1,y_1) > u(x_2,y_2)$ when A is preferred to B, and $u(x_1,y_1) = u(x_2,y_2)$ when A is indifferent to B. That is, the numerical ranking preserves the ordering of market baskets according to the preferences of the consumer.

CARDINAL AND ORDINAL RANKINGS

At first glance, it appears as though utility functions generate a *cardinal* ranking of market baskets. A cardinal ranking is like a score on an examination, where the number itself has significance. If Bill scores 90 and Beth 100, then not only is Bill ranked lower than Beth but also the fact that he is 10 points lower instead of just one is significant. If utility functions were used to generate a cardinal ranking, then this approach to consumer choice would be much more restrictive than the indifference curve approach used in the text. Remember, when we use indifference curves to represent preferences we never require an individual to say by how much one basket is preferred to another but only whether or not it ranks higher.

In fact, using utility functions to assign a numerical value to market baskets need not represent a cardinal ranking but can instead represent an *ordinal* ranking. An ordinal ranking is one for which rank is important but the particular index itself is not. For example, hardness represents an ordinal ranking for geologists who assign the number 1 to the softest material and 10 to the hardest. They do not mean that the hardest material is 10 times harder than the softest. Their scale simply tells them if one material is at all harder than another, *not* how much harder. Any arbitrary assignment of numbers to materials will do as long as higher numbers are assigned to harder materials. Geologists could use randomly selected numbers between 10 and 100, 100 and 1,000, or 1,000 and 10,000, and it would make no difference.

Utility functions provide the same type of ranking of market baskets as the geologists' hardness scale does for materials. It does not matter whether we assign numbers between 1 and 10 or numbers between 10 and 20 as long as the scheme preserves the ranking of the baskets.

As an example of a utility function, suppose that a consumer's preferences, defined over goods x and y, are represented by the function $u = xy$. Indifference curves can be found by determining the different combinations of x and y that yield the same utility index. For example, if $u = 10$, then $y = 10/x$ is the equation describing the indifference curve. This indifference curve is shown in Figure 3–10.

UTILITY FUNCTIONS AND INDIFFERENCE CURVES

The change in utility associated with a change in the level of consumption of one good, holding the consumption of all other goods constant, is called **marginal utility.** Marginal utility is denoted MU and measures the additional utility an individual receives when he or she acquires a little more of one good. For example, the marginal utility of good x is the increase in utility due to a small increase in the amount of good x, holding quantities of all other goods constant.

Oftentimes, we can use the concept of marginal utility to help us understand and interpret changes in the marginal rate of substitution. Since the MU_x measures the change in utility as the quantity of good x changes by a small amount, and MU_y measures the change in utility as the quantity of y changes by a small amount,

FIGURE 3-10 | UTILITY FUNCTIONS AND INDIFFERENCE CURVES

u	x	y
10	1	10
10	2	5
10	5	2
10	10	1

Indifference curves associated with the utility function u = xy are obtained by graphing the equation y = u/x.

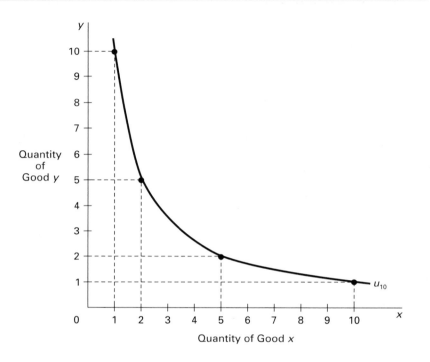

Quantity of Good y

Quantity of Good x

these are the *utility prices* of both goods, and the ratio of the two measures the rate at which the consumer is willing to exchange one good for the other. Thus,

$$MRS_{xy} = MU_x/MU_y.$$

EXAMPLE 3-3

MARGINAL UTILITIES AND THE MARGINAL RATE OF SUBSTITUTION

After extensive research, it has been determined that John's preferences for coffee and tea can be represented by the following utility function: u = xy, where x is the quantity of coffee, y the quantity of tea, and u an index of the level of satisfaction. (a) How would John rank a basket containing three cups of coffee and three cups of tea to a basket containing one cup of coffee and four cups of tea? (b) If John currently is consuming three cups of coffee and three cups of tea per day, would he be willing to exchange two cups of tea for one cup of coffee? Would he be willing to exchange one cup of tea for three cups of coffee? Illustrate. (c) If the marginal utilities associated with this utility function are $MU_x = y$ and $MU_y = x$, calculate John's marginal rate of substitution between x and y if he has three cups of coffee and tea.

■ **SOLUTION** (a) Let market basket A consist of three cups of coffee and three cups of tea and market basket B consist of one cup of coffee and four cups of tea. This question asks how an individual with preferences given by $u = xy$ will rank A and B. To answer, we must calculate the utility associated with each market basket. For basket A we have $u = xy = 3 \cdot 3 = 9$ and for basket B we have $u = xy = 1 \cdot 4 = 4$. Since $9 > 4$, John prefers market basket A to B.

(b) If John currently has three cups of tea and coffee, would he be willing to trade two cups of tea for one cup of coffee? If such a trade occurred, John would end up with four cups of coffee and one cup of tea. If he were better off with this market basket, call it C, he would be willing to make the trade. The utility associated with market basket C is: $u = xy = 4 \cdot 1 = 4$. Since $4 < 9$, he would not trade. Notice that market basket C is in fact on an indifference curve below u_1. This is shown in Figure 3–11, where indifference curve u_1 represents all market baskets indifferent to A. John would be willing to trade if he could obtain any market basket in the shaded area of the graph since he would then be better off.

However, in answer to the second part of (b), John *would* be willing to exchange one cup of tea for three cups of coffee. Such a trade would yield market basket D in Figure 3–11, which consists of six cups of coffee and two cups of tea. To verify that D is on a higher indifference curve, we simply calculate the utility associated with D: $u = xy = 6 \cdot 2 = 12$. Since $12 > 9$, John is better off with market basket D.

(c) Finally, we are asked to calculate the marginal rate of substitution of coffee for tea when John has market basket A. We have

$$MRS_{xy} = MU_x/MU_y = y/x \ 3/3 = 1;$$

that is, the rate at which John is willing to exchange coffee for tea is one. ■

Example 3–3 can be used to illustrate a minor problem that arises when we interpret the MRS as measuring the rate at which an

FIGURE 3–11   JOHN'S PREFERENCES FOR COFFEE AND TEA

John prefers basket A to baskets B and C because it is on a higher indifference curve. However, basket D is preferred to basket A.

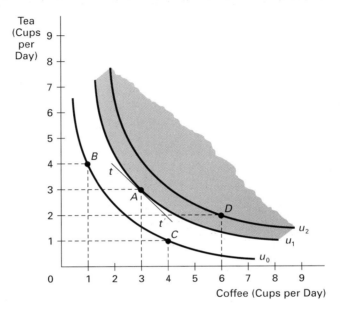

individual is willing to exchange one good for another and then apply it to discrete changes. Looking back at Figure 3–11, if John has market basket A, then the $MRS_{xy} = 1$, which means that minus the slope of tangent line tt' is one. But in answering part (b) of Example 3–3, we found that John would not exchange one cup of tea for one cup of coffee, because he would end up on a lower indifference curve! This is because the MRS becomes smaller as we move down along the indifference curve; that is, it takes more than one cup of coffee to compensate for the loss of one cup of tea. This is a dilemma that we cannot solve but only allow for when explaining discrete changes using marginal concepts.

3.3 CONSUMER CHOICE

■ Indifference curves represent a consumer's preferences for different market baskets. The budget constraint shows which market baskets are affordable. Combining these two concepts, we can determine which market basket the consumer will actually purchase.

MAXIMIZING SATISFACTION

We begin by assuming that the consumer will choose to purchase, from those market baskets that are affordable, the one that *maximizes satisfaction*. In other words, given a limited income and the prevailing prices, the consumer will select the market basket that is on the highest possible indifference curve.

Figure 3–12 depicts this problem. We measure the quantity of food (good x) on the horizontal axis and the quantity of clothing (good y) on the vertical axis. Indifference curves u_0, u_1, and u_2 represent the consumer's preferences. Budget constraint BC_1 represents the economic environment.

Since satisfaction increases as we move in a northeast direction, the consumer maximizes satisfaction by choosing market basket C on indifference curve u_1. This market basket yields the greatest level of satisfaction, given that it must be chosen from the budget constraint, and is called the **optimal market basket.** The optimal market basket consists of x_0 units of food and y_0 units of clothing. Even though the individual would prefer any market basket on u_2, none of these is affordable. Every other market basket on the budget constraint is affordable, but only C yields the greatest level of satisfaction. For example, the consumer can purchase basket H, but this basket is on indifference curve u_0, which represents a lower level of satisfaction.

THE OPTIMAL MARKET BASKET   **FIGURE 3–12**

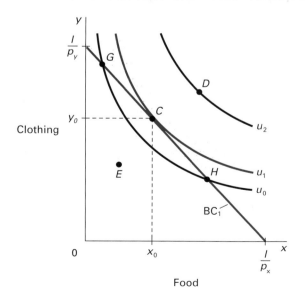

Point C is the market basket that maximizes satisfaction. It is called the optimal market basket. The optimal market basket is the point where Miki's indifference curve is tangent to her budget constraint—that is, where the MRS_{xy} is equal to the price ratio.

When satisfaction is maximized, the highest indifference curve attainable is the one that is tangent to the budget constraint. In Figure 3–12, indifference curve u_1 is tangent to budget constraint BC_1 at C. This means that satisfaction is maximized when the slope of the indifference curve is equal to the slope of the budget constraint. Since these slopes equal minus the marginal rate of substitution and minus the price ratio, respectively, the consumer's optimal market basket must satisfy the following condition:

$$MRS_{xy} = p_x/p_y. \qquad (3.2)$$

Equation (3.2) is very important because it gives us insights into how individuals make decisions. The marginal rate of substitution, on the one hand, is the rate at which an individual is willing to exchange one good for the other. It measures the maximum amount of clothing that the consumer is willing to give up for an additional unit of food or, in other words, the *marginal benefit* of consuming one more unit of food in terms of clothing. The price ratio, on the other hand, is the rate at which an individual can exchange one good for another in the marketplace. It measures the minimum amount of y that must be given up in order to purchase an additional unit of x or, in other words, the *marginal cost* of consuming an additional unit of food in terms of clothing. At point C, marginal benefit is equal to marginal cost.

This line of reasoning can explain why market basket G, for example, does not maximize satisfaction. At point G, the marginal rate of substitution is greater than the price ratio. Thus, at this point the marginal benefit of consuming an additional unit of food is greater than the marginal cost, and the consumer is better off consuming more food and less clothing.

EXAMPLE 3–4

FINDING THE OPTIMAL MARKET BASKET

Kirk Calloway likes to play golf and tennis. His preferences for golf and tennis can be represented by utility function $u = xy$, where x and y are rounds of golf and sets of tennis per month respectively. The associated marginal rate of substitution between golf and tennis along a representative indifference curve is given by $MRS_{xy} = y/x$ (see Example 3–3). Kirk is currently attending dental school and has an income of \$90 per month. The price of one round of golf is $15 and the price of playing one hour of tennis is $1.00. Kirk currently plays one round of golf per month and 75 hours of tennis. Is Kirk maximizing satisfaction, given his budget constraint? If not, explain what he should do.

■ **SOLUTION** We must determine the quantities of golf and tennis Kirk should play if he wants to maximize satisfaction. We already know the equation defining Kirk's MRS along any indifference curve, his budget constraint, and his current "consumption" of both goods. Kirk is doing the best he can do when

$$\text{MRS}_{xy} = p_x/p_y \qquad\qquad \text{or when}$$

$$y/x = 15/1 = 15.$$

Without going any further we can solve part of the problem. From the equation above, Kirk is clearly maximizing satisfaction when he consumes 15 times as much y as x. Thus, his current market basket of one round of golf and 75 hours of tennis is not optimal. When $x = 1$ and $y = 75$, the marginal rate of substitution is greater than the price ratio, $\text{MRS} = 75 > 15 = p_x/p_y$, and Kirk should play more golf and less tennis.

This point is clear in Figure 3–13. Market basket B on indifference curve u_0 is Kirk's initial market basket. At B, the indifference curve is steeper than the budget constraint. In order to maximize satisfaction, Kirk must move down the budget constraint, substituting tennis for golf until he reaches point A.

Now we can determine precisely how much of each good he should consume. Kirk's budget constraint is

$$90 = 15x + 1y.$$

Solving the optimality condition $y/x = 15$ for y gives $y = 15x$. Substituting this into the budget constraint and solving for x gives the optimal number of rounds of golf per month: $x^* = 3$. Plugging this value for x back into the budget constraint gives the optimal hours of tennis per month: $y^* = 45$. Thus, Mr. Calloway should adjust his market basket by increasing his consumption of golf from one to three rounds per month and decreasing his consumption of tennis from 75 to 45 hours per month. ■

We can use the concept of marginal utility to give yet another interpretation of the condition guaranteeing that consumers maximize satisfaction (utility). Recall that the marginal rate of substitution of good x for good y is equal to the ratio of the marginal utilities

MARGINAL UTILITY AND THE OPTIMALITY CONDITION

FIGURE 3–13   KIRK'S OPTIMIZATION PROBLEM

If the MRS is greater than the price ratio, as at point B, then Kirk increases his satisfaction by substituting golf for tennis. This will continue to be true until he attains market basket A.

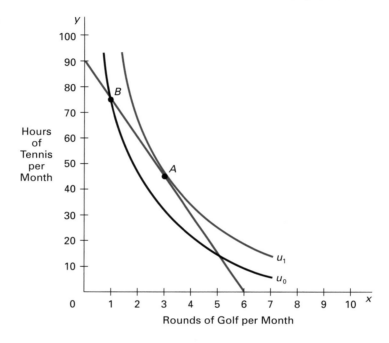

of the goods; that is, $MRS_{xy} = MU_x/MU_y$. Knowing this allows us to write the condition for maximizing satisfaction as follows:

$$MU_x/MU_y = p_x/p_y.$$

Now let us rearrange this equation slightly. Dividing both sides of the equation by p_x and multiplying both sides by MU_y gives

$$MU_x/p_x = MU_y/p_y.$$

That is, the consumer is maximizing satisfaction when the marginal utility of the last dollar spent on good x, MU_x/p_x, is just equal to the marginal utility of the last dollar spent on good y.

If this relation were not true, then the consumer could rearrange his consumption pattern and achieve a higher level of utility. For example, if $MU_x/p_x > MU_y/p_y$ then one dollar less spent on good y causes total utility to fall by MU_y/p_y, and one dollar more spent on good x causes total utility to increase by MU_x/p_x. Since $MU_x/p_x > MU_y/p_y$, total utility increases. Thus spending $1 less on y and $1 more on x achieves higher utility with no extra expenditure.

When preferences are such that a consumer purchases some of both goods, then equality between the MRS and the price ratio characterizes the optimal market basket. However, consumers often do not consume positive amounts of every good. For example, many individuals who would like to take a vacation to Australia or own a chalet in the Alps choose not to purchase these goods. The indifference curve analysis can explain why this is the case.

Figure 3–14 illustrates a situation in which a consumer purchases only one of two available goods. Faced with budget constraint BC_1, the consumer chooses to buy market basket A on indifference curve u_1. This is called a *corner solution* because the optimal market basket appears at the corner of the person's budget set. At A, the MRS is less than the price ratio, which means that if the consumer had more broccoli to give up, he or she would happily trade it for more steak. In other words, at point A the marginal benefit of consuming the first unit of broccoli is less than the marginal cost, and so not even the first unit is worth buying.

When a corner solution arises, the MRS is not necessarily equal to the price ratio. This highlights the importance of *both* preferences *and* relative prices for predicting the effects on consumer behavior of changing economic conditions. If the price ratio is substantially greater than the MRS, then a small reduction in the price of broccoli, holding income and the price of steak constant, will have no impact on the consumer's choice of market basket.

A CORNER SOLUTION

A CORNER SOLUTION   **FIGURE 3–14**

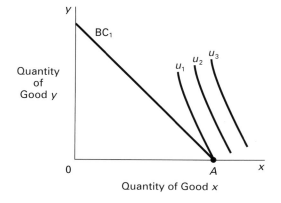

It is possible that the consumer will not purchase any amount of one of the goods. In this case, the optimal market basket lies at one of the intercepts of the budget constraint, with all income being spent on one good. Here A is the optimal market basket— and the consumer purchases only steak.

SUMMARY

1. The theory of consumer choice derives from the assumption that each individual purchases the market basket that maximizes satisfaction, given his or her budget constraint.

2. The budget constraint is the collection of market baskets that can be purchased if all income is spent. The slope of the budget constraint is the negative of the price ratio and it measures the rate at which individuals are allowed to trade one good for another.

3. The budget set is the collection of market baskets that a consumer can purchase with all or part of a given income. The budget set is the area between the budget constraint and the axes.

4. The preferences of an individual consumer are assumed to satisfy the Axioms of Preference and can be represented by a family of indifference curves.

5. An indifference curve is the collection of market baskets that yield the same level of satisfaction. Indifference curves are negatively sloped, they do not intersect, and they are convex to the origin.

6. Minus the slope of an indifference curve is the marginal rate of substitution between goods. The marginal rate of substitution measures the rate at which an individual is willing to exchange one good for another.

7. Utility functions can also be used to describe preferences. Utility is a measure of the level of satisfaction associated with any market basket.

8. The optimal market basket is the combination of goods that maximizes a consumer's satisfaction, given his or her limited income. An individual consumer is maximizing satisfaction when the marginal rate of substitution is equal to the price ratio, provided the budget constraint is satisfied. This optimality condition illustrates the fundamental principle of marginal analysis: individuals maximize satisfaction when the marginal cost of consuming an additional unit of a good is just equal to the marginal benefit.

KEY TERMS

Budget Constraint
Market Basket
Price Ratio
Composite Good
Budget Set
Preferences

Axioms of Preference
Indifference Curve
Marginal Rate of Substitution
Utility Function
Marginal Utility
Optimal Market Basket

1. What is the budget constraint and how does the concept of opportunity cost relate to it.

2. An individual has a fixed income and purchases two goods, x and y, at market prices. The equations below give the budget constraints for four different cases.
   a) Graph each of the budget constraints and label the corresponding budget sets.
   b) For each of the cases, determine the income and prices that are consistent with the budget constraint.

   (i) $10 = 4x + 2y$ (ii) $y = 2 - 6x$
   (iii) $26x = 72 - 72y$ (iv) $x = 5$

3. Suppose a hurricane damages a large portion of the sugarcane crop and as a result the world supply of sugar falls sharply and shortages ensue. In addition, suppose the government of a small country has decided to freeze the price of sugar at its pre-disaster levels and to ration sugar. It issues every citizen 10 coupons and each coupon permits the bearer to purchase one pound of sugar. Assuming that there are only two goods in this country, sugar and potatoes, and that it is illegal to buy and sell coupons, determine the impact of this rationing scheme on a typical individual's budget constraint and budget set.

4. Consider a consumer with a money income of $100. Assume this consumer purchases two goods x and y with prices $p_x = 10 and $p_y = 5 respectively. It is wartime and the government has decided to ration good x. Each consumer receives five ration stamps, one of which is required to purchase one unit of x.
   a) If ration stamps cannot be traded for money, graph the consumer's budget set.
   b) If a black market for stamps develops and the price of stamps on the black market is $10, graph the new budget set.
   c) If the government legalizes stamp trading, what will happen to the budget constraint?

5. An individual with income I has available to him two goods a and b at prices p_a and p_b respectively. Describe his budget constraint and budget set. Now suppose a lump-sum fee is legislated which requires that he pay N dollars when he buys any amount of a. He is not required to pay any fee if he does not buy any of a. Describe the new budget constraint and budget set.

6. Mr. Strange can join a club for an annual fee of $20. If he joins, he can purchase golf balls at 40% off the retail price. Compare Mr. Strange's budget constraints if he joins and if he does not join.

7. "Yesterday I won $1,000 in the lottery. Now I can afford to eat out more often." Evaluate this statement in terms of this individual's budget constraint.

8. Chris belongs to a tennis club.
   a) She pays $100 per month in dues and can play as many hours of tennis per month as she desires at no additional charge. Describe her budget constraint.
   b) Suppose the club discontinues the monthly charge and instead charges $5 per hour for tennis. Describe her new budget constraint and compare it to the old one.

9. Ms. Willis likes to give to charities.
   a) If she can deduct contributions from income to arrive at her taxable income, describe Ms. Willis' budget constraint when the income tax rate is 5%.
   b) Repeat this exercise assuming that the tax rate is 10%. Is the budget set larger or smaller?

10. Assume a two-good world, x and y, with $p_y = \$1$. There is the following quantity discount on good x: for the first 10 units, $p_x = \$4$ for all units bought and for 11 units or more, $p_x = \$2.00$ for all units bought. Illustrate the budget constraint.

11. In many fast-food restaurants, soft drinks are available in small (6 oz.), medium (8 oz.), and large (12 oz.) sizes. In addition, the price per ounce usually falls the larger the size. Describe the budget set of an individual who purchases at most one soft drink per visit, if a small drink costs $.75, a medium costs $.90, and a large costs $1.20.

12. In the mid-1970s, OPEC imposed an oil embargo against the U.S. The flow of oil was temporarily halted and a gasoline shortage ensued. If service stations limited consumers to 15 gallons per visit, illustrate a typical consumer's budget constraint before and after the embargo.

13. Suppose that in order to reduce air pollution, the government imposes an excise tax (that is, a per-unit tax) of $.10 per gallon purchased. Describe an individual's budget constraint and budget set before and after the tax.

14. Discuss a situation where an individual's preferences might violate
    a) Axiom 1;
    b) Axiom 2; or
    c) Axiom 3.

15. Roy drinks one cup of coffee each morning before going to the office. Roy is very particular about his coffee. For each six ounces of coffee he adds exactly one teaspoon of sugar.
    a) Graph Roy's preferences regarding sugar and coffee using indifference curves.
    b) Are Roy's preferences consistent with the Axioms of Preference?

16. Molly enjoys going out each Friday night for pizza and soda. While Molly prefers more soda to less, she doesn't care whether she drinks Coca-Cola or 7-Up as long as it is low-calorie soda. Illustrate Molly's preferences for low-calorie Coca-Cola and 7-Up.

17. In this chapter we have discussed the preferences of individuals and made several general assumptions about these preferences. Since some decisions are made by groups rather than individuals, we might also want to think about the preferences of groups and how they relate to those of individuals. To do so, let us consider three young professionals, Debbie, Donna, and Richard, who get together for dinner once a month. This month they are considering a French, Italian, and German restaurant. They have decided to choose this month's venue by voting on each alternative. Debbie, Donna, and Richard have preferences as follows:

    Debbie: French is preferred to Italian and
              Italian is preferred to German.
    Donna: German is preferred to French and
              French is preferred to Italian.
    Richard: Italian is preferred to German and
              German is preferred to French.

    The group will go to only one restaurant.
    a) If they take a vote on each pair of alternatives, and if majority rule determines the winner, what restaurant will the group visit?
    b) Based on this example, do you think that transitivity is a natural assumption for group preferences?

18. What is the marginal rate of substitution between two goods? In what sense does it measure the rate at which an individual is willing to exchange one good for another?

19. After extensive research it has been determined that Joe's preferences for milk and cookies can be represented by a utility function given by the equation $u = x^2 y$, where x is the quantity

of milk, y is the quantity of cookies, and u is an index of the level of satisfaction.

a) How would Joe rank a basket containing three glasses of milk and three cookies to a basket containing two glasses of milk and four cookies?

b) If Joe currently is consuming two glasses of milk and two cookies per day, would he be willing to exchange one glass of milk for one cookie? Explain.

20. It is a little-known fact that Roy recently graduated from the Nelson–Rogers Academy of Country and Western Dance. After subjecting himself to a series of exhausting interviews, Roy indicates that he is equally ecstatic after indulging in the following combinations of two popular dances:

Two-Step	Cotton-Eye-Joe
12 hours	1 hour
6 hours	4 hours
3 hours	7 hours
1 hours	10 hours

a) Illustrate Roy's preferences with an indifference curve.

b) Is the combination of 7 hours of Cotton-Eye-Joe and 1 hour of Two-Step as pleasing to Roy as any of the above?

c) What about 6 hours of each?

d) How will this indifference curve change if suddenly Roy loses any desire for the Two-Step?

e) How will it change if the price of doing the Two-Step goes up?

f) What does the slope of the curve mean?

21. An individual consumes two goods x and y. The price of x is $5 and the price of y is $7. The marginal rate of substitution of x for y is 10/28. The consumer spends her entire income on x and y. What should the consumer do? Explain.

22. a) State the condition that must hold if an individual maximizes satisfaction given his or her budget constraint.

b) Interpret this condition.

23. Johnny B. Goode purchases two types of records, hard rock and punk. Currently a hard rock LP costs $5 and a punk LP costs $8. Johnny spends all his income on records. If Johnny's MRS between hard rock LPs and punk LPs is 5/2, should he spend more or less on punk music?

Deaton, A., and J. Meullbauer. 1980. *Economics and Consumer Behavior*. Cambridge: Cambridge University Press.

Hicks, J. R. 1946. *Value and Capital*. 2nd ed. Oxford: The Clarendon Press.

Kreps, D. 1990. *A Course in Microeconomic Theory*. Princeton: Princeton University Press.

Varian, H. R. 1992. *Microeconomic Analysis*. 3rd ed. New York: Norton.

REFERENCES

CONSUMER THEORY: A CALCULUS APPROACH

A3.1 INDIFFERENCE CURVES

Suppose the utility function $u = u(x,y)$ represents the preferences of an individual consumer for goods x and y. Given this information, we can use implicit functions to derive the expression given in the text relating the marginal rate of substitution to marginal utilities. First, note that the marginal utility of good x is the partial derivative of the utility function with respect to good x, and the marginal utility of good y is the partial derivative of the utility function with respect to good y:

$$MU_x = \frac{\partial u(x,y)}{\partial x} \text{ and } MU_y = \frac{\partial u(x,y)}{\partial y}.$$

We use partial derivatives here because the marginal utility of one good is calculated holding the other good fixed.

Now, in order to derive the marginal rate of substitution we must first find the function that describes an indifference curve. That is, we must find a function relating y to x for a given level of utility. If we had a specific utility function we could do this by solving it *explicitly* for y as a function of x and u. Since we do not have a specific utility function, however, we can only solve it *implicitly* for y as a function of x. This implicit function is denoted by $y = \phi(x,u^0)$, where u^0 is the utility level associated with the indifference curve in question.

Substituting this function into the utility function yields an identity:

$$u^0 \equiv u[x, \phi(x,u^0)].$$

This is an identity because for each value of x the function $\phi(x,u^0)$ tells us how much y we need to get on indifference curve u^0.

Now we can differentiate both sides of this identity with respect to x. When doing this, however, we must be careful. Notice that x appears in two places in the identity. This means that changing x will change the function in two ways—by changing both the first and the second arguments. Thus, when differentiating we must take account of both changes. This gives

$$0 = \frac{\partial u(x,y)}{\partial x} + \frac{\partial u(x,y)}{\partial y}\frac{\partial y}{\partial x}.$$

Solving this last equation for $\dfrac{\partial y}{\partial x}$ gives the slope of the indifference curve:

$$\frac{\partial y}{\partial x} = -\frac{\partial u(x,y)}{\partial x} \bigg/ \frac{\partial u(x,y)}{\partial y}. \qquad (A3.1)$$

Just as we stated in the text, the marginal rate of substitution is equal to the ratio of marginal utilities.

EXAMPLE A3–1

Suppose that an individual's preferences are represented by the utility function $u = x^a y^b$. This is called a *Cobb–Douglas utility function*. Derive the marginal rate of substitution associated with these preferences.

■ **SOLUTION** We could do this one of two ways. First we could solve the equation $u^0 = x^a y^b$ for y as a function of x and u^0 and then take the derivative of that function with respect to x. Alternatively we could calculate marginal utilities and substitute into the equation derived above. Since the latter seems easier, we will try that approach. We have

$$MU_x = ax^{a-1}y^b \text{ and } MU_y = bx^a y^{b-1} \qquad \text{and}$$

$$MRS_{xy} = -MU_x/MU_y = (a/b)(y/x) \quad ■$$

A3.2 DERIVING THE FIRST ORDER CONDITIONS USING CALCULUS

We can summarize the consumer's optimization as follows:

$$\max_{x,y} u = u(x,y)$$

$$\text{subject to } I = p_x x + p_y y.$$

This is a constrained optimization problem, so we can use the Lagrange multiplier method to derive the optimality conditions.

The Lagrangian for this problem is

$$L = u(x,y) + \lambda(I - p_x x - p_y y).$$

Differentiating this function with respect to x, y, and λ gives the first order conditions:

$$\frac{\partial L}{\partial x} = \frac{\partial u(x,y)}{\partial x} - \lambda p_x = 0, \qquad (A3.2)$$

$$\frac{\partial L}{\partial y} = \frac{\partial u(x,y)}{\partial y} - \lambda p_y = 0, \qquad (A3.3)$$

$$\frac{\partial L}{\partial \lambda} = I - p_x x - p_y y = 0. \qquad (A3.4)$$

Now if we solve equation (A3.2) for λ and substitute into equation (A3.3) we have the optimality condition discussed in the text:

$$\frac{\partial u(x,y)}{\partial x} / \frac{\partial u(x,y)}{\partial y} = p_x/p_y. \qquad (A3.5)$$

INDIVIDUAL AND MARKET DEMAND

LEARNING OBJECTIVES

After completing Chapter 4 you should be able to do the following:

■ Explain how to derive an individual consumer's demand curve using the theory of consumer choice.

■ Discuss how a change in income or prices affects demand.

■ Define normal and inferior and describe the types of goods that might fall into each of these categories.

■ Define substitutes and complements and describe the types of goods that might fall into each of these categories.

■ Compare the income and substitution effects associated with a price change.

■ Aggregate individual demands to obtain market demand.

■ Explain the relation between the price elasticity of demand and total revenue.

■ Illustrate how demand curves can measure the net benefit to consumers of purchasing a good at the market price.

EXAMPLES

■ **4-1** Cobb–Douglas Preferences and Demand Functions

■ **4-2** Excise Taxes and Lump-Sum Taxes

■ **4-3** Market Demand and Revenues

■ **4-4** Using the Price Elasticity of Demand

■ **4-5** Consumer Surplus and the Gasoline Tax

In Chapter 3 we discussed a theoretical model that uses indifference curves and budget constraints to explain consumer choice. We saw that a consumer chooses from among those market baskets that are affordable the one that maximizes satisfaction. In this chapter, we use the theory of consumer choice to investigate demand. We begin by examining the demands of individual consumers. Using indifference curves and budget constraints, we show how to derive a consumer's demand curve for some good and how changes in income or in the prices of other goods affect it. Next, we show how the individual demand curves of all consumers of a particular commodity can be aggregated to obtain the market demand curve. We also discuss how the concept of elasticity measures the sensitivity of market demand to changes in prices or income. Finally, we illustrate how demand curves can measure the net benefit consumers receive when they purchase a product.

INDIVIDUAL DEMAND
■ In order to derive a consumer's demand curve for some good, we begin by examining how a change in the price of that good affects the optimal market basket. Suppose that Ben Bailey, a typical consumer, eats potatoes and meat. Ben currently has an income of I_0 dollars per week and the prices of potatoes and meat are p_x^0 and p_y^0 respectively. Given these prices and Ben's income, his initial budget constraint, BC_0, is given by

$$BC_0: I = p_x^0 x + p_y y,$$

where x denotes the quantity of potatoes and y the quantity of meat. As Figure 4–1(a) shows, given this budget constraint Ben chooses market basket D on indifference curve u_0. Market basket D contains x_0 pounds of potatoes and y_0 pounds of meat.

Now suppose the price of potatoes falls to p_x^1. As a result of this change, the price ratio falls, $(p_x^1/p_y) < (p_x^0/p_y)$, and the budget constraint rotates out about point B to BC_1. Confronted with this new budget constraint, Ben maximizes satisfaction by choosing market basket E on indifference curve u_1, and his consumption of potatoes increases from x_0 to x_1 pounds in response to the lower price. If the price of potatoes falls even further to p_x^2, the budget constraint becomes even flatter, (BC_2 in Figure 4–1(a)), Ben chooses market basket F, and he eats even more potatoes.

Continuing in this manner, we can vary the price of potatoes and determine the market basket that Ben will choose at any price, given his preferences. Remember that a different budget constraint corresponds to every different price and that Ben will always choose the market basket that maximizes satisfaction—that is, the market basket on the highest indifference curve (or the optimal market basket). The curve connecting each of these commodity

THE PRICE–CONSUMPTION CURVE

FIGURE 4–1

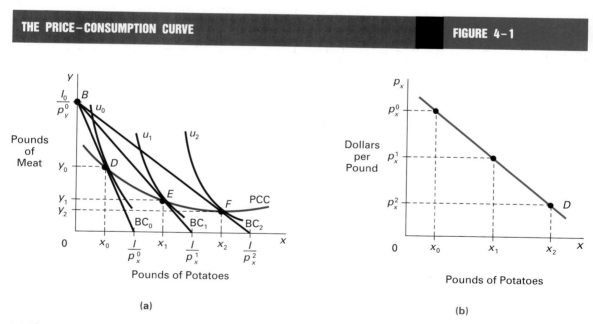

(a)

(b)

(a) The price–consumption curve shows how the optimal market basket changes as the price of one good changes. It contains all the information needed to derive a demand curve. (b) The demand curve relates quantity consumed to market price. For all documented real-world commodities, the Law of Demand holds; that is, demand curves are negatively sloped. As price increases, quantity demanded falls.

bundles, PCC in Figure 4−1(a), is called the price−consumption curve. The **price−consumption curve** shows how the optimal market basket changes as the price of potatoes changes, holding income and the price of meat constant.

THE INDIVIDUAL CONSUMER'S DEMAND CURVE

The price−consumption curve is important because it conveys all the information necessary to derive the individual's demand curve. Recall that a **demand curve** is the graphical representation of demand—it represents the relation between the quantity a consumer is willing and able to purchase and price, when all other factors influencing consumption do not change. In Figure 4−1(b), D denotes the consumer's demand curve for potatoes. This means D shows the quantity of potatoes Ben will purchase at each different price, provided income and the price of meat do not change.

We obtain the demand curve from the price−consumption curve in the following manner. Returning to Figure 4−1(a), we see that, given preferences, income, and the price of meat, the quantity of potatoes purchased varies from x_0 to x_1 to x_2 as the price of potatoes changes from p_x^0 to p_x^1 to p_x^2. If we plot these price−quantity pairs in Figure 4−1(b) and then connect them with a line, we map out the demand curve. It is important to remember that along any particular demand curve, income and prices of other goods are held constant.

THE LAW OF DEMAND

If the price of potatoes changes, holding income and the price of meat constant, we observe movements along the demand curve. We call these changes in *quantity demanded*. The demand curve in Figure 4−1(a) indicates that as the price of potatoes falls (rises), quantity demanded rises (falls). We will demonstrate later in this chapter that it is theoretically possible for a demand curve to be positively sloped. Nevertheless, for nearly every real-world good, quantity demanded is negatively related to price. Economists call this the **Law of Demand.** (Economists reserve the word *law* for phenomena that almost always follow the same pattern.)

THE DEMAND FUNCTION

In addition to representing demand with a graph, we can represent it algebraically with an equation called the **demand function.** In general, we will specify the demand function for good x as follows:

$$x = D(p_x; p_y, I). \qquad (4.1)$$

Equation (4.1) contains the same information as does the graph in Figure 4−1(b). It indicates that the amount of potatoes purchased depends on the price of potatoes, the price of meat, and income. We place a semicolon after p_x to remind us that when we draw a picture of a demand curve, income (I) and the prices of other goods (p_y) are held constant.

■ We have seen how a change in the price of potatoes affects an individual's choice of how many potatoes to purchase. Next, let us see how a change in income or the price of meat affects the demand for potatoes.

4.2 CHANGES IN DEMAND

Figure 4–2(a) shows how a change in income affects Ben's choice of which market basket to purchase. Once again, given BC_0 Ben maximizes satisfaction by choosing market basket D on indifference curve u_0.

CHANGES IN INCOME

THE INCOME–CONSUMPTION CURVE

FIGURE 4–2

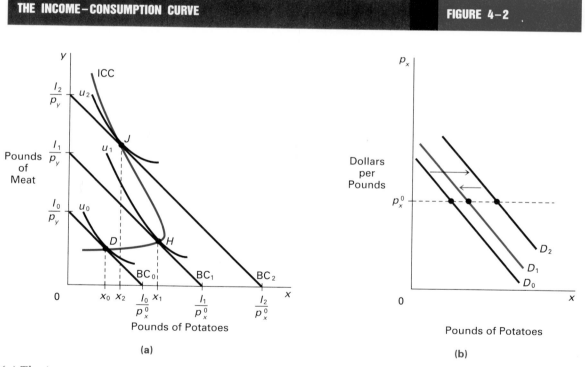

(a)

(b)

(a) The income–consumption curve shows how the optimal market basket changes as income changes, holding prices constant. (b) As income increases from I_0 to I_1, the demand curve shifts out from D_0 to D_1. Over this range, x is a normal good. As income increases from I_1 to I_2 the demand curve shifts in from D_1 to D_2. Over this range, x is an inferior good.

Now suppose Ben's income increases to I_1 dollars per year, while prices remain unchanged. This causes the budget constraint to shift outward from BC_0 to BC_1. Since prices have not changed, these budget constraints are parallel. When faced with budget constraint BC_1, Ben chooses market basket H on indifference curve u_1. His consumption of potatoes increases from x_0 to x_1 pounds and, since indifference curve u_1 is higher than indifference curve u_0, Ben is better off.

If Ben's income rises even further to I_2, his budget constraint shifts out even further and he chooses market basket J on indifference curve u_2. If we continue varying income in this manner, we can determine the market basket that Ben will choose given any level of income. The line connecting these market baskets is called the income–consumption curve. In Figure 4–2(a) the income–consumption curve is line ICC. The **income–consumption curve** shows how the utility-maximizing market basket changes in response to a change in income, holding relative prices constant.

The income–consumption curve is used to determine how a demand curve shifts when income changes. In Figure 4–2(b), D_0 is Ben's demand curve for meat when he has income I_0. If Ben's income increases to I_1, then he buys more potatoes. This means that the demand curve for potatoes shifts to the right from D_0 to D_1. Goods exhibiting this characteristic are called normal goods. A **normal good** is one that consumers purchase more of as income increases, or less of as income falls.

Now if Ben's income increases to I_2, he buys less potatoes, which means that the demand curve for potatoes shifts to the left from D_1 to D_2. Goods that have this characteristic are called inferior goods. An **inferior good** is one that consumers purchase less of as income increases, or more of as income falls. In this instance, potatoes are a normal good for low levels of income and an inferior good for higher levels of income.

Whether a good is normal or inferior depends on the preferences of the consumer and not on the intrinsic nature of the good itself. An inferior good is not a bad; that is, it is not a commodity that makes consumers worse off. For example, some individuals might regard macaroni and cheese as an inferior good. Macaroni and cheese is not a bad because more is preferred to less. However, if income increases, prices and tastes remaining unchanged, then some individuals may choose to consume less rather than more since now they can switch to steak.

While there is no general rule for determining whether a good is normal or inferior, economists have observed some general tendencies. Goods that are very *narrowly* defined within a larger class containing other high quality items are usually inferior goods. For example, low-quality cuts of beef like hamburger or brisket tend to be inferior goods. As incomes increase, consumers tend to substitute away from these meats to better cuts such as T-bone and sirloin steaks.

Goods that are *broadly* defined tend to be normal goods. The category "automobiles" is more likely to be a normal good than is the category "compact cars," and the category "compact cars" is more likely to be a normal good than are "Honda Civics." Since in microeconomics we are often concerned with broadly defined goods, we usually assume that we are dealing with normal goods. However, we must remember that whether or not a good is in fact normal or inferior depends both on preferences and the level of income.

Demand for a good depends not only on income, tastes, and the good's own price, but also on the prices of other goods, especially those closely related to the one under consideration. We would expect, for instance, that a substantial increase in the price of beef would lead to consumers buying more chicken, even though the price of chicken does not change. That is, we would expect an increase in the price of beef to cause the demand curve for chicken to shift to the right. In this example, chicken is a substitute for beef. If two goods are **substitutes,** then an increase in the price of one leads to an increase in demand for the other. Substitute goods can usually replace each other in consumption. Butter and margarine, Coca-Cola and Pepsi, video movie rentals and movie theater movies, and Hondas and Toyotas are examples of substitute goods.

In contrast to substitutes, **complements** are goods that are usually used or consumed together. Automobiles and gasoline, steak and steak sauce, hot dogs and hot dog buns, and night club entertainment and drinks are examples of complements. If two goods are complements, then an increase in the price of one leads to a decrease in demand for the other. By this reasoning, we would expect a sharp increase in the price of coffee to lead to a reduction in demand for cream. That is, we would expect an increase in the price of coffee to cause the demand curve for cream to shift to the left.

Up to this point we have used graphical analysis to investigate demand. In the next example, we represent the consumer's preferences by a Cobb–Douglas utility function and then proceed to derive an explicit algebraic expression for demand. (Paul Douglas was a twentieth-century economist at the University of

COMPLEMENTS AND SUBSTITUTES

Chicago and Charles Cobb was a mathematician at Amherst College. The Cobb–Douglas functional form was first used to study production.) This example is important because a *Cobb–Douglas utility function* is the simplest algebraic expression of preferences that gives rise to typical indifference curves. It therefore is used frequently to present examples of economic ideas. This next example also demonstrates how economists use algebraic models to supplement graphical analysis. Deriving an explicit demand function allows us to say precisely how demand changes when the economic environment changes.

EXAMPLE 4–1

COBB–DOUGLAS PREFERENCES AND DEMAND FUNCTIONS

The owner of Pizzas "Я" Us is thinking about opening a new store. One factor she must consider is demand, so she has hired us to analyze the demand for pizza in the area where the proposed store would be built. Suppose we know from previous surveys that the typical pizza consumer spends $200 per year on pizzas and Big Macs and has preferences that we can represent by the following utility function: $u = xy$, where x is pizzas per year and y is Big Macs per year. The associated MRS is: $MRS_{xy} = y/x$. (a) Derive the typical pizza consumer's demand function for pizzas. (b) Does this demand function satisfy the Law of Demand? (c) Is pizza a normal good? (d) Is pizza a substitute for Big Macs?

■ **SOLUTION** The typical consumer maximizes satisfaction, so we must find the points where $MRS_{xy} = p_x/p_y$. Using information in the problem, we have

$$MRS_{xy} = y/x = p_x/p_y.$$

Solving this equation for y gives us the relation between x and y that must hold if the consumer is maximizing satisfaction: $y = p_x x/p_y$.

(a) To find the demand curve for pizza, we substitute $y = p_x x/p_y$ into the budget constraint and solve for x. This step ensures that the consumer not only maximizes satisfaction but also stays within her means. The appropriate substitution gives: $I = p_x x + p_y(p_x x/p_y)$. Solving for x yields the typical consumer's demand function for pizza: $x^* = I/2p_x$, where the asterisk means the optimal value of x.

(We can also obtain the demand curve for good y by substituting x^* into the budget constraint: $y^* = I/2p_y$.)

Now that we have an algebraic expression of demand we can determine precisely the effects of changes in prices and incomes. (b) This demand curve satisfies the Law of Demand: as p_x increases, x^* falls. (c) Pizza is a normal good: as I increases, x^* increases. (d) The demand for pizza is independent of the price of Big Macs, so pizzas and Big Macs are neither substitutes nor complements. In this instance, the demand for pizzas is independent of the demand for Big Macs, a result that stems directly from the assumption of Cobb–Douglas preferences. ∎

∎ A change in the price of a good has two effects. First, consumption changes because *real purchasing power* changes— that is, there's a change in the amount of the good that consumers can buy with a given income. We call this the **income effect.** When the price of one good falls, for example, consumers realize an increase in real purchasing power. Their budget sets expand and they attain a higher indifference curve. Thus, real incomes increase because money incomes now go further.

Second, consumption changes because *relative prices* change. When the price of one good falls, consumers purchase more of that good because it has become relatively cheaper and less of other goods because they have become relatively more expensive. We call this the substitution effect. The **substitution effect** is the change in quantity (of one good) demanded due to a change in relative prices *when real income is held constant* (when the consumer can move only along his or her original indifference curve). While we usually cannot observe the income and substitution effects separately because they happen simultaneously, it will enhance our understanding of demand if we distinguish between them. Thus, whenever we investigate the effects of a change in the price of one good, holding money income and the prices of all other goods constant, we will *decompose the total effect* into income and substitution effects. (We sometimes call this process the Hicks decomposition of the total effect—named for Sir John Hicks, a contemporary English economist and Nobel laureate.)

To grasp the substitution effect, consider first the total effect of a price change as shown in Figure 4–3. (We use the composite good convention because the analysis focuses on one good only.) The initial budget constraint is line BC_1 and the consumer maximizes

4.3 INCOME AND SUBSTITUTION EFFECTS OF A PRICE CHANGE

THE SUBSTITUTION EFFECT FOR A DECREASE IN PRICE

| FIGURE 4-3 | INCOME AND SUBSTITUTION EFFECTS: A PRICE DECREASE |

The total effect due to a fall in the price of food, $(x_2 - x_0)$, can be decomposed into income and substitution effects. We draw a hypothetical budget constraint, GH, that is parallel to the new budget constraint, BC_2, and tangent to the original indifference curve, u_0. The substitution effect is $(x_1 - x_0)$ and the income effect is $(x_2 - x_1)$.

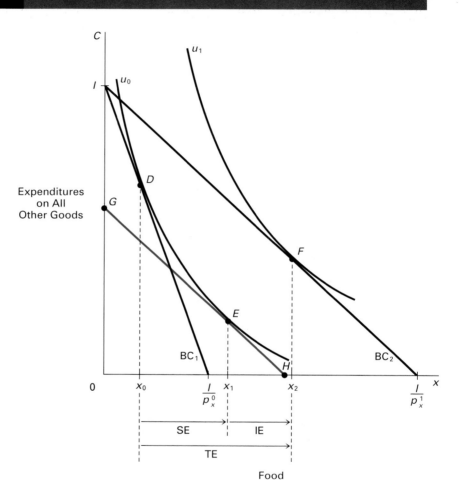

satisfaction by choosing market basket D on indifference curve u_0. Here the individual purchases x_0 units of food.

When the price of food falls, the budget constraint rotates outward to BC_2 and the consumer chooses market basket F on indifference curve u_1. Thus, because the price of food has fallen, the individual is better off, real income has increased, and he or she can purchase more food. The *total effect* (TE) of the price change is an increase in food purchased equal to $(x_2 - x_0)$ units of food.

We can decompose the total effect of this price change into income and substitution effects. To isolate the substitution effect, suppose we ask the following hypothetical question: How much food will a consumer purchase when the price of food falls from p_x^0 to p_x^1 and we adjust money income in such a way that the individual is no better off than before the price change? The answer to this question is the substitution effect.

Graphically we show the substitution effect (SE) by constructing—parallel to BC_2—a hypothetical budget constraint that reflects the new price ratio and is tangent to the original indifference curve u_0, which holds real income constant. In Figure 4–3, the line GH represents this hypothetical budget constraint. Notice that, given this budget constraint, the individual chooses market basket E and purchases x_1 units of food. Thus, the substitution effect is equal to $(x_1 - x_0)$ units of food.

When the price of food falls, the substitution effect always leads to an increase in the quantity of food demanded. This result follows directly from the assumption that indifference curves are negatively sloped. Budget constraint GH must be tangent to indifference curve u_0 at a point below and to the right of the original optimal market basket.

Now consider the income effect. The income effect associated with the reduction in the price of food is the change in consumption due solely to the change in real income, holding relative prices constant. In Figure 4–3 the income effect (IE) is the change in the amount of food consumed as the budget constraint shifts from GH to BC_2. Thus, the increase in food consumption of $(x_2 - x_1)$ units of food is the income effect. Since budget constraint GH is parallel to budget constraint BC_2, relative prices are constant as we move from E to F, which means that $(x_2 - x_1)$ measures the change in quantity demanded due solely to a change in purchasing power (real income).

THE INCOME EFFECT FOR A DECREASE IN PRICE

In this particular case, the price change leads to an *increase* in real income, generating an increase in consumption. This is because food is a normal good. For normal goods the income effect reinforces the substitution effect, which means that the total effect of a decrease in price is an increase in quantity demanded. (For a price increase, the substitution and income effects indicate a decrease in consumption.) Thus, the demand curve for a normal good must be downward-sloping—that is, the Law of Demand must hold.

From the discussion in the previous two sections it should be clear that if the income effect reinforces the substitution effect, the demand curve is negatively sloped. However, one question still remains: Can demand curves ever be positively sloped?

POSITIVELY SLOPED DEMAND CURVES OR GIFFEN'S PARADOX

FIGURE 4-4   **INFERIOR GOODS AND GIFFEN'S PARADOX**

(a) Good x is an inferior good. However, the demand curve for good x is still downward-sloping because the substitution effect outweighs the income effect. (b) Good x is an inferior good. Here the income effect outweighs the substitution effect and the demand curve for good x is upward-sloping. Good x is called a Giffen good in this case.

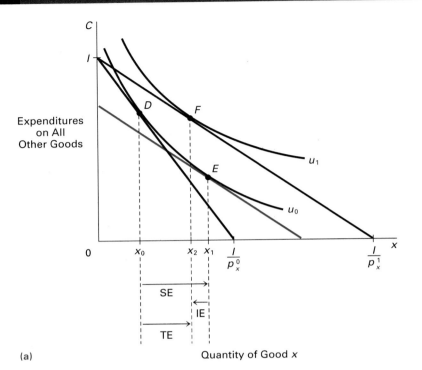

(a)

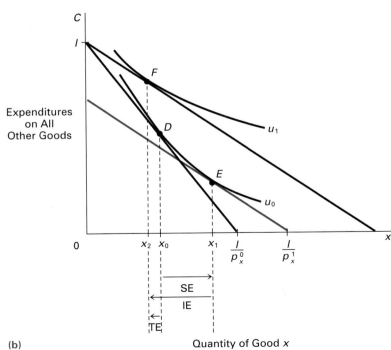

(b)

The only hope we have of generating upward-sloping demand curves is if income effects work *against* the substitution effects. Figure 4–4 illustrates this situation. In both Figures 4–4(a) and 4–4(b), good x is an inferior good. That is, when real income increases, quantity demanded falls. In Figure 4–4(a) the substitution effect (SE) is an increase in quantity demanded of $(x_1 - x_0)$ units of good x and the income effect (IE) is a reduction of $(x_1 - x_2)$ units of good x. In this case, the income effect works against the substitution effect. However, in Figure 4–4(a) the income effect is not large enough to offset the substitution effect so the demand curve for good x is still negatively sloped.

In Figure 4–4(b), however, the income effect is larger than the substitution effect. This results in a positively sloped demand curve or what is called **Giffen's Paradox**, named for the nineteenth-century economist, Robert Giffen, who believed that the demand curve for potatoes in Ireland was upward-sloping. According to Giffen and others, typical Irish peasants in the nineteenth century were so poor they spent almost all their income on potatoes. When the price of potatoes fell, they could spend less on potatoes but still get the same amount of nutrition, so they diverted some of their income to vegetables and meat. Since the latter also provided calories, they could reduce their consumption of potatoes even further. Thus Giffen argued that the income effect was large enough to offset the substitution effect. However, no one has found empirical evidence to support this claim.

Giffen's Paradox is a theoretical possibility but is of little practical interest. In order to violate the Law of Demand, a good must be an inferior good and have an income effect larger than its substitution effect. However, for most goods income effects are small. In fact, large income effects are usually associated with goods that make up a big share of the consumer's budget—goods such as housing and food—and these are normal, not inferior, goods.

Aside from helping us understand the theoretical underpinnings of demand, income and substitution effects can also aid us in evaluating government and business policies. The next example illustrates this type of analysis. We will discuss additional examples in Chapter 5.

EXAMPLE 4–2

EXCISE TAXES AND LUMP-SUM TAXES

An excise tax is a per-unit tax on a particular commodity. In the United States, consumers face excise taxes on automobile tires, gasoline, telephone services, cigarettes, and liquor. Excise taxes are levied both to raise revenues and to discourage consumption of certain goods. For example, while excise taxes on liquor and cigarettes were designed primarily to deter consumption (sometimes these are called the "sin" taxes), they currently generate over 40 billion dollars in revenues for the federal government.

A lump-sum tax, also called a "head" tax or a "poll" tax, is a tax of a fixed number of dollars per person. A lump-sum tax is therefore a tax on general purchasing power. In the United States there are no real lump-sum taxes. In some European countries, however, they are still used to raise revenues. In fact, in 1989 the British government instituted a poll tax; it was so unpopular that it was one of the primary factors that led to the resignation of Prime Minister Margaret Thatcher.

Now let us consider an excise tax on gasoline. In December 1990 the U.S. government increased the federal tax on gasoline by $.05 per gallon. Proponents of the tax argued that it would not only generate additional tax revenues but also would reduce dependence on foreign oil by reducing gasoline consumption.

Suppose we have been asked by a consumer advocate group to evaluate this proposal. In particular, we are (a) to determine how the tax will affect consumers' real income and gasoline consumption; and (b) to compare the proposed tax to a lump-sum tax that would raise the same amount of revenue. According to our staff, gasoline currently costs $1.00 per gallon and is a normal good.

■ **SOLUTION** Consider a representative consumer, C. S. Stratton, who has an income of I dollars per week. C. S. spends his entire income on gasoline and all other goods. His budget constraint prior to the tax is BC_1 in Figure 4–5(a). Given this budget constraint, C. S. maximizes satisfaction by choosing market basket D on indifference curve u_0. Thus, before the tax he purchases x_0 gallons of gasoline.

(a) If the government imposes a $.05 per-gallon tax on gasoline, C. S., like all consumers, pays more at the pumps. (For the moment assume that consumers pay the entire tax. In Chapter 11, we will investigate whether or not this is, indeed, the case.) This causes C. S.'s budget constraint to rotate inward about point I from BC_1 to BC_2 and he now chooses market basket E on indifference curve u_1. His real income falls from u_0 to u_1 and the quantity of gasoline he purchases drops from x_0 to x_1. We know that gasoline consumption must fall, because for normal goods the income and substitution effects work in the same direction.

(b) Suppose instead that the government institutes a lump-sum tax that raises the same amount of revenue as the excise tax. A

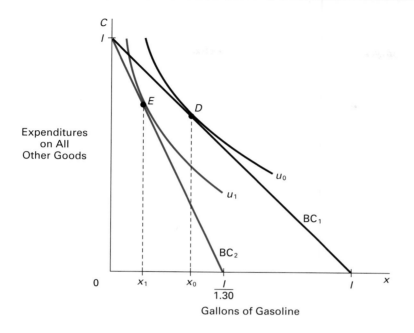

(a)

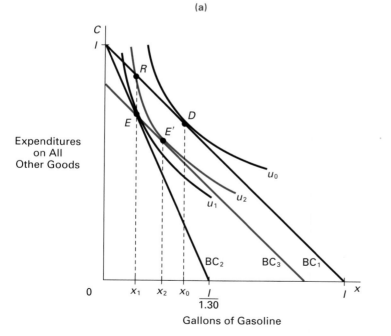

(b)

(a) The tax on gasoline increases the price of gasoline which causes the budget constraint to rotate inward to BC_2. Real income and gasoline consumption both fall. (b) A lump-sum tax that raises the same amount of revenue causes the budget constraint to shift in parallel to BC_3. Real income and gasoline consumption both fall but not as much as they do under the excise tax.

lump-sum tax causes the initial budget constraint to shift in from BC_1 to BC_3 in Figure 4–5(b). These budget constraints are parallel because the tax does not affect relative prices. The fact that BC_3 passes through E means that no matter which market basket on BC_3 he chooses, C. S. will pay the same amount of taxes as he did when faced with a gasoline tax.

To see this last point, note that the vertical distance between E and BC_1 represents the amount C. S. pays in gasoline taxes. (Just compare the budget constraints with and without the excise tax: the difference between them is exactly what C. S. pays in taxes.) If C. S. chooses market basket E, tax revenue is ER. Thus, since we want to raise the same revenue with a lump-sum tax, BC_3 must pass through point E. No matter which commodity bundle C. S. chooses on BC_3, he will pay ER in taxes.

With BC_3, C. S. maximizes satisfaction by purchasing commodity bundle E'. Compared to the excise tax, C. S. is better off, buys less gas, and spends more on other goods. ∎

Why is it that a lump-sum tax reduces consumption and real income less than an excise tax? Both excise and lump-sum taxes cause purchasing power to fall and both have an income effect, tending to reduce consumption and real income. However, the excise tax also has a substitution effect and this tends to reduce consumption and real income even further.

Example 4–2 shows that consumers are generally better off if government taxes general purchasing power rather than single commodities. Why then do we not see widespread use of lump-sum taxes? Why was the British poll tax so unpopular? Actually, these are normative questions that we cannot answer solely by the positive analysis we have undertaken. Our analysis demonstrates that taxpayers are better off with lump-sum taxes but it does not tell us that society as a whole prefers lump-sum taxes to excise taxes. The usual argument against lump-sum taxes is that they are not "fair"; that is, taxing all individuals the same dollar amount whether they are rich or poor is not equitable.

4.4 MARKET DEMAND

∎ Up to this point we have focused our attention on individual consumers. We learned how to construct an individual consumer's demand curve for a commodity using information concerning preferences, prices, and income. In addition, we investigated how changes in prices and income affect an individual's demand for goods. We found that demand curves are negatively sloped except for "Giffen goods," for which quantity demanded increases when price increases and falls when price falls; and we concluded that the Law of Demand prevails at the level of the individual consumer.

Now we turn to market demand. *Market demand* is the aggregate demand of all consumers of a product. It relates the price of a good to the quantity purchased by all individuals.

We obtain the **market demand curve** for a specific good by adding together the quantities demanded by each individual consumer at every possible price. Using Table 4−1, we can construct a market demand curve from information concerning individual demand curves. Here we suppose that there are only two types of consumers, type A and type B, and that this market comprises one consumer of each type. Column 1 of the table gives price, Column 2, individual A's demand for x, Column 3, individual B's demand for x, and Column 4, market demand.

AGGREGATING INDIVIDUAL DEMANDS TO OBTAIN MARKET DEMAND

Figure 4−6 graphs individual and market demand curves from the data in Table 4−1. The demand curve for consumer A is D_a, the demand curve for consumer B is D_b, and D_m is the market demand curve. For prices above \$3 the market demand curve is identical to the individual demand curve for consumer B. This occurs because above \$3 per unit, quantity demanded by consumer A is zero.

When the price falls below \$3, quantity demanded increases for two reasons. First, those consumers already in the market buy more. For example, if the price falls from \$3 to \$2, consumer B increases purchases of good X from 10 to 20 units. Second, there are new entrants into the market. Consumer A now has a positive demand for good X. Both these points are very important to remember:

Quantity demanded at the market level can increase because quantity demanded by individuals already in the market increases and because there are new market participants.

p_x	x_a	x_b	X_m
1	20	30	50
2	10	20	30
3	0	10	10
4	0	0	0

TABLE 4−1

INDIVIDUAL AND MARKET DEMANDS

FIGURE 4-6 | **AGGREGATING INDIVIDUAL DEMANDS TO OBTAIN THE MARKET DEMAND**

We obtain the market demand curve, D_m, by adding together the quantity demanded by each individual consumer at every possible price. As the price falls, two factors work to increase market demand: more consumers enter the market and consumers already in the market purchase more of the good.

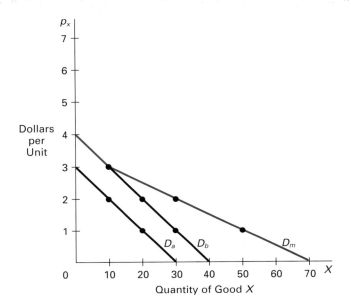

In this instance, the Law of Demand holds both for individuals and for the market as a whole; that is, both individual and market demand curves are downward-sloping. But suppose that for some consumers good X is a Giffen good. Does the Law of Demand prevail at the market level even though it does not for certain individuals? The answer is yes if, when the price of X falls, there are enough new entrants into the market to offset the individuals for whom X is a Giffen good. In this text, when we consider market demand curves, we will assume that the Law of Demand always prevails, even if it is violated for certain individuals. As the price of a good changes, buyers exiting from and entering into the market always generate a negatively sloped market demand curve.

Often we will not have a table to describe the way quantity demanded varies with price. Instead, we will have individual demand functions or sometimes just individual demand curves. Based on this information alone, we must be able to construct not only the graph of the market demand curve but also the *market demand function*.

Suppose that the market for styling mousse is comprised of three individuals: Mary, Mike, and Misty. Mary's demand function is

$$D_1: x = \begin{cases} 20 - 4p_x & \text{if } p_x \le 5 \\ 0 & \text{if } p_x > 5 \end{cases}$$

Mike's demand function is

$$D_2: x = \begin{cases} 40 - 10p_x & \text{if } p_x \le 4 \\ 0 & \text{if } p_x > 4 \end{cases}$$

and Misty's demand function is

$$D_3: x = \begin{cases} 30 - 10p_x & \text{if } p_x \le 3 \\ 0 & \text{if } p_x > 3 \end{cases}$$

where x is the number of bottles of styling mousse purchased per year and p_x is the price per bottle. When we derive market demand functions from individual demand functions, we must distinguish between purchases by individuals and purchases by consumers as a group. Typically economists use lower-case letters to denote quantity demanded by individuals and upper-case letters to denote quantity demanded by consumers as a group. In this instance, we let x denote the number of bottles of styling mousse demanded by an individual and X be the number of bottles demanded by all consumers together.

We have drawn the demand curves associated with each of the three demand functions in Figure 4–7. Letting $x = 0$ in Mary's demand function, D_1, we see that it has a price intercept of 5 and a quantity intercept of 20. Mike's demand curve, D_2, has a price intercept of 4 and a quantity intercept of 40. Misty's demand curve, D_3, has a price intercept of 3 and a quantity intercept of 30.

We obtain the market demand function by aggregating the quantity demanded by each individual at every price. In lay terms, we choose a price, ask how much each consumer would purchase at that price, and sum the results. Note that in the market for styling mousse no one will purchase any mousse that costs over \$5 — for prices above \$5, market demand is zero.

Now suppose the price of mousse begins to fall. When the price falls below \$5, Mary enters the market. If the price remains above \$4, then neither Mike nor Misty purchases any mousse and Mary is the only market participant. For prices between \$4 and \$5 the market demand function is simply Mary's demand function. Thus,

FIGURE 4–7   DETERMINING THE MARKET DEMAND CURVE FOR STYLING MOUSSE

When p_x is greater than $5, quantity demanded is zero and the market demand curve lies along the vertical axis. When p_x is between $4 and $5, the market demand curve is Mary's demand curve. When p_x is between $3 and $4, the market demand curve is the sum of Mike's and Mary's demand curves. When p_x is less than $3, Mary, Mike, and Misty all purchase styling mousse and the market demand curve is the sum of all three demand curves.

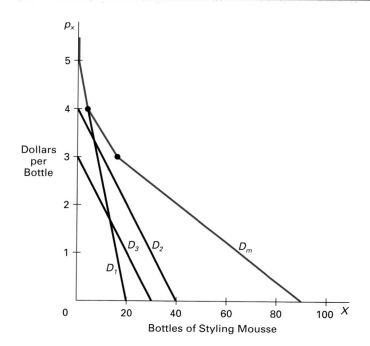

when $4 < p_x \leq 5$, the market demand function is given by: $X = 20 - 4p_x$, where X is quantity demanded.

When the price falls below $4, Mike enters the market. However, as long as the price remains above $3, Misty does not. This means that for prices between $3 and $4 the market demand function is the sum of Mary's and Mike's demand functions—that is, the market demand function is given by: $X = (20 - 4p_x) + (40 - 10p_x) = 60 - 14p_x$. It is important to remember that we add together quantities, not prices, when constructing the market demand function. Since we put quantity on the horizontal axis when we graph demand curves, economists refer to the process of summing individual demand curves to obtain the market demand curve as summing "horizontally."

Finally, when the price falls below $3, Misty enters the market and all three individuals purchase styling mousse. In this instance, the market demand function is given by: $X = (20 - 4p_x) + (40 - 10p_x) + (30 - 10p_x) = 90 - 24p_x$.

Combining these results, we can summarize the market demand function as follows:

$$D_m: X = \begin{cases} 20 - 4p_x & \text{if } 4 < p_x \leq 5 \\ 60 - 14p_x & \text{if } 3 < p_x \leq 4 \\ 90 - 24p_x & \text{if } \quad\;\; p_x \leq 3 \\ 0 & \text{if } 5 < p_x \end{cases}$$

Figure 4–7 shows the market demand curve associated with this market demand function. Again, the Law of Demand prevails.

In the discussion above, market demand for styling mousse depends only on its price. However, market demand for some good will usually depend also on the price of other goods and aggregate income. The next example shows why owners and managers of firms must understand how each of these factors affects market demand.

EXAMPLE 4–3

MARKET DEMAND AND REVENUES

Procter and Gamble (P&G) manufactures and sells Pampers disposable diapers. Suppose P&G's economics division estimates that the demand for Pampers is given by

$$X = 200 - 3000p_x + .01I + 2000p_y,$$

where X is millions of diapers per year, p_x is the price of Pampers, I is average annual income of consumers who purchase Pampers, and p_y is a price index measuring the average price of other disposable diapers. Further, suppose P&G decides to cut the price of Pampers from $.20 to $.15 per diaper. (a) If other disposable diapers sell for $.20 per diaper, and consumers' average income is $20,000, how will this price reduction affect revenues? (b) How will your answer change if other disposable diaper manufacturers respond to P&G's price-cut by cutting their prices from $.20 to $.15? (c) How will your answer change if the economy moves into a recession and average income falls to $18,000?

■ **SOLUTION** At the initial price (with incomes averaging $20,000), P&G will sell $X = 200 - 3000(.20) + 20,000(.01) + 2000(.20) = 200$ million diapers per year and revenue will be $40.0 million per year.

(a) If the price of Pampers falls to $.15, quantity demanded will increase, because the coefficient on p_x is negative. At this price, P&G will sell 350 million diapers per year and revenue will be $52.5 million per year. As a result of the price-cut, sales and revenue both increase.

(b) Now, if rival firms match P&G's lower price, then after its price-cut P&G will sell only 250 million diapers per year. In this instance, revenue falls from $40.0 million to $37.5 million per year. Reducing the price of Pampers tends to increase quantity demanded but the reaction of rival firms tends to decrease demand for Pampers—enough in this case to cause a decline in P&G's revenue. (The effects of one firm's actions on others is discussed in detail in Chapter 14.)

(c) Finally, if the price of Pampers drops just as average income falls from $20,000 to $18,000 per year, P&G will sell 330 million diapers per year and revenue will be $49.5 million per year. Again, quantity demanded tends to increase because of the lower price but now demand tends to decrease because consumers are earning less. However, in this instance, the price-cut still increases revenue. ■

4.5 DEMAND ELASTICITIES

■ As Example 4–3 shows, it is important for firms to understand the factors that affect market demand because market demand determines revenue. To measure the responsiveness of market demand to changes in prices and income, economists use the concept of elasticity. An *elasticity* measures the percentage change in quantity demanded due to a percentage change in a price or income. In this section, we will discuss three important demand elasticities: the price elasticity of demand; the cross-price elasticity of demand; and the income elasticity of demand.

THE PRICE ELASTICITY OF DEMAND

The single most useful demand elasticity is the **price elasticity of demand,** defined as *the percentage change in quantity demanded per 1% change in price.* The price elasticity of demand measures the responsiveness of quantity demanded to changes in the market price.

One of the most important things the price elasticity of demand tells us is how a change in price affects the amount of income consumers spend on a particular good. Knowing how changes in price affect expenditures is important for a number of reasons. For example, from a firm's point of view, consumers' expenditures are the firm's revenues. In order for the firm to make production decisions it is important to know how price changes will affect revenues.

To give a second example, it is essential for local governments to know the impact of price changes on expenditures when they raise revenues by taxing goods bought and sold in their particular jurisdictions. Which goods they choose to tax depends a great deal on how the tax affects prices, the amount bought and sold, and expenditures.

In this text we denote the price elasticity of demand for good X by ϵ_{xx} (ϵ is the Greek letter "epsilon"). The "xx" subscript serves as a reminder that this elasticity is defined for good X with respect to changes in the price of X. If $X = D(p_x, p_y, I)$ is the market demand function for X, then the price elasticity of demand is given by

$$\epsilon_{xx} = -\left[\frac{\Delta X}{X} \Big/ \frac{\Delta p_x}{p_x} \right] = -\left[\frac{p_x}{X} \right] \Big/ \left[\frac{\Delta p_x}{\Delta X} \right]. \qquad (4.2)$$

The term $\left[\dfrac{\Delta X}{X} \right]$ is the percentage change in quantity demanded, $\left[\dfrac{\Delta p_x}{p_x} \right]$ is the percentage change in price, and for small changes $\left[\dfrac{\Delta p_x}{\Delta X} \right]$ is the slope of the market demand curve. When the Law of Demand prevails, the market demand curve is downward-sloping and the price elasticity of demand is a positive number.

Note one point about ϵ_{xx} before continuing. First, since quantity demanded depends on price, the price of other goods, and income, the price elasticity of demand also depends on these variables. This is very important, especially when we are using elasticities estimated from real-world data to predict the impact of a price change on consumption. If income or the price of other goods changes, then the price elasticity of demand may also change.

Economists often find it useful to classify market demand according to whether the price elasticity is less than, equal to, or greater than one.

CLASSIFYING DEMAND ACCORDING TO PRICE ELASTICITIES

Demand is **price-elastic** if $\epsilon_{xx} > 1$. If demand is elastic then for a given percentage change in price, quantity demanded changes by a greater percentage. For example, if $\epsilon_{xx} = 3$, then demand is elastic and a 10% increase in price causes a 30% reduction in quantity demanded.

Demand is **price-inelastic** if $\epsilon_{xx} < 1$. In this instance, a given percentage change in price causes a smaller percentage change in demand. If $\epsilon_{xx} = 1/2$, then a 10% increase in price results in a 5%

reduction in quantity demanded. Demand is less responsive to changes in price than in the first case.

Finally, if $\epsilon_{xx} = 1$, demand is said to be **unit-elastic.** For any given percentage change in price, quantity demanded changes by exactly the same percentage. A 5% increase in price will lead to exactly a 5% reduction in quantity demanded.

CALCULATING THE PRICE ELASTICITY OF DEMAND

Given an equation describing a demand function, we can calculate the price elasticity of demand at any point on the demand curve simply by finding the slope of the demand function at that point and substituting the relevant information into the expression for price elasticity. We call such a calculation a *point elasticity* because it measures the elasticity at a particular point on the demand curve.

Suppose the demand function for good X is given by

$$X = 500 - 6p_x.$$

Since this is a straight line, the slope of this demand function is minus six; that is, $\Delta X/\Delta p_x = -6$. Now suppose we want to calculate the price elasticity of demand when the price of good X is $50 per unit of X and quantity demanded is $500 - 6 \times 50 = 200$ units of good X. We have

$$\epsilon_{xx} = -\left[\frac{p_x}{X}\right] \cdot \left[\frac{\Delta X}{\Delta p_x}\right] = -(50/200) \cdot (-6) = 1.50.$$

Thus, if the price of good X is $50 per unit, market demand is elastic.

Oftentimes there is not an equation available to describe the demand function. Then we must calculate price elasticity from observations of price–quantity points on the demand curve. For example, suppose that when the price of peanut butter is $2.00 per jar, 1,000 jars sell each month and when the price drops to $1.00 per jar, 2,000 jars sell each month. Since price elasticity is the percentage change in quantity divided by the percentage change in price, we must calculate $\Delta X/X$ and $\Delta p_x/p_x$. However, we have a problem. Even though both ΔX and Δp_x are uniquely determined from our data—that is, $\Delta X = (2,000 - 1,000) = 1,000$ and $\Delta p_x = (1.00 - 2.00) = -1$—the values for X and p_x are not. We could use the initial price–quantity pair, 1,000 jars at $2.00 per jar, or we could use the second price–quantity pair, 2,000 jars at $1.00 per jar. Which one should we use?

If we use the initial price–quantity pair, then we obtain

$$\epsilon_{xx} = - \left[\frac{\Delta X}{X} \right] \Big/ \left[\frac{\Delta p_x}{p_x} \right] = -(1{,}000/1{,}000)/(-1/2) = 2.$$

On the other hand, if we use the second price–quantity pair we get

$$\epsilon_{xx} = - \left[\frac{\Delta X}{X} \right] \Big/ \left[\frac{\Delta p_x}{p_x} \right] = -(1{,}000/2{,}000)/(-1/1) = .5.$$

From the first instance we conclude that demand is elastic over this range while from the second case we reckon that demand is inelastic.

We get different values for the price elasticity because it tends to change as we move along the demand curve. This means that for large movements along a demand curve our calculations will be very sensitive to the price–quantity pair we use. As a result, when we deal with large changes in price and quantity we must use what we call the *arc elasticity* formula to calculate the price elasticity of demand:

$$\epsilon_{xx} = - \left[\frac{\Delta X}{.5(X_1 + X_2)} \right] \Big/ \left[\frac{\Delta p_x}{.5(p_x^1 + p_x^2)} \right]. \qquad (4.3)$$

Note that this formula for price elasticity differs from the previous formula only in that the *average* price, $.5(p_x^1 + p_x^2)$, and the *average* quantity, $.5(X_1 + X_2)$, are used to calculate the percentage changes. If we use this formula for the example given above, we have

$$\epsilon_{xx} = - \frac{1{,}000/(.5)(1{,}000 + 2{,}000)}{-1/(.5)(2 + 1)} = 1.$$

Thus, over this range of prices and quantities we now conclude that demand is unit-elastic.

Since the price elasticity of demand reflects the preferences of the multitude of people comprising the market for a particular product, we cannot specify hard and fast rules for determining whether demand for that product will be price-elastic or -inelastic. However, economists have found two primary factors that significantly influence the price elasticity of demand: the availability of substitute goods and the length of time consumers have to adjust to price changes.

DETERMINANTS OF THE PRICE ELASTICITY OF DEMAND

Commodities with many desirable substitutes tend to be price-elastic relative to commodities with only a few poor substitutes. This follows from our discussion of substitution effects. For example, if the price of Coca-Cola increases, people will switch to Pepsi, which is a close substitute for Coca-Cola, and the demand for Coca-Cola will tend to be quite elastic. On the other hand, if the price of cigarettes increases, cigarette smokers have few substitute goods that they can switch to (only cigars and pipes) and the demand for cigarettes will tend to be inelastic.

Table 4–2 reports estimates of the price elasticities associated with several goods. Consider first the column giving the long-run elasticities. An example of a commodity for which there are a variety of good alternatives is intercity bus use. Using the bus system is but one of several ways to get from one city to another. If bus fares increase, individuals can switch to taking a train or a plane, or to driving. As shown in Table 4–2, the demand for intercity bus travel is very price-elastic.

At the other end of the spectrum are goods such as the opera for which there are few adequate substitutes. For an individual who enjoys attending the opera, only opera will do. Movies, night clubs, and other forms of entertainment simply cannot replace opera. The lack of substitute goods means that when the price of opera tickets increases, consumers may go to the opera less frequently but they will be reluctant to give up something for which there is no adequate alternative. As shown in Table 4–2, the demand for theater and opera is very price-inelastic.

TABLE 4–2

ESTIMATED PRICE
ELASTICITIES OF
DEMAND

Commodity Group	Short Run	Long Run
Theater and Opera	.18	.31
Gasoline	.40	1.50
Stationary	.47	.56
Foreign Travel	.14	1.77
Housing	.30	1.88
Household Electricity	.13	1.89
Tobacco Products	.46	1.89
Intercity Bus Travel	.20	2.17
Automobiles and Parts	1.87	2.24
Motion Pictures	.87	3.67

Source: Houthakker, Hendrik, and Taylor, *Consumer Demand in the United States: Analyses and Projections*. (Cambridge: Cambridge University Press, 1970.)

The other important factor that influences the price elasticity of demand is the length of time consumers have to adjust to price changes. In the short run, demand tends to be less elastic than in the long run. Given enough time consumers can find different ways to adjust to price changes. In the long run, more opportunities are available.

Looking again at Table 4–2 we see that in the long run demand is uniformly more elastic. For example, the short-run price elasticity of demand for electricity is less than one tenth the long-run elasticity. If the price of electricity increases, in the short-run consumers might adjust thermostats, check to make sure lights are turned off in rooms not in use, and reduce the use of appliances. While these adjustments will help, in the short run only a limited amount can be done to conserve electricity. In the long run, consumers have many more options. Individuals can switch from electric appliances to gas or solar-powered appliances or they can insulate their homes. In the long run, individuals can find more ways to cut back on consumption of electricity.

One important use of the price elasticity of demand is to determine how total expenditures change in response to a price change. What consumers spend on a particular good represents the revenues producers receive for that good. Many times producers attempt to raise their revenues (incomes) by artificially increasing the price of their product. Farmers have been known to hold back part of their harvest or to destroy livestock in order to increase prices. As a result of such actions, revenues from the sale of these goods may either rise or fall depending on the price elasticity of demand. If demand is elastic, then a 10% increase in price leads to more than a 10% reduction in quantity demanded. This in turn leads to a fall in consumer expenditures on the commodity and a fall in revenues to the farmer. The loss in revenues from lost sales outweighs the gain from a higher price per unit. If demand is inelastic, then revenues increase.

Total expenditure on a good, denoted by TE, is the product of the commodity's price and the quantity purchased. Total expenditure by consumers is equal to total revenue, TR, to sellers of the commodity. We are interested in the relation between the price elasticity of demand and the change in total expenditure on a particular good arising from a change in its price. If demand is price-elastic, total expenditure falls as price increases and rises as price falls. For example, suppose that when the price of a particular cereal is $1.50 per box, individuals purchase 100,000 boxes per month. Total expenditures per month on this good are $150,000.

USING THE PRICE ELASTICITY OF DEMAND TO ANALYZE CONSUMER EXPENDITURES

TABLE 4–3

PRICE ELASTICITY
OF DEMAND AND
EXPENDITURES

	Expenditures		
	$\epsilon_{xx} > 1$	$\epsilon_{xx} = 1$	$\epsilon_{xx} < 1$
Price Increases	fall	remain the same	rise
Price Decreases	rise	remain the same	fall

Further, suppose that for this cereal $\epsilon_{xx} = 2$. If the price increases 10% to $1.65 then quantity demanded falls by 20% to 80,000 boxes per month. Thus, after the price increase, total expenditure—or total revenue to the seller—falls to $132,000 per month.

If demand is price-inelastic, total expenditure rises as price increases and falls as price falls. For example, in the short run the price elasticity of demand for tobacco products is .46 (see Table 4–2). In this case, a 10% increase in price leads to a 4.6% fall in quantity demanded, which in turn leads to an increase in expenditures on tobacco products.

Finally, if demand is unit-elastic, expenditures do not change when price changes. If $\epsilon_{xx} = 1$, then a 10% increase in price leads to a 10% fall in quantity demanded and total expenditures remain unchanged. These results are summarized in Table 4–3.

Now let us see how we can use the relation between the price elasticity of demand and total expenditures to investigate a problem faced by athletic directors at universities across the country—what price to charge for football tickets.

EXAMPLE 4–4

USING THE PRICE ELASTICITY OF DEMAND

Suppose the market demand function for tickets to football games is given by

$$X = 100,000 - 2,000p_x$$

where X is the number of tickets sold per game and p_x is the price of a ticket. (a) Determine an expression giving the price elasticity of demand as a function of ticket price. (b) If the stadium's capacity is 70,000 seats, what price should the university charge for football tickets if the Athletic Director's goal is to fill the stadium to capacity? (c) What price should it charge to maximize revenues from ticket sales?

■ **SOLUTION** (a) Since this is a linear demand function, we have that

$$\Delta X/\Delta p_x = -2,000.$$

Substituting this information into the expression for price elasticity we get

$$\epsilon_{xx} = (p_x/X)(2,000) = [p_x/(100,000 - 2,000p_x)] \cdot 2,000.$$

This equation relates elasticity to price.

(b) Since capacity is 70,000, the ticket price that fills the stadium is given by

$$X = 100,000 - 2,000p_x = 70,000$$

or, solving for price, $p_x = \$15$ per ticket.

(c) We can use the relation between price elasticity and total expenditure to answer question (c). If $\epsilon_{xx} > 1$ then we know that an increase in price increases total expenditures (revenue). If $\epsilon_{xx} < 1$ then we know that an increase in price decreases expenditures which means that a reduction in price increases expenditures (revenue). Thus, revenue must be maximized when $\epsilon_{xx} = 1$; that is, when demand is unit-elastic.

Now we can find the price that maximizes revenue. Setting the price elasticity of demand equal to one we have

$$\epsilon_{xx} = [p_x/(100,000 - 2,000p_x)] \cdot 2,000 = 1$$

or, solving for price, $p_x = \$25$. Notice that at this price $X = 100,000 - 2,000 \cdot 25 = 50,000$ and some seats are left empty. ■

This example illustrates how we can use the price elasticity of demand to analyze market demand. As we progress in economics, we will find that the price elasticity of demand is used time and again to investigate the impact of price changes on quantity demanded and consumer expenditures.

Price elasticity of demand is the most important elasticity used in economics. However, the concept of elasticity can also measure the responsiveness of consumption to changes in income and the prices of other goods.

TWO OTHER DEMAND ELASTICITIES

INCOME ELASTICITY OF
DEMAND

To measure the responsiveness of consumption to changes in income we use the **income elasticity of demand** defined as *the percentage change in quantity demanded per 1% change in income.* It is denoted by

$$\epsilon_{xI} = \left[\frac{\Delta X}{X} \Big/ \frac{\Delta I}{I} \right] = \left[\frac{I}{X} \right] \cdot \left[\frac{\Delta X}{\Delta I} \right]. \qquad (4.4)$$

The income elasticity of demand indicates whether or not a commodity is a normal or inferior good. If ϵ_{xI} is positive then X is a normal good. If ϵ_{xI} is negative then X is an inferior good. In general, the income elasticities of demand for necessities, such as food and health-care services, are smaller than for luxuries, such as new cars and household appliances.

CROSS-PRICE ELASTICITY
OF DEMAND

As we have discussed earlier, the market demand curve depends not only on the price of the good being considered but also on the prices of other goods and income. The **cross-price elasticity of demand** for a good is defined as *the percentage change in quantity demanded of that good per 1% change in the price of another good.*

The cross-price elasticity of demand for good X with respect to the price of good Y, denoted by ϵ_{xy}, is given by

$$\epsilon_{xy} = \left[\frac{\Delta X}{X} \Big/ \frac{\Delta p_y}{p_y} \right] = \left[\frac{p_y}{X} \right] \cdot \left[\frac{\Delta X}{\Delta p_x} \right]. \qquad (4.5)$$

The sign—negative or positive—depends on whether goods are substitutes or complements. If good X is a substitute for good Y, then an increase in the price of good Y leads to an increase in quantity demanded of good X ($\Delta X/\Delta p_x > 0$) and ϵ_{xy} is positive. If good X is a complement for good Y, then an increase in the price of good Y leads to an decrease in the quantity demanded of good X ($\Delta X/\Delta p_x < 0$) and ϵ_{xy} is negative.

Economists use cross-price elasticities primarily as indicators of the availability and strength of substitute goods. Information concerning the number of close substitute goods is used quite frequently in antitrust cases. This is because the number of competitors a firm has can signal how many close substitute goods exist. Cross-price elasticities indicate how various markets interrelate.

4.6 CONSUMER SURPLUS

■ Consumers buy goods and services because the purchase makes them better off. Consumer surplus measures *how much* better off they are. For an individual, consumer surplus is the difference between the maximum amount she is willing to pay for a good and the amount she actually pays for it. Thus, **consumer surplus** measures the net benefit of consuming a certain quantity of a good. For instance, suppose that an individual would be willing to pay $5 per pound for hamburger, even though she has to pay only $2 per pound. The $3 per-pound savings is the net benefit (or consumer surplus) secured by the consumer. If we add the consumer surpluses of all individuals buying a particular good, we obtain an aggregate measure of consumer surplus. For a market, consumer surplus measures the net benefit secured by all individuals.

The easiest way to measure consumer surplus is to use demand curves. Let us initially assume chicken is sold in one-pound packages. Now let us start with a price so high that no one will buy any chicken and gradually lower it until the consumer buys one pound. In Figure 4–8(a), the consumer buys one pound of chicken when the price falls to $5 per pound. Since this is the maximum

CONSUMER SURPLUS   **FIGURE 4–8**

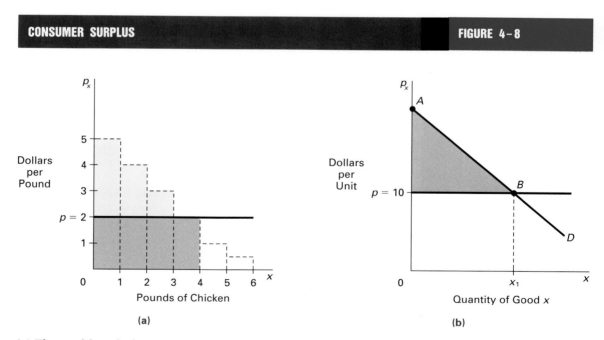

(a) The total benefit from consuming four pounds of chicken is the sum of the four shaded rectangles, or $14. Since the four pounds of chicken cost only $8, consumer surplus is $6, which is the lightly shaded area. (b) Consumer surplus is the area below the market demand curve and above the market price consumers pay for the good. With a smooth demand curve, consumer surplus is area pAB.

price the individual is willing to pay for the first pound of chicken, it is a dollar measure of the marginal benefit, or marginal value, of the first pound of chicken purchased. Lowering the price further, we see that the consumer will buy a second pound of chicken at a price of $4 per pound. This is the maximum amount the individual is willing to pay for the second pound of chicken—or the marginal benefit of the second pound of chicken.

Continuing in this manner, we can generate the demand curve. As shown in Figure 4–8(a), because we have assumed that chicken can only be bought in one-pound packages, the demand curve is a steplike curve. This demand curve is sometimes called a *willingness-to-pay* curve since each point on it represents the maximum amount the consumer is willing to pay for a specific unit of chicken. Notice that because the law of demand holds, the marginal benefit of consuming chicken falls as more chicken is purchased.

The area of each rectangle in Figure 4–8(a) also measures the marginal benefit of consuming a particular unit of chicken. The *total benefit* associated with consuming a certain quantity of chicken is the sum of the marginal benefits. For example, the total benefit of consuming one pound of chicken is $5; the total benefit of consuming two pounds is $5 + $4 = $9; and so on. Thus, the total benefit of consuming a particular quantity of chicken is just the area under the demand curve up to the quantity purchased.

Now suppose the consumer can purchase all the chicken she wants to at a price of $2 per pound. At this price, she buys four pounds of chicken; that is, she buys chicken up to the point where the marginal benefit is equal to the marginal cost. Now notice that the total benefit of consuming four pounds is $14, but she actually pays a total of only $8 for the chicken. This means that consumer surplus is ($14 − $8) = $6. In other words, the net benefit of purchasing four pounds of chicken at a price of $2 per pound is $6.

We now have a convenient way to measure consumer surplus. For an individual, it is the area below her demand curve and above the price she pays for the good. For the market as a whole, it is the area below the market demand curve and above the market price for the good. In Figure 4–8(b), we illustrate consumer surplus using a smooth demand curve. At a price of $10 per unit, consumers buy x_1 units. The total benefit of consuming x_1 units is $0ABx_1$; the total cost is $0pBx_1$; and consumer surplus is pAB.

CONSUMER SURPLUS AND INDIFFERENCE CURVES

We can also represent consumer surplus using indifference curves and budget constraints. Once again, suppose that an individual purchases three pounds of chicken at a price of $2 per pound. Figure 4–9 shows the optimal market basket at point A on

CONSUMER SURPLUS AND INDIFFERENCE CURVES

FIGURE 4–9

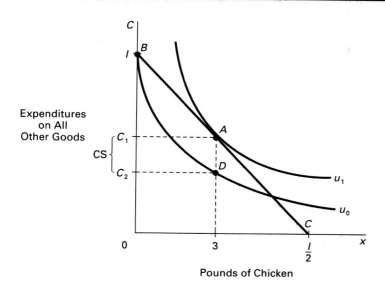

$(I - C_1)$ is the amount of income the consumer must spend to purchase x_1 units of good x. $(I - C_2)$ is the maximum amount the consumer would be willing to pay. Consumer surplus is $(C_1 - C_2)$ or the distance AD.

indifference curve u_1. Now note that this consumer is better off purchasing three pounds of chicken at $2 per pound than purchasing no chicken at all. If he purchased no chicken, the optimal market basket would be point B on indifference curve u_0 which is a lower indifference curve. Thus, the net benefit, or consumer surplus, of purchasing three pounds of chicken at $2 per pound is shown by the increase in real income from u_0 to u_1.

Now let's see if we can measure in dollar terms how much better off the consumer is with basket A than with basket B. Beginning at B, what is the maximum amount the consumer would be willing to pay for three pounds of chicken? In Figure 4–9, this is $(I - C_2)$ dollars because the individual attains the same level of satisfaction with market basket B as with market basket D and D contains three pounds of chicken. That is, $(I - C_2)$ measures the *total benefit* from consuming three pounds of chicken. This corresponds to the area under the demand curve in Figure 4–8(a).

Now to calculate consumer surplus, we must compare the maximum amount the consumer is willing to pay for three pounds of chicken, $(I - C_2)$, to the amount the consumer actually pays. In this instance, the consumer pays $(I - C_1)$ dollars for three pounds of chicken. Consumer surplus is the difference between total benefit, $(I - C_2)$, and total cost, $(I - C_1)$, or $(C_1 - C_2)$ dollars. Since $(C_1 - C_2)$ is also equal to distance AD, consumer surplus is the dollar value of the vertical distance between A and D.

Consumer surplus has many important applications in economics. For a market as a whole, consumer surplus measures the total benefit to society of being able to purchase a good at the market price. Thus, economists can use changes in consumer surplus to evaluate the costs and benefits of different pricing schemes, different market structures, and different public policies that affect consumer choices.

EXAMPLE 4–5

CONSUMER SURPLUS AND THE GASOLINE TAX

In Example 4–2 we used indifference curves and budget constraints to show that a $.05 per-gallon tax on gasoline makes consumers worse off. Now let's use the concept of consumer surplus to measure in dollars *how much* worse off they are.

Suppose that prior to the tax, gasoline sold for $1 per gallon and 100 billion gallons were consumed per year. Using the short-run price elasticity of demand (Table 4–1), determine the reduction in consumer surplus due to the new tax.

■ **SOLUTION** We must first derive the market demand curve for gasoline. Since we know one price–quantity pair and the price elasticity of demand, we can calculate a linear demand curve for gasoline. If the demand curve is linear, then algebraically the demand function is

$$\text{Demand: } X = a - bp_x$$

where X is billions of gallons per year, p_x the price per gallon, a the quantity intercept, and $-b$ the slope. To determine the slope and intercept, recall that we can write the price elasticity of demand as

$$\epsilon_{xx} = -\left[\frac{p_x}{X}\right] \cdot \left[\frac{\Delta X}{\Delta p_x}\right].$$

For linear curves, $(\Delta X/\Delta p_x)$ is constant and in this instance equal to $-b$. Substituting this value for $(\Delta X/\Delta p_x)$ into the elasticity formula gives

$$\epsilon_{xx} = b(p_x^1/X_1)$$

where p_x^1 and X_1 are the price and quantity for which we have data. Substituting the values for ϵ_{xx}, p_x^1, and X_1 into this last equation we can solve for the slope of the demand curve:

$$b = \epsilon_{xx} (X_1/p_x^1) = .4(100/1) = 40.$$

Knowing the slope of the demand curve, we can find the intercept using the demand function:

$$a = X_1 + bp_x^1 = 100 + 40 \cdot 1 = 140.$$

Thus, given the data, the market demand curve is

$$\text{Demand: } X = 140 - 40p_x.$$

Figure 4–10 illustrates this demand curve. When the price is $1 per gallon of gasoline, consumers purchase 100 billion gallons of

CONSUMER SURPLUS AND EXCISE TAXES
FIGURE 4–10

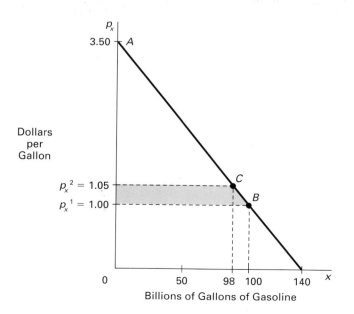

Consumer surplus prior to the tax is area ABp_x^1. After the tax, consumer surplus falls to area ACp_x^2. The tax reduces consumer surplus by area $p_x^2CBp_x^1$.

gasoline each year. Initially, consumer surplus is the area of triangle ABp_x^1, which is $125 billion per year.

Assuming as we did in Example 4–2 that the tax is passed on completely to consumers, the price of gasoline after tax increases to $1.05, demand falls to 98 billion gallons per year $(140 - 40 \cdot 1.05)$, and consumer surplus falls to $122.5 billion per year (area ACp_x^2 in the diagram). Thus the tax makes consumers worse off and the change in consumer surplus, $(125 - 122.5) = \$2.5$ billion per year, is a dollar measure of how much real income has fallen. Put another way, consumers would be willing to pay $2.5 billion to avoid the $.05 per-gallon tax on gasoline. ∎

1. Changing the price of one good while holding all other prices and income constant yields the demand curve. For nearly all goods the Law of Demand prevails. Demand curves are negatively sloped.

2. When income changes, the demand curve shifts. If the quantity purchased increases when income increases and falls when income falls, then the good is a normal good. If the reverse is true, then the good is an inferior good.

3. A change in the price of a related good also causes the demand curve to shift. Goods are substitutes if when the price of one good rises, quantity demanded of the other rises. Goods are complements if when the price of one good rises, quantity demanded of the other falls.

4. In order to investigate price changes in even greater detail, we decomposed the change in demand stemming from a change in price into income and substitution effects. If the income and substitution effects work together then the Law of Demand always holds. If they work against each other, then the Law of Demand holds if the substitution effect is greater than the income effect but fails to hold if the reverse is true.

5. Market demand is the total quantity demanded by all consumers in a particular market. The market demand curve shows the relation between the market price for a good and the amount of the good that people purchase, provided incomes, the prices of all other goods, and tastes do not change. At the market level, the Law of Demand always holds: if the price falls, quantity demanded increase; if the price increases, quantity demanded falls.

6. The price elasticity of demand measures the extent to which quantity demanded by all market participants varies with price changes. We define it as the percentage change in quantity demanded per 1% change in market price. Market demand is elastic if a 1% change in price leads to more than a 1% change in quantity. Market demand is inelastic if a 1% change in price leads to less than a 1% change in quantity.

7. The price elasticity of demand is used to investigate how consumer expenditures vary in response to changes in market prices. If demand is elastic, a price increase leads to lower expenditures. If demand is inelastic, a price increase leads to higher expenditures.

8. The cross-price elasticity of demand measures the percentage change in quantity demanded of one good due to a 1% change in the price of another good. The cross-price elasticity of

demand is positive for substitute goods and negative for complementary goods.

9. The income elasticity of demand measures the percentage change in demand due to a 1% change in income. Income elasticities are positive for normal goods and negative for inferior goods.

10. Consumer surplus is the difference between the maximum amount consumers are willing to pay for a particular quantity of some good and the amount they actually must pay. Consumer surplus represents the net benefit to consumers of being able to trade at the market price. It can be used to represent the economic gains and losses associated with particular economic policies.

KEY TERMS

Price–Consumption Curve
Demand Curve
The Law of Demand
Demand Function
Income–Consumption Curve
Normal Good
Inferior Good
Substitutes
Complements
Income Effect
Substitution Effect

Giffen's Paradox
Market Demand Curve
Price Elasticity of Demand
Price-Elastic
Price-Inelastic
Unit-Elastic
Income Elasticity of Demand
Cross-Price Elasticity of
    Demand
Consumer Surplus

QUESTIONS AND PROBLEMS

1. Using indifference curves and budget constraints, derive two points on a consumer's demand curve for some good x when x is an inferior good and the income effect is less than the substitution effect.

2. Are the following statements true or false? Explain.
   a) Quantity demanded varies directly with price when the consumer is compensated for a price change in such a way that she is forced to remain on her original indifference curve.
   b) Quantity demanded varies inversely with price when money income is held constant.

3. Given the data in the table below, illustrate:
   a) the income–consumption curve;
   b) the price–consumption curve; and
   c) the demand curve for good x.

Time	p_x	p_y	x	y	I
day 1	$2	$ 5	250	100	$1000
day 2	2	10	250	50	1000
day 3	1	10	500	50	1000
day 4	2	5	125	50	500

4. A young man was heard to remark, "I earn $100 dollars a week and spend half of it on golf no matter what the price of golf is." Illustrate this individual's price–consumption curve and his demand curve for golf.

5. a) Explain the effect of a fall in income on an individual's demand curve.
   b) Explain the effect of an increase in the price of tea on the demand curve for coffee.
   c) Explain the effect of an increase in the price of sugar on the demand curve for tea.

6. "Family size in the United States decreased from 1950 to 1980 while per-capita income increased. Assuming constant tastes, we must conclude that children are inferior goods." Evaluate this statement.

7. Suppose that margarine is an inferior good. Describe and illustrate the income and substitution effects associated with an increase in the price of margarine if the demand curve for margarine is downward-sloping.

8. According to observers, some of the elderly on fixed incomes are so poor they spend almost all their income on petfood for their own consumption. If the price of petfood falls, these individuals can get the same amount of nutrition for a smaller expenditure on petfood, which in turn allows them to divert some of their income to vegetables and meat. Since these items also provide calories, they can even reduce their consumption of petfood.
   a) If this is true, is petfood a Giffen good for these consumers?
   b) Illustrate how the income effect dominates the substitution effect for Giffen goods and graph the associated demand curve.

9. The chief executive of Wrapper Inc. has decided to introduce a new type of bubble gum called Grenade. Grenade is sugar-free and contains bits of dried fruit that explode with flavor when chewed. Wrapper's economists expect consumer demand for

Grenade to come from two primary sources: teenagers and health-conscious adults. The following are estimates of the demand for Grenade:

$$X^{teen} = 100 - 25p; \qquad X^{adults} = 30 - .03p$$

where X is quantity and p is price.

a) Find the market demand function for Grenade bubble gum if there are 1,000 teenagers and 500 adults.

b) If Wrapper Inc. wants to sell 10,000 packs of gum, what price must it charge?

10. One of the most famous "paradoxes" in the history of economic thought is the water–diamond paradox: Why is a vital commodity like water very cheap, while diamonds, which are clearly less essential for human existence, are very expensive? Explain this so-called "paradox" by comparing the market price (marginal benefit) of each commodity to the consumer surplus (total net benefit) associated with each commodity.

11. Suppose the government subsidizes the passenger railroad industry. Assume that the subsidy lowers passenger fares one dollar per ticket on average.

a) Illustrate the effect of the policy on consumer surplus.

b) Is the increase in consumer surplus larger or smaller than the cost of the program to the government? Explain.

12. Laser Tag is a new game recently introduced in the U.S. The game is played with a toy Laser Gun. The demand for Laser Guns is given by $X = 500 - 2p$.

a) At what price and quantity will total expenditure be maximized?

b) If the price is increased from $20 to $25, what will be the effect on total expenditures?

c) Over this range of prices what is the price elasticity of demand?

13. As noted in Chapter 1, General Motors has invested over $3 billion in its new Saturn line of automobiles. In deciding whether or not to undertake this investment, GM had to understand the relation between consumer demand for Saturn cars and its price, prices of other competing cars, and consumer incomes. Suppose you were hired by GM to estimate the demand function for Saturn cars and that you determined the following: $X = 600 - 6p_x + .5I + 2p_y$ where X is the number of Saturns per year, p_x the price of a Saturn, I is average annual income, and p_x is a price index measuring the price of comparable imports. In addition, you know that GM plans to

sell the Saturn for $12,000, that the average price of competing imports is $15,000, and that average income is $25,000 per year.

a) How many Saturn cars do you estimate will be sold?

b) If foreign producers cut prices by 10% in response to the introduction of Saturn, how will Saturn sales be affected?

c) If average income falls $5,000, how will Saturn sales be affected?

14. Bytes Inc. manufactures and sells personal computers. Bytes' economists estimate the price elasticity of demand to be 2. Currently PCs are selling for $750 and sales are 100 units per month.

a) If the price increases to $1,000, how many PCs will Bytes sell each month?

b) What will happen to revenues?

15. Demand for good X is estimated to be $X = 100 - .1p$.

a) If the price of X is $300 per unit, what is the price elasticity of demand at this price?

b) If the manufacturers wish to increase total expenditures, should they raise or lower the price?

16. Table 4–1 indicates that at a price of $1, quantity demanded is 50 units. When the price increases to $3, quantity demanded falls to 10 units.

a) Calculate the price elasticity of demand using the price–quantity information before the price change.

b) Calculate the price elasticity of demand using the price–quantity information after the price change.

c) Calculate the arc price elasticity of demand using the average price–quantity formula given on page 111.

17. Illustrate demand curves with the following elasticities:

a) $\epsilon_{xx} = 0$ (perfectly inelastic); and

b) $\epsilon_{xx} = \infty$ (perfectly elastic).

Write an equation for the associated demand functions.

18. An economist estimates the demand for intermediate microeconomics texts to be $p = 10 - X$.

a) Over what range of prices is demand (i) elastic; (ii) inelastic; (iii) unit-elastic?

b) At the current price two units are demanded. If the price increases what will happen to total expenditures?

19. The price elasticity of demand for restaurant meals is estimated to be 2.3 and the income elasticity is 1.6.

a) Are restaurant meals an inferior good? Explain.

b) Are restaurant meals a necessity or a luxury good? Explain.

20. Soul Sound sells 2,000 compact discs annually. Due to a new technical innovation, the price of compact disc players fell from $750 to $400. As a result, Soul Sound's sales of compact discs increased to 3,000 per year.
    a) What is the cross-price elasticity of demand for compact discs and compact disc players?
    b) At what price would you expect sales of discs to double from the original 2,000?
21. You are a member of a local agricultural cooperative. The majority of members favor a plan calling for each farmer to hold half his acres out of production to increase the price of corn. Proponents of the plan argue that the price increase will generate greater revenues for farmers. A consultant to the co-op has informed you that the demand for corn is given by:

$$X = 1,000 - 1,000p_x + .005I + 500p_w$$

where X is bushels of corn per year, p_x the price of corn, and p_w the price of wheat. If corn is currently selling for $.50 per bushel, do you argue for or against the plan?

REFERENCES   Deaton A., and J. Meullbauer. 1980. *Economics and Consumer Behavior*. Cambridge: Cambridge University Press.

Kreps, D. 1990. *A Course in Microeconomic Theory*. Princeton: Princeton University Press.

Varian, H. R. 1992. *Microeconomic Analysis*. 3d ed. New York: Norton.

DEMAND: A CALCULUS APPROACH

In the first section of this appendix we demonstrate how to derive demand functions and investigate their comparative static properties using calculus. In the second section we show rigorously that consumer surplus measures changes in real income.

A4.1 DEMAND FUNCTIONS

A consumer's demand function, sometimes called a Marshallian demand function, gives the quantity of a commodity that an individual will buy as a function of prices and income. We can derive demand functions from the first order conditions associated with the utility maximization problem.

Recall from the Appendix to Chapter 3 that the consumer's optimization problem can be summarized as follows:

$$\max_{x,y} u = u(x,y)$$

subject to $I = p_x x + p_y y$.

The Lagrangian for this problem is

$$L = u(x,y) + \lambda(I - p_x x - p_y y)$$

and the first order conditions are the following:

$$\frac{\partial L}{\partial x} = \frac{\partial u(x,y)}{\partial x} - \lambda p_x = 0 \qquad (A4.1)$$

$$\frac{\partial L}{\partial y} = \frac{\partial u(x,y)}{\partial y} - \lambda p_y = 0 \qquad (A4.2)$$

$$\frac{\partial L}{\partial \lambda} = I - p_x x - p_y y = 0 \qquad (A4.3)$$

Note that these first order conditions consist of three equations and three unknowns: x^*, y^*, and λ^*. The demand functions are obtained by solving this system for the unknowns in terms of the parameters of the model—that is, in terms of prices and income. If we do not have an explicit utility function, then we can only solve these equations implicitly. In particular, we denote the demand functions by:

$$x = x(p_x, p_y, I) \text{ and } y = y(p_x, p_y, I). \qquad (A4.4)$$

This notation is slightly different than in the text because now we are interested in both the demand for x and the demand for y.

EXAMPLE A4-1

Suppose that we can represent an individual's preferences by the utility function $u = 2x^{.5} + 2y^{.5}$. Derive this individual's demand functions and discuss their comparative static properties.

■ **SOLUTION** The Lagrangian for this optimization problem is

$$L = (2x^{.5} + 2y^{.5}) + \lambda(I - p_x x - p_y y)$$

and the corresponding first order conditions are as follows:

$$\partial L/\partial x = x^{-.5} - \lambda p_x = 0,$$

$$\partial L/\partial y = y^{-.5} - \lambda p_y = 0,$$

$$\partial L/\partial \lambda = I - p_x x - p_y y.$$

Solving the first equation for λ and substituting into the second equation gives

$$y^{-.5} - (x^{-.5}/p_x)p_y = 0;$$

solving this equation for y gives

$$y = (p_x/p_y)^2 x;$$

substituting this into the budget constraint gives

$$I - p_x x - p_y(p_x/p_y)^2 x = 0;$$

and solving for x gives the demand function for good x:

$$x = I/(p_x + p_x^2/p_y).$$

The demand function for good y is obtained by substituting for x in the expression $y = (p_x/p_y)^2 x$:

$$y = I/(p_y + p_y^2/p_x).$$

Having derived the demand functions, we obtain the comparative static properties simply by differentiating with respect to p_x, p_y, and I. Consider first a change in the price of good x. We have

$$\frac{\partial x}{\partial p_x} = -[I/(p_x + p_x^2/p_y)^2] \cdot (1 + 2p_x/p_y) < 0 \qquad \text{and}$$

$$\frac{\partial y}{\partial p_x} = -[I/(p_y + p_y^2/p_x)^2] \cdot (-p_y^2/p_x^2) > 0.$$

The first inequality indicates that the demand curve for good x is negatively sloped; that is, an increase in the price of good x, holding the price of good y and income constant, leads to a decrease in the amount of x purchased. The second inequality indicates that good y is a substitute for good x; that is, an increase in the price of good x, holding the price of good y and income constant, leads to an increase in the amount of y purchased. Note that we have used the partial derivative notation. This is because we are analyzing the effect of a change in one variable holding all others constant.

Next consider a change in the price of good y. We have

$$\frac{\partial x}{\partial p_y} = -[I/(p_x + p_x^2/p_y)^2] \cdot (-p_x^2/p_y^2) > 0 \qquad \text{and}$$

$$\frac{\partial y}{\partial p_x} = -[I/(p_y + p_y^2/p_x)^2] \cdot (1 + 2p_y/p_x^2) < 0.$$

Thus, good x is also a substitute for good y and the demand curve for good y is negatively sloped.

Finally, consider a change in income. Differentiating the demand functions with respect to I we have

$$\frac{\partial x}{\partial I} = 1/(p_x + p_x^2/p_y) > 0 \qquad \text{and}$$

$$\frac{\partial y}{\partial I} = 1/(p_y + p_y^2/p_x) > 0.$$

These inequalities indicate that both x and y are normal goods over all ranges of income; that is, an increase in income shifts both demand curves to the right. ∎

A4.2 CONSUMER SURPLUS

As we noted in the text, the price at which a consumer is willing to purchase an amount of good x depends in general on how much money income she has to spend. This means that using CS to measure real income is exactly correct only when a consumer's willingness to pay is independent of income—in other words, only when there are no *income effects*.

When preferences can be represented by a quasilinear utility function, there are no income effects and CS is an exact measure of real income. The general form of a *quasilinear utility* function is as follows:

$$u = v(x) + C.$$

The indifference curves associated with this utility function are vertically parallel—all the curves are vertically shifted versions of one curve. This is easily seen by noting that the slope of an indifference curve is independent of the value of C ($dC/dx = -v'(x)$).

Now consider the problem of maximizing quasilinear utility subject to a budget constraint:

$$\max_{x,C} u = v(x) + C$$

$$\text{subject to } I = p_x x + C.$$

In this instance, it is easy to convert this problem to an unconstrained optimization problem by eliminating C from the optimization problem. Substituting from the budget constraint, we have

$$\max_x u = v(x) + I - p_x x.$$

The first order condition for this problem is

$$v'(x) - p_x = 0. \tag{A4.5}$$

Thus, the inverse demand curve is given by $p_x = p(x) = v'(x)$. This means that the price the consumer is willing to pay to consume x is exactly equal to marginal utility.

Since the inverse demand function is the derivative of the utility function, we can integrate to find the utility function:

$$v(x) = \int_0^x v'(s)ds = \int_0^x p(s)ds. \tag{A4.6}$$

Hence, for quasilinear preferences the utility associated with consuming good x is exactly the area under the demand curve and consumer surplus measures exactly the net benefit of purchasing good x at price p_x: $CS = v(x) - p_x x = \int_0^x p(s)ds - p_x x$.

EXAMPLE A4–2

Suppose that an individual's preferences can be represented by the quasilinear utility function $u = 16x^{.5} + C$. Derive the demand function of good x and use consumer surplus to determine the welfare loss associated with a price increase from $1 to $5.

■ **SOLUTION** In this instance, the first order condition gives the following inverse demand function:

$$p_x = v'(x) = 8x^{-.5}.$$

In order to determine the change in real income associated with the stated increase in price, we need to calculate the change in the area under the demand curve, in this instance:

$$\int_0^x 8s^{-.5}ds = 16s^{.5}\Big|_0^x = 16x^{.5}.$$

Note that when $p_x = 1$, $x = 64$ and when $p_x = 2$, $x = 16$. Thus, before the price increase $CS = 16 \cdot 8 - 1 \cdot 64 = 64$ and after the price increase $CS = 16 \cdot 4 - 2 \cdot 16 = 32$, so consumer surplus falls by $32. This price increase therefore results in a $32 reduction in real income. ■

APPLICATIONS USING CONSUMER THEORY

After completing Chapter 5 you should be able to do the following:

◼ Analyze the effects of price discounts, nonprice rationing, excise subsidies, and fixed quantity subsidies on the choices consumers make.

◼ Use the theory of consumer choice to explain whether or not workers will work longer or shorter hours if income tax rates are lowered.

◼ Use the theory of consumer choice to explain why some individuals borrow while others save and how lower interest rates affect saving.

EXAMPLES

◼ **5–1** Clipping Coupons

◼ **5–2** Using Queues to Ration Gasoline

◼ **5–3** Eliminating the Deduction for Charitable Contributions

◼ **5–4** The Food Stamp Program

◼ **5–5** Income Taxes and Work Effort

◼ **5–6** Lower Interest Rates and Borrowing

By now, we know that one of the most important uses of the theory of consumer choice is to help us understand demand. We also know that once we grasp why demand curves satisfy the Law of Demand and how they shift when the economic environment changes, we can address many problems using demand curves without going behind the scenes and looking specifically at consumer choice.

Nevertheless, indifference curves and budget constraints—the principal tools we have acquired for analyzing consumer choice—are essential for solving some interesting and important economic problems. In this chapter we apply the theory of consumer choice to a variety of real-world problems. We see why "clipping coupons" can make some individuals better off and increase sales; why lower income taxes can lead people to work less rather than more; and why lower interest rates will lead to more borrowing, greater current demand for goods and services, but, possibly, a reduction in future demand. This chapter aims chiefly to demonstrate how the theory of consumer choice can help us understand the effect of corporate and public policies on economic decision making.

■ Firms often try to stimulate sales by using different types of price-discounting schemes. We have all encountered offers such as "Buy one get one free!" or "Two for the price of one," discounts for large bulk purchases, and "blue light specials," where customers receive a percentage discount off the listed price for a given amount of time.

5.1 PRICE DISCOUNTS

When consumers face **price discounts** of one form or another, two questions arise: Are they better off or worse off? and, Do they purchase more of the discounted item? Both of these questions are important from the firm's point of view. If consumers are not better off—if real income does not increase—the discount will be irrelevant. If consumers are better off yet do not purchase more of the discounted good, revenues will not increase.

One popular method of price discounting is to distribute discount coupons. Usually these coupons allow the bearer to purchase a fixed quantity of a particular item at a discount. If consumers desire more units of the commodity, they must purchase them at the market price. In the United States, almost every Sunday newspaper has one entire section devoted to coupons offering discounts on a variety of items such as toothpaste, breakfast cereal, laundry detergent, and other groceries.

EXAMPLE 5-1

CLIPPING COUPONS

The Kellogg Company, one of the largest manufacturers of breakfast cereals, often issues coupons that allow the bearer to purchase Kellogg's cereal at a discount, usually $.25 to $.50 off the usual price. (a) If consumers can use only one coupon per visit to the store, does this pricing strategy make consumers of breakfast cereals better off or worse off? (b) If cereal is a normal good, do consumers purchase more cereal? (c) Would consumers prefer a smaller *price* discount to coupons?

■ **SOLUTION** (a) Let us begin by considering a typical consumer, Michelle, who has an income of I dollars per week and spends it on cereal and all other goods. Michelle's pre-coupon budget constraint, BC_1, is illustrated in Figure 5-1(a) where we measure boxes of cereal on the horizontal axis and expenditures on all other goods on the vertical axis. Given BC_1, Michelle maximizes satisfaction by consuming market basket E on indifference curve u_0. The optimal market basket contains one box of Kellogg's cereal.

Now suppose Michelle clips out of the newspaper a coupon that allows her to purchase up to two boxes of Kellogg's cereal at a discount of $.50 per box. This coupon shifts Michelle's budget constraint to AFD. For the first two boxes of cereal, the price is $.50 less per box which means that this portion (AF) of her new budget constraint is flatter than the original. If Michelle wants to purchase more than two boxes, however, she must pay the market price and so the remaining part (FD) of the new budget constraint is parallel to the original. Given budget constraint AFD, Michelle's budget set has expanded so we know she is better off than before.

(b) Kellogg's cereal is now cheaper relative to other goods so the substitution effect indicates an increase in sales. Real income has also increased, and since cereal is a normal good, the income effect reinforces the substitution effect. Thus, Michelle purchases more boxes of Kellogg's cereal. In Figure 5-1(a), Michelle now chooses market basket F which contains two boxes of cereal.

(c) Consider Figure 5-1(b). (BC_1, AFD, E, and F are as before.) Now suppose that instead of issuing coupons, Kellogg simply reduces the price of its cereal. This would rotate budget constraint BC_1 outward about point A. Whether or not the consumer is better off depends on how much the price drops. The slope of the budget constraint given by AG—call it p_x^1—reflects the exact price that would make the consumer indifferent between coupons and a price

CLIPPING COUPONS   **FIGURE 5–1**

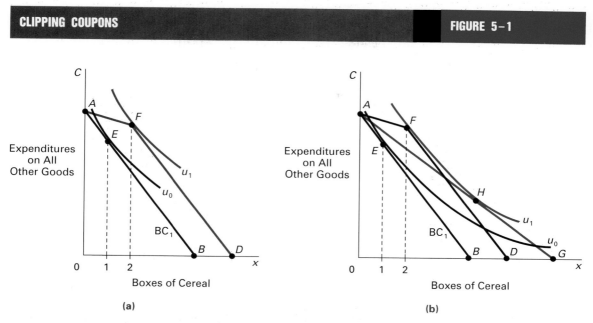

(a)   **(b)**

(a) A coupon offering a $.50 per-box discount for up to two boxes of cereal gives rise to budget constraint AFD. The optimal market basket is F. Real income is higher and the consumer buys more cereal. (b) A consumer is indifferent between a price reduction on all units of good x that rotates BC_1 outward to AG and the coupons. Any further price reduction would be preferred to coupons.

reduction. If Kellogg lowers the price of cereal below p_x^1, the budget constraint rotates even further and Michelle would prefer the price discount. However, as long as the discounted price remains greater than p_x^1, she would prefer coupons. ■

Before we move on, we should discuss briefly why firms might offer coupons rather than simply reduce prices. We will show in Chapter 13 that under certain circumstances firms can increase profits by segmenting buyers into two or more distinct classes and charging each class a different price. Such price discrimination is commonplace. Restaurants, movie theaters, and golf courses usually offer reduced prices for senior citizens and children; campus bookstores charge faculty and students different prices for books and supplies (faculty are usually given a discount); and nightclubs often arrange special evenings when women pay less for food and drinks.

Issuing coupons is another type of price discrimination. Coupons effectively segment buyers according to how they value time. On the one hand, individuals who value time highly—young urban professionals for example—will not take the time to clip coupons and shop for bargains. To save time, they are willing to pay the retail price for goods and services. On the other hand, individuals who do not value time very highly will "clip" coupons and shop for "bargains." By segmenting the market in this fashion, firms can increase profit.

5.2 NONPRICE RATIONING

■ As we noted in Chapter 1, prices in free markets serve a rationing function: they allocate goods among consumers. Sometimes, however, firms and governments use **nonprice rationing**—that is, they step in and organize the allocation of a good among consumers. Usually, nonprice rationing takes effect when supplies of a product are limited and it seems more equitable—fairer—than allowing price to perform the rationing task.

Nonprice rationing can take various forms. *Governments* usually ration goods by issuing a fixed number of ration coupons. When purchasing a rationed good, each consumer must also turn in a coupon. In many countries basic commodities such as sugar, salt, and gasoline were rationed during World War II because supplies were scarce.

Firms, on the other hand, sometimes ration goods either by making people wait in line or by restricting the number of units an individual can purchase per visit, or by a combination of these two. In the U.S., service stations rationed gasoline in this fashion during the 1979 oil embargo. In fact, most of us have probably experienced this type of nonprice rationing. Anyone who has waited in long lines to purchase items in short supply such as popular toys (Cabbage Patch dolls in 1983–1984) or tickets to musical concerts (New Kids on the Block, Michael Jackson) and sporting events (Super Bowl, NCAA basketball tournament), or anyone who has queued to eat in a popular restaurant that doesn't take reservations or to register for college classes, is familiar with this type of nonprice rationing.

EXAMPLE 5–2

USING QUEUES TO RATION GASOLINE

In 1974 and 1979 the nations of OPEC (Organization of Petroleum Exporting Countries) were successful in reducing the supply of oil to importing countries and, as a result, a shortage of gasoline arose. In the U.S. the federal government imposed price ceilings on gasoline in order to prevent prices from soaring. This measure led to long lines at the pumps.

Suppose that local service stations are open from 8 A.M. to 5 P.M. so that the typical consumer, Kathy, must take time off work to purchase gasoline. (a) If there are no restrictions on the number of gallons she can purchase per visit, will Kathy wait in line? (b) If she waits will she buy more or less gasoline than she would buy if there were no shortage? (c) If service stations decide to limit each customer to 10 gallons per visit, will Kathy wait in line? (d) Would retirees be more or less likely than Kathy to wait in line to purchase gasoline? Explain.

■ **SOLUTION** Let's begin by illustrating what Kathy would do if she did not have to wait in line to buy gasoline. In Figure 5–2(a), BC_1 represents Kathy's budget constraint, and $0AB$ the budget set in the absence of any type of nonprice rationing. Given this budget constraint, Kathy maximizes satisfaction by purchasing market basket E on indifference curve u_3. This optimal bundle contains x_0 gallons of gasoline.

(a,b) On the one hand, once nonprice rationing goes into effect, Kathy must decide whether or not to wait in line. If she chooses not to, she is left with market basket A on indifference curve u_1. On the other hand, if she takes time off from work to queue, she forfeits income and her budget constraint shifts inward. As long as there are no restrictions on the number of gallons she can purchase after waiting in line, her budget constraint is BC_2. The budget set associated with BC_2 is area $0CD$. Since this is smaller than $0AB$, we know that whether she waits or not, Kathy is worse off than she was before rationing.

Kathy will wait in line to buy gasoline only if she can attain a higher level of real income by doing so—that is, if she can attain a level of real income greater than that represented by the indifference curve passing through market basket A. This curve is u_1, which represents Kathy's real income if she does not wait in line.

Given budget constraint BC_2, Kathy maximizes satisfaction by consuming market basket F on indifference curve u_2. This curve represents Kathy's maximum level of satisfaction if she waits in line. In this instance, u_2 is further to the northeast than u_1, so Kathy is better off waiting in line and she buys fewer gallons of gasoline ($x_1 < x_0$).

The indifference curves shown in Figure 5–2(a) are just one possible representation of a consumer's preferences. In Figure 5–2(b), we have illustrated another family of indifference curves

FIGURE 5-2   **WAITING TO BUY GASOLINE**

(a) Having to wait in line to purchase gasoline shifts the budget constraint inward to BC$_2$. The optimal market basket is F since the alternative, not buying gasoline, is on a lower indifference curve. If, in addition, consumers are limited to 10 gallons per visit, the budget constraint becomes CG, and real income falls even further. (b) Here, the individual will not wait in line. Market basket A is on a higher indifference curve compared to bundle F.

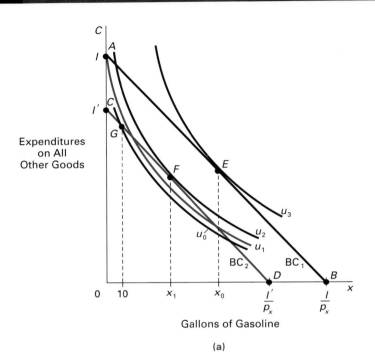

(a)

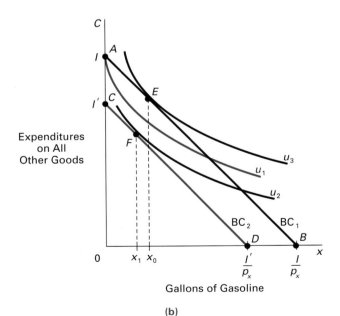

(b)

that are flatter than Kathy's. An individual with these preferences would not wait since the real income associated with market basket A (indifference curve u_1) is greater than that associated with bundle F (indifference curve u_2). This consumer would be worse off waiting.

The difference between Kathy's preferences and those depicted in 5–2(b) is the relative preference for gasoline. Even though each consumer faces the same economic conditions, Kathy has a stronger preference for gasoline relative to other goods, so she waits while the other individual does not.

(c) Next we must consider the case where consumers are allowed to purchase only, say, 10 gallons of gasoline. In this instance, Kathy's budget constraint is the line segment CG (see Figure 5–2(a)). Since bundle A is on a higher indifference curve $(u_1 > u_0)$, Kathy does not wait. Instead, she spends all her income on other goods (which includes taking the bus to work). In this instance, the quantity restriction alters behavior. Kathy no longer finds it in her best interest to wait.

(d) If Kathy is retired, then her wage rate is zero and the opportunity cost of waiting in line, in money terms, is zero. Waiting in line has no effect on her budget constraint so she will wait and purchase market basket E. Thus, other things being equal, retired individuals tend to spend more time waiting in lines to purchase goods. ∎

There are two lessons to be learned from Example 5–2. First, when evaluating the effect of nonprice rationing on the well-being of individual consumers, it is important to consider not only the money cost of purchasing the rationed good but also any other costs imposed on consumers by the rationing mechanism itself. In this example, there is an opportunity cost to waiting in line—lost income—which reduces the market baskets available to the consumer. A study by economists Robert Deacon and John Sonstelie has indicated that during the shortages in the 1970s, the opportunity cost of waiting in line to purchase gasoline was lowest for part-time workers ($3.52–$5.30) and students ($7.15–$10.96) and that it increased with income. In light of our discussion, this seems quite reasonable. Part-time workers and students can wait in line when it doesn't conflict with their jobs or classes, respectively, while higher incomes mean greater lost earnings per unit of time. (Robert T. Deacon and John Sonstelie, "Rationing by Waiting and the Value of Time: Results from a Natural Experiment." *Journal of Political Economy*, 93 [1985]: 627–47.)

Second, an individual's relative preference for the good he or she is waiting to purchase also affects the decision to wait in line. Those who have a strong preference for driving their own cars—and hence a strong preference for gasoline—tend to wait; those willing to use other means of transport tend to opt out of waiting.

5.3 EXCISE SUBSIDIES

■ An **excise subsidy** is just the opposite of an excise tax in that the government *pays* part of the per-unit price of a good and allows consumers to purchase as many units of the good as desired at the lower, subsidized, price. For example, if the government pays 25% of a household's food or clothing costs, then this effectively lowers the prices of these goods for that household.

In the U.S., some of the most interesting and important excise subsidies are the tax deductions in the income tax code. Tax deductions are excise subsidies in that the government reduces the taxpayer's burden when certain items are purchased, a measure which in effect lowers the prices of these items just as a direct excise subsidy would do. Some examples of deductible expenses are medical expenses above 7.5% of adjusted gross income, mortgage interest payments, charitable contributions, fringe benefits, and moving expenses.

Since tax deductions reduce the size of the tax base, they also reduce the revenue that can be collected at a given tax rate. The primary goal of the Tax Reform Act of 1986 was to reduce income tax rates while maintaining tax revenues by reducing and eliminating tax deductions. The legislature cut the amount of medical expenses that taxpayers could claim, eliminated the deduction for charitable contributions for those not itemizing deductions, and eradicated all deductions for personal interest expenses on automobiles, credit cards, and educational loans.

EXAMPLE 5–3

ELIMINATING THE DEDUCTION FOR CHARITABLE CONTRIBUTIONS

Prior to the Tax Reform Act of 1986, everyone could deduct all contributions to charity. Now only those taxpayers who itemize deductions on their federal return can claim for charitable contributions. Suppose that the Red Cross has hired us to investigate how taxpayers will adjust their donations to charity after this change if: (a) the income tax rate remains the same and (b) the income tax rate is lowered so that tax revenues are held constant.

■ **SOLUTION** First we must determine how much the typical consumer, Sally, gives to charity (the Red Cross) prior to the change in the tax code. If Sally has an adjusted gross income of I dollars per year, and her income tax rate is t, then her initial budget constraint is

$$BC_1: I - t(I - x) = x + C$$

where x is the amount spent on charity, C is the amount spent on all other goods, and $(I - x)$ is her taxable income. Budget constraint BC_1 is shown in Figure 5–3(a). The slope of BC_1 is $-(1 - t)$ and reflects the relative price of giving to charity. Given budget constraint BC_1, Sally maximizes satisfaction by consuming market basket D on indifference curve u_0 and she contributes x_0 dollars to charity. (We are simplifying the true tax rate structure by assuming that the tax rate t does not vary with income. This is called a proportional tax. In the U.S. the income taxes are progressive; that is, t increases with income. However, the conclusions we reach in this example are valid for a progressive tax as well.)

(a) If the deduction for charitable contributions is eliminated, the cost of giving to charity increases because individuals no longer get a tax-break. If the deduction is eliminated and the income tax rate does not change, then Sally's budget constraint swings inward from BC_1 to BC_2 ($BC_2: I - tI = x + C$). The slope of BC_2 is -1 which reflects the increased price of giving $(1 > 1 - t)$.

Given BC_2, Sally's budget set is smaller which means that whatever market basket she chooses, she is worse off than before: her real income has fallen. But does she give more or less to charity? To answer this question, we must check the income and substitution effects.

The price of charity has gone up relative to the price of other goods. The substitution effect indicates that charitable contributions should decrease. In addition, real income has fallen, so given that charitable contributions are normal goods, the income effect also indicates that contributions should fall. Since both the substitution and income effects work in the same direction, the total effect is a reduction in charity. In Figure 5–3(a), the new optimal market basket is bundle E on indifference curve u_1. Eliminating the deduction while holding the tax rate constant makes Sally worse off and reduces the amount she gives to charity from x_0 to x_1 dollars.

(b) In order to consider tax revenues, we must first add to our diagram a pretax budget constraint. In Figure 5–3(b), BC_0 is the pretax budget constraint. It has the same slope as BC_2. The vertical distance between BC_0 and BC_1, DG, represents tax payments with

FIGURE 5-3   ELIMINATING THE DEDUCTION FOR CHARITY

(a) Eliminating the deduction for charity increases the price of giving to charity which shifts the budget constraint to BC₂. Real income falls as does the amount individuals give to charity. (b) If the tax rate is simultaneously changed to maintain constant tax revenues, consumers are better off than they were with the tax deduction and higher tax rates.

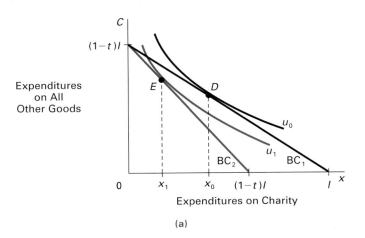

(a)

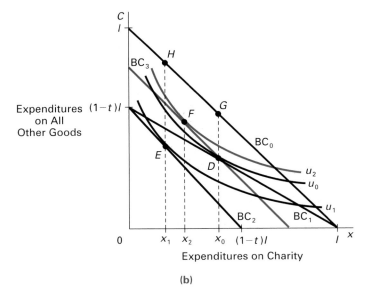

(b)

the deduction, while the vertical distance between BC_0 and BC_2, EH, represents tax payments without the deduction. Clearly, Sally's tax bill increases when the deduction is eliminated but the tax rate is unchanged (see above).

Now we want to construct the budget constraint associated with a tax rate that, in the absence of any deduction for charity, raises the same revenue as was raised when the deduction was allowed—that is, that raises DG dollars in revenue. To do this, we must lower the tax rate. This causes the budget constraint to shift outward, parallel to BC_2. It should shift so that no matter which market basket Sally chooses she pays DG dollars in taxes. In Figure 5–3(b), this new budget constraint is BC_3, which passes through point D—the vertical distance between BC_0 and any point on BC_3 is precisely DG.

Given BC_3, is Sally better off? Maximizing satisfaction subject to BC_3, Sally consumes market basket F on indifference curve u_2. Sally's real income increases even beyond the level it was at when the deduction for charity was allowed! That is, eliminating the deduction and simultaneously reducing the tax rate to maintain revenue makes her better off.

In addition, note that Sally gives more to charity than she did before the tax rate changed—$x_2 > x_1$, but less than she did when the deduction was allowed—$x_2 < x_0$. This is why Sally is better off with a lower tax rate and no deduction rather than a higher tax rate with a deduction. The deduction lowers the price of charity relative to other goods and generates both income and substitution effects; a cut in the tax rate generates only an income effect. Both result in the same amount of tax savings but consumers are better off if they realize those savings irrespective of how much they give to charity. ∎

The analysis in this example implies that consumers are better off with lump-sum rather than excise subsidies. (We learned the same thing from Example 4–2 about excise and lump-sum taxes.) If given cash, consumers can purchase a preferred market basket. However, this *positive* analysis does not imply that cash grants are a *desirable* way to subsidize everyone. It only demonstrates that recipients would be better off according to their own preferences. Whether or not cash grants are better is a *normative* issue.

5.4 FIXED-QUANTITY SUBSIDIES

■ In the United States there are a variety of government spending programs designed to aid the poor. These *transfer programs* are a way of providing goods and services to low-income individuals to help them maintain some minimal standard of living. For example, Medicaid provides medical care for individuals under 65; the Housing Assistance program offers subsidized housing; and the Food Stamp program supplies food and other basic items.

Each of these transfer programs provides poorer people with fixed-quantity subsidies. When the government arranges a **fixed-quantity subsidy,** it makes a certain quantity of a good available to consumers at no cost or at a cost below the market price. The important difference between a fixed-quantity subsidy and an excise subsidy is that the quantity of the good being subsidized is fixed and beyond the control of the recipients.

In the next example, we illustrate how consumer choice theory can help us understand the effects of a fixed-quantity subsidy on consumer behavior.

EXAMPLE 5–4

THE FOOD STAMP PROGRAM

A food stamp program supplies eligible low-income families with food stamps at a cost below the market value of the stamps. Recipients can use these just like money to buy food and other basic items.

Suppose that Mark qualifies for the food stamp program. If he chooses to participate, Mark pays $50 and receives a booklet of food stamps that he can use to purchase up to $250 worth of food per month. (This is how the federal food stamp program operated prior to 1979. Shortly we'll discuss how the program has altered since then.) (a) Assuming Mark has a monthly income of $500 per month, and that the price of food is $5 dollars per unit, will he enroll in the program? (b) If he chooses to participate, will he increase his food consumption? (c) Would Mark prefer a cash grant that costs the government the same amount of money? Explain.

■ **SOLUTION** In Figure 5–4(a), BC_1 represents Mark's pre-subsidy budget constraint. Prior to receiving food stamps, Mark maximizes satisfaction by purchasing market basket A on indifference curve u_0; thus, he consumes x_0 units of food. (a,b) If Mark chooses to participate in the program, his budget constraint shifts to JKL. The food stamps cost Mark $50, which reduces the amount he can spend on other goods from $500 to $450, but he can use the stamps to purchase up to $250 of food without spending any more of his own cash. Effectively, the price of food is zero as long as he has stamps. This means that the first part of his budget constraint, JK, is horizontal. If Mark uses all his food stamps, he can purchase $x_2 = 250/5 = 50$ units of food. Should he want to buy more food, he must use his own money and pay the market price. This means that the second part of his budget constraint, KL, is parallel to his original budget constraint. In this case, the budget constraint is kinked at point K where the $250 in food stamps is used up.

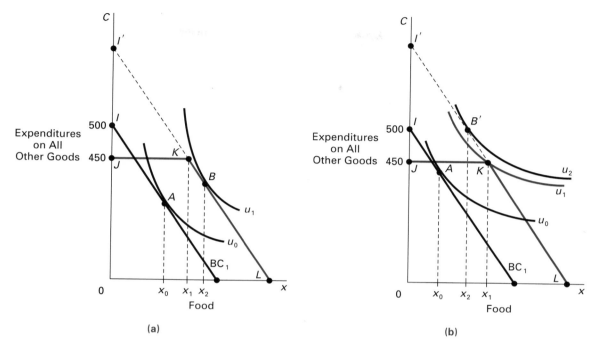

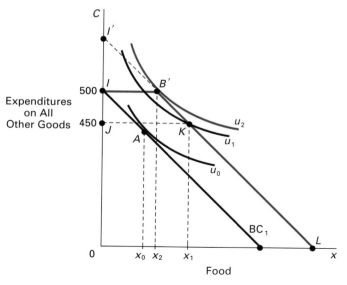

(a) The food stamp program shifts the budget constraint to JKL by allowing the consumer to purchase $250 of food stamps, JK, for only $50, IJ. In this instance, the result is identical to giving the consumer a $200 cash grant. (b) A consumer with preferences like these would prefer the cash grant. (c) If the purchase price requirement is eliminated and the consumer is given $200 in free food stamps, more people will be indifferent between food stamps and a $200 cash grant.

Given budget constraint *JKL* in Figure 5–4(a), Mark chooses market basket *B* on indifference curve u_1. Since he is better off with this basket, he enrolls in the program and his food consumption increases from x_0 to x_2. From the policy maker's perspective, these are desirable results because the government's goals in providing food stamps are to increase real income and food consumption of poorer people.

Question (c) asks whether or not Mark would prefer a $200 cash grant to the food stamps. With a $200 cash grant, Mark's budget constraint would shift outward from BC_1 to *I'KL*. The cash grant budget constraint differs from the food stamp budget constraint in that the market baskets on *I'K* are now available to Mark. This is because cash can purchase food *or* other goods while food stamps can purchase food *only*.

Given budget constraint *I'KL*, there are two possibilities. In Figure 5–4(a), Mark maximizes satisfaction by purchasing market basket *B*, the same one he chose under the food stamp subsidy. In this instance, Mark is indifferent between receiving a $200 cash grant and paying $50 for $250 worth of food stamps; the effects are the same either way. The reason for this is that Mark wants to consume *more than* $200 worth of food, $x_2 > x_1$. Under the food stamp program, Mark uses all his food stamps *and* spends some of his own money to buy more food.

Figure 5–4(b) shows the other possibility. In this case, another consumer, Misty, would prefer the $200 cash grant. If given $200 in cash, Misty maximizes satisfaction by purchasing market basket *B'* on indifference curve u_2. Notice that this market basket contains less than $200 worth of food, $x_2 < x_1$. Misty prefers other goods over food more than Mark does (or, put another way, Mark is a bigger food lover than Misty). The food stamp program, however, does not allow her to purchase this market basket because the stamps can only be used to buy food; she can only choose from those market baskets on *JKL*. Faced with this budget constraint, the best Misty can do is choose market basket *K* on indifference curve u_1 (a corner solution). ∎

Example 5–4 illustrates how economists use consumer theory to understand the effects of a fixed-quantity subsidy; however, it can also help us design a better food stamp program. There is a problem if the situation shown in Figure 5–4(b) occurs: if individuals are better off with a cash grant, then they have an incentive to sell some of their food stamps and use the proceeds to buy other goods; as a result there is a tendency for an illegal black market for food stamps to arise. We would like to design a program in which most recipients are like Mark and as few as possible are like Misty.

One way to reform the food stamp program with this aim in mind might be to eliminate the $50 purchase price and simply give out $200 worth of food stamps free. This, in effect, would extend the food stamp budget constraint from K back along the cash grant budget constraint to B'. As shown in Figure 5–4(c), the food stamp budget constraint would be $IB'L$. Comparing this design to the one discussed above, the market baskets on $B'K$ are now available to recipients and the number of individuals who would prefer a cash grant has decreased. In the late 1970s, economists used this line of reasoning to argue for a change in the food stamp program and in 1979 just such a change was implemented. Currently in the U.S., food stamps are provided at no cost to recipients and, while there is still a black market for stamps, economist agree that most recipients are indifferent between the stamps and a cash grant.

■ Up to this point, we have assumed that the consumer's income is fixed. For most people, however, this is not the case. Income varies depending on such factors as how much time is spent working. The indifference curve/budget constraint apparatus that we used to develop the theory of consumer choice can also be used to investigate an individual worker's decision about how many hours to work and to analyze how changes in the economic environment affect that decision.

Let's begin by writing down an equation characterizing the budget constraint of a typical worker, Frances. We assume that Frances earns a fixed hourly wage and can work any number of hours at that wage. Let C denote consumption expenditures (this is just like the composite commodity only now it includes *all* goods), L denote hours of work, and w, the wage rate. Frances' budget constraint must reflect the fact that the amount she spends on goods must equal her income. Thus, her budget constraint is

$$BC_1: C = wL. \qquad \text{(5.1)}$$

Is something missing from this budget constraint? Does Frances have an unlimited amount of time to spend working? Of course she does not. She has only 168 hours a week (24 hours a day, seven days a week). Thus we must incorporate this *time constraint* into her budget constraint.

In order to do this, we divide the total time available, denoted by T, into two mutually exclusive categories: work and leisure. Here the term leisure simply refers to the portion of time for which

5.5 THE CONSUMPTION– LEISURE CHOICE AND WORK EFFORT

Frances does not receive compensation from an employer. Letting H denote leisure time, Frances' time constraint is given algebraically by $H + L = T$. That is, working time plus leisure time must equal the total time available.

Incorporating the time constraint into Frances' budget constraint by substituting $L = T - H$ into equation (5.1) gives

$$\text{BC}_1: C = w(T - H) = wT - wH. \qquad (5.2)$$

Figure 5–5 illustrates this budget constraint. We measure consumption expenditures on the vertical axis and leisure time on the horizontal axis. The budget constraint is a straight line and its slope is equal to minus the wage rate.

Now recall that previously the slope of a budget constraint reflected relative prices—that is, the rate at which consumers could exchange goods. It does so here as well. The wage is the opportunity cost of not working and hence represents the relative price of leisure time. When consumers must earn income in the labor market, the slope of the budget constraint reflects the rate at which they can exchange leisure time for income.

FIGURE 5–5   **CONSUMPTION-LEISURE CHOICE AND WORK EFFORT**

If read from left to right, the horizontal axis measures leisure time. If read from right to left it measures hours of work. The slope of budget constraint BC_1 is minus the wage rate. The optimal market basket is A. This individual works $(T-H_1)$ hours and earns C_1 dollars which he spends on consumption goods.

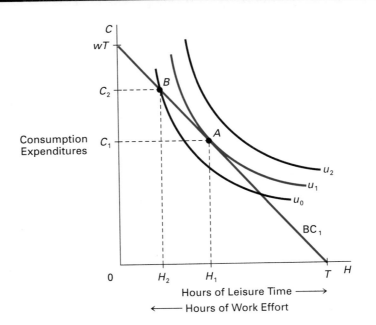

Given her budget and time constraints, we want to know how Frances will divide her time between leisure and work. To the worker, leisure time is an economic good, just as are apples and oranges—for a given level of consumption more leisure time is preferred to less. We can represent an individual's preferences for consumption expenditure and leisure with a family of indifference curves. In Figure 5–5, we have drawn three such indifference curves.

Recall that the slope of an indifference curve represents the rate at which a consumer is willing to exchange one good for another. In this instance the goods are consumption and leisure time. The slope measures the relative importance of leisure and consumption to the individual.

Given BC_1, Frances maximizes satisfaction by consuming market basket A on indifference u_1. This market basket consists of H_1 hours of **leisure time** and C_1 dollars of income to be spent on consumption. **Work effort** is $L_1 = (T - H_1)$ hours. Once again, the consumer maximizes satisfaction by choosing the market basket corresponding to the point where an indifference curve is tangent to the budget constraint. That is, Frances maximizes satisfaction when the rate at which she is willing to exchange leisure time for consumption— the marginal rate of substitution between consumption and leisure time—is just equal to the wage rate—or the opportunity cost of not working.

Note that Frances *does not* maximize her income. She could earn more money choosing market basket B which represents working longer hours: $(T - H_2) > (T - H_1)$. However, the additional amount of goods and services that she can purchase with this added income, $(C_2 - C_1)$, is not worth the leisure time she must sacrifice, $(H_1 - H_2)$, to obtain it; that is, market basket B is on a lower indifference curve than market basket A.

Using indifference curves and budget constraints to investigate work effort is a straightforward and important extension of consumer choice theory. To take one example, we can use this model to analyze how a change in income tax rates will affect work effort and tax revenues.

EXAMPLE 5–5

INCOME TAXES AND WORK EFFORT

During the 1980s a wave of fiscal conservatism rolled through the United States. One of the primary concerns of the Reagan administration (1980–1988) was tax reform. During his two terms in office, President Reagan advocated reducing the income tax rate for most Americans. To promote such a reduction in the face of rising government expenditures, President Reagan adopted an argument first made by an American economist, Arthur Laffer: the president argued that lower taxes would actually increase tax revenues because individuals would now have a greater incentive to work. Opponents of the president's plan argued that tax cuts would not necessarily increase work effort and that they certainly would not increase revenues.

Suppose that a newly elected member of the House of Representatives has hired us as consultants to work on tax reform. (a) First we must analyze the impact of a tax cut on the work effort of a typical American. (b) Second we need to determine whether or not tax revenues will increase or decrease when the tax rate changes.

Our initial research indicates the following: Dave Webster, the typical American, faces an income tax rate of 30% and works 2,000 hours per year. We also know from previous studies that leisure time is a normal good.

■ **SOLUTION** Dave Webster's budget constraint prior to the proposed tax cut is

$$BC_1: C = wL - t_1wL = (1 - t)_1w(T - H) = \hat{w}_1T - \hat{w}_1H,$$

where t_1 is the initial tax rate, $\hat{w}_1$ is the initial net (after-tax) wage, and T is the total hours per year available for work or leisure (accountants usually take T to be 5,840 hours).

Figure 5–6(a) shows budget constraint BC_1. Given this budget constraint we know that Dave Webster maximizes satisfaction by working 2,000 hours per year, or by using $H_0 = T - 2,000$ hours for leisure time, market basket E on indifference curve u_0.

(a) Now suppose the tax rate is cut from t_1 to t_2. As a result, Dave's budget constraint shifts to BC_2 in the diagram. It is steeper because the new net wage, $\hat{w}_2 = (1 - t_2)w$, is greater than the initial net wage, $\hat{w}_1$. Given budget constraint BC_2, does Dave work more or less? Since the slope of the budget has changed, relative prices have changed and we must consider income and substitution effects.

The reduction in the tax rate increases the net wage or the per-hour amount each individual takes home. This means that the cost of not working an additional hour increases; that is, the opportunity cost of staying at home increases (or leisure time is now relatively more expensive). Since the price of leisure time increases, the substitution effect indicates that Dave should consume fewer hours of leisure and work more.

INCOME TAXES AND WORK EFFORT

FIGURE 5–6

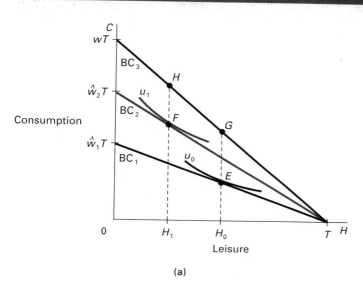

(a)

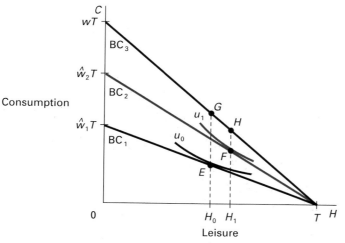

(b)

(a) A reduction in the income tax rate increases the net wage and swings the budget constraint up to BC_2. Leisure time is more expensive and real income is higher. If the substitution effect dominates the income effect, then the optimal market basket is F and work effort increases. In this instance, tax revenues may either increase or decrease. (b) If the income effect dominates, then the optimal market basket is F and work effort falls. In this instance, tax revenues always fall.

The increase in the net wage also causes real income to rise. No matter which market basket Dave chooses on budget constraint BC_2, he is better off. We know that leisure is a normal good so the income effect indicates that Dave should consume more leisure time and work less.

The total effect of the tax cut is the sum of the income and substitution effects. Since the substitution effect indicates that work effort should increase, while the income effect signals that it should decrease, the total effect is ambiguous. Although we know that leisure is a normal good, the income and substitution effects work in opposite directions and we cannot be sure whether the tax cut will increase or decrease work effort. The end result depends on preferences.

This result is different from the one we obtained in Chapter 4. There we found that the income and substitution effects reinforce each other for normal goods. The reason for this difference is that when the price of leisure time—the wage rate—increases, real income also increases; however, for other normal goods an increase in price leads to a fall in real income.

Figure 5–6(a) illustrates the case where the substitution effect outweighs the income effect. In this instance, Dave Webster increases his work effort in response to the increase in the net wage: $H_1 < H_0$. Figure 5–6(b) illustrates the case where the income effect is greater than the substitution effect and Dave works less: $H_1 > H_0$. The impact of the tax on work effort depends crucially on the preferences of the individuals affected by the change.

(b) In order to determine the impact of the tax cut on tax revenues we must be able to compare the tax payments Dave made before and after the change. Dave's tax payment when the tax rate is t_1 is $t_1 w L_1$. Can we illustrate this payment in Figure 5–6(a)? As it stands now we cannot; but, can we think of a hypothetical budget constraint that, if added to the diagram, would allow us to depict tax payments?

The budget constraint that will do the trick is the "no tax" budget constraint. In Figure 5–6(a), this is BC_3, which is steeper than either of the budget constraints with taxes since the net wage is higher.

Adding BC_3 to our analysis allows us to illustrate tax payments, which in turn are tax revenues. Consider first the initial tax rate. In Figure 5–6(a), draw a vertical line from point E up to G on BC_3. The distance GH_0 is the amount Dave could spend on other goods if he worked 2,000 hours per year and paid nothing in taxes. The distance EH_0 is the amount Dave is actually able to spend given the initial tax rate. The difference between these, GE, is the amount of income that Dave must forego to pay income taxes; thus, *GE* represents tax revenues when the tax rate is t_1. Similarly, *HF* is Dave's tax payment after the tax cut.

Can we say which is larger? The way Figure 5–6(a) is drawn, Dave pays less after the tax cut; that is, tax revenues fall. Note, however, that the further to the left point *F* is along BC_2, the greater are tax payments after the tax cut. Eventually a point could be reached where tax payments would actually increase. However, such a result is not necessarily the case. It occurs only if the work effort increases a great deal or, in other words, if the substitution effect is substantially larger than the income effect.

Finally, consider tax revenues when work effort falls as a result of the tax cut. In this case, *HF* is always less than *GE* (see Figure 5–9[b]) and tax revenues always fall.

We conclude, then, that in general the tax cut will have an ambiguous impact on work effort and tax revenues. The results depend crucially on the preferences of the individuals affected. If income effects dominate, then a tax cut reduces work effort. If substitution effects dominate, then a tax cut increases work effort. The effect of the tax cut on tax payments depends in its turn on the change in work effort. ∎

A word of caution is in order here. In Example 5–5 we are focusing on an individual, not the economy as a whole, so our conclusion concerning tax cuts is somewhat more pessimistic than is probably warranted. To see this, note that in each case discussed above, the individual increases consumption following the tax cut. Thus, even if one individual reduces work effort someone else must increase work effort to produce the additional goods and services that the first individual is buying after the tax cut. This does not necessarily mean that tax revenues actually increase, but only that it is not as remote a possibility as Example 5–5 seems to indicate.

∎ In the last section we used indifference curves and budget constraints to model an individual's choice between leisure time and consumption expenditures when he or she had to work for a living. We can also use this same apparatus to investigate the factors that influence the way consumers rearrange consumption over time by saving or borrowing.

Saving involves spending less than one's current income, so that future consumption can be greater than future income. **Borrowing**, on the other hand, involves spending more than one's current income by reducing future consumption below future income. By

5.6 INDIVIDUAL CHOICES OVER TIME

borrowing and saving, we rearrange consumption between different time periods.

To make the model as simple as possible, suppose that Bruce, a typical consumer, has a two-period time horizon. He earns I_1 dollars in period 1 (today) and I_2 dollars in period 2 (tomorrow). The interest rate at which he can borrow or lend is r% per year. Further, we assume that there is no inflation in the general price level—that a dollar today buys the same amount of goods as a dollar tomorrow. We can relax this assumption if we use the real rate of interest instead of the nominal rate but, for our purposes now, it is easier to assume no inflation. (The nominal rate of interest is the actual rate at which an individual can borrow and lend. We can think of the real rate of interest as the nominal rate less the inflation rate. Interest rates are discussed in greater detail in Chapter 17.)

Now let's begin by writing an equation representing Bruce's lifetime budget constraint. Letting C_1 and C_2 stand for expenditures on present and future consumption respectively, Bruce's lifetime budget constraint can be written as

$$BC_1: C_1 + C_2 = I_1 + I_2 + r(I_1 - C_1),$$

where $r(I_1 - C_1)$ is interest earned if Bruce saves, $(I_1 - C_1) > 0$, or the interest that must be repaid if Bruce borrows, $(I_1 - C_1) < 0$. Combining like terms, we have

$$BC_1: C_1(1 + r) + C_2 = I_1(1 + r) + I_2.$$

This equation indicates that lifetime expenditures on consumption measured in tomorrow's dollars, $C_1(1 + r) + C_2$, must be equal to lifetime income measured in tomorrow's dollars, $I_1(1 + r) + I_2$. (If we divided both sides of the budget constraint by $1 + r$, then expenditures on consumption and incomes would all be measured in today's dollars.)

Figure 5–7(a) illustrates this budget constraint. We measure consumption in period 2 on the vertical axis and consumption in period 1 on the horizontal axis. The budget constraint is a straight line and its slope is equal to $-(1 + r)$ which reflects the relative price of present to future consumption. To make this last point clear, note that $(1 + r)$ is the opportunity cost of spending a dollar today. If Bruce spends one dollar of his current income then he has one less dollar to spend tomorrow and, in addition, he foregoes the interest he could have earned by saving the dollar. Thus, $(1 + r)$ presents the relative price of current consumption. In the two-

INDIVIDUAL CHOICES OVER TIME   FIGURE 5-7

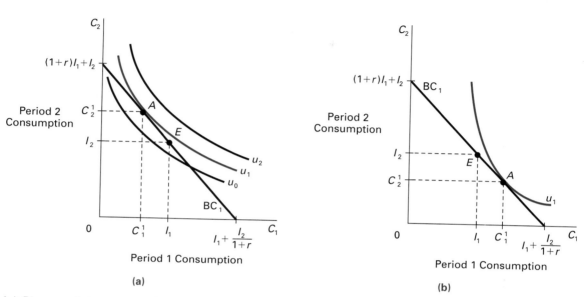

(a)

(b)

(a) Given an interest rate of r percent per year, earnings of I_1 dollars in period 1, and I_2 dollars in period 2, the budget constraint relating consumption today to consumption tomorrow is BC_1. The slope of BC_2 is $-(1 + r)$. The optimal market basket is A. Since C_1^1 is less than I_1, this consumer saves in period 1 to finance consumption in period 2. (b) Here, C_1^1 is greater than I_1 and this consumer borrows in period 1 which reduces consumption in period 2.

period model, the slope of the budget constraint reflects the rate at which consumers can exchange consumption today for consumption tomorrow.

There is one point on Bruce's lifetime budget constraint that deserves special attention—market basket E. This is called the *endowment market basket* and represents the situation where Bruce neither borrows nor lends. If Bruce chooses to purchase the endowment market basket, then he spends all his current income today and all his future income tomorrow. This means that the endowment market basket is always available to Bruce no matter what the interest rate is.

Given his budget constraint, we want to know how much Bruce purchases in each period. The indifference curves in Figure 5–7(a) represent Bruce's preferences for present and future consumption.

In this case, the slope of an indifference curve measures the rate at which a consumer is willing to exchange present consumption for future consumption.

Given BC_1, Bruce maximizes satisfaction by consuming market basket A on indifference u_1. This market basket consists of C_1^1 dollars of present consumption and C_2^1 dollars of future consumption. As we know, the consumer maximizes satisfaction by choosing the market basket corresponding to the point where an indifference curve is tangent to the budget constraint; thus, Bruce maximizes satisfaction when the marginal rate of substitution between present and future consumption is just equal to $(1 + r)$, the opportunity cost of spending money today.

The consumer depicted in Figure 5–7(a) is a saver; that is, Bruce postpones present consumption to increase future consumption. In the first year, his expenditures on consumption are less than his earnings $(C_1^1 > I_1)$ while in the second year his expenditures on consumption are greater than his earnings $(C_2^1 > I_2)$. This means that Bruce takes part of his first-period income, puts it in the bank, and uses it, plus the interest earned on it, to increase second-period consumption.

The consumer depicted in Figure 5–7(b), on the other hand, is a borrower. In the first year, expenditures on consumption are greater than earnings $(C_1^1 > I_1)$ while in the second year expenditures on consumption are less than earnings $(C_2^1 < I_2)$. This means that the individual borrows against future income in order to increase current consumption which, in turn, means that part of his or her second-period income must go to repay the loan, including interest.

Now let's use the model outlined above to see why a lower interest rate does not necessarily mean that people will borrow more.

EXAMPLE 5–6

LOWER INTEREST RATES AND BORROWING

In the fourth quarter of 1990, most economists conceded that the U.S. economy had fallen into a recession. As a result, the Federal Reserve Board began a series of policy changes designed to bring about lower interest rates, the goal being to stimulate the economy by increasing borrowing and hence augmenting the demand for goods and services. Consider Ginger, a typical consumer, who at the current rate of interest borrows $1,000. (a) If as a result of the

Fed's policies the interest rate on personal loans falls, will Ginger borrow more? (b) Will she be better off or worse off as a result?

■ **SOLUTION** Suppose Ginger earns I dollars in each period. Her lifetime budget constraint is given by

$$BC_1\colon C_1(1 + r_1) + C_2 = I(1 + r_1) + I,$$

where r_1 is the current interest rate. As shown in Figure 5–8, given this budget constraint Ginger maximizes satisfaction by consuming market basket F on indifference curve u_0. At the current rate of interest Ginger borrows $1,000 which means she consumes $C_1^1 > I$ today and $C_2^1 < I$ tomorrow.

(a) When the interest rate falls, Ginger's lifetime budget constraint becomes BC_2 in Figure 5–8. Notice that we obtain BC_2 by rotating BC_1 counterclockwise about the endowment market basket. Given BC_2, does Ginger borrow more? Because the relative price of present consumption has changed, we must investigate the income and substitution effects. The price of present consumption

LOWER INTEREST RATES AND BORROWING   FIGURE 5–8

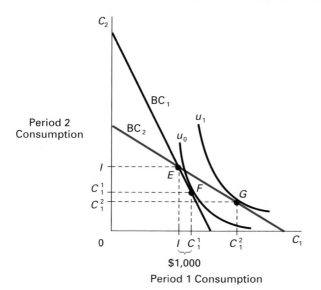

A lower interest rate gives rise to budget constraint BC_2. As a result, real income increases, first-period consumption and borrowing increase, and second period consumption falls.

relative to future consumption has fallen because foregone interest is now lower. This means that the substitution effect causes current consumption to rise (and future consumption to fall) which, in turn, means borrowing tends to increase. (b) In addition, Ginger's real income is higher—she is better off—because she can consume a market basket on a higher indifference curve. (This is true for all borrowers. Assuming that consumption is a normal good, the income effect indicates that both present and future consumption should increase. The total effect is an increase in present consumption, because the income and substitution effects work together.) Figure 5–8 shows Ginger's new optimal market basket. Given BC_2, she maximizes satisfaction by consuming market basket G on indifference curve u_2. She is better off and borrows more so she can consume more in period 1: $C_1^2 > C_1^1$. ∎

Examples 5–4 and 5–5 illustrate the importance of understanding income and substitution. Example 5–4 shows that lower income tax rates will actually reduce an individual's work effort if the income effect dominates the substitution effect. Example 5–5 shows that even though a lower interest rate will lead to increased borrowing, this does not necessarily mean that demand for goods and services will increase *both now and in the future*. Even though present consumption increases, future expenditures may increase or decrease because the income and substitution effects work against each other. If the substitution effect dominates, future consumption will fall whereas if the income effect dominates, future consumption will rise. Whenever we analyze the effects of a change in relative prices on consumer behavior we must be aware of all possibilities; the income and substitution effects help us understand what these possibilities are.

1. The theory of consumer choice is important because it can be used not only to help us understand demand but also to analyze a wide variety of real world economic situations. Specific examples that we have examined include price discounts, non-price rationing, excise subsidies, and fixed quantity subsidies.
2. In each case, indifference curves and budget constraints are used to predict the effects of a particular corporate or public policy on consumer behavior. We found that when the policy under consideration affects relative prices, then the magnitudes of both the income and substitution effects are important.
3. We also used the theory of consumer choice to explain why lower income taxes can lead people to work less rather than more and why lower interest rates lead to more borrowing, greater current demand for goods and services, and, possibly, less future demand. Again, income and substitution effects play a central role in obtaining these results.

SUMMARY

Price Discounts
Nonprice Rationing
Excise Subsidy

Fixed-Quantity Subsidy
Leisure Time and Work Effort
Saving and Borrowing

KEY TERMS

1. Illustrate the effect of the following on real income:
   a) The government gives an individual $500 (this is called a lump-sum subsidy).
   b) The government levies a $.10 excise tax on cigarettes.
   c) The government levies a proportional tax on nonlabor income only.
   d) The interest rate falls 50%.
2. Many nightclubs offer two-for-one specials at various times during the week. How do these specials affect a representative customer's real income and demand for drinks?
3. Determine the impact of the quantity-rationing scheme discussed in Problem 3−3 on real income and the quantity of sugar consumed.
4. Penny's Pizzeria is offering a special this month. If you buy one large 16-inch pizza you get a second one free. Illustrate the effect of this special on real income and pizza consumption.
5. Consider the following type of discount frequently offered by retailers: each unit of good x purchased over 10 units is half

QUESTIONS AND PROBLEMS

price. How does this discount affect real income and consumption of good *x*? Be sure to consider all possibilities.

6. Suppose two individuals, Smith and Jones, spend all their incomes on Colombian coffee and food. Smith is a certified financial planner and earns $100 per hour. Jones is an economic consultant and earns $200 per hour. Suppose a severe drought damages a large portion of the Colombian coffee crop, causing a shortage.
   a) If U.S. retailers ration the available supply by allowing consumers to purchase at most two pounds of coffee, will Smith be better off or worse off?
   b) If lines form to buy Colombian coffee, will Smith or Jones be more inclined to wait? Explain using indifference curves and budget constraints.

7. Assume that an individual earns $8 per hour, receives $40 of nonlabor income per week, and works 40 hours per week. If this individual receives a 10% raise, will work effort rise or fall? Explain.

8. Suppose that Ed qualifies for a public housing program. If he chooses to participate, he can move to a three-room apartment and pay $50 per room per month in rent.
   a) If Ed can rent a nongovernment-subsidized apartment at a market rental rate of $100 per room per month and if he currently rents a four-room apartment, will he enroll in the program? (Assume rooms are the same size and quality.)
   b) Would Ed prefer a cash grant that costs the government the same amount of money as the public housing program? Explain.

9. What is the impact of a sales tax on a typical individual's level of real income and the consumption of goods and services?

10. Consider the gasoline tax discussed in Example 4–2. Suppose that while the government wants to reduce demand it also wants to maintain the standard of living. This being the case, consumers who are taxed are also given a lump-sum rebate just large enough to maintain their level of real income prior to the tax increase. Illustrate how you would determine the size of the rebate for an individual consumer.

11. At times local governments give free food to the low-income individuals. Illustrate and discuss the impact of such a program on real income and the demand for food of a typical individual qualifying for the program.

12. In order to stimulate sales, Dippin' Donuts is offering a special deal on doughnuts purchased in the month of May. If an

individual purchases one dozen doughnuts he or she pays half price for any additional doughnuts purchased. Will this pricing strategy increase sales?

13. Currently a local golf club charges individuals $12 per round of golf. Under these conditions Phil plays four rounds per month. The club now offers him an alternative price package: he can pay a fee of $80 per month and play as much golf as he wants. Given this option, does Phil play more than four times a month?

14. Given the situation described in Problem 6 of Chapter 3, does Mr. Strange join the club? Explain.

15. Ms. Willis gives $100 each year to a local charity. Currently the income tax rate is 5% and contributions to charities are deductible.

    a) If the government increases the income tax rate to 10% will Ms. Willis be better off or worse off?

    b) Will she give more or less to charity?

16. Suppose the government introduces a Negative Income Tax program. Under this program, participants receive a guaranteed income of G dollars per week. The guarantee is reduced by $t\%$ of any earnings. One of the primary concerns with welfare programs is that they cause participating individuals to reduce work effort. Determine the impact of the N.I.T. program on work effort if, prior to enrolling, an individual (a) is unemployed and (b) is employed.

17. Discuss the impact on work effort of a welfare program that gives participants a guaranteed hourly wage, g.

18. Mr. Smith recently turned 62 and is eligible for Social Security. If he decides to retire, he will receive $500 per month. If he remains employed he can earn $1,000 per month but he must work at least 40 hours per week.

    a) Will Mr. Smith retire?

    b) Would your answer change if he could work as much as he would like to? Explain.

19. Assume that an individual has a two-period time horizon. She receives two equal incomes, one in each period. The market rate of interest is 5%. At this rate the consumer is neither a borrower nor a lender.

    a) If the market rate of interest increases to 10%, will this individual be better off or worse off?

    b) Will she now be a borrower? Explain.

20. City Consumer Bank of Huntsville is offering its customers the opportunity to purchase certificates of deposit (CD) that pay

twice the current market rate of interest (the usual rate on 90-day T-bills). The certificate requires a deposit of at least $10,000.

a) Determine when an individual will purchase a CD and when he or she will not.

b) By purchasing a CD, does the typical customer save more or less than before?

REFERENCES

Aaron, H. J., and J. A. Pechman. 1981. *How Taxes Affect Economic Behavior*. Washington, D.C.: The Brookings Institution.

Becker, G. S. 1981. *A Treatise on the Family*. Cambridge: Harvard University Press.

Levitan, S. A. 1985. *Programs in Aid of the Poor*. 5th ed. Baltimore: Johns Hopkins University Press.

MEASURING CHANGES IN REAL INCOME

A5.1 COMPENSATING AND EQUIVALENT VARIATION

In general, consumer surplus only approximates the exact change in real income caused by a price change. For most practical applications, this approximation is good enough; however, in some instances it is useful to have an exact monetary measure. Here we will discuss two such measures and show how they relate to consumer surplus.

One exact measure of change in real income is the compensating variation, denoted by CV. For an increase in price, the *compensating variation* is the amount of money we would have to give an individual *after* the price change to make him or her just as well off as *before* the price change. Similarly, the CV associated with a decrease in price is the amount of money we would have to take away from an individual *after* the price change to make him or her just as well off as *before* the price change.

In order to learn how to calculate CV, consider a simple example. Suppose that Calley faces the following budget constraint:

$$BC_1: I_1 = p_x^1 x + C.$$

This budget constraint is shown in Figure A5−1(a). Given BC_1, Calley maximizes utility by purchasing market basket E on indifference curve u_1.

Now suppose the price of good x increases to p_x^2. Calley's new budget constraint is

$$BC_2: I_1 = p_x^2 x + C.$$

Calley is now worse off. She purchases market basket F, which is on a lower indifference curve.

How much worse off is Calley? If we use CV to answer this question, then we must determine how much money we would have to give Calley to compensate her for the price increase; that is, how much money would she need at the new price to be as well off as she was in the first place?

In Figure A5−1(a), this amount of money is I_2 dollars. Budget constraint BC_3 is parallel to BC_2, which means that its slope reflects the new price for good x and is tangent to u_1. Thus I_2 is the amount of income, given the new price for x, needed to attain u_1, and CV is the difference between I_2 and I_1; that is, $CV = I_2 - I_1$.

(a) CV is the amount of money it would take to restore the individual to his or her original level of satisfaction. (b) EV is the amount of money an individual would be willing to pay to avoid the price increase.

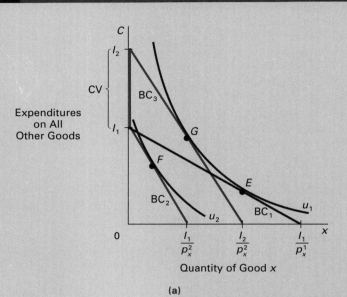

(a)

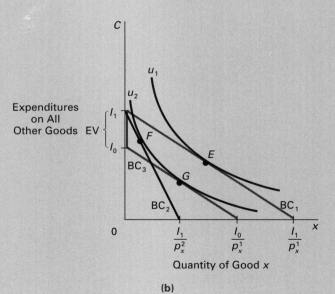

(b)

Another exact measure of a change in real income is the equivalent variation. The *equivalent variation*, denoted EV, measures how much an individual would be willing to pay to avoid a price change; that is, how much money would an individual need at the original price of good x to be as well off as he or she would be after the price change?

In Figure A5–1(b), I_0 is the amount of money Calley needs at the original prices to attain u_2. Budget constraint BC_3 is parallel to BC_1 and tangent to u_2. Having income I_0 and paying the original price p_x^1 allows Calley to purchase a market basket equivalent to bundle F (on the same indifference curve). Thus the EV is the difference between I_1 and I_0; that is, $EV = I_1 - I_0$. The EV is the amount Calley is willing to pay to keep the price at p_x^1, rather than having it change to p_x^2.

Both CV and EV are exact measures of a change in real income. Both are equally valid and which we use depends on the particular situation we are studying. Geometrically they measure the distance between two indifference curves. In general, they will be different because the prices that construct them are different. However, if the indifference curves are vertically parallel, CV and EV are the same. In this instance, the distance between any two indifference curves is the same no matter where we measure it. This means that CV, EV, and CS all give the same money measure of a change in real income.

EXAMPLE A5–1

Suppose a consumer has preferences that we can represent by the utility function $u = xy$. Initially, the price of x is $5 per unit of good x, the price of y is $5 per unit of good y, and income is $100. If the price of x increases to $10, what are the compensating and equivalent variations and how do they compare to consumer surplus?

■ **SOLUTION** From Example 4–1 we know that the demand functions for this utility function are

$$x = I/2p_x \text{ and } y = I/2p_y.$$

Thus, when the price of x increases from $5 to $10, quantities demanded change from $x_1 = 10$ and $y_1 = 10$, to $x_2 = 5$ and $y_2 = 10$.

To calculate CV we ask how much money would make the consumer as well off at the new prices as she was initially. Let I stand for this amount of money. At the original prices, the consumer's level of real income is given by $u = x_1 y_1 = 10 \cdot 10 = 100$. At the new prices and an income of I, the consumer's level of real income would be $u = (I/20)(I/10) = I^2/200$. Setting this equal to the initial level of real income and solving for I gives $I = 100\sqrt{2} \cong 141$. This means that if the consumer had an income of $141, at the new prices she would be just as well off as she was facing the old prices with an income of $100; that is, CV $\cong$ $41.

To calculate EV we ask how much money would make the consumer as well off at the old prices as she is now. At the new prices, the consumer's level of real income is given by $u = x_1 y_1 = 5 \cdot 10 = 50$. At the old prices and an income of I, the consumer's level of real income would be $u = (I/10)(I/10) = I^2/100$. Setting this equal to the new level of real income and solving for I gives $I = 50\sqrt{2} \cong 70$. Thus, if the consumer had an income of $70 at the initial prices she would be just as well off as she would be facing the new prices with an income of $100; that is, EV = $31.

Finally, let us compare these calculations to consumer surplus. CS is the area under the demand curve minus the expenditures on good x:

$$CS = \int_0^x (I/2s)ds - p_x x$$

Since expenditures on good x are the same before and after the price change, the change in consumer surplus is given by

$$\Delta CS = \int_{x_2}^{x_1} (I/2s)ds = (I/2)[ln(x_1) - ln(x_2)] = 50 \cdot ln(2) \cong \$35.$$

Note that consumer surplus lies between compensating and equivalent variations; that is, EV < CS < CV. Using advanced methods, this can be verified for a wide range of circumstances. (See Robert Willig, "Consumer's Surplus without Apology." *American Economic Review*, 66 [1976]: 589–97.) ∎

A5.2 REVEALED PREFERENCE AND THE CONSUMER PRICE INDEX

Consumer surplus can measure changes in real income if we know the demand curve. Oftentimes, however, this is not available. Instead, we only have observations at different points in time concerning purchases of various market baskets. Fortunately, we can still measure changes in real income by applying the idea of *revealed preference* and using *price indices*.

REVEALED PREFERENCE

A diagram will best demonstrate the idea of revealed preference. In Figure A5–2, suppose BC_1 is the budget constraint the consumer faces in year one and BC_2 is the budget constraint she faces in year two:

$$BC_1: I = p_x^1 x + p_y^1 y \quad \text{and} \quad BC_2: I = p_x^2 x + p_y^2 y.$$

REVEALED PREFERENCE   **FIGURE A5–2**

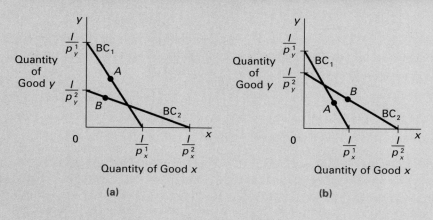

(a)

(b)

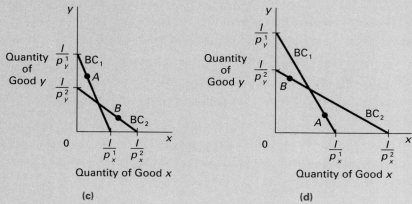

(c)

(d)

(a) Market basket A is revealed preferred to market basket B. (b) Market basket B is revealed preferred to market basket A. (c) Neither A nor B is revealed preferred to the other. (d) If A is chosen given BC_1 and B is chosen given BC_2, then this consumer is not maximizing satisfaction.

Further, suppose that given these budget constraints, the consumer purchases basket A the first year and basket B the second. If we assume that this consumer is maximizing satisfaction, then what can we say about the consumer's preferences between A and B?

Consider Figure A5−2(a) first. Since market basket B is in the budget set associated with BC_1, the consumer could have purchased it in year one had she wanted to. However, the consumer chose bundle A rather than bundle B; thus, she must have preferred bundle A. In this instance, we say that bundle A *is revealed preferred* to bundle B: the consumer reveals his or her preference by purchasing market basket A. If bundle A is revealed preferred to bundle B, then the consumer must be worse off in year two.

Next consider Figure A5−2(b). In this instance, market basket A is in the budget set associated with BC_2 and could have been purchased in year two. Since bundle B was purchased in year two, bundle B is revealed preferred to bundle A and the consumer is better off in year two.

Finally, consider Figure A5−2(c). Neither bundle A nor B is revealed preferred to the other and we cannot say if real income is greater in year one or two. This shows that in some instances we cannot tell whether the consumer is better off in year one or in year two without knowing his or her preferences.

We can use the idea of revealed preference to check whether the consumer is actually maximizing satisfaction subject to her budget constraint. Consider Figure A5−2(d). If she maximizes satisfaction could she choose both market baskets A and B? From this diagram we can conclude: (i) if the consumer chooses market basket A when she faces budget constraint BC_1, then A is revealed preferred to B; (ii) if she chooses market basket B when she faces budget constraint BC_2, the B is revealed preferred to A. Clearly, these two statements contradict one another: any consumer making such choices cannot be maximizing satisfaction or else something has changed that we have not yet taken into account.

THE CONSUMER PRICE INDEX

We now can construct an index number that can measure changes in real income. There are two basic types of index numbers: quantity index numbers and price index numbers. Here we will focus on one particular type of price index that receives much attention in the popular press, the consumer price index (CPI). The *consumer price index* measures changes in the overall price level or, in other words, changes in the *cost of living*. The CPI has many functions but its primary use is to determine whether or not real income changes over time. For example, in order to determine whether consumers' real incomes change over time, we compare the change in money incomes to the change in the CPI. If money incomes increase more than the CPI, we say real incomes have increased.

In order to understand the logic of the CPI and to see how it can measure changes in real income, suppose that Carl consumes food, good x, and clothing, good y. In the current year, year one, he faces the following budget constraint:

$$BC_1: I = p_x^1 x + p_y^1 y.$$

This budget constraint is shown in Figure A5–3. Given BC_1, Carl maximizes satisfaction by consuming market basket A. His real income corresponds to indifference curve u_1.

THE CONSUMER PRICE INDEX

FIGURE A5–3

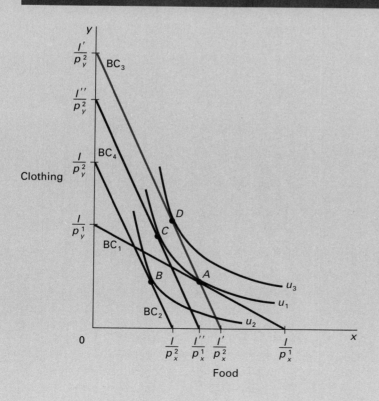

BC_3 represents the cost of purchasing market basket A after prices have changed. If the CPI is used to measure the change in real income we would say that real income has fallen by $(I' - I)/1\%$ which overstates the reduction in real income.

Now suppose that in year two, prices change. If all prices change at the same rate, then it will be easy to determine the overall change in the price level. A 5% increase in all prices means that the price level has increased 5%. However, prices rarely change at the same rate. Some may increase 5% while others decrease 2%. When such a situation occurs, we calculate a price index to estimate the average (overall) change in prices.

Suppose, then, that the prices of goods x and y both change but perhaps at different rates. Carl's new budget constraint is

$$BC_2: I = p_x^2 x + p_y^2 y.$$

In Figure A5–3, we see that Carl now purchases market basket B and—since A is revealed preferred to B—his real income has fallen.

One way to calculate the overall change in prices associated with BC_1 and BC_2 is to compare the cost of market basket A, the optimal market basket in year one, at year-one prices and year-two prices. This is basically how the CPI is calculated. The CPI is the ratio of the cost of purchasing some base-year market basket at current prices to the cost of purchasing the same bundle at the next year's prices. A price index using year-one quantities is called a *Laspeyres price index*, after the nineteenth-century statistician E. Laspeyres. (When year-two quantities are used, it is called an H. Paasche price index.)

For Carl, the cost of purchasing market basket A in year one is

$$I = p_x^1 x_1 + p_y^1 y_1$$

and in year two it is

$$I' = p_x^2 x_1 + p_y^2 y_1.$$

Thus, the consumer price index is

$$\text{CPI} = \frac{p_x^2 x_1 + p_y^2 y_1}{p_x^1 x_1 + p_y^1 y_1} = \frac{I'}{I}. \qquad (A5.1)$$

We can also illustrate the calculation of the CPI graphically. To do this we must add a hypothetical budget constraint to Figure A5–3 to show the cost of purchasing market basket A at year-two prices. In the diagram, this is BC_3. Notice that BC_3 has the same slope as BC_2 and passes through market basket A. Comparing BC_3 to BC_2 shows how much more money income Carl needs to purchase market basket A at year-two prices and gives the CPI, I'/I.

We can now see how accurately the CPI measures the change in real income—that is, the difference between u_1 and u_2. In year one, the CPI is equal to 1 since $p_x^2 = p_x^1$ and $p_y^2 = p_y^1$. If in year two the CPI is equal to, say, 1.2, the cost of living has increased 20%. We would like this also to mean that for a consumer whose money income does not change, real income has fallen 20%—or, put another way, that if a consumer's income also increased 20% he or she would be just as well off in period two as in period one. However, Figure A5−3 shows that if in fact the consumer faces BC_3, he or she will be better off: $u_3 < u_1$. Thus the CPI overstates the rate of inflation because money incomes need not rise as fast as the CPI for individuals to maintain their real income.

We can make this point even clearer by contrasting the CPI with an "ideal" measure of the change in price levels. An ideal price index would show just how much money income a consumer needs to attain the same real income in period 2 as in period 1. In Figure A5−3, I'' is the income the consumer needs to attain u_1 when facing year-two prices. Offered BC_4 he would choose market basket C on indifference curve u_1. An ideal price index, then, would be I''/I, which is less than the CPI measure, I'/I. If market basket C had been used to calculate the CPI then the index would measure precisely the change in real income. However, this is an ideal situation; in the real world, market basket A is used, which means that the CPI overstates the reduction in real income.

THE COMPETITIVE FIRM: OUTPUT SUPPLY AND INPUT DEMAND

■ *Part 3 investigates the production and supply of goods and services. Our primary goal in this part is to determine the level of output a competitive firm will supply, the inputs they will use, and how a change in the economic environment affects their choices. The material in Part 3 will help us understand business decisions.*

■ *Chapter 6 begins by discussing the business firm, why the goal of most business firms is to maximize profit, and what economists mean by profit. This discussion provides a solid foundation upon* tion upon which we can build our theoretical model. The second half of the chapter examines a firm's technology, which represents the relation between inputs used and the level of output produced. It develops the concepts of a production function (which represents the technology algebraically) and isoquants (which represent the technology graphically).

■ Chapter 7 investigates the relation between the cost of using inputs and the level of output produced. The chapter shows how to derive both short- and long-run cost curves and to see how they might shift when the economic environment changes. A thorough understanding of the relation between input costs, the technology, and the cost curves is very important because it will help us understand, for example, how payroll taxes or E.P.A. regulations affect a firm's production costs.

■ Chapter 8 uses the cost curves developed in the previous chapter to investigate a perfectly competitive firm's output supply and input demand decisions. The model presented in this chapter assumes that, given the market it faces, the firm aims to maximize profit. The chapter discusses both short- and long-run decisions. Chapter 8 provides the principles used in the next two chapters to complete the supply and demand model of the market economy.

FIRMS, ECONOMIC PROFIT, AND PRODUCTION

6

In the last three chapters we focused on the demand side of the product market—that is, on the behavior of consumers. Now we turn to the supply side and investigate the behavior of producers. In the next few chapters we will study firms' employment and production decisions. Our goal is to develop a theory that will help us answer two basic questions: (i) How much of each factor of production should a firm use to produce a good or service? and (ii) How much of the good or service should the firm produce and sell to consumers?

In this chapter we begin by discussing the nature of firms, profit maximization as the objective of the decision-making unit within the firm, and the meaning of economic profit. Then we investigate the firm's technology—that is, the means by which physical and human resources, such as capital and labor, are transformed into goods and services. One particular concern will be the distinction economists make between production in the short run and production in the long run.

6.1 THE NATURE OF FIRMS

■ Recall from Figure 1−1 (the circular flow of economic activity) that we divide the economy into two sectors: households and firms. Households, on the one hand, are the consumers of goods and services as well as the owners of the resources used in the production process. Households make up the demand side of the product market and the supply side of the resource market. Firms, on the other hand, make up the supply side of the product market and the demand side of the resource market. **Firms** are the economic entities that convert resources into goods and services.

Firms employ inputs, or *factors of production*, that are used to produce outputs. *Inputs* are the resources used in the production process to manufacture goods or to provide services. *Outputs* are the goods and services produced and sold to individual consumers or to other firms.

For convenience, economists usually classify inputs into four broad groups: land, natural resources, labor, and capital. The land input is the soil used in the production process or the property where the firm is located. Natural resources are the raw materials used in the production process. Labor inputs are the hours of work effort and the skills supplied by a firm's employees. Capital inputs include the buildings, machines, and other equipment used to produce goods and services.

Consider a hypothetical firm, U.S. Seating, that manufactures filing cabinets. Land, natural resources, labor, and capital are all necessary to produce filing cabinets. The land input is the property where the firm's buildings are located. The natural resource is the metal used to build the filing cabinets. The labor inputs are the hours of work put in by engineers who design the product, by supervisors, by machinists who build and operate the machines that manufacture the filing cabinets, and by assembly line workers who put together the final product. The capital inputs include the factories or plants in which the cabinets are produced, the presses that stamp out the various parts, assembly tools and typewriters, pencils, pens, and other office supplies used throughout the firm.

Why, in modern economies, does production take place primarily through firms? At first this may seem a silly question—firms obviously exist to make money by selling goods. Why, though, has the particular type of economic organization we call a firm come into being?

WHY DO FIRMS EXIST?

The primary reason is that firms can reduce the transaction costs associated with production. **Transaction costs** arise when resources are needed to gather information about prices or potential trading partners, to negotiate contracts, and to insure that contracts are honored. Firms exist because such costs are generally lower when production takes place within a business firm.

For example, in order to manufacture and sell television sets, drafting experts, electronics specialists, cabinet makers, salespersons, and suppliers of parts could all get together and agree upon a series of contracts specifying which resources each individual would provide, which task each would perform, and how each would share in the revenues from sales. The time and effort it would take to negotiate and enforce these contracts would be extremely high and the finished product would thus be extremely expensive. However, if a firm is created, many of these transaction costs drop substantially or even disappear. Once a firm is formed, each resource owner deals only with a single entity, the firm.

In a market economy such as the United States has, firms are legal entities owned by individuals. A firm's *owners* are responsible for its actions. They are the individuals who bear the risks and reap the rewards associated with the firm's actions.

TYPES OF FIRMS

In general, firms assume one of three forms: sole proprietorship, partnership, or corporation.

The simplest structure is the *sole proprietorship*, a business owned by one individual and in most cases managed by that same individual. Sole proprietorships include physicians, lawyers, small service-type businesses, and small retail establishments. The owner is responsible for all debts and the firm ceases to exist when

SOLE PROPRIETORSHIP

the owner dies. There are no legal contracts involved in organizing a sole proprietorship and the initial investment is usually small.

PARTNERSHIP

A more complicated type of firm is the *partnership*—a business owned by two or more individuals and managed according to a contractual agreement between them. The latter usually includes such things as each partner's initial investment, his or her duties, how profits or losses will be shared, and the settlement should a partner die or withdraw from the firm. Partnerships include certain retail establishments and professional practices such as CPA firms. Each partner is responsible for all the firm's debts and the partnership ends if any member withdraws or dies.

THE MODERN
CORPORATION

The third type of firm is the *corporation*, in which the owners of the firm are the stockholders. Each stockholder is responsible for the firm's debt only up to the limit of his or her own investment in the enterprise. The corporation continues to exist even if a stockholder dies or shares of stock are sold from one individual to another. The stockholders usually do not manage the firm directly. They elect a board of directors to represent their interests and select the officers of the corporation who, in turn, manage the firm.

In the United States the vast majority of businesses, in terms of numbers of firms, are sole proprietorships. However, in terms of sales, U.S. corporations dominate nearly every major industry.

The sole proprietorship, the partnership, and the corporation are classifications based on ownership. The proprietorship has a single owner, the partnership has two or more owners, and the corporation usually has many owners. However, we can also classify firms according to the type of business activity they perform.

There are three major groups: service, merchandising, and manufacturing. *Service companies* perform services for a fee. They include businesses such as accounting firms, law firms, repair shops, physicians, and a variety of others. *Merchandising companies* purchase goods that are ready for sale. Automobile dealers, appliance stores, department stores, and supermarkets are examples of merchandising firms. *Manufacturing companies* purchase raw materials, convert them into various products, and then sell the products to other firms or consumers. Examples of manufacturing firms are computer manufacturers, stereo manufacturers, and manufacturers of wine coolers.

In accounting, manufacturing firms are the most difficult to handle due to their complex nature. In economics, however, manufacturing firms are the easiest to discuss because it is usually clear how they combine resources to produce their product. Many of the examples you will encounter in the next several chapters involve manufacturing firms but the entire analysis is equally well suited for any type of firm.

■ In this book we will assume that the firm's sole objective is to maximize profit. The **profit maximization** assumption is usually used in microeconomics because it explains and predicts the behavior of producers quite well. However, profit maximization is not universally accepted as the sole objective of business firms; thus, some discussion of this assumption is warranted.

In the case of a sole proprietorship or a partnership, where the owners of the firm also manage its day-to-day operation, it seems fairly clear that the firm will be operated to maximize profit. Since the owners' income corresponds to the firm's profit, owners will naturally strive to attain the greatest profit possible.

In a corporation, however, profit maximization may not be the sole goal of the managers making the day-to-day decisions. In a large firm, the managers usually interact very little with the owners (that is, with the stockholders). This being the case, managers may seek to achieve goals other than profit maximizing. For example, managers of a large corporation may be more concerned with maximizing the size of their staff to increase their influence within the firm, or with maximizing sales and revenues to achieve growth, or with maximizing dividend payments to pacify stockholders.

Nonetheless, the fundamental behavioral assumption that economists use to model the decision-making process of firms is profit maximization. This is because even large corporate enterprises are owned by stockholders and, just as the owners of a small proprietorship are concerned with the income they receive from the firm, so too are stockholders. If stockholders exercise effective control over the hiring and firing of managers, the latter must operate as their agents and strive to maximize profit. If a manager makes decisions that lead to less-than-maximum profit, the stockholders will replace that person.

Even if stockholders do not exercise this strict control, they can always sell their stock if the firm does not maximize profits. This, in turn, lowers the market price of the stock and makes the firm a primary target for takeover bids by other corporations. If the firm is taken over, the old managers will be replaced by new managers who, presumably, will pursue a strategy more consistent with profit maximization.

In the real world there are forces at work tending to eliminate firms that follow strategies consistently deviating from profit maximization. But we should remember that even if profit maximization cannot explain every decision made by owners and managers of firms, the goal of the theory of the firm is to explain, in general, firms' output and employment decisions. Profit maximization does very well in explaining and predicting the behavior of firms.

6.3 THE MEANING OF ECONOMIC PROFIT

■ Since profit is simply revenue minus cost, if we are to understand what economists mean by profit we must understand precisely what economists mean by the costs of production.

DEFINING THE COSTS OF PRODUCTION

The owner of any firm must make two basic decisions—what combination of inputs to use to produce any given level of output and how much output to produce. In making these decisions, the owner of a firm must consider the cost of acquiring the inputs. Few important employment and production decisions are reached without a careful analysis of costs. For example, a profit-maximizing firm's decision to increase production will depend on the relation between the revenues generated by the additional output and the costs associated with employing more factors of production. Likewise, the optimal input mix will depend on the relative prices of the inputs used to produce output.

Production costs are therefore important factors in determining how much of a good or service a firm will offer for sale; but how do we reckon these costs? There are a variety of answers to this question depending on the way we define the term "costs." In many circumstances, a firm's production costs are equated with the monetary expenditures on the factors of production; in other words, the cost of manufacturing a particular good is the amount of money the firm must pay to obtain the inputs needed for the production process. However, *to an economist* the cost of undertaking any particular activity may include much more than monetary outlays.

OPPORTUNITY COSTS

The costs that are relevant for decision making are whatever the decision maker must give up to undertake a particular action. Economists call these costs the opportunity costs or economic costs of using resources in one way rather than another.

The **opportunity** or **economic cost** of using resources to undertake a chosen enterprise is the value of those resources measured in terms of their next best alternative use. For example, suppose you are paying your own way to go to college. Your annual expenses—including tuition, registration fees, books, and supplies—may total $6,000 per year. These expenses are one component of the opportunity cost of going to college. If you had not spent $6,000 on your education you could have spent these monies on other goods and services. You cannot use the resources expended on your education to purchase or produce something else.

However, these are not the only opportunity costs of going to school. If you spend a year in college, that is one year less that you can spend working. The income you forego by not working is another component of the opportunity cost of college. In deciding whether or not to attend college you must consider not only out-of-pocket expenses, but also foregone earnings. Combined, these are the opportunity (economic) costs of obtaining a college education.

For a firm, the economic costs of production include the monetary outlays associated with using resources to produce goods. These production costs represent the opportunity cost of employing these resources; that is, they reflect the value of the resources measured in terms of their next best alternative use.

In addition to direct monetary expenses, the economic costs of production include any other opportunity costs incurred while owning and operating the firm. For example, the opportunity cost of the labor hours that the owner spends operating the business equals the earnings that are foregone by not working for someone else. Similarly, the opportunity cost of investing money in a business is the highest return which that money could have earned had it been invested somewhere else. Thus, just as for an individual going to college, a firm's "costs" are all of the opportunity costs associated with the production process.

Perhaps the best way to understand what economists mean by the economic cost of production is to compare the accountant's definition of cost to the economist's. Consider Sara Pound, an independent business woman who has invested $61,000 in a retail store specializing in stuffed animals. Sara has no employees and her income statement for the year as prepared by the reputable accounting firm F.A.O., Inc., is as follows:

EXPLICIT AND IMPLICIT COSTS

Sales:		$71,000
Less: Cost of goods sold		35,000
Gross profit		$36,000
Less: Advertising	$ 5,000	
Utilities	1,000	
Property Tax	2,000	
Rent	15,000	
Other expenses	3,000	$26,000
Net accounting profit		$10,000

Notice that the accountant includes only the explicit costs of production in the firm's income statement. **Explicit costs** are those costs involving an actual monetary payment to another party. Cost of goods sold, advertising, utilities, taxes, rent, and miscellaneous expenses are all explicit costs.

Explicit costs are one component of the opportunity cost associated with Sara's business. For economists, however, explicit costs do not tell the whole story. Economists would include some additional costs, called implicit costs of production, as part of Sara's operating expenses. **Implicit costs** are those costs associated with the use of resources that belong to the firm's owner. Explicit and implicit costs together equal the opportunity, or economic, cost of production.

In the example above there are two implicit costs not considered by the accountant. First, since Sara operates the store herself she contributes her time and talents to the business. This contribution represents a cost because if Sara did not run the store she could work for someone else managing another store. By running her own retail business Ms. Pound foregoes the wages she could earn elsewhere.

One obvious question is, How do we measure this implicit cost? Typically we ask what Sara could earn in the next best job alternative. If she has a B.S. in economics and could earn $40,000 working for someone else, then $40,000 measures one implicit cost of running her stuffed animal business.

The second implicit cost involves the $61,000 that Sara has invested in the operation. Had she not invested in this particular business, Sara could have invested her money elsewhere. If the best alternative use of her funds is a savings account paying 10% in interest per year, then the implicit cost of investing in her retail store is the $6,100 she could have earned by putting her money in the bank. Put another way, the rate of return that she could have obtained from investing elsewhere is another implicit cost of operating this business.

An economist would revise Sara's income statement as follows:

Sales:		$71,000
Less: Cost of goods sold		35,000
Gross profit		$36,000
Less: Other Explicit Costs:		
Advertising	$ 5,000	
Utilities	1,000	
Property Tax	2,000	

Rent	15,000	
Other expenses	3,000	
Total Other Explicit Costs		$26,000
Net accounting profit		$10,000
Less: Implicit costs:		
Foregone wages	$40,000	
Foregone interest	6,100	
Total Implicit Costs		$46,100
Net economic profit (loss)		($36,100)

When only explicit costs are considered, Sara's production costs total $61,000; however, when implicit costs are included, Sara's production expenses increase to $107,000.

Profit is revenue minus cost but, as we saw earlier, the accountant considers only explicit production costs while the economist considers both explicit and implicit costs. It is this distinction between costs that gives rise to a distinction between accounting profit and economic profit. Accounting profit is the difference between revenue and explicit costs. For Sara Pound's firm, accounting profit is $10,000. **Economic profit** is defined as *the difference between revenue and both explicit and implicit costs—* that is, the difference between revenue and the opportunity or economic costs of production. For Sara Pound's firm, economic profit is a loss of $36,000.

ECONOMIC PROFIT

Throughout the remainder of this book, the term profit will refer to economic profit since it is the relevant concept for making economic decisions. If firms were to base production and employment decisions on accounting profit, they would exclude implicit costs from consideration and hence make economically unprofitable decisions. The next example illustrates this point.

EXAMPLE 6-1

ACCOUNTING PROFIT, ECONOMIC PROFIT, AND DECISION MAKING

Fly Rite, a small manufacturer of silk kites, is considering using its inventory of silk to make a new line of box kites for sale to retailers at $35 per kite. The silk for the new kites cost Fly Rite $10 per yard but now sells for $30 per yard. If it takes one yard of silk, $1 of labor services, and $9 of other materials to manufacture one kite, should Fly Rite introduce the new line of kites?

■ **SOLUTION** We will assume that the owners of Fly Rite aim to maximize profit and so we must calculate profit. If our calculations predict a positive profit, the company should introduce the new line of kites; if a loss, it should abandon the project.

Remember that the explicit costs are the monies actually paid to other parties. Here the explicit costs are the labor costs, the cost of materials other than silk, and the cost of the silk itself. The explicit costs of producing one kite are $20.

Now remember that implicit costs are the costs associated with the use of resources that belong to the firm's owners. Since the silk was purchased in a previous period, it is now a resource owned by the firm. Silk is currently selling for $30 per yard, so the implicit cost of using a yard of silk to make a box kite is $20. That is, rather than use the silk to make kites, Fly Rite could sell off their inventory at $30 per yard and realize a gain of $20 per yard. By using the silk for kites, Fly Rite foregoes this $20 gain.

If the owners of Fly Rite ignore the implicit costs of production they will base their decision on accounting profit, and reckoning that the kites will earn them $35 − $20 = $15 per kite, they will choose to introduce the new line. However, if the owners take into account both explicit and implicit costs, they will realize that Fly Rite's profit on this venture will be −$5 per kite (a loss of $5 per kite) and they will abandon the project. ■

So far we have discussed profit maximization as the goal of the firm, but what does it mean for a firm to be earning a positive profit (economic profit)? Since the profit belongs to the owner of the firm, a positive profit means that the owner is receiving, as his or her reward for bearing the associated risks, more than he or she could earn in the next best job alternative. This is a very important point. To make it clear, consider a simple example. Suppose a self-employed plumber does a job that nets $300 for a day's work. The plumber's accounting profit for the job is $300. Further, suppose this same plumber could earn $250 per day working for a custom-home builder. Then the implicit cost of working as an independent contractor is $250 and the positive, or economic, profit for the job is $50; that is, the plumber earns $50 more than he could earn in the next best alternative.

If a firm earns a negative economic profit, its owner receives less than he or she could in the next best alternative. This does not mean that accounting profit is necessarily negative but simply that the opportunity costs of being in this particular business outweigh the revenues or benefits. Finally, as we will see in later chapters, the case where firms earn a zero economic profit plays a central role in determining prices and output for an industry as a whole. When a firm is earning a zero profit the owner receives exactly what he or she could earn in the next best alternative. That is, accounting profit is positive and equal to what the owner of the firm could earn elsewhere. In this instance economists say that the firm is earning a *normal accounting profit*.

The concept of economic profit takes into account all the costs associated with a particular economic activity. Therefore, it is the relevant concept for decision making within firms. If a firm is to survive and prosper, owners and managers alike must make decisions that are, for the most part, consistent with the maximization of economic profit.

■ Every firm is constrained by the technology currently available. By **technology** we mean the way in which inputs, or resources, must be combined to yield output, or product; we mean the existing state of the art or the existing technical know-how concerning the way goods can be produced.

While, in general, many inputs are used in the production process, we can illustrate the essential ingredients of production and cost theory by considering only two types of inputs. In this text we will usually assume that firms produce goods using capital and labor. We introduce this simplification for the same reason that we considered only two goods when discussing the theory of consumer choice: by restricting our analysis to at most two inputs, we can use graphs to illustrate many of the principles at work.

How can we describe the technology facing an individual firm? One way is with a production table. A **production table** is a menu indicating the maximum amount of output that can be obtained from given amounts of inputs per unit of time. It tells the owner of the firm which combinations of capital and labor can be used to produce output and how much output is actually produced, given those combinations.

For example, the data in Table 6–1 represent the technology of the All American Sporting Goods Corporation, a firm that uses labor, L, and capital, K, to produce official major league baseballs, y. The labor input is measured in person-hours per day, the capital input is the number of machine-hours per day, and output is the number of baseballs produced per day. According to this table, if one person operates one machine for 10 hours, 100 baseballs are manufactured; if two persons and two machines are employed for 10 hours each, 200 balls are produced; and so on.

6.4 DESCRIBING A FIRM'S TECHNOLOGY: PRODUCTION TABLES AND PRODUCTION FUNCTIONS

THE PRODUCTION TABLE

TABLE 6-1

THE PRODUCTION
TABLE FOR THE
ALL-AMERICAN
SPORTING GOODS
CORPORATION:
BASEBALLS PER
YEAR

		Labor (Person-Hours Per Day)				
		10	*20*	*30*	*40*	*50*
Capital (Machine-Hours Per Day)	10	100	141	173	200	224
	20	141	200	245	283	316
	30	173	245	300	346	387
	40	200	283	346	400	447
	50	224	316	387	447	500

**THE PRODUCTION
FUNCTION**

When economists are discussing theoretical models of production they often use a production function to describe the technology. A **production function** is an equation showing the maximum amount of output that a firm can produce from any specified amounts of inputs. If labor and capital are the only two inputs used to produce a particular good, then the production function is written as follows:

$$y = F(K,L); \qquad (6.1)$$

where y is the maximum amount of good y that can be produced with any given combination of capital, K, and labor, L.

For example, the technology may be represented by the production function

$$y = 10(K \cdot L). \qquad (6.2)$$

According to equation (6.2), the maximum output produced using 5 units of capital and 5 units of labor is $y = 10(5 \cdot 5) = 250$ units of good y; using 9 units of capital and 4 units of labor, it is $y = 10(9 \cdot 4) = 360$ units of good y; and so on.

In this text, we will assume that the available technology is a given fact of whatever economic environment is facing the owners of firms. We will make no attempt to explain why a particular technology exists or how it might change over time. Assuming that the technology is a parameter is analogous to assuming that consumers' preferences are a given. This is not to say that the effect of changes in tastes and technologies on economic decisions is unimportant. Rather, we must postpone such considerations until we have a basic understanding of microeconomic theory.

Whether the technology is represented by a production table or a production function we assume that firms know the existing technology and always produce the maximum output possible given any combination of inputs. This is called *technological efficiency*. (If a firm is technically inefficient, then it is wasting resources. It could obtain more output using the same inputs.)

◼ In the theory of consumer choice we used a family of indifference curves to graph an individual's preferences. In the production theory we can use a family of isoquants to graph the technology facing an individual firm.

An **isoquant** is a curve showing all the ways a firm can combine capital and labor to produce a specified level of output. Figure 6–1 shows three isoquants. On the vertical axis we measure units of capital and on the horizontal axis, units of labor. Each point in this diagram represents a particular input bundle. An **input bundle** is just a particular combination of inputs. For example, point A represents an input bundle consisting of L_1 units of labor and K_1 units of capital.

Along any one isoquant, output is held constant. For instance, each input bundle on the isoquant that passes through bundle A,

6.5 DESCRIBING A FIRM'S TECHNOLOGY: ISOQUANTS

ISOQUANTS

FIGURE 6–1

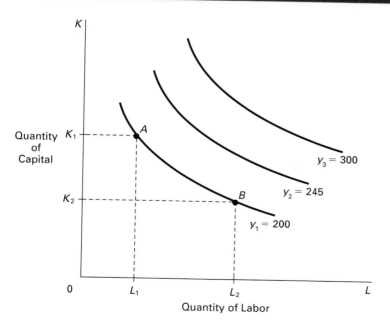

An isoquant is a curve in input space showing all the input bundles that are physically capable of producing a given level of output. Isoquants are a representation of a firm's technology.

Quantity of Labor

isoquant y_1, can produce 200 units of output. If the firm operates at point A, it employs K_1 units of capital and L_1 units of labor to produce 200 units of output. The firm can also produce the same output at B by reducing capital to K_2 and increasing labor to L_2.

The isoquants in Figure 6−1 illustrate an important assumption economists make when studying the theory of production: technologies are such that a firm can generally combine inputs in a variety of ways to produce a specified amount of output. The firm can produce 200 units of output by using any input bundle on isoquant y_1 or 300 units of output by using any input bundle on isoquant y_3.

When a firm can produce a given level of output using different combinations of inputs, the technology is called a *variable proportions technology*. If this kind of technology characterizes production, then one input can be substituted for another in such a way as to maintain a constant level of output. The family of isoquants in Figure 6−1 represents a variable proportions technology.

Although economists consider variable proportions to be the most common type of technology, there are some products that can be produced only when inputs are used in certain proportions. In the manufacture of most medications, for example, the chemicals must be combined in very precise proportions. Likewise, in the production of many durable goods, it is essential to use certain inputs in fixed proportions: the production of a television set requires one picture tube and one cabinet; the production of a Mercedes-Benz requires an engine, one steering wheel, and four wheels; the production of a stereo turntable requires one tonearm and one needle cartridge; and so on. This type of technology is called a *fixed proportions technology* because the inputs must be used in fixed proportions.

We represent a fixed proportions technology by isoquants that are L-shaped as shown in Figure 6−2. With this technology it is not possible to substitute one input for another and maintain the same level of output.

While fixed proportions technologies certainly exist, input substitution is normally possible. This is especially true when we are concerned with inputs such as capital and labor. A firm can almost always substitute machine-hours for person-hours and vice versa and still maintain a constant level of production. Therefore, in this text we will assume that firms face variable proportions technologies.

PROPERTIES OF TYPICAL ISOQUANTS

Isoquants provide us with a convenient graphical representation of technologies. Up to this point, however, the only thing we have assumed is that firms are technically efficient—that is, firms use a

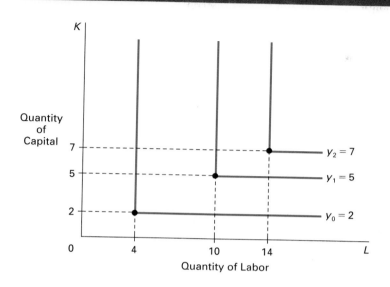

ISOQUANTS FOR A FIXED PROPORTIONS PRODUCTION FUNCTION

FIGURE 6-2

A fixed proportions production function is one that requires a certain fixed amount of inputs to produce a specified output. Here, two units of labor must be used with each unit of capital.

technology that yields the maximum possible output for any combination of inputs. Since isoquants can have almost any shape, if we are to make further progress, we must specify more precisely the nature of the technology. This in turn will determine the properties of the isoquants.

We assume that isoquants have four characteristics considered typical of most technologies. First, we assume that an isoquant passes through every input bundle. This means that any input bundle can be used to produce some output. Thus, a technology can be represented by a family of isoquants.

Second, we assume that isoquants do not intersect. If two isoquants were to intersect, the input bundle corresponding to the intersection point could be used to produce two different technologically efficient outputs. Logically, this is impossible.

Third, we assume that both inputs are productive; that is, if input bundle A contains as many units of every input as does bundle B and more units of at least one input, then bundle A yields more output than bundle B. This assumption is analogous to the assumption that more is preferred to less in consumer theory.

Note that if both inputs are productive, then isoquants lying further to the northeast correspond to higher levels of output. As a firm employs more of both inputs, its output must increase. In addition, if both inputs are productive, then isoquants are negatively sloped and one input can be substituted for another without changing output. For example, if a firm employs more labor, output increases and the firm is operating on a higher isoquant. If it wants to keep output unchanged (remember that along an isoquant, output is held constant), then it must input less capital.

The last assumption we make concerning technologies is stated in terms of the shapes of isoquants themselves: isoquants are convex to the origin. Convexity of isoquants, like convexity of indifference curves, is not an irrefutable fact but instead a property that economists have found to be typical of many technologies. Essentially, this assumption implies that as one input—say, labor—becomes more abundant while another input—say, capital—becomes scarce, it becomes more difficult for labor to replace capital in the production process.

ISOQUANTS AND INDIFFERENCE CURVES

Isoquants appear to have very similar properties to indifference curves but there is one important difference that we must keep in mind. When we studied the preferences of consumers, we could not measure an individual's satisfaction in units. As we moved from one indifference curve to another we knew whether an individual was better off or worse off but not by how much. However, when we move from one isoquant to another we can say exactly by how much output changes. We can associate with each isoquant a certain level of production that is measurable in units of output. Thus, if a firm is producing compact disc players, then each isoquant characterizing the firm's technology corresponds to a certain number of compact disc players.

In a sense, being able to measure output makes the theory of production less complicated than consumer theory since it allows us to compare directly two firms producing the same good but doing so using different technologies.

6.6 THE LONG AND SHORT RUNS

■ Isoquants represent the technology that is currently available to owners of firms. They show all the different ways firms can combine inputs to produce a given level of output.

If there are no restrictions on which input bundles a firm can use in the production process, isoquants represent the long-run production opportunities available to the firm. The **long run** is the period of production during which the firm can vary all inputs. In the long run, changes in output levels can be accomplished by altering the employment levels of any factor of production.

However, in many circumstances the owner of a firm may not be able to adjust all inputs to meet desired changes in output levels. The levels of some inputs may be fixed. The period of production during which some inputs cannot be varied is called the **short run.**

In the short run, changes in output can be accomplished by changing only the variable inputs. Generally, economists assume that when capital and labor are the only two inputs, capital is fixed in the short run and labor is variable.

For example, suppose that a firm is currently producing 100 bottles of soda by employing K_1 units of capital and L_1 units of labor, or input bundle A on isoquant y_1 in Figure 6–3. Next, suppose that the owner of the firm wants to increase production to 150 bottles by the end of the month. In this short period of time, the owner of the firm may not be able to purchase additional units of all inputs. In particular, she may not be able to build another plant, or add another assembly line, or replace existing machines with new, more efficient ones. The input bundles that point C represents in the diagram are not available in the short run.

If some inputs are fixed, the owner of the firm must increase production in the short run by employing more of the variable input, which, in this case, is labor. She can ask workers to work

PRODUCTION IN THE SHORT RUN

FIGURE 6–3

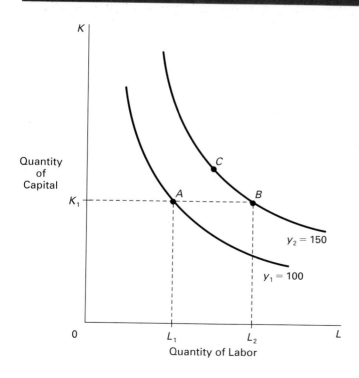

In the short run, the capital input is fixed. If the owner of the firm wants to expand production from 100 to 150 units, he or she must use K_1 units of capital and will have to increase labor from L_1 to L_2.

longer hours and hire more workers. In the short run, however, the firm is still constrained to operate with K_1 units of capital. If production is to be increased to 150 bottles, then the firm must use input bundle B in Figure 6–3.

Clearly, no input is absolutely fixed no matter how short the production period. What economists mean by a fixed factor of production is that the cost of changing the quantity of such an input is prohibitively high. For example, in the short run it would be quite costly to build new production facilities, to purchase machines that are central to the production process, or to hire workers whose tasks require having specific training not easily transferable to other workers.

Similarly, firms can rarely vary any inputs costlessly in the long run. Frequently, contracts exist that prohibit changes in variable inputs on a moment's notice. However, variable inputs are far less costly to alter than are fixed inputs.

6.7 PRODUCTION IN THE SHORT RUN

■ Economists distinguish between the short and long runs because short-run changes in output are accomplished differently from long-run changes.

In the short run the firm is constrained to use the capital it has on hand. If we let $\overline{K}$ denote the quantity of capital a firm currently employs then the short-run production function is denoted by

$$y = F(\overline{K},L). \qquad (6.3)$$

The short-run production function is also called the *total product function*. For a given quantity of capital, the total product function gives the maximum amount of output that a firm can produce with any quantity of labor.

THE TOTAL PRODUCT CURVE

A **total product curve** is the graph of a total product function. It shows how output varies as more or less of the variable input is used along with the fixed inputs. Figure 6–4(a) illustrates a typical total product curve.

Along the curve labeled TP_1 in the diagram, a firm can increase output by increasing the amount of labor relative to the fixed amount of capital. Notice that TP_1 shows that when some inputs are fixed, there is a maximum amount of output the firm can produce. This occurs at point C when L_3 units of labor are used with $\overline{K}$ units of capital. If more than L_3 units of labor were used, output would actually decrease. Of course a profit-maximizing firm never would operate on this portion of the total product curve since it could produce more output with less labor.

TOTAL, AVERAGE, AND MARGINAL PRODUCT CURVES

FIGURE 6–4

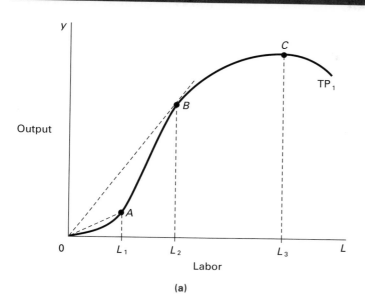

(a)

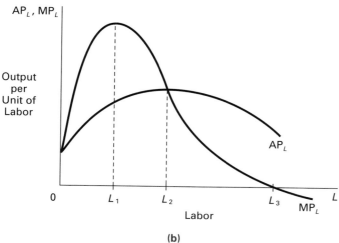

(b)

(a) The total product curve, TP$_1$, is the graphical representation of the short-run production function. (b) The average product of labor, AP$_L$, is the slope of a ray drawn from the origin to a point on the total product curve. The marginal product of labor is the slope of the total product curve.

The **average product** of a variable input is total product divided by the amount of that input used. For example, the average product of labor, denoted AP$_L$, is total product divided by the amount of labor employed: AP$_L = \dfrac{\text{TP}}{L}$.

THE AVERAGE PRODUCT CURVE

We can obtain the *average product curve* directly from the total product curve. In Figure 6−4(a), the average product of labor is simply the slope of a ray drawn from the origin to a point on the total product curve. For example, the slope of OA is y_1/L_1, which is the average product of labor when L_1 units of labor are used.

Notice that the AP_L also rises to a maximum and then falls. The maximum average product of labor is attained when L_2 units of labor are employed. At this point, the ray from the origin, OB in Figure 6−4(a), is tangent to the total product curve. The AP_L curve is graphed in Figure 6−4(b), where the vertical axis measures output per unit of labor.

THE MARGINAL PRODUCT CURVE

The **marginal product** of a variable input is the change in output per unit change in its use, holding all other inputs constant. For example, the marginal product of labor, denoted MP_L, is the change in output per unit change in the amount of labor used, holding capital constant.

We can also obtain the *marginal product curve* directly from the total product curve. In Figure 6−4(a), the marginal product of labor is simply the slope of the total product curve. Notice that once again, this curve rises to a maximum and then falls. The maximum marginal product of labor is attained when L_1 units of labor are employed. On the total product curve this corresponds to point A, which is the inflection point of the curve.

The MP_L curve is graphed in Figure 6−4(b). Note that the MP_L curve peaks before the AP_L curve does. In addition, note that marginal product is greater than average product when average product is rising; marginal product is less than average product when average product is falling; and marginal product is equal to average product when average product attains its maximum. These results are true of any average and marginal curves. (Think of your grade point average. If your marginal grade per course is higher than your average grade, your GPA will rise. If your marginal grade is less than your average, your GPA will fall.)

THE LAW OF DIMINISHING MARGINAL PRODUCTIVITY

Economists usually assume that as the employment of one input increases, holding all other inputs constant, a point is reached beyond which the marginal product of that input falls. This **Law of Diminishing Marginal Productivity** is an assumption economists make restricting the shape of the technology in the short run. They justify this assumption by noting that it is a property common to most real-world production functions. As we will see in the next chapter, the Law of Diminishing Marginal Productivity is important because it plays a crucial role in determining the shape of the firm's short-run cost curve.

In Figure 6–4(a), the point of diminishing marginal productivity of labor is A on TP_1. It is the point corresponding to the maximum marginal product of labor; if more than L_1 units of labor are used, the MP_L falls.

■ Just as the rate at which a consumer is willing to substitute one good for another, the marginal rate of substitution, played a central role in modeling the choices made by individual consumers, in the long run the rate at which one input can be substituted for another in production, called the **marginal rate of technical substitution,** will play a central role in modeling the choices made by owners of firms.

As we have seen, the essential feature of a variable proportions technology is that along an isoquant different combinations of inputs yield the same level of output. Now suppose a firm uses capital and labor to produce compact disc (CD) players. Figure 6–5 shows the isoquant representing all input bundles that can pro-

6.8 PRODUCTION IN THE LONG RUN

THE MARGINAL RATE OF TECHNICAL SUBSTITUTION

THE MARGINAL RATE OF TECHNICAL SUBSTITUTION

FIGURE 6–5

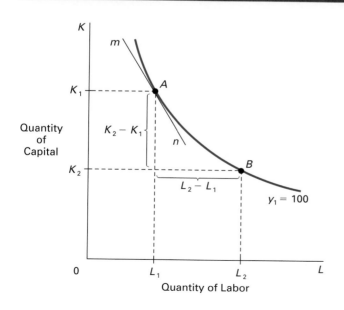

The marginal rate of technical substitution of labor for capital is minus the slope of the isoquant. When L_1 units of labor and K_1 units of capital are used to produce 100 units of output, the $MRTS_{LK}$ is minus the slope of tangent line mn.

duce 100 CD players. Both input bundle A, consisting of L_1 units of labor and K_1 units of capital, and bundle B, consisting of L_2 units of labor and K_2 units of capital, lie on this isoquant.

Let's assume that the firm currently employs K_1 units of capital and L_1 units of labor to produce 100 CD players. If we were to reduce the quantity of capital available to this firm from K_1 to K_2 units, how many more units of labor would it have to hire to keep on producing 100 CD players? Since input bundle B is on isoquant y_1, it can also produce 100 CD players. Thus, the firm would need to increase employment from L_1 to L_2 units of labor to maintain production at 100 units.

Now suppose we take the ratio of $(K_2 - K_1)$ to $(L_2 - L_1)$. This will measure the average rate at which the firm technically can substitute one input for another and still maintain the same level of production. (Note that this ratio is a negative number since, as we move from A to B, capital is falling while labor is rising.) If we let bundle B approach bundle A along isoquant y_1, the ratio $(K_2 - K_1)/(L_2 - L_1)$ approaches the slope of the tangent line, mn, at point A. Thus, the slope of the tangent line measures the marginal rate at which the firm technically can substitute capital for labor and still maintain the same level of production.

We define the marginal rate of technical substitution of L for K, denoted MRTS_{LK}, as the number of units of capital that can be sacrificed per unit of labor gained so as to maintain the same level of production. Just as with the MRS, economists define the MRTS_{LK} as a positive number, so the marginal rate of technical substitution is equal to *minus* the slope of the isoquant. It measures the rate at which a firm technically is able to substitute inputs in production.

Since isoquants are convex, the MRTS_{LK} diminishes as labor is substituted for capital. Essentially, this means that, as labor becomes more abundant relative to capital, it takes more units of labor to replace each unit of capital and still maintain the same output rate.

The primary reason for a **diminishing marginal rate of technical substitution** is that inputs are not perfect substitutes but, rather, tend to complement each other. Each input has attributes that make it capable of doing something other inputs cannot do as well. Thus, as labor becomes more abundant relative to capital it makes sense that it becomes increasingly difficult to replace capital with labor.

MARGINAL PRODUCTS AND THE MARGINAL RATE OF TECHNICAL SUBSTITUTION

When we look at the cost-minimizing choice of inputs in the next chapter, it will be useful to understand how the marginal rate of technical substitution of labor for capital relates to marginal products of labor and capital.

   The marginal rate of technical substitution measures the rate at which one input can be substituted for another while maintaining a given level of output. Marginal products, on the other hand, measure the change in output due to a unit change in one input, holding the other constant. Since MP_L measures the change in output as the quantity of labor changes by a small amount and MP_K measures the change in output as the quantity of capital changes by a small amount, the ratio of the two measures the rate at which labor can be substituted for capital, holding output constant. Thus, we have this equation:

$$MRTS_{LK} = MP_L/MP_K. \qquad\qquad (6.4)$$

EXAMPLE 6–2

THE RELATION BETWEEN MARGINAL PRODUCTS AND THE MARGINAL RATE OF TECHNICAL SUBSTITUTION

Suppose a firm that produces concrete has a production function given by

$$y = \sqrt{LK}$$

where y is tons of concrete produced per week. The marginal products associated with this production function are

$$MP_L = .5\sqrt{(K/L)} \quad \text{and} \quad MP_K = .5\sqrt{(L/K)}.$$

(a) Calculate the $MRTS_{LK}$ when the firm uses 10 units of capital and 5 units of labor. (b) Does this technology exhibit the Law of Diminishing Marginal Productivity for both inputs? (c) Are the isoquants associated with this technology convex?

■ **SOLUTION** (a) Since the marginal rate of technical substitution of labor for capital is equal to the ratio of the marginal products, we have

$$MRTS_{LK} = MP_L/MP_K$$

$$= [.5\sqrt{(K/L)}]/[.5\sqrt{(L/K)}] = K/L = 10/5 = 2;$$

that is, the rate at which labor can be substituted for capital while maintaining the same level of production is 2 units of capital per 1 unit of labor.

(b) The Law of Diminishing Marginal Productivity states that a point is reached beyond which the marginal product of an input declines as more of the input is used, holding all other inputs constant. In this instance, the Law of Diminishing Marginal Productivity holds for both inputs. Illustrating for the marginal product of labor, $MP_L = .5\sqrt{(K/L)}$. Holding K fixed, notice that as L increases, MP_L always decreases which means that the Law of Diminishing Marginal Productivity holds immediately.

(c) If isoquants are convex, then the $MRTS_{LK}$ falls as labor is substituted for capital. In this instance, the marginal rate of technical substitution of labor for capital is equal to the capital–labor ratio. Now as labor is substituted for capital, the capital–labor ratio must fall; therefore, the $MRTS_{LK}$ must also fall which means that the isoquants are convex. ∎

RETURNS TO SCALE

How output varies in response to a change in the scale of operation—that is, in response to a proportionate change in all inputs—has important implications for practical decision making. Imagine, for example, that an analysis has revealed that automobile manufacturers can distribute new cars to dealers at a lower cost if they use several regional assembly plants rather than one large, central plant. Such information very likely will influence their decisions about where to locate their plants. Whatever the industry, owners who want to alter production levels must know how output will respond to a change in the scale of the operation.

In the long run, as we know, a firm can vary all of its inputs. If it increases all inputs in the same proportion, three possibilities arise. Assume that it increases all inputs by 10%. If as a result output also increases by 10% then there are **constant returns to scale.** If output increases by more than 10%, then there are **increasing returns to scale.** Finally, if output increases by less than 10%, then there are **decreasing returns to scale.**

Figure 6–6 illustrates constant, increasing, and decreasing returns to scale indicating how a firm's isoquants are spaced along a ray from the origin. In each of the panels in Figure 6–6 we have drawn in a ray labeled OT. Along this ray capital and labor are changing in the same proportions; that is, the capital–labor ratio (K/L) is constant. In each of these diagrams $K/L = 1/2$ along OT.

Suppose initially that a firm employs 5 units of capital and 10 units of labor, and produces 100 units of output. What happens to output if the firm doubles both inputs? In Figure 6–6(a) output doubles when both inputs double (constant returns to scale). Using this as our benchmark, let us compare Figure 6–6(b) and (c). In (b)

RETURNS TO SCALE   **FIGURE 6-6**

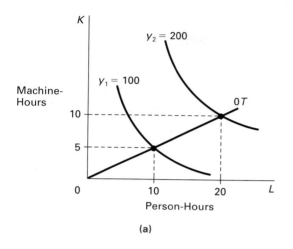

(a)

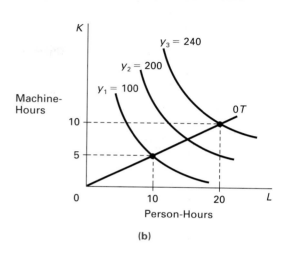

(b)

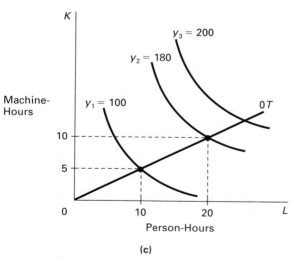

(c)

A production function exhibits increasing, panel (a), constant, panel (b), or decreasing, panel (c), returns to scale according to whether, when all inputs are doubled, output more than doubles, doubles, or increases by less than two-fold, respectively.

output increases from 100 to 240 when both inputs double (increasing returns to scale). This means that the isoquant corresponding to an output of 200 units is closer to the $y = 100$ isoquant than it is in (a). The isoquants are closer together. In (c) we have decreasing returns to scale and the isoquants are further apart.

In theory we easily can identify production functions that exhibit increasing, constant, or decreasing returns to scale as long as we can specify an explicit production function. Without such a function, however, it is much more difficult and in fact, many production functions have all three of the characteristics—increasing, constant, and decreasing returns to scale—depending on the quantities of inputs used. The returns to scale in any particular firm are an empirical issue.

Nonetheless, we can point out what factors are likely to affect the returns to scale. They include the specialization and division of labor. As a firm initially expands its scale of operation, it can assign workers specific tasks. This increases the productivity of workers since it allows them to concentrate on one particular job rather than having to perform many tasks. For example, consider a firm that manufactures dollhouses. Initially the firm may employ one worker who must assemble, finish, and package the dollhouses. As output increases and it becomes profitable to hire additional inputs, the firm can increase productivity by dividing workers into groups, each specializing in one of the three tasks. The modern-day assembly line is a good example of increasing returns to scale.

With constant returns to scale, average and marginal products are independent of the size of the plant. If a firm can double its production by building another factory identical to the one currently in operation, then constant returns to scale are guaranteed. Both factories would use the same production process and produce exactly the same output. Fast food restaurants and video rental stores are examples of firms that, most likely, operate under constant returns to scale.

Decreasing returns to scale set in as inefficiencies in managing a large organization arise. As the size of the business increases, coordinating and monitoring the operation of many plants and employees becomes difficult. Communication channels between workers, supervisors, and management become distorted and often broken. Production and employment decisions can no longer be made or implemented quickly, often leading to ineffective management. The end result is that to double production, more than twice the management input is needed; this, in turn, leads to decreasing returns to scale.

1. In this chapter we have discussed the concepts upon which the theory of production and employment rest. Firms are economic entities that convert resources into goods and services. Firms exist because the transaction costs associated with the production process are lower if production takes place within firms.

2. Economic cost plays a fundamental role in the theory of the firm. The economic cost, or opportunity cost, of using resources to undertake some action is the value of those resources measured in terms of the next best alternative. Economic costs include both the explicit and implicit costs associated with a particular endeavor.

3. In microeconomics we assume firms operate to maximize economic profit. Economic profit is the difference between revenue and economic cost. A firm earns a positive economic profit if the owners receive more than they could earn in the next best alternative and an economic loss if the owners receive less. Economists have found that a theory based on profit maximization does exceedingly well in predicting the way in which owners and managers make employment decisions.

4. Production is the process of employing inputs to produce goods and services. A firm's technology, or the existing technical know-how, can be represented by a production table, a production function, or a family of isoquants. No matter how we choose to depict a firm's technology, we always assume that the firm operates in a technologically efficient way; that is, we assume that inputs are combined to yield the maximum possible output.

5. An isoquant shows all the combinations of inputs that can be used to produce a given level of output. Isoquants and indifference curves have the same geometrical properties although they represent very different concepts. Minus the slope of an isoquant is called the marginal rate of technical substitution. It measures the rate at which a firm technically is able to substitute inputs and still maintain the same level of production.

6. We also distinguished between production in the short run, when some inputs cannot be varied, and the long run, when all inputs can be varied. Economists have found that many short-run production functions satisfy the Law of Diminishing Marginal Productivity. According to this law, a point is reached beyond which the marginal product of the variable input declines as more of that input is used, holding all other inputs constant.

7. Finally, in the long run we discussed how output changes as a result of proportionate changes in all inputs. If output increases in greater proportion than input use, then production is said to exhibit increasing returns to scale. Constant and decreasing returns to scale are defined similarly. In general, we expect increasing returns to scale to prevail at low output levels and decreasing returns to scale at higher output levels.

KEY TERMS

Firms
Transaction Costs
Profit Maximization
Opportunity or Economic Cost
Explicit and Implicit Cost
Economic Profit
Technology
Production Table and
  Production Function
Isoquant
Input Bundle
Long and Short Runs

Total Product Curve
Average Product
Marginal Product
Law of Diminishing Marginal
  Productivity
Marginal Rate of Technical
  Substitution
Diminishing Marginal Rate of
  Technical Substitution
Increasing, Constant, and
  Decreasing Returns to Scale

QUESTIONS AND PROBLEMS

1. a) Explain why firms exist.
   b) If you want to have French pastries for breakfast, why might you purchase them at a bakery rather than make them yourself?
2. Discuss whether or not profit maximization is an appropriate behavioral assumption for the three types of firms discussed in this chapter.
3. a) Define explicit and implicit costs.
   b) Why do economists worry about implicit costs?
4. Last year a well-known accountant, Mr. Smith, billed his clients a total of $200,000 for services rendered by his firm. Mr. Smith rented office space for $5,000, employed a staff consisting of a C.P.A, a bookkeeper, and a secretary for $50,000, spent $900 on subscriptions to various newspapers and professional journals, and rented a shredding machine that is used to destroy unwanted documents for $1,000.
   a) If Mr. Smith could earn $100,000 per year working for another accounting firm, determine accounting profit and economic profit for his operation. Be sure to specify which costs are explicit and which are implicit.
   b) At what salary would Mr. Smith be willing to leave his business to work for another firm?
5. Carrie is considering going to a four-year college. She estimates

that out-of-pocket expenses for attending college will be $4,000 per year for tuition, books, and supplies. She can earn $10,000 per year working for her father if she does not go to college. If Carrie plans to work for 30 years, what is the minimum amount Carrie must expect to earn after graduation to make college financially worthwhile? (Assume a zero rate of interest.)

6. a) Kirk recently graduated from dental school. In order to set up his own practice, Kirk must invest $50,000 in equipment and an office. He can either borrow the money from the bank at 9% per year or use his own money. What should Kirk do? Explain.

   b) Suppose that Kirk has established his practice and has married Kathy, a dental hygienist. Kirk argues that Kathy should work for him because it would save money since he would not have to hire a hygienist. Kathy, on the other hand, argues that the cost to them is the same regardless. With whom do you agree? Explain.

7. Fred recently graduated from medical school. After completing his residency work, Fred turned down a $40,000 per year position with a hospital to start his own pediatrics practice. Fred invests $130,000 that he borrows from the bank at 10% per year. Revenue during the first year was $150,000, and expenses were:

Rent	$20,000
Taxes	5,000
Employees' Salaries	45,000
Medical Supplies	50,000
Other Supplies	10,000

   a) Calculate both accounting and economic profit.
   b) How would your calculations change if instead of borrowing $130,000 Fred invests his own money?

8. Compucenter previously purchased 3,000 PC/XT systems boards for $200 each. Currently these processors sell for $100. One Compucenter manager has suggested that each processor be combined with $700 worth of labor and other supplies to produce a PC that would be sold for $850. Should the owners of Compucenter follow this plan of action? Explain.

9. a) Explain the concept of a production function or a production table.
   b) How are these related to the technology?
   c) Explain what is meant by technological efficiency.
   d) Is information concerning the production function alone adequate for determining the profit-maximizing rate of output?

10. Using the production function

$$y = 10\sqrt{KL},$$

construct a production table where capital and labor range from 1 to 10 units each.

11. a) Explain the Law of Diminishing Marginal Productivity.
    b) What variables must be held constant if this law is to apply?

12. Farmer Green grows corn on two identical acres of land that are adjacent to one another. Green has a fixed amount of time to allocate to farming each day. Within each acre, growing corn is subject to diminishing marginal productivity. If corn sells for $2.50 per bushel, find a rule that explains how long Green should spend working each acre if he wants to maximize revenue from the sale of corn.

13. a) Define the short and long runs.
    b) Why is it important to distinguish between the short and long runs?
    c) Give an example of a firm for which the short run might be very short (days or weeks) and one for which it might be very long (months or years).

14. In the nineteenth century, the British economist Thomas Malthus reasoned that, since the amount of land is in fixed supply, the marginal productivity of labor in food production would fall as the world population increases and more labor works the land. Therefore, the amount of food per person would always fall over time, leading to a shortage of food and widespread famine. Explain why Malthus' line of reasoning is incorrect.

15. Suppose that the Mass Transit Authority (MTA) of a large city must produce a certain amount of passenger service per year. MTA finds that the following combinations of maintenance personnel and buses can be used to provide the required output.

Input Bundle	Number of Buses	Number of Maintenance Personnel
1	100	50
2	101	41
3	102	37
4	103	33
5	104	30

a) Suppose MTA currently is using 100 buses and 50 maintenance persons. If one more bus is purchased, how many workers can MTA lay off and still maintain the required output of bus services? Is this the marginal rate of technical substitution between buses and maintenance personnel? Explain.

b) Using this data, graph an isoquant. Be sure to label your graph carefully.

c) Do these data illustrate the Law of Diminishing Marginal Productivity? Do they illustrate a diminishing $MRTS_{LK}$? Explain.

16. a) For the production function

$$y = 5K^{.5}L^{.5}$$

determine three input bundles that will yield isoquants corresponding to 320 and 500 units of output.

b) Use this information to sketch the isoquants.

17. Two students enrolled in intermediate microeconomics are having a debate concerning production in the long run. Ed argues that output can only be increased if a firm employs more of every input. Mary maintains that Ed is right if the production function exhibits fixed proportions but is wrong otherwise. Comment on this debate.

18. Suppose that the production function for Wheels, Inc., a manufacturer of unicycles, is

$$y = L^{.5} + K^{.5}$$

with marginal product functions

$$MP_L = 1/2L^{.5} \quad \text{and} \quad MP_K = 1/2K^{.5}$$

where y is output of unicycles per month, L is the labor input and K is the capital input.

a) Determine output and the $MRTS_{LK}$ when $L = 100$ and $K = 64$.

b) If both labor and capital double, determine the new output and $MRTS_{LK}$.

c) Does this production function exhibit the Law of Diminishing Marginal Productivity?

d) Does this production function exhibit increasing, constant, or decreasing returns to scale?

REFERENCES   Alchian, A., and H. Demsetz. 1972. "Production, Information Costs, and Economic Organization." *American Economic Review* (Dec.): 777–95.

Coase, R. 1937. "The Nature of the Firm." *Economica* (Nov.): 386–408.

Gold, B. 1971. "Changing Perspectives on Size, Scale, and Returns: An Interpretive Survey." *Journal of Economic Literature* (March): 5–33.

Kreps, D. 1990. *A Course in Microeconomic Theory*. Princeton: Princeton University Press.

PRODUCTION THEORY: A CALCULUS APPROACH

A6.1 ISOQUANTS

Suppose the production function $y = F(K,L)$ represents the technology for a firm using capital and labor to produce good y. Given this information, we can derive the expression given in the text relating the marginal rate of technical substitution to marginal products using implicit functions. First, note that the marginal product of labor is the partial derivative of the production function with respect to labor and the marginal product of capital is the partial derivative of the production function with respect to capital:

$$MP_L = \frac{\partial F(K,L)}{\partial L} \quad \text{and} \quad MP_K = \frac{\partial F(K,L)}{\partial K}.$$

We use partial derivatives here because the marginal product of one input is calculated holding the other input fixed.

Now, in order to derive the marginal rate of technical substitution we must first find the function that describes an isoquant. That is, we must find a function relating K to L for a given level of production. If we had a specific production function we could do this by solving it *explicitly* for K as a function of L and y. Since we do not have a specific production function, however, we can only solve it *implicitly* for K as a function of L. This implicit function is denoted by $K = \psi(L,y^0)$, where y^0 is the output level associated with the isoquant in question.

Substituting this function into the production function yields an identity:

$$y^0 \equiv F[\psi(L,y^0),L].$$

This is an identity because for each value of L the function $\psi(L,y^0)$ tells us how much K we need to produce y^0.

Now we can differentiate both sides of this identity with respect to L. When doing this, however, we must be careful. Notice that L appears in two places in the identity. This means that changing L will change the function in two ways: by changing the first argument and by changing the second argument. Thus, when differentiating we must take account of both changes. This gives

$$0 = \frac{\partial F(K,L)}{\partial L} + \frac{\partial F(K,L)}{\partial K}\left(\frac{\partial K}{\partial L}\right).$$

Solving this last equation for $\frac{\partial K}{\partial L}$ gives the slope of the isoquant:

$$\frac{\partial K}{\partial L} = \frac{\partial F(K,L)}{\partial L} \Big/ \frac{\partial F(K,L)}{\partial K}.$$

Just as we stated in the text, the marginal rate of technical substitution is equal to the ratio of marginal products.

EXAMPLE A6–1

Suppose that a firm's technology is represented by the production function $y = K^a L^b$. This is called a *Cobb–Douglas production function*. Derive the marginal rate of technical substitution associated with this production function.

■ **SOLUTION** In this instance, marginal products are given by

$$MP_K = aK^{a-1}L^b, MP_L = bK^a L^{b-1} \qquad\qquad \text{and}$$

$$MRTS_{LK} = -MP_L/MP_K = (b/a)(K/L). \blacksquare$$

THE THEORY OF COST

LEARNING OBJECTIVES

After completing Chapter 7 you should be able to do the following:

■ Discuss the relation between the Law of Diminishing Marginal Productivity and the shape of the total variable cost curve.

■ Determine the slope of an isocost line and interpret its economic significance.

■ Show graphically and algebraically how to find a firm's cost-minimizing input bundle.

■ Explain intuitively the conditions characterizing a firm's choice of which input bundle to use.

■ Explain how the long-run total cost curve is derived from the expansion path.

■ Discuss the relation between economies and diseconomies of scale and the shape of the long-run average cost curve.

■ Compare short- and long-run total and per-unit cost curves.

■ Analyze the impact of input taxes and input restrictions on long-run costs.

EXAMPLES

■ **7–1** Short-Run Costs and a New Product Line

■ **7–2** Determining the Cost-Minimizing Input Bundle

■ **7–3** Payroll Taxes and Cost Minimization

■ **7–4** Pesticide Regulation and Cost Minimization

Up to this point we have focused on the physical relation between inputs and outputs. However, if we are to understand how profit-maximizing firms decide how much to produce and how much of each factor of production to employ, then not only must we understand the physical relation between inputs and outputs but we must also understand how production costs vary with output. In this chapter we will investigate the relation between cost and output in both the short and long runs. This is called *cost theory*. Once we master cost theory, we can move on to Chapter 8 where we explore how revenue and cost together determine the profit-maximization level of outputs and inputs for price-taking firms.

7.1 PRODUCTION COSTS IN THE SHORT RUN

■ Recall that in the short run the firm cannot vary all of its inputs. Some inputs are fixed and some are variable. This means that in the short run we must distinguish between costs arising from the use of fixed inputs and costs arising from the use of variable inputs.

FIXED COSTS

Total fixed costs (TFC) are the costs the firm bears independent of the output it produces; they are associated with the inputs that the firm cannot vary in the short run. Fixed costs cannot be avoided in the short run even if the owner of the firm decides to produce zero output. In our two-input model, the owner's expenditures on capital are fixed costs in this sense.

Fixed costs usually arise for one of two reasons: either the transaction costs associated with renegotiating previous contractual arrangements are very large or the firm employs very specialized factors of production. One example of a fixed cost arising because of transaction costs is a monthly lease or mortgage payment. If a firm has a long-term lease on a rented building or a mortgage on an owned one, and if the cost of renegotiating the lease or mortgage is high, then the firm must make its rental or mortgage payment each month even if no output is produced. This type of fixed cost is also an explicit cost.

An example of a fixed cost arising because of specialization would be payments for machines designed to stamp out parts that are used only in the production of a certain good. Such machines will have little value outside their current use and firms will be reluctant to dispose of them to meet temporary declines in demand or to purchase more of them to meet temporary increases in demand. This too is an explicit fixed cost.

Other examples of more common short-run fixed costs are property taxes, insurance premiums, interest paid on borrowed funds, foregone wages and foregone interest. The first three of these are explicit costs while the last two are implicit costs. All of them are fixed costs because they are independent of the firm's level of production.

In later chapters we will also need to distinguish between two other types of fixed costs called *quasi-fixed costs* and *sunk costs*. Quasi-fixed costs are independent of how much the firm produces but do not have to be paid if owners decide to produce zero output. One example of a quasi-fixed cost would be the electricity used to light a factory. If a firm closes down its factory, it uses no electricity for lights; however, if it produces any positive amount of output, it must turn on the lights and purchase a fixed amount of electricity.

QUASI-FIXED COSTS AND SUNK COSTS

Sunk costs are fixed costs in that they are independent of the level of output but, in addition, they are costs that must be paid even if the owners of the firm liquidate and go out of business. Sunk costs are inescapable even in the long run. For example, suppose the owner of a firm purchases a machine for $10,000. Further, suppose that after taking possession of the machine the owner can resell it for only $8,000 (meaning that it has depreciated already). Fixed costs for this firm would be $10,000 but sunk costs would be $2,000 since, if the machine is sold, the owner can recover only $8,000 of the $10,000.

The distinction between fixed costs and quasi-fixed costs will be important for the short-run, shut-down decision (Chapter 8). The distinction between fixed costs and sunk costs is important for the long-run decision to enter and exit an industry (Chapter 9).

Total variable costs (TVC) are the costs associated with the employment of the variable inputs used in the production process. Since the quantity of a variable input changes with output, total variable costs depend on how much output a firm produces. For example, in order to increase production in the short run, more of

VARIABLE COSTS

the variable inputs must be used which leads to an increase in total variable costs.

TOTAL COST

Short-run total cost (STC) is the sum of total variable cost and total fixed cost; that is, STC = TFC + TVC. Short-run total cost represents the cost of all fixed and variable inputs used in the production process. How does total cost vary with output? Since total fixed cost is constant, the total cost curve increases with output and has the same shape as the TVC curve.

OVERHEAD COSTS

The concept of overhead costs is often a source of confusion in intermediate economics courses. In order to avoid this problem, we give here a brief discussion of the relation between overhead costs, variable costs, and fixed costs.

Our definitions of TFC and TVC classify costs by how they respond to changes in the volume of manufacturing activity. TFC are costs that are not affected by the volume of production activity while TVC vary directly with changes in the volume of production activity. This type of classification is useful because employment and production decisions depend on how revenues and costs vary with the level of production.

An alternative means of classifying costs is also popular with businesspersons. They classify costs by their relation to the manufacturing process. For example, *manufacturing direct costs* are the costs of materials clearly and easily traceable to the finished product and the costs of all employees actually working with materials to convert them into finished goods. *Manufacturing overhead costs,* on the other hand, are costs that cannot be traced conveniently or directly to specific products. Overhead costs include such things as taxes, insurance premiums, supervisors' salaries, base fees charged by utility companies, the cost of lubricants for machines, the cost of miscellaneous supplies used in the production process, and the cost of the electricity used to operate machines. Classifying costs by their relation to the manufacturing process is useful to owners and managers who use such information to help monitor different operations within the firm.

The point we want to emphasize is that overhead costs can be either fixed or variable. Taxes, insurance premiums, supervisors' salaries, and the base fees charged by utility companies are fixed costs. They must be paid regardless of how much output is produced. Lubricants for machines, miscellaneous supplies used in the production process, and the electricity used to operate machines are variable costs since they depend on how much output the firm produces. In economics, whether or not costs are direct or overhead is not important. What is important is whether or not costs are fixed or variable.

As we will see in the next chapter, most economic analysis of profit-maximizing firms relies on per-unit costs—that is, on average and marginal cost. First, let us consider the firm's average cost curves.

In the short run we distinguish between three types of average cost: average fixed cost, average variable cost, and average total cost. **Average fixed cost** (AFC) is total fixed cost divided by output; that is, AFC = TFC/y. We measure average fixed cost in dollars per unit of output. Since fixed costs do not vary with changes in output, AFC is very large for low output rates and very small for high output rates. As output increases, AFC declines continuously.

Average variable cost (AVC) is total variable cost divided by output; that is, AVC = TVC/y. Unlike AFC, AVC need not be a decreasing function of output over the entire range of production possibilities. The shape of the AVC curve depends on the shape of the total variable cost curve which, in turn, depends on the shape of the short-run production function.

The last measure of average cost in the short run is short-run average total cost (SATC). **Short-run average total cost** is short-run total cost divided by output; that is, SATC = STC/y. Notice that the SATC is also related to AFC and AVC in a very simple way. Recalling that the STC is the sum of TFC and TVC, we have, SATC = AFC + AVC.

Short-run marginal cost (SMC) is the change in total cost per unit change in output. Since, in the short run, any change in total cost is a change in variable cost, SMC is also the change in total variable cost per unit change in output. Thus, SMC = ΔSTC/Δy = ΔTVC/Δy. SMC is measured in dollars per unit of output.

A firm's technology and the prices it pays for inputs determine its production costs. In the short run, the total product curve, or short-run production function, represents the technology so that, to a large extent, the Law of Diminishing Marginal Productivity determines short-run costs. Consider Figure 7–1(a), which shows a representative total product curve, labeled TP. This total product curve reflects the Law of Diminishing Marginal Productivity; that is, a point is reached beyond which the marginal product of the variable input declines. As labor input increases from zero to 400, output increases at an accelerating rate which means that the MP_L

is increasing. As labor increases beyond 400, output increases but at a decreasing rate which means that the MP_L is decreasing. Thus, diminishing marginal productivity begins when labor increases beyond 400 units.

Using Figure 7–1(a), we can construct the relation between

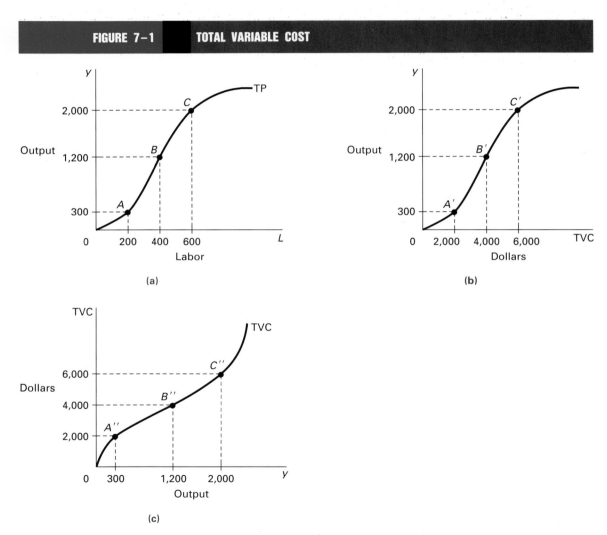

FIGURE 7–1   **TOTAL VARIABLE COST**

(a)

(b)

(c)

The total variable cost curve is constructed from the total product curve. The law of diminishing marginal productivity determines the shape of the total cost curve.

variable cost and output. Suppose that the firm produces 300 units of a particular good. According to the total product curve, this requires 200 units of labor. If labor is paid $10 per hour then the variable cost of producing 300 units of output is $2,000; that is, TVC = $2,000. Similarly, if output is 1,200 then TVC = $4,000 and if output is 2,000 then TVC is $6,000.

These cost–output pairs are plotted in Figure 7–1(b). Notice that the resulting curve has exactly the same shape as the short-run production function! The two diagrams differ only in the units of measurement on the horizontal axis. In (a) we have units of labor input; in (b) we have dollars.

We still do not have our total variable cost curve. However, Figure 7–1(b) contains all the information we need to determine it. We want variable cost as a function of output. To get this, all we have to do is reverse the axes in (b). This is shown in Figure 7–1(c). The curve labeled TVC is the total variable cost curve. Remember, this curve is derived for a given amount of the fixed input and given input prices. If either of these were to change, then a new TVC curve would arise.

Reviewing the construction of the TVC curve it is clear that the shape of the short-run production function, the technology, determines the shape of the TVC curve. Input prices have no effect on the shape of the TVC curve because they are constant. However, the price of the variable factor of production does determine the location of the TVC curve. For example, if labor costs doubled what would happen to the TVC curve in Figure 7–1(c)? It would cost more to produce every level of output (except zero of course) and the TVC curve would rotate up about the origin.

■ Most economic analysis of profit-maximizing firms relies heavily on average and marginal cost curves so it is important to understand (a) how they derive from the total cost curves and (b) how they relate to each other. Figure 7–2(a) shows the total cost curves that economists feel are typical of most technologies and Figure 7–2(b) illustrates the associated per-unit cost curves. The TFC curve is horizontal because these costs are independent of output. As we demonstrated in the last section, the shape of the TVC curve is implied by the technology and, in particular, by the extent to which production involves diminishing returns to variable factors. The STC curve is simply the TVC shifted up vertically by the TFC.

Now let's take a closer look at the relationship between total costs and per-unit costs.

7.2 SHORT-RUN COST CURVES

| FIGURE 7-2 | THE SHORT-RUN COST CURVES |

(a) We obtain the STC curve by adding total fixed costs to the TVC curve. (b) AFC declines continuously. AVC, SATC, and SMC are all U-shaped. SMC is equal to AVC and SATC at their respective minimum points.

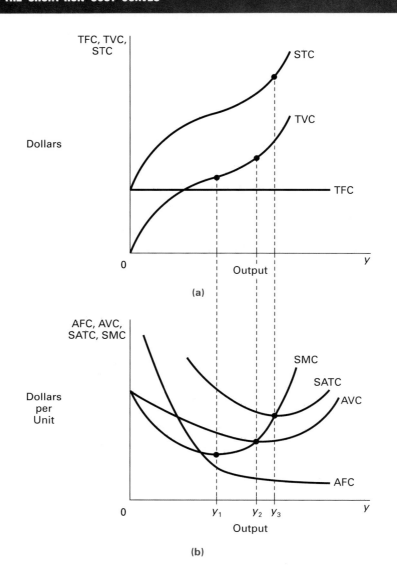

THE AVERAGE COST CURVES

Let us begin with the AFC curve. Figures $7-3$(a) and (b) show a firm's TFC and AFC cost curves respectively. Since AFC = TFC/y, AFC is given by the slope of a ray from the origin to a point on the TFC curve. For example, for output y_1, AFC is $TVC_1/y_1 = AD/0D$

which is the slope of the ray labeled 0A. For output y_2, AFC = TFC_1/y_2 which is the slope of 0B and for output y_3, AFC = TFC_1/y_3 which is equal to the slope of 0C. Since total fixed cost does not vary with output, AFC declines as output increases.

Next consider the AVC curve. Figures 7−3(c) and (d) show how we determine AVC from the TVC curve. Since AVC = TVC/y, average variable cost is the slope of a ray from the origin to a point on the TVC curve. For example, when output is equal to y_1 units, AVC = TVC_1/y_1 = AD/0D which is the slope of ray 0A. In order to see how AVC changes as output increases, place your I.D. card along the ray labeled 0A in Figure 7−3(c), let output increase, and note how the slope of the edge of your I.D. card changes as it moves up along the TVC curve from A to B to C. For production levels between 0 and y_2, AVC falls. At y_2 the ray from the origin to point B is tangent to the TVC curve, which means that at this output AVC attains its minimum. Beyond y_2, AVC begins to rise.

We derive the SATC curve in exactly the same way as the AVC curve. As shown in Figures 7−3(e) and (f), SATC falls to a minimum at output level y_3 and then rises. In addition, note that the minimum point of the SATC curve occurs at an output level greater than the output level where AVC attains its minimum; that is, $y_3 > y_2$.

Finally, consider the SMC. Recall that marginal cost is the change in total cost, which is also the change in total variable cost, per unit change in output. This means that we can measure SMC as the slope of either the STC curve or the TVC curve. Figures 7−3(g) and (h) show the derivation of the SMC curve. As output increases and we move up along the total cost curve (either the STC curve or the TVC curve), SMC falls (check it out with your I.D. card) until production is at y_1. This is the inflection point of both the STC and TVC curves, it is where the marginal product of labor begins to decline, and it corresponds to the minimum point of the SMC curve. As production increases beyond y_1, SMC begins to rise. Also, note that at y_2 the slope of the TVC curve is equal to the slope of a ray from the origin to point B' on the TVC curve and at y_3 the slope of the STC curve is equal to the slope of a ray from the origin to point C on the STC curve. This means that when production is y_2 units of output, SMC and AVC are equal and when production is y_3 units of output, SMC and SATC are equal.

The shape of the SMC curve depends on the shape of the TVC curve, which in turn depends on the shape of the short-run production function. (Recall Figure 7−1.) Since the Law of Diminishing Marginal Productivity guarantees that there is a point beyond which the marginal product of labor falls, it also guarantees

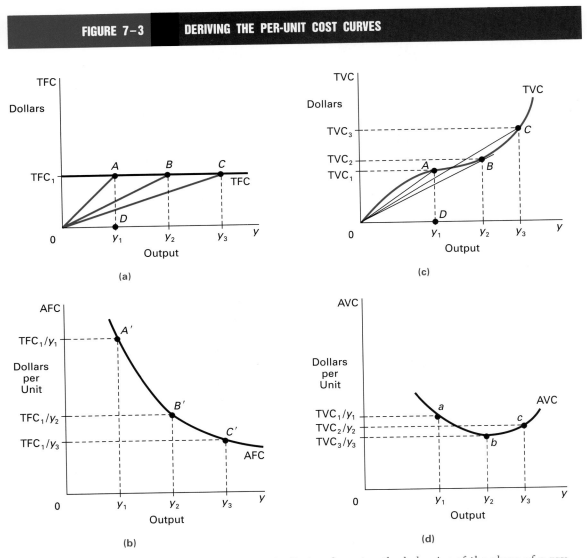

FIGURE 7-3   DERIVING THE PER-UNIT COST CURVES

The average cost curves are obtained geometrically by observing the behavior of the slope of a ray from the origin to a point on the appropriate total cost curve. The marginal cost curve is obtained by observing the behavior of the slope of the TVC curve or the STC curve.

that there is a point beyond which short-run total cost increases at an increasing rate. For example, in Figure 7-3(g) the marginal product of labor increases as output expands to y_1 units and then begins to decline. The Law of Diminishing Marginal Productivity implies that short-run marginal cost eventually must increase.

CONTINUED

FIGURE 7–3

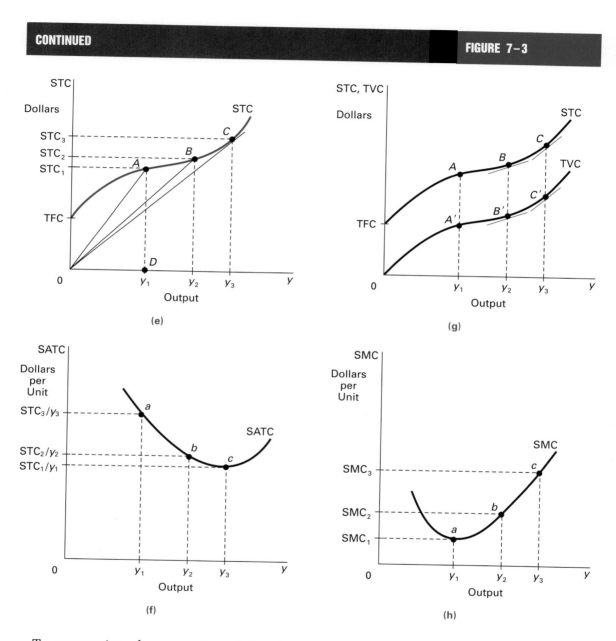

(e)

(g)

(f)

(h)

To summarize, the properties of the short-run, per-unit cost curves are as follows (refer to Figure 7–2[b]): (i) AVC falls, reaches a minimum, and then increases. (ii) SATC falls, reaches a minimum, and then increases. The minimum point of the SATC curve occurs at a level of production greater than that corresponding to the minimum point of the AVC curve. (iii) SMC falls, reaches a minimum, and then increases. SMC equals AVC and SATC when these curves attain their minimums. SMC is less than average cost when average cost is falling and greater than average cost when it is rising.

It is easy to become all wrapped up in learning how to derive three total cost curves, three average cost curves, and one marginal cost curve. Moreover, understanding how they relate geometrically may seem to be an arduous task. However, while mastering these points, it is important not to lose sight of the two economic concepts involved: the Law of Diminishing Marginal Productivity and the firm's ability to employ additional inputs at constant prices.

In microeconomics, we use short-run cost curves primarily to help us understand profit maximization. The next example gives us a preview of some of the issues discussed in Chapter 8 and illustrates how short-run cost curves can help owners and managers of firms make wise business decisions.

EXAMPLE 7-1

SHORT-RUN COSTS AND A NEW PRODUCT LINE

Suppose the research and development department of Gerber Foods, Inc., has developed a new line of baby food. Management has decided to introduce the new line if anticipated revenues cover variable costs. (In Chapter 8, we will discuss whether or not this is the appropriate criterion.) The economics department of Gerber has provided management with the following cost estimates:

$$STC = 5000 + 500y - .5y^2 + .0005y^3 \qquad \text{and}$$

$$SMC = 500 - y + .0015y^2$$

where y is thousands of jars of baby food produced per month. (a) If the firm expects to sell the new product to retailers for \$.30 per jar, should it introduce the new line? (b) What if the price is \$.50 per jar?

■ **SOLUTION** If revenues are going to cover variable costs, then per-unit price must be greater than per-unit or average variable cost. Since we do not know how many jars Gerber expects to sell, we cannot determine precisely whether or not the firm should introduce the new line; however, we can provide management with a range of production levels for which price is greater than average variable cost.

(a) First, let's find the minimum point of the AVC curve. If price is below this level, then the firm definitely should not introduce the new line. We know that average variable cost attains its minimum when AVC and SMC are equal. In this instance, TFC = 5,000, TVC = $.0005y^3 - .5y^2 + 500y$, and AVC = $.0005y^2 - .5y + 500$. Setting AVC equal to SMC gives

$$.0005y^2 - .5y + 500 = .0015y^2 - y + 500.$$

Solving this equation for y yields the output where AVC attains its minimum, $y = 500$, and substituting this output into the equation for AVC gives: AVC(500) = $375 per thousand jars or $.375 per jar. Since $.30 is less than minimum AVC, at this price (or any price below $.30) revenues will never cover variable costs and the firm should not introduce the line.

(b) Since $.50 is greater than minimum AVC, there is a range of outputs for which revenues *will* cover variable costs. To find this range, simply find where AVC is equal to .50; that is, find where $.0005y^2 - .5y + 500 = 500$. Solving this equation for y, we find that $y = 1,000$. Thus, if Gerber anticipates selling one million or more jars per month, it should introduce the new line. ■

■ In the long run, a firm can adjust all inputs. In this section, we address a fundamental problem faced by all firms: how to choose the combination of inputs that minimizes the cost of producing a given level of output. In the next section, we will investigate the relation between long-run costs and output.

7.3 PRODUCTION COSTS IN THE LONG RUN

Up to this point, we have addressed the theory of production from a purely technical standpoint. We have said that a firm is operating in a technically efficient manner if it uses a production process that, for a given quantity of inputs, produces the maximum possible output.

The assumption of technical efficiency is purely a physical problem that can be dealt with by physicists and engineers. It says nothing about which input bundle firms should use to produce a given level of output. However, profit-maximizing owners of firms are concerned not only with technical efficiency but also with maximizing output in the *cheapest* possible way.

The prices of inputs are determined by the fluctuations of supply

INPUT PRICES AND ISOCOST LINES

and demand in the resource market. In Chapter 10 we will investigate precisely how this happens. For the moment, however, we will suppose that producers can purchase any quantity of inputs at given market prices.

Once again, we assume that there are only two inputs, capital and labor. We can denote the prices of these two inputs as w and r respectively (where w is the wage rate and r, the rental rate for capital). Remember, these prices reflect the opportunity cost of using labor and capital. The total cost to the firm of using any input bundle, denoted by C, is the sum of the firm's expenditures on capital and labor:

$$C = rK + wL. \qquad (7.1)$$

For a given level of expenditures (for a given C), economists call equation (7.1) an isocost line. Given input prices, an **isocost line** is an equation that relates a specified total cost to the quantities of capital and labor a firm employs.

Notice that for a given C, an isocost line has exactly the same form as a budget constraint. (Replace C with income, inputs with goods, and input prices with the prices of goods.) This gives us another interpretation of an isocost line. Suppose that, in the current production period, a firm has decided to spend C dollars on capital and labor; that is, the firm's outlay in the current period is C dollars. In this instance, the isocost line gives us all the different combinations of capital and labor that the firm can purchase with C dollars.

An isocost line is the equation of a straight line. To graph a representative isocost line, we follow the same steps we used to graph a budget constraint. We begin by solving the isocost line equation for capital as a function of labor. This gives

$$K = C/r - (w/r)L.$$

The first term on the right-hand side of this equation is the K-intercept. If the company hires no workers, then $L = 0$ and C/r is the capital that it can purchase with C dollars.

The slope of an isocost line is given by the coefficient on L, or $-w/r$. It is the negative of the input price ratio and measures the rate at which one input can be traded for another.

In Figure 7–4 we have illustrated an isocost line. We measure labor on the horizontal axis and capital on the vertical axis. This isocost line shows the different combinations of capital and labor that C dollars can purchase.

AN ISOCOST LINE

FIGURE 7-4

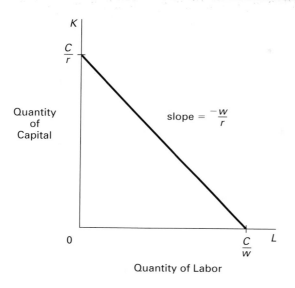

An isocost line is a collection of input bundles that can be purchased for a given level of expenditure. The slope of an isocost line is minus the input price ratio.

MINIMIZING PRODUCTION COSTS

Suppose that Swingthru, Inc., manufactures golf clubs. If the owners of Swingthru decide to produce 100,000 clubs per year, how can they minimize cost? Figure 7-5 illustrates the solution to this problem. We measure labor on the horizontal axis and capital on the vertical axis. Isoquant y_1 represents a production level of 100,000 clubs; that is, isoquant y_1 shows all the combinations of capital and labor that can produce 100,000 golf clubs. Isocost lines IC_0, IC_1, and IC_2 correspond to expenditures of C_0, C_1, and C_2 dollars respectively. Since cost declines as we move in a southwest direction, we know that $C_0 < C_1 < C_2$. The slopes of these isocost lines are the same because input prices are constant, regardless of how many units of capital and labor are employed.

Since cost decreases as we move in a southwest direction, the firm minimizes cost by choosing input bundle R on isoquant y_1. R represents the least expensive combination of capital and labor that can produce 100,000 clubs per year. This cost-minimizing input bundle consists of K_1 units of capital and L_1 units of labor and the cost of employing these inputs is C_2. Of course the firm would rather spend less, for example only C_0, on inputs. However, since isoquant y_1 lies entirely above IC_0, with this level of expenditure,

FIGURE 7–5   THE COST-MINIMIZATION PROBLEM

The point of tangency between an isoquant and an isocost line indicates the least costly way of producing a given level of output. In this case, using L_1 units of labor and K_1 units of capital is the cheapest way to produce 100,000 golf clubs per year.

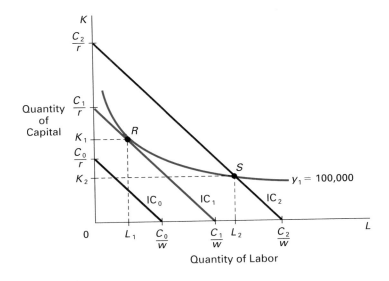

the firm cannot purchase any input bundle that will allow it to produce its desired output. Furthermore, any other input bundle on y_1 costs more to use. Consider input bundle S. It contains enough capital and labor to produce output y_1, (K_2 units of capital and L_2 units of labor), but the cost of using these inputs is greater than the cost of using R: $C_2 > C_1$.

The point where isocost line IC_1 is tangent to isoquant y_1 determines the cost-minimizing choice of capital and labor. At this point, the slopes of the isocost line and the isoquant are equal. Thus, the firm minimizes costs by choosing the input bundle on isoquant y_1 that satisfies the following condition:

$$\text{MRTS}_{LK} = w/r. \qquad (7.2)$$

Equation (7.2) indicates that Swingthru will adjust its employment of inputs in such a way that the rate at which labor can be traded for capital in production, MRTS_{LK}, is equal to the rate at which labor can be exchanged for capital in the factor markets: w/r.

We can use the notion of marginal products to help us understand why this equality must hold. Recall that the marginal rate of technical substitution equals the ratio of the marginal products of inputs; that is, $\text{MRTS}_{LK} = \text{MP}_L/\text{MP}_K$. Knowing this allows us to write the cost-minimizing condition as follows:

$$\text{MP}_L/\text{MP}_K = w/r.$$

Rearranging slightly gives

$$\text{MP}_L/w = \text{MP}_K/r. \tag{7.3}$$

Equation (7.3) shows that costs are minimized when the marginal product of the last dollar spent on labor, MP_L/w, is equal to the marginal product of the last dollar spent on capital, MP_K/r.

If the cost-minimization condition does not hold, the firm is not producing as much output as it could given its costs, or, equivalently, the firm is not producing the current level of output at the lowest possible cost. For example, if $\text{MP}_L/w > \text{MP}_K/r$, then one dollar less spent on capital causes output to fall by MP_K/r, and one dollar more spent on labor causes output to increase by MP_L/w. Since $\text{MP}_L > \text{MP}_K/r$, output increases. Spending \$1 less on capital and \$1 more on labor achieves a higher level of production without increasing costs or, equivalently, the firm achieves the same level of production at a lower cost.

It is important for owners and managers to know if they are using the cost-minimizing input combination. If they are not, they should reallocate inputs in such a way that their firm will produce the same output at a lower cost which, in turn, leads to greater profit. They can use the condition derived above to determine whether or not their firm is operating with the cost-minimizing combination of capital and labor. The next example illustrates such an application of cost theory.

EXAMPLE 7–2

DETERMINING THE COST-MINIMIZING INPUT BUNDLE

Eastwick Polystyrene, Inc., produces polystyrene cups. Suppose we can represent Eastwick's technology by the production function: $y = 50\sqrt{KL}$, where y is the number of polystyrene cups produced each week. The associated marginal product functions are

$$\text{MP}_L = 25\sqrt{(K/L)} \text{ and } \text{MP}_K = 25\sqrt{(L/K)}.$$

Currently Eastwick produces 100,000 cups per week using 2,000 units of labor and 2,000 units of capital per week. The price of capital is $40 per unit and the price of labor is $10 per unit. (a) Is Eastwick using the cost-minimizing input bundle? If not, explain carefully what Eastwick can do to increase production without increasing cost. (b) How many units of labor and capital should the owners of the firm employ if they want to produce 100,000 cups as cheaply as possible?

■ **SOLUTION** (a) We know that MRTS $= MP_L/MP_K = w/r$ if Eastwick is minimizing costs. In this instance, $w/r = 10/40 = 1/4$ and $MRTS_{LK} = MP_L/MP_K = K/L$. Currently Eastwick employs $K = 2,000$ units of capital and $L = 2,000$ units of labor to produce 100,000 polystyrene cups. Given this combination of capital and labor, the $MRTS_{LK}$ is equal to 1 and, because $1 > 1/4$, Eastwick is not minimizing costs.

We must now calculate whether Eastwick should hire more labor and use less capital or vice versa. Let's begin by drawing a diagram illustrating the current situation. The isoquant drawn in Figure 7–6 gives all the input bundles that can produce 100,000 cups per week. Eastwick must be using an input bundle on this isoquant.

Isocost line IC_1 is the isocost line that minimizes the cost of producing 100,000 cups per week. It is tangent to the isoquant y_1. If Eastwick were minimizing costs, it would be using input bundle A. At this point $MRTS_{LK} = w/r = 1/4$.

FIGURE 7–6	EASTWICK COST-MINIMIZATION PROBLEM

Initially, Eastwick is using input bundle B to produce 100,000 cups per week. This is not the least-cost combination of inputs. Eastwick should substitute labor for capital until it is using input bundle A.

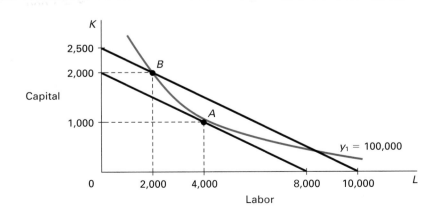

However, we know that Eastwick is not using A because, given the current input bundle, $\text{MRTS}_{LK} > w/r$; that is, when 2,000 units of labor and 2,000 units of capital are used, isoquant y_1 is steeper than the isocost line. This means that Eastwick's current input bundle must lie somewhere to the northwest of bundle A on isoquant y_1. In Figure 7–6 we have labeled this input bundle B which consists of 2,000 units of capital and 2,000 units of labor.

The isocost line passing through input bundle B is IC_2. Notice that at point B the isoquant is steeper than the isocost line. This is the situation we wanted to illustrate. Now what should the firm do? From the diagram it is clear that if the firm moves along isoquant y_1 towards A, substituting labor for capital, cost will fall. For example, at point B, $\text{MP}_L/\text{MP}_K > w/r$ or $\text{MP}_L/w > \text{MP}_K/r$. If one dollar less is spent on capital then output falls by MP_K/w. In order to get back to isoquant y_1 Eastwick must use more labor; however, since $\text{MP}_L/w > \text{MP}_K/r$ at point B, it can increase output by the required amount if it spends less than one dollar more on labor. Thus, cost falls and output remains constant at 100,000 cups per week.

(b) Finally, we must determine the cost-minimizing input bundle. We know that Eastwick is minimizing when

$$\text{MRTS}_{LK} = K/L = 1/4$$

or when $L = 4K$. Substituting this information into the production function, we have

$$y = 100{,}000 = 50\sqrt{4K^2} = 100K.$$

Solving this last equation for K gives the cost-minimizing quantity of capital: $K^* = 1{,}000$. Since $L = 4K$, we also know that $L^* = 4{,}000$. That is, given a production level of 100,000 cups per week, the firm minimizes its costs when it employs 4,000 units of labor and 1,000 units of capital. ■

Whenever $\text{MP}_L/w < \text{MP}_K/r$, Eastwick, Inc., can reduce costs without reducing output by shifting from labor, where the marginal product of a dollar spent on labor is low, to capital, where the marginal product of a dollar spent on capital is high. Similarly, when $\text{MP}_L/w > \text{MP}_K/r$, the firm can reduce costs without reducing output by shifting from capital to labor. Only when $\text{MP}_L/w = \text{MP}_K/r$ will the firm be minimizing costs.

FIGURE 7-7   THE EXPANSION PATH

The expansion path shows the least costly way of producing each level of output when all inputs can be varied, assuming w/r is constant. It is found by connecting all tangency points.

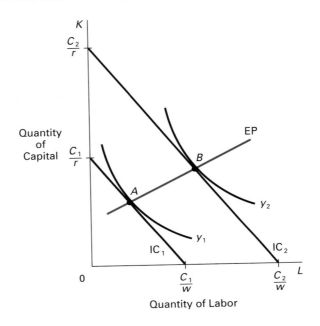

THE EXPANSION PATH

Now let us examine how the cost-minimizing input bundle changes in response to a change in the output rate. Suppose we begin with a firm producing y_1 units of output. Input bundle A in Figure 7–7 represents the cost-minimizing input bundle. Now suppose the owner of the firm wants to expand production to y_2 units of output. Input bundle B represents the new cost-minimizing input bundle. Note that B contains more of both inputs.

If we continue varying output, we can determine the cost-minimizing input bundle associated with each output rate. The line connecting the input bundles that minimize cost is called the **expansion path**. In Figure 7–7, the expansion path is line EP. The expansion path shows how the cost-minimizing input bundle changes as output changes, holding relative prices constant.

7.4 LONG-RUN COST CURVES

■ The long-run total cost (LTC) curve is the graph of the relation between output and minimum cost. In the long run, for any given level of output a firm will use the input bundle that minimizes production costs; thus, associated with each possible output rate, there is a minimum cost or outlay. If the owners of firms are concerned about maximizing profit in the long run, then the relevant cost for decision making is the minimum cost necessary to produce any particular level of output, or **long-run total cost.**

The LTC curve is derived from the firm's expansion path. Recall that the expansion path shows how the cost-minimizing input bundle varies as output changes. However, the expansion path also allows us to ascertain how LTC varies with output.

To see this, suppose we start out with a firm producing an arbitrary amount of output, y_1. The isoquant representing this level of production is shown in Figure 7–8(a). The cost-minimizing input bundle is given by point R on isocost line IC_1. At this point do we have enough information to find a point on the LTC curve? We know the firm is producing y_1 units of output and we know that whatever expenditure is associated with isocost line IC_1 is the minimum cost we are looking for. Let C_1 be this level of

DERIVING THE LONG-RUN TOTAL COST CURVE

FIGURE 7–8

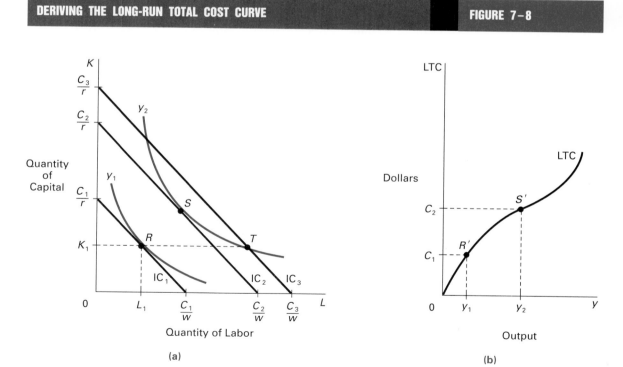

(a)

(b)

The long-run total cost curve derives from the isocost-isoquant diagram. It shows the minimum cost necessary to produce each rate of output.

expenditure. Then, when output is y_1, LTC is C_1. In Figure 7−8(b) this cost−output pair is plotted as a point on the LTC curve.

To get a second point on the LTC curve, let output increase to y_2 and let the firm minimize costs again. We find a new optimal input bundle, point S on isocost line IC_2. If C_2 represents the expenditure associated with IC_2, then $C_2 > C_1$ since IC_2 is further away from the origin. Thus, as output increases, long-run total cost increases as well. This second cost−output pair is also plotted in Figure 7−8(b).

If we were to repeat this exercise for every possible level of production, we could map out the entire LTC curve. In Figure 7−8(b) we have drawn in a representative long-run total cost curve.

LONG-RUN AVERAGE AND MARGINAL COSTS

We will use two additional cost curves to analyze production decisions in the long run: the **long-run average cost** (LAC) curve and the **long-run marginal cost** (LMC) curve. Figure 7−9 shows the LAC and LMC curves associated with the typical LTC illustrated in Figure 7−8(b).

Notice that the average and marginal cost curves fall to a minimum and then rise. LMC is less than LAC for output rates below y_1 and greater for output rates above y_1. LMC and LAC are equal when LAC attains its minimum. (Remember that average cost is the slope of a ray from the origin to a point on the total cost curve and marginal cost is the slope of the total cost curve.)

ECONOMIES AND DISECONOMIES OF SCALE

We have drawn the LTC curve to imply a U-shaped LAC curve. Now we must explain why LAC curves might have this shape. In the long run, the shape depends on the physical relation between inputs and outputs; that is, it depends on the firm's technology. In particular, increasing and decreasing returns to scale are the factors determining the shape of the LAC curve.

Over the range of outputs where LAC is falling, a firm is said to experience economies of scale. In Figure 7−9, economies of scale are evident for production levels up to y_1 units of output. Over this range, a firm can lower LAC by expanding production and adjusting all inputs optimally.

Economies of scale arise when a firm's production function exhibits increasing returns to scale; that is, when expanding all inputs proportionally leads to a greater proportional increase in output. To see this more clearly, consider a specific example. Suppose that 20 workers and 2 machines produce 100 units of output. Given increasing returns to scale, a doubling of all inputs will more than double output: hence, forty workers and 4 machines

LONG-RUN AVERAGE AND MARGINAL COST CURVES

FIGURE 7-9

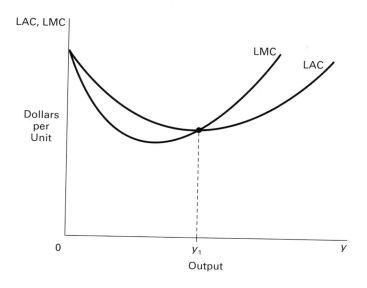

The long-run average and marginal cost curves are U-shaped. When LAC is falling, economies of scale are evident; when LAC is rising, diseconomies of scale are evident.

might increase output to 300 units. What has happened to average cost? A doubling of inputs doubles total cost when input prices are constant. Since LAC is total cost divided by output, LAC must fall when total cost doubles and output more than doubles. Thus, increasing returns to scale lead to economies of scale.

A firm is likely to experience increasing returns to scale for lower output rates. As the scale of its operation expands, it may realize substantial gains by division of labor and through specialization. This, in turn, implies that LAC falls for lower output rates.

Using the same line of reasoning, constant returns to scale imply a constant LAC and decreasing returns to scale imply an increasing LAC. When the LAC is rising, the firm is said to experience **diseconomies of scale.** Increasing returns to scale are usually the result of management inefficiencies that arise as the scale of operation expands. In Figure 7−9, diseconomies of scale set in for output levels above y_1.

Economists have examined the long-run cost structure of many industries. Most of these studies have found that long-run average costs decrease early on, remain nearly constant over a range of outputs, and then, possibly, increase.

7.5 PUBLIC POLICY AND LONG-RUN COSTS

■ The long-run average and marginal cost curves play a very important role in the theory of production. In this section we will see how taxes on inputs and input restrictions affect these long-run cost curves.

INPUT TAXES AND LONG-RUN COSTS

In the United States, firms often must pay taxes based on the quantities of certain inputs they employ. For example, the federal government requires that firms make payments to unemployment compensation funds and social security based on their total wage bill. (This is called a payroll tax.) Some states also levy an excise tax on energy use.

When government levies a tax on an input, the price of the taxed input relative to the price of other inputs increases. If owners are cost minimizers, then the tax may cause them to look for new ways of combining their inputs—ways that will still produce their desired output but keep costs at the pretax minimum. In the next example, we will investigate precisely how a tax on labor can affect the cost-minimizing input mix as well as the long-run cost curves.

EXAMPLE 7–3

PAYROLL TAXES AND COST MINIMIZATION

McPheters, Inc., is a manufacturer of high-definition televisions. McPheters uses capital and labor to produce their televisions and the technology is such that the long-run average and marginal cost curves are U-shaped. In the U.S., the federal government requires firms to pay up to \$7,000 per worker into an unemployment compensation fund. How does this affect the firm's long-run cost curves? Illustrate.

■ **SOLUTION** We begin by illustrating the cost-minimizing choice of inputs, the LAC curve, and the LMC curve as they look before law requires the firm to pay into the fund. In Figure 7–10(a), isoquant y_1 represents the output rate associated with the minimum point of the LAC curve. Isocost line IC_1 indicates the different combinations of capital and labor that McPheters can purchase for a given total expenditure, C_1. The slope of this isocost line is $-w/r$.

Suppose that, prior to the payroll tax, the firm was producing y_1 television sets using the cost-minimizing input bundle, A. This input bundle consisted of K_1 units of capital and L_1 workers and the cost of employing these inputs was C_1 dollars. In Figure 7–10(b) we

INPUT TAXES AND LONG-RUN COSTS   **FIGURE 7–10**

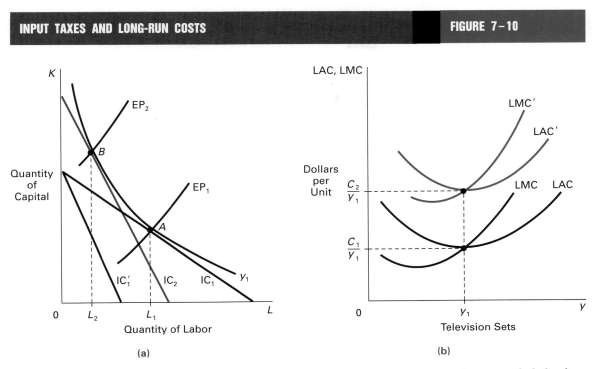

(a)   (b)

A payroll tax increases the price of labor which, in turn, increases long-run total costs and shifts the LAC and LMC curves up.

have drawn the firm's LAC and LMC curves. They are U-shaped and the minimum point of the LAC curve occurs when the firm is producing y_1 televisions.

Now suppose that the government requires McPheters to pay a tax of $T = \$7,000$ per worker. What will be the new least-cost combination of inputs that can produce y_1 televisions? The tax increases the cost of labor and consequently, the isocost line rotates in about the capital intercept. In Figure 7–10(a), IC_1' is the new isocost line. It represents all the combinations of capital and labor that C_1 dollars can purchase after the tax has been paid. The slope of this isocost line is $-(w - T)/r$. (Verify this by writing down the equation for IC_1'.)

Notice that once the firm is required to pay into the fund, an outlay of only C_1 dollars is not sufficient to allow the firm to employ enough capital and labor to produce y_1 television sets; that is, IC_1' lies below isoquant y_1. Thus, if the firm were to continue producing y_1 units of output, expenditures would have to increase.

In this instance, input bundle B on isoquant y_1 and isocost line IC_2 is the new cost-minimizing input bundle. B consists of K_2 units of capital and L_2 units of labor—more capital and less labor than before. The tax causes the firm to substitute capital for labor.

Notice also that we can determine from Figure 7–10(a) how the payroll tax affects the long-run average and marginal cost curves. All input bundles on isocost line IC_1 require an expenditure of C_1 dollars. Since isocost line IC_2 is further to the northeast, all input bundles on IC_2 must require a greater level of expenditure. This expenditure level is denoted C_2 in the diagram. Thus, when the firm has to pay a payroll tax, the minimum cost of producing any level of output increases; that is, long-run total, average, and marginal costs increase. In Figure 7–10(b), this is shown as an upward shift in the LAC and LMC curves. (The way the picture is drawn, the minimum point of the new LAC curve remains at y_1; this need not be the case). ■

In general, an increase in the price of an input causes firms to substitute away from that input. This seems common sense. However, remember that we cannot infer from Figure 7–10 that the firm actually will use less labor and more capital. This is because here we have not yet determined what the new profit-maximizing rate of output will be.

Prior to the payroll tax, the firm produced y_1 units of output and employed an input bundle on expansion path EP_1. After the tax, the firm's expansion path changes to EP_2. However, there is no reason to suppose that the firm will operate at point B on this expansion path; that is, there is no reason to suppose that y_1 is still the profit-maximizing rate of production. In fact, we will show in the next chapter that the profit-maximizing output rate actually falls.

INPUT RESTRICTIONS AND LONG-RUN COSTS

In Example 7–2 we saw how policies that alter relative input prices lead to a change in the amounts of capital and labor a firm employs and to a change in long-run costs. Other important government policies that alter factor intensities and long-run costs are *various input restrictions*. In the United States, either federal or state governments may impose these restrictions. For example, many states have attempted to keep hospital costs from escalating by prohibiting hospitals from adding new beds without permission of the appropriate state agency; the federal government has attempted to reduce air and water pollutants by restricting emissions of pollutants; and the federal government often restricts the amounts of pesticides that manufacturers can use in the production of agricultural products. In the next example, we will investigate how this latter type of input restriction affects a firm's long-run production costs.

EXAMPLE 7-4

PESTICIDE REGULATION AND COST MINIMIZATION

Suppose that the Environmental Protection Agency imposes a limit on the amount of insecticide that cotton growers can use. Assuming that the technology used to produce cotton is such that the long-run average and marginal cost curves are U-shaped, what effect will this restriction have on a firm's long-run cost curves? Illustrate.

■ **SOLUTION** We begin by illustrating the optimal choice of inputs, the LAC curve, and the LMC curve as they look before the restriction goes into effect. In Figure 7−11(a), we measure insecticide on the horizontal axis and labor on the vertical axis. Prior to the restriction, the representative cotton grower is producing y_1 units of cotton using cost-minimizing input bundle A. This input bundle consists of L_1 units of labor and I_1 units of insecticide and the cost of using these inputs is C_1 dollars. Figure 7−11(b) shows the firm's initial LAC and LMC curves.

If this firm were to increase output to y_2 units of cotton per year, it would move along expansion path EP_1 from A to B. The minimum cost of producing y_2 units of cotton is C_2 dollars per year.

Now suppose the government restricts the use of insecticides to I_0 units per year. With this restriction, the firm cannot produce y_1 units of cotton using the cost-minimizing input bundle A because this bundle contains more insecticide than the law permits. The firm can, however, produce y_1 units of cotton by using input bundle D, which consists of I_0 units of insecticide and L_2 units of labor. Notice that now an outlay of C_1 dollars is not sufficient to allow the firm to produce y_1 units of cotton. Since D is on a higher isocost line, outlays will have to increase. In this instance, the firm must spend C_2 dollars to purchase input bundle D on isocost line IC_2.

The effect of this type of input restriction on LAC and LMC is shown in Figure 7−10(b). LAC′ and LMC′ represent the firm's long-run cost curves after the restriction is imposed. We can see that both average and marginal costs increase for cotton growers once the restriction becomes law. ■

FIGURE 7–11   INPUT RESTRICTIONS AND LONG-RUN COSTS

Limiting the use of insecticides in such a way that the cost-minimizing input bundle cannot be employed increases long-run total costs and shifts the LAC and LMC curves up.

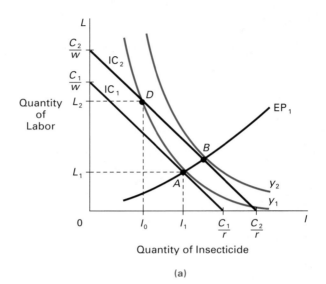

(a)

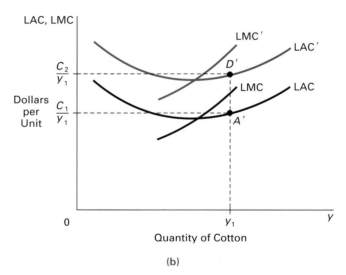

(b)

■ When we discuss the way in which firms and industries adjust production levels to changes in the demand for their products, the relation between the short-run and long-run cost curves will play a very important role. We can think of the long run as the firm's planning horizon. Long-run considerations determine what types of investments owners of firms will make and, in particular, what quantities of fixed inputs they will use in the short run. Once the owners have decided on the scale of operation, the firm is constrained in the short run to operate within these bounds. Thus, the relation between short- and long-run costs is very important.

In discussing the relation between short- and long-run cost curves, it is convenient to imagine plant or factory size as representing the fixed factors of production. That is, each particular quantity of capital corresponds to a particular plant size.

Let us begin by comparing short- and long-run total costs. Suppose that a cost-minimizing firm is currently using K_1 units of capital and L_1 units of labor to produce y_1 units of output. Further, suppose that this combination of inputs is the optimal input bundle for producing y_1 units of output, given current input prices. Figure 7–8(a) illustrated this situation. There, isocost line IC_1 was tangent to isoquant y_1 at point R, implying that C_1 was the minimum cost of producing y_1 units of output.

Now suppose the firm builds a plant with capital stock K_1. We say that this is the optimal plant size for producing y_1 since it corresponds to the cost-minimizing input bundle. In the short run, the firm must use this plant.

If y_1 units is the short-run output, what is the corresponding short-run total cost (STC)? Since this plant is designed to produce y_1 optimally, STC is C_1; that is, short-run and long-run total costs are equal for an output rate of y_1. Thus, point R' in Figure 7–12(a) is a point on both the long-run total cost curve *and* the short-run total cost curve corresponding to a capital stock of K_1 units.

Now suppose the firm wants to increase output to y_2. Figure 7–8(a) showed us that, in the long run, the firm would employ input bundle S, which consisted of more labor and more capital. Isocost line IC_2 represented the minimum cost of producing y_2, denoted as C_2. This gives us another point on the firm's LTC curve, point S' in Figure 7–12(a).

We want to know whether the cost of producing y_2 will be larger or smaller in the short run than in the long run. In the short run, the firm is constrained to use K_1 units of capital to produce this larger output. Input bundle T in Figure 7–8(a) represented the combination of capital and labor that would produce y_2 units of output,

STC AND LTC

FIGURE 7–12   **COMPARING THE SHORT- AND LONG-RUN TOTAL COST CURVES**

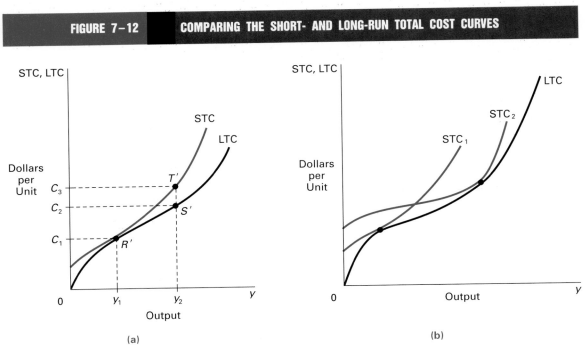

(a) Short-run total cost is equal to long-run total cost at the output rate for which the fixed factor of production is optimal: y_1 in the diagram. At every other output rate, short-run costs are greater. (b) There is a short-run cost curve associated with each level of the fixed factor of production. Economists sometimes refer to the LTC curve as the "envelope" of the short-run cost curves.

given K_1 units of capital. Is this input bundle more or less expensive to employ than bundle S? Note that the isocost line through T, labeled IC_3, is further away from the origin and therefore represents a greater expense. Denoting this higher cost as C_3 gives us another point on the STC curve, point T' in Figure 7–12(a). Thus, short-run cost is greater than long-run cost.

Each point on the LTC curve is a point where costs are minimized. In the short run, firms cannot adjust the input mix to minimize costs; thus, costs must be higher in the short run. Figure 7–12(b) shows two short-run total cost curves: STC_1 and STC_2. Each of these cost curves corresponds to a different plant size (a different capital stock) and each has one point in common with the LTC curve. For the output rates where the short-run and long-run curves touch, the size of the plant corresponds to the quantity of capital that can produce these levels of output optimally.

The relation between short- and long-run average costs can be
inferred from the discussion above: short-run average cost must be
at least as great as long-run average cost at every level of
production. However, it is more useful to explain the relation
between short- and long-run average costs in terms of the cost
curves themselves.

Let us suppose that there are only three sizes of plant the firm
can build. Corresponding to each of these is an SATC curve. In
Figure 7−13, curves $SATC_1$, $SATC_2$ and $SATC_3$ represent the three
plants. Notice that, as the scale of operation expands from $SATC_1$ to
$SATC_2$, the short-run average cost curves shift down. Over this
range of outputs, the firm experiences economies of scale. As the
scale of operation expands from $SATC_2$ to $SATC_3$, the short-run
average cost curves shift up. Over this range of outputs, the firm
experiences diseconomies of scale.

Suppose the firm decides to produce y_1 units of output. (Why the
firm chooses any particular output rate is discussed further in
Chapter 9.) The firm could build the smallest plant, represented by
$SATC_1$ and produce y_1 at C_1 dollars per unit or it could build the

LAC AND SATC

SHORT- AND LONG-RUN AVERAGE COST CURVES   **FIGURE 7−13**

*The long-run average
cost curve is the
"envelope" of the short-
run average cost curves.*

next largest plant, represented by $SATC_2$, and produce the same output at C_2 dollars per unit. Since the firm is a cost minimizer, it will build the plant associated with $SATC_1$ and produce y_1 at the lowest per-unit cost (which implies the lowest total cost).

Long-run average cost is, by definition, the lowest average cost attainable when any plant size is possible—that is, when all inputs are variable. When only three plant sizes are possible, the long-run average cost curve consists of all points on the solid, scalloped section of the SATC curves. Each of these portions of the SATC curves represents the lowest possible per-unit cost for the corresponding level of output.

In general, a firm will have many more plant sizes to choose from. If there are a large number of options, then the LAC curve is, effectively, the smooth curve shown in Figure 7–13. Each short-run average cost curve has one point in common with the LAC curve, which we can call the "envelope" of the SATC curves. Each point on the LAC corresponds to a different short-run scale of operation that a firm can choose.

A BRIEF COMMENT ON CAPACITY

When businesses talk about the scale of operation or plant size, they often refer to the *capacity* of the plant or operation. This term can give rise to some confusion, so it is best to state now what we mean by it. For a given plant (or capital stock), the **capacity** is that output rate which is optimal for that plant; that is, a plant is operating at capacity if the firm is currently using the cost-minimizing input bundle. For example, the capacity of the plant represented by $SATC_3$ in Figure 7–13 is y_3 units of output. This is the notion of capacity that we shall use in the remainder of this book.

1. In this chapter, we have examined the way in which the costs of production vary with output in both the short and long runs. Understanding the relation between costs and output is important because, for profit-maximizing firms, costs play a central role in determining the supply of goods and services.

2. In the short run, firms cannot change the quantities of certain fixed inputs. The Law of Diminishing Marginal Productivity dictates the shapes of short-run cost curves. In particular, marginal cost declines in the short run until the point of diminishing marginal productivity sets in, and then it increases.

3. Short-run marginal cost intersects the U-shaped average variable cost and average total cost curves at their minimum points.

4. In the long run, all inputs are variable and, for any given output, the firm can use the input bundle that minimizes costs. In an isocost–isoquant diagram, the optimal input bundle corresponds to the point where the marginal rate of technical substitution of labor for capital is equal to the input price ratio.

5. The expansion path obtained from the isocost–isoquant diagram shows how the optimal input combination varies with output. It conveys all the information necessary to derive the long-run total cost curve, which graphs the relation between output and minimum cost.

6. The shape of the long-run average cost curve is determined by returns to scale. The curve is U-shaped if returns to scale are decreasing for low output rates and increasing for high output rates. The firm is experiencing economies of scale if the long-run average cost curve is declining and diseconomies of scale if it is rising. The long-run marginal cost curve is also U-shaped and intersects the minimum point of the long-run average cost curve.

7. All cost curves, short- and long-run, are drawn for given input prices and a given technology. If any input price changes or if the technology changes, then the cost curves will also change.

SUMMARY

Total Fixed Costs
Total Variable Costs
Short-Run Total Cost
Average Fixed Cost
Average Variable Cost
Short-Run Average Total Cost
Short-Run Marginal Cost

Isocost Line
Expansion Path
Long-Run Total Cost
Long-Run Average Cost
Long-Run Marginal Cost
Economies and Diseconomies
  of Scale

KEY TERMS

1. Explain the role played by the Law of Diminishing Marginal Productivity in determining the shape of the short-run marginal cost curve.

QUESTIONS AND PROBLEMS

2. a) Explain the relation between average cost and marginal cost.
   b) Why are they equal at the minimum point of the average cost curve?
3. a) If the marginal product of labor declines over the entire range of production, what will the SMC curve look like? The SATC curve? The AVC curve?
   b) Repeat the exercise if the marginal product of labor is initially constant and then decreasing.
4. Larry's Lobster Den, a small firm that raises and sells lobsters, has cost curves given by

$$STC = 200 + 5y + y^2 \quad and \quad SMC = 5 + 2y$$

where y is the number of lobsters produced each month.
   a) In a single diagram, graph the STC, TVC, and TFC curves.
   b) In another diagram, graph SATC, AVC, AFC, and SMC.
   c) Does the Law of Diminishing Marginal Productivity hold in this case? Explain.
5. Complete the following table:

Output	TFC	TVC	STC	AFC	AVC	SATC	SMC
1	$100	$10.00					
2					$8.00		
3							$5.00
4						$31.50	
5			$130.00				

6. Suppose that the price of labor is $20 per man-hour and the price of capital is $20 per machine-hour. Since both capital and labor have the same per-hour cost, a cost-minimizing firm will employ equal amounts of the two inputs. Comment on this argument.
7. If the government passes a law requiring firms to provide health insurance for all employees, what impact will this law have on the cost-minimizing input bundle?
8. Smith, Jones, and Weston is a small firm in east Texas that restores antique china cabinets. Currently the company is operating at a point where $MP_L = 10$ and $MP_K = 24$. If the wage rate is $15 per person-hour and the price of capital is $24 per machine-hour, is the firm employing the optimal input combination? If not, explain carefully what the owners should do. Illustrate your answer.

9. Suppose the owner of a firm is employing the cost-minimizing quantity of capital and labor. If the price of labor and the price of capital double, what happens to the long-run cost curves?

10. a) Define economies and diseconomies of scale.
    b) Illustrate an LAC curve that exhibits only economies of scale.
    c) Illustrate an LAC that exhibits only diseconomies of scale.

11. Explain why the SATC curve shifts down as capacity increases.

12. A constant cost firm is one for which the LAC is horizontal. A decreasing cost firm is one for which LAC falls and an increasing cost firm is one for which LAC increases. Illustrate LMC and LAC for each of these cases.

13. Suppose a hospital uses two inputs, beds and labor, to produce medical services. Some states have attempted to contain health care costs by adopting laws prohibiting hospitals from increasing the number of hospital beds. Does such a regulation accomplish this objective? Explain.

14. Determine how a government regulation requiring safety glasses for workers will affect a firm's long-run cost curves.

15. Robinson Crusoe has found that the production function for gathering coconuts is given by

$$y = 10\sqrt{L}$$

where y is the number of coconuts gathered per week and L is the number of hours per week that Man Friday spends gathering coconuts.
    a) If Crusoe pays Man Friday one dollar per hour, calculate his total and average cost curves.
    b) Graph Crusoe's average cost curve.
    c) What will the associated marginal cost curve look like?

16. A firm produces peanut butter using capital and labor. The firm has a production function given by

$$y = 10\sqrt{K \cdot L}$$

where y is pounds of peanut butter produced per month, K is the quantity of capital employed, and L is the amount of labor employed.
    a) If the firm currently is operating with 5 units of capital, calculate the SATC and AVC curves and graph them.
    b) If capital doubles, explain what will happen to the short-run cost curves.

17. Suppose a firm has a constant returns to scale technology.
    a) Illustrate its long-run cost curves.
    b) How will these cost curves change if the price of labor falls?

REFERENCES   Hicks, J. 1946. *Value and Capital.* 2nd ed. Oxford: Clarendon Press.

Kreps, D. 1990. *A Course in Microeconomic Theory.* Princeton: Princeton University Press.

Varian, H. 1992. *Microeconomic Analysis.* 3d ed. New York: Norton.

SHORT- AND LONG-RUN COST FUNCTIONS: THE CALCULUS APPROACH

A7.1 DERIVING THE LONG-RUN TOTAL COST FUNCTION

The cost-minimization problem discussed in the text can be summarized as follows:

$$\min_{L,K} C = rK + wL$$
$$subject\ to\ y = F(K,L).$$

This is a constrained minimization problem so we can use the Lagrange multiplier method to derive the optimality conditions.

The Lagrangian for this problem is

$$V = (rK + wL) + \lambda[y - F(K,L)].$$

Differentiating this function with respect to L, K, and λ gives the first order conditions:

$$\frac{\partial V}{\partial L} = r - \lambda\frac{\partial F}{\partial L} = 0$$

$$\frac{\partial V}{\partial K} = w - \lambda\frac{\partial F}{\partial K} = 0$$

$$\frac{\partial V}{\partial \lambda} = y - F(K,L) = 0$$

Now if we solve the first equation for λ and substitute into the second equation we have the optimality condition discussed in the text:

$$\frac{\partial F(K,L)}{\partial L} \Big/ \frac{\partial F(K,L)}{\partial K} = w/r.$$

Note that the first order conditions consist of three equations and three unknowns: L, K, and λ. We can solve this system of equations for the unknowns in terms of the parameters of the model—that is, in terms of prices and the given level of output. If we do not have an explicit production function, then we can only solve these equations implicitly. In particular, the firm's *conditional input demand functions* are given by:

$$L = L(w,r,y) \quad and \quad K = K(w,r,y).$$

The conditional input demand functions give the cost-minimizing levels of employment, given input prices *and* a particular level of production. We must be careful to remember that the conditional input demand functions are not the profit-maximizing levels of input usage.

Now, to obtain the long-run total cost function, we simply substitute the conditional input demand functions into the objective function. This gives

$$\text{LTC} = C(w,r,y) = wL(w,r,y) + rK(w,r,y).$$

EXAMPLE A7–1

Suppose that a Cobb–Douglas production function $y = K^{1/4}L^{1/4}$ represents a firm's technology. Derive the conditional factor demand functions and the long-run total cost function.

■ **SOLUTION** The Lagrangian for this optimization problem is

$$V = wL + rK + \lambda(y - L^{1/4}K^{1/4})$$

and the corresponding first order conditions are

$$\partial V/\partial L = w - \lambda(1/4)L^{-3/4}K^{1/4} = 0$$

$$\partial V/\partial K = r - \lambda(1/4)L^{1/4}K^{-3/4} = 0$$

$$\partial L/\partial \lambda = y - K^{1/4}L^{1/4} = 0.$$

Solving the first equation for λ and substituting into the second equation gives

$$w/r = K/L.$$

Solving this equation for K gives

$$K = (w/r)L.$$

Substituting this into the production function gives

$$y - L^{1/4}[(w/r)L]^{1/4} = 0$$

and solving for L gives the conditional input demand function for good L:

$$L = (r/w)^{1/2}y^2.$$

Substituting for L into the expression $K = (w/r)L$ gives the conditional input demand function for K:

$$K = (w/r)(r/w)^{1/2}y^2 = (w/r)^{1/2}y^2.$$

By expressing costs when the firm uses cost-minimizing levels of inputs, we can obtain the long-run total cost function. That is,

$$\text{LTC} = C(w,r,y) = [w(r/w)^{1/2} + r(w/r)^{1/2}]y^2$$

$$= 2(w \cdot r)^{1/2}y^2.$$

Notice that, in this instance, the long-run total cost function is an increasing and convex function of output. This result makes sense, because the production function given exhibits decreasing returns to scale. ■

A7.2 SHORT- AND LONG-RUN COST FUNCTIONS

The discussion in the text concerning the relation between the short- and long-run cost functions seems pretty clear geometrically. Using calculus, however, we can gain additional insights.

Let $\text{STC} = C^S(y,K)$ denote the short-run total cost function given capital stock K. If we substitute the conditional capital demand function into the short-run cost function we have the following identity:

$$\text{LTC} = C(y) \equiv C^S[y,K(y)] = \text{STC}.$$

This is just the mathematical way of saying that each short-run cost curve has one point in common with the long-run cost curve. Mathematicians say that the long-run cost function is the *envelope* of the short-run cost functions.

Differentiating this identity with respect to y gives

$$\frac{\partial \text{LTC}}{\partial y} = \frac{\partial \text{STC}}{\partial y} + \frac{\partial \text{STC}}{\partial K} \cdot \frac{\partial K}{\partial y}$$

This says that we can think of long-run marginal cost as having two parts: the change in short-run cost, holding capital fixed, and the change in short-run cost when capital stock adjusts.

Now notice that if capital is chosen optimally—that is, to minimize cost, then it must be the case that $\partial K/\partial y = 0$. Thus, long-run marginal cost and short-run marginal cost must be the same when cost is minimized.

PROFIT MAXIMIZATION: THE COMPETITIVE FIRM

LEARNING OBJECTIVES

After completing Chapter 8 you should be able to do the following:

■ Explain the meaning of perfect competition.

■ Describe how to determine the profit-maximizing output rate and level of employment for a perfectly competitive firm.

■ Derive input demand and output supply curves.

■ Compare profit maximization in the short and long runs.

■ Analyze how price changes affect a firm's output supply and input demand curves.

8

EXAMPLES

The discussion of production and cost in Chapters 6 and 7 applies to all business firms, regardless of the type of market in which they operate. Any firm's cost curves are affected by the same factors: the productivity of inputs and their prices. However, knowing the structure of costs alone does not allow us to determine how much output a firm should produce or how much of each input it should employ.

In this chapter, we focus on the output and employment decisions of individual firms operating in a *perfectly competitive market*. First, we examine how a competitive firm chooses its level of output and how changes in prices and costs affect that choice. This analysis leads to the firm's output supply curve. Second, we determine the quantities of inputs that maximize profit and how changes in prices and costs affect those quantities. This analysis leads to the firm's input demand curves.

8.1 THE MEANING OF PERFECT COMPETITION

■ The concept of perfect competition, or a perfectly competitive market, is one of the most useful models of market structure. Perfect competition is a benchmark case that can offer us many important insights into how producers and consumers interact to determine market prices and quantities. Understanding perfect competition will allow us to tackle many of the important economic problems that society faces every day.

To a businessperson, *competition* usually means the rivalry between firms in a particular industry. For example, companies that manufacture and sell personal computers compete in this sense. Each firm decides whether or not to introduce a new line of computers, develop add-ons for existing computers, or expand its advertising campaign only after considering how its competitors are likely to respond to its decisions.

In microeconomics, *perfect competition* means something very different from the businessperson's notion of competition. The primary characteristic distinguishing a perfectly competitive market from others is that the market is totally impersonal. As buyers and sellers make decisions, they do not have to take into account the actions of other buyers and sellers, nor do they have to consider how their actions will affect other market participants. **Perfect competition** occurs when anonymous market forces determine the prices and quantities of goods bought and sold in the marketplace.

THE REQUIREMENTS FOR PERFECT COMPETITION

There are four essential requirements that must be met if a market is to be perfectly competitive. First, any one economic agent must be so unimportant relative to the entire market that it cannot affect prices by its actions. Every economic agent is a *price taker*. In both product and resource markets, this means that individual buyers are so small relative to the entire market that their purchases have no perceptible effect on market demand and that sellers can sell all the output they want to at the market price.

The second requirement for perfect competition is that in any one market, the product or resource being traded must be homogeneous across sellers. This means that, in any one product market, the output of one firm is indistinguishable from that of any other firm; that is, there is no product differentiation. This also means that in any one input market the services of one seller are indistinguishable from those of another. This condition guarantees that consumers are indifferent about which firm they buy from and firms are indifferent about which resource owner they buy from.

The third requirement for perfect competition is that buyers and sellers have perfect information concerning all prices relevant to the decision-making process. This guarantees a single price for each good, or factor of production, traded in the marketplace. Consumers with perfect information about the prices of the goods they wish to purchase will always buy at the lowest price. Producers, on the other hand, need perfect information about the prices of the goods they sell and the costs of the inputs they use if they are to attain the most profitable level of production.

Finally, for perfect competition to exist, all resources must be perfectly mobile in the long run. This means that buyers and sellers of commodities, as well as factors of production can enter and exit markets costlessly in the long run. Labor must be able to move freely from one job to another and firms able to exit and enter markets easily. Perfect mobility rules out factors of production that are so firm or industry-specific that they are of little value outside their current employment. Perfect mobility also rules out entry barriers such as patents, copyrights, and large start-up costs. As we will see, free entry and exit is the single most important requirement for perfect competition but, as you may have surmised, it is also the most difficult to realize in practice.

It should be clear to you that there are few perfectly competitive markets. Perfect information and free mobility of all resources are conditions that seldom, if ever, exist in the real world. But if perfect competition is merely a theoretical construct, why are we interested in studying it at all?

As with any theoretical model, we can obtain general hypotheses only if we abstract from specifics. We can build a model to describe with great accuracy a certain real-world phenomenon, but then it is of little value in describing any other. Remember that, in devel-

WHY STUDY PERFECT COMPETITION?

oping any theoretical model, we test its predictions against reality and not against the assumptions upon which we construct the model. Thus, the primary reason economists study the competitive model is because it is simple; even more important, it is quite often a reliable means of explaining and predicting real-world behavior. In a great many instances, perfect competition is a theoretical device that works. This is why we have referred to it as a benchmark model. We can learn a great deal from it about the way markets work.

ALTERNATIVE TYPES OF MARKETS

Perfect competition is one important type of market structure; however, there are several other types that we will consider in later chapters. To help us put the competitive model in perspective, we will briefly discuss these alternative market types here.

A *pure monopoly* exists if there is only one seller in some well-defined market. This seller faces a given, downward-sloping demand curve representing the demands of numerous buyers who cannot negotiate collectively with the monopolist. Monopoly is at the other extreme from perfect competition but, as is the case for the latter, there are few real-world markets that satisfy the conditions for its existence in a pure form. Nonetheless, many markets can approximate monopoly, and quite often the implications of the monopoly model can explain observed behavior. Both perfect competition and monopoly are benchmark examples from which we can learn a great deal.

Perfect competition and pure monopoly lie at the two extremes of the market spectrum. Perfect competition is characterized by price-taking firms producing a homogeneous product and the perfect mobility of resources between industries. Monopoly, on the other hand, is characterized by a single firm producing a product for which there are no close substitutes. Both are benchmark cases that yield a great many useful insights into the way markets operate.

Between these two extremes lies a more common form of market structure called *oligopoly*. Markets of this type consist of relatively few firms producing either a homogeneous or a differentiated product. In an oligopoly, a firm can have some control over the price it receives for its product, because it produces a relatively large share of the total output. Also, strategic behavior is very important; that is, each firm in the industry must take into account how its rivals will react to any decision it makes. If we consider that oligopolies include markets such as steel, automobiles, aluminum, and soft drinks, to name just a few, it is clearly important to understand the basic oligopoly models.

■ In order to determine the output rate that maximizes profit (economic profit), we must first investigate how profit varies with output. *Profit* is defined as *total revenue minus total cost* (economic cost). If we denote total revenue by TR, profit by the Greek letter π (read "pie"), and total cost by TC, then profit is given by

$$\pi = \text{TR} - \text{TC}. \qquad (8.1)$$

(We use TC to denote total cost since the analysis is relevant for both the short and long runs.)

We want to know how π, the difference between revenue and cost, varies with output. In the last chapter, we investigated the way in which cost varied with output for the typical firm. Our first task now is to investigate how revenues vary with output for a competitive firm.

We calculate a firm's total revenue by multiplying the price of its product by the quantity of it that is sold. A firm that sells output in a perfectly competitive market is a *price taker*; that is, the market price is assumed to be unaffected by how much output any one firm produces. This implies that whatever the price, as determined by market supply and demand, the owner of each firm assumes that he or she can sell as many units of output as desired at the going market price. Thus, the demand curve for a competitive firm's output is a horizontal line.

To see this, consider a simple example. Suppose Pauline is the owner of a firm that manufactures and sells collegiate ruled notebook paper. If there are 3,000 firms in the paper industry, each currently producing and selling 500 reams of paper per day at $2.00 per ream, then Pauline will be a price taker. She assumes that because her firm supplies only .033% of the market, any change in her output rate will have no perceptible effect on price and, thus, she can sell all the paper she produces at $2.00 per ream.

Figure 8–1 illustrates this situation. As shown in Figure 8–1(a), supply and demand determine the market price for paper. At $2.00 per ream, 1.5 million reams of paper are bought and sold each year. Since each firm produces only a small portion of this total amount, a change in any one firm's output rate will have a negligible effect on total market supply and, thus, a negligible effect on market price. The demand curve for a competitive firm's output is shown in Figure 8–1(b).

For an individual price-taking firm, the price per unit of output is independent of how much is sold. In this case, total revenue is

$$\text{TR} = py \qquad (8.2)$$

FIGURE 8-1   THE DEMAND CURVE FACING A PERFECTLY COMPETITIVE FIRM

The market price of paper is $2. A competitive firm can sell all the reams of paper it wants to at this price. The demand curve for a competitive firm is a horizontal line at the market price.

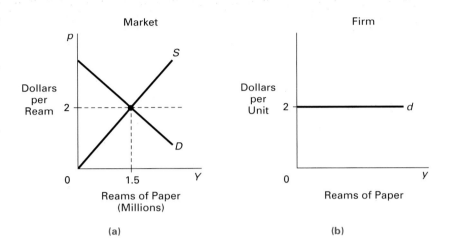

where p is a constant. Notice in Figure 8–2(a) that equation (8.2) is a straight line emanating from the origin with a slope of p. The line labeled TR is the total revenue curve for a price-taking firm that sells its output for $2 per unit.

Marginal revenue (MR) is the change in total revenue per unit change in output. Marginal revenue is the slope of the total revenue curve. For a price-taking firm, marginal revenue is equal to the price of the good being produced. Each additional unit of output can be sold without reducing the price, meaning that each additional unit sold increases total revenue by an amount equal to the price. The MR curve shown in Figure 8–2(b) corresponds to the TR curve in Figure 8–2(a). The MR curve for a price-taking firm is a horizontal line at the market price. From the firm's perspective, the MR curve is the demand curve for its product.

Before turning to the profit-maximizing output, we need to reiterate one point. Even though each firm assumes a constant price, this does not mean that the price simply falls from the sky. The market price is determined by the interaction of buyers and sellers; it is this price that each firm takes as a given.

DETERMINING THE PROFIT-MAXIMIZING OUTPUT RATE: THE TOTAL REVENUE –TOTAL COST APPROACH

A firm can increase or decrease the rate of output by varying the quantity of inputs used in the production process. (If we are considering the short run, then only the variable inputs can be adjusted.) Our goal in this section is to determine the output rate that makes the difference between revenue and cost as large as

TOTAL AND MARGINAL REVENUE FOR THE PRICE-TAKING FIRM   FIGURE 8–2

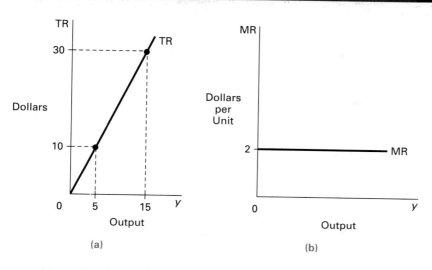

(a)

(b)

(a) Total revenue is price times quantity. For the competitive firm, total revenue is a straight line emanating from the origin. (b) Marginal revenue is the change in total revenue when there is a one-unit change in output. For the competitive firm, marginal revenue is equal to the market price.

possible—that is, to determine the output level that maximizes profit.

Perhaps the best way to see how firms determine the profit-maximizing level of production is to consider an example. Suppose that Henry Higgins owns and manages the Pygmalion School of Etiquette (PSE), a finishing school for young urban professionals. Students enroll for a six-month session and tuition for each session is $5,000 per student. Utilities, rent, and property taxes for the school are $4,000 per session. The school provides room and board, books, and supplies for the students. Table 8–1 gives these variable

TABLE 8–1

VARIABLE COSTS FOR THE PYGMALION SCHOOL OF ETIQUETTE

Enrollment	Total Variable Cost
1	$ 1,400
2	3,600
3	6,600
4	10,400
5	15,000
6	20,400
7	25,600
8	33,600
9	41,400
10	50,000

costs for output levels ranging from 1 to 10 students. Given this information, Higgins must determine the profit-maximizing number of students to graduate each session (assuming that every student who enrolls graduates).

One way for Higgins to determine the profit-maximizing number of students is to calculate profit for every possible output rate. Table 8–2 gives these calculations and Figure 8–3 shows the results graphically. The first two columns in the table give output (enrollment) and price (tuition) respectively. Higgins can enroll as many students as he desires at the market price of $5,000 per student.

Columns 3 and 4 reflect the revenue and cost data respectively. Total revenue is price times quantity. Total cost is the sum of fixed and variable costs. Column 5 gives profit which is the difference between TR and STC. As column 5 indicates, profit is negative if fewer than 2 students are enrolled or if more than 8 are enrolled, and is positive when between 2 and 8 students are enrolled. As is clear from the table, maximum profit is $6,000 when output is 5 students. Thus, Higgins should enroll 5 students per session.

The straight line in Figure 8–3(a), labeled TR, is a graph of the total revenue curve generated by the data in column 3 of Table 8–2. For price-taking firms, the total revenue curve is always a straight line emanating from the origin. Price does not change with output and the slope of the TR curve, marginal revenue, is the market price. In this example $MR = p = \$5,000$.

The short-run total cost curve corresponding to the data for PSE is labeled STC in the diagram. Notice that the STC curve in this example has the shape that gives rise to U-shaped average and marginal cost curves.

TABLE 8–2

PROFIT FOR THE PYGMALION SCHOOL OF ETIQUETTE WHEN TUITION IS $5,000

Enrollment	Price	TR	STC	Profit
1	$5,000	$ 5,000	$ 5,400	$ −600
2	5,000	10,000	7,600	2,400
3	5,000	15,000	10,600	4,400
4	5,000	20,000	14,400	5,600
5	5,000	25,000	19,000	6,000
6	5,000	30,000	24,400	5,600
7	5,000	35,000	29,600	5,400
8	5,000	40,000	37,600	2,400
9	5,000	45,000	45,400	−400
10	5,000	50,000	54,000	−4,000

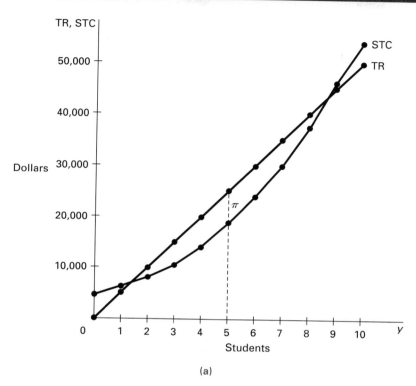

(a)

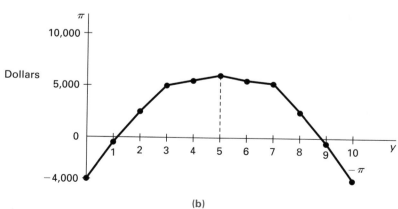

(b)

(a) Profit in the short run is the difference between TR and STC. (b) In this instance, profit is negative for low output rates, increases to a maximum, and then declines. Profit is maximized when the school enrolls 5 students.

Figure 8–3(b) is a graph of PSE's profit for each output rate. As the table indicates, profit is initially negative. As output increases, profit becomes positive and eventually turns negative again. Profit is at its maximum when the difference between TR and STC is as large as possible or when we are at the top of the profit hill. Again, this occurs when 5 students are enrolled.

Since in this instance we are considering a short-run profit-maximizing decision, Higgins must also consider whether or not PSE should remain open or shut down. (We will discuss this decision in detail later in the chapter.) Recall that in the short run firms must pay fixed costs regardless of the output rate. If Higgins were to shut down the school he would incur a loss of $4,000 per session. Since operating the firm at the profit-maximizing output rate yields a profit, Higgins certainly does better by staying open.

Suppose, however, that tuition dropped to $3,200. Table 8–3 shows that, in this instance, it would be impossible for Higgins to earn a profit: for every output rate STC is greater than TR and Higgins incurs a loss. In this case, the profit-maximizing output rate is three students; that is, losses are minimized when three students are enrolled in the program.

Since he is incurring a loss, Higgins must consider whether or not to shut down his operation. If he shuts down, he must pay the fixed costs and will incur a loss of $4,000. If he remains open and operates at the profit-maximizing level, he incurs a loss of $1,000. Therefore, since Higgins' loss is less if he remains open, he will not shut down the school.

Now suppose the price falls even further to $2,500. Again, as Table 8–4 shows, a loss is unavoidable. However, in this case the

TABLE 8–3

PROFIT FOR THE PYGMALION SCHOOL OF ETIQUETTE WHEN TUITION IS $3,200

Enrollment	Price	TR	STC	Profit
1	$3,200	$ 3,200	$ 5,400	$ −2,200
2	3,200	6,400	7,600	−1,200
3	3,200	9,600	10,600	−1,000
4	3,200	12,800	14,400	−1,600
5	3,200	16,000	19,000	−3,000
6	3,200	19,200	24,400	−5,200
7	3,200	22,400	29,600	−7,200
8	3,200	25,600	37,600	−12,000
9	3,200	28,800	45,400	−16,600
10	3,200	32,000	54,000	−22,000

Enrollment	Price	TR	STC	Profit
1	$2,500	$ 1,000	$ 5,400	$ −4,400
2	2,500	2,000	7,600	−5,600
3	2,500	3,000	10,600	−7,600
4	2,500	4,000	14,400	−10,400
5	2,500	5,000	19,000	−14,000
6	2,500	6,000	24,400	−18,400
7	2,500	7,000	29,600	−22,600
8	2,500	8,000	37,600	−29,600
9	2,500	9,000	45,400	−36,400
10	2,500	10,000	54,000	−44,000

TABLE 8−4

PROFIT FOR THE PYGMALION SCHOOL OF ETIQUETTE WHEN TUITION IS $2,500

profit-maximizing output rate is one student which results in a loss of $4,400. If Higgins stays in business, the best he can do is to suffer a loss of $4,400, because any other positive level of production would yield even greater losses. Here, then, Higgins maximizes profit (minimizes losses) by shutting down. If he closes the school he incurs a $4,000 loss, which is better than a $4,400 loss.

The TR−TC approach to profit maximization gives us a way of determining the profit-maximizing or optimal level of production. However, for economists this approach is not entirely satisfactory since it gives very little insight into the decision-making process. Remember that one of our goals is to understand how to make the decisions that will maximize profit.

When we studied the theory of consumer behavior, we found that individuals were doing the best they could do when the marginal benefit of a particular action was equal to the marginal cost. We also hinted that this is a general principle that can be applied to any economic agent. Therefore, we must now ask if the owner of a profit-maximizing firm determines the level of production by equating the marginal benefit to the marginal cost of production.

Finding the output rate that maximizes profit is an unconstrained optimization problem that we can solve using the technique discussed in Chapter 2. In Figure 8−4 we have drawn the TR and TC curves and the profit function, assuming that output can be varied continuously. Given these TR and TC curves, how can we characterize the point where profit is maximized? Profit is maximized when the firm is producing an output rate corresponding to

DETERMINING THE PROFIT-MAXIMIZING RATE OF OUTPUT: THE MARGINAL REVENUE−MARGINAL COST APPROACH

FIGURE 8–4   PROFIT AS A FUNCTION OF OUTPUT

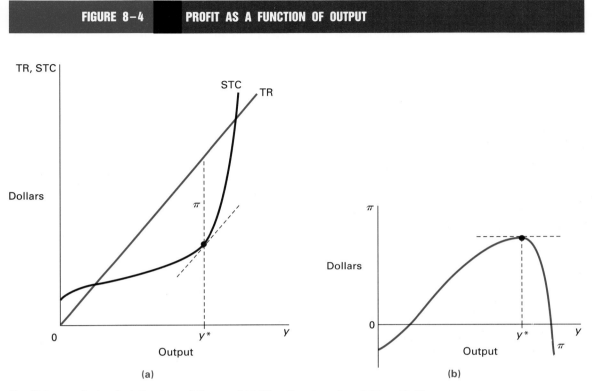

(a)   (b)

Profit is maximized at the top of the profit hill—that is, when MR = SMC.

the top of the profit hill, y^* in Figure 8–4. At this point the slope of the profit function is zero, meaning that the *marginal profit* is just zero. Furthermore, since to the left of y^* the profit function has a positive slope and to the right of y^* it has a negative slope, we know that we have found a maximum and not a minimum (Figure 8–4[b]).

Now recall the definition of profit: $\pi = \text{TR} - \text{TC}$. If output changes a little bit, what happens to profit? As output changes, both revenue and costs change. Since marginal revenue measures the change in revenue per unit change in output, and marginal cost measures the change in cost per unit change in output, we can express marginal profit as follows:

$$\text{marginal profit} = \text{MR} - \text{MC};$$

that is, the change in profit is equal to marginal revenue minus marginal cost.

If we want to be at the top of the profit hill, marginal profit must be zero. This means that profit is maximized when

$$\text{marginal profit} = MR - MC = 0 \qquad \text{or when}$$

$$MR = MC. \tag{8.3}$$

Equation (8.3) is the profit-maximizing condition. The owner of a firm should choose that output rate for which MR is equal to MC.

If we look back at Table 8–2, we see that MR = MC at an output rate of 5, which is precisely the profit-maximizing level of production we determined earlier. However, it is now clear what economic principle gives rise to Higgins' decision to enroll 5 students. This is just another example of economic agents equating the marginal benefits and marginal costs of undertaking a particular action. For the owner of a firm, the marginal benefit of producing an additional unit of output is simply the change in revenue, while the marginal cost is the change in production costs. Profit-maximizing producers are doing the best they can do when marginal benefit is equal to marginal cost.

Notice that to this point our solution to the profit maximization problem has not used the perfect competition assumption. That is, any profit-maximizing firm, whether a price taker or not, will always choose the output rate for which marginal revenue is equal to marginal cost. But can we say anything more if we are considering a perfectly competitive firm?

We know that for a price-taking firm, marginal revenue is equal to the price of the product being produced and sold. This means that a perfectly competitive firm is maximizing profit when the level of production is such that price is equal to marginal cost; that is, when $p = MC$.

(Throughout this discussion we have not mentioned fixed costs. The reason for this is that in the short run fixed costs determine only whether or not a firm should shut down. The business decision regarding production in the short run is not affected by fixed costs. The profit-maximizing output is determined by setting marginal revenue equal to marginal cost. Fixed costs are irrelevant when deciding how much to produce in the short run; that is, after fixed costs are paid, they have no bearing on the production decision.)

It is very important that we understand why finding the production level where price (marginal revenue) is equal to marginal cost yields the profit-maximizing output rate (provided, of course, that it is worthwhile to produce anything at all). To make sure we understand why profit is maximized when MR = p = MC, let's try to demonstrate this result using a graph depicting the marginal revenue and marginal cost curves of a typical firm.

Figure 8–5 illustrates the marginal revenue and marginal cost curves for such a firm. Since price is equal to marginal revenue, this is a competitive firm. We find the profit-maximizing level of production by equating MR and MC. In Figure 8–5, p = MC when the firm produces y^* units of output.

How can we prove that y^* maximizes profits? Suppose that the firm were operating at a lower output rate such as y_1. At y_1, MR is greater than MC, which means that producing another unit of output would increase revenue more than it would increase cost, and profit would be greater. At any output rate where marginal revenue is greater than marginal cost, the firm can increase profit by increasing output.

At an output rate greater than y^*, y_2 for example, MR is less than MC, which means that reducing output by one unit would lower cost more than it would lower revenue, and profit would again be greater. At any output rate where marginal revenue is less than marginal cost, the firm can increase profit by reducing output.

If it is worthwhile for a competitive firm to produce a positive amount of output, then the firm will maximize profit by operating at the level where price is equal to marginal cost. At any other level

FIGURE 8–5	PROFIT MAXIMIZATION: THE MARGINAL REVENUE–MARGINAL COST APPROACH

For output rates less than y^*, MR > SMC and profit can be increased by increasing production. For output rates greater than y^*, MR < SMC and profit can be increased by reducing production. When output is equal to y^*, MR = SMC and profit is maximized.

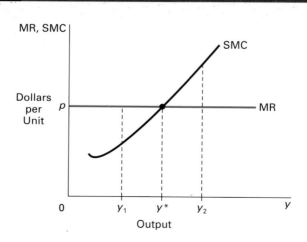

of output, profit will be lower. This is just another example of the fundamental optimization principle: marginal benefit equals marginal cost.

EXAMPLE 8–1

EXCISE TAXES AND PROFIT MAXIMIZATION

Suppose that Llama, Inc., manufactures and sells cigarettes in the U.S. Llama cigarettes are manufactured using a synthetic tobacco that has no tar or nicotine and currently sells for p_1 dollars per pack. Llama is a price taker. Suppose the federal government decides to impose an excise tax of T dollars per pack on producers of cigarettes. (In the U.S. cigarette manufacturers face both federal and state taxes). (a) How will this excise tax affect Llama's profit-maximizing level of production in the short run? (b) What will be the effect on the short-run profit-maximizing output level if, instead of levying an excise tax, the government requires manufacturers of cigarettes to buy a license?

■ **SOLUTION** Figure 8–6 illustrates the marginal cost curve for producing cigarettes. Prior to the tax, the firm maximizes profit if it produces the output level for which marginal revenue—price in this example—is equal to marginal cost. In this instance, the optimal output rate is y^* packs of cigarettes per year.

(a) First we must consider what happens when the owner of the firm must pay a T dollar per-pack tax. After the tax is levied, the cost of producing and selling one additional pack of cigarettes is equal to the marginal cost of production plus the tax that must be paid. In Figure 8–6 we have added a new line to the graph and labeled it SMC + T. It is the marginal cost curve with the tax added on. Since the tax is a per-unit tax, the SMC + T curve is simply the original marginal cost curve shifted up exactly T dollars.

From the diagram, it is clear that output must fall. Profit is maximized when marginal revenue is equal to SMC + T; that is, the profit-maximizing output rate falls from y^* to y_1. The excise tax increases the cost of producing and selling the good and, as a result, reduces the profit-maximizing output rate.

(b) Next consider what happens when the government requires firms in the cigarette industry to purchase a license. If any cigarettes are produced and sold, the firm must buy the license. As a result, the marginal cost of producing cigarettes, provided some

An excise tax increases the marginal cost of production which, in turn, causes the profit-maximizing level of production to fall.

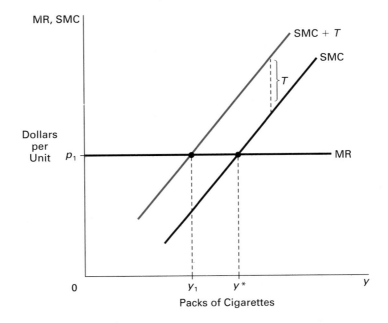

Packs of Cigarettes

cigarettes are produced, does not change. Thus, the profit-maximizing level of production does not change! The license has no impact on the firm's profit-maximizing production decision in the short run. ■

One word of caution is in order here. In Example 8–1 we are implicitly assuming that the price of cigarettes remains at p_1 dollars per pack. If we were to allow for the interaction of supply and demand forces, then the market price might change and we would have to modify our analysis appropriately. Such issues are considered in Chapters 9 and 11.

8.3 SHORT-RUN SUPPLY FOR A PERFECTLY COMPETITIVE FIRM

SHORT-RUN PROFIT OR LOSS

■ So far we have learned how to describe the way individual producers decide how much output to produce. Our next task is to derive the output supply curves for an individual firm.

For a price-taking firm, equating price and marginal cost guarantees that profit is maximized, provided it is worthwhile to produce anything at all; however, this does not guarantee that a firm is earning a positive profit. (See the discussion of the Pygmalion School of Etiquette earlier in this chapter.) The firm could be incurring a loss, which is a negative profit.

In order to determine whether a firm is making a profit or incurring a loss, we must compare total revenue to total cost or, what amounts to the same thing, average revenue to average cost. Average revenue, denoted AR, is just TR/y. Writing short-run profit in terms of AR and SATC, we have

$$\pi = \text{TR} - \text{STC} = y(\text{AR} - \text{SATC}). \qquad (8.4)$$

If AR > SATC, then the firm is earning a profit, and if AR < SATC, it is making a loss. For a price-taking firm, AR = TR/y = py/y = p. Thus, a price-taking firm earns a positive profit if price is greater than average cost and makes a loss if price is less than average cost.

Figure 8–7(a) illustrates the case where a firm is making a profit. The market price for this product is p_1 dollars per unit, which means that the marginal revenue curve for the firm is the horizontal line labeled MR_1. The short-run profit-maximizing level of pro-

PROFIT OR LOSS IN THE SHORT RUN   **FIGURE 8-7**

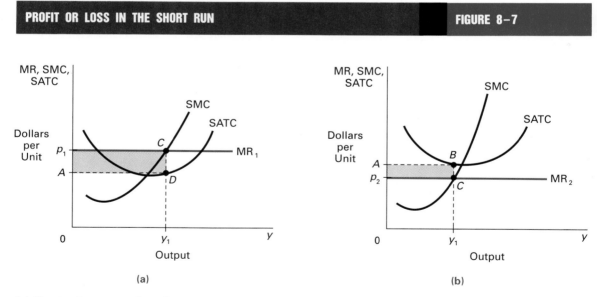

(a) If price is greater than the minimum of the SATC curve, then owners make a profit. (b) If price is less than the minimum of the SATC curve, then owners incur a loss.

duction is y_1 units of output. At this output rate, average total cost is A dollars per unit of output. Since average revenue (price) is greater than SATC, the firm makes a profit.

Using Figure 8–7(a) we can show profit by comparing total revenue and total cost. Total revenue is price, represented by distance $0p_1$, times quantity, represented by distance $0y_1$, or area $0p_1Cy_1$. Total cost is SATC times quantity or area $0ADy_1$. Profit is the difference between total revenue and total cost and is represented by area Ap_1CD.

Figure 8–7(b) shows the case where the firm incurs a loss. Here the market price, p_2, is low enough that there is no way for the firm to make a profit. The profit-maximizing output rate is y_1 units. Price is less than SATC so the firm suffers a loss. Total revenue is $0p_2Cy_1$, total cost is $0ABy_1$, and the loss is represented by the area p_2ABC.

In this instance, producing the profit-maximizing level of output, y_1, results in a loss. This means that if the firm is operated at any other positive output rate, losses would be even greater. However, the owner of the firm may be able to reduce its loss by shutting down (see the discussion of the Pygmalion School of Etiquette)—that is, by producing nothing.

OPERATING AT A LOSS IN THE SHORT RUN

If the owners of a business make a profit, clearly they will continue to produce a positive amount of output. If, on the other hand, they incur a loss at the profit-maximizing output rate, then in the short run they may decide to close down the operation and produce nothing if the losses incurred by shutting down are smaller.

THE SHUTDOWN POINT WHEN THERE ARE NO QUASI-FIXED COSTS

A firm incurs loss if the market price is less than SATC for all output levels. When this happens, the owner must decide whether to produce a positive output or none at all. Notice that we are not saying that the firm goes out of business; that would be a long-run question, for the owner would have to dispose of all fixed factors of production. Here we are saying that it may be a better strategy in the short run to produce zero output in order to incur only those fixed costs that are inescapable.

The **shutdown point** is defined as *the price that yields a loss just equal to the firm's fixed costs.* If there are no quasi-fixed costs then the shutdown point is the output rate that generates just enough revenue to cover all of the firm's variable costs. We can show the shutdown point algebraically simply by noting that

$$\pi = py^* - \text{TVC} - \text{TFC} = -\text{TFC} + y^* (p - \text{AVC}) \qquad (8.5)$$

where y^* is the profit-maximizing output level. If $p > AVC$, then at least some of the firm's fixed costs are covered and the firm should continue to operate. If $p < AVC$, then producing y^* results in a loss that is greater than fixed costs and the firm should shut down.

The **breakeven point** is defined as *the price that yields zero profit*. At the breakeven point, TR = STC. If the firm operates above the shutdown point but below the breakeven point, it incurs a loss; however, revenues are large enough to cover all of the firm's variable costs with some left over to apply to fixed costs. The loss is therefore smaller than the fixed costs and the firm will continue to operate. If the firm operates below the shutdown point, revenues are not large enough to cover all of the variable costs and the loss is greater than the fixed costs. In this case the firm is shut down.

Figure 8−8 shows the breakeven and shutdown points. If the market price is p_1, then the profit-maximizing output is y_1 and economic profit is zero. Notice that when the market price is below the SATC curve a loss is incurred; however, revenues are still large enough to cover all of the variable costs of production. As long as the market price is above AVC, some revenues are left over after paying all variable costs; these can be applied to the fixed costs. In this case the firm does better by continuing the operation of the plant.

THE BREAKEVEN AND SHUTDOWN POINTS   **FIGURE 8−8**

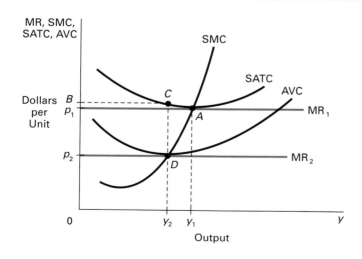

If the market price is p_1, total revenue is just equal to total cost and the firm breaks even. If the market price is p_2, total revenue is just equal to total variable cost and the firm incurs a loss equal to fixed costs.

If the market price is p_2, then the profit-maximizing output is y_2 and the firm incurs a loss equal to its fixed costs. In this case the owner of the firm is indifferent between operating the business and shutting down. If the market price is below p_2 then the firm will not earn enough revenue to cover all of its variable costs and it should shut down.

In the next example, we know explicit price and cost data and must determine the profit-maximizing output rate for various market prices. Remember, here we are assuming that there are no quasi-fixed costs.

EXAMPLE 8–2

SHORT-RUN SUPPLY

Vanderkamps is a firm that produces Edam cheese, a mild, yellow, Dutch cheese. The owner of Vanderkamps estimates that monthly total and marginal cost will be

$$STC = 500 + y + .0005y^2 \text{ and } SMC = 1 + .001y,$$

where y is pounds of Edam produced per month. Edam cheese is currently selling for $3.00 per pound. (a) If Vanderkamps wants to maximize profit, how many pounds of cheese should it produce each month? (b) If the price of Edam cheese falls to $1.50 per pound, how many pounds of cheese should the firm produce each month? (c) One of Vanderkamps' managers recommends that the quantity of Edam produced each month should be such that per-unit costs are as low as possible. She argues that, regardless of the price, producing at the level where average cost is minimized will obviously result in the greatest profit. Is she right?

■ **SOLUTION** (a) First we must find the profit-maximizing rate of output when the price of cheese is $3.00. Setting price (marginal revenue) equal to marginal cost and solving for output we have

$$3 = 1 + .001y \hspace{4cm} \text{or}$$

$$y^* = (3 - 1)/.001 = 2,000.$$

The profit-maximizing quantity of cheese to produce is therefore 2,000 pounds per month. In this instance, total revenue is

$3 \cdot 2{,}000 = \$6{,}000$, total cost is $500 + 2{,}000 + .0005(2{,}000)^2 = \$4{,}500$, and profit is \$1,500 per month. Since it is earning a positive profit, the firm should continue to operate in the short run.

(b) If the price falls to \$1.50, then the profit-maximizing rate of output falls to 500 pounds per month ($1.50 = 1 + .001y$ implies that $y = (1.50 - 1)/.001 = 500$). Total revenue is now \$750, total cost is \$1,125, and the firm incurs a loss of \$375 per month. Since a loss is incurred, we must compare the loss to fixed costs. In this example, total fixed costs are \$500 per month and the firm should not shut down. The loss incurred by producing 500 pounds of cheese per month is less than the loss the firm would incur if it shut down.

(c) Finally, let us consider the manager's proposition that Vander-Kamps should produce at the level where SATC is as small as possible (see Figure 8–9). In this instance, $SATC = (500/y) + 1 + .0005y$. We know from Chapter 7 that at the minimum point of the SATC curve, $SMC = SATC$. Equating these two expressions yields

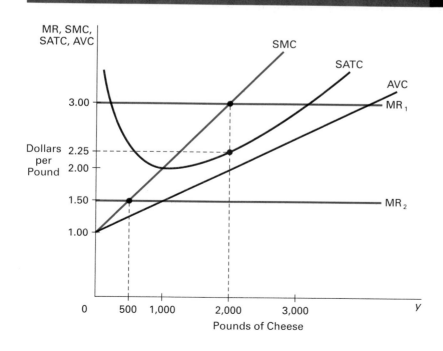

PROFIT MAXIMIZATION FOR VANDERKAMPS

FIGURE 8–9

If the price of cheese is \$3, profit is maximized when 2,000 pounds of cheese are produced per month, and the firm earns a profit. If the price of cheese is \$1.50, then profit is maximized when 500 pounds of cheese are produced each month, and the firm incurs a loss. However, since revenues are large enough to cover variable costs and some fixed costs, the firm continues to operate in the short run.

$$1 + .001y = (500/y) + 1 + .0005y.$$

Combining like terms we have

$$(500/y) = .0005y \text{ or } y^2 = 500/.0005 = 1{,}000{,}000.$$

Taking the square root of both sides of this last equation, we find that SATC attains its minimum when $y = 1{,}000$.

At this output rate, short-run average and marginal cost are

$$SATC(1{,}000) = SMC(1{,}000) = 1 + .001(1{,}000) = \$2 \text{ per pound.}$$

If the market price of cheese is greater than \$2 per pound, then MR > SMC and Vanderkamps can increase its profit by producing more. If the market price is less than \$2 per pound, then MR < SMC and Vanderkamps can increase its profit by producing less. Only if the market price of cheese is \$2 per pound will the minimum point of the SATC curve represent the profit-maximizing level of production. ■

The manager's suggestion in this previous example is one that some real-world managers purport to follow. It is commonly called maximizing profit margin. A firm's *profit margin* is defined as *profit per unit of output* or simply *average profit*. For a price-taking firm, average profit is maximized when per-unit cost is minimized. We can see this by writing down the equation for average profit:

$$\pi/y = (TR/y) - (STC/y) = p - SATC.$$

Since price does not depend on output, average profit is maximized when SATC is as small as possible.

If a manager follows a strategy that maximizes profit margin or, what amounts to the same thing, minimizes per-unit costs, she will not necessarily maximize profit. It is important to understand why this is so. Remember, both revenues and costs determine profit and it is the marginal change in these two components, not the average change, that is key to deciding how much to produce.

THE SHUTDOWN POINT
WHEN THERE ARE QUASI-
FIXED COSTS

When there are quasi-fixed costs, the shutdown point is the output rate that generates just enough revenue to cover all of the firm's variable costs as well as its quasi-fixed costs. This means that when there are quasi-fixed costs, the shutdown point must be an output rate greater than the one corresponding to the minimum point of the average variable cost curve.

In the next example we are asked to analyze the short-run production decision of a firm that incurs both fixed and quasi-fixed costs. Remember, the firm can avoid quasi-fixed costs in the short run by producing nothing but it cannot avoid fixed costs.

EXAMPLE 8-3

SHORT-RUN SUPPLY WHEN THERE ARE QUASI-FIXED COSTS

Textbook, Inc., is a small firm that manufactures and sells textbooks. Its owners currently publish an intermediate microeconomics textbook that sells for $30 per book. Textbook's accounting department has supplied the following information concerning annual development and production costs for the book.

Fixed Costs:
Annual lease payments for the equipment used to produce the book	$25,000

Quasi-Fixed Costs:
Text development	$20,000
Text preparation for printing	15,000
Advertising	20,000
Total	$55,000

Variable and marginal costs are estimated to be

$$TVC = 20y + .0005y^2 \text{ and } SMC = 20 + .001y.$$

If the owners of Textbook, Inc., are profit maximizers, how many books should they print?

■ **SOLUTION** First we need to find the number of books that must sell if the owners of the firm are to maximize profit. To find the profit-maximizing output rate, we find the output rate for which marginal revenue, price in this instance, is equal to marginal cost:

$$30 = SMC = .001y + 20.$$

Solving this equation for y gives the profit-maximizing output rate: $y^* = 10,000$ books per year. If 10,000 books are produced, total revenue will be $10,000 \cdot 30 = \$300,000$. Since TVC $= 20 \cdot 10,000$ $+ .0005(10,000)^2 = \$250,000$, quasi-fixed costs are $55,000, and fixed costs are $25,000, the firm incurs a loss of $30,000 per year. (The revenues generated from sales of the book are large enough to cover all of the firm's variable costs, part of the quasi-fixed costs, and none of the fixed costs.)

Since a loss is incurred, we must ask if the firm can do better by shutting down. If the firm does not print any books, then it must pay only the $25,000 in fixed costs. Thus, the firm does do better by shutting down. ∎

Notice that in Example 8–3, if we had included quasi-fixed costs as a fixed cost, we would not have made the correct profit-maximizing decision. If we had treated quasi-fixed costs as fixed costs, we would have recommended that the firm stay in operation, since at 10,000 books per year the firm would have a total revenue of $350,000 and variable costs of $300,000, leaving $50,000 to be applied to fixed costs. Thus, if we had mistakenly included quasi-fixed costs, we would have recommended keeping the operation going—the wrong decision.

DERIVING A FIRM'S SUPPLY CURVE

The **short-run supply curve** is defined as *the relation between quantity sold and price, when input prices and the capital stock (or plant size) are held constant.* The short-run supply curve shows how sellers of a particular good or service react to short-run changes in the price of that good or service.

The point we must keep in mind is that in the short run a firm supplies a positive amount of output only if its revenues are large enough to cover all its variable costs (and quasi-fixed costs if there are any). For simplicity, we will assume that there are no quasi-fixed costs so that a positive output is supplied only if the market price is above the minimum point of the AVC curve.

Keeping the shutdown point in mind, we can derive an individual firm's short-run supply curve, which we denote by SS. The double "S" is to remind us that we are talking about the *short-run* supply curve rather than the long-run supply curve.

Figure 8–10(a) shows the short-run marginal and average variable cost curves for a competitive firm. When the market price is below p_1 the firm supplies no output since the producer does better if the plant closes down. In Figure 8–10(b), we plot the profit-maximizing price–output pairs which give rise to the short-run supply curve. From zero to p_1 the supply curve is a

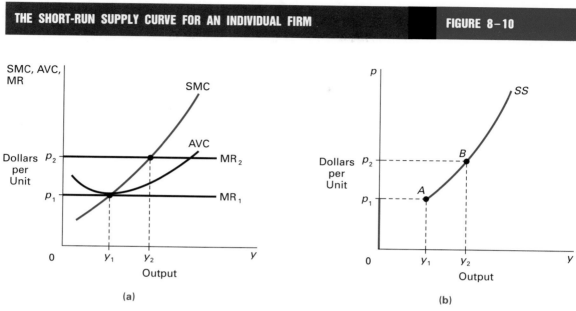

THE SHORT-RUN SUPPLY CURVE FOR AN INDIVIDUAL FIRM   FIGURE 8–10

(a) *Profit maximization for a perfectly competitive firm requires the firm to produce the output rate for which price equals marginal cost. Below p_1, the firm shuts down and produces nothing. (b) The short-run supply curve for a competitive firm is positively sloped. Higher prices lead to higher production levels.*

vertical line along the p-axis. Over this range of prices, nothing is produced.

At price p_1 the firm is indifferent between producing y_1 units of output or shutting down. We assume that the owner always chooses to produce in this situation so that when the market price is p_1, supply is y_1. This corresponds to point A in Figure 8–10(b). If the market price increases to p_2, the profit-maximizing output is y_2 units. Thus, when the price is p_2, supply increases to y_2, point B in the diagram. Continuing in this manner, we can plot the short-run supply curve for a perfectly competitive firm.

In Figure 8–10, the supply curve is positively sloped; that is, as the price of good y rises (falls) quantity supplied rises (falls). Naturally, this is because the firm's SMC curve is also positively sloped. This positive relation between quantity supplied and price is called the **Law of Supply**.

THE LAW OF SUPPLY

THE SHORT-RUN SUPPLY
FUNCTION

The short-run supply curve can also be represented by a function. This *short-run supply function* has two pieces to it and is written as

$$y = \begin{cases} 0 & \text{if} \quad \pi < -\text{TFC} \quad \text{or} \quad p < \min \text{AVC} \\ \text{SS}(p,w,r,\overline{K}) & \text{if} \quad \pi \geq -\text{TFC} \quad \text{or} \quad p \geq \min \text{AVC} \end{cases}. \quad (8.6)$$

The firm is shut down if profit is less than minus fixed costs; that is, it produces no output if price is less than the minimum AVC. Output is equal to a function that depends on price, factor costs, and the fixed capital stock, if profit is greater than or equal to minus fixed costs. This means that when price is greater than or equal to the minimum AVC, the firm supplies a positive amount of output.

Once again, a warning is in order. Recall that when we discussed demand functions and demand curves, we had to be careful to note that while economists write the demand function with quantity as the dependent variable, they graph the demand curve with price plotted on the vertical axis and quantity on the horizontal axis. Economists do the same thing when they discuss supply functions and supply curves. They graph the supply curve with price on the vertical axis and quantity on the horizontal axis but write the supply function with quantity as the dependent variable.

Having determined a firm's short-run supply curve, we can now ask how changes in input prices affect supply.

**A CHANGE IN THE PRICE
OF A VARIABLE INPUT**

Consider first the impact of a change in the price of a variable input on the profit-maximizing output rate. The curve labeled MC_1 in Figure 8–11(a) is the marginal cost curve for a competitive firm. If the market price for good y is p_1, then the profit-maximizing output rate is y_1.

Now suppose that the price of a variable input rises. As we saw in Chapter 7, an increase in factor prices leads to an upward shift in the SMC curve; that is, for each rate of output, marginal cost is higher. The result is a new marginal cost curve, MC_2, located to the northwest of MC_1.

Given the new marginal cost curve, marginal revenue is equal to marginal cost when y_2 units are produced. Thus, an increase in factors prices leads to a reduction in the optimal level of production and an upward shift in the short-run supply curve.

**A CHANGE IN THE PRICE
OF A FIXED INPUT**

A change in the price of a fixed input affects total fixed costs as well as average total cost. However, it has no effect on total variable cost or marginal cost. This means that a change in the price of a fixed input will have no effect on a firm's supply curve other than

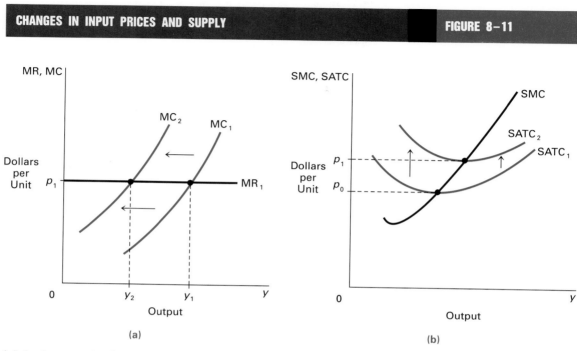

CHANGES IN INPUT PRICES AND SUPPLY

FIGURE 8–11

(a)

(b)

(a) An increase in the price of a variable input causes the marginal cost curve to shift up which, in turn, leads to an upward shift in the short-run supply curve. (b) An increase in the price of a fixed input causes the average cost curve to shift up; however, since the marginal cost curve is unchanged, this has no effect on the supply curve except to increase the shutdown point.

to change the shutdown point. For example, as is shown in Figure 8–11(b), an increase in the price of a fixed factor increases the price at which the firm shuts down from p_0 to p_1 dollars per unit of output.

■ In the long run all inputs are variable. Owners of firms can now attain the profit-maximizing rate of output by adjusting plant size. In Figure 8–12 we illustrate this adjustment process for a firm already established in a particular business.

Suppose that the market price for good y is p_1 and the firm currently is operating with a plant, or capital stock, for which $SATC_1$ and SMC_1 are the average and marginal cost curves respectively. Faced with these cost curves, the profit-maximizing firm will choose to operate where $p_1 = SMC_1$. Production is y_1 units of output in the short run. At this output rate, the producer earns a positive profit.

8.4 LONG-RUN SUPPLY FOR A PERFECTLY COMPETITIVE FIRM

FIGURE 8–12	PROFIT MAXIMIZATION IN THE LONG RUN

Long-run profit maximization requires owners to choose the output rate for which MR = LMC. If y_1 units of output are being produced in the short run, then the owner should expand capacity and produce y_2 units of output in the long run.

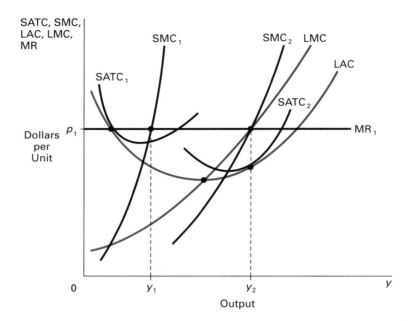

In the long run the owner should produce the rate of output for which price is equal to LMC. For the marginal revenue and marginal cost curves shown in Figure 8–12, the firm maximizes profit in the long run when production is y_2 units of output per period. That is, the owner should expand plant size or capacity and utilize the capital stock associated with the cost curves labeled SMC_2 and $SATC_2$. Here the firm is maximizing profit, since $p_1 = $ LMC, and $SATC_2$ and SMC_2 represent the optimal plant size.

LONG-RUN PROFIT OR LOSS

In the short run, a firm stays in operation even when it incurs a loss, as long as the owners can cover all of the variable costs and at least some of the fixed costs. That is, even if the firm makes a loss it may pay to stay in business in the short run. In the long run, on the other hand, there are no fixed costs and if the owners of a firm incur a loss, they are not doing as well as they could in the next best alternative. This being the case, the owners will shut down the firm, sell all resources used in the production process, and exit the business. (The firm can simply transfer any resources that it can use in the next best alternative to the appropriate business.)

As long as the market price is above the minimum point of the long-run average cost curve, the firm makes a profit and the owners will operate it at the profit-maximizing level of production. If the market price falls below the minimum point of the long-run average cost curve, the firm incurs a loss and the owners will go out of business. Thus, the **long-run supply curve** for a competitive firm is simply the LMC curve for output rates equal to or greater than the output rate associated with the minimum LAC.

■ We have examined the implications of profit maximization for the output decision of the price-taking firm. Now we will examine the implications of profit maximization for the input demand decision of the firm.

Given that the owners of a firm decide to produce a positive amount of output, profit maximization implies that they should choose the output rate that will cause marginal revenue to equal marginal cost; that is, they should increase output until the marginal benefit of producing one more unit (marginal revenue) is just equal to the marginal cost. Quite naturally, a similar condition holds for the hiring of inputs.

Let us begin by considering a firm that uses only one input, labor. In order to determine the quantity of labor that maximizes profit, we must investigate how profit varies with the use of labor. Writing profit in terms of the quantity of labor used we have

$$\pi = pF(L) - wL.$$

We want to know the level of L that maximizes profit. Once again, this is an unconstrained optimization problem. Profit is maximized when the profit per unit change in labor is zero. If the quantity of labor used changes a small amount, how does profit change?

First consider the change in revenues. If the firm uses more labor in the production process, then output increases by an amount equal to the marginal product of labor. For a perfectly competitive firm, the revenue generated by this increase in output is equal to the market price times how much more output is produced; that is, revenue increases by $p \cdot MP_L$. Economists call this the **marginal revenue product** of labor (or the value of the marginal product of labor), and it is denoted by MRP_L. The marginal revenue product of labor is the change in revenue due to a small change in labor usage, when all other inputs are constant.

8.5 PROFIT MAXIMIZATION AND THE EMPLOYMENT OF INPUTS

PROFIT MAXIMIZATION WHEN ONLY ONE INPUT IS USED

Next consider the change in costs. For a perfectly competitive firm, the owners must pay the market wage for each additional unit of labor used, meaning that each additional unit of labor increases costs by w dollars. Economists call this the **marginal factor cost** of labor, and it is denoted MFC_L. The marginal factor cost of labor is the change in cost due to a small change in labor usage, when all other inputs are constant. For a price-taker, $MFC_L = w$.

Profit is maximized when the change in profit per unit-change in labor is equal to zero; that is, when

$$\text{marginal profit} = pMP_L - w = 0.$$

Thus, profit is maximized when $pMP_L = w$ or when $MRP_L = MFC_L$.

Once again, we can use a simple diagram to show why this must be the profit-maximizing rule. In Figure 8–13 we have illustrated the MRP_L curve. We have drawn it negatively sloped, reflecting the Law of Diminishing Marginal Productivity. Given a wage rate w_1, we want to show that profit is as large as possible when a firm employs L^* workers. To accomplish this, we use the same argument we used to demonstrate that $p = SMC$ is the profit-maximizing rule for determining the output rate.

Suppose that the owner of the firm employs L_1 workers instead of L^*. By adding one more unit of labor, revenue increases by MRP_L

FIGURE 8–13	OPTIMAL INPUT DEMAND

Profit maximization for the competitive firm requires that the firm hire labor up to the point where the MRP_L is equal to the wage rate, or L^* units of labor. If the firm employs L_1 units of labor it can increase profit by hiring more labor. If it employs L_2 units, it can increase profit by reducing employment.

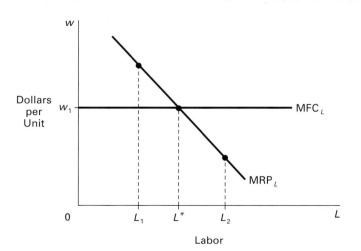

and costs increase by w_1. Since, when L_1 units of labor are employed, $MRP_L > w_1$, profit must increase and the firm should employ one more unit of labor. How long can we make this argument? Clearly it holds as long as $MRP_L > w_1$ or until the firm uses L^* units of labor in the production process.

Next, suppose that the owner of the firm employs L_2 workers instead of L^*. By reducing the quantity of labor employed by one unit, revenue decreases by MRP_L and costs decrease by w_1. Since, when L_2 units of labor are employed, $MRP_L < w_1$, profit must increase and the firm should employ one less unit of labor. How long can we make this argument? Clearly, it holds as long as $MRP_L < w_1$ or until the firm uses L^* units of labor in the production process.

In Example 8–4, we are asked to determine the profit-maximizing quantity of labor to hire for a firm using only labor in the production process. Then we are asked to investigate how both employment and production vary as the output price and the wage rate vary.

EXAMPLE 8–4

DERIVING A FIRM'S DEMAND FOR LABOR

H. R. Montag, Inc., manufactures and sells hand-crafted stereo cabinets. The quantity of cabinets that this firm can craft per year is $y = 400\sqrt{L}$ where L is the number of workers hired per year. The marginal product of labor is: $MP_L = 200/\sqrt{L}$. The market price for stereo cabinets is currently \$1,000 per cabinet. (a) Assuming that Montag is a price-taking firm, determine the profit-maximizing number of workers it should employ if the wage rate is \$25,000 per worker per year. (b) If the wage rate falls to \$20,000 per worker per year, will Montag hire more workers? Explain. (c) If the price of cabinets doubles, will the firm hire more workers (use the original wage rate)? Explain and illustrate.

■ **SOLUTION** (a) We begin by finding the profit-maximizing level of employment for arbitrary prices. Let p denote the price of toothpicks and w, the wage rate. Then profit maximization implies that

$$MRP_L = p \cdot 200/\sqrt{L} = w.$$

Solving this equation for L gives the profit-maximizing level of employment. We have: $L^* = (p \cdot 200/w)^2$.

(b) Next, we substitute the values for p and w given in the problem. When $p = 1{,}000$ and $w = 25{,}000$, $L^* = (1{,}000 \cdot 200/25{,}000)^2 = 64$ workers per year. Figure 8–14 illustrates this calculation. MRP_L^1 is the marginal revenue product curve when the price of cabinets is $1,000. When the wage rate is $25,000 per worker per year, the profit-maximizing number of workers to employ corresponds to the intersection of the marginal revenue product curve and the horizontal marginal factor cost curve.

If the wage rate falls to $20,000 per worker per year, employment increases to $L^* = 100$ workers. That is, the wage reduction lowers marginal factor costs, which in turn leads to an increase in the number of workers the firm hires.

(c) If the price of cabinets doubles and $w = \$25{,}000$, then $L^* = 256$ workers. The increase in output price increases the marginal revenue product of labor since each cabinet produced now generates more revenues for the firm. In Figure 8–14, a higher output price causes the MRP_L^1 curve to shift up to MRP_L^2. ■

| FIGURE 8–14 | H. R. MONTAG'S DEMAND FOR LABOR |

When the wage rate is $25,000 per worker per year and the price of stereo cabinets is $1,000 per cabinet, 64 workers are hired. If the wage rate falls to $20,000 per worker per year, employment increases to 100 workers. When the wage rate is $25,000 per worker per year, an increase in the price of cabinets shifts the MRP_L curve to the right and employment increases from 64 to 256 workers.

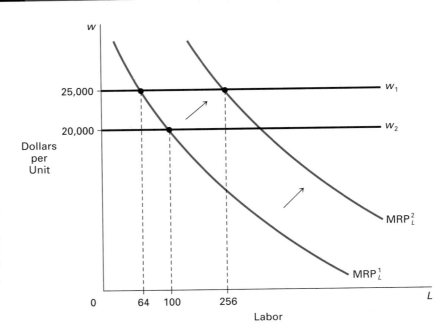

We have determined the profit-maximizing condition for a firm that uses only one input. Now we must generalize this rule to the case where a firm uses more than one input in the production process.

PROFIT MAXIMIZATION WHEN MORE THAN ONE INPUT IS USED

When a firm uses more than one input in the production of a good or service, the profit maximization rule derived above for one input must hold for all inputs. For example, if capital and labor are used to produce some good, then profit is given by

$$\pi = pF(K,L) - wL - rK.$$

A firm maximizes profit when the marginal change in profit per unit change in labor, holding capital constant, is zero *and* the marginal change in profit per unit change in capital, holding labor constant, is zero. Thus, profit is maximized when

$$MRP_L = pMP_L = w = MFC_L \qquad (8.7)$$

and

$$MRP_K = pMP_K = r = MFC_K. \qquad (8.8)$$

That is, the firm maximizes profit when the marginal revenue product of each input is equal to the marginal factor cost.

Notice that one implication of these conditions is that a profit-maximizing firm must also be a cost minimizer. To see this, simply solve one of the conditions for p and substitute into the other. This gives:

$$MP_L/MP_K = w/r,$$

which is the cost minimization condition we derived in Chapter 7. Profit-maximizing firms hire inputs up to the point where marginal revenue product is equal to marginal factor cost; this, in turn, implies that the firms are minimizing costs.

■ Having derived the short- and long-run supply curves for a competitive firm, we can now turn our attention to deriving a producer's short- and long-run input demand curves.

8.6 INPUT DEMAND CURVES FOR A PERFECTLY COMPETITIVE FIRM

DERIVING THE SHORT-RUN INPUT DEMAND CURVE FOR A COMPETITIVE FIRM

We call the demand for inputs a *derived demand*: it is derived from the demand for the product produced by the firm that employs the input. If there were no demand for the product, then there would be no demand for the factors of production used to produce the product.

The **short-run input demand curve** is defined as *the relation between quantity demanded and input price, when all other input prices, output price, and the capital stock are held constant.* In this section, we investigate the factors that determine the properties of short-run input demand curves for a perfectly competitive firm.

The first question we must address is, When will the owner of a firm choose to employ a positive amount of an input in the short run? Clearly, if a business makes a profit, it will supply a positive amount of output and, hence, employment will be positive. However, if the owners of the firm incur a loss, then they might shut the firm down. In this case, we assume that input demand is zero. In the remainder of this chapter we assume that output price is such that firms always choose to stay in business and, thus, always supply a positive amount of output. Given this assumption, firms will always demand positive amounts of the variable inputs.

SD_L will denote an individual firm's short-run demand curve for labor. The "S" is to remind us that we are talking about the *short-run* input demand curve rather than the long-run curve. To determine the firm's short-run input demand curve, consider Figure 8–15: (a) shows the marginal revenue product curve,

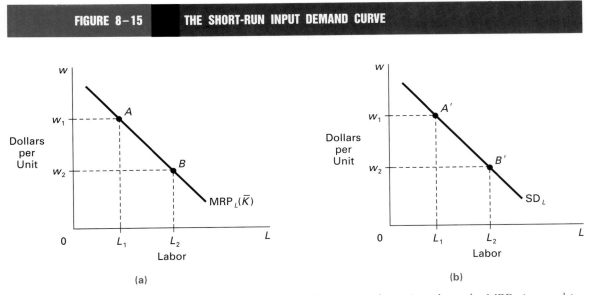

FIGURE 8–15   **THE SHORT-RUN INPUT DEMAND CURVE**

(a)

(b)

(a) Profit maximization requires that the firm hire workers up to the point where the MRP_L is equal to the wage. (b) The short-run input demand curve represents the relation between quantity employed and input price, given all other input prices, output price, and the quantity of capital used.

denoted MRP$_L$, for a typical firm with capital stock $\overline{K}$; in (b), we plot the profit-maximizing price–input pairs which give rise to the input demand curve.

Recall that profit maximization requires the firm to hire labor up to the point where the wage rate is equal to the MRP$_L$. If the wage rate is w_1, then the profit-maximizing quantity of labor to employ is L_1. This corresponds to point A' in Figure 8–15(b). If the wage rate falls to w_2, a profit-maximizing producer will choose the level of employment corresponding to the point where $w_2 = $ MRP$_L$, or L_2 in Figure 8–15(a); that is, when the wage is w_2, the demand for workers is L_2. This corresponds to point B' in Figure 8–15(b). Continuing in this manner, we can plot the short-run input demand curve. Notice that, in the short run, an individual firm's demand curve for labor is downward-sloping—that is, the lower the price of labor, the greater the quantity demanded. In addition, note that the short-run input demand curve has precisely the same shape as the marginal revenue product curve.

A function can also represent the short-run input demand curve. This *short-run input demand function* has two pieces to it and is written as

$$L = \begin{cases} 0 & \text{if} \quad \pi < -\text{TFC} \\ SD_L(w,r,p,\overline{K}) & \text{if} \quad \pi > -\text{TFC} \end{cases}. \qquad (8.9)$$

That is, employment is equal to a function that depends on the wage rate, other factor costs, the output price, and the fixed capital stock.

The **long-run input demand curve,** denoted D_L, illustrates the relation between input price and the level of employment, holding the prices of other inputs and output price constant but allowing the level of capital to adjust optimally. In the long run all inputs can be varied and, for this reason, we must take into account the fact that a change in the price of one input affects not only how much of that input is used but also the amounts of the other inputs that are used.

In order to derive the long-run input demand curve, we must determine how the long-run profit-maximizing quantity of an input varies as the price of the input changes. Once again, we will focus on labor, but the analysis is relevant for any factor of production.

Suppose the price of labor falls. What happens to the profit-maximizing amount of labor? We saw in Chapter 4 that we could decompose a change in the price of a good consumed by indi-

THE SHORT-RUN INPUT
DEMAND FUNCTION

DERIVING THE LONG-RUN
INPUT DEMAND CURVE
FOR A COMPETITIVE FIRM

viduals into income and substitution effects. We can undertake a similar decomposition here; that is, we can decompose the change in the price of one input into a substitution effect and an output effect. The *substitution effect* is the change in the quantity of an input used due to a change in relative input prices, holding output constant. The *output effect*, sometimes called the *scale effect*, is the change in the quantity of an input used due to the implied change in the long-run marginal cost curve and, hence, the optimal output rate.

Figure 8–16(a) shows the substitution effect. The initial output rate is y_1 and the initial amount of labor and capital used are L_1 and K_1 respectively. This information is represented by input bundle A on expansion path EP_1. When the price of labor falls, the isocost curve rotates about the K-axis and gets flatter. If the firm is constrained to produce y_1 units of output, it will now use input bundle B; that is, it will substitute labor for capital. This increase in the quantity of labor used by the firm is the substitution effect. In Figure 8–16(a), the substitution effect is $(L_2 - L_1)$ units of labor.

The adjustment from A to B in Figure 8–16(a) is also shown in Figure 8–16(b) as the move from A' to B'. When the price of labor falls, the entire marginal cost curve shifts down from LMC_1 to LMC_2. This means that at an output rate of y_1 units, marginal revenue is greater than marginal cost and the profit-maximizing firm has an incentive to increase production. Thus, as a result of the lower price of labor the firm expands output to y_2. In Figure 8–16(a), this is represented by the movement along the new expansion path EP_2 from B to C. (Remember, an expansion path is drawn for given input prices.) As the firm produces more output, it moves to a higher isocost line and uses more of both inputs. The scale effect is the increase in the amount of labor used, given by $(L_3 - L_2)$ in the diagram.

The long-run input demand curve indicates the full response of labor to an input price change. In Figure 8–16, both the substitution and output effects imply that the firm will employ more units of labor at a lower input price (and less at a higher input price). This means that the firm's long-run input demand curve is negatively sloped, as shown in Figure 8–16(c).

When an increase in the profit-maximizing level of output leads to an increase in the amount of an input a producer employs, we say that the input is a *normal input*. In Figure 8–16, both capital and labor are normal inputs since, as the firm moves from B to C, more of both inputs are used. We call an input an *inferior input* if an increase in the profit-maximizing level of output leads to a decrease in the amount of the input the producer employs. Using

OPTIMAL EMPLOYMENT AND CHANGES IN FACTOR PRICES **FIGURE 8–16**

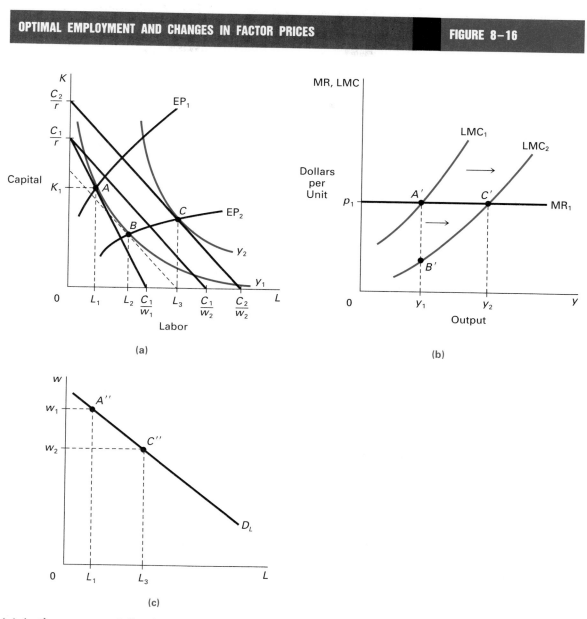

(a) As the wage rate falls, the LMC curve shifts to the right and the profit-maximizing output rate increases to y_2. (b) In order to increase output to y_2 units, the firm now expands along the new expansion path EP_2. When it produces y_2 units, it employs L_3 units of labor. (c) The long-run input demand curve for a competitive firm is negatively sloped; that is, quantity demanded increases as the wage rate falls.

mathematics beyond the scope of our current discussion, it is possible to show that input demand curves are negatively sloped for both normal and inferior inputs; that is, for example, a profit-maximizing firm will always employ more labor at a lower wage and less at a higher wage.

MARGINAL REVENUE
PRODUCT AND THE LONG-
RUN INPUT DEMAND
CURVE

How does the long-run input demand curve compare with the marginal revenue product curve? To demonstrate the relation between the MRP_L and D_L, let's suppose a firm is initially using the profit-maximizing quantities of capital and labor. As shown in Figure 8–17, given a wage of w_1 dollars per unit of labor, this firm employs L_1 units of labor, corresponding to point A on MRP_L^1. Note also that the firm is using K_1 units of capital.

Now let's suppose that the wage rate falls to w_2 dollars per unit of labor. If capital were to remain constant at K_1 units, then the firm would increase its use of labor to L_2; that is, the firm would move along MRP_L^1 from A to B. This, however, does not represent the

FIGURE 8–17	MARGINAL REVENUE PRODUCT AND THE LONG-RUN INPUT DEMAND CURVE

When all inputs are variable, the MRP_L curve shifts with changes in the quantity of capital used in the production process. The long-run input demand curve for labor, D_L, takes into account the change in the amount of capital the firm employs.

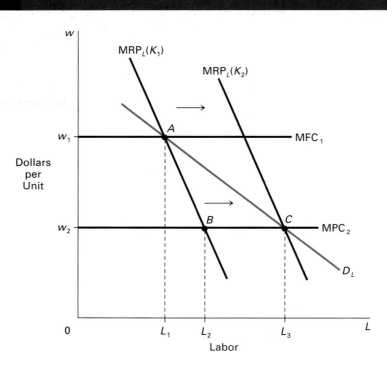

firm's complete adjustment to the change in the wage rate; usually the firm *will* change the amount of capital it uses.

There are two possibilities to consider. The first possibility arises when inputs are *technical complements*. This is the case if an increase in the quantity of one leads to an increase in the marginal product of the other. This is thought to be typical of most real-world technologies.

If capital and labor are technical complements, then when the firm uses more labor (the move from A to B in Figure 8–17), the marginal product of capital increases *and* the firm uses *more* capital. An increase in the quantity of capital, however, causes the marginal revenue product curve to shift from MRP_L^1 to MRP_L^2; since the marginal product of labor has increased. This, in turn, leads to a further increase in the labor force (the move from B to C in the diagram). Thus, the full adjustment to the lower wage is an increase in the labor force from L_1 to L_3. Connecting points A and C gives the firm's long-run demand curve for labor. At each point on this curve, the firm increases its labor force up to the point where the marginal revenue product of labor is equal to the marginal factor cost; however, along this demand curve we are also allowing the firm to adjust its use of capital to the profit-maximizing level.

The second possibility arises when inputs are *technical substitutes*. This is the case if an increase in the quantity of one leads to a decrease in the marginal product of the other. If capital and labor are technical substitutes, then when the firm uses more labor (the move from A to B in Figure 8–17), the marginal product of capital decreases and *less* capital is used. However, when inputs are technical substitutes, a reduction in the quantity of capital increases the marginal product of labor so that the MRP_L curve shifts to the right just as before. Thus, in either case the long-run input demand curve is negatively sloped.

What can cause a firm's input demand curve to change? Input demand curves will shift when the price of the firm's output, the prices and quantities of other inputs, or the technology change. Here we will consider the most important variable affecting input demand—that is, output price.

CHANGES IN OUTPUT PRICE

Focusing our attention on normal inputs, we see in Figure 8–18(a) a price-taking firm's long-run marginal cost curve for given factor prices. The profit-maximizing output rate is y_1.

In Figure 8–18(b), the isoquant and isocost curve illustrate the cost-minimizing combination of inputs to employ if a firm wants to produce y_1 units of output. The firm minimizes its costs when it uses L_1 units of labor and K_1 units of capital in the production process.

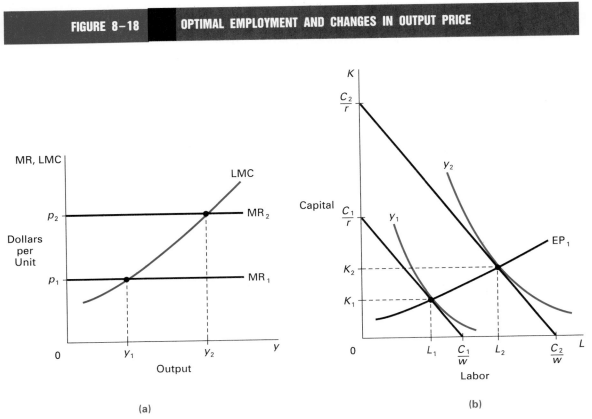

FIGURE 8-18   OPTIMAL EMPLOYMENT AND CHANGES IN OUTPUT PRICE

(a) As output price increases from p_1 to p_2, the profit-maximizing output rate increases from y_1 to y_2. (b) The firm increases output by moving out along expansion path EP_1. When production is at y_2, it employs K_2 units of capital and L_2 units of labor.

Now suppose the price of the product produced and sold by this firm increases to p_2. The profit-maximizing output will increase from y_1 to y_2, as the diagram shows. Given this new profit-maximizing output level, the firm expands production along expansion path EP_1. The owners minimize their costs when they employ the input bundle consisting of L_2 units of labor and K_2 units of capital. An increase in the output price increases the amount of each input the firm employs which, in turn, shifts the input demand curves to the right as is shown in Figure 8-18(c).

Another way to see this is to remember that MRP is simply the product price times marginal product. If the product price rises, this leads to an increase in the marginal revenue product of each input and the MRP curves shift to the right. That is, given factor costs, the firm will use more of each input because its value to the firm has increased. As a result of the shift in the MRP curves, both the short- and long-run input demand curves will also shift to the right.

SUMMARY

1. Four properties characterize a perfectly competitive market: all producers and consumers are price-takers; products or resources are homogeneous across sellers; buyers and sellers have perfect information; and all resources are perfectly mobile.

2. For the output decision, profit maximization requires that the owners of firms choose the output rate for which marginal revenue—price for the competitive firm—is just equal to marginal cost.

3. For the input decision, profit maximization requires that firms use inputs up to the point where marginal revenue product is equal to marginal factor cost.

4. The optimal output supply and input demand in the short run are not affected by fixed costs. However, fixed costs do affect the level of profit or loss and are used to determine shutdown output rate. The shutdown point is the rate of output that yields a loss just equal to fixed costs.

5. The firm's short-run supply curve is the short-run marginal cost curve, provided the firm produces a positive amount of output.

6. In the long run, the supply curve is the long-run marginal cost curve above the minimum point of the long-run average cost curve. In both the short and long runs the law of supply prevails; that is, the supply curve is positively sloped.

7. The firm's short-run input demand curve is the marginal revenue product curve, provided the firm produces a positive amount of output. In the long run, an input demand curve is found by equating marginal revenue product to marginal factor cost while allowing the firm to adjust all inputs optimally. In both the short and long runs, input demand curves are negatively sloped.

KEY TERMS

Perfect Competition

Marginal Revenue

Shutdown and Breakeven
  Points

Short- and Long-Run Supply
  Curves

Law of Supply

Marginal Revenue Product

Marginal Factor Cost

Short- and Long-Run Input
  Demand Curves

QUESTION AND PROBLEMS

1. For a competitive firm, explain why marginal revenue is equal to price.

2. For a price-taking firm, explain why profit maximization implies that $p = SMC$ in the short run and that $p = LMC$ in the long run.

3. Compucenter purchased 3,000 PC/XT systems boards for $200 each. Currently these boards sell for $100. One Compucenter manager has suggested that the firm combine each board with

$700 worth of labor and other supplies to produce a PC it could sell for $900. Should the owners of Compucenter follow this plan of action? Explain.

4. Suppose that a competitive firm has cost curves given by

$$STC = 200 + 5y + y^2 \quad \text{and} \quad SMC = 5 + 2y.$$

a) If the market price for good y is $25, what is the profit-maximizing output rate?

b) How large is profit?

c) If the price doubles, how do your calculations change?

5. An economic consultant for the Peabody Manufacturing Corporation, a manufacturer of yoyos, has determined that the total and marginal cost functions for the company are

$$STC = 200 + 5y - .2y^2 + .01y^3 \quad \text{and}$$

$$SMC = 5 - .4y + .03y^2$$

where y is the number of yoyos produced each year.

a) What are fixed costs?

b) Determine the rate of output corresponding to minimum average variable cost (remembering that SMC = AVC at the minimum point).

c) Determine the profit-maximizing output rate as a function of the market price.

d) Explain why profit is not maximized at the rate of output corresponding to minimum average total cost.

6. Harry's Hack Sack, Inc., has the following cost functions:

$$STC = 400 + 2.5y - 3y^2 + .002y^3 \quad \text{and}$$

$$SMC = 2.5 - 6y + .006y^2$$

where y is the number of Hack Sacks produced each month. Currently Harry is producing 2,000 hack sacks per month. If the price of a Hack Sack is $2.50, is Harry maximizing profit? Explain.

7. Sure Cook, Inc., manufactures and sells microwave ovens in the Phoenix metropolitan area. The average price of a microwave oven in the Phoenix area is $300. The owner of Sure Cook estimates that short-run total and marginal costs are given by

$$STC = .004y^3 - .9y^2 + 300y + 750 \quad \text{and}$$

$$SMC = .012y^2 - 1.9y + 300$$

where y is the number of microwaves produced each month.

    a) Find the shutdown point.

    b) What is the profit-maximizing output rate?

8. a) Compare quasi-fixed costs, fixed costs, and sunk costs.

    b) Do any of these costs affect the profit maximization decision? Explain.

9. Hi-Tech, Inc., is a small California-based firm that produces a scientific word-processing software package for PCs called EROS. The owners of the firm are profit maximizers. The accounting department has prepared the following estimates of fixed and variable costs of the new version.

Fixed Costs:		
Mortgage payments	$100,000	
Equipment	9,000	
Property taxes	2,000	
Total		$112,000
Quasi-Fixed Costs:		
Program development	$520,000	
Manual revisions	15,000	
Advertising	10,000	
Total		$545,000
Variable costs per unit:		
Eight floppy disks	$8	
Packaging costs	1	
Shipping costs	1	
Printing of manual	5	
Total		$15

EROS sells for $450. Given the current level of fixed inputs, Hi-Tech can produce a maximum of 5,000 units.

    a) What is the profit-maximizing output rate?

    b) Find the market price that would just make it worthwhile to manufacture EROS.

10. Suppose that the government institutes a regulation requiring firms to provide safety glasses for workers.

    a) Show how this regulation will affect a firm's short-run cost curves.

    b) Determine this regulation's effect on the short-run profit-maximizing output rate and the profit-maximizing quantity of labor.

11. Determine the impact of a profit tax on the profit-maximizing output rate in the short run and the long run.

12. a) Define marginal revenue product.

    b) "If the MRP_L is less than the wage rate, the firm should lower the wage rate until the two are equal." Does this statement explain the way a price-taking firm maximizes profit?

13. Window Specialists, Inc., is a window-cleaning firm. The number of windows that it can clean per day is $y = 500\sqrt{L}$, where L is the number of window washers hired per day. The marginal product of labor is $MP_L = 250/\sqrt{L}$. The market price for window cleaning is \$5 per window.

    a) Assuming that Window Specialists is a perfect competitor, determine the profit-maximizing number of workers if the wage rate is \$50 per day.

    b) If the wage rate doubles, does the firm hire more workers? Explain.

14. Kelly's Plastics manufactures dishwasher safe plastic dinnerware. Kelly's long run total and marginal cost curves are given by

$$LTC = 500y - 20y^2 + y^3 \quad \text{and} \quad LMC = 3y^2 - 40y + 500.$$

    a) If the price of the good is \$500, how much output should Kelly's produce?

    b) At this output rate, will Kelly's stay in business? Explain.

15. Suppose the owners of a firm are maximizing profit in the long run.

    a) What happens to the average and marginal cost curves if the government imposes an excise tax of \$$t$ per unit sold on producers?

    b) What happens to the short-run supply curve?

    c) What happens to the input demand curves?

16. Repeat Problem 15 when the government imposes a tax on capital of \$$q$ per unit of capital employed.

17. Explain the substitution and output effects associated with an increase in the wage rate.

18. a) Analyze the impact of a payroll tax on the quantity of labor employed by a price-taking firm in the long run. (A payroll tax is a tax levied on firms per dollar spent on labor.)

    b) What does this tell you about how the tax affects the long-run demand curve for labor?

REFERENCES

Baumol, W. 1977. *Economic Theory and Operations Analysis.* 4th ed. Englewood Cliffs: Prentice-Hall.

Kreps, D. 1990. *A Course in Microeconomic Theory.* Princeton: Princeton University Press.

Varian, H. 1992. *Microeconomic Analysis.* 3rd ed. New York: Norton.

PROFIT MAXIMIZATION: A CALCULUS APPROACH

APPENDIX

A8.1 PROFIT MAXIMIZATION AND OUTPUT

Using calculus makes profit maximization problems very simple. We can summarize the profit maximization problem discussed in Section 7.2 as follows:

$$\max_{y} \pi = py - TC(y).$$

The first order condition for this unconstrained optimization problem is

$$\frac{\partial \pi}{\partial y} = p - \frac{\partial TC}{\partial y} = 0$$

and the second order condition is

$$\frac{\partial^2 \pi}{\partial y^2} = -\frac{\partial^2 TC}{\partial y^2} = -\frac{\partial MC}{\partial y} < 0.$$

The first order condition implies that price equals marginal cost and the second order condition says that the marginal cost must be increasing (thus guaranteeing that we have a maximum and not a minimum). Solving the first order condition for y gives the profit-maximizing output y^* as a function of price or, in other words, the firm's supply function. Of course, this discussion assumes that $y^* > 0$. If price is less than AVC at y^*, the firm should shut down and produce no output.

A8.2 PROFIT MAXIMIZATION AND INPUTS

We can summarize the profit maximization problem discussed in Section 8.5 as follows:

$$\max_{L,K} \pi = pF(K,L) - wL - rK.$$

The first order conditions for this unconstrained optimization problem are

$$\frac{\partial \pi}{\partial L} = p\frac{\partial F}{\partial L} - w = 0 \quad \text{and} \quad \frac{\partial \pi}{\partial K} = p\frac{\partial F}{\partial K} - r = 0.$$

These first order conditions imply that a firm should hire inputs up to the point where marginal revenue product is equal to marginal factor cost. Solving these two equations for L and K gives the profit-maximizing inputs L^* and K^* as functions of prices or, in other words, the firm's input demand functions.

EXAMPLE A8–1

Suppose the production function $y = F(K,L) = L^{1/2} + K^{1/2}$ represents a competitive firm's technology. In this instance, the first order conditions are

$$(p/2)L^{-1/2} - w = 0 \quad \text{and} \quad (p/2)K^{-1/2} - r = 0.$$

Solving these equations for K and L gives

$$L^* = (p/2w)^2 \quad \text{and} \quad K^* = (p/2r)^2.$$

These are the firm's input demand functions. Notice that factor demands are negatively related to factor prices and positively related to output price.

To obtain the firm's supply function, we substitute L^* and K^* into the production function:

$$y^* = (L^*)^{1/2} + (K^*)^{1/2} = (p/2)[(1/w) + (1/r)].$$

Thus, output is postively related to output price (the supply curve is upward-sloping) and negatively related to factor prices. ■

MARKET STRUCTURE AND PRICE

■ *Part 4 brings together the analyses of consumers and producers to explain how prices are determined. The first three chapters in this part focus on the perfectly competitive model. Here we assume that buyers and sellers are price takers; that is, they make their decisions based on the belief that they cannot affect market prices. Essentially, these chapters complete the supply and demand model of a market economy and provide invaluable insights into how markets work.*

■ Many markets, however, are dominated by a few firms. In these instances, the competitive model does not always explain and predict market behavior very well. The last three chapters in this part investigate the implications of dropping the price-taker assumption. The material in these chapters will help us understand business firms' pricing strategies.

■ Chapter 9 shows how the supply and demand model can explain the way market prices and quantities are determined in competitive output markets. Once again, economic profit takes center stage and much of the chapter is devoted to explaining the role it plays in encouraging firms to enter or exit a market. Chapter 9 also investigates how equilibrium prices and quantities change when economic conditions change.

■ Chapter 10 shows how the supply and demand model can explain the way market prices and levels of employment are determined in competitive input markets. While this chapter focuses on one of the most important factors of production—labor—much of the theory applies to any input. After completing this chapter we will have a better understanding of such important issues as how an increase in the Social Security payroll tax will affect wage rates and employment, why professors are typically paid less than their private sector counterparts, and why some resources earn large economic rents.

■ Chapter 11 applies the competitive model to a variety of economic issues. This chapter investigates the effects of taxes, wage and price controls, technological innovations, and trade restrictions on producers, consumers, and resource owners. This chapter brings to full light the significance and power of the supply and demand model.

■ Chapter 12 begins our investigation of markets for which the competitive model does not apply. The first part of the chapter analyzes the case of a single seller, called a monopoly. A monopoly faces the market demand curve and can choose on it whichever price–quantity combination maximizes profit. The second part of the chapter examines the case of a single buyer, called a monopsony. A monopsony faces the market supply curve and can choose on it whichever price–quantity combination maximizes profit. Monopoly and monopsony are the most extreme forms of market power.

■ Chapter 13 applies the theory of monopoly to several real-world economic problems. This chapter examines the consequences of regulating monopolies such as electric companies. It also shows how a monopoly can increase profit by charging different types of buyers different prices and how a monopoly can increase profit and efficiency by charging different prices at different times. Finally, Chapter 13 investigates the most important type of monopoly in an input market — the labor union.

■ Chapter 14 considers cases where there are only a few sellers. This makes things considerably more complicated because, in general, each seller's demand curve then depends to a certain extent on its rivals' behavior — the demand curve for Apple personal computers, for instance, depends on what IBM and COMPAQ do. This chapter explores a variety of models based on different assumptions about how one firm believes its rivals will behave. These types of models have many applications to the real world. For example, they can help us understand why, in deciding what prices to charge for its new Saturn line of cars, it was important for General Motors to consider how Japanese car manufacturers would respond to the Saturn. Chapter 14 also examines situations where firms collude in an attempt to extract monopoly profits. The OPEC cartel is an important example of this type of market structure.

THE THEORY OF PRICE FOR COMPETITIVE OUTPUT MARKETS

9

LEARNING OBJECTIVES

After completing Chapter 9 you should be able to do the following:

■ Compare short- and long-run competitive equilibrium.

■ Derive the short-run market supply curve and explain how to determine the equilibrium price and quantity.

■ Explain why the long-run market supply curve is horizontal for a constant cost industry, positively sloped for an increasing cost industry, and negatively sloped for a decreasing cost industry.

■ Discuss economic rent and why it can be used to measure the gains from trade accruing to resource owners.

EXAMPLES

■ **9–1** Short-Run Competitive Equilibrium: The Lettuce Market

■ **9–2** Deriving the Long-Run Market Supply Curve

■ **9–3** Rising Mortgage Rates and Economic Rents

So far we have focused on the individual elements of the supply and demand model of a market economy. In Chapters 3−5 we were concerned with the behavior of consumers. In Chapters 6−8 we focused on the behavior of producers. Now it is time to put the two together to complete the supply and demand model. In the next three chapters we concentrate on the competitive industry. We will use what we learned in the preceding chapters to understand how the interaction of buyers and sellers determines market prices and quantities in competitive markets.

In this chapter, we will explain how market demand and supply interact to determine equilibrium prices and quantities for *outputs*. This is called the *neoclassical theory of value* and it is concerned with the way in which supply and demand determine the values, or prices, of goods and services and the quantities of goods and services that are bought and sold.

■ Our first task in this section is to determine the short-run market supply curve. The **short-run market supply curve** gives the total quantities supplied by all firms in an industry at each possible price. In order to derive the short-run market supply curve we will make two additional assumptions: (i) each firm in the industry under consideration has exactly the same cost curves; and (ii) firms in the industry can purchase (or rent) the needed amounts of variable inputs without bidding up their prices.

9.1 SHORT-RUN COMPETITIVE EQUILIBRIUM

If the prices of the variable inputs are constant, deriving the short-run market supply curve is a straightforward task. In the short run a competitive firm operates at the output rate corresponding to the point where price is equal to marginal cost, provided price is greater than the minimum of the average variable cost curve. As we demonstrated earlier, the short-run supply curve for an individual firm is simply that portion of the short-run marginal cost curve above the average variable cost curve.

In Figure 9−1(a) we have drawn the SMC curve for a representative firm in the lettuce industry. Price p_0 corresponds to the minimum of the AVC curve. If the price of lettuce falls below p_0, the firm cannot cover all of its variable costs and shuts down. Now suppose there are 100 identical lettuce growers. They are identical in the sense that they operate using the same technology and, hence, the same cost curves. If the price is just equal to p_0, then each firm in the industry produces y_0 bushels of lettuce. Market supply is in this instance $Y_0 = 100y_0$; that is, market supply is the sum of the quantities produced by each firm.

THE SHORT-RUN MARKET SUPPLY CURVE

FIGURE 9–1   **THE SHORT-RUN MARKET SUPPLY CURVE**

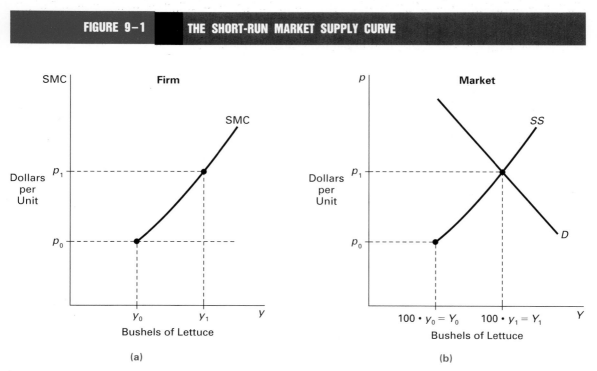

(a) SMC is the short-run marginal cost curve above the minimum point of the AVC curve. At a price of p_0, output for the typical firm is y_0 bushels of lettuce; at a price of p_1, output is y_1 units. (b) The short-run market supply curve is the horizontal sum of the individual firms' supply curves. In the short run, the equilibrium price and quantity are determined by equating supply and demand.

If the price increases to p_1, each firm expands production to y_1. Since input costs do not change, the marginal cost curve does not change, and market supply is $Y_1 = 100y_1$. Repeating this process for all possible prices, we map out the short-run market supply curve shown in Figure 9–1(b). This curve, labeled SS in the diagram, is upward-sloping and is usually equal to the horizontal sum of the individual firms' supply curves. The short-run market supply curve shows the amount of output that the industry will produce in the short run for every possible price.

The short-run market supply curve is not always the sum of the individual firms' supply curves. As output price rises, all profit-maximizing firms expand production, causing demand for inputs to rise. If this increase in demand for inputs causes input prices to rise, then each firm's marginal cost curve shifts up. For any given market price, the upward shift in marginal cost curves lowers each firm's profit-maximizing output level. As a result, the market supply curve is less responsive to changes in output price than it would be if input prices were constant. Nonetheless, even in this instance the short-run market supply curve will be positively sloped.

We have now arrived at the point where many Principles courses begin: supply and demand analysis. Supply and demand analysis offers significant insights into the way in which real-world market economies function. It is a tool that has withstood the test of time as a paradigm capable of explaining and predicting the changes in price and quantity that arise when competitive markets are subjected to a change in the economic environment.

Before we can determine equilibrium price and quantity, we must understand what economists mean by competitive equilibrium. An *equilibrium point* is defined as *a state of nature which, if attained, will be maintained*. It is a point from which there is no tendency for change. In the short run a perfectly competitive market is said to be in equilibrium if three conditions are satisfied: consumers are maximizing satisfaction; producers are maximizing profit; and supply is equal to demand. **Short-run competitive equilibrium** is an allocation of resources corresponding to the intersection of the short-run market demand and supply curves. In the short run we determine the equilibrium price and quantity by equating supply and demand.

In Figure 9–1(b) we have included the market demand curve for lettuce, labeled D. Given this demand curve, the equilibrium price and quantity are p_1 and Y_1 respectively. In this instance, each individual firm will produce at the point where $p_1 = SMC$. Thus, each firm will produce y_1 bushels of lettuce. This is also assumed to be a stable equilibrium point. For any price below p_1, quantity demanded is greater than quantity supplied, there is excess demand for lettuce, and the price is bid up. For any price above p_1, quantity supplied is greater than quantity demanded, there is an excess supply of lettuce, and the price is bid down. The market is in balance again when quantity supplied is equal to quantity demanded, or when y_1 bushels are traded at p_1 dollars per bushel.

The mechanics of supply and demand analysis are indeed straightforward; however, using these tools to gain insights into the functioning of real-world markets requires practice and more practice! Example 9–1 below illustrates how to determine the short-run equilibrium price and quantity and how they change in response to a change in the economic environment.

PRICE AND QUANTITY IN THE SHORT RUN

EXAMPLE 9–1

SHORT-RUN COMPETITIVE EQUILIBRIUM: THE LETTUCE MARKET
Suppose that the market demand curve for lettuce is given by

$$Y = D_1(p) = 150,000 - 5,000p$$

where Y is the number of bushels of lettuce demanded per year and
p is the price per bushel. In addition, suppose that the lettuce
industry is a perfectly competitive industry consisting of 10
identical firms with cost curves given by

$$STC = .001y^2 + 10y + 1000 \qquad \text{and}$$

$$SMC = .002y + 10.$$

where y represents the number of bushels of lettuce produced by
the representative firm. (a) Determine the short-run market supply
curve, graph the supply and demand curves, and illustrate
graphically the equilibrium price and quantity. (b) Determine
algebraically the equilibrium price and quantity, the output rate for
each firm, and profit for each firm, (or, in other words, for the
representative firm). (c) In the 1970s a consumer boycott of the
lettuce industry in the U.S. was organized to protest the treatment
of migrant workers. Suppose that such a boycott led to less
demand. If the resulting demand curve was

$$Y = D_2(p) = 100,000 - 5,000p,$$

determine the new equilibrium price and quantity, the new output,
and the new profit for each firm.

■ **SOLUTION** (a) Since this is a competitive industry, the short-run
market supply curve is the horizontal sum of the individual firms'
supply curves. To find the supply curve for the representative firm
we must (i) find the shutdown point and (ii) set price equal to
marginal cost and solve for output. The shutdown point is
determined by the minimum point of the average variable cost
curve. In this case, $AVC = .001y + 10$. Both SMC and AVC are
shown in Figure 9–2(a). They are both straight lines that intersect
the vertical axis at 10. This means that the shutdown point is $10;
that is, if the price of lettuce falls below $10 per bushel, the firm
will supply no output.

EQUILIBRIUM IN THE LETTUCE MARKET　　　　　**FIGURE 9–2**

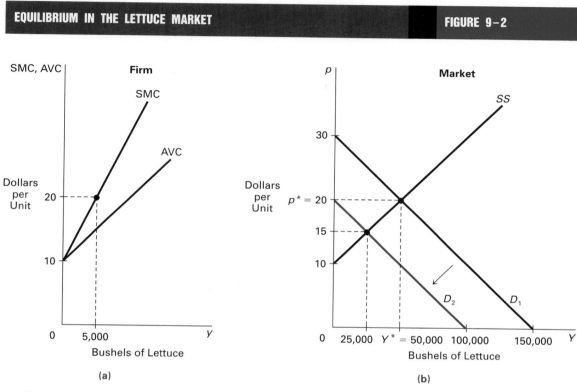

(a) When the market price is $20 per bushel, each firm in the lettuce industry produces 5,000 bushels per year and earns positive economic profit. (b) In the short run, the equilibrium price and quantity are $20 per bushel and 50,000 bushels per year. The consumer boycott shifts the market demand curve in from D_1 to D_2. The equilibrium price falls from $20 to $15 per bushel and the equilibrium quantity falls from 50,000 to 25,000 bushels per year.

Now we know that for prices greater than or equal to $10 per bushel, the representative firm's supply curve is found by setting price equal to marginal cost and solving for output. Here we have $p = .002y + 10$ or $y^* = 500p - 5,000$, which is the short-run supply curve for all prices greater than $10.

Each of the 10 firms in this industry are identical, meaning that the market supply curve is simply 10 times an individual firm's supply curve. Thus, the market supply curve is

$$Y = SS(p) = 10(y^*) = 5,000p - 50,000.$$

The market supply and demand curves are shown in Figure 9–2(b). The demand curve has a price intercept of $30 while the supply curve has a price intercept of $10. The equilibrium price and quantity are determined by the intersection of the supply and demand curves. In Figure 9–2(b) the equilibrium price and quantity are denoted p^* and Y^* respectively.

(b) Next we are asked to find algebraically the equilibrium price and quantity, the output rate for each firm, and profit for each firm. To find the equilibrium price and quantity, we set supply equal to demand and solve for price:

$$D_1 = 150{,}000 - 5{,}000p = 5{,}000p - 50{,}000 = SS \qquad \text{or}$$

$$10{,}000p - 200{,}000 = 0.$$

Solving this for price gives $p^* = \$20$ per bushel of lettuce; that is, when the market is in equilibrium lettuce will trade at $20 per bushel.

We find the equilibrium quantity by substituting $20 into either the demand or supply curves and solving for Y. Using the demand curve we find $Y^* = 150{,}000 - 5{,}000 \cdot 20 = 50{,}000$ bushels of lettuce.

Output and profit for an individual firm follow directly from there. Since all firms are the same, each firm supplies one tenth of the market or 5,000 bushels of lettuce. We can verify this by noting that when the price of lettuce is $20 per bushel, each firm supplies $y^* = 500 \cdot 20 - 5{,}000 = 10{,}000 - 5{,}000 = 5{,}000$ bushels of lettuce. Profit is revenue minus total costs, meaning that each firm earns a positive economic profit equal to $100{,}000 - 76{,}000 = \$24{,}000$.

(c) Our last task is to determine the impact of a boycott on the equilibrium price and quantity. The boycott shifts the demand curve but does not change the short-run market supply curve. Setting demand equal to supply now gives

$$100{,}000 - 5{,}000p = 5{,}000p - 50{,}000.$$

Solving this equation for p gives the new market price for lettuce: $p_1 = \$15$ per bushel of lettuce. Substituting into the shifted demand curve gives the new quantity: $Y_1 = 100{,}000 - 5{,}000 \cdot 15 = 25{,}000$ bushels of lettuce. Each firm in the industry will now produce 2,500 bushels of lettuce and earn a positive economic profit of $2{,}500 \cdot 15 = 37{,}500 - 32{,}250 = \$5{,}250$.

These calculations are illustrated in Figure 9–2(b). The boycott shifts the demand curve inward, which leads to a reduction in price, industry output, firm output, and profit. ■

■ One of the conditions for perfect competition is that resources are perfectly mobile; that is, resources can be moved costlessly from one industry to another. Up until this point we have not used this condition in our discussions of competitive equilibrium. In the long run, costless entry and exit of firms into and out of an industry in response to profit incentives is the condition guaranteeing long-run competitive equilibrium.

9.2 LONG-RUN COMPETITIVE EQUILIBRIUM

Recall that in the short run a perfectly competitive market is in equilibrium if three conditions are met: consumers maximize satisfaction; producers maximize profit; and quantity supplied is equal to quantity demanded. In the long run one additional condition must be added to the list: firms earn zero economic profit.

THE ZERO PROFIT CONDITION

Suppose you are the owner of a firm that is currently earning zero economic profit. If firms in other industries are also earning zero economic profit, this means that you are doing as well as you could do in the next best alternative. However, what will you do if firms in another industry are earning positive economic profit? If this is the case, then the resources employed in that industry are earning a greater return than you are currently earning. If resources are perfectly mobile, you will liquidate your current business and transfer your resources to the industry that is realizing a positive profit. Alternatively, if firms in a particular industry are making economic losses, then there is an incentive to move out of that industry and into one which is earning at least zero economic profit.

The discussion above suggests what economists mean when they refer to long-run competitive equilibrium. In the long run a market or industry is in equilibrium only when entry and exit cease, and entry and exit will cease only when firms in the industry are earning zero economic profit. If a positive profit is realized, firms will be encouraged to enter the industry. If a loss is incurred, firms will be encouraged to exit. Only when profit is zero will firms have no incentive to exit or enter the industry. Thus, in addition to the conditions needed to attain a competitive equilibrium in the short run, in the long run profit must be zero. **Long-run competitive equilibrium** is an allocation of resources such that supply is equal to demand and economic profit is zero.

There seems to be one problem, however, with the competitive model discussed above. If firms know that eventually they will earn zero economic profit, why do they ever enter or exit a market? Of course, the answer is that in the short run there are substantial profits, or losses, to be made and it may take a long time for the market to reach a long-run competitive equilibrium. The first firm to enter a market where positive profits can be made will make a much greater short-run profit than firms entering later. Similarly, the first firm to exit a market where losses are being incurred will save much more than those exiting later.

Before leaving our discussion of the zero profit condition, it is important to remember the distinction between accounting profit and economic profit discussed in Chapter 6. Accounting profit is the difference between revenues and the explicit costs of production. Economic profit takes account of implicit costs as well. A firm earning zero economic profit may, in fact, be earning positive accounting profit. For example, suppose the owner of a firm develops a process that allows him or her to produce the same quality product as all the other firms in the industry at a lower average cost. In long-run equilibrium, this firm earns zero economic profit, just as does every other firm in the industry; however, it will earn a positive accounting profit. If the new process gives the firm a cost advantage, then other firms will be willing to pay for permission to use the process. As a result, there is an opportunity cost associated with exclusive use of the process; that is, the firm could sell the new process to another firm rather than keep it exclusive. This opportunity cost is an implicit cost of production and is not considered when calculating accounting profit. Thus, even though economic profit is zero in equilibrium, accounting profit is greater than zero.

The zero profit condition is essential for the attainment of long-run competitive equilibrium. Positive economic profit encourages entry since firms can do better than in the next best alternative. Positive accounting profit, however, does not necessarily encourage entry. It may simply indicate that a firm already in the industry has a valuable resource that other firms do not have.

9.3 THE LONG-RUN MARKET SUPPLY CURVE

■ Perhaps the best way to illustrate an industry's adjustment to long-run competitive equilibrium is to determine the long-run market supply curve. The **long-run market supply curve** is the collection of price–quantity pairs that satisfy the conditions for long-run competitive equilibrium. The precise shape of the long-run market supply curve depends on the assumptions we make about the shape of individual firms' cost curves, about the mobility of resources, and about the impact that changes in industry output have on factor prices. In the next three sections, we will derive the long-run market supply curve for three different types of industries by investigating how changes in the economic environment impact on the equilibrium price and quantity, and on the number of firms.

A **constant cost industry** is one in which input prices remain constant as industry output expands or contracts. Usually an industry is characterized by constant costs if it is a small employer relative to the entire input market or if it employs inputs that are not industry-specific. For example, consider the lettuce industry. Firms that produce lettuce use farmhands (oftentimes migrant workers) and farm machinery—inputs which the asparagus, bean, or onion industries can use just as easily. If output in the lettuce industry increases, then lettuce growers will need to employ more workhands and more tractors. In order to obtain these additional factors of production, lettuce growers will have to bid these resources away from asparagus, bean, and onion growers. If the lettuce industry is a constant cost industry, then this means that lettuce growers can obtain the additional farmhands and machinery they need without increasing the wage rate or price of tractors in any measurable way.

To derive the long-run market supply curve, we must specify precisely the type of industry we are considering. We begin with the simplest type of industry but, nonetheless, one that proves to be a very useful example. This type of industry exhibits three essential ingredients: it consists of several identical firms with U-shaped average cost curves; entry into and exit from it are costless; and it is a constant cost industry.

Figure 9–3 illustrates the process of determining the long-run market supply curve. Figure 9–3(a) illustrates the supply and demand conditions for the market as a whole; Figure 9–3(b) shows the cost curves for the representative firm. D_1 denotes the initial market demand curve and SS_1, the initial short-run market supply curve. The short-run competitive equilibrium in this market yields the price of p_1 dollars per unit of good Y and total output of Y_1 units. Given this price, the representative firm (see Figure 9–3[b]) maximizes profit by producing y_1 units of output. This short-run equilibrium is also a long-run competitive equilibrium since output price, p_1, is equal to LAC for each firm in the industry.

Now suppose demand for good Y increases. In Figure 9–3(a) the new demand curve is labeled D_2. What happens to the equilibrium price in the short run? As the demand curve shifts to the right, price rises to p_3 and firms already in the business increase production to meet the extra demand. This is represented by the movement from A to B in Figure 9–3(a) and from A' to B' in Figure 9–3(b). In the short run, therefore, price rises as demand increases.

Firms already in the business now earn positive economic profit when they operate at the new profit-maximizing output rate since

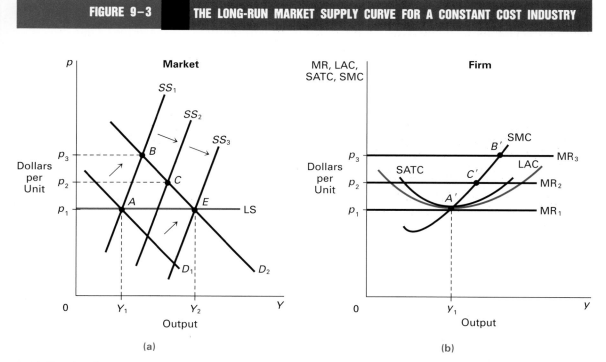

FIGURE 9–3   **THE LONG-RUN MARKET SUPPLY CURVE FOR A CONSTANT COST INDUSTRY**

Initially, the short-run equilibrium price and quantity are p_1 and Y_1 respectively. When demand increases from D_1 to D_2, both price and quantity increase in the short run as the movement from A to B shows. As a result of the higher price, firms earn positive economic profit which, in turn, leads to entry. As firms enter the market, the short-run supply curve shifts to the right until each firm earns zero economic profit once again. In the long run, quantity increases but the market price remains the same; that is, the long-run market supply curve is horizontal at p_1.

price, p_3, is greater than average cost. However, even though the owners of each firm are doing the best they can, the industry is not in long-run equilibrium. Resources employed in this industry are earning a greater return than in the next best alternative. Because firms are earning a profit, owners of firms in other industries are attracted to the good Y industry and entry occurs. As firms enter the market, industry output increases and the short-run supply curve shifts to the right. As industry output increases, price begins to fall. This is represented by the movement from B to C in Figure 9–3(a).

In Figure 9–3(a), SS_2 represents the new short-run industry supply curve. If entry ceases, the new short-run equilibrium price would be p_2, but still this would not represent a long-run equilibrium. If the market price for good Y were p_2 then each profit-maximizing firm would still earn a profit. This, in turn, would cause additional entry and the short-run supply curve would shift even further to the right.

How long does entry occur? Firms enter the market until any positive profit is eliminated. In Figure 9–3(a), SS_3 is the final short-run supply curve. The equilibrium price and quantity are now p_1 and Y_2 respectively. The industry has now attained an allocation of resources that characterizes long-run competitive equilibrium. As Figure 9–3(b) shows, when the market price is p_1 and production is y_1, each individual firm earns zero economic profit because price is equal to LAC. Thus, each firm is doing as well as it could do in the next best alternative, and its owners have no incentive to move their resources out of this business and into a different one.

Since this is a constant cost industry, the cost curves do not shift as industry output expands, and minimum long-run average cost remains unchanged. Thus, while in the short-run the market price rises in response to an increase in demand, the price falls to its original level when the industry is once again in long-run competitive equilibrium.

We can repeat this line of reasoning when demand falls rather than rises. When demand falls, short-run price and quantity also fall. Firms already in the business now incur economic losses. Resources employed in this industry are earning less than in the next best alternative. As a result, exit occurs. Owners of firms now have an incentive to move their resources out of this business and into a more profitable one.

The exiting firms cause the short-run supply curve to shift to the left which, in turn, causes the market price of good Y to rise. Price continues to rise until the industry is in long-run competitive equilibrium. Since this is a constant cost industry, cost curves are not affected by the fall in industry-wide output and the long-run equilibrium price is unchanged.

Thus, while in the short run the market price falls in response to a decrease in demand, the price rises to its original level when the industry is once again in long-run competitive equilibrium. For a constant cost industry, no matter if demand increases or decreases, in the long run the market price returns to its original level.

The adjustment process discussed above is the essence of long-run competitive equilibrium. We can add two important observations concerning the conditions that satisfy this equilibrium. First, it is *costless* entry and exit that drives economic profit to zero. If for some reason entry and exit are not costless—if resources are not perfectly mobile—then entry and exit can be restricted and long-run equilibrium will not be characterized by zero economic profit for all firms participating in the business. Second, when the zero economic profit condition is met, each firm in the industry is operating at the minimum point of their long-run average cost curves. This means that if we know or can estimate the LAC curve, then we know the equilibrium price that will emerge for a perfectly competitive industry. It is the price that corresponds to the minimum of the LAC curve.

We can use these results to illustrate the long-run market supply curve (also called the long-run industry supply curve). The long-run market supply curve indicates the relation between the market price and industry output when the market is in long-run equilibrium. In Figure 9–3, this curve is a horizontal line at p_1 dollars per unit of good Y. If entry is costless, firms are identical, and costs are constant, then the long-run market supply curve is always a horizontal line; that is, the industry can increase output without increasing the market price.

Note one final point here. Even when the short-run market supply curve is the horizontal summation of the individual firms' short-run supply curves, the long-run market supply curve is not the horizontal summation of the individual firms' long-run supply curves.

DETERMINING THE LONG-RUN MARKET SUPPLY CURVE FOR AN INCREASING COST INDUSTRY

An **increasing cost industry** is one for which input prices rise as industry output expands and fall as industry output contracts. Industries characterized by increasing costs are usually large employers of inputs or firms that employ industry-specific inputs. For example, consider the cotton industry. Firms that produce cotton use industry-specific machines to pick and gin cotton; that is, the machines are designed to perform only these highly specialized tasks and have little or no value in other industries. If output in the cotton industry increases, then cotton growers will need to employ more machines. In order to obtain these additional factors of production, input prices must rise to induce suppliers of cotton-farming equipment to supply more machines.

For a constant cost industry with identical firms and free entry, the long-run market supply curve is horizontal. However, for an increasing cost industry with identical firms and free entry, the long-run market supply curve is upward-sloping.

In order to demonstrate this result, consider A. M. LeVelle Microprocessor, Inc., a firm that develops, manufactures, and markets high-performance memory chips for personal computers. It is well known that the success of any company in this industry depends on whether or not the firm can attract and retain highly skilled scientists. This being the case, the memory chip industry is an increasing cost industry. Assume in this instance that the market for memory chips is perfectly competitive and consists of firms identical to A. M. LeVelle.

Now suppose that, during the past year, recent developments in the manufacturing of PCs reduces the price of these machines by 30%. A lower price for PCs leads to an increase in demand for memory chips since they are complementary goods. What will be the impact of this increase in demand on the equilibrium price and quantity of memory chips?

Figure 9−4(a) illustrates the supply and demand conditions for the market as a whole; Figure 9−4(b) shows the cost curves for the representative firm, A. M. LeVelle. SS_1 is the initial short-run supply curve and D_1 is the market demand curve.

THE LONG-RUN MARKET SUPPLY CURVE FOR AN INCREASING COST INDUSTRY

FIGURE 9−4

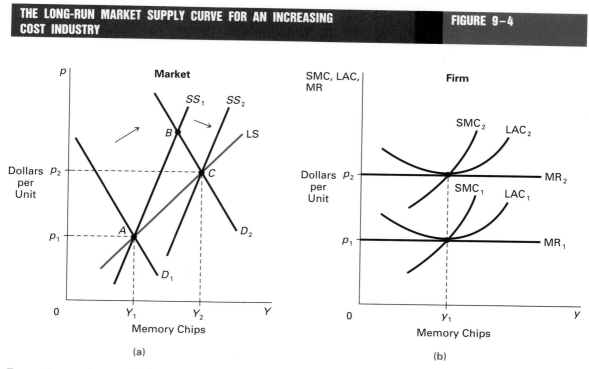

For an increasing cost industry, the long-run market supply curve, LS, is positively sloped since, as output expands, each firm's cost curves shift up.

The long-run equilibrium price and quantity are p_1 and Y_1 respectively and each firm in the business maximizes profit by producing y_1 memory chips. (Notice that firms are earning zero economic profit.)

Now suppose demand increases. In Figure 9–4 the new demand curve is labeled D_2. As with a constant cost industry, when the demand curve shifts to the right, price begins to rise in the short run as firms already in the business increase production to meet the extra demand. This short-run price increase is the movement from A to B in Figure 9–4(a).

As the price rises, firms in the business earn positive economic profit when they operate at the new profit-maximizing output rate. This means that the memory chip business attracts new firms and the short-run market supply curve shifts to the right. As industry output increases, prices begin to fall until firms are earning zero economic profit. This is the movement from B to C. However, since this is an increasing cost industry, price does not fall to the original level of p_1 dollars per chip. As industry output increases, firms must bid away firm-specific factors of production—in this case, highly skilled scientists—either from other firms in this business or from a closely related business. This, in turn, means that the prices of these factors of production increase, leading to an upward shift in each firm's cost curves.

In Figure 9–4(b), an upward shift in LeVelle's cost curves represents the increase in factor costs. In particular, the LAC curve shifts from LAC_1 to LAC_2. Notice that, in this instance, the minimum points of LAC_1 and LAC_2 both occur at an output rate of y_1 units. This need not be the case. The LAC curve could have shifted up and to the left or up and to the right. The only difference would have been in the optimal output rate for firms that continue to produce memory chips.

As we can see from the diagram, the new long-run equilibrium price is p_2 which is higher than it was before the change in demand. Thus, for an increasing costs industry the market price increases if demand increases and falls if demand falls: price does not return to its original level as it did for a constant cost industry.

The long-run market supply curve, LS in Figure 9–4(a), is a positively sloped line. If entry is costless, firms are identical, and costs are increasing, then the long-run market supply curve is always upward-sloping. The industry produces more output in response to an increase in demand but only if the market price of the good being examined increases. (The appendix to this chapter illustrates how to calculate the equilibrium price, quantity, and number of firms for an increasing cost industry.)

FIGURE 9–5   **THE LONG-RUN MARKET SUPPLY CURVE FOR A DECREASING COST INDUSTRY**

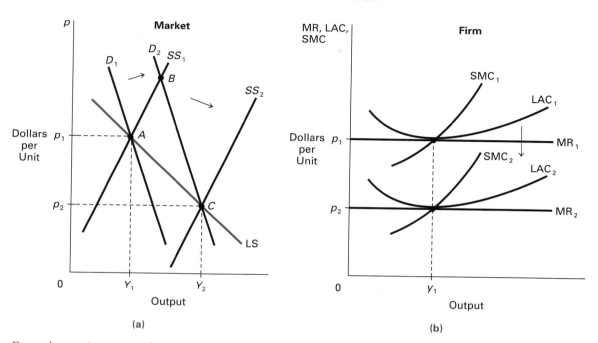

For a decreasing cost industry, the long-run market supply curve, LS, is negatively sloped, since each firm's cost curves shift down as output expands.

A **decreasing cost industry** is one in which input prices fall as industry output expands and rise as industry output contracts. The long-run market supply curve is downward-sloping for a decreasing cost industry.

While a negatively sloped long-run market supply curve is a theoretical possibility, it is a vary rare occurrence in the real world. This being the case, we will discuss it only briefly.

The case of a decreasing cost industry is shown in Figure 9–5, which, like earlier graphs in this chapter, illustrates the market first and then the representative firm. Initially, the long-run equilibrium price and quantity are p_1 and Y_1 respectively. Now suppose demand increases from D_1 to D_2. When the demand curve shifts to the right, price begins to rise in the short run as firms already in the business increase production to meet the extra demand. This short-run increase in price is the movement from A to B in Figure 9–5(a).

THE LONG-RUN MARKET SUPPLY CURVE FOR A DECREASING COST INDUSTRY

As the price rises, firms in the business earn positive economic profit and the industry expands. As industry output increases, the prices of some inputs used in the production process actually decline leading to a downward shift in the cost curves of each firm. The new long-run equilibrium price is p_2, which is lower than it was before the change in demand. Thus, for a decreasing cost industry the market price falls if demand increases and increases if demand falls. The long-run market supply curve, *LS* in Figure 9–5(a), is negatively sloped. The industry produces more output in response to an increase in demand and does so for a lower market price.

The difficult part of this analysis is to explain why a firm's cost curves would ever shift down as industry output expands. Remember, if we observe a fall in price and an increase in quantity in the long run, this is not necessarily evidence that we have found a decreasing cost industry. In a decreasing cost industry, price falls as a direct result of the effect of industry-wide expansion on input prices. However, it may be the case that the long-run average cost curve is shifting down because of technological innovations. This phenomenon occurred in the television market in the 1970s and in the personal computer market in the 1980s. Decreasing cost industries, like Giffen goods, are a theoretical possibility, but if they do exist, they are very rare. Thus, the constant cost and increasing cost cases are used almost exclusively for analyzing real-world markets.

The next example illustrates how to determine the long-run market supply curve for a constant cost industry, given particular cost curves for firms in that industry.

EXAMPLE 9–2

DERIVING THE LONG-RUN MARKET SUPPLY CURVE

Franco Brothers, Inc., manufactures and sells bicycles. Franco's total and marginal cost functions are given by

$$LTC = .0005y^3 - .5y^2 + 500y \qquad \text{and}$$

$$LMC = .0015y^2 - y + 500$$

where y is the number of bicycles produced and sold each year. The market for bicycles is a perfectly competitive constant cost industry consisting of firms identical to Franco Brothers. (a) Determine the long-run equilibrium price, quantity, and number of firms if the market demand curve is given by

$$Y = D_1(p) = 57{,}500 - 20p.$$

(b) In the last few years, individuals have become health conscious. As a result, the demand for bicycles has increased. Determine the long-run equilibrium price, quantity, and number of firms if the new market demand curve is

$$Y = D_2(p) = 107{,}500 - 20p.$$

(c) Illustrate each of your calculations with a graph and show that the long-run market supply curve is a horizontal line at the long-run equilibrium price.

■ **SOLUTION** (a) Since all firms in the industry are identical and there is free entry, the industry is in long-run competitive equilibrium when each firm earns zero economic profit. Each firm earns zero economic profit when the market price of bicycles is equal to the minimum of the LAC curve. Thus, if we can find the minimum of the LAC curve we will know what the equilibrium price must be.

We begin by finding the output rate corresponding to the point where LAC attains its minimum value. Recall that LMC = LAC when LAC is a minimum. Setting LMC equal to LAC gives:

$$.0015y^2 - y + 500 = .0005y^2 - .5y + 500.$$

Solving this equation for y we have

$$.001y^2 - .5y = y(.001y - .5) = 0$$

or $y^* = 500$. Hence, in equilibrium each firm produces 500 bicycles per year since LAC attains its minimum value at that output rate.

In order to determine the equilibrium price, we must determine average cost when output is 500. Substituting 500 into the equation for LAC gives

$$\text{LAC}(500) = .0005(500)^2 - .5 \cdot 500 + 500 = \$375 \text{ per bicycle.}$$

When this industry is in long-run equilibrium, $p = \text{LAC}(500)$. Each firm produces 500 bicycles per year and sells them at a price of $375 per bike.

Our next tasks are to determine the equilibrium output rate (quantity) for the industry as a whole and the number of firms in the business. These are easy calculations to make since, in equilibrium, quantity supplied must equal quantity demanded. When the market price is $375, quantity demanded is

$$Y^* = D_1(375) = 57,500 - 20 \cdot 375 = 50,000 \text{ bicycles.}$$

Since each firm in the business produces 500 bicycles per year there must be 50,000/500 = 100 firms in this industry.

In Figure 9–6(a) we have illustrated the supply and demand curves for the market as a whole. In Figure 9–6(b) we have illustrated the long-run equilibrium point for Franco Brothers, Inc. SS_1 is the short-run supply curve corresponding to the plant that optimally produces 500 bicycles per year. D_1 is the initial demand

FIGURE 9–6   **THE LONG-RUN MARKET SUPPLY CURVE FOR THE BICYCLE INDUSTRY**

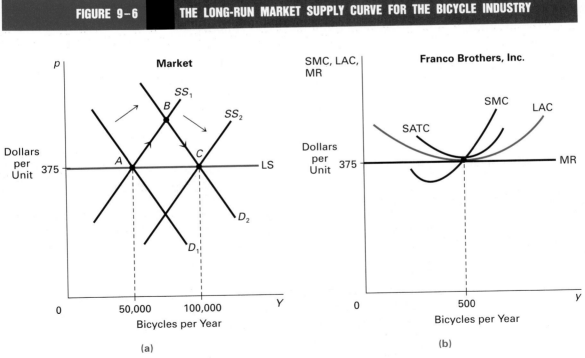

The long-run market supply curve, LS, is a horizontal line at the minimum point of the representative firm's LAC curve.

curve. Since the equilibrium price is $375 and quantity is 50,000, SS_1 must intersect D_1 at point A in the diagram.

(b) Next we are asked to investigate how a change in demand affects the equilibrium price, quantity, and number of firms. In Figure 9–6(a) the new demand curve is labeled D_2. What happens to the equilibrium price in the short run when the demand for bicycles increases? As the demand curve shifts to the right, price begins to rise as firms already in the business increase production to meet the extra demand. This is represented by the movement from A to B. That is, in the short run the price rises as demand increases.

As the price rises, firms in the business earn positive economic profit when they operate at the new profit-maximizing output rate, since price is greater than long-run average cost. The fact that firms in the bicycle business are earning a profit attracts new firms into the industry. This, in turn, shifts the short-run market supply curve to the right. As industry output increases, prices begin to fall until, once again, firms are earning zero economic profit. Since this is a constant cost industry, the cost curves do not change as industry output expands: minimum LAC is still $375. Thus, the long-run equilibrium price remains at $375 per bicycle.

As before, each firm produces 500 bicycles per year. However, because there are now more firms in the business, industry-wide production has increased to

$$Y^{**} = D_2(375) = 107,500 - 20 \cdot 375 = 100,000 \text{ bicycles.}$$

The number of firms increases to 100,000/500 = 200 firms. This new long-run equilibrium point is represented by C in Figure 9–6(a). ■

■ In Chapter 11 we will investigate how various policies impact on equilibrium prices and quantities, and on the economic welfare of market participants. In these discussions, it will be helpful if we know how to use supply and demand curves to measure the gains from trade. We already know from our earlier work that consumer surplus measures the gains that consumers accrue from being able to trade at the market price and that profit measures the gains earned by owners of firms. We now must develop a measure of the gains that accrue from trade resource owners.

We will use economic rent to measure the gains that resource owners accrue from trade. **Economic rent** is defined as *any payment made to owners of resources over and above the minimum payment necessary to induce owners to keep these*

9.4 ECONOMIC RENT

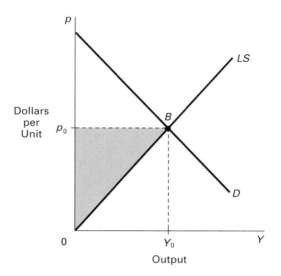

FIGURE 9-7 **ECONOMIC RENT**

The area above the long-run market supply curve and below the market price represents economic rent. It is the difference between revenues received by owners of firms and the minimum amount required to keep inputs in their current employment.

resources in their current employment. In the output market, economic rent is the area above the long-run supply curve and below the market price. In Figure 9-7, economic rent is area $0p_0B$.

To understand why this area does indeed represent economic rent, we must think a little about the long-run market supply curve. Each point on the long-run market supply curve represents the minimum price that consumers would have to pay for a specific unit of output to enable owners of firms to hire the inputs they need to produce that unit of output. This means that the *area* under the long-run market supply curve represents the minimum amount consumers must pay for a certain quantity of output to enable owners of firms to hire the inputs they need to produce that quantity of output. For example, Figure 9-7 shows that owners of firms need to be paid a minimum of $0BY_0$ dollars to have enough money to hire the inputs needed to produce Y_0 bushels of wheat.

Now suppose the market price of wheat is p_0 dollars per bushel. In this instance, wheat producers receive revenues of $0p_0BY_0$ dollars. Since this is a competitive industry, owners of firms earn zero economic profit—they earn what they could earn in the next best alternative to wheat farming—which means that all revenues generated by the sale of wheat are paid to resources owners. Thus, when the market price is p_0 dollars per bushel, resource owners receive $0p_0BY_0$ dollars and earn $0p_0B$ ($0p_0BY_0 - 0BY_0$) dollars above the minimum amount that it would take to keep these factors employed in the wheat industry.

Economic rent measures the gains that resource owners accrue because firms can sell the output produced using their input services at the market price. It is important to remember that economic rent is not economic profit. At any point on the long-run market supply curve, economic *profit* is zero but, at that same point, economic *rent* may be greater than zero. Economic rent represents a payment above and beyond what is needed to keep resources in the industry.

One final point concerning economic rent. If the industry under consideration is a constant cost industry, then the long-run market supply curve is horizontal, and economic rent is zero. For a constant cost industry, resources are paid exactly what it takes to keep them in their current employment. This result gives us another way to characterize a constant cost industry: if the prices of inputs do not rise when industry output expands, then resource owners supplying inputs to this industry are paid exactly their opportunity costs.

EXAMPLE 9–3

RISING MORTGAGE RATES AND ECONOMIC RENTS

Residential construction is an example of an increasing cost industry since it accounts for much of the demand for inputs such as lumber and plumbing equipment and employs labor with industry-specific skills such as electricians and plumbers. When residential housing construction expands, input prices are bid up and when it contracts, input prices fall.

Between 1980 and 1984, interest rates on home mortgages increased from 9.3% to 11.7% in the U.S. This dramatic rise in interest rates caused demand for new-home construction to fall substantially. Determine the impact of rising mortgage rates on the price and quantity of new homes bought and sold and on economic rents earned by owners of inputs employed in the residential construction industry.

■ **SOLUTION** Figure 9–8(a) illustrates the supply and demand curves for the residential construction industry and Figure 9–8(b) shows the cost curves for a representative firm. SS_1 is the initial short-run

FIGURE 9–8   **MORTGAGE RATES AND ECONOMIC RENT**

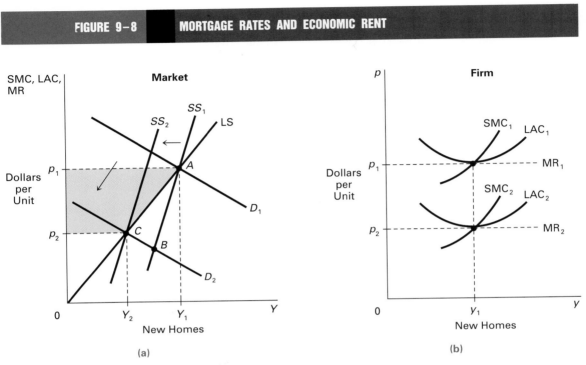

As a result of increasing interest rates, the demand for new homes falls. This, in turn, causes price to fall from p_1 to p_2 and quantity to fall from Y_1 to Y_2. Thus, economic rent is lower by area p_1ACp_2.

supply curve and D_1 is the market demand curve. The long-run equilibrium price and quantity are p_1 and Y_1 respectively and each firm in the business maximizes profit by producing y_1 homes.

Now suppose mortgage interest rates increase and demand for new homes falls. In Figure 9–8(a) the new demand curve is labeled D_2. When the demand curve shifts to the left, price falls in the short run as firms already in the business produce fewer new homes. The short-run decrease in price is the movement from A to B.

As the price falls, firms in the business incur economic losses when they operate at the new profit-maximizing output rate. This means that firms exit the industry and the short-run market supply curve shifts to the left. As industry output falls, price begins to rise until firms are earning zero economic profit once again. This is the movement from B to C. However, since this is an increasing cost industry, price does not rise to the original level of p_1 dollars per home. As industry output decreases, firms bid down the price of firm-specific factors of production, which in turn leads to a downward shift in the cost curves of each firm. In Figure 9–8(b) a downward shift in the LAC curve from LAC_1 to LAC_2 represents the decrease in factor costs.

The new long-run equilibrium price and quantity are p_2 and Y_2 respectively. Both are lower than they were before the change in demand. For an increasing cost industry, price and quantity both fall when demand falls.

Now what happens to economic rent? Before the rise in mortgage interest rates, economic rent is area $0p_1A$. Afterwards, it is area $0p_2C$. Thus, economic rent has fallen by area p_2p_1AC. As a result of the increase in interest rates, owners of resources employed in the residential construction industry are worse off. ■

■ Recall that there are four requirements for perfect competition: firms are price takers; firms in an industry produce a homogeneous product; firms have perfect information; and resources are perfectly mobile in the long run. While it is fairly obvious that there are few real-world markets satisfying all of these requirements, the competitive model is still extremely useful, because many markets are almost perfectly competitive. In particular, firms in many real-world markets face highly elastic demand curves, so that they behave as price takers, and entry and exit are relatively easy.

Oftentimes economists use the number of firms in an industry to indicate whether or not an industry is perfectly competitive. Industries with a large number of firms are competitive while those with a small number are not. Unfortunately, this rule for classifying industries can be very misleading. For example, a market with a large number of firms, say more than 20, cannot be characterized as perfectly competitive if these firms collude to set price. A market with four or five firms, on the other hand, may be analyzed using the competitive model if the market demand curve is very elastic. In this instance, each individual firm faces a demand curve that is nearly horizontal and each will behave like a price taker.

9.5 WHEN CAN WE USE THE COMPETITIVE MODEL?

SUMMARY

1. Short-run market supply is the sum of the quantities produced by each firm in a particular industry at any price. In the short run, the market demand and supply curves determine price and quantity; that is, in the short run a competitive equilibrium is an allocation of resources corresponding to the intersection of the short-run market demand and supply curves.

2. In the long run, a competitive equilibrium requires one additional condition: economic profit must be zero. Only then will entry and exit cease. Only then will the industry be in equilibrium.

3. The long-run market supply curve is the collection of price–quantity pairs that satisfy the conditions for long-run competitive equilibrium. The precise shape of the long-run market supply curve depends on the assumptions we make concerning individual firms' cost curves, the mobility of resources, and the impact of changes in industry output on factor prices.

4. For a constant cost industry, the long-run market supply curve is horizontal at the minimum point of the long-run average cost curve; for an increasing cost industry, it is positively sloped; and for a decreasing cost industry, it is negatively sloped.

5. Economic rent is any payment made to resource owners over and above the minimum payment necessary to keep the resources in their current employment. In the output market economic rent is the area above the long-run market supply curve and below the price producers receive for their goods.

KEY TERMS

Short-run Market Supply
  Curve
Short-run Competitive
  Equilibrium
Long-run Competitive
  Equilibrium

Long-run Market Supply
  Curve
Constant Cost Industry
Increasing Cost Industry
Decreasing Cost Industry
Economic Rent

QUESTIONS AND PROBLEMS

1. Define competitive equilibrium for both the short and long runs and explain the difference between your two definitions.

2. Suppose the short-run market demand and supply curves for water beds are given by

$$Y = D(p) = 20{,}000 - 15p \qquad \text{and}$$

$$Y = SS(p) = 10{,}000 + 10p.$$

a) Graph the demand and supply curves and show the equilibrium price and quantity.
b) Determine the equilibrium price and quantity algebraically.
c) Suppose that an increase in the price of conventional mattresses increases the demand for water beds and that the resulting demand curve is

$$Y = D(p)_1 = 25,000 - 10p.$$

Find the new equilibrium price and quantity.

3. Sleeptight Water Beds is one firm in the water bed industry. The market demand and supply curves are the original ones given in Problem 2. The industry is perfectly competitive. Sleeptight's cost curves are

$$STC = 100 + 100y + 2y^2 \qquad \text{and}$$

$$SMC = 100 + 4y.$$

Find the short-run profit-maximizing output rate for Sleeptight and the profit earned, if any.

4. Clothes "Я" Us is a franchise specializing in the retail sale of clothing for children of all ages. Both the retail and wholesale markets for clothing are perfectly competitive increasing cost industries. The clothing sold by Clothes "Я" Us is manufactured in Korea and Taiwan. Suppose the U.S. Garment Workers Union convinces the federal government to reduce U.S. dependence on foreign clothing by imposing a $2 per-garment tariff on all clothes imported by wholesalers.
a) Determine the short-run effect of the tariff on the wholesale price and the quantity of children's clothing sold to retailers. (Hint: What affect does the tariff have on the supply of foreign clothing to Clothes "Я" Us?).
b) Determine the short-run effect of the tariff on retail price and on the quantity of children's clothing sold to consumers.

5. How would your answers in (4) change if, instead of a tariff, the government imposed an import quota on foreign clothing?

6. "One characteristic of long-run competitive equilibrium is that each firm in the industry earns zero economic profit. Obviously, such a situation cannot persist, since firms earning zero profit will go out of business." Evaluate this statement.

7. Jersey Joe's Gymnasium currently earns an economic profit.
a) If the market for gymnasium services is a perfectly competitive constant cost industry, explain what will happen to this profit in the long run.

b) Suppose that Jersey Joe's cost curves are given by

$$LTC = .00005y^3 - .05y^2 + 500y \qquad \text{and}$$

$$LMC = .00015y^2 - .1y + 500$$

where y is the number of hours patrons use the gym per year. Calculate the long run equilibrium price for an hour's worth of gym services if all other firms in the industry have the same cost curves.

8. Moll Flanders owns and operates a small boutique specializing in creating and selling wedding dresses. The cost curves associated with Moll's firm are given by

$$LTC = .00025y^3 - .01y^2 + 250y \qquad \text{and}$$

$$LMC = .00075y^2 - .02y + 250$$

where y is the number of dresses produced and sold per year. The market for wedding dresses is a perfectly competitive, constant cost industry consisting of boutiques identical to Moll Flanders.

a) Determine the equilibrium price, quantity, and number of firms if the market demand curve is

$$Y = D_1(p) = 5,000 - 2p.$$

b) How many dresses will Moll sell?

c) Recently the trend has been towards informal weddings. This has caused demand for wedding dresses to fall. Determine the equilibrium price, quantity, and number of firms if the new market demand curve is

$$Y = D_2(p) = 2,000 - 2p.$$

9. Assume that the popcorn industry is a perfectly competitive increasing cost industry. Illustrate and explain the effects of the following on price and quantity:

a) an increase in attendance at movie theaters across the country;

b) an infestation of insects that destroy young popcorn plants;

c) the imposition of a law requiring all firms in the popcorn industry to provide free medical insurance to all popcorn pickers.

10. Compare and contrast how an excise subsidy impacts on price, quantity, and economic rent for increasing and constant cost industries.

11. Explain the difference between accounting profit, economic profit, and economic rent.

12. Bud's Suds, Inc., is one of several firms located in Happy Hollow, a rural community in central Colorado, that manufactures and sells root beer. The Happy Hollow root beer firms are famous for a soda made with water from natural artesian wells located on each firm's property. These are the only wells of their kind west of the Mississippi river. Root beer produced from the water is especially rich and flavorful, possessing qualities that can be matched only in other root beers that have undergone an extra, quite costly, process. This high-quality root beer is sold in Colorado and bordering states for p_H dollars per case.

a) Illustrate the economic rent that is attributable to the artesian water.

b) Bud's Suds is currently owned and operated by Alphonse Wellington who rents the facility from its owner on a two-year lease arrangement. Mr. Wellington hires a crew of ten assistants and a salesperson on a monthly basis (with wages renegotiable each month). He buys his supplies of raw materials, root extract, sugar, hops, etc. from various Colorado wholesalers, but without contracts of any kind. Who of the following will garner the bulk of the economic rent attributable to the artesian water over one year? Over two years? Over three years? Will it be the owner of the firm, the ten assistants, the salesperson, the land owner, or the suppliers of raw materials?

Kreps, D. 1990. *A Course in Microeconomic Theory*. Princeton: Princeton University Press.

Stigler, G. 1985. "Perfect Competition, Historically Contemplated." In *Microeconomics: Selected Readings,* ed. E. Mansfield. 5th ed. New York: Norton.

Varian, H. 1992. *Microeconomic Analysis*. 3d ed. New York: Norton.

REFERENCES

APPENDIX   **EXAMPLE A9-1**

CALCULATING THE LONG-RUN COMPETITIVE EQUILIBRIUM FOR AN INCREASING COST INDUSTRY

A consultant hired by the owner of A. M. LeVelle Microprocessor, Inc., estimates that the firm's total and marginal cost functions are given by

$$\text{LTC} = .0005y^3 - .5y^2 + 500y + .0001y \cdot Y \qquad \text{and}$$

$$\text{LMC} = .001^2 - y + 500 + .0001Y$$

where y is the number of chips produced by LeVelle each year and Y is industry output. (Allowing long-run costs to depend on industry-wide output is one way to model increasing costs. As industry output increases, long-run costs increase as a result of escalating factor prices. As industry output falls, long-run costs fall as a result of falling factor prices.) (a) Determine the long-run equilibrium price, quantity, and number of firms if the market demand curve is given by

$$Y = D_1(p) = 53,400 - 20p.$$

(b) How many chips will A. M. LeVelle manufacture and sell each year? (c) Determine the new long-run equilibrium price, quantity, and number of firms if the market demand curve becomes

$$Y = D_2(p) = 99,300 - 20p.$$

■ **SOLUTION** Since all firms in this industry are identical and there is free entry and exit, long-run competitive equilibrium is attained when each firm earns zero economic profit or when the market price is equal to the minimum of the LAC curve. The difference between this example and Example 9–2 is that LAC and LMC depend on Y and therefore the minimum of the LAC curve changes as industry output changes.

(a,b) We begin by finding the output rate corresponding to the point where LAC attains its minimum value. Given the LTC curve for LeVelle's, $\text{LAC} = .0005y^2 - .5y + 500 + .0001Y$. Setting LMC equal to LAC we have

$$.0015y^2 - y + 500 + .001Y = .005y^2 - .5y + 500 + .0001Y.$$

Solving this equation for y gives

$$.001y^2 - .5y = y(.001y - .5) = 0$$

or $y^* = 500$. Thus, LAC attains its minimum value when the output rate is 500 memory chips per year.

In order to find the long-run equilibrium price, we must determine LAC when $y = 500$. Substituting 500 into the equation for LAC gives

$$LAC(500) = .0005(500)^2 - .5(500) + 500 + .001Y$$
$$= 375 + .0001Y \text{ dollars per memory chip.}$$

When this industry is in long-run equilibrium, $p = 375 + .0001Y$ dollars per chip. Notice that, since each firm's LAC curve depends on industry-wide output, the long-run equilibrium price also depends on industry-wide output. How, then, can we find the long-run equilibrium price?

First, since all firms in this industry are identical, we know that industry output is the output rate of each firm times the number of firms in the business. Let n be the number of firms. Then industry output must be $500n$ memory chips. Substituting this into the expression for the long-run equilibrium price we have

$$p^* = 375 + .5n.$$

Next, we can substitute p^* into the market demand curve to obtain the total number of memory chips that the industry must produce each year. This gives

$$Y^* = D_1(p^*) = 53.400 - 20(375 + .5n)$$
$$= 53,400 - 7,500 - 10n = 45,900 - 10n.$$

Setting Y^* equal to market supply, $n(500)$, and solving for n gives us the long-run equilibrium number of firms in the business:

$$45,900 - 10n = 500n$$

or $n^* = 45,900/510 = 90$ firms. That is, when entry and exit cease, there will be 90 firms in the memory chip industry.

Now we can find the long-run equilibrium price and quantity. We find the former by substituting 90 into the expression for the price:

$$p^* = 375 + .5(90) = \$420 \text{ per chip.}$$

Since each firm in the business produces 500 memory chips per year, the long-run equilibrium output rate for the industry as a whole is Y^* 90(500) = 45,000 chips per year. Summarizing our findings, we conclude that, when this industry is in long-run equilibrium, there are 90 firms in the industry, each producing 500 memory chips per year and selling them for $420 each.

(c) Our final task is to determine how a change in demand impacts on the long-run equilibrium price, quantity, and number of firms. Setting demand equal to supply when n firms are operating gives

$$Y^{**} = D^2(p^*) = 99{,}300 - 20(375 + 5p)$$
$$= 91{,}800 - 10n = 500n$$

or $n^* = 180$ firms. When entry and exit cease, there will be 180 firms in the business.

Substituting 180 into the appropriate expressions gives

$$p^* = 375 + .5(180) = \$465 \text{ per memory chip} \qquad \text{and}$$

$$Y^* = 180(500) = 90{,}000 \text{ memory chips per year.}$$

As a result of the increase in demand, price and quantity both increase. ∎

THE THEORY OF PRICE FOR COMPETITIVE INPUT MARKETS

10

LEARNING OBJECTIVES

After completing Chapter 10 you should be able to do the following:

■ Describe the long-run industry and market input demand curves.

■ Explain how to derive the long-run market labor supply curve.

■ Discuss long-run competitive equilibrium in the labor market and explain why wage rates tend to equalize across industries.

■ Define and illustrate economic rent for a single input.

EXAMPLES

■ **10–1** The Social Security Payroll Tax

■ **10–2** Are Professors Underpaid?

■ **10–3** The Jacksons' Victory Tour

In the preceding chapter we used the supply and demand model to explain how prices and quantities are determined in *output* markets. Now we can turn our attention to *input* markets—that is, the markets for labor, capital, natural resources, and land. In this chapter we discuss the basic principles common to all input markets; in particular, we focus on the factors that determine the level of employment and price of any input. The analysis of input markets is very similar to that of output markets since both involve the interaction of buyers and sellers. The difference, of course, is that now firms are the demanders and households are the suppliers.

As indicated by the circular flow of economic activity shown in Figure 1–1, households supply productive resources to firms and, in return, receive payments from firms for the use of these resources. These payments determine the level and distribution of income, which is why economists often refer to the material covered in this chapter as the *neoclassical theory of distribution*. Understanding how input markets operate will help us understand, for example, why physicians earn so much more than secretaries and how the Social Security payroll tax or a legal minimum wage affects employment. These are important issues and they generate a great deal of interest in input markets.

In this chapter we continue to refer to the competitive model. It is particularly useful here because many input markets comprise a large number of demanders and suppliers which means they tend to be price takers. We shall begin by analyzing industry and market demand for inputs, then focus on the supply of inputs, and, finally, examine the interaction of demand and supply.

10.1 INDUSTRY AND MARKET DEMAND FOR INPUTS

■ In Chapter 8 we saw that the input demand curve of an individual competitive firm is negatively sloped. Now we must aggregate the demands of individual firms to obtain the industry and market demand curves. In this chapter we will be concerned exclusively with the long-run. This is not to say that the short run is not important; however, most of the interesting problems that arise when analyzing input markets are best handled by allowing firms to adjust all inputs optimally.

INDUSTRY DEMAND FOR INPUTS

The **long-run industry input demand curve** depicts the total quantity of an input employed by firms in a given industry. It illustrates the collection of price–input pairs representing all states that satisfy the conditions for long-run competitive equilibrium. In particular, all points on the long-run industry demand curve correspond to situations where firms maximize profit and earn zero economic profit.

In order to find the industry input demand curve, we must aggregate the long-run input demand curves of all firms. However, there are two complications: output price and the number of firms can vary as industry employment changes. This means that the industry input demand curve is not necessarily the horizontal sum of all the individual firms' input demand curves.

Figure 10−1 shows the process of determining the long-run industry demand curve for labor. In Figure 10−1(a), LS_1 is the long-run market supply curve, given current input prices. For simplicity, we shall assume that this is a constant cost industry. The initial equilibrium output price and quantity are p_1 and Y_1 respectively.

In Figure 10−1(b), ΣD_L^1 is the summation of each firm's demand curve for labor when output price is p_1. The initial equilibrium wage and level of employment are w_1 and L_1 respectively.

Finally, in Figure 10−1(c) the representative firm's long-run demand curve for labor, given an output price of p_1, is $D_L^1(p_1)$. If the wage rate is w_1 dollars per unit of labor, each firm employs l_1 units of labor. (We use a lower case l to stand for the quantity of an input hired by an individual firm.)

Now suppose the wage rate falls to w_2. Individual firms already in the business now earn positive economic profits because costs are lower. As a result, firms currently in the industry increase production to the new profit-maximizing level. If the price of good Y remained at p_1 dollars per unit, each firm would increase employment along $D_L^1(p_1)$ from A'' to B''.

But what in fact happens to the price of the output that this industry is producing? As a result of the decrease in the price of labor, firms already in the industry increase production. In addition, the industry attracts new firms because now business is profitable. As a result, the long-run supply curve shifts from LS_1 to LS_2 and output price falls from p_1 to p_2.

A lower price for the product also impacts on each firm's long-run demand for labor. Remember, input demand curves are derived demand curves and are affected by changes in output price. As output price falls, marginal revenue product falls and the firm's demand curve shifts from $D_L^1(p_1)$ to $D_L^2(p_2)$. Given this new long-run demand curve for labor, each firm in the industry (remember there are now more firms in the industry) employs l_3 units of labor, and industry demand is $\Sigma D_L^2(p_2)$ units of labor. In Figure 10−1(b), the industry begins expanding from A' towards B' but, because output price falls, ends up expanding only to point C'.

In Figure 10−1(b) D_L represents the long-run industry demand curve for labor. It is not the sum of the individual firms' demand

FIGURE 10-1 THE INDUSTRY INPUT DEMAND CURVE

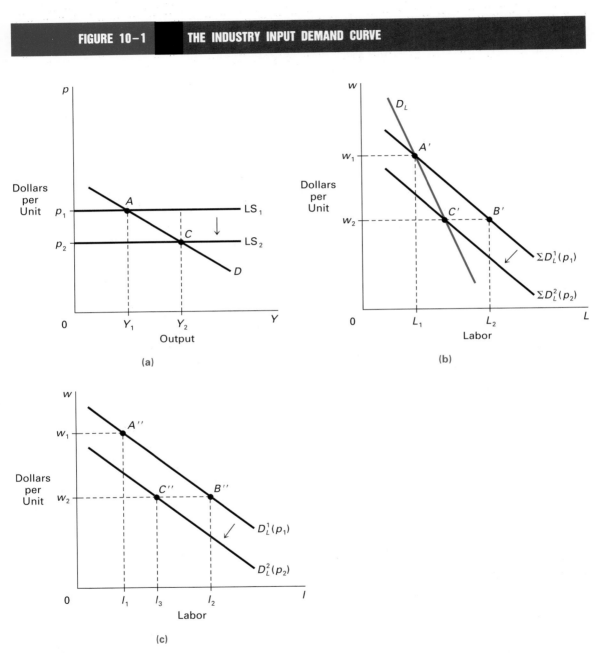

(a)

(b)

(c)

As all firms expand, employment along input demand curve D_L^1, output increases. This causes output price to fall and the input demand curve to shift in to D_L^2. D_L is the long-run market demand curve for labor. It is steeper than the sum of all the individual firms' demand curves because, as employment increases, supply increases and output price falls.

curves, because it takes into account the change in output price that results when industry-wide supply changes. In general, the long-run industry demand curve for an input is steeper than the sum of the individual firms' demand curves.

Market input demand is the sum of the quantities demanded by all industries using the input. For example, the market demand curve for machinists is the sum of the demands of the automobile industry, the electronics industry, and all other industries that use machinists.

Figure 10−2 illustrates how to construct the market demand curve for machinists if we assume for convenience that they are employed only by the automobile and electronics industries. In Figure 10−2(a), the automobile and electronics industry demand curves for machinists are D_L^A and D_L^E respectively. In Figure 10−2(b), D_L is the market demand curve for machinists, or the sum of the quantities demanded by both industries at any wage. Just as we obtained the market demand curve for an output, the market demand curve for an input is the horizontal sum of individual input demand curves.

It is important that owners and managers of firms understand input demands. For example, managers of steel companies use

MARKET DEMAND FOR INPUTS

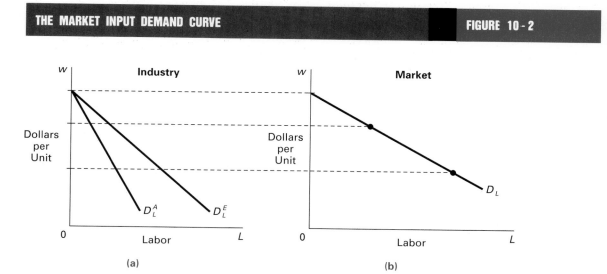

THE MARKET INPUT DEMAND CURVE   **FIGURE 10 - 2**

The market input demand curve is the horizontal sum of all the individual industries' input demand curves.

information concerning the demand for steel to decide how much steel to produce and managers of automobile companies use the same information to estimate how their steel purchases and costs will change if the price of steel changes. An understanding of input demand is also important for evaluating government policies. For example, the impact of an increase in the legal minimum wage on employment of low-wage workers will depend crucially on the characteristics of the demand for unskilled workers.

DETERMINANTS OF THE PRICE ELASTICITY OF DEMAND FOR AN INPUT

The price elasticity of demand for an input is defined in the same way as it is for a good (see Chapter 4). It measures the responsiveness of quantity demanded to changes in price. For example, if the price elasticity of demand for unskilled labor is 2, then this means that a 10% increase in the wage rate will cause a 20% reduction in quantity of labor demanded by firms. How large the price elasticity of demand is for an input can be important. The impact of an increase in the legal minimum wage or the social security payroll tax, for instance, will depend on how responsive the demand for labor is to changes in wage rates.

There are four primary factors that affect the price elasticity of demand for an input: the substitutability of inputs in production, the price elasticity of demand for the product that the input helps to produce, the price elasticity of supply of other inputs, and the length of time allowed for adjustment.

Input demand curves will be more elastic the easier it is to substitute one input for another in production. When a firm's technology allows it readily to substitute machines for workers, for example, a small increase in the wage rate may cause the firm to increase its use of machines and reduce its use of labor substantially. On the other hand, when machines are not good substitutes for workers, even a large increase in the wage rate may not cause much of a decline in labor. When it is easy to substitute inputs, the substitution effect associated with an input price change is large, and this tends to make input demand more elastic.

The input demand curve will also be more elastic the greater the price elasticity of demand for the product being produced. Remember that the demand for an input is derived from the demand curve for the product it helps produce. If demand for the product is elastic, then consumers will purchase substantially more of the good at a slightly lower price, so that when an input price falls, firms will produce much more and, as a result, employment of that input will rise sharply. An elastic product demand curve gives rise to a large output effect which, in turn, makes the input demand curve more elastic.

The price elasticity of demand for an input will be larger, the greater the price elasticity of supply of other inputs. If, say, the supply of machines is very elastic, then this encourages firms to switch from workers to machines because the price of machines will not rise very much.

Finally, the input demand curve will be more elastic the longer the time allowed for adjustment. For example, if the price of skilled workers rises, it may not be possible to lay off skilled workers immediately without reducing output a lot. However, as time passes the firm will be able to build new production facilities that will allow it to switch from skilled workers to machines.

■ Having discussed the demand for inputs used in the production of goods and services, we must now investigate the supply side of input markets. As we begin this discussion, we should take care to distinguish between the amount of inputs in existence at any given point in time—called the stock of resources—and the amount that resource owners are willing to offer for sale or rent. For example, at any point the total amount of land that can be used to produce goods is fixed; however, the amount of land that landowners are willing to supply to producers will depend on the price the producers are willing to pay. It is this latter relation that, along with the demand for inputs, determines prices and quantities.

Industry input supply is the total amount of input supplied by resource owners to a particular industry at any price. Recall that, for a constant cost industry, on the one hand, firms can obtain all the inputs they desire at a given price. This means that the industry input supply curves for a constant cost industry are horizontal at the market price. The firms making up a constant cost industry purchase only a small portion of the total amounts of inputs supplied to all industries. Any change in quantity demanded does not measurably affect input prices. Firms making up an increasing cost industry, on the other hand, purchase substantial amounts of inputs and must pay higher prices in order to attract more inputs. This means that the industry input supply curves for an increasing cost industry are upward-sloping.

Market input supply is the sum of the quantities of that input supplied by resource owners to all industries at any price. The shape of any one market input supply curve will depend on how broadly or narrowly we define the input. For example, the market input supply curve for highly skilled chemists researching new drugs for the treatment of cancer will have a very different shape compared to the market input supply curve for all chemists.

10.2 INDUSTRY AND MARKET SUPPLY OF INPUTS

We can, however, make some general statements as to the shape of input supply curves. Inputs that one firm produces and other firms buy or rent to produce final goods and services have positively sloped market input supply curves. These types of inputs are called *intermediate goods*. They are outputs for certain firms and inputs for others. For example, oil is the output of the oil industry but an input for many other industries. Since we have shown that supply curves for competitive firms are either upward-sloping or horizontal, it follows that the market supply curves for intermediate goods are also upward-sloping or horizontal.

One of the most important inputs, labor, is fundamentally different from other inputs in that it is a human resource and therefore can never be owned by a producer. Labor must always be rented. The remainder of this section focuses on the unique case of labor supply.

AN INDIVIDUAL WORKER'S LABOR SUPPLY CURVE

While the shape of the labor supply curve depends crucially on how we define labor, several factors influence the position of the curve. As the age composition of the work force changes, as individuals move from one area to another, or as individuals undertake education that enables them to move into other occupations, the supply of particular types of labor to various firms, industries, and economies may change drastically. These changes represent shifts in the labor supply curve as opposed to movements along the labor supply curve.

Here, we are going to simplify our analysis of labor supply as much as we can without losing the essential features of the supply side of input markets. This will allow us to focus on questions of general interest to all labor markets.

To derive a well-defined labor supply curve we will begin by assuming that the size of the labor force and its occupational distribution are constants. This allows us to focus on a labor supply curve that measures labor in hours of work effort.

In Chapter 5 we investigated an individual's consumption–leisure choice. There we determined the level of work effort that maximized satisfaction given the wage rate and the prices of all other goods. In this section we will begin by briefly reviewing the discussion in Chapter 5 and then use the analysis of an individual's consumption–leisure choice to derive the labor supply curve.

Recall that our basic hypothesis is that workers choose how much time to spend in leisure activities by maximizing satisfaction given their time and budget constraints. In Figure 10–3(a), the horizontal axis measures hours of leisure. T represents the total amount of time available to the individual. If we read from right to

AN INDIVIDUAL WORKER'S LABOR SUPPLY CURVE

FIGURE 10–3

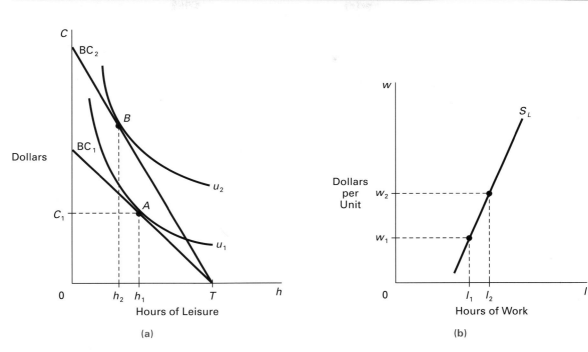

(a) Given BC_1, the individual supplies $I_1 = (T - h_1)$ hours of work. When the wage rate increases, work effort may increase or decrease depending on the income and substitution effects. Here the substitution effect dominates and work effort increases to $I_2 = (T - h_2)$. (b) S_L is the individual's labor supply curve. In this instance, the labor supply curve is positively sloped.

left, the horizontal axis also measures hours of work. The vertical axis measures expenditures on all goods, or consumption. The slope of each of the budget constraints shown in the diagram is minus the wage rate.

Given a budget constraint, we want to know how many hours an individual will spend in leisure activities; this, in turn, will tell us how many he will spend working. Given BC_1, the individual whose preferences are depicted in Figure 10–3(a) maximizes satisfaction by consuming commodity bundle A on indifference curve u_1. This commodity bundle consists of l_1 hours of leisure time and C_1 dollars of income to be spent on consumption. Work effort is $h_1 = (T - l_1)$ hours.

Now let the wage rate increase, as is shown by the slope of BC_2. When the wage increases, the price of leisure and real income both increase also. The substitution effect indicates that the individual should reduce leisure and increase work effort while the income effect indicates just the opposite. The total effect is ambiguous. In Figure 10−3(a), we have illustrated the situation where the substitution effect dominates and hours of work increase as the wage increases. As Figure 10−3(b) shows, this means that this individual's labor supply curve is upward-sloping. (If the income effect dominates, then the labor supply curve is negatively sloped.)

THE MARKET LABOR SUPPLY CURVE

The **market labor supply curve,** denoted by S_L, depicts the relation between the wage and the amount of labor supplied by all market participants. While we cannot say for certain whether an individual's labor supply curve is positively or negatively sloped, the long-run market supply curve is always either horizontal or positively sloped.

To grasp this, consider first the short-run market supply curve. When we are discussing the supply side of the labor market, the short run means that period of time during which the stock of human capital or skills is fixed. Human capital is the embodiment of the productive skills possessed by workers. Suppose we consider one type of labor, say mechanical engineers. In the short run we can say nothing definitive about the shape of the labor supply curve for mechanical engineers. Since the number of mechanical engineers is fixed, a change in the wage rate can only lead to a change in the number of hours worked by those individuals already employed as mechanical engineers. In the short run the labor supply curve may be positively or negatively sloped depending on whether or not substitution effects dominate income effects.

In the long run, however, the stock of human capital is not fixed. Entry into and exit from occupations can take place. An English teacher may become a mechanical engineer if the financial rewards are great enough. Students planning their careers can choose the occupations offering the highest financial returns. In the long run, if the wage rate increases, workers currently employed may adjust their work effort in either direction; however, in almost every instance, entry into the occupation will more than offset any reduction in work effort. In the aggregate, the long-run market labor supply curve will be positively sloped.

10.3 LONG-RUN COMPETITIVE EQUILIBRIUM IN THE INPUT MARKET

■ Firms use inputs to produce goods and services. Input demand curves reflect the impact of input prices on the employment decisions of owners of firms. Resource owners supply inputs to firms. Input supply curves reflect the impact of input prices on the amounts resource owners supply. Combining the long-run market demand and supply curves for inputs, we can determine the long-run equilibrium price and employment of inputs.

Figure 10−4 shows the market demand and supply curves for labor. Here we assume that all labor is homogeneous and is measured in person-hours per year. What will be the wage and level of employment when this labor market is in long-run equilibrium? Long-run equilibrium requires that quantity supplied is equal to quantity demanded. Thus, the intersection of the demand and supply curves determines the long-run equilibrium wage. In Figure 10−4, w^* is the long run equilibrium wage rate and L^* is the long-run equilibrium level of employment.

To demonstrate why w^* and L^* do, in fact, represent a long-run competitive equilibrium, suppose that workers are currently receiving a wage lower than w^*. Suppose that the wage rate is w_1 dollars per person-hour. Figure 10−4 shows clearly that at this lower wage rate workers will supply only L_1 units of labor services; that is, since the labor supply curve is positively sloped, they will supply fewer units of labor services at lower prices. Firms, however, will now demand L_2 units of labor services. Lower factor costs give rise to an increase in the profit-maximizing level of input demand. Since quantity of labor demanded by firms, L_2, is greater

COMPETITIVE EQUILIBRIUM IN THE LABOR MARKET **FIGURE 10−4**

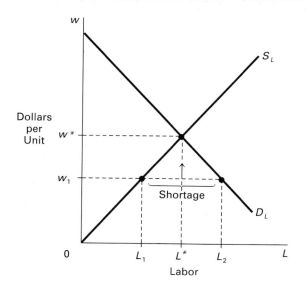

The intersection of the demand and supply curves determines the long-run equilibrium wage and level of employment, w^* and L^* respectively. If the market wage is below w^*, an excess demand for workers arises and the wage rate is bid up. If the market wage is above w^*, there is an excess supply of workers and the wage rate is bid down.

than the quantity supplied by workers, L_1, there is a shortage of workers when the wage rate is w_1.

At a wage rate of w_1 dollars per unit of labor, firms will not be able to hire all the workers they need and the wage rate will be bid up. In order to meet firms' production needs, owners must attract workers from other firms in the industry or from other firms outside the industry. However, workers can be persuaded to leave their current employment only if owners offer them a higher wage rate. Thus, if the wage rate is below w^*, market forces will cause the price of labor to rise. This process will continue until the wage rate—the price of labor—is such that the quantity of labor services supplied by workers just equals the quantity of labor services that firms are willing to employ.

INPUT PRICE EQUALIZATION ACROSS INDUSTRIES

Oftentimes, several different industries will use the same input. For example, most manufacturing industries employ some engineers, semiskilled workers, and unskilled workers. When these widely used inputs are identical, competition between industries tends to make the prices received by owners of these inputs the same no matter which industry employs them. That is, just as competition tends to make identical goods sell for the same price no matter which firm produces them, competition tends to equalize the prices of identical inputs across industries.

To see that this is indeed the case, consider the labor market depicted in Figure 10–5. Suppose that there are only two industries, industry I and industry II, that employ a certain type of worker. Initially we begin from a point where all markets are in long-run equilibrium; in particular, the long-run equilibrium wage rate in both industries is w^*. It is determined by the intersection of the supply and demand curves for labor in each industry.

Now suppose that for some reason tastes change and the demand for the output produced by industry I increases. The increase in demand for output in industry I will cause the price of that industry's good to increase. Since the demand for labor is a derived demand, the increase in output price will increase the profit-maximizing quantity of inputs employed at any wage rate; this in turn causes the labor demand curve for industry I to shift to the right. In Figure 10–5(a), D_I^1 shifts out to D_I^2.

In the short run, before entry and exit occur in the labor market, the equilibrium wage rate and level of employment in industry I rise to w_I^1 and L_I^1 respectively. The increase in employment is due to an increase in work effort by those workers already employed in industry I. In Figure 10–5(a) this is the move from A to B.

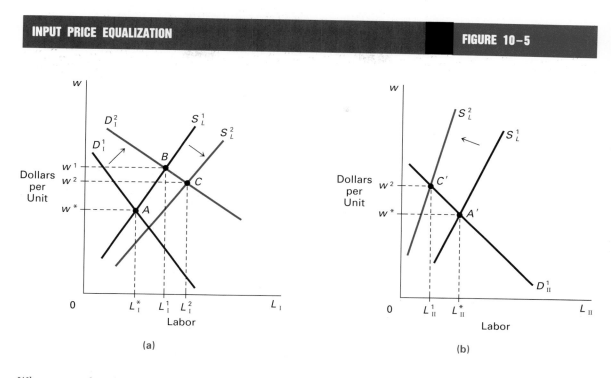

INPUT PRICE EQUALIZATION

FIGURE 10–5

(a)

(b)

When more than one industry employs the same factor of production, competition requires that the input be allocated across industries so that the price is the same no matter where the input is employed. If inputs have a higher price in industry I, then input owners have an incentive to supply more inputs to industry I which, in turn, tends to lower the price.

Does this new state represent a long-run equilibrium situation for the labor market? It does not. Since both industries are employing the same type of labor, the price difference between labor used in industry I and labor used in industry II will cause exit and entry. Industry I will attract workers currently employed in industry II. This will cause workers to exit industry II and enter industry I and, in turn, industry I's labor supply curve shifts to the right and industry II's labor supply curve shifts to the left. This process will continue until wage rates are equalized. The final long-run equilibrium point is represented by C in Figure 10–5(a) and point C' in Figure 10–5(b). Once again, supply is equal to demand and wage rates are equal.

The next example illustrates how the competitive model of input markets can help us understand the impact of the Social Security payroll tax on employment and wage rates.

EXAMPLE 10–1

THE SOCIAL SECURITY PAYROLL TAX

In the U.S. the Social Security payroll tax is divided equally between employees and employers. In 1990 the tax rate was 7.65% so that, for a worker earning $30,000 per year, both the worker and the employer paid $2,295 in Social Security taxes. Every year when federal budget negotiations take place, the U.S. Congress debates whether or not to increase the Social Security payroll tax rate. Suppose the Congress is considering changing the tax rate from 7.65% to 8.00% and has hired us as economic consultants to evaluate the impact of the tax hike on the wage rate and on the level of employment of low-income, semiskilled, workers.

FIGURE 10–6   **THE SOCIAL SECURITY PAYROLL TAX**

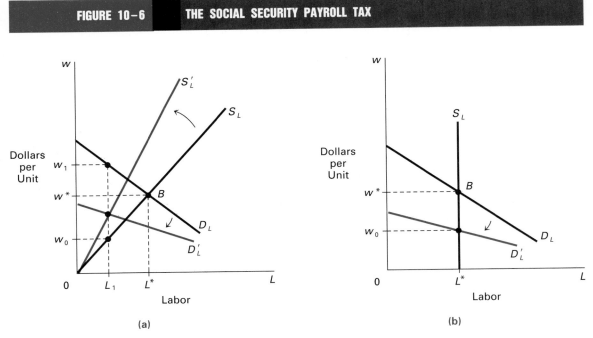

(a)

(b)

(a) A payroll tax levied on workers and firms shifts the supply curve upward to S'_L and the demand curve downward to D'_L. Employment is reduced to L_1, firms pay a higher wage, w_1, and workers receive a lower net wage, w_0. (b) When the labor supply curve is vertical, workers bear the entire cost of the payroll tax in the form of reduced wages.

■ **SOLUTION** In Figure 10–6 S_L and D_L represent the supply and demand curves for semi-skilled workers prior to the tax rate increase. The equilibrium wage rate and level of employment are w^* and L^* respectively. In addition, income for semiskilled workers as a group is given by area $0w^*BL^*$.

Now suppose the tax increases. What impact does this have on the demand and supply curves? Recall that the demand curve for labor shows the maximum amount employers are willing to pay for each unit of labor. For example, in Figure 10–6, employers are willing to pay w^* dollars per hour for L^* units of labor. If firms must pay an additional $.035 per dollar earned by its employees in taxes, the maximum amount they are willing to pay for L^* units of labor is still w^* dollars per hour; however, $.035 \cdot w^*$ of this now goes to the government. Thus, with the tax in place firms will be willing to pay workers only $.965 \cdot w^*$ per hour for L^* units of labor. In effect, the tax shifts the demand curve D_L downward by the amount of the tax to D_L' in Figure 10–6. This means that firms will pay workers less at each level of employment.

Since the tax is paid by both employers and employees, it also affects the supply curve. As a result of the tax, the supply curve shifts upward from S_L to S_L'. Workers must receive more per hour to get them to supply a given amount of work effort since they must pay an additional .035 per dollar earned to the government. For example, workers will continue to supply L^* units of work effort only if they are paid $1.035 \cdot w^*$ per hour which, after taxes, is w^* per hour.

The intersection of S_L' and D_L' determines the new equilibrium level of employment, L_1. At this level of employment, the wage rate firms pay is w_1 (read off the original demand curve for labor) and the wage rate received by workers after taxes is w_0. In this instance, the tax rate increase causes per-unit labor costs to rise, $w_1 > w^*$, the after-tax wage to fall, $w_0 < w^*$, and employment to fall. ■

In this example, firms and workers share the burden of the payroll tax. However, most public finance economists believe that workers, in fact, bear nearly all of the cost of a payroll tax in the form of reduced wages. (Problem 14 asks you to show that the real effects of a payroll tax are independent of how it is legally divided between workers and firms.) Figure 10–6(b) illustrates this situation. Again, in the absence of the tax, the equilibrium wage and level of employment are w^* and L^* respectively. Now suppose the government levies a payroll tax. To simplify the discussion, let's assume that employers pay the entire tax. The demand curve shifts downward by the entire amount of the tax from D_L to D'_L. Employment remains at L^* because the labor supply curve is vertical; however, the net wage that workers receive falls from w^* to w_0, the full amount of the tax. Thus, when the labor supply curve is vertical, workers bear the full cost of the payroll tax even though firms are legally obligated to pay the tax. This point is commonly misunderstood. A highly inelastic labor supply curve means that the employer's portion of the payroll tax reduces net wages just as much as the employee's portion.

As this discussion indicates, precisely how much of the payroll tax the workers bear depends crucially on the elasticity of the labor supply curve. Since the Social Security payroll tax applies to almost every job and industry in the economy, the appropriate supply curve for analyzing this type of tax is the aggregate supply curve for all hours of work and most empirical evidence suggests that this supply curve tends to be quite inelastic.

10.4 COMPENSATING WAGE DIFFERENTIALS

■ The preceding discussion concerning the equalization of input prices across industries assumes that the workers employed in each industry are identical in that they have the same skills and they evaluate the desirability of jobs only in terms of money incomes. Given these assumptions, competitive pressures guarantee that input prices will tend to equalize across industries. However, in the real world we observe a wide variation in the wage rates that firms pay to different individuals. Wage rates differ between occupations and they differ between individuals employed in the same occupation. Thus, the next question we must ask is why do wage rates differ in a world of price-takers?

Individuals differ both with respect to the skills they possess and with respect to the types of jobs they are willing to do. These differences affect the supply side of the input market and lead to differences in wage rates. While wages can differ for many reasons, here we will focus on two of the most important: differences in tastes and differences in skills.

WAGE DIFFERENTIALS AND TASTES

In general, different workers attain different levels of satisfaction from the same type of work. Such differences in tastes or preferences manifest themselves in wage differentials that reflect the relative desirability of one job over another. When monetary compensation is not the only factor influencing an individual's choice of jobs, he or she will be willing to trade off income for nonmonetary compensation. Some individuals may be willing to take jobs in certain desirable locations for less pay than they could earn doing the same job elsewhere; others may be willing to take on jobs that are intrinsically less desirable in return for higher pay. For example, many people will sacrifice pay if they can live in an area with a nice climate or a low crime rate; and individuals who paint suspension bridges receive higher wages than those who paint one-story homes.

In these types of situations, a long-run competitive equilibrium will cause the full price rather than the money price of inputs to equalize. Typically, the full price of an input means the money price plus the nonmonetary compensation associated with employing the input in a particular use. When supply and demand forces work to equate full prices, then differences in money prices arise. These differences, called **compensating wage differentials**, are the differences in money prices that compensate for differences in nonmonetary prices or differences in money prices that equalize full prices.

**WAGE DIFFERENTIALS
AND SKILLS**

The second important reason wage differences arise is that individuals have different skills. Workers in a given occupation may not all be homogeneous; some may be more productive than others. That is, two groups of workers doing the same job may have different marginal products. Since profit maximization requires that input price be equal to marginal revenue product, those workers who are less productive will receive a lower wage rate.

In addition to differences within an occupation, substantial wage differences exist between occupations. Doctors and lawyers have much higher wage rates than do factory workers. Once again, these differences arise because doctors and lawyers have skills different from those of factory workers. Such skill differentials arise because some individuals choose to augment their initial stock of skills by going to school or obtaining other types of training. Since the additional skills needed for certain jobs are costly to acquire, individuals who make such an investment must receive compensation at least large enough to cover expenses and any foregone earnings. If this were not the case, people would not spend time or money to acquire the skills needed to become doctors or lawyers.

When there are many different occupations, each requiring different skills, our model of long-run equilibrium will imply that the return from being employed in any one occupation should be equal to the return from being employed in any other, where the returns are net of the costs of acquiring the necessary skills. Only then will entry and exit into and out of various occupations cease. This means that jobs requiring large investment costs must also pay higher wages.

EXAMPLE 10–2

ARE PROFESSORS UNDERPAID?

The average university professor's salary is typically much lower than what he or she could earn in the private sector, yet universities seem able to retain their faculty. Assuming that the market for professors (Ph.D.s) is perfectly competitive, is this situation consistent with long-run equilibrium?

■ **SOLUTION** If the market for professors (Ph.D.s) is perfectly competitive, then we would expect salaries to be the same no matter where the individual is employed. Since this is not the case, it must be the case that university professors have a "taste" for the university life-style over the private sector life-style; that is, private sector jobs are, in some sense, less desirable to them than university jobs. It follows that individuals who decide to go into academics may enjoy teaching to the extent that they are willing to forego income to be in a position where they can teach. As a result, in long-run equilibrium, private sector employers must pay a compensating wage differential to individuals with Ph.D.s. If they do not, then these factors of production will move to the universities. ■

10.5 ECONOMIC RENT FOR A SINGLE INPUT

■ Recall that economic rent is any payment made to owners of resources over and above the minimum payment necessary to induce them to keep these resources in their current employment. In the output market, economic rent is the area above the long-run market supply curve and below the market price. This area represents the economic rent that firms in a given industry are paying to ensure future supplies of all factors of production.

We can also determine the economic rent that firms pay to suppliers of a particular input that can contribute to the production of a variety of goods and services. Figure 10–7 illustrates the economic rent earned by workers employed in a competitive labor market. The equilibrium wage and level of employment are w^* and L^* respectively. In this market workers as a group earn w^*L^*; that is, the total payment owners of firms make to these workers is w^*L^*.

From the workers' perspective, the labor supply curve represents the marginal cost of supplying their labor services. The labor supply curve represents the minimum amount workers must earn if they are to receive a payment equal to the opportunity costs they

ECONOMIC RENT FOR A SINGLE INPUT

FIGURE 10-7

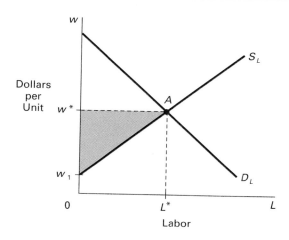

The portion of economic rent going to workers is the area above the labor supply curve and below the wage rate.

incur by staying in their current employment. This being the case, what is the minimum payment necessary to keep all L^* workers in their current employment?

Consider the first worker hired. For any input price below w_1, no one can be induced to work. Thus, the minimum payment necessary to induce this first worker to remain in his or her current employment is w_1 dollars per hour. As the wage increases above w_1, more individuals choose to work because they now earn enough to cover their opportunity costs. In total, the minimum payment needed to induce all L^* individuals to work is given by area $0w_1AL^*$.

The economic rent these workers earn is the difference between what they are actually paid and area $0w_1AL^*$—that is, area $0w^*AL^*$ − $0w_1AL^*$, or $w_1w^*AL^*$. This area represents the payment made to workers above the opportunity costs of their employment. This area represents the workers' share of the economic rents earned by all inputs employed in a particular industry.

We have talked about economic rent as measuring the payments to resource owners above the minimum amount necessary to keep inputs in their present employment. However, in the history of economic thought the term *economic rent* was associated with total payments to owners of fixed factors of production. In this section we want to investigate this historical notion of economic rent and

A HISTORICAL NOTE ON ECONOMIC RENTS

compare it with the modern definition. This investigation will help
to reinforce the meaning of economic rent.

RICARDIAN RENT

Two of the earliest economists to write on the topic of economic
rent were David Ricardo and Henry George. In their writings,
Ricardo and George assumed that the supply of land to an economy
is fixed so that its supply curve is vertical. A vertical supply curve
simply means that landowners will supply the same amount of
land no matter what the price of land is. If S represents the supply
of land in Figure 10–8, and D_1 represents the demand curve, then
the equilibrium price of land will be p_1. If the demand curve shifted
for some reason, then the equilibrium price would change, but
quantity would remain at Q_1 units of land.

Now suppose the equilibrium price for land is p_1. Then, in
Figure 10–8, area $0p_1AQ_1$ represents the income landowners
receive for the use of their land. Ricardo and George considered this
area to represent economic rents. Today economists refer to this
income as *Ricardian rent*.

But are Ricardian rents—landowners' incomes—economic

FIGURE 10–8   **RICARDIAN RENT**

*If an input is in fixed
supply, then all
payments to owners of
that factor are economic
rents. These rents are
called Ricardian rents.*

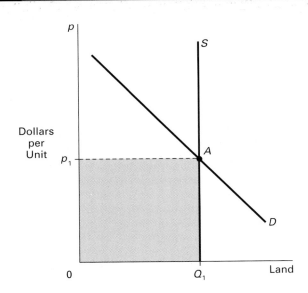

rents as we have defined them? In fact they are. Because the supply curve for land is assumed to be vertical, there is no opportunity cost associated with using the land; that is, even at a price of zero, landowners will supply Q_1 units of land. This being the case, the minimum payment necessary to keep land in its current employment is also zero and any revenue collected from the sale of land will be above the minimum amount necessary to keep it in its current use.

EXAMPLE 10-3

THE JACKSONS' VICTORY TOUR

One of the most successful American entertainers of the 1980s was Michael Jackson. His "Thriller" was the top-selling record album in history. In 1984 Michael and his four brothers gave several concerts on a highly successful "Victory Tour" around the U.S. In order to make sure that everyone wanting to purchase a ticket for one of the concerts would be treated fairly, Michael insisted that all tickets be sold for $30 per ticket. However, even at this price there was excess demand for the tickets as evidenced by scalpers' prices in excess of $500. (a) Assuming that, on average, each concert stadium seats 80,000 people and that the long-run equilibrium price of tickets is $80, illustrate the economic rents going to the Jacksons for one of their concerts. (b) Illustrate the rents going to scalpers.

■ **SOLUTION** (a) Figure 10-9(a) shows the supply and demand curves for concert tickets. The supply curve is vertical at 80,000 seats, which is the average capacity of stadiums on the Victory Tour. In the absence of any price controls, the equilibrium ticket price is $80. If the Jacksons artificially set a price of $30 per ticket, they will receive economic rents equal to area $0CEF$ or $2,400,000 per concert.

(b) At a price of $30 per ticket, there is excess demand. If scalpers sell tickets at the equilibrium price of $80, then they will collect area $BGEC$, or $4,000,000, in rents. However, if scalpers can identify concertgoers who place the highest value on tickets, they can charge what each individual is willing to pay (area $AGF0$) and collect $AGEC$ in rents. By restricting ticket prices to $30, Michael has essentially created a windfall in rents to scalpers.

FIGURE 10-9 **SCALPERS RENTS FOR THE JACKSON'S VICTORY TOUR**

If ticket prices are set below the market price, scalpers reap much of the economic rents. If they charge the market clearing price, rents are represented by area BGEC. If they charge what concertgoers are willing to pay, rents are given by area AGEC. ■

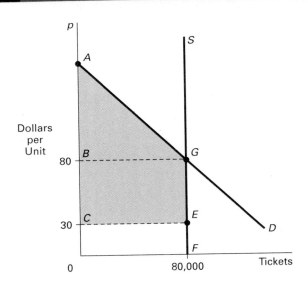

1. For inputs we must distinguish between industry and market demand. The long-run industry input demand curve is the sum of all the quantities employed by each firm in an industry. It takes into account the change in output price that results when industry-wide supply changes.

2. The long-run market input demand curve is the sum of the quantities demanded by all industries using the input. The market input demand curve is the horizontal sum of individual firms' input demand curves.

3. Inputs that one firm produces and other firms buy or rent to use in the production of final goods and services have positively sloped market input supply curves. Even though individual labor supply curves may be positively or negatively sloped, the market labor supply curve is positively sloped.

4. When we are dealing with input markets, long-run competitive equilibrium requires that firms earn zero profit and that the input market clears. The intersection of the long-run supply and demand curves determines the equilibrium price and level of employment.

5. When we are studying the labor market, long-run equilibrium also implies that wage rate differences across occupations must reflect the costs of acquiring the skills necessary for the job. In particular, wage differences must be such that the return—net of investment costs—from being employed in one occupation should be equal to the return from being employed in any other occupation.

6. Economic rent is any payment made to resource owners over and above the minimum payment necessary to keep inputs in their current employment. In the input market, it is the area above the market input supply curve and below the price that input owners receive for their services.

SUMMARY

Long-run Industry Input
   Demand Curve
Market Input Demand
Industry Input Supply

Market Input Supply
Market Labor Supply Curve
Compensating Wage
   Differentials

KEY TERMS

QUESTIONS AND PROBLEMS

1. Helen's Harley Haven sells motorcycles. Currently, the number of motorcycles the firm can sell per month is given by

$$Y = L - .05L^2$$

where L is the number of workers the firm employs per month. The marginal product of labor is

$$MP_L = 1 - .1L.$$

The market price for motorcycles is currently $5,000.
a) Assuming that Helen's is a price-taking firm, determine the profit-maximizing demand for labor if the wage rate is $3,000 per month.
b) Derive the short-run labor demand curve and illustrate it with a graph.

2. a) If the productivity of workers increases, what will happen to the long-run market demand curve for workers? Explain.
b) If the demand for red dye #5 falls, what will happen to the long-run industry demand curves for inputs employed in the dye-making industry?

3. a) Explain the effect of a 10% increase in the legal minimum wage on employment if the price elasticity of demand for semiskilled labor is 2.0.
b) How does your answer change if the price elasticity of demand is .2?

4. a) If the supply of workers to a particular industry increases, what will happen to wages and employment?
b) Does this increase in supply benefit workers, employers, consumers? Explain.

5. Evaluate the following statement: "The supply curve of neuro-surgeons is vertical because few people have the ability to be neurosurgeons."

6. In order to gain a cost advantage over his rivals, Rocky Raccoon has decided to cut wages to his employees by 20%. Will this work? Explain.

7. Suppose that the demand and supply functions for computer analysts in the U.S. are given by

$$L = D_L(w) = 20 - .1w$$

and
$$L = S_L(w) = 12 + .1w$$

where L is thousands of person-hours per year and w is the wage rate per hour.
a) Determine the equilibrium wage rate and level of employment.

b) If the government imposes a payroll tax equal to 10 dollars per hour on employers of computer analysts, what will be the new equilibrium wage rate and level of employment?

8. Suppose that the demand for quarterbacks on NFL football teams is given by

$$L = D_L(w) = 100 - .0001w$$

and the supply of quarterbacks is

$$L = S_L(w) = .0001w$$

where L is the number of players and w is the annual salary.

a) Graph the supply and demand curves.

b) Determine the equilibrium wage rate for quarterbacks.

c) Do quarterbacks collect any economic rents?

d) If attendance at NFL games drops because of increased interest in college football, what will happen to the quarterbacks' equilibrium wage and level of employment?

9. a) If a decrease in the demand for oranges results in an increase in the demand for apples, how will this affect the prices of factors of production employed in the apple industry?

b) Who benefits from the increase in the demand for apples?

10. Recently, automobile manufacturers in the U.S. replaced some assembly line workers with robots. Some U.A.W. activists vehemently opposed this move, arguing that such labor-saving technologies are the source of many of the problems confronting U.S. workers. Management, on the other hand, argued that introducing the new technology would actually make workers better off. With whom do you agree? Explain carefully.

11. a) Why are doctors paid more than janitors?

b) Does this mean that society values doctors more than janitors? Explain carefully.

12. Upon graduation, accounting students typically receive higher starting salaries than do those who graduate with a marketing major. This being the case, are these two labor markets in equilibrium? Be sure to discuss both the short and long runs.

13. Explain the meaning of economic rent as it applies to resource owners. It is often argued that government should tax land rents since this would not affect supply. Do you agree? Explain.

14. "The government really has no control over who bears the cost of a payroll tax, because the real effects of the tax are the same

whether the tax is collected from employers, employees, or both." Using the competitive model, verify or refute this statement.

15. Proponents of national health insurance have argued for financing the program with revenues generated by an additional payroll tax levied on firms. Does this mean that firms would, effectively, bear the cost of national health insurance? Explain carefully.

REFERENCES   Kreps, D. 1990. *A Course in Microeconomic Theory*. Princeton: Princeton University Press.

Varian, H. 1992. *Microeconomic Analysis*. 3d ed. New York: Norton.

APPLICATIONS USING THE COMPETITIVE MODEL

11

LEARNING OBJECTIVES

After completing Chapter 11 you should be able to do the following:

■ Show how to use consumer surplus and economic rent to evaluate the gains and losses stemming from government policies.

■ Analyze the economic effects of excise taxes, income taxes, price ceilings, price floors, minimum wages, cost-saving innovations, quotas, and tariffs using the competitive model.

EXAMPLES

In this chapter we show how the supply and demand model can be applied to a wide variety of economic issues. The examples in this chapter deal with recent U.S. economic phenomena. In particular, we will analyze the tax on cigarette producers, the personal income tax, the gasoline crises of 1973–1974 and 1979, agricultural price supports for corn, the minimum wage law, the dramatic decline in prices of videocassette recorders, and import quotas on memory chips for personal computers.

Even though at this point we should all know how supply and demand interact to determine prices and quantities, understanding the competitive model well enough to use it to investigate specific policies takes practice. The more problems we practice, the easier it will be for us to use the competitive model to analyze new issues.

11.1 USING CONSUMER SURPLUS AND ECONOMIC RENT TO EVALUATE THE GAINS AND LOSSES FROM GOVERNMENT POLICIES

■ When we evaluate a particular government policy that affects equilibrium prices and quantities, we consider how the policy affects the well-being of consumers, producers, resource owners, and society as a whole. In order to determine whether or not various groups are better off or worse off, we need a way to measure the gains and losses caused by the government policy. We do this by calculating the *changes* that the policy causes in consumer surplus, economic rent, and economic profit.

Recall that consumer surplus measures the net benefit consumers obtain from a competitive market, economic rent measures the net benefit to resource owners, and economic profit measures the net benefit to producers. Thus, observing how each of these changes in response to a change in the economic environment will tell us who benefits from the latter and who is harmed by it. In addition, observing how the sum of consumer surplus, economic rent, and economic profit, which we call **total economic surplus,** changes will tell us whether or not society as a whole is better off or worse off.

To give an example, Figure 11–1 shows total surplus for a competitive market in long-run equilibrium. Consumer surplus is the area below the demand curve and above the price consumers pay for the good, or area p^*AC. Economic rent is the area above the long-run industry supply curve and below the price producers receive for the good, or area $0p^*C$. Economic profit is zero, because the industry is in long-run equilibrium. Thus, total surplus is area $0AC$.

Now suppose that a government policy restricts output to Y_1 units. Consumers are willing to pay p_1 for this quantity of good y so that consumer surplus falls to p_1AC. Consumers are now worse off; p^*p_1BC, the reduction in consumer surplus, is a measure of how

FIGURE 11–1

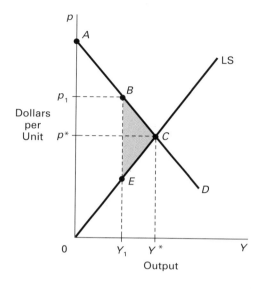

A government policy restricting output to Y_1 units causes aggregate surplus to fall from 0BC to 0ABE. The deadweight loss associated with the policy is BCE.

much worse off. Economic rent is now $0p_1BE$, which may be either larger or smaller than before government intervention, so we cannot say whether resource owners are better off or worse off. Producers continue to operate along the long-run industry supply curve earning zero economic profit, so the policy has no effect on owners of firms in this industry. Total surplus, on the other hand, has fallen to $0ABE$, so society as a whole is worse off (compared to the competitive equilibrium it was in with no government intervention); area BCE measures how much worse off society is. Economists call this the **deadweight loss** or **inefficiency** associated with the policy. (Chapters 15 and 16 discuss economic efficiency at length.)

■ Table 11–1 gives data on the various sources of U.S. government revenues for 1988. The data show that federal government revenues amounted to $1,012.343 billion in fiscal 1988 and that tax receipts accounted for over 87% of these revenues. Individual income taxes are the most important source of federal government tax revenues. In 1988 individual income taxes generated over $400 billion or 39% of federal government revenues. Payroll taxes, which are used to finance Social Security, accounted for 32% of revenues. The

11.2 TAXATION

TABLE 11-1

GOVERNMENT
REVENUE IN THE
U.S.: 1987-88
(BILLIONS OF
DOLLARS)

	Federal Government	State and Local Governments
Total revenue	1,012.343	884.500
Intergovernmental revenue	2.859	117.602
Taxes	882.388	540.515
Property	—	132.240
Sales, gross receipts, customs	52.604	156.257
Individual income taxes	401.181	88.349
Corporate net income	94.195	23.741
Payroll taxes	319.788	104.840
Other taxes	14.620	35.088
Miscellaneous revenue	127.096	226.384

Source: Bureau of the Census, U.S. Department of Commerce.

corporate income (profit) tax generated approximately $94 billion or 9% of revenues.

Table 11-1 also indicates that state and local governments raised $884.5 billion in fiscal 1988 and that taxes accounted for 60% of these revenues. The most important sources of tax revenues for state and local governments are sales taxes, property taxes, individual income taxes, and payroll taxes.

Since taxes are such an important source of government revenues, it is important to understand the economic effects of different types of taxes. If you take a course in public finance, you will spend a great deal of time analyzing each of the taxes shown in Table 11-1. Here we will demonstrate how to use the competitive model to analyze two important types: excise taxes and personal income taxes.

EXCISE TAXES

Excise taxes are selective taxes levied on either the consumption or production of certain goods. In the U.S., federal, state, and local governments impose excise taxes on a variety of goods such as alcoholic beverages, cigarettes, automobile tires, gasoline, and selective retail sales.

There are two basic types of excise taxes. A *per-unit excise tax* requires a payment of a fixed amount of money for every unit of a particular commodity bought or sold. The excise taxes on alcoholic beverages, cigarettes, automobile tires, and gasoline are examples of per-unit excise taxes. An *ad valorem excise tax* is a tax levied as a percentage of the market price of a good. Retail sales taxes are examples of ad valorem excise taxes. The economic effects of per-unit excise taxes and ad valorem excise taxes are the same.

In the next example, we will use the competitive model to determine the economic impact of a per-unit excise tax. We are interested in how the tax is shared between producers and consumers; how it affects prices, production, consumption, and employment; and how it affects economic welfare.

EXAMPLE 11–1

THE CIGARETTE TAX

During the Reagan administration, 1981–88, domestic policy makers made two issues their primary concerns: controlling the federal deficit and reducing the personal income tax burden. Some advisors suggested that both objectives could be met by increasing federal excise taxes on alcoholic beverages and cigarettes. Currently, President Bush's economic advisors are also weighing the pros and cons of increasing federal excise taxes to raise more revenues. Suppose that the Bush administration has hired us to analyze the economic effects of the current $.10 per-pack excise tax levied on producers of cigarettes. In particular, we are to determine the impact of the tax on producers, consumers, and resource owners, and on long-run equilibrium prices and quantities.

■ **SOLUTION** We begin our investigation by assuming that the cigarette industry is characterized by perfect competition, that the firms in the cigarette business have identical U-shaped average cost curves, and, at least initially, that this is a constant cost industry. After examining the constant cost case, we can then see whether our analysis changes substantially if, in fact, the cigarette industry is an increasing cost industry.

CASE 1: A CONSTANT COST INDUSTRY Suppose that, prior to the tax increase, the industry is in long-run equilibrium. Industry output is Y_0 packs of cigarettes per year and the market price is p_0 dollars per pack. Each firm in the business maximizes profit by producing y_0 packs of cigarettes per year and earns zero economic profit. We have shown this situation graphically. Figure 11–2(a) illustrates the representative firm's per-unit cost curves. Price is equal to the minimum of the long-run average cost curve, labeled LAC. In Figure 11–2(b) D is the market demand curve for cigarettes, SS_1 is

FIGURE 11–2   EFFECTS OF AN EXCISE TAX: A CONSTANT COST INDUSTRY

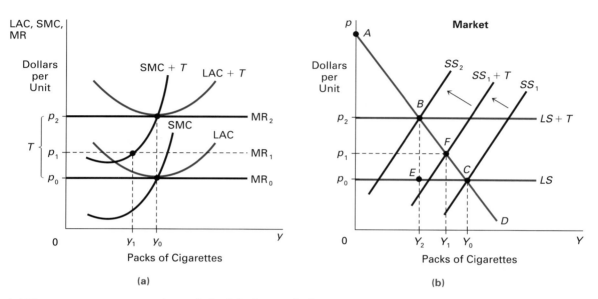

(a) Firms earn zero economic profit both before and after imposition of the tax. (b) An excise tax shifts LS up by the amount of the tax to LS + T. Output falls, and price rises by the amount of the tax.

the short-run market supply curve, and LS is the long-run market supply curve. The market clears at price p_0 and quantity Y_0.

Now suppose the government levies a tax on cigarettes equal to $T = \$.10$ per pack. Consider first what happens at the firm level. For every unit produced, cost increases by T dollars; that is, for each pack of cigarettes they produce, owners of cigarette firms must pay not only the production costs but also the tax. Thus, from the producer's perspective the per-unit cost of producing cigarettes has increased to $LAC + T$ dollars and the short-run marginal cost of producing cigarettes has increased to $SMC + T$. In effect, the tax shifts the cost curves up vertically by the amount of the tax (and all other per-unit cost curves shift as well). These after-tax cost curves are shown in Figure 11–2(a).

In the short run how will a firm already in the business react to the tax? Since at every level of output the marginal cost of production is higher by T dollars per unit of output, the short-run market supply curve shifts up by the amount of the tax, $SS_1 + T$ in

Figure 11-2(b). When the short-run market supply curve shifts, output price begins to rise until the market reaches the short-run equilibrium point where supply is equal to demand, point F in the diagram. In this instance, the new short-run equilibrium price and quantity are p_1 and Y_1 respectively.

The profit-maximizing firm will now produce at the point where price, p_1, is equal to marginal costs. In Figure 11-2(a), profit is maximized in the short run when SMC $+ T = p_1$ or when the output rate is y_1 packs per year. Therefore, each firm currently in the business reduces production from y_0 to y_1 packs per year.

At this price, however, each firm in the industry incurs a loss since price is now less than average cost: $p_1 <$ LAC $+ T$ at y_1. This means that owners of firms in the cigarette industry are doing worse than they could do in the next best alternative and some will exit the industry. As this happens, the short-run market supply curve shifts to the left even further and the market price rises once again. As long as some firms in the industry are incurring losses, some firms will continue to exit the business.

How long will this continue? Since we have assumed that the cigarette industry is a constant cost industry, the cost curves do not change as output falls. Thus, exit continues until the market price increases to the minimum of the LAC $+ T$ curve or until the price increases to $p_2 = p_0 + T$ dollars per pack. At this price firms produce y_0 packs per year and again earn zero economic profit. Total revenue is $p_2 y_0$, total production cost is $p_0 y_0$, total tax liability to the government is $T y_0$, and profit is given by

$$\pi = \text{TR} - \text{LTC} - \text{Tax Liability} = (p_2 - p_0 - T) y_0 = 0.$$

THE MARKET FOR INPUTS USED IN THE CIGARETTE INDUSTRY After the tax increase, the new long-run competitive equilibrium results in higher prices for cigarettes and lower levels of production and consumption. But what effect does the tax increase have on employment and factor prices?

In Figure 11-3, we have drawn the long-run market supply and demand curves for labor employed in the cigarette industry. The long-run market supply curve is horizontal because we have assumed that this is a constant cost industry; that is, we have assumed that a change in industry-wide output, which leads to a change in industry-wide employment, does not affect input prices. Demand curve D_L^1 represents firms' demand for labor when cigarettes are selling for p_0 dollars per pack. Given these supply and demand curves, the equilibrium wage rate and level of employment are w_1 and L_1 respectively.

In the short run, the tax increase lowers the marginal revenue product of labor because each additional worker hired now generates less after-tax revenue than before: $(p_1 - T)MP_L < p_0MP_L$. As the marginal revenue product of labor falls, the market demand curve for labor shifts to the left. In the long run, as firms exit the industry this also causes a reduction in the demand for labor since there are now fewer firms in the cigarette business. Consequently, the market demand for labor shifts even further to the left.

In Figure 11–3, D_L^2 is the new long-run market demand curve for labor. After the tax increase, the long-run equilibrium wage rate remains at w_1 (remember, this is a constant cost industry) and the equilibrium level of employment falls to L_2.

WINNERS AND LOSERS Next we can ask who wins and who loses as a result of the tax. First, consider consumers. Prior to the tax, consumer surplus is area ACp_0 in Figure 11–2(b). After the government levies the tax, the quantity of cigarettes bought and sold falls from Y_0 to Y_2 and the price consumers pay increases to

FIGURE 11-3	EFFECTS OF AN EXCISE TAX ON WAGES AND EMPLOYMENT FOR A CONSTANT COST INDUSTRY

In the long run the excise tax causes the demand curve for labor to shift from D_L^1 to D_L^2. As a result, for a constant cost industry the wage rate remains the same and employment falls.

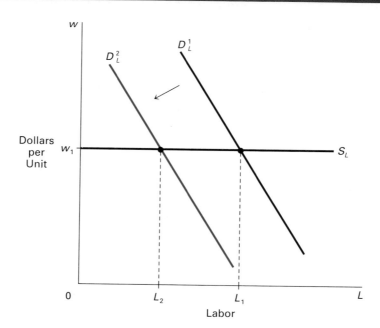

p_2. The result is that consumer surplus falls to ABp_2; that is, the tax increase makes cigarette consumers worse off.

Second, consider producers. Since profit is zero in the long run both before and after the tax, producers are neither worse off nor better off. This is a commonly misunderstood result. Even though the producer has "passed on" 100% of the tax to consumers— consumers now pay $p_2 = p_0 + T$ for cigarettes—quantity sold falls until profit is zero.

Finally, consider the owners of the resources used to produce cigarettes. Resources owners include workers, owners of capital, and owners of any other inputs that contribute to the production of cigarettes. Recall that, in the long-run, economic rent—the area between the long-run industry supply curve and the price that producers receive for their goods—is a measure of the returns over and above the minimum needed to keep these factors in their current employment. In this instance, the long-run supply curve is horizontal and economic rent is zero. Thus, the resource owners who keep their resources in the cigarette industry after the tax neither win nor lose.

What about the firms that left the industry? Do those individuals who supplied resources to these firms win or lose? Since we are assuming all markets are perfectly competitive, resources released when firms exit an industry find employment in other industries. Hence, in the long run these resource owners are neither better off nor worse off than before.

So far, we have found that consumers are worse off and that producers and resource owners are neither better off nor worse off. Does anyone benefit from the tax? Of course, the winners are those who will eventually benefit from the government's expenditures of the revenues generated by the tax. After the government levies the tax, revenues increase. In Figure 11–2(b) area p_2BEp_0 represents this increase. We use this area to measure the gains to individuals benefiting from government expenditures of tax revenues.

CASE 2: AN INCREASING COST INDUSTRY If the cigarette industry is an increasing cost industry, the analysis proceeds in the same manner as for the constant cost case but the impact of the tax is quite different.

Once again, suppose that prior to the tax the industry is in long-run equilibrium. Industry output is Y_1 packs of cigarettes per year and the market price is p_1 dollars per pack. Each firm in the business maximizes profit and earns zero economic profit. This situation is shown in Figure 11–4(a). The long-run market supply curve is upward-sloping because we have assumed that, in this

FIGURE 11–4   EFFECTS OF AN EXCISE TAX: AN INCREASING COST INDUSTRY

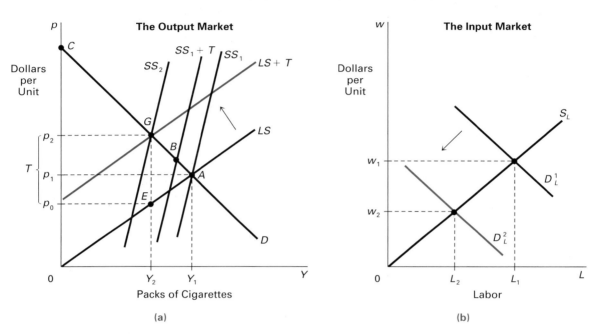

(a) An excise tax shifts LS up by the amount of the tax to LS + T. Output falls and price rises; however, now price increases by less than the tax. (b) The excise tax reduces the demand for labor in the long run, which, in this instance, lowers employment and the wage rate.

instance, the cigarette industry is an increasing cost industry. The market clears at price p_1 and quantity Y_1.

Now suppose the government imposes a tax on cigarettes of T dollars per pack. First, consider what happens at the firm level. As before, cost has increased by T dollars for every unit produced; in effect, the tax shifts the cost curves up vertically by the amount of the tax.

In the short run, the industry is in equilibrium when supply is equal to demand, point B in Figure 11–4(a). Price is higher, output is lower, and, since price is less than average cost, each firm in the industry incurs a loss.

We still have not reached the new long-run equilibrium point. Firms already in the business are making losses and, as a result, some firms will exit the industry. As this happens, industry output continues to fall. Since here we are assuming that the cigarette industry is an increasing cost industry, the reduction in output lowers factor costs which, in turn, shifts the cost curves down.

How long does this continue? Exit continues until firms again earn zero profit after taxes have been collected; that is, until the after-tax price is p_0. We can determine the final long-run equilibrium price and quantity by shifting the long-run industry supply curve up by the amount of the tax. The new long-run industry supply curve, $LS + T$ in the diagram, intersects the demand curve at a price of p_2 dollars per pack. Industry output falls to Y_2. At the new market price, firms in the industry once again earn zero economic profit.

THE MARKET FOR INPUTS USED IN THE CIGARETTE INDUSTRY After the tax, the new long-run competitive equilibrium results in higher prices for cigarettes and lower levels of production and consumption. But what effect does the tax have on employment and factor prices?

In Figure 11–4(b), we have drawn the long-run market supply and demand curves for labor employed in the cigarette industry. The long-run market supply curve is positively sloped because we are assuming that this is an increasing cost industry—that is, that an increase (decrease) in industry wide output, which leads to an increase (decrease) in industry wide employment, increases (decreases) some input prices. Demand curve D_L^1 represents firms' demand for labor when cigarettes are selling for p_1 dollars per pack. Given these supply and demand curves, the equilibrium wage rate and level of employment are w_1 and L_1 respectively.

In the short run, the tax lowers the marginal revenue product of labor since each additional worker hired now generates less after-tax revenue than before. As the marginal revenue product of labor falls, the market demand curve for labor shifts to the left. In the long run, as firms exit the industry this also causes a reduction in the demand for labor since there are now fewer firms in the cigarette business. Consequently, the market demand for labor shifts even further to the left.

In Figure 11–4(b), D_L^2 is the new long-run market demand curve for labor. After the tax is levied, the long-run equilibrium wage rate falls to w_2 (because this is an increasing cost industry) and the equilibrium level of employment falls to L_2.

WINNERS AND LOSERS Once again we can ask who wins and who loses as a result of the tax. Notice that in an increasing cost industry producers and consumers "share" the tax. Before the tax, consumers are paying p_1 dollars per pack, all of which producers are pocketing. After the tax, consumers pay a higher price of p_2 dollars per pack. Producers receive p_2 dollars from consumers but from this they must deduct the payment to the tax collector. Producers now pocket only $p_2 - T = p_0$ dollars per pack. Thus, both consumers and producers share the tax.

Now we can determine who wins and who loses. First, consider consumers. Prior to the tax, consumer surplus is area CAp_1 (Figure 11–4[a]). After the tax, the quantity of cigarettes bought and sold falls to Y_2 and the price consumers pay increases to p_2. As a result, consumer surplus falls to CGp_2. Just as before, the tax makes cigarette consumers worse off.

Next, consider producers. Since profit is zero in the long run both before and after the tax, producers are neither worse off nor better off. Even though the producer has not "passed on" 100% of the tax to consumers, quantity sold falls until profit is zero.

Third, consider the owners of the resources used to produce cigarettes. Economic rent before the tax is $0Ap_1$. After the tax increase, economic rent falls to $0Ep_0$. Because economic rent has fallen, the owners of resources whose supply curves are positively sloped are worse off. (The owners of factors of production with perfectly elastic supply curves are neither worse off nor better off.) Thus, by reducing output, the tax lowers the return to owners of those resources employed in the cigarette business that have positively sloped supply curves.

Finally, let us look at the government. As before, the government collects additional tax revenues and those individuals who will benefit from government expenditures of these revenues are better off. In Figure 11–4(a), tax revenues increase by p_2GEp_0. Thus, when we have an increasing cost industry, both consumers and resource owners are worse off as a result of the tax increase and those benefiting from government expenditures generated by the tax are better off. ∎

We have seen how an excise tax benefits some individuals and harms others, but what has happened to the total well-being of all economic agents affected by such a tax? A complete theoretical answer to this question would require an analysis of each market directly or indirectly affected by the tax. This is called *general equilibrium* analysis and it will be discussed in Chapter 16. However, at this point we can cite some empirical evidence suggesting that excise taxes result in a substantial reduction in total surplus.

As a practical matter, policy makers need to know if the inefficiencies generated by excise taxes are large enough to be important. Recently, three economists, C. Ballard, J. Shoven, and J. Whalley, estimated the inefficiency associated with the excise taxes that are levied on U.S. consumers and producers (C. Ballard, J. Shoven, and J. Whalley, "General Equilibrium Computations of the Marginal Welfare Costs of Taxes in the United States," *The American Economic Review* 75 [March 1985]). They concluded that the inefficiencies are substantial: each additional dollar of tax revenues generated by excise taxes causes an inefficiency of between $.26 and $.39. This means that if excise taxes are to finance government expenditures, then the benefits generated by the expenditures must be at least 26% greater than the revenues needed to fund the program.

As shown in Table 11–1, **personal income taxes** represent the major source of revenue for both federal and state governments in the United States. In Chapter 5 we investigated the economic effects of income taxes from an individual's perspective. Here we will use the competitive model to determine the economic impact of income taxes from a market perspective.

PERSONAL INCOME TAXES

EXAMPLE 11–2

INCOME TAXES

The Tax Reform Act of 1986 represents one of the most dramatic overhauls of the United States' income tax system. The most basic change in the tax code is a new tax rate structure that moves the U.S. closer to levying a single tax rate. For most individual taxpayers, the new tax rate structure will have only two tax brackets (while prior to 1987 there were 16 tax brackets). For example, in 1988 the marginal tax rates for all single individuals were 15% on the first $17,850 of taxable income and 28% on taxable income in excess of that amount.

Suppose we have been asked to explain the economic effects of a 28% income tax on single taxpayers. In particular, we are asked to examine how this tax affects the equilibrium wage and level of employment, and how it affects producers, consumers, and resource owners.

■ **SOLUTION** For simplicity let us begin by assuming that all workers are identical in all relevant aspects so that in equilibrium there is a single wage rate. (We could also think of this as focusing on one particular labor market in the economy.) Suppose that prior to the tax the labor market is in long-run equilibrium. In Figure 11−5(a), D_L is the long-run demand curve for labor and S_L is the long-run labor supply curve prior to the imposition of the income tax. The equilibrium wage rate and level of employment are w_1 and L_1 respectively.

Now suppose the government levies an income tax of $t = 28\%$. Consider what this means from the worker's perspective. For any given wage rate, the net after-tax wage falls. This means that, in order to get workers to supply any given amount of labor, employers must pay them a higher wage. For example, in Figure 11−5(a) workers initially would have been willing to supply L_0

FIGURE 11−5   **THE EFFECTS OF AN INCOME TAX**

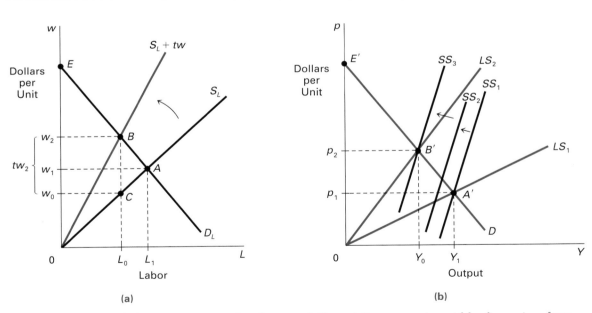

(a) An income tax shifts S_L to $S_L + tw$. Employment falls and the wage rate paid by firms rises from w_1 to w_2; however, the net (after-tax) wage received by workers falls from w_1 to w_0. (b) The income tax increases production costs as shown by the shift in the long-run supply curve. As a result, output falls and price rises.

units of labor per year when the wage rate was w_0 dollars per unit. After the tax, workers must be paid w_2 dollars per unit to get them to supply L_0 units of labor per year, where $w_2 - tw_2 = w_0$. That is, employers must pay workers a wage that yields a net after-tax wage of w_0.

Thus, from the worker's perspective the income tax is like an ad valorem excise tax on labor supply and it shifts (rotates) the labor supply curve from S_L to $S_L + tw$. Notice that the tax does not cause a *parallel* shift in the labor supply curve. This is because, for a given tax rate, the amount paid in taxes per unit of labor supplied—the vertical distance between S_L and $S_L + tw$—increases with the wage rate. The new equilibrium point is B. The market wage increases from w_1 to w_2 and employment falls from L_1 to L_0 hours per year.

THE MARKET FOR GOODS AND SERVICES After the imposition of the income tax, the new long-run competitive equilibrium results in higher wage rates and fewer hours worked per year. But what effect does the tax have on the prices and quantities of goods and services?

In Figure 11–5(b), we have drawn the long-run market supply and demand curves for good Y. Supply curve LS_1 represents the supply of good Y when the wage is w_1 dollars per hour. Given these supply and demand curves, the equilibrium price and quantity are p_1 and Y_1 respectively.

When the government imposes the income tax, the wage rate increases to w_2 and this, in turn, increases the marginal cost of production. As a result of the increase in marginal costs, the short-run supply curve shifts up from SS_1 to SS_2, price begins to rise, and output begins to fall. In the long run, firms employing workers subject to the income tax make losses and some exit the industry, thus reducing supply even further. In Figure 11–5(b), LS_2 is the new long-run market supply curve. After the tax is levied, the long-run equilibrium price increases to p_2 while quantity falls to Y_0.

WINNERS AND LOSERS Who benefits from and who is harmed by an income tax? Notice that, because the labor supply curve is positively sloped, employers and workers share the tax. Before the tax, firms were paying w_1 dollars per hour of labor employed and workers were receiving w_1 dollars per hour worked. After the tax, firms pay a higher wage of w_2 dollars per hour. Workers receive w_2 dollars per hour from producers but from this they must pay income taxes. They now take home only $w_0 = w_2 (1 - t)$ dollars per worker. Hence, both workers and employers share the tax.

Now we can determine who wins and who loses. First, consider workers. Prior to the tax, economic rent going to workers is given by area w_1A0 in Figure 11–5(a). After the income tax is levied, employment falls to L_0 hours per year and the net wage workers receive falls to w_0 dollars per hour. The result is that economic rent falls to w_0C0. The tax, therefore, makes workers worse off.

Next, consider consumers, producers, and all resource owners employed in this industry. When we want to examine the impact of some policy on producers and consumers, it is always easiest to look at the output market (shown in Figure 11–5[b]). From the diagram, we find that consumers of goods and services, on the one hand, are worse off: consumer surplus before the tax is given by area $p_1E'A'$; after the tax, it falls to $p_2E'B'$. Producers, on the other hand, earn zero economic profit both before and after the tax and are neither worse off nor better off. Even though firms must pay a higher wage, quantity falls and price rises until profit is zero once again. The effect of the tax on resource owners as a group is ambiguous. Economic rent changes from $0p_1A'$ prior to the tax to $0p_2B'$ after the tax. We cannot say, in general, which of these areas is larger. We do know, though, that suppliers of labor are worse off, so that if resource owners as a whole are actually better off, it must be because the economic rent going to owners of capital increases. However, this can only occur if there is a substantial substitution of capital for labor when the cost of labor increases.

Finally, consider the government. The government collects additional tax revenues. In Figure 11–5(a), workers' income before taxes are paid is area $0w_2BL_0$; after tax, income is area $0w_0CL_0$; thus, tax revenues increase by $w_2BCw_0 = 0w_2BL_0 - 0w_0CL_0$ dollars. (Those individuals benefiting from government expenditures of these revenues are better off.) ∎

Income taxes also lead to economic inefficiencies. Ballard, Shoven, and Whalley estimate that each additional dollar of tax revenues generated by income taxes causes an inefficiency of between \$.16 and \$.31. This means that if income taxes are used to raise revenues, then the benefits generated by spending these tax revenues must be at least 16% greater than the revenues collected if the inefficiency is to be overcome.

11.3 WAGE AND PRICE CONTROLS

∎ Governments often intervene in certain markets by imposing wage and price controls. Perhaps the most famous (or infamous) use of wage and price controls in recent times was when President Nixon imposed nationwide wage and price controls in 1971. In the following section we will use the competitive model to determine the economic effects of various types of wage and price controls that have been used in the U.S.

Price ceilings are restrictions imposed by the government to prevent prices from rising to their long-run equilibrium levels. Throughout the history of the U.S. there have been several instances when the government has imposed price ceilings in an attempt to keep prices below their market clearing levels. During the 1970s the federal government kept both the price of natural gas and the price of gasoline far below their equilibrium levels. During World War II many U.S. cities imposed a variety of price ceilings. One of the most common was the rent control ordinance, which was nothing more than a price ceiling on rental rates for housing units. In fact, many U.S. cities still use some form of rent control today.

In the next example, we investigate the economic effects of a price ceiling imposed on the market for gasoline. This example will highlight how useful the concepts of consumer surplus and economic rent can be for evaluating economic policies.

PRICE CEILINGS: THE U.S. GASOLINE CRISES

EXAMPLE 11-3

A PRICE CEILING FOR GASOLINE

Recall from Example 5-2 that in 1973-74 and again in 1979 the nations of OPEC (Organization of Petroleum Exporting Countries) were successful in reducing the supply of oil to importing countries. As a result, gasoline prices in the countries affected by the shortage rose dramatically. However, as we learned in the earlier example, the U.S. federal government imposed a price ceiling on gasoline. The goal of this policy was to return the price of gasoline to pre-shortage levels so that owners of resources employed in the gasoline industry would not realize additional economic rents.

Let us suppose that, after gasoline prices rise in response to the oil shortage, the government imposes a price ceiling, fixing the price of gasoline at its pre-shortage level. How will this regulation impact on the quantity of gasoline bought and sold and the well-being of producers, consumers, and resource owners?

■ **SOLUTION** First we must determine the pre-shortage and post-shortage prices and quantities of gasoline in the absence of government regulation. In Figure 11-6, LS_1 and D are the

FIGURE 11–6   **A PRICE CEILING**

With a maximum price of p_1 dollars set below the equilibrium price of p_2 dollars, quantity supplied falls to Y_1, quantity demanded increases to Y_4, and a shortage of gasoline arises.

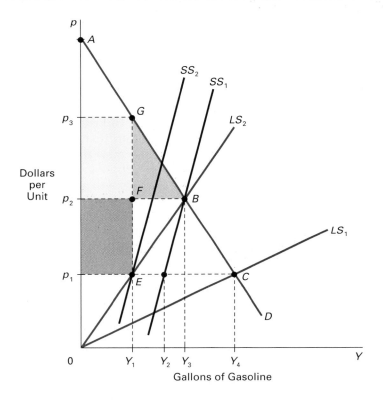

pre-shortage long-run supply and demand curves for gasoline. In this instance, the equilibrium price and quantity are p_1 dollars per gallon and Y_4 gallons respectively.

When OPEC limits the supply of oil, the long-run supply curve for gasoline shifts from LS_1 to LS_2 since it is now more costly to produce and sell any given quantity of gasoline. In the absence of a price ceiling, the post-shortage equilibrium price would be p_2 and the equilibrium quantity would be Y_3.

Now consider a government-imposed price ceiling equal to p_1 dollars per gallon; that is, owners of service stations are not allowed to charge a price exceeding p_1. What impact does this restriction have on quantity supplied, compared to the post-shortage equilibrium? Using Figure 11–6, we see that in the short run firms already in the business will reduce the supply of gasoline to Y_2. However, established firms incur losses at this price and begin exiting from the industry. This causes the short-run supply curve to shift from

SS_1 to SS_2. As a result, quantity supplied is reduced even further to Y_1 gallons of gasoline.

Given the ceiling price, quantity supplied is reduced; however, quantity demanded increases to Y_4. Since p_1 is below the market clearing price, a shortage of gasoline arises. Consumers demand Y_4 gallons but producers supply only Y_1 gallons so there is a shortage of $(Y_4 - Y_1)$ gallons.

WINNERS AND LOSERS Those who argue in favor of price ceilings maintain that they make consumers better off by returning prices to their original levels. It is clear from our analysis that the price ceiling does return the price of gasoline to its original level but who in fact benefits and who is harmed?

Here, we must consider consumers, producers, and resource owners. (Since the government is not collecting taxes or paying out subsidies, it does not enter the picture.)

Let us begin by examining consumers. It is commonly believed that price ceilings make consumers better off. Is this true? Let us compare consumer surplus with and without the price ceiling. In the absence of a price ceiling, consumer surplus would be area ABp_2 in Figure 11–6. With a price ceiling of p_1 dollars per gallon of gasoline, consumer surplus is $AGEp_1$. Which is larger? The answer is that we do not know for sure. Some consumers gain because they can buy gasoline at a lower price, but others lose because less gasoline is available for consumption and even though they would be willing to pay the price there is not any gasoline left to buy. The gain to consumers is represented by area p_2FEp_1; it is simply a transfer of surplus from resource owners to consumers. Area FBG represents the loss.

Whether or not consumers as a whole are better off or worse off depends on the sizes of these areas and these, in turn, depend on the elasticities of the supply and demand curves. If demand is relatively elastic, consumers are better off, but if demand is relatively inelastic, consumers are worse off.

In the discussion above, area $AGEp_1$ identified consumer surplus after the government imposed a price ceiling. This representation of consumer surplus implicitly assumes that the gasoline being bought and sold is allocated to the most valued customers; that is, to those willing to pay the most for it. However, since there is a shortage of gasoline, it is more likely that the available supply of gasoline is rationed by some other, nonprice, means.

As we discussed in Chapter 5, one common type of nonprice rationing requires individuals to wait in line to purchase the scarce good. During the U.S. gasoline crises of 1973–74 and 1979 this is precisely how gasoline was allocated. When individuals must wait in line to obtain a good they must pay not only a money price for the good but also the additional *waiting time price*.

From Figure 11–6 we see that gasoline consumers are willing to pay p_3 dollars per gallon to obtain Y_1 gallons. However, they pay only p_1 dollars per gallon because of the price ceiling. If gasoline is rationed by waiting in line, then the difference between what consumers are willing to pay and the money price they actually pay is the waiting time price for gasoline. In this example, the waiting time price is $(p_3 - p_1)$ dollars per gallon.

Now, if consumers must pay a money price of p_1 dollars per gallon and a waiting time price of $(p_3 - p_1)$ dollars, then in fact they are paying a total price of p_3 dollars per gallon. With nonprice rationing, therefore, consumers are paying in total what they are willing to pay. This means that consumer surplus when the price ceiling is in effect is really only area AGp_3. The price ceiling makes consumers worse off! Consumers lose GBF because output has decreased and they lose p_3GFp_2 because they must now pay a higher total price for gasoline.

What about producers? Since both with and without the price ceiling we assume that competition leads to a zero profit allocation of resources, producers are in the same position in both circumstances. They are earning what they could earn in the next best alternative.

Finally, consider the owners of the resources used to produce gasoline. Economic rent without the ceiling would be area p_2B0. With a maximum price of p_1, economic rent is p_1E0. Economic rent has definitely fallen as the result of the price ceiling; that is, resource owners are worse off. Because of the price ceiling, the return to factors of production employed in this industry falls. ■

Price ceilings result in a welfare loss to consumers and resource owners. But are these losses large enough to be important to policy makers? A study by contemporary economists Frech and Lee has indicated that the inefficiency associated with the price ceilings imposed during the oil crises of 1973–74 and 1979 were substantial (H.E. Frech, III, and W.C. Lee, "The Welfare Cost of Rationing-by-Queuing across Markets: Theory and Estimates from the U.S. Gasoline Crises," *The Quarterly Journal of Economics*, 102 [Feb. 1987]. Reprinted by permission of The MIT Press, Cambridge, Mass. Copyright © 1987 by the President and Fellows of Harvard College and the Massachusetts Institute of Technology.). Frech and Lee estimated that the loss in consumer surplus due to waiting time costs and due to the reduction in the quantity of gasoline bought and sold in California alone was $1,176,008,000 during the 1973–74 crisis and $798,618,000 during the 1979 crisis.

Price floors are government restrictions preventing the price of some good from falling to its equilibrium level. Examples of price floors imposed on U.S. markets include the former regulation of the airlines by the Civil Aeronautics Board (CAB), the minimum wage law, and a variety of agricultural price support schemes. Until 1978, the CAB set most airline fares well above those that would have prevailed in an unregulated environment; the federal government sets minimum wages that are designed to keep the wage rate above the market clearing wage; and price support schemes, many of which originated in the 1930s, are designed to keep the price of farm products above the market clearing price. The next section will examine minimum wage laws, and the problems at the end of the chapter will address the issue of airline regulation. Here we focus on U.S. agricultural policy.

Since the 1930s the U.S. government has played a dominant role in the nation's agriculture. The Food and Security Act of 1985 is the most recent comprehensive farm law. As Example 1–1 explained, the objective of this legislation is to support the incomes of producers of commodities such as dairy products, tobacco, wheat, cotton, rice, and corn by keeping the prices of these products above their market clearing levels. The proponents of these federal programs usually argue that price supports are necessary to ensure adequate food supplies, to protect small farms, to reduce price instability, and to reduce dependence on imports.

The competitive model can be used to analyze the economic impact of agricultural price support programs (and to answer some of the questions raised in Example 1–1). In Example 14–4 we will use the competitive model to analyze the government's policy to support the price of corn.

PRICE FLOORS: U.S. AGRICULTURAL POLICY

EXAMPLE 11–4

THE PRICE SUPPORT PROGRAM FOR CORN

In recent years Congress has mandated two support levels for corn: a *loan rate* and a *target price*. The loan rate is the price at which an eligible farmer can take out a price support loan. The unique feature of price support loans is that they do not have to be repaid. In order to take out a loan, the farmer uses his or her crops as collateral. If the market price of corn rises above the loan rate, then the farmer may sell the stored corn and repay the loan. If the market price of corn remains below the loan rate, then the farmer will keep the loan money and the government will take title to the corn that the farmer has used for collateral.

The target price is used to determine when farmers should receive *deficiency payments*. These payments are excise subsidies and are computed as the difference between the target price and the higher of the loan rate or the market price. When the market price falls below the target price, farmers begin receiving deficiency payments from the government.

In 1985 the market price of corn was approximately $1.50 per bushel. At this same time, the target price of corn was $3.00 and the loan rate was $2.40. Given these price support levels, determine the effect of this price support program for corn on the quantity of corn bought and sold and on the well-being of producers, consumers, and resource owners.

■ **SOLUTION** We begin by illustrating the long-run supply and demand curves for corn in the U.S. As Figure 11−7 shows, we assume that the corn industry is an increasing cost industry primarily because the price of land used to produce corn rises as industry-wide production of corn rises. In the absence of a price support program, the equilibrium price is $p_c = \$1.50$ per bushel of corn and the equilibrium quantity is Y_2 bushels.

Now suppose the government implements the price support program described above. Consider first the loan rate of $2.40 per bushel. Farmers can borrow $2.40 per bushel from the government as long as they place their corn in storage for collateral. Although farmers can take their corn out of storage at any time and sell it to repay the loan, they will not do this, since the market price for corn is below the loan rate. Thus, from a farmer's perspective the demand curve for corn is horizontal once the market price falls to $2.40. In Figure 11−7, the farmer's demand curve for corn is effectively *ABD'*.

In addition to price support loans, the government also makes deficiency payments equal to the target price minus the loan rate, or $.60 per bushel. From the farmer's perspective this lowers the marginal cost of production. In Figure 11−7, this is represented by a shift in the long-run industry supply curve from *LS* to *LS* + *S*, where $S = \$.60$ is the per-bushel subsidy.

What impact does this program have on quantity supplied? In the short run firms already in the business will increase their supply of corn. However, because each farmer now receives $3.00 per bushel, established firms make a profit and entry into the industry occurs. This causes the short-run supply curve to shift to the right. Now, how far does the short-run supply curve shift? Entry

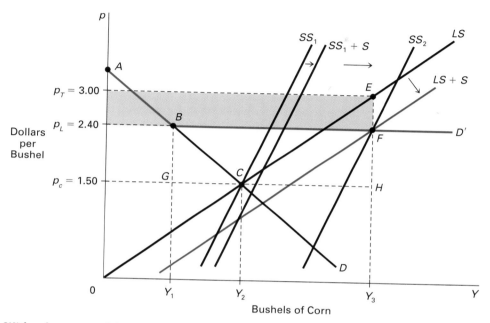

SUPPORTING THE PRICE OF CORN

FIGURE 11–7

With a loan rate of $2.40 per bushel and a deficiency payment of $.60 per bushel, the price consumers pay for corn rises from $1.50 to $2.40 per bushel and quantity demanded falls from Y_2 to Y_1. Producers receive $2.40 from consumers, and $.60 from the government, or a total of $3.00 per bushel of corn, and production increases from Y_2 to Y_3. The result is a surplus of corn, $(Y_3 - Y_1)$, which the government must buy to maintain the price support program.

occurs until each firm in the corn business earns zero economic profit and supply is equal to demand—that is, until industry output expands to Y_3 bushels of corn.

Given the support price program, quantity supplied increases, the price of corn increases to $2.40, and quantity demanded by consumers falls to Y_1. Since $2.40 is above the market clearing price, a surplus of corn arises. Consumers demand only Y_1 bushels but farmers supply Y_3 bushels and the government must buy up the surplus if the price floor is to be maintained.

WINNERS AND LOSERS Those who argue in favor of a price floor maintain that it will keep farmers in business and raise their standard of living. It is clear from our analysis that the price floor does keep farmers in business; in fact, it encourages more firms to enter the industry. But who wins and who loses?

Again, we must consider consumers, producers, resource owners, and the government. Let us begin with consumers. In the absence of the price support, consumer surplus is area ACp_c in Figure 11–7. With the price support program, consumer surplus falls to ABp_L. Consumers are worse off because the price is higher and consumption is lower.

What about producers? Since we are dealing with an agricultural business, oftentimes the owner of the firm and the owner of the resources used to produce the good are both the farmer. Nonetheless, we need to distinguish between the farmer as the owner of the firm and the farmer as a resource owner. Both with and without the price support we assume that competition leads to a zero profit allocation of resources. Farmers, as owners of firms, are in the same position in both circumstances. They are earning what they could earn in the next best alternative.

Now consider the farmer as owner of the resources used to produce corn. Economic rent without the price support would be area p_cC0. This is a measure of the return to farming or a measure of the farmer's standard of living. With the price support program, farmers effectively receive $3.00 per bushel, and economic rent increases to p_TE0. Owners of farming industry resources that have positively sloped supply curves are better off because the price support program increases the price of corn and increases the amount of corn produced.

Finally, we must consider the government. Under this particular scheme, the government must make deficiency payments equal to area p_TEFp_L in Figure 11–7 and must purchase $(Y_3 - Y_1)$ bushels of corn at $2.40 per bushel. This means that, in addition to the deficiency payments, the government must spend $2.40(Y_3 - Y_1)$ dollars on corn. Since the market price of corn is p_c dollars in the absence of price controls (the "world" price for corn), if the government can sell the corn it buys from farmers at this price to other countries around the world, then it will be able to generate $p_c(Y_3 - Y_1)$ dollars of revenues. (The government might also give the surplus to poor peoples around the world, thus increasing worldwide consumer surplus.)

Since the government finances price support programs with tax revenues, taxpayers are worse off by the difference between what they pay in taxes and what is generated in revenues. This loss is represented by $p_TEFp_L + BFHG$ in Figure 11–7. (If the government

Commodity	Consumer Loss	Taxpayer Cost	Producer Gain	Net Loss
Corn	0.5–1.1	10.5	10.4–10.9	0.6–0.7
Sugar	1.8–2.5	0	1.5– 1.7	0.3–0.7
Milk	1.6–3.1	0	1.0– 1.4	1.1–1.7
Wheat	0.1–0.3	4.7	3.3– 3.6	1.4–1.5

Source: Annual Report of the President: 1985, President's Council of Economic Advisors.

TABLE 11–2

ANNUAL GAINS AND LOSSES FROM PRICE SUPPORT PROGRAMS: 1985 (BILLIONS OF DOLLARS)

cannot sell its stock of corn, then the loss to taxpayers will be even greater.) ∎

Does the price support program lead to inefficiencies? That is, do the economic costs outweigh the benefits? The inefficiencies associated with price support programs are quite large. Table 11–2 gives estimates of the losses associated with several price support programs in effect in 1985. For the corn market alone, the president's Council of Economic Advisors estimates a net loss to society of $600–$700 million.

If price support programs give rise to such large inefficiencies, why does the government use them? Recall that the motivation for this particular policy is to increase farmers' incomes (and hence keep farmers in business). In fact, price support programs are usually touted as primarily benefiting the small farmer since he or she is the one most likely to go out of business as the result of low prices. As we demonstrated above, the program does increase incomes provided the farmer is the owner of the resources used to produce the corn. In many instances, this is the case and price support programs do increase the farmers' standard of living.

Even this argument is flawed, however, because the distribution of program benefits is very inequitable. The benefits of price support programs go primarily to those producers suffering the smallest financial hardship and not to those suffering the greatest financial hardship. According to the 1986 Annual Report of the President, government payments in 1985 went mostly to *large* farming operations. The average payment to all farmers with sales over $500,000 annually was almost $40,000 while the average payment to all farmers having sales of $10,000 to $20,000 is less than $1,000.

EXAMPLE 11–5

THE MINIMUM WAGE LAW

The federal minimum wage was established in 1938 when Congress passed the Fair Labor Standards Act (FLSA). The intended purpose of the minimum wage has always been the maintenance of a minimum standard of living. The minimum wage was initially set at $.25 and covered only about 43% of the work force. In 1991 the minimum wage was $4.45 and covered almost 90% of the work force. The primary groups not covered by the federal minimum wage law are employees of small retail firms, household workers, employees in certain recreational industries, and agricultural workers.

At first glance the **minimum wage law** seems a straightforward way to increase the living standards of the working poor; however, by this stage in our study of economic theory we should realize that what appears to be true on the surface may not, in fact, be the case at all. In this example we will use the competitive model to determine the economic impact of a minimum wage. (a) Analyze the affect of a $4.00 per-hour uniform minimum wage on employees covered by the minimum wage, and on producers, consumers, and other resource owners. (b) Teenage workers make up a large portion of the low-income workers in the U.S. and, as a result, are one group of individuals affected by minimum wage legislation. In an attempt to lessen any adverse impact of the minimum wage on teenagers, the Reagan administration proposed a special subminimum wage of $2.50 per hour for teenagers. Determine the economic impact of this proposed policy change on teenage employment.

■ **SOLUTION** In order to simplify our analysis, we begin by assuming that all workers affected by the minimum wage are identical in all respects except age. For convenience, we will divide these individuals into two groups: teenagers and adults. In Figure 11–8(a), S_L^T represents the supply of teenage workers measured in person-hours while D_L^T represents the demand. In Figure 11–8(b), S_L^A and D_L^A represent the supply and demand for adult workers covered by the minimum wage law.

In the absence of a minimum wage, let us assume that the equilibrium wage rates would be $2.00 per hour for teenagers and $3.00 per hour for adults and that the equilibrium level of employment would be L_2^T units of labor for teenagers and L_2^A units of labor for adults.

THE MINIMUM WAGE LAW

FIGURE 11—8

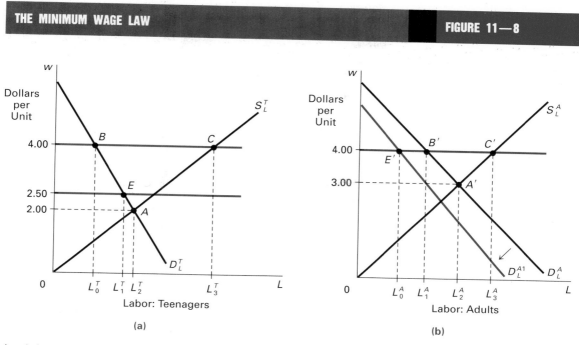

(a)

(b)

A minimum wage of $4.00 per hour reduces employment of teenage and adult workers. Incomes of those employed rise if demand is inelastic and fall if demand is elastic. A subminimum wage for teenagers increases teenage employment but also decreases demand for adult workers.

(a) Now suppose that Congress passes a minimum wage law that requires all employers in the covered sectors to pay a wage of at least $4.00 per hour. What will be the impact of this legislation?

The first prediction we can make based on economic theory is that employment in the covered sectors will fall. A minimum wage above the market clearing wage causes employers to hire fewer workers. In Figure 11–8(a), employment of teenagers falls from L_2^T to L_0^T and employment of adults falls from L_2^A to L_1^A. (Economists refer to the reduction in employment as the *disemployment effect* of the minimum wage).

A second, although less certain, prediction of the theory is that unemployment will rise. As a result of a higher minimum wage, there are more teenagers and adults looking for jobs. For example, at the $4.00 per-hour minimum wage, teenage employment is only L_0^T but the quantity of teenage labor supplied is now L_3^T. The minimum wage causes an excess supply of workers and if all these individuals continue to search for jobs, unemployment will increase. The reason we cannot state this result with certainty is that some or all of the unemployed may give up searching for a job and, as a result, will not show up in unemployment statistics. (You might argue that we are violating the assumptions of perfect competition since we now allow resources to be unemployed. If the competitive assumption held world wide, then those individuals without jobs could find employment in another country that does not have a minimum wage.)

Does the minimum wage law achieve its stated goal of raising incomes of the working poor? The answer depends on the elasticity of the demand curve for labor. If the demand for labor is inelastic, then the percentage decline in employment is smaller than the percentage increase in the wage, and incomes rise. If the demand for labor is elastic, then the percentage decline in employment is greater than the percentage increase in the wage, and incomes fall.

WINNERS AND LOSERS It is clear that the winners from the minimum wage law are those workers who kept their jobs and are earning a higher wage than before. However, there are several groups who are losers. First, workers laid off by employers because of the wage increase lose. If these workers remain unemployed, then their economic rent falls to zero. If they find employment outside the covered sectors, then their economic rent still falls but not all the way to zero. Second, consumers of goods produced by firms employing workers covered by the minimum wage law are worse off. The minimum wage law increases production costs. This, in turn, shifts firms' average and marginal cost curves up, reduces supply, and results in higher long-run equilibrium prices for outputs. Consumers now pay higher prices and consume less; thus, consumer surplus falls and consumers are worse off. (Can you illustrate this result?) Thirdly, consider resource owners. As we have shown, some workers are better off and some are worse off. What about owners of other inputs used in the production process? The extent to which other resource owners are affected by the minimum wage law depends on how inputs are substituted in production. A higher price for labor will reduce demand for inputs that are technical complements and thus reduce economic rents going to owners of these inputs. The reverse is true for technical substitutes. In total, the most likely case will be a decline in economic rents making resource owners another group that is worse off.

Producers are neither better off nor worse off in the long run since they earn zero economic profit both before and after the minimum wage law goes into effect.

A SUBMINIMUM WAGE FOR TEENAGERS (b) What will happen to employment in the two labor markets pictured in Figure 11–8 if the government legislates a subminimum wage of $2.50 for teenagers? The impact on the teenage labor market is clear: employment increases from L_0^T to L_1^T. However, we can expect employment in the adult labor market to fall, because firms hire more teenagers now that the price of this input has fallen. Since, in many instances, the teenagers and adults covered by the minimum wage law are substitutes in production, more jobs for teenagers means fewer jobs for adults. Figure 11–8(b) shows this change as an inward shift in the labor demand curve. As a result, employment of adults falls from L_1^A to L_0^A. ■

Economists have undertaken a substantial amount of empirical research to determine the effects of minimum wage laws. Perhaps the most important conclusion that can be drawn from this research is that, as predicted by the theory, minimum wage laws do lead to a substantial reduction in employment. This disemployment effect is larger for teenagers and smaller for adult men and women. For example, Brown, Gilroy, and Kohen conclude that a 10% increase in the minimum wage reduces teenage employment by about 1% (Charles Brown, Curtis Gilroy, and Andrew Kohen, "Time-Series Evidence on the Effect of the Minimum Wage on Youth Employment and Unemployment," *Journal of Human Resources*, 18 [Winter 1983]: 3–31). In addition, the demand elasticities are such that the minimum wage causes incomes of adult men and women as a group to rise while incomes of teenagers fall. One empirical study also considered the subminimum wage issue. The study found that a subminimum wage would increase teenage employment by up to 430,000 and reduce adult employment by up to 107,000 (Daniel Hamermesh, "Minimum Wages and the Demand for Labor," *Economic Inquiry*, 20 [July 1982]: 365–80).

■ **Cost-saving innovations**—technological advances that result in lower production costs—play a major role in the growth and development of any economy. If we look at the economic history of the U.S., examples abound. One classic example is Henry Ford's introduction of mass-produced Model Ts in 1915. Recently, hi-tech industries such as the electronics industry and the computer industry have offered the most visible cost-saving innovations.

In this section, we use our theory of competitive markets to predict how cost-saving innovations will effect prices, quantities, and the economic well-being of market participants. We will show

11.4 COST-SAVING INNOVATIONS

that innovations giving rise to lower production costs not only generate short-run positive economic profit for the owners of firms that are first in the field, but also lead to lower prices, cause consumption to increase, and improve the economic welfare of consumers and resource owners in the long run.

EXAMPLE 11-6

VIDEOCASSETTE RECORDERS

In the late 1970s, technological advances in the electronics industry drastically lowered the cost of manufacturing videocassette recorders (VCRs). Suppose that Video-tech, Inc., is one of the first firms to implement the new technology. Using the competitive framework, present a detailed economic analysis of the impact of these technological advances on the market for VCRs.

■ **SOLUTION** Let us begin by assuming that the VCR industry is in long-run equilibrium prior to the development of the new technology. In Figure 11–9(a), LAC_1 and SMC_1 represent Video-tech's cost curves before the firm implements the cost-saving innovation. In Figure 11–9(b), D is the market demand curve for VCRs, LS_1 is the initial long-run industry supply curve, and SS_1 is the initial short-run supply curve.

The intersection of the supply and demand curves determines the equilibrium price and quantity. In this instance, the equilibrium price is p_1 and the equilibrium quantity is Y_1. Given this market clearing price, Video-tech produces y_1 VCRs and earns zero economic profit.

Now suppose Video-tech implements the new cost-saving technology. In Figure 11–9(a) this innovation is represented by a downward shift in the firm's cost curves, from LAC_1 and SMC_1 to LAC_2 and SMC_2. What happens to production of VCRs and to profit?

In the short run, before all firms in the business implement the new technology, the price of VCRs remains at p_1. The profit-maximizing level of production for Video-tech increases to y_2 VCRs per year. At this output rate, the firm earns an economic profit equal to area $ABCD$ in Figure 11–9(a).

Video-tech's profit has two effects. First, it encourages established firms to use the new technology or develop a comparable one

COST-SAVING INNOVATIONS

FIGURE 11–9

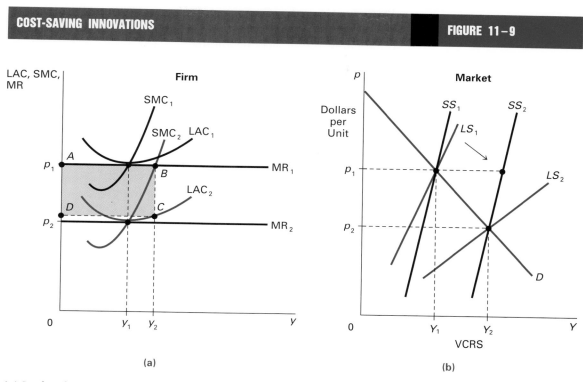

(a) In the short run, a new cost-saving technology generates positive economic profit; however, once a new long-run equilibrium emerges, firms earn zero economic profit. (b) The innovation shifts long-run supply from LS_1 to LS_2. Output increases and price falls.

of their own. Second, it attracts new firms to the industry. Both of these changes cause the long-run industry supply curve to shift to the right until profit for each firm in the industry is zero. In Figure 11–9(b) this is shown as the shift from LS_1 to LS_2. When long-run equilibrium is reestablished, the price of VCRs falls to p_2 dollars per VCR and the quantity bought and sold increases to Y_2.

When their product is selling at the new price, firms once again earn zero economic profit. Video-tech no longer garners any benefit from being the first to introduce the new technology. Furthermore, Video-tech cuts production of VCRs back to y_1 units per year.

WHO BENEFITS FROM THE INNOVATION? Next, we must consider how the innovation affects consumers and owners of resources employed in the VCR industry. Consumers of VCRs are certainly better off. The cost-saving innovation has resulted in more VCRs being produced and sold at a lower price, so consumer surplus definitely increases.

What about the owners of the inputs used to produce VCRs? In the short run, firms using the new technology earn a positive profit, which is shared among resource owners in a way consistent with any binding contracts that may have been agreed upon. In the long run, once all firms have implemented the technology, economic rent is still positive but we cannot say whether it is larger or smaller than before. Thus, the long run effect of the cost-saving innovation on resource owners is ambiguous. ■

The basic conclusion of the analysis presented above is that, in the long run, cost-saving innovations lead to more goods being bought and sold at lower prices. Table 11−3 shows annual sales and prices of videocassette recorders sold in the U.S. from 1975 to 1987. During this time period, quantity sold grew from 40,000 units in 1975 to more than 13 million in 1987. Over this same time period, the average price fell from $850 in 1975 to $385 in 1987.

11.5 TRADE RESTRICTIONS

■ The U.S., like most countries, uses a variety of trade restrictions to protect domestic producers against foreign competition; two of the most important are import quotas and tariffs. An **import quota**

TABLE 11−3

THE VCR MARKET: 1975−87

Year	Quantity (Thousands)	Average Price
1975	40	$850
1976	70	929
1977	250	720
1978	415	786
1979	488	797
1980	802	774
1981	1,471	766
1982	2,020	645
1983	4,127	524
1984	7,881	455
1985	11,786	402
1986	13,533	389
1987	13,231	385

Source: EIA Electronic Market Data Book (various years).

is a restriction on the number of units of a particular good that can be imported from foreign countries. A **tariff** is an excise tax on foreign goods.

Since the Smoot–Hawley Tariff of 1930, the U.S. has reduced its tariff barriers substantially. However, over the years the U.S. has also imposed several trade restrictions designed to give special protection to various manufacturing and agricultural sectors. For example, special protection was obtained by Presidents Eisenhower and Kennedy for the textile and oil industries, by President Johnson for the meat industry, by President Nixon for the steel industry, by President Carter for the textile, steel, and footwear industries, and by President Reagan for the sugar, textile, automobile, and steel industries. The purpose of special protection, simply put, is to insulate domestic firms from foreign competition.

In the next example we use the competitive model to determine the economic effects of the trade restriction imposed by the U.S. government on foreign producers of sugar.

EXAMPLE 11–7

THE SUGAR QUOTA

Import quotas control foreign sales of sugar to the U.S. (a) Analyze the effects of this trade restriction on the domestic price of sugar, domestic consumption, and domestic production. (b) Determine who benefits and who is harmed by the import quota.

■ **SOLUTION** (a) In order to analyze the economic effects of an import quota, we must take care to distinguish between domestic and foreign producers. In Figure 11–10, LS_{us} represents the domestic supply curve, LS_f represents the foreign supply curve, LS_T is the total supply curve, and D_{us} is the domestic demand curve. The total supply curve is obtained by horizontally summing the foreign and domestic supply curves.

The equilibrium price and quantity correspond to the point where total supply is equal to demand, or point A in the diagram. In the absence of any quota, the equilibrium price is p_1 dollars per pound of sugar, and the equilibrium quantity, which is domestic consumption, is Y_T pounds. Given this price, foreign sales, which are imports, will be Y_f pounds of sugar and domestic sales will be Y_{us} pounds. Note that $Y_T = Y_{us} + Y_f$.

FIGURE 11–10   **THE IMPORT QUOTA ON SUGAR**

The quota limits foreign supply to Y'_F pounds of sugar, thus causing the total supply curve to shift from LS_T to LS'_T. Price and domestic production rise but consumption falls.

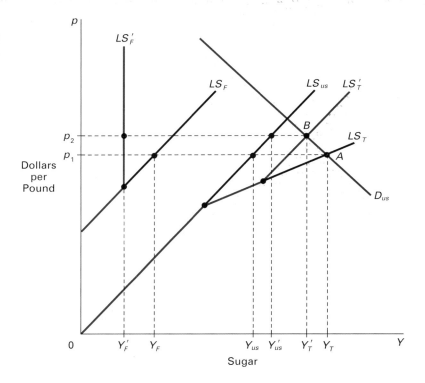

Now suppose the government limits imports to Y'_f pounds of sugar per year. What impact does this restriction have on the total supply curve? Effectively, this makes the foreign supply curve vertical at Y'_f. This, in turn, causes the total supply curve to shift to LS'_T in Figure 11–10 (since now the total supply curve is the horizontal sum of LS'_f and LS_{us}). The new equilibrium price rises to p_2 and domestic consumption falls to Y'_T.

What impact does the quota have on domestic firms? In the short run, the rise in the price of sugar causes profit-maximizing domestic firms to increase production. In addition, each domestic firm already in the sugar industry now earns positive economic profit. New firms enter the sugar industry until, once again, firms earn zero economic profit. The end result is that domestic production increases to Y'_{us}. Domestic producers now sell more sugar at a higher price.

THE MARKET FOR INPUTS USED IN THE SUGAR INDUSTRY After the quota goes into effect, the new long-run competitive equilibrium results in higher sugar prices and a higher level of domestic production. What effect does this have on domestic resource owners? An increase in the price of sugar causes the marginal revenue product of inputs to increase. Each additional unit of capital or labor employed now generates more revenue than before. As marginal revenue products rise, the market demand curves for inputs shift to the right. Equilibrium input prices and the level of employment both increase. (You should be able to illustrate what is happening here.)

WINNERS AND LOSERS (b) First let us consider domestic consumers of sugar. Since the price of sugar has gone up and quantity consumed has fallen, consumer surplus falls as a result of the quota. Consumers are worse off. In Figure 11–10, area p_1p_2BA represents the reduction in consumer welfare.

Next, consider domestic producers. According to our analysis, both before and after the quota goes into effect, domestic producers earn zero economic profit. Thus, they are neither better off nor worse off. But if producers are not better off, then has the quota achieved its objective of protecting domestic firms? Paradoxically, the answer is yes. Remember, the reason the quota was imposed in the first place was because policymakers feared that domestic firms would not survive foreign competition; that is, they feared that as imports increased, the price of sugar would fall, causing domestic firms to incur economic losses and exit the industry. The quota has prevented this from happening. Domestic firms remain in the sugar business because they are still able to earn zero economic profit.

Foreign firms also benefit, since they can sell sugar in the U.S. at a higher price. This conclusion presumes that lost sales to the U.S. are made up for by exports to other countries or more sales at home.

Finally, consider owners of the resources used to produce sugar. Since we have assumed that this is an increasing cost industry, resource owners are better off. Input prices and employment have both increased; hence, economic rents increase too. ■

We now know who benefits from and who is harmed by the quota but again we must ask if the costs outweigh the benefits. In a report prepared in 1984 for the United States Federal Trade Commission, Tarr and Morkre estimated the costs and benefits of U.S. trade restrictions for four different industries, including the sugar industry (David Tarr and Morris Morkre, "Aggregate Costs to the United States of Tariffs and Quotas on Imports: General Tariff Cuts and Removal of Quotas on Automobiles, Steel, Sugar, and Textiles." *Bureau of Economics Staff Report to the Federal Trade Commission* [December 1984]). For fiscal year 1983, they found that the sugar quota reduced consumer surplus by $735 million and increased economic rents to domestic resource owners by $414 million. Thus, the sugar quota resulted in a net loss in well-being of $321 million.

1. This chapter has shown how the competitive model can be used to analyze a wide variety of real-world economic problems. Supply and demand analysis is one of the most important tools available to economists, who can gain a great many insights if they can reduce a problem to a question about supply and demand.

2. Consumer surplus and economic rent are used to evaluate the gains and losses associated with particular government policies and, in one instance, the gains associated with technological change. We found that government intervention in competitive markets redistributes income so that some groups are better off and some are worse off and leads to a reduction in total economic surplus.

3. In general, taxes result in (i) a reduction in output; (ii) higher prices; (iii) a reduction in employment of inputs; (iv) lower prices paid to resource owners; (v) a reduction in consumer surplus; and (vi) a reduction in economic rents. The only individuals who benefit from taxes are those who benefit from the government's expenditures of the tax revenues.

4. Price ceilings lead to shortages and, thus, result in a welfare loss to consumers and resources owners. Price support programs lead to surpluses. As a result, resources owners are better off, while consumers and taxpayers are worse off. A minimum wage law reduces employment, increases incomes of the working poor if the demand for labor is inelastic, results in higher prices and less output (so consumers are worse off), and, most likely, reduces economic rent.

5. Cost-saving technological innovations lead to lower prices and an increase in output, so consumers definitely benefit. In the short-run, economic rent increases. In the long-run economic rent is positive but we cannot say whether it is larger or smaller than before.

6. Like taxes, trade restrictions generally lead to higher prices. As a result, domestic production rises, domestic consumption falls, consumers are worse off, and resource owners are better off. Even though owners of firms still earn zero economic profit, the domestic industry has expanded.

SUMMARY

KEY TERMS

Total Economic Surplus
Deadweight Loss or
 Inefficiency
Excise Tax
Personal Income Tax
Price Ceiling

Price Floor
Minimum Wage Law
Cost-Saving Innovation
Import Quota
Tariff

QUESTIONS AND PROBLEMS

1. a) If an excise tax is imposed on a product for which there are few good substitutes, who will pay the tax? Explain.
   b) Does your answer have anything to do with why goods such as cigarettes and liquor are taxed in the U.S.? Explain.

2. Suppose that the market demand and supply curves for calculators are given by

$$Y = D(p) = 600 - 10p \qquad \text{and}$$

$$Y = LS(p) = 200 + 40p$$

   where Y is quantity and p is the price of calculators.
   a) Determine the equilibrium price and quantity.
   b) If an excise tax of $4 per calculator is imposed on the seller, what will be the new equilibrium price and quantity?
   c) What proportion of the tax is paid by consumers?
   d) If, instead, the $4 excise tax is imposed on the consumer, what will be the new equilibrium price and quantity?

3. The Social Security payroll tax consists of two equal tax rates, one levied on employees and one levied on employers (in 1989 each tax rate was 7.65%). Using the competitive model, analyze the economic effects of the Social Security payroll tax. In particular, examine how this tax affects the equilibrium wage and level of employment, producers, consumers, and resource owners.

4. Housing assistance programs are designed to provide subsidized housing to low-income families. In the U.S., most of these programs require the recipient to move into specially constructed housing units supplied by the government. Suppose the government makes three-room apartments available at a rental rate of $100 per month. If, prior to implementation of this transfer program, the market rental rate for the same size and quality of apartment is $500 per month, determine the affect of this program on the equilibrium rental rate and on the quantity of housing available, and discuss who wins and who loses as a result of this program. (Hint: consider two markets, the market for housing supplied by the government and the market for privately supplied housing.)

5. Medicaid is a health insurance program for poor people under 65 years of age. Financed by the government, it is the most expensive transfer program in the U.S. Essentially, for those individuals who qualify, it reduces the cost of medical services to zero.

a) Analyze the effect of such a program on consumption of medical services by the poor. Who wins and who loses?

b) Illustrate the inefficiency of this program.

6. Price controls limiting the rents that owners of rental housing may charge are called rent controls. Since the 1970s, rent controls have become popular in many U.S. cities including New York, Los Angeles, and Boston. Suppose your local city council has hired you to study the economic impact of rent controls. Present a detailed economic analysis of the impact of rent controls on the community. Be sure to discuss who benefits from the rent controls. Will rent controls lead to lower-quality housing? Explain.

7. Oftentimes, black markets arise when price ceilings are imposed on particular goods. A *black market* is a market in which products are sold at prices above the legal maximum. How do the existence of black markets affect the total quantity bought and sold *and* what is the black market price if

a) suppliers caught engaging in black market activities go to jail?

b) consumers caught engaging in black market activities go to jail?

8. Some people argue that price controls are desirable because they prevent producers from earning huge windfall profits. Do you agree or disagree with this statement? Explain using the competitive model.

9. a) Explain and illustrate the inefficiency associated with price ceilings and floors.

b) If price contols give rise to inefficiencies, why are they used?

10. The Civil Aeronautics Board (CAB) regulated the airline industry from 1938 to 1978. During that time, the CAB kept airline fares substantially above the levels that would have prevailed in a free market.

a) Determine how this price floor affects the quantity of airline services bought and sold.

b) Who benefits and who is harmed by this type of regulation?

c) During this period of time, would you expect the quality of airline services to improve or deteriorate? Explain.

11. In order to deal with the growing dairy surpluses generated by the government's price support program, the Reagan administration offered dairy farmers the option of selling their cows for slaughter in return for substantial government payments. Anyone taking advantage of this program had to agree not to produce milk for a period of five years. Explain

carefully the economic effects of this program. Be sure to consider both the dairy and beef industries.

12. The market supply and demand curves for corn are given by

$$Y = LS(p) = 10,000p \qquad \text{and}$$

$$Y = D(p) = 30,000 - 500p$$

where Y is bushels of corn and p is the price per bushel.

a) Determine the equilibrium price and quantity.

b) What is income for farmers as a group? Be sure to distinguish between gross income or total revenue, and net income.

c) If the government guarantees corn growers $4 per bushel, determine the surplus of corn that the government must purchase.

d) Determine the increase in income for farmers as a group, if any.

13. "In the long run, economic profit is zero; thus, there is no incentive for firms to introduce cost-saving innovations." Discuss this statement.

14. Engineers at the I.M. Brighter Corporation have developed a cost-effective way of producing light bulbs with an average life twice as long as bulbs currently on the market. Discuss the impact of this innovation on prices, quantity, and profit in both the short and long runs. Who benefits from this new technology? (Hint: "Cost-effective" means that the cost per hour of light supplied is lower, not the cost of a light bulb.)

15. Analyze the affect of a sales tax levied on consumers on total economic surplus.

16. Recently, some automobile manufacturers have replaced human welders with robots. Ignoring the presence of labor unions in the auto industry, use the competitive model to explain how a move toward a fully automated production line affects the equilibrium wage and level of employment in the automobile industry.

17. a) Discuss the difference between using tariffs and using quotas to reduce foreign imports.

b) Who would be in favor of eliminating trade restrictions? Explain in terms of who benefits and who loses as a result of tariffs and quotas.

c) Who would oppose eliminating trade restrictions?

18. In the early 1980s the U.S. and Japan agreed to limit the export of automobiles to the U.S. Analyze the effects of this import quota on the domestic market for automobiles. Be sure to be

explicit about who benefits and who loses as a result of the quota.

19. The market demand and supply curves for shoes are given by

$$Y = LS(p) = 1{,}000 + 20p \qquad \text{and}$$

$$Y = D(p) = 3{,}000 - 5p$$

where Y is quantity in thousands and p is the price per pair of shoes.

a) Determine the equilibrium price and quantity.

b) Suppose foreign producers are willing to sell shoes in the U.S. for $50 per pair. Determine domestic demand, domestic production, and imports.

c) Suppose that U.S. shoe producers convince the government to impose a $2 tariff on imported shoes. What will be the new equilibrium price, domestic demand, domestic production, and imports.

20. "A uniform minimum wage is wholly unsuited for raising the incomes of the working poor since the individuals who are harmed are, in fact, the least productive workers." Do you agree or disagree with this statement? Explain your position using the competitive model.

REFERENCES

Aaron, H. J., and J. A. Pechman. 1981. *How Taxes Affect Economic Behavior.* Washington, D.C: The Brookings Institution.

Harberger, A. C. 1974. *Taxation and Welfare.* Boston: Little, Brown.

Parsons, D. O. 1980. *Poverty and the Minimum Wage.* Washington, D.C.: American Enterprise Institute for Public Policy Research.

Pechman, J. A. 1985. *Who Paid the Taxes: 1966–1985?* Washington D.C.: The Brookings Institution.

Robinson, K. L. 1989. *Farm and Food Policies and their Consequences.* New Jersey: Prentice-Hall.

THE THEORY OF PRICE UNDER IMPERFECT COMPETITION: MONOPOLY

LEARNING OBJECTIVES

After completing Chapter 12 you should be able to do the following:

- Discuss the meaning of the terms *market power*, *monopoly*, and *monopsony*.

- Explain why the demand curve facing a monopoly is the market demand curve.

- Describe the marginal revenue curve associated with a monopoly's demand curve.

- Determine the profit-maximizing price and quantity for a monopolist and compare them to the profit-maximizing price and quantity in perfect competition.

- Explain why the supply curve facing a monopsony is the market supply curve.

- Describe the marginal factor cost curve associated with a monopsony's supply curve.

- Determine the profit-maximizing price and quantity for a monopsony and compare them to the profit-maximizing price and quantity in perfect competition.

EXAMPLES

- **12-1** Licensing Monopolies and Profit Maximization

- **12-2** Determining Short- and Long-Run Quantities for a
  Monopoly

- **12-3** Excise Taxes: Monopoly and Competition Compared

- **12-4** Determining Prices and Quantities for a Monopsony

The competitive model is useful for analyzing economic problems when buyers and sellers do not have substantial market power. **Market power** refers to the ability of individual economic units to affect market prices. In a competitive market, buyers and sellers are assumed to have no control over market prices or, in other words, no market power. In many real-world markets, however, individual buyers and sellers do have some degree of market power. Thus, it is important for us to understand how market power works and how it affects producers, consumers, and resource owners.

In this chapter we explain the profit-maximizing behavior of a firm that has market power and compare it to that of firms in a competitive market.

■ A **monopoly** is a market structure characterized by only one seller of a particular good. A monopoly, being the sole producer, has market power. It need not worry about rivals who might charge lower prices and thereby increase their market share at the expense of the monopoly. A monopoly is the entire market and has complete control over the amount of output produced and offered for sale. If we classified market structure by the degree of market power, perfect competition and monopoly would lie at opposite ends of the spectrum.

12.1 MONOPOLY

If other firms begin producing the same product as the monopoly produces, or one that is a close substitute, then the monopoly's market power will be diluted or even eliminated completely. A monopoly can persist only if there is some factor that prevents other firms from entering the market and if there are no good substitutes for the product being produced by the monopoly. If either of these conditions is not satisfied, then eventually the monopoly will be unable to maintain its market power.

SOURCES OF MARKET POWER

One source of market power is the exclusive ownership of a scarce resource required for the production of a particular commodity. One well-known example of a monopoly that existed because of this type of market power was the Aluminum Company of America (Alcoa). For many years prior to World War II, Alcoa owned virtually every source of bauxite in the United States. Since bauxite is a necessary ingredient for the production of aluminum, exclusive ownership of this input gave Alcoa a monopoly of the aluminum market.

Other important sources of market power are legal restrictions prohibiting entry into a market. In the United States these restrictions often take the form of patents. There are many examples of firms that have had a substantial degree of market power because of patents prohibiting other firms from producing their product: E.I. du Pont de Nemours & Co. had a patent for cellophane; Polaroid patented their cameras; and Minnesota Mining and Manufacturing (Three M) had a patent for their scotch tape, to name just a few.

The awarding of an exclusive franchise or license to serve a particular market is also a common source of market power in the U.S. In this instance, the local, state, or federal government gives a business the exclusive right to market a good or service within a particular jurisdiction. Examples of businesses that have been granted these types of licenses or franchises are public utilities, cable television companies, the post office, university and college bookstores, and some airline routes.

A third type of entry barrier giving rise to market power is economies of scale. If, for the relevant range of demand, per-unit cost is falling, then an established firm will have lower costs than a new firm entering on a smaller scale. As a result, new firms will not be able to earn positive profit at the price charged by the existing firm. This type of situation is called a *natural monopoly*. Examples of natural monopolies are public utilities such as municipal waterworks, electrical power companies, telephone companies, and sewage disposal systems. (Natural monopoly is discussed in detail in the next chapter.)

As we will show later in this chapter, a monopoly, because it has market power, can earn a positive economic profit even in the long run. Understanding why monopoly power exists gives rise to an important interpretation of monopoly profit: the profit generated by a monopoly in the long run can be thought of as the economic rent or return to whatever gives rise to the monopoly in the first place. For example, what would an entrepreneur have been willing to pay to purchase the property rights to the bauxite mines held by Alcoa? The value of these property rights would be the value of all current and future monopoly profits generated by having exclusive use of the mines. A similar line of reasoning applies to patents, copyrights, and licenses.

Like perfect competition, examples of *pure*, or *absolute*, monopoly are rare in the U.S. Very few markets have just one seller. However, as the preceding discussion indicates, many firms do have some degree of market power, even if they are not the only producers of a product. Thus, it is important for us to understand the monopoly model because, quite often, it does a very good job of explaining and predicting the behavior of firms with market power. Remember, theoretical models need not be precise descriptions of reality in order to help explain the way real-world markets work.

■ Even though a monopoly has complete control over the amount of output that is produced and offered for sale, this does not mean it can charge as high a price as it wants to. A monopoly is constrained by the the market demand curve for the product it produces. For example, suppose Go Video, a small American firm, owns a patent giving it the exclusive right to produce and sell a dual deck videocassette recorder. It is therefore a monopoly producer. Suppose that this product currently sells for about $1,000 per machine. If Go Video is a monopoly, why doesn't it charge $5,000, $10,000, or $15,000 per machine? The answer is simple: If dual deck videocassette recorders cost $15,000, not many people would buy them and Go Video would earn a much lower profit. Go Video can decide how many machines to sell and let market demand determine price, or choose how much to charge and let market demand determine quantity sold, but it cannot do both.

Because a monopoly is constrained by market demand, the amount of output it wishes to sell varies negatively with the price it charges. If a monopoly wants to sell more output, it must lower price. If it chooses to sell less, then it can increase price. This stands in direct contrast to the horizontal demand curve faced by a competitive firm and is the primary reason for the difference between output and price in a monopoly and output and price in a competitive industry.

Any firm concerned with profit must also be concerned with the way output relates to revenue—in other words, with marginal revenue. As we saw in Chapter 8, for a perfect competitor marginal revenue is equal to price. For a monopoly, however, this is not the case. Whether the monopoly is a university bookstore or Polaroid, the owner faces a downward-sloping demand curve, which means that marginal revenue is always less than price.

12.2 DEMAND AND MARGINAL REVENUE FOR A MONOPOLY

To see why marginal revenue is less than price when a firm faces a downward-sloping demand curve, consider once again the definition of marginal revenue. Marginal revenue is the change in total revenue, price times quantity, due to a unit change in output. For a competitor, price is independent of output so that marginal revenue is equal to price; however, for a monopoly price is not independent of the amount of output sold.

In Figure 12–1 we have drawn the market demand curve facing Hi-Tech, Inc., the only firm that manufactures and sells VCRs in its immediate area. The demand curve reflects the prices consumers are willing to pay to purchase particular quantities of VCRs. This tells us that if Georgette, the owner of Hi-Tech, wants to sell, say, 1,000 VCRs, then she can charge $200 per VCR. Total revenue from the sale will be $200,000.

Suppose the owner of Hi-Tech decides to increase production and sales of VCRs to 2,000 units. What will happen to revenues? In order to increase sales to 2,000, Georgette must lower the price of VCRs to $150 per unit. In this instance, total revenue will increase from $200,000 to $300,000.

Now let us take a closer look at what happens to total revenue as output increases. Since the demand curve is downward-sloping

---

FIGURE 12–1   **THE DEMAND CURVE FACING HI-TECH**

The market demand curve is the monopolist's demand curve. If Hi-Tech increases sales from 1,000 to 2,000 VCRs per year, then the price of VCRs must fall from $200 to $150 per VCR. As a result of the decrease in price, total revenue on the first 1,000 VCRs falls by $50,000. As a result of the increase in sales, total revenues increase by $100,000. In this instance, total revenue increases.

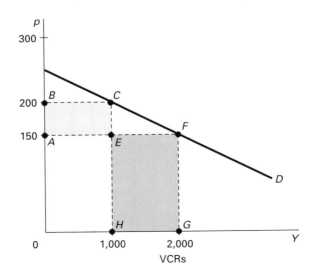

there are two effects. First, when the price is lowered, it is lowered on all units that are sold. This means that the revenue generated on the first 1,000 VCRs is lower than it was before. When the price falls from \$200 to \$150 per VCR, revenue on the first 1,000 VCRs sold falls \$50,000 from \$200,000 to \$150,000. Area *ABCE* in Figure 12–1 represents this change in revenue. This area is equal to the change in price, Δp, of −\$5 times 1,000 units of good Y. Second, when the price is lowered, sales of VCRs increase by 1,000 units. This increase in sales tends to increase total revenue since the new sales are of VCRs that were not selling prior to the price reduction. In this instance, the additional revenue generated is \$150,000, or area *EFGH* in the diagram. This area is equal to the change in output, ΔY, of 1,000 times \$150 per unit of good Y. Thus, total revenue after the price is lowered is the sum of these two components, or \$300,000, and the overall change in total revenue is an increase of \$100,000.

It will be useful to have an algebraic expression for marginal revenue when we discuss the monopoly's output decision. From the discussion above, we know that the change in total revenue, ΔTR, due to a change in output, is given by

$$\Delta TR = Y \cdot \Delta p + p \cdot \Delta Y.$$

We can obtain the marginal revenue, $\Delta TR/\Delta Y$, by dividing this equation by ΔY:

$$MR = \Delta TR/\Delta Y = Y(\Delta p/\Delta Y) + p. \qquad (12.1)$$

The first term on the far right of equation (12.1), $Y(\Delta p/\Delta y)$, represents the change in revenues per unit change in output arising because the price of the good being produced must be changed. This term is negative, because the demand curve is negatively sloped. For example, if output increases, then $Y(\Delta p/\Delta Y)$ represents the reduction in total revenue on the units of output that were initially sold at a higher price. The second term, p, is the market price, which represents the change in revenue arising because quantity produced and sold changes. If output increases, then the increase in revenue per unit change in output due to additional sales is just the market price.

From the equation given above, it is clear that when the demand curve is negatively sloped, marginal revenue is equal to price as long as $Y = 0$ and is always less than the market price as long as output is positive. Thus, the marginal revenue curve begins at the

LINEAR DEMAND CURVES AND MARGINAL REVENUE

same point on the price axis as the demand curve does, and as output increases it must always lie below the demand curve.

When the demand curve is linear, we can be even more specific about the relation between demand and MR. In particular, given this condition we can show that the slope of the MR curve is twice the slope of the demand curve. For example, suppose the demand curve for Ford Mustangs is given by the equation $Y = 40 - (1/20)p$. This demand curve is labeled D in Figure 12–2(a). Notice that since the demand curve is a straight line, its slope, $\Delta p/\Delta Y$, is -20.

Now, in order to determine the marginal revenue curve associated with this demand curve, we must first solve for p: $p = 800 - 20Y$. We call this the *inverse demand function*. Using the definition of marginal revenue, we can say that MR $= Y(\Delta p/\Delta Y) + p = Y(-20) + (800 - 20Y) = 800 - 40Y$. Thus, the marginal revenue curve is twice as steep as the demand curve.

The associated MR curve is also shown in Figure 12–2(a). When output is zero, both MR and price are equal to $800. As output increases, both price and MR fall, but MR falls twice as fast as price.

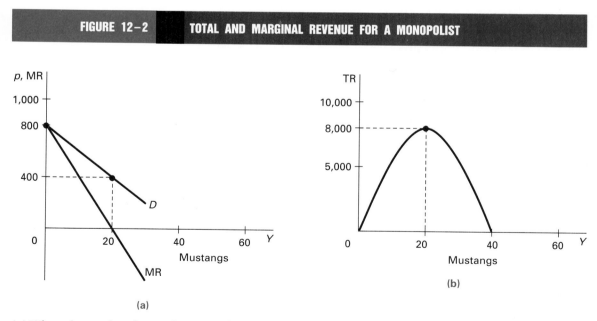

| FIGURE 12–2 | TOTAL AND MARGINAL REVENUE FOR A MONOPOLIST |

(a) When the market demand curve is linear, the marginal revenue curve is linear and has twice the slope of the demand curve. (b) For a monopolist, total revenue increases to a maximum and then falls. The maximum point of the total revenue curve occurs when marginal revenue is zero.

When output is between 0 and 20 Mustangs, MR is positive, which means that as output increases, total revenue increases. When output is greater than 20, MR is negative, which means that as output increases, total revenue falls. When output is exactly 20, MR is zero and price is $400 per car. Figure 12–2(b) graphs the total revenue curve for a firm facing the demand curve in Figure 12–2(a). We can see that total revenue increases, reaches a maximum of $8,000 at an output rate of 20 units per year, and then declines. The maximum point on the total revenue curve is attained at the rate of output for which marginal revenue is zero.

For many applied problems, being able to express marginal revenue in terms of the elasticity of the demand curve is very helpful. We can use the expression for marginal revenue given above to express the relation between MR and price in terms of the elasticity of the demand curve. Recall that the price elasticity of demand for some good Y is given by

ELASTICITY AND MARGINAL REVENUE

$$E_{YY} = -(\Delta Y/Y)/(\Delta p/p) = -(\Delta Y/\Delta p)(p/Y);$$

or, in other words, the price elasticity of demand is the percentage change in quantity demanded per percentage change in price.

Rewriting the expression for marginal revenue in terms of E_{YY} we have

$$MR = Y(\Delta p/\Delta Y) + p = p[1 + (Y/p)(\Delta p/\Delta Y)]$$

$$= p[1 - (1/E_{YY})]. \qquad (12.2)$$

For a particular output, equation (12.2) relates marginal revenue to the price elasticity of demand. Using this expression we can ascertain several interesting relations that will be very useful when we study price discrimination.

First, notice that if the demand curve facing a monopolist were horizontal as it is for a perfect competitor, then $E_{YY} = \infty$ and MR = p since, as E_{YY} approaches infinity, $1/E_{YY}$ approaches zero. In this instance a monopoly would behave just like a perfect competitor. Second, if demand is elastic, $E_{YY} > 1$ and MR is positive. Third, if demand is unit-elastic, $E_{YY} = 1$, and MR = 0. Finally, if demand is inelastic, $E_{YY} < 1$, and MR is negative.

■ We can begin our investigation of a monopoly's pricing and output decisions by making two assumptions. First, we assume that the goal of the monopoly is to maximize profit. In the competitive

12.3 PROFIT MAXIMIZATION FOR A MONOPOLY

model, profit maximization seems a reasonable goal because forces at work tend to eliminate firms that consistently deviate from it (see Section 6.2). For a monopoly, this assumption may seem less reasonable because a monopoly may be able to generate an economic profit without earning the maximum profit possible. Once again, however, a monopoly model based on profit maximization does very well at explaining and predicting most behavior. For this reason, we retain the profit maximization assumption.

Second, we assume that the monopoly hires inputs in competitive markets; that is, the monopoly has no market power in its input markets. The monopoly can hire as much of any input it wants without affecting the price of the input. Thus, the monopoly's cost curves will have the same general properties as those cost curves discussed in Chapter 7.

Given these assumptions, what quantity of its good should the monopoly produce and offer for sale? As we saw in Chapter 8, any firm maximizes profit when output is such that marginal revenue equals marginal cost. This means in the short run output is such that MR = SMC and in the long run it is such that MR = LMC.

FIGURE 12–3	PROFIT MAXIMIZATION FOR A MONOPOLIST

Profit is maximized when marginal revenue is equal to marginal cost. At any other output rate, profit can be increased by moving towards Y^*.

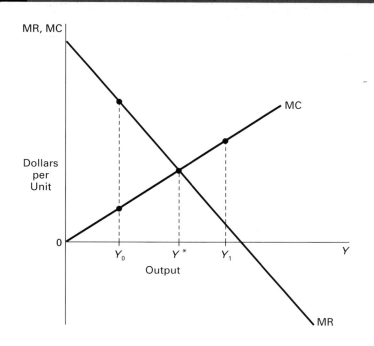

Figure 12–3 shows the marginal revenue and marginal cost curves for a monopoly. The firm maximizes profit when it is producing Y^* units of output. At Y^*, MR = MC. If the owner of the firm operates at a lower output, such as Y_0, then MR < MC and the firm can increase its profit by increasing production. Similarly, if the firm operates at an output rate greater than Y^*, such as Y_1, then it can increase its profit by cutting back on production. The monopolist is doing the best he or she can do by operating at Y^*.

One immediate result of profit maximization is that the firm will never operate at an output rate where the market demand curve is inelastic. To understand this, recall that when the price elasticity of demand is less than one, MR is negative. Since MC is always positive or zero, MR can never be equal to MC at an output rate where MR is negative.

While it is commonly believed that a monopoly, by its very nature, must earn a profit, in the short run this is not necessarily true. Figure 12–4(a) depicts a monopoly that earns a positive economic profit and Figure 12–4(b), a monopoly that incurs a loss. In the first instance, the profit-maximizing output rate is Y^*. Given this quantity, the monopoly charges p^* per unit of Y. Total revenue,

SHORT-RUN PROFIT AND LOSS

SHORT-RUN PROFIT AND LOSS FOR A MONOPOLIST

FIGURE 12–4

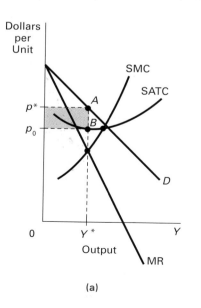

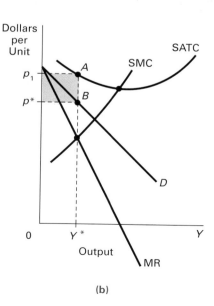

(a) Given the profit-maximizing output of Y^* units of good Y, the monopolist charges p^* dollars per unit per year and earns positive economic profit. (b) In this case, the profit-maximizing price is less than SATC and the monopolist incurs a loss.

(a)

(b)

then, is represented by area $0p^*AY^*$. If the monopoly produces Y^* units of good Y then SATC is p_0 and STC is represented by area $0p_0BY^*$. In this instance the monopoly makes a profit equal to p_0p^*AB.

In the second instance, the profit-maximizing output rate is also Y^*. However, by producing this quantity, the monopoly incurs a loss. Total revenue is $0p^*BY^*$, total cost is $0p_1AY^*$, and the loss incurred is represented by the difference between these two, or p^*p_1AB.

Whether or not the owner of the monopoly continues to operate in the short run if he or she is incurring a loss depends on fixed and variable costs. As is the case for a perfect competitor, if revenue is large enough to cover all of the firm's variable costs then the monopoly will not shut down, but if revenue does not cover all variable costs then the firm will be shut down.

EXAMPLE 12-1

LICENSING MONOPOLIES AND PROFIT MAXIMIZATION

Marysville Gas and Electric is the sole supplier of electricity to the community of Marysville. The economics division of the firm estimates that the inverse demand function for electricity is given by

$$p = 100 - 10Y$$

and that short-run marginal cost is given by

$$SMC = 5Y$$

where Y is measured in thousands of kilowatt-hours per day. (a) If Marysville Gas and Electric is not regulated, meaning that the owners of the firm have full control over price, determine the quantity of electricity they should deliver and the price they should charge in order to maximize profit. Illustrate your answer. (b) Marysville Gas and Electric is currently earning a positive economic profit. Suppose the local government institutes an ordinance requiring all utility companies to purchase a $60 license. How will this affect the profit-maximizing output rate and price? Illustrate.

■ **SOLUTION** (a) Profit is maximized when MR = SMC. Since the demand curve is linear, the marginal revenue curve has the same price intercept as the demand curve and twice the slope. The latter is given by

$$MR = 100 - 20Y.$$

Setting marginal revenue equal to marginal cost we have

$$100 - 20Y = 5Y.$$

Solving this equation for Y gives the profit-maximizing output rate: $25Y = 100$ or $Y^* = 4,000$ kilowatt-hours per day.

Now how do we find the price that the monopolist charges for electricity? Since the market demand curve tells us how much consumers are willing to pay for various quantities of electricity, we substitute the profit-maximizing output rate into the equation for demand. This gives: $p^* = 100 - 10(4) = \$60$ per 1,000 kilowatt-hours.

Our next task is to illustrate these calculations. Figure 12–5(a) illustrates the demand, marginal revenue, and marginal cost

PROFIT MAXIMIZATION FOR MARYSVILLE GAS AND ELECTRIC   FIGURE 12–5

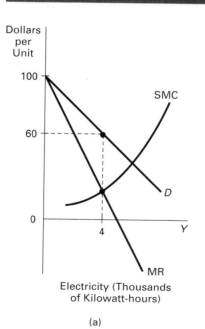

(a)

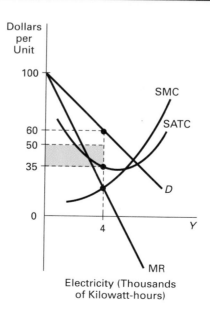

(b)

(a) Profit is maximized when the firm produces 4,000 kilowatt-hours per day. Given this output rate, the price of electricity is $60 per 1,000 kilowatt-hours. (b) Requiring the monopolist to purchase a license leaves the profit-maximizing output rate unchanged but reduces profit by the cost of the license.

curves. Demand and marginal revenue both have a price intercept of 100. Marginal revenue is equal to zero when the output rate is 5,000 kilowatt-hours per day. It is equal to marginal cost when $Y = 4$. Going vertically up to the demand curve from $Y = 4$ gives the market price for electricity.

(b) Now let us consider how the local government's ordinance affects price and quantity. From the monopolist's perspective, the license fee is a fixed cost. The firm must pay it regardless of how many kilowatt-hours it is producing and selling. Therefore, the new ordinance has no effect on the monopolist's marginal cost curve.

The impact of the license fee is shown in Figure 12−5(b). The firm maximizes profit by choosing the output rate where MR = SMC. Before the license is required for operation, the profit-maximizing price and quantity are $60 per 1,000 kilowatt-hours and 4,000 hours respectively. The owner of the power company earns a profit of $25 \cdot 4 = $100 per day.

The license fee leaves the SMC curve unchanged. If the firm continues to operate, the profit-maximizing output rate will still be 4,000 kilowatt-hours per day and the corresponding output price will be $60. However, profit will be lower by the amount of the fee. In Figure 12−5(b), where the fee is given by the shaded area, profit falls to $40 per day. Requiring a monopolist to purchase a license has no effect on the profit-maximizing output rate or price in the short run. It simply reduces monopoly profit. ■

12.4 LONG-RUN EQUILIBRIUM FOR A MONOPOLY

■ Under perfect competition, an industry's long-run competitive equilibrium is characterized by firms maximizing profit and by firms entering and exiting the business until those operating are earning zero economic profit. Do these same conditions hold for a monopolist? We have already assumed that a monopolist will maximize profit; however, under monopoly entry into the industry is not possible. If the sole operator is earning a profit in the short run, no other firms can enter the market in response to this incentive. Therefore, long-run equilibrium does not require that a monopolist earn zero economic profit.

In the long run two possibilities arise. First, if the firm incurs a loss in the short run and if there is no plant size that will generate a positive or zero economic profit in the long run, then the firm will go out of business. If it cannot make a positive economic profit in the long run, then the owner of the monopoly can do better by taking his or her resources and employing them elsewhere.

The second possibility that arises is when the firm *can* earn a positive profit in the long run. In this case, the owner of the monopoly must decide whether profit can be increased in the long run by changing plant size. Figure 12−6 shows the situation where the owner should increase plant size in the long run. In this diagram D and MR are the market demand and marginal revenue curves facing the monopolist. LAC and LMC are the long-run cost curves. SAC and SMC are the short-run cost curves representing the current plant size.

In the short run, profit is maximized when MR = SMC. In Figure 12−6 the profit-maximizing output rate is given by Y_0. Given this level of production the monopolist charges p_0 dollars per unit of good Y. Total revenue is represented by area $0p_0CY_0$, total cost is $0AEY_0$, and profit is Ap_0CE.

Now the owner of the monopoly must determine whether or not to change capacity in the long run. Long-run profit maximization requires that MR = LMC, or an output rate of Y_1 units of good Y. Any other rate of output results in lower profit. (In particular, if the firm were to continue to produce Y_0 units, then it could increase profit by increasing production, since at this point LMC would be less than MR.) Thus, in the long run the owner of this firm can increase profit by increasing plant capacity (which gives rise to a new set of short-run cost curves), and by lowering the price of the

LONG-RUN EQUILIBRIUM FOR A MONOPOLIST   **FIGURE 12−6**

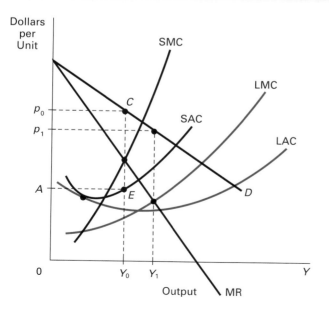

In the long run, profit is maximized when MR = LMC. The difference between perfect competition and monopoly, however, is that for the monopolist long-run profit need not be zero.

product to p_1 dollars per unit. However, note that in the long run there are no forces driving the monopolist to the minimum point of the firm's long-run average cost curve.

EXAMPLE 12–2

DETERMINING SHORT- AND LONG-RUN PRICES AND QUANTITIES FOR A MONOPOLY

Suppose that the Pautauxant Mining Co. is the sole supplier of plutonium to the National Center for the Development of Nuclear Energy. The manager of P.M.C. estimates that the demand for plutonium is given by

$$Y = 4,000 - 2p$$

where Y is pounds of plutonium per year and p is the market price. In addition, the firm's accounting department estimates short- and long-run costs to be

$$STC = 100 + 20Y + .5Y^2 \quad \text{and} \quad SMC = 20 + Y$$

$$LTC = 30Y + .25Y^2 \quad \text{and} \quad LMC = 30 + .5Y.$$

Given this information, determine the following for (a) the short run and (b) the long run: the profit-maximizing output rate; the market price for plutonium; the profit earned, if any.

■ **SOLUTION** (a) Profit maximization in the short run requires that MR = SMC. In order to determine marginal revenue we must first solve the demand function for price as a function of quantity. This gives $p = 2,000 - .5Y$. Since the inverse demand function is linear, the marginal revenue curve has the same price intercept and twice the slope: MR = $2,000 - Y$.

Setting MR = SMC and solving for output we have

$$2,000 - Y = 20 + Y$$

or $Y^* = 990$ pounds of plutonium per year.

Now what price can P.M.C. charge for plutonium? Substituting the profit-maximizing output into the demand curve gives $p^* = 2,000 - .5(990) = \$1,505$ per pound of plutonium. Thus, P.M.C.

will produce 990 pounds of plutonium and sell it for $1,505 per pound.

Given this price and quantity, TR = (1,505)(990) = $1,489,950 per year, STC = $100 + 20(990) + .5(990)^2 = $509,950$ per year, and profit is equal to $980,000 per year. Since it is earning a positive profit, the firm will continue to operate in the short run.

(b) In the long run the owners of P.M.C. must decide whether to expand or contract production. Profit maximization in the long run requires MR = LMC which gives

$$2,000 - Y = 30 + .5Y$$

or, solving for Y, $Y^* = 1,313$ pounds of plutonium per year (rounded to the nearest pound). The long-run price will be $p^* = 2,000 - .5(1313) = \$1,343$ per pound. That is, in the long run the owners should increase production by 323 pounds and lower the market price by $162 per pound.

We can also show that profit in the long run increases. Given the long-run price and quantity we can say that TR = (1,343)(1,313) = $1,763,359 per year, LTC = $30(1,313) + .25(1,313)^2 = \$470,382$ per year, and π = TR − LTC = $1,292,977 per year. ■

■ Under perfect competition, on the one hand, competitive equilibrium implies that firms produce at the level where price is equal to marginal cost. Under monopoly, on the other hand, equilibrium implies that the firm produces at a level where price is greater than marginal cost. In this section we will discuss the important economic implications of this difference.

When we analyzed perfectly competitive markets, we focused on the interaction between supply and demand. However, for markets characterized by monopoly we cannot use this type of analysis, because a monopoly has no supply curve. When firms are price takers, the market supply curve relates industry output to price. Given any price, the supply curves indicate how much of the product firms in a particular industry will produce. For a monopolist, there is no such relation between price and output.

To understand this point, consider the monopoly depicted in Figure 12−7. With demand curve D_1, the profit-maximizing output is Y_1 and price is p_1. Now suppose the demand curve shifts to D_2. The new marginal revenue curve is MR_2, which intersects the LMC curve at the same output level as before. This means that, given D_2, the profit-maximizing output is still Y_1 but the price has fallen to p_2. That is, two different prices can be associated with the same

12.5 PERFECT COMPETITION AND MONOPOLY COMPARED

THE NONEXISTENCE OF SUPPLY CURVES

FIGURE 12–7   **NONEXISTENCE OF SUPPLY CURVES**

A monopolist does not have a supply curve. Both p₁ and p₂ are associated with the same profit-maximizing level of production.

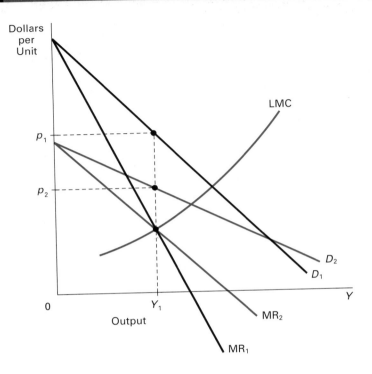

profit-maximizing output rate. Thus, a monopoly does not have a supply curve of the type we associate with a competitive industry.

HIGHER PRICE, LOWER OUTPUT

One of the most important concerns of economists is the way in which alternative market structures affect prices and output. In fact, most of the antitrust laws in the U.S. have arisen because of operational differences between a monopoly and perfect competition. This being the case, we now turn to a careful comparison of prices and output under monopoly and under competition.

Suppose that an industry is initially a perfectly competitive, constant cost industry. In Figure 12–8, LS is the long-run market supply curve, D is the market demand curve, and MR is the marginal revenue curve associated with the market demand curve. Under perfect competition, the long-run equilibrium price and quantity are p_1 and Y_1 respectively. Notice that MR is irrelevant for determining price and quantity in a perfectly competitive industry.

OUTPUT AND PRICE: MONOPOLY AND PERFECT COMPETITION COMPARED   FIGURE 12–8

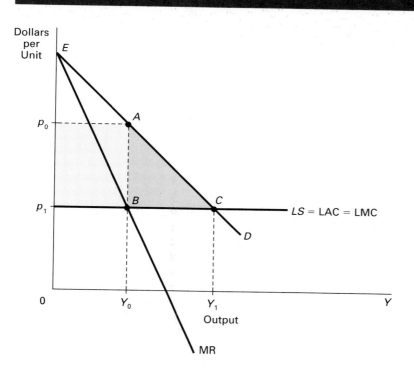

A monopolist produces less output than a perfect competitor, $Y_0 < Y_1$, and charges a higher price, $p_0 > p_1$. As a result, consumer surplus falls and the monopolist earns a monopoly profit (area p_0ABp_1). The monopoly leads to an inefficiency that is represented by area ABC.

This is because each firm in the industry is a price taker and, thus, each firm acts as if it faces a horizontal marginal revenue curve.

Now suppose this industry becomes a monopoly. What will happen to price, output, and employment? Before we can answer this question we must be sure we understand the seemingly innocuous statement that the competitive industry becomes a monopoly. In moving from perfect competition to pure monopoly, it is clear that the market demand curve now becomes the firm's demand curve and that marginal revenue is MR in Figure 12–8. But what about the cost curves? If we assume that the monopoly simply is endowed with each of the plants previously operated by one of the many perfect competitors, and if we assume that the monopoly operates these plants at the same costs as did the individual firms, then the long-run industry supply curve is the monopoly's long-run average cost curve. Since we have assumed that this is a constant cost industry, the monopoly's LAC curve is also its LMC.

Given these assumptions, we can compare price and output under competition and monopoly. The monopoly maximizes profit by producing where MR = LMC. The monopoly in Figure 12−8 produces Y_0 units of output, charges a price of p_0, and earns p_0ABp_1 dollars in monopoly profit. Thus, given the same demand and cost conditions as firms in a competitive industry, the monopolist will produce less output and charge a higher price.

That a monopoly produces less and charges more is one of the most cited results of microeconomic theory. However, remember that this discussion was based on the assumption that the monopoly operated under the same cost conditions as did the competitive industry. In the last section of this chapter, when we consider various ways of regulating monopolies, we shall discuss whether or not this is, in fact, a legitimate assumption to make.

INCOME REDISTRIBUTION

If a competitive industry becomes a monopoly, then there will be a redistribution of resources and some individuals will gain and some will lose. Again, refer to Figure 12−8. Consumers are worse off under monopoly because they consume less at a higher price. We can measure just how much worse off consumers are by considering consumer surplus in the two situations. When the price is p_1 and output Y_1, consumer surplus is area p_1EC; however, when the price is p_0 and output Y_0 consumer surplus is p_0EA. Thus, consumer surplus falls by p_1p_0AC, which is a measure of how much worse off consumers are.

Now who gains? Of course the owner of the monopoly does. The monopoly profit is a measure of the monopoly's gain, since it represents a payment over and above the minimum necessary to keep resources in their current employment. In Figure 12−8, monopoly profit is given by area p_1p_0AB. Notice that this area represents a transfer of consumer surplus from consumers of the product to the monopoly. This is why we often hear people say that monopolies are exploiting consumers and should be regulated.

THE INEFFICIENCY OF MONOPOLY

In Chapter 11, we found that government policies that interfere with the competitive process often give rise to economic inefficiencies: any gains in well-being are more than offset by the losses. Since monopoly leads to less output and higher prices than perfect competition, we can also show that monopolies give rise to economic inefficiencies.

To see why this is the case, refer again to Figure 12−8. Under perfect competition, firms produce Y_1 units of output and sell them at p_1 dollars per unit. Under monopoly, output falls to Y_0 units and price increases to p_0. As shown above, this means that consumers lose consumer surplus equal to $p_1 p_0 AC$. Part of this loss in well-being is offset by the monopolist's profit, area $p_1 p_0 AB$. The remainder, area ABC, is a net loss to society.

Economists use area ACB as a measure of the **inefficiency of monopoly**. It is sometimes called the *deadweight loss* or *welfare cost* of a monopoly that is endowed with the same demand and cost curves as a competitor. It arises because under monopoly output is lower and price higher than under competition. Of course, as before, these conclusions are based on the assumption that the monopolist operates with the same cost structure as does the competitive industry.

In recent decades, economists have tried to estimate the inefficiency of monopoly in the U.S. As yet, there is no clear consensus as to its size. Most estimates indicate it is somewhere between .1 and 2% of gross national product (GNP). (In 1989, GNP was over $5 trillion, which would put the inefficiency of monopoly between $5 and $100 billion.) (F. M. Scherer and D. Ross, *Industrial Market Structure and Economic Performance*, 3d. ed. Copyright © 1990 by Houghton Mifflin Company. Used with permission.).

In the next example, we will compare and contrast the economic effects of an excise tax levied on a monopoly and one levied on a perfectly competitive industry. In particular, we want to know if the price to consumers increases more when the industry is monopolistic or when it is competitive.

EXAMPLE 12-3

EXCISE TAXES: MONOPOLY AND COMPETITION COMPARED

Suppose that Video Video, Inc., is the sole supplier of VHS video movies in the town of Clarksville. The marginal cost of providing VHS movies is constant at $30 per movie. (a) If an excise tax of $6 per tape is imposed on the seller, how will this affect output and price? (b) What portion of the tax will consumers pay? (c) Does monopoly profit increase or decrease? (d) Will the price to consumers rise more if the industry is competitive or monopolistic?

■ **SOLUTION** (a) In Figure 12–9(a), the equilibrium price and quantity prior to the tax are p_1 and Y_1 respectively. Now suppose the government levies a tax of $6 per movie on Video Video, Inc. From the producer's perspective the long-run marginal cost curve shifts up by the amount of the tax to LMC + 6 in the diagram.

FIGURE 12–9   THE EFFECT OF AN EXCISE TAX ON VIDEO VIDEO, INC.,'S PROFIT-MAXIMIZING OUTPUT RATE AND PRICE

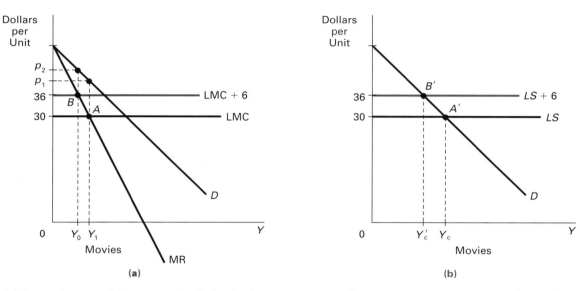

(a) An excise tax of $6 per movie shifts the long- run marginal cost curve up to LMC + 6. The profit-maximizing output level falls and price increases but by less than the tax. The tax is shared between the monopolist and consumers. (b) Under perfect competition, an excise tax levied on firms in a constant cost industry causes output to fall and price to rise by an amount equal to the tax.

Clearly, the profit-maximizing output falls and price increases. In this particular instance, the new profit-maximizing output is Y_0 tapes and the price is p_2 dollars per tape.

(b) Since we know that the marginal revenue curve is steeper than the demand curve, price rises by less than the tax. As we move from A to B in Figure 12–9(a), marginal revenue increases by $6. However, because the marginal revenue is steeper than the demand curve, price increases by less than $6. If the demand curve is a straight line, then price increases exactly half as much as marginal revenue, or $3 in this example.

(c) The monopoly could have charged any price before the tax was imposed. It chose to charge p_1 because this was the price associated with the profit-maximizing quantity; any other price would have resulted in lower profit. Therefore, gross (pre-tax) profit must be lower at p_2 than at p_1 and net (after-tax) profit must be lower still. The tax reduces monopoly profit.

(d) Our final task is to determine whether the price to consumers rises more or less if the industry is a competitive one. To compare monopoly with competition, we must assume that the demand and cost conditions are the same for both market structures. This being the case, we will assume that the competitive industry is a constant cost industry and that the minimum point of the typical firm's LAC curve is $30. The competitive case is shown in Figure 12–9(b).

Before the tax is imposed on producers, the long-run equilibrium output rate is Y_c tapes per month and they sell for $30 each. An excise tax of $6 per tape causes the long-run market supply curve to shift up by $6 to $LS + 6$. The new equilibrium quantity is Y_c' tapes per month and the price to consumers rises to $36 per tape. In a competitive industry the tax causes the price to consumers to rise by the amount of the tax.

We conclude, then, that an excise tax on monopoly raises price less than does the same excise tax on a competitive industry. Why? It is because the monopoly pays for some of the tax out of monopoly profit. (Remember, profit went down because of the tax.) Competitive firms earn zero economic profit and, hence, cannot use profit to pay for some of the tax. ∎

∎ We have examined the implications of profit maximization for the output and pricing decisions of a monopoly. Now we will examine the implications of profit maximization for the input demand decision of a monopoly.

12.6 MONOPOLY AND THE EMPLOYMENT OF INPUTS

As we saw in Chapter 8, in the long run a profit-maximizing firm employs an input up to the point where the marginal revenue generated by hiring one more unit of the input, the marginal revenue product (MRP) of the input, is just equal to the marginal factor cost. This result holds whether the firm is a perfect competitor or a monopoly. The only requirement is that the firm maximizes profit.

If a monopolist is a perfect competitor in the input market, then the price it must pay for inputs is the marginal factor cost of hiring one more unit of the input. That is, just like a perfect competitor, a monopoly assumes that it can hire all the inputs it desires at the market price.

The difference between the competitor's employment decision and the monopoly's results from the way in which additional units of inputs affect revenues. Consider the employment of labor. For a perfect competitor, on the one hand, marginal revenue product— the additional revenue generated by hiring one more worker—is equal to the marginal product of labor times the market price of the output produced by the firm; that is, $MRP_L = MR \cdot MP_L = pMP_L$. For a monopoly, on the other hand, marginal revenue is always less than price, which means that marginal revenue product is always less than it is for a competitor. Thus, the monopoly will hire fewer workers than the competitor.

This discussion is illustrated in Figure 12–10. For simplicity, suppose that all inputs but labor are fixed for the firm. Given a wage rate of w_1 dollars per unit of labor, a profit-maximizing firm that is a price taker in both the input and output markets will employ L_1 units of labor. A profit-maximizing firm that is a monopoly in the output market but a competitor in the input market will employ L_2 units of labor. Thus, for a given input price, employment of labor (or any input) is lower under monopoly than it is under perfect competition.

We should have anticipated this result given our earlier discussion of the output supply decision under monopoly. There we

FIGURE 12–10	MONOPOLY AND EMPLOYMENT

Given a wage rate of w_1 dollars per unit of labor, a profit-maximizing monopolist employs labor up to the point where $MRP_L = w_2$, or L_2 units of labor. Thus, for a given wage a monopolist employs fewer units of labor than does a perfect competitor ($L_2 < L_1$).

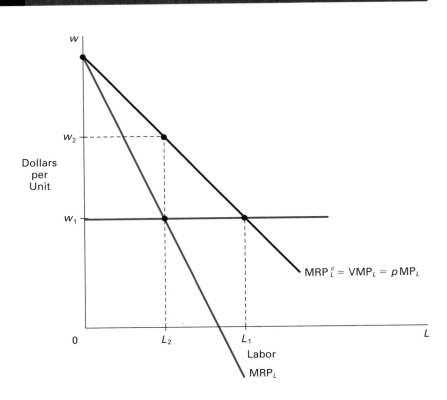

found that a monopolist facing the same demand and cost conditions as a competitive industry produces less output. To accomplish this, the monopolist uses fewer inputs. Figure 12–10 simply illustrates this lower output using the input market.

Using Figure 12–10, we can illustrate one final point. A monopolist employs labor up to the point where marginal revenue product is equal to the wage rate, L_2 in the diagram. Given this level of employment, the market value of the additional output produced by one more unit of labor is $p \cdot MP_L = w_2$ in the diagram. Since the value of the marginal product of labor measures how consumers value the additional output produced by one more unit of labor, a monopolist pays workers less than their value to consumers; that is, $w_1 < w_2$. Consumers are willing to pay more for another unit of labor than it costs the monopoly. The marginal benefit to consumers of hiring another worker is greater than the marginal cost; thus, all gains from trade are not realized and the monopoly results in an inefficient allocation of inputs. Clearly, this is just the argument we made above with respect to the output market. The only difference is that here we are focusing on the input market.

■ Our discussion of monopoly dealt with market power on the seller side of the market. Now we turn to market power on the buyer side. A **monopsony** is a market with only one buyer of a particular good. It is just the opposite of monopoly. As the only buyer, a monopsony has market power because it need not worry about other buyers who might offer to pay a higher price and thereby increase their purchases at the monopsony's expense. As a result of its market power, a monopsony can purchase a good at less than the price that would prevail in a competitive market.

The easiest way to understand monopsony is to think in terms of input markets, and so, for the remainder of our discussion, we will use firms rather than individuals as our examples of monopsony. The primary reason that a firm may have market power as the buyer of an input is that some inputs are highly specialized and, as a result, have few substitutes. For example, automobile firms have market power as buyers of brake pads, computer manufacturers have market power as buyers of disk drives for personal computers, and major league baseball franchises have market power as buyers of professional baseball players. In each of these instances, the input has few, if any, substitute uses.

Consider a monopsony in the market for labor services. Labeled S_L, the labor supply curve in Figure 12–11 indicates the wage rate that the monopsonist must pay to obtain a given quantity of labor

12.7 MONOPSONY

SUPPLY AND MARGINAL FACTOR COST FOR A MONOPSONY

FIGURE 12-11	MONOPOSONY

A profit-maximizing monopsonist hires labor up to the point where the $MRP_L = MFC_L$. In this instance, L_1 units of labor are employed at w_2 dollars per unit of labor. A monopsonist employs fewer workers, $L_1 < L^*$, and pays a lower wage, $w_1 < w^*$, then does a perfect competitor.

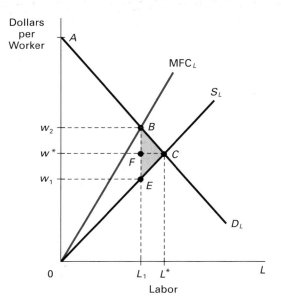

services. An upward-sloping labor supply curve means that the firm must pay a higher wage rate to increase employment.

If the labor supply curve is upward-sloping, then the marginal cost of hiring an additional unit of labor, called the *marginal factor cost* of labor, is not equal to the wage rate. In Figure 12–11, MFC_L represents the marginal factor cost curve.

The wage rate measures the average cost of labor to the firm, but it does not measure the marginal cost. In this instance, the marginal factor cost of labor is greater than the wage, because to obtain more units of labor the firm must pay a higher wage rate to all the units of labor it already employs. Put differently, the average factor cost curve is increasing and, thus, the marginal factor cost curve must lie above the average factor cost curve.

To demonstrate this more clearly, we can use the same line of reasoning that we used to explain the difference between price and marginal revenue for a monopolist. If a monopsony hires an additional worker, then total cost associated with the employment of labor, ΔTFC, increases. Since the labor supply curve is upward-sloping, we can decompose this increase in cost into two parts. Factor costs increase because the wage is higher, $L\Delta w$, and because more workers are employed, $w\Delta L$. Therefore, the change in total factor cost is

$$\Delta TFC = w\Delta L + L\Delta w.$$

Dividing this equation by ΔL gives

$$MFC_L = \Delta TFC/\Delta L = w + L(\Delta w/\Delta L). \qquad (12.3)$$

Since the labor supply curve is upward-sloping, $\Delta w/\Delta L > 0$ and $MFC_L > w$.

From equation (12.3) given above, it is clear that when the supply curve is positively sloped, marginal factor cost is equal to the wage rate as long as $L = 0$ and greater than the wage rate when employment is positive. Thus, the marginal factor cost curve begins at the same point on the wage axis as does the supply curve; as employment increases, it must always lie above the supply curve.

When the supply curve is linear, we can be even more specific about the relation between supply and MFC. In particular, we can show that the slope of the MFC curve is twice the slope of the supply curve when the supply curve is linear. Suppose, for example, that the supply curve for labor is given by $L = 2 + .25w$. Solving this equation for w gives the inverse supply function; that is, $w = 4L - 8$. Notice that, since the supply curve is a straight line, its slope, $\Delta w/\Delta L$, is -4.

Now using the definition of marginal factor cost, we can say that $MFC = w + L(\Delta w/\Delta L) = (4L - 8) + 4L = 8L - 8$. Thus, the marginal factor cost curve is twice as steep as the supply curve.

LINEAR SUPPLY CURVES AND MARGINAL FACTOR COST

A monopsony, like a perfect competitor, maximizes profit when its level of input usage is such that marginal revenue product equals marginal factor cost. In Figure 12–11, MFC_L is the marginal factor cost curve associated with the labor supply curve S_L, and D_L is the firm's long run demand curve for labor, which reflects the marginal revenue product of labor. The firm maximizes profit by employing L_1 units of labor. At that point, the marginal factor cost of labor is equal to the marginal revenue product of labor. Note, however, that in order to hire L_1 units of labor the firm does not have to pay w_2. Rather, the firm must pay only w_1 dollars per unit of labor. The intersection of MFC_L and D_L determines the level of employment, while the labor supply curve determines the wage rate.

PROFIT-MAXIMIZATION FOR A MONOPSONY

EXAMPLE 12–4

DETERMINING PRICES AND QUANTITIES FOR A MONOPSONY

Suppose that The Thai Room is the sole employer of Thai-speaking waiters. The restaurant's demand for waiters is given by $w = 116 - 4L$ and the supply of waiters by $w = 16 + 8L$, where w is the daily wage rate and L is the number of waiters employed. Determine the profit-maximizing level of employment and the corresponding wage rate.

■ **SOLUTION** We determine how many waiters The Thai Room hires by equating the labor demand and marginal factor cost functions. In this instance, marginal factor cost is given by

$$\text{MFC}_L = 16 + 16L.$$

Setting this equal to demand we have

$$16 + 16L = 116 - 4L$$

and solving for L: $L^* = 5$ workers. The wage rate is found by substituting $L = 5$ into the labor supply function:

$$w = 16 + 8(5) = \$56 \text{ per worker per day.} \quad ■$$

Most economists agree that monopsony is far less common than monopoly and that market power in labor markets is, in fact, quite rare. Few workers have employment opportunities limited to just a single firm or group of firms. Large firms like General Motors, Ford, and Chrysler would find it difficult to retain employees if they tried to pay a wage below the competitive rate. Nevertheless, there are input markets where monopsony power is evident, so it is important to understand what can give rise to it.

PERFECT COMPETITION AND MONOPSONY COMPARED

If we compare a labor market characterized by monopsony to a competitive labor market, we find that employment and the wage rate are lower in the former. If the labor market were competitive, then, in Figure 12–11, the restaurant would hire L^* units of labor and the wage rate would be w^*. These results are analogous to those obtained for a monopoly. A monopoly, facing a downward-sloping demand curve, restricts output and obtains a higher price; a monopsony, facing an upward-sloping supply curve, restricts employment and pays a lower wage rate.

Since, compared to perfect competition, monopsony power results in lower prices and fewer input purchases, we can also show that monopsony leads to economic inefficiencies. Once again, consider Figure 12–11. Under monopsony, the wage rate is lower, $w_1 < w^*$, and fewer workers are employed, $L_1 < L^*$. As a result, economic rent going to owners of labor services falls by $w_1 w^* CE$ from $0w^*C$ to $0w_1E$ and workers are worse off.

Next let's consider consumers of the good produced by the monopsony. If the monopsony is a perfect competitor in the output market, then at every point on the long-run labor demand curve, the firm's economic profit is zero and payments to labor are just equal to the value of the output produced by labor. Now just as the long-run supply curve represents the marginal cost to society of producing a particular good or service, the labor demand curve represents the marginal value to society of employing workers in this particular business. Thus, we can interpret the area below the labor demand curve and above the wage rate as a measure of the consumer surplus going to those individuals purchasing the good or service being produced by labor. At the competitive wage rate and level of employment, consumer surplus is represented by area w^*AC. Under monopsony consumer surplus is w_1ABE. Thus, compared to perfect competition consumers may be better off or worse off. They lose area FBC because employment, and hence output, falls but gain area $w_1 w^* FE$ because labor costs fall which, in a competitive output market, means that price will also fall.

Finally, consider how monopsony affects aggregate economic surplus. Economic rent received by workers falls by $w_1 w^* CE$. Consumer surplus falls by FBC and increases by $w_1 w^* FE$. Therefore, area BCE is a net loss to society and, as such, represents the inefficiency of monopsony.

SUMMARY

1. A monopoly is a market structure where there is only one seller of a product with no close substitutes. Since a monopoly supplies the entire market, the demand curve faced by the firm is the market demand curve. A downward-sloping market demand curve means that a monopolist must lower price to increase sales; thus, marginal revenue for the monopolist is always less than price.

2. A monopolist maximizes profit by producing the output rate for which marginal revenue is equal to marginal cost. One implication of profit maximization is that a monopolist will never operate where demand is inelastic.

3. In the short run a monopolist may make a profit or incur a loss. Monopoly power does not guarantee economic profit; however, in the long run, a monopoly always earns an economic profit, called monopoly profit, which can be interpreted as the return to whatever gives rise to the firm's market power.

4. A monopoly produces less output than a perfectly competitive industry and sells its product at a higher price. By restricting output, a monopoly creates economic inefficiencies. Since, at the profit-maximizing point, price is greater than marginal cost, society would be better off with more of the good than is produced and sold by the monopolist. The inefficiency of a monopoly is represented by the triangular area between the demand and marginal cost curves.

5. A monopolist, like a perfect competitor, must purchase inputs for use in the production of its goods and services. A monopolist employs factors of production up to the point where the marginal revenue product of the factor is equal to the input price. For a monopolist marginal revenue is less than price, which means that fewer resources will be employed under monopoly.

6. Monopsony is a market structure with a single buyer, which means that the supply curve faced by the buyer is the market supply curve. An upward-sloping market supply curve means that a monopsonist must pay a higher price to increase purchases; thus, marginal factor cost for the monopsonist is always greater than price.

7. A monopsonist maximizes profit when quantity is such that marginal factor cost equals demand. As a result, a monopsonist employs less of an input and pays a lower price than does a perfect competitor. Further, since society would be better off with a greater level of employment, monopsony leads to inefficiency.

Market Power   Inefficiency of Monopoly
Monopoly   Monopsony

1. Are monopolies more likely in local markets or national markets? Explain.
2. Authors of textbooks typically receive a certain percentage of the wholesale price for each book sold. These payments are called royalties. Suppose you have written a textbook and have agreed to a 10% royalty.
   a) Explain why you are interested in maximizing revenues from the sale of your book while your publisher is interested in maximizing profit.
   b) If demand for your text is estimated to be

$$Y = 10,000 - 50p,$$

   where Y is the number of books sold per year and p is the price, what price would you like the publisher to charge?
   c) If you were allowed to set the price, what price would you choose and how many books would you sell?
   d) Suppose a used book market develops for your book. How does this affect the equilibrium price and quantity of new books?
3. "As sole supplier of a good, a monopolist can gouge consumers by charging a very high price." Is this statement true or false? Explain.
4. Suppose Sally's Sod Farm is the sole supplier of bermuda grass to the community of Bakersfield. The manager of the sod farm estimates that the demand for sod is given by

$$Y = 100 - 4p$$

where Y is square yards of sod and p is the price per square yard. In addition, the firm's accounting department estimates long-run costs to be

$$LTC = 15Y + .125Y^2, \quad \text{and} \quad LMC = 15 + .25Y.$$

Given this information, determine the profit-maximizing output rate, the market price for sod, and the profit earned, if any. Illustrate your answer.

5. Suppose that in the long run the residents of Bakersfield substitute other landscaping materials, such as rocks, for grass. This causes the demand curve for sod to become more elastic. What impact will such a change in demand have on the price of sod?

6. Illustrate a monopoly that
   a) makes a short-run profit;
   b) makes a short-run loss but does not shut down;
   c) shuts down.

7. Firms in a perfectly competitive industry operate at the minimum point of their long-run average cost curves.
   a) Explain why this is not the case for a monopolist.
   b) Does this mean that, in the long run, competitive firms always produce at lower per-unit costs than monopolies?

8. Suppose that the M.S.U. Bookstore is the sole supplier of the intermediate microeconomic textbook currently used at M.S.U. The bookstore estimates that in the coming semester demand for this book is given by

$$Y = 500 - 10p.$$

   The bookstore purchases intermediate microeconomic textbooks from the publisher for $25 per book.
   a) Illustrate the profit-maximizing price and quantity as well as the inefficiency associated with this monopoly.
   b) Is this inefficiency eliminated if the university regulates the bookstore and forces it to sell the textbooks for $25 per book? Explain.

9. A *cartel* is an agreement between producers to coordinate their production and pricing decisions so that each of them earns monopoly profit. Illustrate and explain how a group of firms in a competitive industry can earn monopoly profits by acting together. (Hint: Assume that the industry is initially in long-run equilibrium and show that if each firm agrees to reduce output to attain a higher price, then each firm will earn a profit.)

10. a) What is a monopsony?
    b) Do monopsonies cause unemployment?
    c) Do monopolies cause unemployment? Explain.

11. Most U.S. cities regulate taxis by requiring them to have licenses issued by the city in order to operate. (These licenses are called medallions.)
    a) If cities issue a fixed number of licenses, discuss the effect of this regulation on the taxi industry.

b) Suppose you are considering operating a taxi. How much would you be willing to pay to get a license? Does your answer say anything concerning the amount cities can charge for licenses?

12. The effective life of a patent in the U.S. is about ten years. Suppose you have just been granted a patent for a new product you have invented. Using a diagram, show the minimum amount you would accept from someone wishing to buy your patent.

13. In 1985 Go Video Inc., a small U.S. firm based in Phoenix Arizona, was granted a patent for a dual deck VCR. At that time Go Video was ready to produce and sell the dual deck VCR. However, Japanese firms holding patents to many basic VCR parts refused to do business with Go Video and, as a result, Go Video has not produced or sold one machine. Currently, Go Video is suing several major Japanese VCR producers for damages. Suppose Go Video has hired you to estimate the damages done to the firm. Explain and illustrate how you would go about this task. (Hint: Assume you can estimate the demand and cost functions facing Go Video.)

14. Suppose American Business Machines (ABM) is the sole purchaser of disk drives for personal computers, and that the supply and demand curves facing ABM are given by the equations

$$(\text{supply}) \ X = 6 + .9p$$

$$(\text{demand}) \ X = 10 - .5p$$

where X is thousands of disk drives and p is the price per disk drive.
a) Determine the equilibrium price and number of disk drives purchased by ABM.
b) Compare your answer to part (a) to the competitive price and quantity.
c) Determine the inefficiency associated with this monopsony.

15. Suppose a firm is both a monopolist in the output market and a monopsonist in the input market. Graphically, illustrate the equilibrium input price and quantity and compare these to the competitive solution.

16. Problem 9 asks you to investigate the implications of a cartel among sellers in an output market. It is also possible to have a

cartel among buyers in an input market. Illustrate and explain how a group of firms in a competitive industry can lower costs (and, thus, earn monopsony profit) by acting together as a cartel.

REFERENCES   Kreps, D. 1990. *A Course in Microeconomic Theory*. Princeton: Princeton University Press.

Varian, H. 1992. *Microeconomic Analysis*. 3d ed. New York: Norton.

PROFIT MAXIMIZATION AND MONOPOLY: A CALCULUS APPROACH

A12.1 PROFIT MAXIMIZATION AND OUTPUT FOR A MONOPOLY

Once again, using calculus makes the profit maximization problem very simple. The profit maximization problem discussed in Section 12.3 can be summarized as follows:

$$\max_{Y} \pi = TR(Y) - TC(Y)$$

where $TR(Y) = p(Y) \cdot Y$ is the total revenue function. The first order condition for this unconstrained optimization problem is

$$\frac{\partial \pi}{\partial Y} = \frac{\partial TR}{\partial Y} - \frac{\partial TC}{\partial Y} = 0$$

which implies that marginal revenue equals marginal cost at the optimal level of output. Solving the first order condition for Y gives the profit-maximizing output Y^*, and substituting this into the inverse demand function gives the price the monopolist must charge in order to sell Y^* units of output; that is, $p^* = p(Y^*)$.

The second order condition for this optimization problem is

$$\frac{\partial^2 \pi}{\partial Y^2} = \frac{\partial^2 TR}{\partial Y^2} - \frac{\partial^2 TC}{\partial Y^2} < 0$$

which implies that the slope of the marginal cost curve is larger than the slope of the marginal revenue curve.

For a monopoly, the profit-maximizing price is always greater than marginal cost. To see this, note that

$$MR = p(Y) + \frac{\partial p(Y)}{\partial Y} \cdot Y.$$

Since the demand curve is negatively sloped, the second term is negative so that $p > MR = MC$ at the optimal level of output.

A12.2 INPUT DEMANDS FOR A MONOPOLY

The profit maximization problem discussed in Section 12.6 can be summarized as follows:

$$\max_{L,K} \pi = TR[F(K,L)] - wL - rK.$$

The first order conditions for this unconstrained optimization problem are

$$\frac{\partial \pi}{\partial L} = \frac{\partial TR}{\partial Y} \cdot \frac{\partial F}{\partial L} - w = 0 \qquad \text{and}$$

$$\frac{\partial \pi}{\partial K} = \frac{\partial TR}{\partial Y} \cdot \frac{\partial F}{\partial K} - r = 0.$$

These first order conditions imply that inputs should be hired up to the point where marginal revenue product is equal to marginal factor cost. Solving these two equations for L and K gives the profit-maximizing inputs L^* and K^* as functions of prices or, in other words, the firm's input demand functions.

A12.3 PROFIT MAXIMIZATION AND MONOPSONY

To simplify the exposition, let's assume that the firm uses only one input, labor. In this instance, the profit maximization problem discussed in Section 12.7 can be summarized as follows:

$$\max_{L} \pi = pF(L) - w(L) \cdot L$$

where $w(L)$ is the inverse input supply function. The first order condition for this unconstrained optimization problem is

$$\frac{\partial \pi}{\partial L} = pMP_L - MFC_L = 0$$

which implies that the value of marginal product equals marginal factor cost at the optimal level of employment. Solving the first order condition for L gives the profit-maximizing quantity of labor to hire—L^*—and substituting this into the inverse input supply function gives the wage the monopolist must pay in order to be able to hire L^* units of labor; that is, $w^* = w(L^*)$.

For a monopsony, the profit-maximizing input price is always less than the value of marginal product. To see this, note that

$$MFC = w(L) + \frac{\partial w(L)}{\partial L} \cdot L.$$

Since the supply curve is positively sloped, the second term is positive so that $w < MFC = pMP_L$ at the optimal level of employment. Thus, the monopsonist employs fewer units of labor and pays a lower wage than would a firm that behaved competitively in the input market.

APPLICATIONS USING THE MONOPOLY MODEL

LEARNING OBJECTIVES

After completing Chapter 13 you should be able to do the following:

■ Discuss government regulation of both monopoly and natural monopoly.

■ Explain how first, second, and third degree price discrimination can be used to increase monopoly profit.

■ Discuss the use of peak-load pricing to increase efficiency.

■ Analyze how labor unions can affect wages and employment in both the union and nonunion sectors of the economy.

13

EXAMPLES

■ **13–1** Regulating an Electric Company

■ **13–2** Pricing Airline Tickets

■ **13–3** Pricing Computer Time

■ **13–4** Unions, Wages, and Employment

In this chapter we use the monopoly model to analyze several important economic problems. We begin by discussing how government can increase efficiency by regulating monopoly. One of our primary concerns is the effect of government regulation on a natural monopoly. In the second section we discuss the profitability of various pricing strategies available to firms with market power when markets can be segmented into different groups of buyers—that is, when sellers can discriminate between buyers. In the third section we discuss a pricing strategy that can be used to increase profit and economic efficiency when demand varies across time. Finally, in the fourth section we investigate how labor unions, one of the most important types of market power, influence factor markets. These applications will demonstrate how useful the monopoly model can be in helping us understand the way markets operate in the presence of market power.

13.1 REGULATING MONOPOLIES

■ In the last chapter we concluded that, when confronted with the same demand and cost conditions, monopolies restrict output more, charge higher prices for their products, and employ fewer inputs than do perfectly competitive markets. In addition, we found that monopolies earn monopoly profits even in the long run.

Historically, the United States government has argued that since price is greater than marginal cost under monopoly, the price a monopoly can charge should be regulated in some way. Regulating the price a monopolist can charge for its product simply amounts to imposing a price ceiling on the monopoly. In this section, we want to investigate the impact of a price ceiling on output, consumer welfare, and monopoly profit. We will find that, unlike a competitive market where a price ceiling causes a shortage, a monopoly might actually increase output in response to a price ceiling.

PRICE CEILINGS AND MONOPOLY

Figure 13–1 illustrates a typical monopoly. Prior to regulation, the profit-maximizing price and quantity are p_1 and Y_1 respectively. Now suppose that the government imposes a price ceiling of p_{max} per unit of output on the monopoly. If the price ceiling is to be effective, it must be lower than the initial price of p_1.

As a result of the price ceiling, the effective demand curve facing the monopolist becomes horizontal at the ceiling price from the vertical axis to the demand curve, and then is the original demand curve once again. In the diagram, $p_{max}CD$ is the effective demand curve. For output rates between zero and Y_3 the firm cannot charge more than the ceiling price, so the relevant demand curve for the monopoly is $p_{max}C$. For output rates beyond Y_3, the demand price is less than the ceiling price so CD is the relevant demand curve.

PRICE CEILINGS AND MONOPOLY   **FIGURE 13-1**

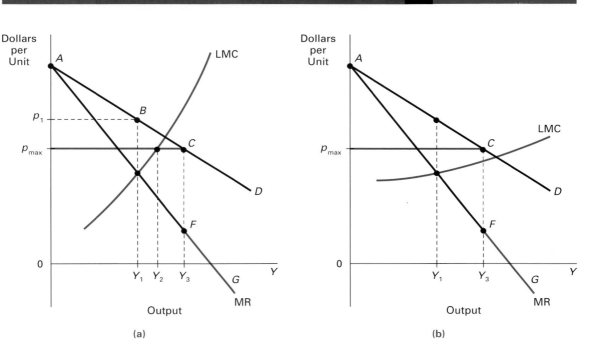

(a) In the absence of a price ceiling, the profit-maximizing price and quantity are p_1 and Y_1 respectively. A price ceiling equal to p_{max} results in an effective marginal revenue curve equal to $p_{max}CFG$ and the profit-maximizing output increases to Y_2. There is a shortage of $(Y_3 - Y_2)$ units of good Y. (b) In this instance, LMC = MR at an output level of Y_3 units of good Y and there is no shortage.

If the effective demand curve changes as a result of the price ceiling, so does the effective marginal revenue curve. When output price is constant, marginal revenue is equal to price so, for output rates between zero and Y_3, the effective marginal revenue curve coincides with the horizontal segment of the effective demand curve, or $p_{max}C$. Beyond Y_3 the effective MR curve is the same as the old MR curve since the demand curve is, once again, negatively sloped. There is a vertical gap in the effective marginal revenue curve at Y_3; that is, the effective marginal revenue curve is given by $p_{max}CFG$.

The price ceiling has two possible consequences. The first is illustrated in Figure 13-1(a). In this instance, the LMC curve intersects the horizontal segment of the effective MR curve. The profit-maximizing output rate is Y_2 and the price is the ceiling price. Output increases, price is lower, and monopoly profit falls. Consumers are better off but, as was true for the competitive industry, the price ceiling leads to a shortage: quantity demanded at p_{max} is greater than quantity supplied.

The second possibility is shown in Figure 13–1(b). In this instance, the LMC curve passes through the gap in the effective marginal revenue curve. The profit-maximizing output rate is now Y_3. Once again, output increases, the price is lower, monopoly profit falls, and consumers are better off; however, now there is no longer a shortage. Quantity demanded equals quantity supplied.

Regulating a monopoly by imposing a price ceiling essentially forces the monopoly to behave as a price-taking firm and adjust quantity in order to maximize profit. One question remains, however: What ceiling price should the regulators choose?

MARGINAL COST PRICING

Suppose that Valerie's Boutique is the only store in Newton Center that sells designer jeans. (Valerie has an exclusive contract with the manufacturers.) The Newton Center city council has decided to regulate this monopoly by imposing a ceiling price on the monopoly. If the city council's objective is to eliminate the inefficiency of the monopoly, what ceiling price should it impose?

The demand, marginal revenue, and marginal cost curves facing Valerie's Boutique are shown in Figure 13–2. Prior to the price control, Valerie sells Y_1 pairs of jeans per year and charges p_1 dollars per pair.

The inefficiency, or welfare cost, associated with this monopoly is area BCE in Figure 13–2. To eliminate this area, the city council must impose a price ceiling that increases production to the point where LMC $= D$; that is, it must choose a ceiling price that makes the firm behave as if it were a perfect competitor. Thus, the council should set a price ceiling of p_0 dollars per pair of jeans. At this price Y_2 pairs of jeans will be bought and sold each year and the inefficiency will be eliminated.

Regulating a monopoly by imposing a price ceiling such that price is equal to marginal cost is called **marginal cost pricing**. Marginal cost pricing eliminates the inefficiency generated by the monopoly.

REGULATING A NATURAL MONOPOLY

When we state that price is higher and output is smaller in a monopoly than in a perfectly competitive industry, we are assuming that costs are identical given either market structure. As we have seen, these results are used as a basis for arguing in favor of

REGULATING A MONOPOLY: MARGINAL COST PRICING

FIGURE 13–2

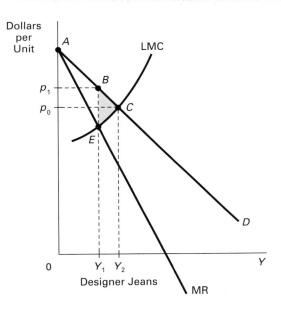

Dollars per Unit

Designer Jeans

Prior to regulation, Valerie sells Y_1 pairs of jeans per year at p_1 dollars per pair. The shaded area represents the monopoly's inefficiency. When the firm is required to sell at marginal cost, p_0 dollars per pair, Valerie sells more pairs of jeans and the inefficiency is eliminated.

regulation. In fact, some individuals take the argument even further and conclude that all monopolies should be broken up into many smaller competitive firms. However, oftentimes the assumption that costs are the same for a single supplier and many smaller suppliers is unrealistic. As we noted in the last chapter, one reason for the existence of monopoly is that a monopolist can take advantage of economies of scale. In this instance, breaking up the monopoly may actually lead to undesirable results.

A **natural monopoly** arises when one large firm can produce at a lower per-unit cost than many smaller firms can. Natural monopolies come about when the technology is such that the LAC falls over the relevant range of market demand—that is, when economies of scale extend to very large output rates. In this instance, one firm can always undersell smaller firms and will eventually take over the entire market.

Natural monopolies typically arise with public utilities firms such as electric, water, gas, and telephone companies. These firms all have one feature in common: by supplying electricity or telephone services through one set of cables and water or gas

NATURAL MONOPOLY

through one set of pipes, their per-unit costs are lower than if many small firms ran their own independent lines to each consumer.

Consider the natural monopoly shown in Figure 13–3. The LAC curve is declining over the entire range of market demand. In this type of situation, one firm will take over the entire market. If one small firm was producing Y_1 units of output at an average cost of p_1, then this firm could expand output, reduce per-unit costs, sell at a lower price, and eventually drive all other firms out of the market. A monopoly arises naturally. In fact, this is why we did not consider firms with declining LAC curves in our discussion of long-run competitive equilibrium (Chapter 9). Such a technology gives rise to a market structure that is incompatible with perfect competition.

AVERAGE COST PRICING

When a market is characterized by natural monopoly, breaking up the monopoly and imposing a competitive structure will

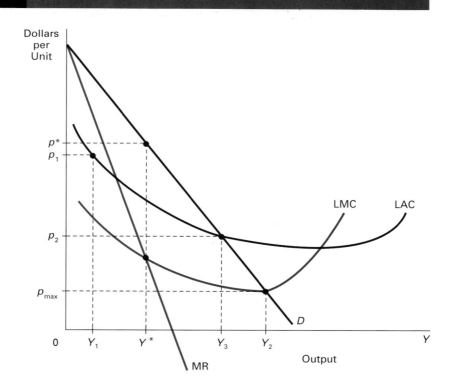

FIGURE 13–3   **NATURAL MONOPOLY**

A natural monopoly arises when LAC falls over the relevant range of market demand. In this instance, one large firm can always undersell smaller firms and will eventually take over the market. If a natural monopolist is required to sell at marginal cost, p_{max}, then it incurs a loss. A viable alternative is to require the firm to sell at average cost, p_2, in which case profit is zero.

actually lead to higher service costs. Naturally, this is an undesirable outcome, so we must consider regulation via price controls.

When the LAC declines over the relevant range of market demand, using marginal cost pricing causes a problem. Returning to Figure 13–3, we find that the profit-maximizing output rate is Y^* and the corresponding price is p^*. At this output rate, price is greater than average cost and the monopoly earns positive monopoly profit.

Now suppose the regulatory board imposes a maximum price for the monopoly's product, equal to p_{max} in the diagram. This is an example of marginal cost pricing since the profit-maximizing output rate is now Y_2 and, at that level of production, price is equal to marginal cost. As we saw above, marginal cost pricing eliminates the welfare cost associated with the monopoly. There is, however, a problem with this pricing scheme. Since the ceiling price is below LAC at Y_2, the firm makes a loss and will go out of business. The only way out of this dilemma is to subsidize the firm; however, this solution usually is prohibitively costly, may be politically unsatisfactory, and may cause undesirable incentives for inefficiency.

An alternative to marginal cost pricing is average cost pricing. **Average cost pricing**, sometimes called rate-of-return pricing, means setting a ceiling price at the level where the LAC curve intersects the demand curve, or price p_2 in Figure 13–3. Given this price, the profit-maximizing output is Y_3. Now the monopolist makes no monopoly profit, which means he or she earns a normal rate of return.

CRITICISMS OF AVERAGE COST PRICING

There are two primary problems that arise when regulators use price ceilings to control natural monopolies. The first problem is how to determine the appropriate ceiling price. In order to implement average cost pricing (or marginal cost pricing for that matter), regulators must have an estimate of the demand and cost curves facing the monopoly—but accurately estimating these curves is a complex and controversial task.

The second problem concerns the incentives that average cost pricing establishes. If the regulated price is pegged to the average cost of production, then a monopoly has no incentive to minimize production costs. Rising costs do not affect profit since the regulated price rises when costs rise. This can lead to waste and mismanagement. Simultaneously, average cost pricing also gives firms an incentive to provide lower quality services over the period of time when the regulated price is not allowed to rise. This is because the monopoly can lower production costs by lowering product quality when the price of its good or service is fixed, and this, in turn, increases monopoly profit.

EXAMPLE 13-1

REGULATING AN ELECTRIC COMPANY

Suppose the Arizona Corporation Commission has hired you to recommend a ceiling price for electricity supplied to the city of Phoenix by APS, a local utility company. The demand for electrical power in Phoenix is estimated to be

$$p = 100 - .05Y$$

and the total and marginal costs of providing electrical power are estimated to be

$$LTC = 30Y - .005Y^2 \quad \text{and} \quad LMC = 30 - .01Y$$

where Y is thousands of kilowatt-hours per day and p is price per 1,000 kilowatt-hours. (a) What are the profit-maximizing quantity and price? (b) What price ceiling will you recommend if your goal is to achieve efficiency? (c) Explain any problems that might arise as a results of the price you recommend.

■ **SOLUTION** (a) If left unregulated, APS would deliver the profit-maximizing quantity of electricity and charge the corresponding price. Setting marginal revenue equal to marginal cost, we have

$$100 - .1Y = 30 - .01Y$$

and solving for Y gives the profit-maximizing quantity: $Y^* = 778,000$ kilowatt-hours per day. The profit-maximizing price is found by substituting Y^* into the demand function, which gives: $p^* = 100 - .05(778) = \$61$ per 1,000 kilowatt-hours.

(b) If our goal is to achieve economic efficiency, then the price ceiling must be such that the monopoly produces at the level where demand is equal to marginal cost. In this instance, we have

$$100 - .05Y = 30 - .01Y$$

or $Y = 1,750,000$ kilowatt-hours. Substituting this quantity into the demand function gives $p = 100 - .05(1,750) = \$13$ per 1,000 kilowatt-hours. That is, if APS is forced to charge $13 per 1,000 kilowatt-hours, then output will be such that price is equal to marginal cost, and the inefficiency of the monopoly will be eliminated.

(c) Unfortunately, a price of $13 per 1,000 kilowatt-hours will result in a loss for APS. To see this, substitute $Y = 1,750$ into the total cost equation: LTC $= 30(1,750) - .005(1,750)^2 = \$72,625$. At $13 per 1,000 kilowatt-hours, total revenue is $13(1,750) = \$22,750$ and the firm makes a loss of $22,750 - 72,625 = -\$49,875$. Thus, the price ceiling guaranteeing efficiency will put APS out of business.

To remedy this, we can recommend either a subsidy to APS that will allow the firm to earn zero economic profit or an alternative price. Since average cost pricing increases efficiency and allows the firm to earn zero economic profit, this is a viable alternative. Setting average cost equal to demand, we have

$$\text{LAC} = 30 - .005Y = 100 - .05Y \qquad \text{or}$$

$$Y = 1,556.$$

Substituting this quantity into the demand function gives

$$p = 100 - .05(1556) = \$22 \text{ per 1,000 kilowatt-hours.}$$

Thus, if APS is forced to charge $22 per 1,000 kilowatt-hours, then consumers are better off than they were with the profit-maximizing price and output, and the utility company earns zero economic profit. ■

■ In the last chapter we saw that a profit-maximizing monopoly charging a uniform price to all customers earns positive economic profit in the long run. We also saw that this monopoly profit arises because a firm with market power can capture some consumer surplus. By charging a higher price for its product and selling fewer units than would a perfect competitor with the same cost curves, the monopoly transfers consumer surplus from consumers to the firm.

Charging a uniform price for its product is one *pricing strategy* that a firm with market power might use; however, this may not be the strategy that maximizes monopoly profit. Sometimes a firm with market power can increase profit by charging different prices to different groups of buyers. For example, firms might increase profit by charging adults one price for a particular good or service while simultaneously offering children and senior citizens discounts for the same good or service.

In this section, we investigate one of the most common ways owners and managers of firms with market power increase monopoly profit, namely, price discrimination. *Price discrimination* is the

13.2 PRICE DISCRIMINATION

practice of charging different groups of buyers different prices for the same good or service when the different prices are not associated with differences in costs.

CONDITIONS FOR PRICE DISCRIMINATION

Three conditions must be met for a firm to practice price discrimination successfully. First, the seller of the product must have some degree of market power. If the firm cannot exert some control over the price of its product, then it cannot practice price discrimination.

Second, the seller must be able to separate buyers into two or more distinct groups, each having different price elasticities of demand; moreover, the cost of doing so must be small. For example, it is relatively cheap for a movie theater to distinguish senior citizens and children from other movie goers. Typically, senior citizens simply must show some type of I.D. and children are asked their age. If buyers cannot be segmented, then price discrimination cannot occur.

Finally, there can be no resale market of the good sold by the monopolist. This is a very important condition. It is also the one most frequently violated. For example, if a computer store offers senior citizens a lower price for a personal computer, then individuals who do not qualify for the discount can have their grandparents purchase a computer and then buy it from them at the lower price. Typically, nondurable goods or services cannot be resold.

TYPES OF PRICE DISCRIMINATION

There are many forms of price discrimination, but the standard method of classification identifies three basic types or degrees of discrimination: first, second, and third degree price discrimination. The common characteristic of each of these types of discrimination is that they allow the firm to capture all or part of the consumer surplus that would have resulted from uniform pricing.

FIRST DEGREE PRICE DISCRIMINATION

First degree price discrimination, also called perfect price discrimination, occurs when a monopolist charges each consumer the maximum price that he or she is willing to pay for each unit bought. If this can be accomplished, then the monopolist increases profit by transferring *all* consumer surplus to the firm.

Suppose Dr. Hart is the only physician in a small town. Anyone living in this town who wants a physical examination must go to Dr. Hart. In this instance, it is possible for Dr. Hart to engage in price discrimination since each of the three conditions are met: first, she has monopoly power; second, she can distinguish between patients simply by having them fill out a form requesting financial and other data that will allow her to estimate each one's willingness to pay; and third, physical examinations cannot be resold.

Figure 13–4 illustrates the demand and cost curves facing Dr. Hart. Recall that the market demand curve represents the maximum price that can be obtained for each additional unit of output. In the absence of price discrimination, Dr. Hart produces at the level where marginal revenue is equal to marginal cost. If she charges each of her patients a uniform price per physical, then she maximizes profit when she performs Y_4 physical examinations per year and charges a fee of p_4 dollars per physical. Monopoly profit is given by area p_5p_4BC and consumer surplus is p_4AB.

First degree price discrimination involves charging the maximum price possible for each unit of output: the patient who attaches the greatest value to health care is identified and charged p_1; the patients willing to pay p_2 and p_3 are identified and charged accordingly, and so on. Thus, if Dr. Hart practices first degree price discrimination, the demand curve reflects the marginal revenue she

FIRST DEGREE PRICE DISCRIMINATION

FIGURE 13–4

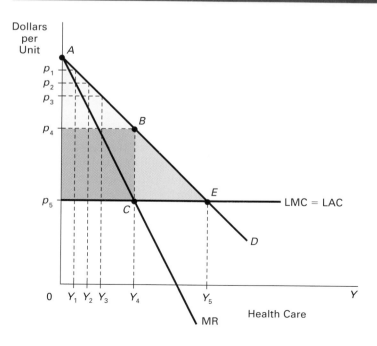

If a monopolist practices first degree price discrimination, then it charges each consumer the maximum he or she is willing to pay. This means that the demand curve is the marginal revenue curve and Dr. Hart will perform Y_4 physicals. Monopoly profit is now area p_5AE and consumer surplus is zero.

earns for the basic service she provides. In addition, the revenue she earns for each examination she performs is simply the price she charges for that visit.

If Dr. Hart is a profit maximizer, output will expand until marginal revenue equals marginal cost or, in this instance, until she performs Y_5 physical examinations. At Y_5, demand is equal to marginal cost. Producing any more or less reduces profit.

Still we have not confirmed that profit is larger than it was before price discrimination. Then, monopoly profit was given by area p_5p_4BC. When the firm price discriminates, however, total profit is the area between the demand and average cost curve, or area p_5AE. (Total revenue is $0AEY_5$ and total cost is area $0p_5EY_5$.) From Figure 13–4 it is clear that profit is larger than before. Furthermore, note that, since each consumer is paying the maximum amount he or she is willing to pay, consumer surplus is zero. First degree price discrimination allows Dr. Hart to capture all consumer surplus in the form of higher profit.

Perfect price discrimination increases monopoly profit. It also makes consumers as a whole worse off. Those individuals who are willing to pay between p_4 and p_1 are worse off since, under uniform pricing, they paid only p_2 per physical examination but now must pay more. Those consumers who are willing to pay between p_5 and p_4 are neither better off nor worse off. These patients now choose to purchase a physical examination but, because they must pay the maximum amount they are willing to pay, the monopolist captures all of their consumer surplus as well. Thus, consumers as a whole are worse off. Even though output is the same as it would be under perfect competition, consumer surplus is redistributed from consumers to the monopolist. What would be consumer surplus under competition, area p_5AE in Figure 13–4, becomes monopoly profit under first degree price discrimination.

Real-world examples of first degree price discrimination are difficult to find because it requires the seller have complete knowledge of both market demand and each individual's willingness to pay. Sometimes, however, firms can discriminate imperfectly by charging several different prices based on estimates of their customers' demand. In the U.S., doctors, lawyers, accountants, salespersons and other producers who know their customers reasonably well often practice this type of price discrimination. For example, a salesperson can often vary the price of a good according to his or her perception of the buyer's willingness to pay. (Have you ever dealt with a car salesperson?) Markets where the product is sold via an auction can also approximate first degree price discrimination. For example, in the U.S. the federal government conducts the sale of Treasury bonds using a sealed bid auction. All bids exceeding a predetermined minimum are accepted and all bidders are obligated to honor their bids in full. Through this type of process, the seller can extract the maximum price each buyer is willing to pay.

Second degree price discrimination is an imperfect form of first degree price discrimination. Instead of setting different prices for each unit, it involves charging different prices for different quantities or "blocks" of the same good or service. In the U.S., utility companies often use this type of pricing strategy.

Figure 13–5 illustrates second degree price discrimination for a monopolist with constant marginal and average cost curves. A profit maximizer charging a single uniform price would produce Y_1 units and charge p_1 dollars per unit. In this instance, monopoly profit is given by area $p_3 p_1 CK$ and consumer surplus is $p_1 AC$.

SECOND DEGREE PRICE
DISCRIMINATION

SECOND DEGREE PRICE DISCRIMINATION

FIGURE 13–5

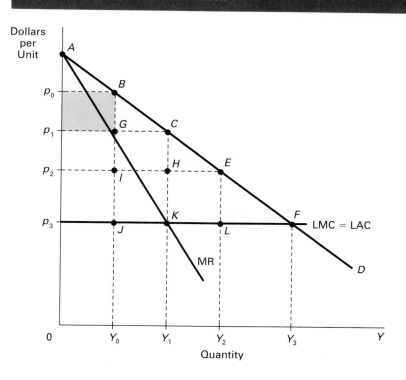

If a monopolist practices second degree price discrimination, then it changes different prices for different blocks of the same good or service. If HCE + LEF is greater than $p_1 p_0 BG$, then consumers as a whole are better off than they would be if a single uniform price were charged.

Now suppose that, instead of charging a single price for all units purchased, the monopolist charges four different prices, based on the quantity purchased. The first block is priced at p_0, the second at p_1, the third at p_2, and the fourth at p_4. Given this pricing strategy, monopoly profit associated with the first block is given by area p_3p_0BJ, the second block by area p_3p_1CK, and the third block by area p_3p_2EL. Thus, total monopoly profit is now larger.

Notice that, even if a monopoly uses second degree price discrimination, it is possible for consumers as a whole to be better off than they would be if a single price were charged. This is because, for certain blocks, price is lower than it would be if a single price were charged. Block pricing generates some consumer surplus for those individuals who were not willing to pay p_1 but who are willing to pay p_2 or p_3. If there are enough new market participants, consumer surplus as a whole can increase.

In Figure 13–5, consumer surplus is p_1AC when a single price is charged. If the monopolist uses block pricing, then consumer surplus is the sum of areas p_0AB, GBC, HCE, and LEF. If $HCE +$ LEF, the sum of which is the consumer surplus going to new market participants, is greater than p_0p_2BG, the portion of consumer surplus that is transferred to the producer, then consumers as a whole are better off.

The most common type of price discrimination is **third degree price discrimination**, which occurs when the total market can be segmented into different groups of buyers, each having its own price elasticity of demand curve. In this instance, the monopoly can increase profit by charging a higher price in the market where demand is less elastic.

Figure 13–6 shows price discrimination in a segmented market. In Figures 13–6(a) and (b) we have drawn the demand curves associated with the two groups of buyers, group A and group B, and the associated marginal revenue curves. Group A has demand curve D_A and marginal revenue curve MR_A. Group B has demand curve D_B and marginal revenue curve MR_B. Demand is assumed to be less elastic in market A than in market B.

The monopoly must make two decisions. It must decide first how much output to produce in total and then how to allocate the output between the two markets. In order to maximize profit, the firm should produce at the level where total marginal revenue is equal to long-run marginal cost. This decision is illustrated in Figure 13–6(c). D_T is the sum of the demand curves given in diagrams (a) and (b) and MR_T is the corresponding marginal

THIRD DEGREE PRICE DISCRIMINATION   **FIGURE 13–6**

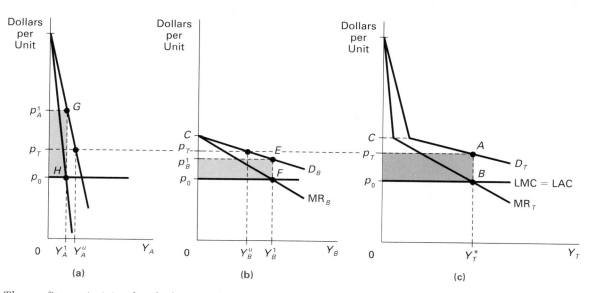

The profit-maximizing level of output for the monopolist is Y_T^* in diagram (c). This output should be allocated across markets so that $MR_A = MR_B = P_o$, or Y_A^1 and Y_B^1 in diagrams (a) and (b) respectively.

revenue curve. For prices above C, D_T corresponds to D_A, since none of the group B buyers are in the market. When the price falls below C, group B enters the market and D_T is equal to $D_A + D_B$. The profit-maximizing level of output is Y_T^* with $LMC = p_0$. In the absence of price discrimination, the monopolist charges p_T per unit of output and earns $p_0 p_T AB$ in monopoly profit.

If the monopoly is going to price discriminate, then once it has determined the profit-maximizing output, its next step is to determine the output rates and prices in each market. The decision rule for allocating output is that the marginal revenue of selling in market A should be equal to the marginal revenue of selling in market B and both should be equal to the profit-maximizing marginal cost; that is, $MR_A = MR_B = p_0$. If these equalities do not hold, then output could be redistributed between the two groups of consumers in such a way that profit would be higher. For example, if $MR_A > MR_B$ then, since marginal cost is the same no matter where the output is sold, selling one less unit in the B market and one more unit in the A market will increase profit.

In Figure 13–6, the profit-maximizing outputs are Y_A^1 and Y_B^1 and the corresponding prices are p_A^1 and p_B^1. Since $p_A^1 > p_B^1$, profit maximization implies that sellers charge a higher price in the market where demand is less elastic. This result is true in general and can be easily explained. Where demand is less elastic, on the one hand, buyers are less sensitive to changes in price, which means that sellers can charge a relatively high price without reducing the quantity demanded too much. In Figure 13–6(a), increasing price from p_T to p_A^1 causes quantity demanded to fall a little from Y_A^u to Y_A^1. Where demand is more elastic, on the other hand, quantity demanded is more sensitive to price, which means that if sellers charge a lower price, quantity demanded increases substantially. In Figure 13–6(b), lowering price from p_T to p_B^1 causes quantity demanded to increase substantially from Y_B^u to Y_B^1.

Compared to a firm that practices uniform pricing, a discriminating monopoly sells fewer units and charges a higher price in the market where demand tends to be inelastic and sells more units and charges a lower price in the market where demand tends to be elastic. As a result, profit increases, since now the average price charged has gone up. The shaded area in Figure 13–6(c) indicates monopoly profit under uniform pricing, while the sum of the shaded areas in diagrams (a) and (b) represents monopoly profit under price discrimination.

Like second degree price discrimination, third degree price discrimination does not necessarily make consumers as a whole worse off. When compared to uniform pricing, price discrimination benefits those who consume more at a lower price, that is, those with elastic demands, and harms those who consume less at a higher price. Whether or not consumers as a whole are better off or worse off depends on how big these effects are.

Examples of price discrimination in segmented markets are easy to find in the real world. Many stores offer quantity discounts to "large" buyers, college bookstores give faculty discounts, movie theaters offer children and senior citizens discounted ticket prices, airlines have regular fares and discount fares, telephone companies charge different rates for residential and business customers, and many firms offer discount coupons or rebates for purchasing their products. In all these cases, firms are selling the same good to different groups of buyers at different prices.

EXAMPLE 13-2

PRICING AIRLINE TICKETS

Suppose the economics division of a major airline company estimates that the demand and marginal revenue functions for first class and excursion fares from Los Angeles to Paris are as follows:

Market A: First Class

$p_A = 4{,}200 - 2Y_A$

$MR_A = 4{,}200 - 4Y_A$

Market B: Excursion

$p_B = 2{,}200 - .25Y_B$

$MR_B = 2{,}200 - .5Y_B$

(a) If the marginal cost of production is \$200 per passenger and the airline uses third degree price discrimination, what fare and what number of passengers will maximize profit in each market? (b) Show that greater profits result from price discrimination than would have resulted from uniform pricing.

■ **SOLUTION** (a) With price discrimination, profit maximization requires that $MR_A = MR_B = LMC$. Since marginal cost is constant at \$200 per passenger, the optimal quantities are the solutions to the equations:

$$MR_A = 4{,}200 - 4Y_A = 200, \text{ which implies that } Y_A = 1{,}000,$$

and

$$MR_B = 2{,}200 - .25Y_B = 200, \text{ which implies that } Y_B = 4{,}000.$$

We obtain optimal prices by substituting the profit-maximizing quantities into the demand equations. This gives $p_A = \$2{,}200$ per passenger and $p_B = \$1{,}200$ per passenger.

(b) Profit in each market is equal to total revenue minus total cost. Thus, $\pi_A = 2{,}200{,}000 - 200{,}000 = \$2{,}000{,}000$ and $\pi_B = 4{,}800{,}000 - 800{,}000 = \$4{,}000{,}000$. Hence, combined profit for the two markets is \$6 million.

To calculate profit in the absence of price discrimination, we must determine the total market demand and marginal revenue functions. The first step is to express the demand equations in terms of quantities. This gives

$$Y_A = 2{,}100 - .5p \quad \text{and} \quad Y_B = 8{,}800 - 4p$$

where the subscript on price has been dropped because both markets are charging the same price. Adding demands gives

$$Y_T = 10,900 - 4.5p.$$

The marginal revenue function associated with this demand curve is obtained by solving for p and noting that the marginal revenue function for a linear demand curve has the same intercept and twice the slope. Thus

$$p = (10,900/4.5) - (1/4.5)Y_T \qquad \text{and}$$

$$MR_T = (10,900/4.5) - (2/4.5)Y_T.$$

Equating marginal revenue and marginal cost gives $Y_T = 5,000$ passengers. Substituting this into the total demand function yields $p = 5,900/4.5 \cong \$1,311$. Thus, if a single uniform price is charged, profit is $\pi_T = 6,555,556 - 1,000,000 = \$5,555,556$, which is less than the profit obtained under price discrimination. ■

Airlines often practice third degree price discrimination. In fact, in a study of the North Atlantic market J.M. Cigliano estimates the price elasticity of demand for air travel between the U.S. and Europe to be -0.45 for first class passengers and -1.83 for excursion passengers (J.M. Cigliano, "Price and Income Elasticities for Airline Travel: The North Atlantic Market." *Business Economics* 15 [Sept. 1980]: 17–21). That is, the price elasticity of demand for excursion fares is about four times as great as that for first class fares and, hence, first class fares should be, and are, substantially higher.

13.3 PEAK-LOAD PRICING

■ As we saw in the last section, a monopolist selling in many markets at the same time can increase profit by practicing price discrimination when demand elasticities differ. Similarly, a firm that uses the same plant or facility to supply a good or service demand for which varies at different points in time can increase profit, as well as economic efficiency, by using peak-load pricing. **Peak-load pricing** involves charging a higher price to customers who purchase the product during periods of "peak" demand and a lower price to those who purchase it during periods of "off-peak" demand.

The pricing of long-distance telephone calls is a good example of peak-load pricing. Most long-distance calls are placed by businesses on weekday afternoons; fewer calls are placed late at night and on weekends. While demand for telephone calls differs with the time of day, so does the cost of producing them. The switching facilities and lines that telephone companies provide are designed to meet demand during peak times. As a result, marginal cost is low during off-peak times when much of a firm's capacity sits idle and it is high during peak times when capacity is strained. Thus, to encourage efficient use of their production facilities, telephone companies should, and do, offer lower rates for off-peak use.

For peak-load pricing to be a successful strategy, not only must demand vary over time, but so too must the cost of producing the product. For example, if a telephone company could store phone calls at negligible cost for later use, then the marginal cost of providing phone calls during peak and off-peak times would be the same. The telephone company could operate at a constant rate of production throughout the day by storing (recording) some calls made during peak hours and then selling them (playing them back) during off-peak hours. However, this practice would not be acceptable. An executive in Los Angeles would not be willing to substitute a call from an associate on Wall Street during peak hours for a recorded call during off-peak hours. Since telephone calls cannot be stored, a successful firm must have the operating capacity to meet demand during peak periods. As a result, marginal cost is high during peak periods, when the firm is operating at or near capacity, and low during off-peak periods.

PROFIT MAXIMIZATION

We can illustrate peak-load pricing using Figure 13–7. There are two periods when demands differ, period 1 and period 2. In Figure 13–7 we have drawn the demand curves associated with the two periods as well as the corresponding marginal revenue curves. D_1 and MR_1 represent demand and marginal revenue during period 1, which is the peak time of day. D_2 and MR_2 represent demand and marginal revenue during period 2, which is the off-peak period.

First, suppose the monopoly ignores the variation in demand over time and charges a single uniform price, p. At this price the monopoly will provide an output of Y_1^1 during the peak period and Y_2^1 during the off-peak period. Notice that, as we would expect, output is substantially greater during the peak period.

Now suppose that, instead of charging a single price, the monopolist uses a peak-load pricing strategy. The monopoly must decide what quantity of output to produce during each period and what price to charge. In order to maximize profit in each period, the firm should produce the level of output for which marginal revenue is equal to marginal cost. In Figure 13–7, the profit-maximizing

FIGURE 13-7   **PEAK-LOAD PRICING**

D_1 and D_2 represent demand during peak and off-peak times respectively. In this instance, a profit-maximizing monopolist will sell Y_1^* units at a price of p_1^* during the peak period and Y_2^* units at a price of p_2^* during the off-peak period. This results in the efficiency gains shown by the shaded areas.

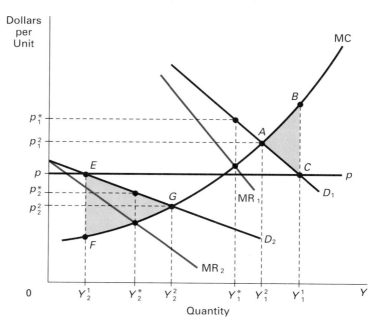

outputs are Y_1^* and Y_2^* and the corresponding prices are p_1^* and p_2^*; that is, during peak times the firm sells Y_1^* units of output at a relatively high price, p_1^*, and during off-peak times the firm sells Y_2^* units at a relatively low price, p_2^*. Output is still greater during the peak period, but now it is much more evenly distributed throughout the day. As a result of using a peak-load pricing strategy, the firm's monopoly profit is greater, because production in each period corresponds to the level where marginal revenue is equal to marginal cost.

It is important to note that peak-load pricing is different from third degree price discrimination. If a monopoly uses third degree price discrimination, then marginal revenue must be equal for each market and equal to marginal cost, the reason being that the costs of providing the good or service to different markets depends on *total* output. (For example, in order to determine the number of movie theater tickets to sell at regular and discounted prices, a theatre owner first determines the quantity of ticket sales for which marginal revenue is equal to marginal cost, independent of whether or not the ticket is a discount or a regular price ticket, and then decides how to allocate these tickets between the two markets.) However, this is not the case with peak-load pricing. Since firms use the same facilities to produce the good or service during peak and off-peak times, costs are independent. Selling more tickets for a matinee show does not affect the cost (wages, heating and lighting, etc.) of selling tickets for an evening show. As a result, price and quantity in each period are determined independently by setting marginal revenue equal to marginal cost for each period.

One advantage peak-load pricing has over uniform pricing is that it leads to a more efficient distribution of output between peak and off-peak times. During the peak period, when production is more costly, people reduce their consumption, as is shown in Figure 13–7 by the movement from Y_1^1 to Y_1^*, and during the off-peak period, when production is cheaper, they increase their consumption, as is shown by the movement from Y_2^1 to Y_2^*.

EFFICIENCY AND PEAK-LOAD PRICING

The easiest way to illustrate the efficiency gains is to consider a regulated monopolist, an electric company for example. Efficiency is achieved if the regulatory agency sets prices corresponding to the point where the demand curves intersect the marginal cost curve. In Figure 13–7, price would be p_1^2 during the peak period and p_2^2 during the off-peak period. Faced with these prices, consumers would reduce use in the peak period from Y_1^1 to Y_1^2 and increase use in the off-peak period from Y_2^1 to Y_2^2.

When use in the peak period falls, costs fall by the area under the marginal cost curve, $Y_1^2 ABY_1^1$, and benefits fall by the area under the demand curve, $Y_1^2 ACY_1^1$. Since costs fall by more than benefits, there is a net gain equivalent to the shaded area ABC. Likewise, when use in the off-peak period rises, costs rise by $Y_2^1 FGY_2^2$, and benefits rise by $Y_2^1 EGY_2^2$. Since benefits rise by more than costs, there is a net gain equivalent to the shaded area EFG. Thus, peak-load pricing results in greater efficiency.

EXAMPLE 13–3

PRICING COMPUTER TIME

The central processing unit (CPU) is the "brain" of a computer. It manages the transmission of information to and from the computer and processes the data. Suppose that you are the manager of a large computational facility and that one of your primary duties is to determine the price or prices to charge for use of CPU time.

Demand for CPU time varies throughout the day and, according to your best estimate, is as follows:

Monday–Friday, 8 A.M.–midnight $p_1 = .1 - .0001Y_1$

All other days and times $p_2 = .05 - .0001Y_2$

where Y is seconds of CPU time and p is the price per second. If the marginal cost of providing CPU time is given by

$$MC = .02 + .0001Y,$$

what are the profit-maximizing prices to charge for the use of CPU time?

■ **SOLUTION** First note that the three conditions for successful peak-load pricing are met: the same facility is used to provide CPU time at different hours of the day; CPU time cannot be stored; and demand varies across time. Thus, peak-load pricing is a viable strategy.

The profit-maximizing prices are determined by setting MR equal to marginal cost for each period. This gives

$$MR_1 = .1 - .0002Y_1 = .02 + .0001Y_1 \qquad \text{and}$$

$$MR_2 = .05 - .0002Y_2 = .02 + .0001Y_2.$$

Solving each of these equations for output yields $Y_1^* = 267$ and $Y_2^* = 100$. Finally, substituting each of these quantities into the relevant demand function gives the profit-maximizing prices; that is, $p_1^* = \$.07$ per second and $p_2^* = \$.04$ per second. Thus, CPU time during peak hours should cost almost twice as much as during off-peak hours. ■

To encourage the use of off-peak hours, nearly all university computer facilities use some type of peak-load pricing scheme. Typically, the price of CPU time during peak hours—weekdays from 1 to 5 PM, for example—is 10 to 30 times higher than during off-peak hours—weekdays from 1 to 8 AM, for example. As a result, computer usage is much lower during peak periods and higher during off-peak periods than it would be if a single uniform price were charged. (When do you do your work on the university computer? Who do you suppose uses the facilities during peak periods?)

■ Sellers of inputs, just like sellers of goods and services, can have monopoly power. For example, a firm that has a patent or some other type of exclusive right to produce an input that is used in the production of other goods and services is a monopolist seller of that input.

Perhaps the most important example of monopoly power in input markets is the labor union. A **labor union** is an organization of workers that can effectively control the supply of labor services to a particular firm or industry. Thus, a labor union can have monopoly power over the sale of labor services.

In Figure 13–8 we have illustrated the market for labor services. The market labor demand curve, D_L, represents the maximum amount firms are willing to pay for each additional worker, while the market labor supply curve, S_L, represents how much labor union workers would supply at each wage if the union had no monopoly power. In the absence of monopoly power in the labor market, L^* workers would be employed at a wage rate of w^* dollars per worker.

If the union does have monopoly power, however, then it can choose any wage rate and corresponding level of employment, just as a monopoly in an output market can choose any price and the corresponding quantity of output. But which wage–employment combination will the union choose?

Just as with any decision-making problem, the answer will depend on the decision maker's objective. When we examined a firm with monopoly power in an output market, we assumed that the firm's objective was to maximize profit. This led to a condition characterizing the optimal price–output combination. For a union, maximizing the economic rent that its workers receive is analogous to maximizing profit for a firm. While profit to a firm is revenue less economic costs, rent to a union represents the wages its members receive less their opportunity costs. (Recall from our earlier discussion of economic rent that graphically it is the area above the labor supply curve and below the wage rate.)

If the union's objective is to maximize the economic rent that its workers receive, then it must hire the number of workers that will make the marginal revenue equal to marginal cost. Marginal revenue to the union is the additional amount its membership earns in wages for each additional worker employed. In Figure 13–8, MR_L represents marginal revenue to the union. Notice that, for any given level of employment, marginal revenue is less than the wage rate. This is because the union is a monopolist in the labor market and any increase in employment lowers the wage to all workers in the union.

FIGURE 13–8   **LABOR UNIONS**

The labor union's supply curve for labor is given by S_L and the firm's demand for labor by D_L. MR_L is the marginal revenue curve facing the labor union. If the goal of the labor union is to maximize economic rent, then L^u workers will be employed at a wage of w^u dollars per worker.

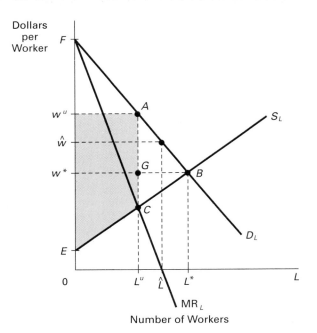

Marginal cost to the union is the additional cost to its membership of employing each additional worker. Since the labor supply curve represents the opportunity cost of workers being employed, to the union it also represents the marginal cost of inducing an additional worker to work.

In Figure 13–8, the union maximizes economic rent if it restricts employment to L^u workers. At L^u, $MR_L = S_L$. If the union restricted membership to fewer workers than this, then $MR_L < S_L$ and the union could increase rent by hiring more workers. Similarly, if the union expanded employment beyond L^u workers, then it could increase rent by hiring fewer workers.

Given L^u, the rent-maximizing level of employment, firms will pay a wage rate of w^u per worker. As a result, area $0w^uAL^u$ represents total wages paid to union members, area $0ECL^u$ gives total opportunity cost, and area Ew^uAC represents total economic rent. Notice that compared to the competitive wage and level of employment, w^* and L^* respectively, the union restricts membership and charges a higher wage.

In the preceding discussion, we assume that the goal of the union is to maximize the economic rent its members receive. However, this is not the only conceivable objective of a labor union. Alternatively, the union may want to maximize the number of workers firms hire, or it may want to maximize the aggregate income of its membership.

To analyze the implication of these alternative goals, consider once again Figure 13–8. If, on the one hand, the goal of the union is to maximize its membership, then it will choose the competitive solution; that is, it will bargain for a wage rate of w^*. If, on the other hand, the goal of the union is to maximize aggregate income, then the union will want to restrict employment to $\hat{L}$, which is the point where marginal revenue is zero. The wage rate associated with this level of employment is $\hat{w}$.

There are still other objectives the union leaders may have, such as maintaining their power within the union. However, most empirical evidence suggests that unions do use whatever monopoly power they still have (it seems to be declining) to restrict employment and raise the wage rate above the competitive level. Economists estimate that in the United States union wages are 10 to 15% higher than comparable nonunion wages. (Richard Freeman and James Medoff, *What Do Unions Do?* New York: Basic Books. 1984).

When unions use their monopoly power to restrict employment and increase their members' wages, the number of nonunionized workers rises. Thus, it is important to understand the impact of labor unions on the nonunionized sector of the labor market.

To illustrate this impact, let's suppose that the total supply of union and nonunion workers is fixed. In Figure 13–9 the market supply of labor in both the union and nonunion sectors is given by S_L. The demand for labor in the union sector is D_u, the demand for labor in the nonunion sector is D_{nu}, and the total market demand for labor is the horizontal sum of the demands in the two sectors, given by D_L.

Now suppose the union decides to increase the wage rate above w^*, the competitive wage rate, to w^u. At the new wage, employment in the union sector falls from L_u^* to L_u^1. (Which union members lose their jobs is a difficult problem facing the union leaders. Typically, they lay off those with the least seniority and lowest skills.) If the workers no longer employed in the union sector become employed in the nonunion sector, the wage rate in the nonunion sector falls until the labor market is in equilibrium once again. In Figure 13–9, the wage rate in the union sector falls from w^* to w_{nu}. The new

FIGURE 13-9   UNIONS AND NONUNION WORKERS

If the total supply of workers is fixed as a result of the labor union's restricting membership $(L_u^1 < L_u^*)$ and raising the wage $(w^u > w^*)$, the nonunion wage falls from w^* to w^{nu}.

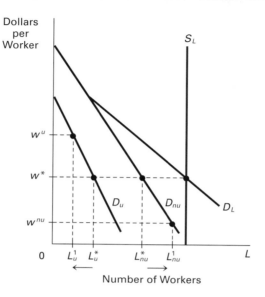

wage, w_{nu}, is the wage at which firms in the nonunion sector will be willing to employ workers leaving the union sector. Thus, as a result of the labor union's restricting membership and raising the union wage, the nonunion wage falls. Union workers benefit at the expense of nonunion workers.

EXAMPLE 13-4

UNIONS, WAGES, AND EMPLOYMENT

Suppose that the industry demand and supply curves for labor are given by

$$L = D_L(w) = 100 - .5w \quad \text{and} \quad L = S_L(w) = w,$$

where w is the daily wage rate and L is the number of workers employed in thousands. Assuming that all workers belong to a labor union and that the labor union can effectively control employment, determine the wage rate, level of employment, and aggregate income of workers if (a) the union maximizes economic rent, (b) the union maximizes aggregate income, and (c) the union maximizes employment. Compare these calculations to the competitive solution.

■ **SOLUTION** (a) If the union's objective is to maximize economic rent, then we find the quantity of labor hired by setting marginal revenue equal to supply and solving for L. Solving the supply and demand functions for w gives

$$(demand) \; w = 200 - 2L$$

$$(supply) \; w = L.$$

Since the demand function is linear, the marginal revenue function has the same intercept and twice the slope: $MR_L = 200 - 4L$. Equating marginal revenue and supply gives

$$200 - 4L = L \qquad\qquad \text{or}$$

$$L = 40,000 \text{ workers.}$$

The wage rate is determined by substituting $L = 40$ into the demand function:

$$w = 200 - 2(40) = \$120 \text{ per worker.}$$

Aggregate income is $120 \cdot 40,000 = \$4,800,000$.

(b) Now suppose that, instead of maximizing economic rent, the union maximizes aggregate income. In this instance, we determine the number of workers hired by setting marginal revenue equal to zero and solving for L. This gives

$$MR_L = 200 - 4L = 0 \qquad\qquad \text{or}$$

$$L = 50,000 \text{ workers.}$$

The wage rate corresponding to this level of employment is

$$w = 200 - 2(50) = \$100 \text{ per worker.}$$

If the union's objective is to maximize aggregate income, employment rises, the wage rate falls, and aggregate income increases to $100 \cdot 50,000 = \$5,000,000$.

(c) Finally, suppose that the union is interested in maximizing employment. In this case, the number of workers hired is determined by equating demand and supply and solving for L—that is, by finding the competitive solution:

$$200 - 2L = L \qquad\qquad \text{or}$$

$$L = 67,000 \text{ workers.}$$

The corresponding wage rate is

$$w = 200 - 2(67) = \$166 \text{ per worker}$$

and aggregate income is $166 \cdot 67,000 = \$4,422,000$. Thus, the competitive solution results in the highest level of employment, the lowest wage, and the lowest aggregate income. ∎

SUMMARY

1. If a monopoly is regulated by marginal cost pricing, which requires that price be equal to marginal cost, the inefficiency of monopoly is eliminated. For most practical matters, marginal cost pricing is difficult to implement. Often regulators use average cost pricing as an alternative. While average cost pricing does not eliminate all the inefficiency of monopoly, it does guarantee that monopoly profit is zero.

2. A monopolist can increase profit through price discrimination as long as the market can be segmented into different buyers with different tastes. The extreme case, called first degree, or perfect, price discrimination, occurs when each buyer is charged the maximum he or she is willing to pay. In this instance, the monopolist captures all consumer surplus.

3. Second degree price discrimination is an imperfect form of first degree price discrimination. It involves charging different prices for different blocks of the same good or service. This pricing scheme generates some consumer surplus for individual buyers, which means that consumers as a whole may be better off.

4. Third degree price discrimination is the most common type of price discrimination. It occurs when buyers can be segmented into two or more distinct groups. A monopolist using this pricing strategy charges a higher price in the market where demand is relatively inelastic and a lower price in the market where demand is relatively elastic.

5. Peak-load pricing is another way a monopolist can increase profit. Peak-load pricing involves charging a higher price to customers who purchase the product during periods of high demand. In addition to increasing profit, peak-load pricing increases efficiency.

6. Labor unions are monopolists in the labor market. If the union's objective is to maximize the economic rent its members receive, then workers will be hired up to the point where marginal revenue to the union is equal to marginal cost. If the union's objective is to maximize aggregate income, then workers will be hired up to the point where marginal revenue is equal to zero. Finally, if the union's objective is to maximize employment, then the competitive solution will prevail.

KEY TERMS

Marginal Cost Pricing
Natural Monopoly
Average Cost Pricing
First Degree Price
   Discrimination
Second Degree Price
   Discrimination
Third Degree Price
   Discrimination
Peak-load Pricing
Labor Union

1. a) If a monopoly is regulated using marginal cost pricing, will it remain in business?
   b) Does your answer have any relevance for the regulation of public utilities companies?
2. a) Would an unregulated natural monopoly be preferable to a regulated natural monopoly? (Hint: Examine both average and marginal cost pricing and determine who benefits and who does not as a result of regulation.)
   b) Does your answer explain the recent trend towards deregulation?
3. a) Define price discrimination and discuss when it might be a profit-maximizing strategy.
   b) Is peak-load pricing a form of price discrimination? Explain.
4. a) As we discussed in Chapter 5, producers of consumer goods often issue coupons that let consumers purchase products at lower prices. Using the theory of price discrimination, explain why issuing coupons can increase profit.
   b) Do you think consumers who use coupons have a more or less elastic demand function than those who do not use coupons. Explain.
5. Many firms offer rebates for the purchase of their products, provided the consumer mails in one or more proof-of-purchase seals. For example, Disney recently offered a three dollar rebate with proof of purchase of the *Sleeping Beauty* videotape. Explain why Disney did not just lower the price of the video by three dollars.
6. Pete's Distributing sells compact discs in two separable markets. The marginal cost of each disc is $2. Demand in each market is given by

$$X_A = 40 - 10p_A \quad \text{and} \quad X_B = 40 - 2p_B,$$

   where X is thousands of compact discs.
   a) If the firm uses third degree price discrimination, how much output should it produce and what price should it charge in each market? What is its profit?
   b) How does your answer change if the firm cannot prevent resale of compact discs? What will its profit be in this case?
   c) Do your answers to (a) and (b) have any implications for markets that are spatially separated? Explain.
7. Many airlines have discount fares if you travel midweek (Tuesday to Thursday). Is this an example of price discrimination, peak-load pricing, or neither? Explain.

8. Suppose that without price discrimination, the profit-maximizing price for an unregulated electric company is $.10 per kilowatt-hour and, at this price, consumers purchase 20,000 kilowatt-hours. Now consider a block pricing scheme in which the price is $.20 per kilowatt-hour for the first 10,000 kilowatt-hours purchased and $.10 thereafter.
   a) Show that this pricing strategy reduces consumer surplus and increases monopoly profit.
   b) Can you think of a block pricing strategy that would actually increase consumer surplus and profit? (Hint: Consider block prices above and below $.10.)
9. Many amusement parks charge a fixed fee when you enter the park and another fee for each ride you go on (that is, a two-part tariff—another way to extract consumer surplus).
   a) Determine the entry fee and price per ride that maximizes profit.
   b) Disneyland now charges an entry fee but the rides are free. Is this a better pricing strategy?
10. The Korean government often grants monopoly rights to firms producing goods that are exported to the U.S. A recent example is a Korean-made automobile called the Hyundai. Assuming that the goal of the Korean monopolist is to maximize profit, would you expect the price of a Hyundai to be higher in Korea or the U.S.? Explain in terms of a model of price discrimination.
11. Firms sometimes charge more for their products in their home country than abroad (net of transportation costs). Using the theory of monopoly, explain when this is feasible and why the good is cheaper abroad.
12. a) Explain why peak-load pricing yields a more efficient distribution of output.
    b) Does this have any implications for the regulatory agency that sets rates for electric companies? (Hint: What rates would you set for an electric company if you were interested in efficiency?)
13. Demand for notebook paper peaks at the beginning of each semester and is very low during the summer months. Why is peak-load pricing not used for notebook paper?
14. The demand for electricity varies greatly during a day. Peak demand is typically during the daytime hours when most businesses are operating. Suppose that demand for electricity is estimated to be

$$\text{(peak)} \quad p_1 = 100 - .01Y_1$$
$$\text{(off-peak)} \quad p_2 = 50 - .01Y_2$$

where Y is thousands of kilowatt-hours per day and p is the price per 1,000 kilowatt-hours. Suppose also that the marginal cost of providing electricity is given by

$$MC = 20 + .01Y.$$

a) Is peak-load pricing a feasible pricing strategy? Explain.
b) What are the profit-maximizing prices to charge for the use of electricity?
c) If the government decides to regulate the utility company providing electricity, what prices would you recommend as the ceiling prices if the government's goal is efficiency?

15. a) Movie theaters typically charge less for matinees than for evening shows. Is this an example of price discrimination or peak-load pricing?
b) Some theaters suspend their matinee discount for "special engagements." Can this be the profit-maximizing strategy? Explain.

16. The demand for labor by an industry is given by

$$L = 1,000 - 5w,$$

where L is the labor demanded per day and w is the wage rate. The supply of labor is given by

$$L = 20 + 2.5w.$$

a) What is the equilibrium wage rate and quantity of labor employed?
b) What is the economic rent earned by union members?
c) If labor is controlled by a monopolistic labor union that wishes to maximize economic rent, what is the quantity of labor employed and the wage rate? Compare this to your answer in part (a).

17. In the U.S., major league baseball prior to 1975 was exempt from the antitrust laws. This allowed baseball team owners to act like a monopsonistic cartel. After 1975 the cartel was effectively broken via a series of lawsuits. As a result, players' salaries increased dramatically. Explain this phenomenon using the monopsony model.

18. Suppose that teams representing the United Automobile Workers labor union and management of all U.S. automobile producers are negotiating a new labor contract. Assume that these two teams represent virtually all workers and all firms.

Determine the wage rate and level of employment that will result from these negotiations if

a) management is able to dominate the negotiations and dictate the terms of the contract

b) the union is able to dominate the negotiations and dictate the terms of the contract

c) you are an arbitrator appointed by the government to set a "fair" wage rate. (This is called a bilateral monopoly case.)

REFERENCES

Kreps, D. 1990. *A Course in Microeconomic Theory*. Princeton: Princeton University Press.

Philips, L. 1983. *The Economics of Price Discrimination*. Cambridge: Cambridge University Press.

Tirole, J. 1988. *The Theory of Industrial Organization*. Cambridge, Mass.: MIT Press.

THE THEORY OF PRICE UNDER IMPERFECT COMPETITION: MONOPOLISTIC COMPETITION, OLIGOPOLY, AND CARTELS

14

LEARNING OBJECTIVES

After completing Chapter 14 you should be able to do the following:

■ Compare monopolistic competition to perfect competition and monopoly.

■ Explain what economists mean by oligopoly, strategic decision making, and a Nash equilibrium.

■ Use the prisoners' dilemma to illustrate the problems that arise in oligopolistic markets.

■ Discuss the Cournot, kinked demand curve, price leadership, and entry limit pricing models of oligopoly.

■ Compare oligopoly to perfect competition and pure monopoly.

■ Explain how to determine the profit-maximizing allocation of output among members of a cartel.

EXAMPLES

■ **14–1** Pricing the Saturn

■ **14–2** Advertising and the Prisoners' Dilemma

■ **14–3** The OPEC Cartel

Recall that perfect competition and pure monopoly lie at opposite ends of the market spectrum. Perfect competition, on the one hand, is characterized by many firms, unrestricted entry, and a homogeneous product. Monopoly, on the other hand, is characterized by a single seller producing a good for which there are no close substitutes. In this chapter, we examine three other types of market structures that lie between these two extremes: *monopolistic competition, oligopoly,* and a *cartel.*

Monopolistic competition is like perfect competition in that there are many firms and entry is not restricted; however, it differs from perfect competition in that each firm produces a differentiated product. A monopolistic competitor is the sole producer of its own brand of a product and that brand differs from other brands in quality, appearance, or reputation. For example, shampoo manufacturers may be viewed as monopolistic competitors. They produce and sell the same general product, shampoo, but many consumers would maintain that Head & Shoulders is "different" from Prell.

Oligopoly, explained briefly in Section 8.1, is closer to pure monopoly. In oligopolistic markets, only a few firms compete with each other and entry is deterred to some extent. The product sold by oligopolistic firms may be differentiated, like automobiles, or homogeneous, like steel; however, owners and managers of firms in any oligopolistic industry must take into account their rivals' reactions to any decisions they might make.

The last type of market structure we examine is a cartel, which is very much like a pure monopoly. The firms making up the cartel explicitly collude to set prices and quantities to maximize their joint profits. However, a cartel differs from a pure monopoly in that it rarely controls an entire market and so must consider how its pricing decisions affect noncartel producers. The most famous, or infamous, cartel is the OPEC cartel.

14.1 MONOPOLISTIC COMPETITION

■ In **monopolistic competition,** firms in a particular business do not produce and sell a product that is homogeneous in every respect. Firms differentiate their products through trade names, advertising, and packaging. In such an industry, firms produce products that are close substitutes; however, by differentiating their product, firms create a barrier to entry for potential competitors. Thus, each firm has some monopoly power, since buyers no longer view firms, or their products, as indistinguishable.

There are many examples of industries in which one firm's output is a close substitute for that of any other firm and in which products are differentiated. The clothing, cigarette, toothpaste, and liquor industries are all markets characterized by monopolistic competition. Take the cigarette industry for example. Many cigarettes have virtually identical contents and, thus, are perfect substitutes for one another. However, through advertising and packaging each manufacturer of cigarettes differentiates its own product and so generates some degree of monopoly power, since firms cannot use the trade name of a rival.

CHARACTERIZING MONOPOLISTIC COMPETITION

The theory of monopolistic competition attempts to describe the behavior of firms in an industry where product differentiation occurs. This theory was developed in the late 1920s and early 1930s by an American economist, Edward Chamberlin, and an English economist, Joan Robinson.

A monopolistically competitive market has three main characteristics. First, there are many firms that compete by selling differentiated products that are close, but not perfect, substitutes for each other. Second, each firm ignores the effects of its actions on the decisions made by other firms in the industry. Third, there is free entry into and exit from the industry. Thus, monopolistic competition has aspects of both monopoly and competition. Each firm has some monopoly power arising from product differentiation, yet each firm is a competitor in that entry is costless and owners of firms assume their actions do not affect the decisions made by other firms.

Product differentiation arises because of advertising, packaging, product design, different types of service arrangements, geographical location, and real or perceived differences in quality. Product differentiation is a source of monopoly power because it creates a barrier to entry. For one reason or another, potential competitors cannot produce an exact replica of any other firm's product but, instead, can produce only a close substitute. On the one hand, product differentiation allows a firm to raise its price without losing all of its customers; on the other hand, if the firm decreases its price, sales will increase because the goods are close substitutes.

Previously we have used the term *industry* to mean a group of firms, each producing a homogeneous product. Strictly speaking, then, when there is product differentiation each firm would be an industry in and of itself. We can get around this problem by modifying somewhat our definition of an industry. When we are considering monopolistic competition, an industry means a group of firms producing goods that are very close substitutes. Often, economists refer to these as *product groups*. Clothing, cigarettes, toothpaste, and liquor are all product groups.

In the short run there is essentially no difference between monopolistic competition and monopoly. Each producer chooses a profit-maximizing price and output, taking the prices and outputs of other firms as given. This means that, knowing the demand for his or her product, each producer determines the output rate for which MR = SMC.

Suppose Figure 14–1(a) shows the demand and cost curves facing a particular firm in the toothpaste product group. Output is the number of tubes of toothpaste produced each year. Profit maximization requires that MR = SMC or that Y_1 tubes of toothpaste are produced each year. In this instance, the firm earns economic profit equal to area Ap_1BC.

Product differentiation means that, in the short run, firms face a downward-sloping demand curve for their products. This is the aspect of monopolistic competition that makes it like a monopoly.

SHORT- AND LONG-RUN MARKET EQUILIBRIUM

MONOPOLISTIC COMPETITION

FIGURE 14–1

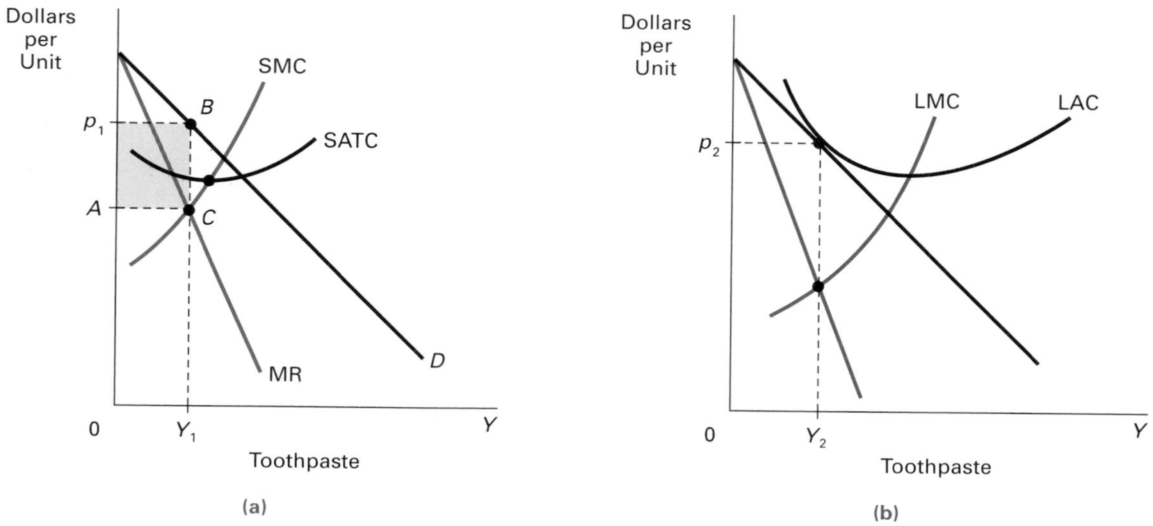

(a) In the short run, the profit-maximizing output rate is Y_1 tubes of toothpaste, which are sold for p_1 dollars per tube. Economic profit is the shaded area. (b) In the long run, free entry into the toothpaste business leads to zero economic profit. Each firm produces at a point where its demand curve is tangent to the LAC curve.

In the long run, other firms are free to enter the market and produce close substitute goods. In the long run we must consider the entry of rivals into the business.

As Figure 14–1(a) shows, the representative firm earns positive economic profit in the short run. This encourages other firms capable of producing close substitutes to enter the market. A monopolistically competitive industry attains long-run equilibrium when entry and exit cease, that is, when economic profit is zero. This is the aspect of monopolistic competition that makes it like perfect competition. Long-run equilibrium is characterized by zero economic profit.

Figure 14–1(b) illustrates the situation where the representative firm in a monopolistically competitive industry earns zero economic profit. For profit to be zero, price must be equal to LAC. Since the demand curve dictates the market price corresponding to any particular output level, and since the demand curve is negatively sloped, long-run equilibrium requires the demand curve to be tangent to the LAC curve. At such a point, total revenue is equal to total cost and profit is zero. In Figure 14–1(b), the demand curve faced by the firm is tangent to the LAC curve at point E.

How does this adjustment take place? If the typical firm earns a positive economic profit, rival firms enter the market. As rivals enter, the number of firms that must share the market increases; thus, demand falls for each individual firm and the demand curve facing each firm shifts to the left. As the demand curve shifts, it also becomes more elastic. This is because a greater number of substitute goods become available as more firms enter the industry. The demand curve continues to shift inward until all economic profit is eliminated.

MONOPOLISTIC COMPETITION AND PERFECT COMPETITION COMPARED

Under perfect competition, profit-maximizing firms produce at the level where price is equal to marginal cost and entry and exit cause economic profit for any one firm to fall to zero. The equality of price and marginal cost means, under perfect competition, that the benefit to consumers of an additional unit of output is just equal to the cost of producing that additional unit of output. The zero profit condition means that firms produce at the lowest possible per-unit cost so that consumers of a product pay the lowest possible price.

Under monopolistic competition, neither of these results holds. As Figure 14–1 shows, under monopolistic competition price is *greater* than marginal cost, even in the long run. This means that the value to consumers of additional units of the product exceeds the cost of producing those units, which is the same result we get under monopoly. Thus, because of the limited market power being exercised by each firm in the business, under monopolistic competition price is higher and output is lower than under perfect competition.

Notice also that, even though profit is zero in the long run, as long as products are differentiated, firms never produce at the output rate associated with minimum long-run average cost. This is because each firm's demand curve is negatively sloped and the tangency point between the demand curve and the LAC curve can occur only at output levels below the minimum point. The difference between the output rate corresponding to the minimum point of the long-run average cost curve and the output rate of a monopolistically competitive firm is called *excess capacity.*

Economists often debate whether or not excess capacity is a disadvantage of monopolistic competition. On the one hand, it can be argued that excess capacity is bad because the same total output can be obtained with fewer firms, each producing more. This would result in lower per-unit costs as each firm could exhaust all economies of scale and produce at capacity. On the other hand, it can be argued that excess capacity is not bad because the alternative—fewer firms, each producing more—means fewer products and therefore less choice for consumers. In this instance, we must weigh the cost of excess capacity (higher per-unit costs) against the benefits (greater product variability). If the benefits outweigh the costs, then excess capacity is not really an undesirable characteristic of monopolistic competition.

For several years after its development, economists considered the theory of monopolistic competition very important in the analysis of market structures lying between perfect competition and monopoly. Recently, however, enthusiasm for the theory has waned.

One of the most damaging criticisms of monopolistic competition is that even though it may describe some real-world markets more realistically, it predicts the effects of changes in the economic environment no more accurately than the competitive model does.

Another criticism of the theory is that it is extremely difficult to use to study the effects of excise taxes, wage and price controls, or trade restrictions, all of which are relatively easy to analyze using the competitive model. For example, suppose the government levies a per-unit excise tax on firms in a monopolistically competitive industry. Some firms in the business will incur losses and exit the industry. This will cause the demand curves facing each of the remaining firms to shift. However, we have no way of knowing how

SHORTCOMINGS OF THE THEORY OF MONOPOLISTIC COMPETITION

each firm's demand curve actually shifts and, thus, we cannot determine the new long-run equilibrium prices and quantities.

Essentially, the theory of monopolistic competition departs from the competitive model in two basic ways: individual firms produce slightly differentiated products and they each face negatively sloped demand curves. The result of these departures is a theory that is extremely difficult to use for practical purposes; on the other hand, understanding monopolistic competition may help us find better models of the middle ground between perfect competition and monopoly.

14.2 OLIGOPOLY MODELS

■ A market structure in which there are a few large firms producing either a homogeneous or a differentiated product is called an **oligopoly**. It is one of the most common types of market structure. Oligopolistic industries in the United States are especially plentiful in manufacturing; they include the automobile, steel, breakfast cereal, and computer industries. In an oligopoly, firms can earn positive economic profits even in the long run, because barriers to entry make it difficult for new firms to enter the market.

Determining the profit-maximizing price and output for an oligopolistic firm is a difficult task because each firm must take into account the behavior and response of its rivals in the market. In other words, a firm's strategy for handling rivals, or its *strategic behavior*, becomes important. The owners of a firm operate strategically if, in making decisions, they consider how other firms in the market are likely to act. It is because an oligopolistic market consists of a few large firms that strategic behavior is important. For example, suppose IBM is considering a 15% cut in prices of personal computers in order to stimulate sales. In making their decision, IBM's managers must consider carefully how Apple will react. It might do nothing; it might cut prices a little; it might match IBM's price-cut; or it might cut prices even more than IBM. Each of these responses will have a different impact on IBM's profit as well as Apple's. Likewise, any action Apple takes to counter IBM's move will impact on IBM's subsequent decisions. Thus, when making pricing decisions, and, in fact, when making any major economic decision such as production levels, advertising expenditures, or the introduction of a new product line, each firm must take into account the probable reactions of its competitors.

Recall that in building an economic theory our goal is to find a model we can use to analyze a variety of situations. For oligopoly this is difficult because the equilibrium prices and quantities that arise depend crucially on how owners of firms expect rivals to react to their decisions. If we change our assumption concerning how firms are likely to respond to their rivals' decisions then we might need to change our estimates of the equilibrium prices and quantities.

Generally there can be no unified, single theory of oligopoly behavior. Most models are designed to address specific business problems rather than describe general behavior. In this section we examine several oligopoly models. Their implications differ because each is based on different assumptions concerning the behavior of rival firms.

Before we discuss any model of oligopoly, we must be sure to understand what strategic decision making is all about and just what economists mean by long-run equilibrium when strategic behavior is allowed.

Oligopolistic firms make decisions without knowing precisely how their rivals will respond, which means that strategic decision making is crucial to their survival. **Strategic decision making** is concerned with the answer to the following question: If the owner of a firm believes her rivals act to maximize their own profits, then how should she take her rivals' actions into account when making her own profit-maximizing decisions? Once we have answered this question, in principle we can go on to determine the equilibrium price and quantity.

Unfortunately, answering this question and determining an equilibrium price and quantity is not always easy. The final equilibrium price and quantity will depend on the number of firms in the market, the information available to each firm, the payoffs, the strategies each rival selects, and whether or not owners of firms act independently or collude. (The body of literature that analyzes strategic decision making is called *game theory*. In microeconomics, we can use game theory to analyze the output and pricing decisions of oligopolistic firms.)

When strategic considerations are important, the return to any one firm will, in general, depend on the decisions made by other firms participating in the market. Therefore, we need an equilibrium concept that is more general than the long-run equilibrium concept we used earlier in the competitive and monopoly models. The concept that fills this need is the **Nash equilibrium** (named after John Nash, a mathematician who first formally discussed the concept). In economics we assume that a Nash equilibrium, like a competitive equilibrium, is characterized by firms maximizing

STRATEGIC DECISION MAKING AND LONG-RUN EQUILIBRIUM IN OLIGOPOLY MODELS

STRATEGIC DECISION MAKING

LONG-RUN EQUILIBRIUM IN OLIGOPOLISTIC MARKETS

profits and by markets clearing. In addition, however, a Nash equilibrium depends on a set of strategies that imply that each firm believes, correctly, that it is doing the best it can do given the actions of its rivals. Put another way, given the decisions made by the owners of all other firms in the market, the remaining owner acts to maximize profit. As a result, no firm has any incentive to change its behavior.

How does a competitive equilibrium compare to a Nash equilibrium? Actually, a competitive equilibrium is one type of Nash equilibrium. When a competitive market is in equilibrium, each firm is doing the best it can do, given the actions of all other market participants. As we will see, the concept of a Nash equilibrium is very useful for analyzing behavior in oligopoly markets.

THE COURNOT MODEL

The oligopoly model we shall study first was developed in the late 1830s by the French economist A.A. Cournot. While the Cournot model is now considered naive and unrealistic, it does provide us with the insights needed to understand the fundamentals of oligopoly markets and strategic decision making. The **Cournot model of oligopoly** is a good model to begin with because it is fairly simple to understand and it can show how uncoordinated decision making by rival firms can produce an outcome that lies between perfect competition and pure monopoly.

DUOPOLY: QUANTITY-SETTING FIRMS

Let us begin, as Cournot did, by assuming that there are two firms each selling mineral water. The mineral water flows from two springs located side by side. When there are only two firms in the market, we have what is termed a *duopoly*. Fundamentally, duopoly and oligopoly are the same so we can focus on the simpler case of duopoly without losing any basic insights into oligopoly behavior. The question we wish to answer is what are the equilibrium price and quantity for this industry?

To analyze this duopoly, we follow Cournot and make several simplifying assumptions. First we assume that firms in the industry produce a homogeneous product; that is, there is no product differentiation. In the context of the mineral springs example, this means that each spring provides identical water. The implication of this assumption is that firms choose the quantity they will produce and allow price to be determined by market demand. Second, we assume that firms face the same cost conditions and that the marginal cost of producing water is constant. (Cournot assumed that the mineral springs were artesian wells, which are wells from which water flows naturally without pumping, and that buyers of mineral water had to supply their own containers. From these assumptions he inferred that the marginal cost of producing water was zero.) Third, we assume that each firm knows the market demand curve and that the demand curve is linear. Finally, we must make a behavioral assumption about how each owner expects his or her rival to act. Such assumptions are fundamental in any oligopoly model. In the Cournot model we assume that each entrepreneur expects his or her rival never to change output; that is, each firm makes its output decision assuming that its competitor's output level is fixed.

Given these assumptions, we can consider the output decisions of each firm. Each firm maximizes profit by producing where MR = LMC. Suppose the two firms in this market are owned by Mr. Adams, firm A, and Ms. Bellview, firm B. Let Y^A and Y^B denote the output of firms A and B respectively. Industry output is $Y = Y^A + Y^B$ gallons of water.

Now let us consider firm A's output decision. From Adams' perspective the output of firm B, Y^B, is a constant. This means that every possible value of Y^B gives rise to a different demand curve for firm A. In Figure 14–2(a), we have drawn two such demand curves and the corresponding marginal revenue curves. The demand curve labeled $D^A(O)$ represents the demand curve facing Adams if Belleview produces no output. It is the market demand curve for water. The corresponding marginal revenue curve is $MR^A(O)$. The demand curve labeled $D^A(Y_1^B)$ represents the demand curve facing firm A if firm B produces Y_1^B gallons of water. It is the market demand curve shifted to the left by Y_1^B gallons. The corresponding marginal revenue curve is $MR^A(Y_1^B)$.

Now suppose Adams believes that Bellview will produce no water; that is, only firm A is in the market. What output would Adams choose to maximize profit? In this instance, Adams behaves just like a monopolist since the market demand curve is firm A's demand curve. In this instance, profit is maximized when $MR^A(O) = LMC$ or when firm A produces Y_1^A gallons of water.

Now suppose, instead, that Adams believes that Bellview will produce Y_1^B gallons of water. Firm A's demand and marginal revenue curves become $D^A(Y_1^B)$ and $MR^A(Y_1^B)$ respectively and profit is maximized when firm A produces Y_2^A gallons of water.

If we continue in this manner we can map out the relation between firm A's profit-maximizing output rate and the amount of output produced by firm B. If Adams thinks Bellview will produce nothing, firm A produces Y_1^A gallons of water; if Adams thinks Bellview will produce Y_1^B gallons of water, firm A produces only Y_2^A gallons of water; and so on. Thus, firm A's profit-maximizing level of output is a decreasing function of how much output Adams thinks firm B will produce.

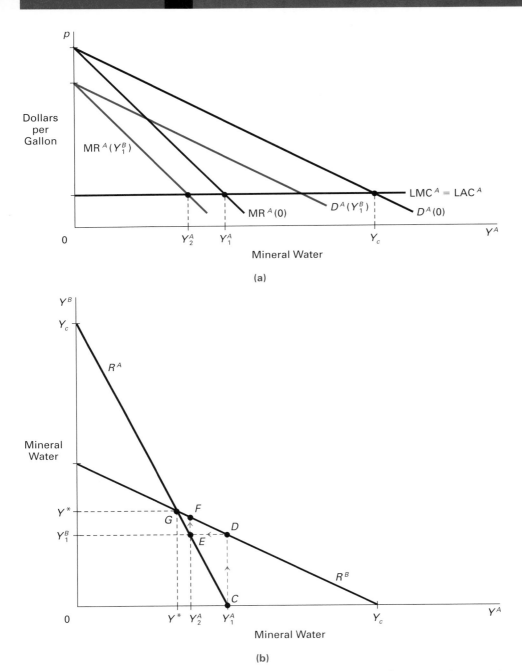

(a) In the Cournot model, each firm maximizes profit, assuming that its rival never changes output.
(b) Equilibrium in the Cournot model of oligopoly corresponds to the intersection of the reaction curves, point G. In equilibrium, each firm produces Y* gallons of mineral water.

In Figure $14-2$(b), R^A represents the negative relation between firm A's profit-maximizing output and what it thinks firm B will produce. R^A is called firm A's reaction curve (and the equation that represents this curve is called the *reaction function*) because it indicates how firm A reacts to a change in the output rate of firm B.

Using a similar argument, we can derive firm B's reaction curve. In Figure $14-2$(b), R^B represents the negative relation between firm B's profit-maximizing output and what it thinks firm A will produce. R^B indicates how firm B reacts to a change in the output rate of firm A.

Equilibrium in this market requires that these two reaction curves be satisfied simultaneously; that is, in equilibrium the intersection of the two reaction curves gives the output levels of each firm. In this instance, when the industry is in equilibrium firm A and firm B both produce Y^* gallons of water.

The equilibrium solution to the Cournot problem is a Nash equilibrium. In equilibrium, neither firm can increase profit, given the decisions of the other firm. Neither firm has an incentive to change its output or price as long as it believes that the other firm will maintain production at Y^* gallons of water.

DUOPOLY:
PRICE-SETTING FIRMS

In the Cournot model discussed above we assumed that each firm produced a homogeneous product and, therefore, chose to set quantity rather than price. However, in most oligopolistic industries firms produce slightly differentiated products and firms choose to set price rather than quantity (often the former situation is referred to as quantity competition and the latter as price competition).

The Cournot model can also be used to analyze the behavior of price-setting firms. The only difference is that now we assume each firm expects its rival's price to remain fixed.

Given this assumption, we proceed in the same manner as before. Let us begin by considering firm A's pricing decision. From Adams' perspective the price firm B charges, p^B, is a constant. This means that every possible value of p^B gives rise to a different demand curve for firm A. In Figure $14-3$(a), we have drawn two such demand curves and the corresponding marginal revenue curves. The demand curve labeled $D^A(p_1^B)$ represents the demand curve facing Adams if Belleview charges p_2^B dollars per gallon of water. The demand curve labeled $D^A(p_2^B)$ represents the demand curve facing firm A if firm B charges a lower price, p_2^B dollars per gallon, for water. Note that the demand curve facing firm A shifts down if firm B lowers its price. The corresponding marginal revenue curves are $\mathrm{MR}^A(p_1^B)$ and $\mathrm{MR}^A(p_2^B)$ respectively.

FIGURE 14–3   **PRICE-SETTING FIRMS**

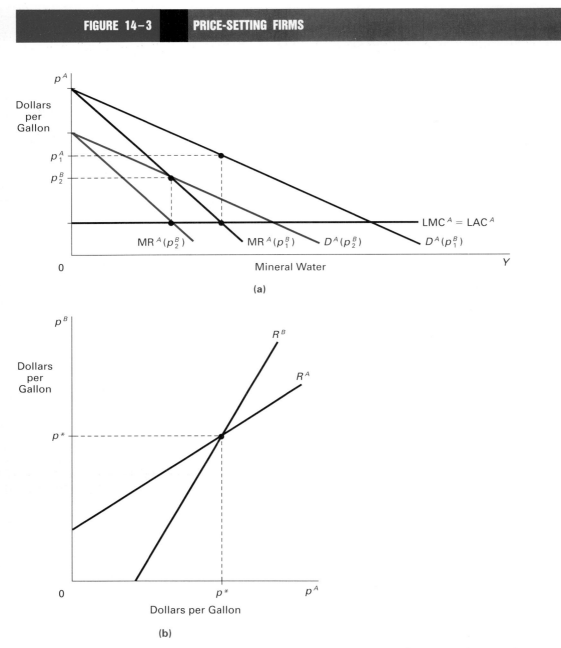

(a) In the price-setting model, each firm maximizes profit, assuming that its rival never changes the price it charges. (b) Equilibrium again corresponds to the intersection of the reaction curves. In equilibrium, each firm charges p* dollars per gallon.

Now suppose Adams believes that Bellview will charge p_1^B dollars per gallon. What price would Adams choose in order to maximize profit? In this instance, profit is maximized when $MR^A(p_1^B) = LMC$ or when firm A charges p_1^A dollars per gallon of water.

Now suppose, instead, that Adams believes that Bellview will charge $p_2^B < p_1^B$ dollars per gallon of water. Firm A's demand and marginal revenue curves become $D^A(p_2^B)$ and $MR^A(p_2^B)$ respectively and profit is maximized when firm A charges p_2^A dollars per gallon. That is, if firm B lowers price then firm A also lowers price.

If we continue in this manner we can map out the relation between firm A's profit-maximizing price and the price set by firm B. In Figure 14–3(b), R^A represents the positive relation between firm A's profit-maximizing price and what it thinks firm B will charge. R^A is firm A's reaction curve and it indicates how firm A reacts to a change in the price set by firm B.

Using a similar argument, we can derive firm B's reaction curve. In Figure 14–3(b), R^B represents the positive relation between firm B's profit-maximizing price and what it thinks firm A will charge. R^B indicates how firm B reacts to a change in the price set by firm A.

Equilibrium in this market requires that these two reaction curves be satisfied simultaneously; that is, in equilibrium the intersection of the two reaction curves gives the prices set by each firm. In this instance, when the industry is in equilibrium firm A and firm B both charge p^* dollars per gallon of water.

Another way of looking at the Cournot problem will help us understand why the Cournot equilibrium is a Nash equilibrium and how the Cournot equilibrium compares to the competitive equilibrium and monopoly.

In Figure 14–4(a), we have drawn the market demand curve, the associated marginal revenue curve, and the long-run marginal cost curve for the mineral water industry. The competitive output level is found by setting price equal to marginal cost. At this output level each firm in the industry maximizes profit and earns zero economic profit. In this case, the competitive equilibrium price and quantity are p_c and Y_c respectively.

The monopoly output level is found by setting marginal revenue equal to marginal cost. In this case, a monopolist would produce Y_m gallons of water and charge p_m dollars per gallon. Also note that, since the demand curve is linear, the marginal revenue curve intersects the marginal cost curve at a point equal to half Y_c; that is, $Y_m = (1/2)Y_c$.

COMPETITION, MONOPOLY, AND THE COURNOT MODEL

FIGURE 14-4   **COMPETITION, MONOPOLY, AND THE COURNOT MODEL**

The equilibrium quantity in the Cournot model is greater than it is under monopoly but less than it is under competition. The equilibrium price is greater than the competitive price but less than the monopoly price.

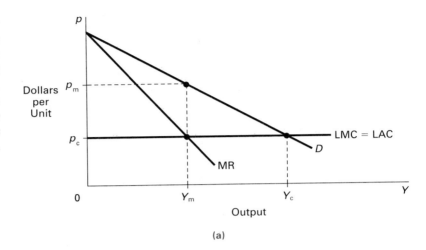

(a)

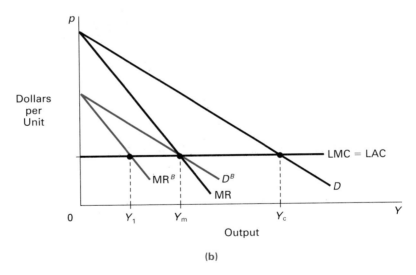

(b)

Now let us consider the Cournot equilibrium. As before, suppose initially that firm *A* is the only firm in the market and is producing $Y_m = (1/2)Y_c$ gallons of water (point *C* in Figure 14-2[b]).

Now suppose firm *B* enters the market. We must derive the demand curve that firm *B* faces. Since each owner expects that rivals never change output, when Ms. Bellview enters the market, she expects that firm A will always supply $(1/2)Y_c$ gallons of water. Thus, firm B's owner views her demand curve as the market demand curve less the amount produced by firm A, $(1/2)Y_c$ gallons of water, or demand curve D^B in Figure 14–4(b). To maximize profit, Ms. Bellview produces where MR = LMC and sells Y_1 gallons of water (point D in Figure 14–2[b]). Again, since the D^B is linear, MR^B intersects the LMC curve at $Y_1 = (1/2)[Y_c - (1/2)Y_c] = (1/4)Y_c$; that is, firm B subtracts firm A's production from Y_c and produces half of that.

With firm B in the market, Adams must now decide what he should do. If he expects firm B always to produce Y_1 gallons of water, firm A's new demand curve is now the market demand curve less $(1/4)Y_c$ gallons of water. The new profit-maximizing rate of output for firm A is half the difference between Y_c and firm B's level of production, which is equal to $(1/2)[Y_c - (1/4)Y_c] = (3/8)Y_c$ gallons of water (point E in Figure 14–2[b]). Given this new output rate for firm A, firm B must adjust. Firm B's new profit-maximizing output rate will be $(1/2)[Y_c - (3/8)Y_c] = (5/16)Y_c$ (point F in Figure 14–2[b]). This adjustment process continues with Adams gradually decreasing production and Bellview gradually increasing production. Equilibrium, in the sense of a Nash equilibrium, is attained when neither party, acting alone, has any incentive to change price or quantity; that is, when each firm produces exactly half the difference between total quantity demanded and the output of the other firm. This occurs when total output is equal to $(2/3)Y_c$ gallons of water with each firm producing $(1/3)Y_c$ gallons.

Thus, the equilibrium quantity in the Cournot model is greater than the amount a monopolist would produce but less than the competitive quantity. This implies that the equilibrium price in the Cournot model is less than the monopoly price but greater than the competitive price, and that total industry profit is less than monopoly profit. (Remember that for a given market demand curve, p_m and Y_m are, respectively, the profit-maximizing price and quantity for a monopolist and that any other price–quantity pair satisfying the demand curve must yield a lower total profit.) We can conclude, then, that the Cournot model yields a better outcome for firms than competition does but a worse one than monopoly does.

We have covered a great deal of ground up to this point. The next example gives us a chance to determine the equilibrium price and quantity when we know explicit demand and cost functions. This example should reinforce our understanding of the Cournot model and its relation to perfect competition and monopoly.

EXAMPLE 14-1

PRICING THE SATURN

When General Motors, Inc., planned to build the Saturn, a car designed to compete head-on with Japanese imports, it had to determine the right price to charge. This was difficult because GM had to consider how Japanese car manufacturers would respond.

To illustrate how we can use the Cournot model to help us understand GM's pricing problem, let's suppose that one of the Saturn model's targets is Honda's Accord, that both GM's Saturn plant and Honda's Accord plant face fixed overhead costs of $240,000 per month, a variable cost of $9,000 per car, and that the market demand curve for this type of automobile is estimated to be

$$Y = 48,000 - 4p$$

where Y is the number of cars sold per month and p is the market price. (a) If GM were the sole supplier of this type of car, what price would it charge and how many Saturns would it sell? (b) If the market for this type of car were perfectly competitive, what would be the equilibrium price and quantity? (c) Using the Cournot model of duopoly, determine the equilibrium price and quantity. (d) Compare GM's profit under (a) and (c).

■ **SOLUTION** (a) Under monopoly, the demand curve facing GM is the market demand curve. Solving for price as a function of quantity gives the inverse demand curve

$$p = 12,000 - .25Y$$

and marginal revenue is given by

$$MR = 12,000 - .5Y.$$

Profit maximization requires that marginal revenue be equal to marginal cost: $MR = 12,000 - .5Y = 9,000$ implies that $Y_m = 6,000$ Saturns per month. Substituting Y_m into the demand curve gives $p_m = \$10,500$.

(b) The long-run competitive equilibrium price in this instance is $p_c = \$9,000$. To find the equilibrium quantity we simply substitute $9,000 into the demand function. This gives $Y_c = 12,000$ (remember, $Y_m = (1/2)Y_c$).

(c) Now consider the Cournot equilibrium. From the discussion given above, we know that in equilibrium industry output will be $Y^* = (2/3)Y_c = 8,000$ which lies between the competitive and monopoly outcomes. Substituting Y^* into the inverse demand function gives the equilibrium price: $p^* = 12,000 - .25(8,000) = \$10,000$. The oligopoly price is greater than the competitive price but less than the monopoly price.

(d) Finally, let us compare monopoly profit and oligopoly profit. Monopoly profit in this example is: $\pi_m = (10,500 - 9,000)(6,000) - 240,000 = \$8,760,000$. Oligopoly profit is: $\pi^* = (10,000 - 9,000)(8,000) - 240,000 = \$7,760,000$ or $\$3,880,000$ per firm. As we noted above, monopoly profit is greater than oligopoly profit. ■

The behavioral assumption used in the Cournot model has been criticized as being too restrictive. In the model, firms expect that their rivals will not adjust output (or price), but in the real world firms repeatedly observe that their rivals do, in fact, change output (or price). Nonetheless, the Cournot model is useful because it does provide a determinate equilibrium and it does illustrate the importance of interdependence in oligopolistic markets.

The Cournot model yields a determinate equilibrium price and quantity. In addition, like a competitive equilibrium, a Cournot equilibrium is a *noncooperative* equilibrium: each firm maximizes profit, given the actions of its rivals. The resulting profits earned by each firm are higher than they would be under perfect competition but lower than they would be if the firms colluded and operated as a monopoly. This latter observation raises an interesting question. If firms can collude and increase profits, why don't they?

In the United States, antitrust legislation makes *explicit* collusion between firms illegal. However, if coordinated decision making between oligopolistic firms can lead to higher profits, then it would seem that the optimal strategy for such firms would be to collude *implicitly*—that is, for each firm to maximize profit by charging the price and producing the quantity that they would if they did collude. If each firm did this, then profit would be greater for each firm in the industry.

The problem with implicit collusion is that any one firm can do better by not cooperating. In game theory this type of situation is called the prisoners' dilemma. The **prisoners' dilemma** is used to demonstrate how two decision makers, acting independently, may choose a strategy that makes them both worse off than they would be if they were to merge and choose a joint strategy. Owners and

COLLUSION AND THE PRISONERS' DILEMMA

managers of oligopolistic firms often find themselves facing the prisoners' dilemma. They must decide whether to "cooperate" with other firms in the industry or to operate independently and attempt to capture greater profits at the expense of their rivals.

THE CLASSIC PRISONERS'
DILEMMA

Consider the following prisoners' dilemma. Jesse James and Cole Younger are arrested for a bank robbery. Each suspect is placed in a separate cell and is not allowed to talk to the other. Without a confession, there is not enough evidence to convict either of them for the robbery; however, there is enough evidence without a confession to convict them of unlawful possession of firearms.

During questioning, each prisoner is told the following:

1. If you confess and your partner doesn't, you will receive a suspended sentence for turning state's evidence.
2. If you do not confess and your partner does, you will be sentenced to 15 years in the state penitentiary.
3. If you both confess, both of you will be sentenced to 10 years in the state penitentiary.
4. If neither of you confesses, both of you will be sentenced to 5 years for unlawful possession of firearms.

The *payoff matrix* shown in Table 14–1 illustrates these outcomes or payoffs. It shows the "payoff" to each player given his decision and the decision of the other player. Each player in the game must choose a strategy—confess or do not confess—without consulting his partner, but the payoff of the decision depends on what his partner does. This is a noncooperative game because the prisoners cannot collude.

In this setting, what should Jesse and Cole do? Herein lies the dilemma. The prisoners know that had they been allowed to communicate prior to being questioned (in which case this would

TABLE 14–1

THE PAYOFF
MATRIX FOR JESSE
AND COLE

		Jesse			
		Confesses		*Does Not Confess*	
Cole	*Confesses*	Jesse: Cole:	10 years 10 years	Jesse: Cole:	15 years 0 years
	Does not Confess	Jesse: Cole:	0 years 15 years	Jesse: Cole:	5 years 5 years

be a *cooperative game*) then it would have been in both their self-interests to reach a collusive agreement not to confess, because by doing so they would both receive the lightest prison sentence. Does this mean that, even though they cannot collude explicitly, they will collude implicitly? Probably not. Even if they reached such a collusive agreement, when the men are separated for questioning it is in the self-interest of each to cheat on the agreement, turn state's evidence, and confess. If Cole does not confess, then Jesse can take advantage of this by confessing and he will go free. Likewise, if Jesse does not confess, Cole is better off confessing himself. Thus, even though it is in their joint interests not to confess, both prisoners probably will confess and go to jail for ten years.

OLIGOPOLY AND THE PRISONERS' DILEMMA

The prisoners' dilemma can be used to analyze the decisions owners of oligopolistic firms must make. For example, suppose two breakfast cereal manufacturers, Brandon Sweet, Inc., and the T.R. Crane Co., are considering two pricing options: charge either the monopoly price of $3 per box or the Cournot price of $1 per box. If both firms choose to charge the monopoly price, then they split the market and profit is $50,000 for each firm. If one firm chooses to charge $3 per box and the other charges only $1 per box, then the firm charging the lower price captures a larger share of the market and earns a profit of $100,000, while the firm charging the higher price looses customers and earns only $25,000. Finally, if both firms charge the Cournot price, then they split the market and earn a profit of $30,000 each. The question we want to answer is, What price will each firm set?

Table 14−2 illustrates the payoff matrix associated with these different pricing strategies. If the firms collude and charge the

TABLE 14−2

THE PAYOFF MATRIX FOR BRANDON SWEET, INC., AND THE T.R. CRANE CO.

		Brandon Sweet			
		High Price		*Low Price*	
T.R. Crane	*High Price*	B.S.: T.R.C.:	$ 50,000 $ 50,000	B.S.: T.R.C.:	$100,000 $ 25,000
	Low Price	B.S.: T.R.C.:	$ 25,000 $100,000	B.S.: T.R.C.:	$ 30,000 $ 30,000

monopoly price, their profit is $50,000 each. However, each firm always makes a greater profit by charging $1, no matter what its rival does. If T.R. Crane charges $1, Brandon Sweet does best by charging $1. If T.R. Crane charges $3, Brandon Sweet still does best by charging $1 (and vice versa). Thus, unless there is an enforceable agreement between the two firms to charge $3, neither firm can trust its rival to charge the monopoly price and both will charge the Cournot price.

The prisoners' dilemma arises whenever an oligopolistic firm must make a decision that affects its position in the market relative to its rivals. In the next example, we will use the prisoners' dilemma to examine the interdependence of advertising decisions.

EXAMPLE 14–2

ADVERTISING AND THE PRISONERS' DILEMMA

Suppose IBM and Apple are considering their advertising budgets for the upcoming summer campaign. Each firm is introducing a new machine with enhanced graphics capabilities. This being so, advertising expenditures are expected to have a dramatic effect on profit. Each firm has two options: a large advertising budget or a small one. If both firms choose small advertising budgets, then they split the market and profit is $150,000,000 for each. If one firm chooses a large budget while the other chooses a small one, then the firm with the large budget captures the bigger share of the market and increases the overall size of the market more than its competitor does. In this case, the former makes a profit of $200,000,000, while the latter makes a profit of $25,000,000. Finally, if both firms choose a large advertising budget they once again split the market; however, since advertising costs are higher, profit falls to $130,000,000 for each firm.

(a) Using the prisoners' dilemma, discuss the strategy that each firm is most likely to follow in the absence of collusion. (b) How does this compare to the collusive solution?

■ **SOLUTION** (a) First we must construct a payoff matrix. The payoffs for this game are shown in Table 14–3. The diagonal elements of the matrix represent the strategies where both firms choose either a small or large advertising budget while the off-diagonal elements represent one firm choosing a large budget and the other choosing a small budget.

TABLE 14-3

THE PAYOFF
MATRIX FOR IBM
AND APPLE

		IBM			
		Large Budget		Small Budget	
Apple	Large Budget	IBM: Apple:	$130,000 $130,000	IBM: Apple:	$ 25,000 $200,000
	Small Budget	IBM: Apple:	$200,000 $ 25,000	IBM: Apple:	$150,000 $150,000

Consider IBM's decision first. If IBM chooses a small advertising budget, then profit will be either $150,000,000 or $25,000,000. If it chooses a large advertising budget, then profit will be either $200,000,000 or $130,000,000. Since, in the latter case, profit is higher for each alternative that IBM might choose, IBM will most likely choose a large budget. The same is true for Apple. Thus, both firms will choose large advertising budgets and profit will be $130,000,000 for each firm.

(b) If the firms were to collude and agree to hold down advertising outlays, then profit for both would be $150,000,00 each. Collusion would allow the firms to reduce costs and thus increase profits. ∎

Our discussion to this point illustrates the difficulties faced by owners and managers of oligopolistic firms. Even though profits are higher if oligopolistic firms cooperate, these firms are in a prisoners' dilemma. No one firm can expect its competitors to follow a strategy that would maximize joint profit, which means that all firms adopt a strategy that leads to lower profits. However, as we shall illustrate below, this does not mean necessarily that collusion, explicit or implicit, must fail.

In our discussion of the prisoners' dilemma, we implicitly assumed that firms made their output and pricing decisions only once. However, in most real-world markets characterized by oligopoly, firms are repeatedly revising their output and price decisions over time as they continually observe the behavior of their rivals. This allows firms to determine if their rivals can, in fact, be trusted. As a result, implicit as well as explicit (when it is legal) collusion can prevail even in the face of the prisoners' dilemma.

**IMPLICATIONS OF THE
PRISONERS' DILEMMA FOR
OLIGOPOLY**

Nonetheless, in many instances implicit collusion tends to be very fragile and does not last for very long. Oftentimes firms have an inherent distrust of all rivals, and price wars explode as soon as competitors suspect any firm of "cheating" by cutting prices or increasing advertising. Because of this, firms operating in an oligopolistic market have a desire for price stability.

PRICE RIGIDITY AND THE KINKED DEMAND CURVE MODEL

Because oligopolistic firms want to avoid price wars and maintain stability, *price rigidity* is often a characteristic of oligopolistic markets. If cost or market demand declines, firms are usually reluctant to cut prices for fear that this will bring on a price war with its rivals. However, if cost or market demand rises, firms are reluctant to raise prices for fear that their rivals will not also raise prices.

The **kinked demand curve model of oligopoly** developed in the 1930s by Paul Sweezy, was designed to explain why prices in oligopolistic industry tend to be rigid despite changes in cost or demand. The behavioral assumption we make concerning each firm's expectations of its rivals' actions is not the same in the kinked demand curve model as it is in the Cournot model. In the kinked demand curve model, the owner of each firm expects that rivals *will* match any price-cut below the current market price in order to maintain their market share but *will not* match any price increase. Effectively, this means that the oligopolist faces a demand curve that is kinked at the current market price.

Figure 14−5 shows the *kinked demand curve* model. We begin with an oligopolistic industry already in equilibrium. The market price is currently p_1 dollars per unit and each firm produces Y_1 units of output. Point B in Figure 14−5 represents this initial situation. The behavioral assumption made above means that the owner of firm A always expects the worst possible outcome. If, on the one hand, firm A increases price above p_1, it expects its rivals to ignore the change; this would lead to a substantial reduction in quantity demanded for this oligopolist. Thus, the demand curve to the left of point B is relatively elastic. If firm A cuts price below p_1, on the other hand, it expects its rivals to do the same, which would mean that quantity demanded for this oligopolist would increase only slightly. To the right of B, the demand curve is relatively inelastic. The end result is that firm A faces demand curve ABD, which has a kink at point B.

If the demand curve is kinked, then, as Figure 14−5 shows, the corresponding marginal revenue curve is discontinuous at the kink. The top part of the marginal revenue curve corresponds to the relatively elastic portion of the demand curve. At B the slope of

THE KINKED DEMAND CURVE MODEL OF OLIGOPOLY

FIGURE 14-5

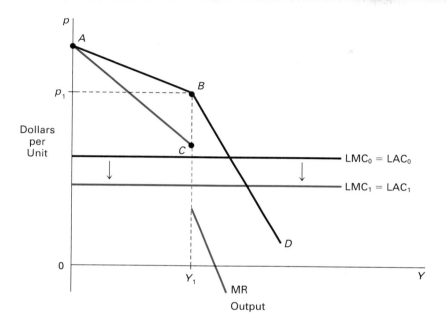

A kinked demand curve at output Y_1 leads to a marginal revenue curve with a gap at Y_1. The profit-maximizing output rate is Y_1 as long as LMC is less than p_1 dollars per unit of output.

the demand curve changes abruptly, causing a discontinuity (a "gap") in the marginal revenue curve. This is the dashed portion of the marginal revenue curve. The bottom part of the marginal revenue curve corresponds to the less elastic portion of the demand curve.

As a result, the firm's costs can change without leading to a price change. As the diagram shows, marginal cost could increase but it would still be equal to marginal revenue at the same output level, and that price does not change.

When it was developed, the kinked demand curve model appeared to explain a wide range of oligopoly behavior. However, one of the main objectives of microeconomic theory is to explain how prices and outputs are determined and the kinked demand curve model cannot do this. Furthermore, the model has also been criticized on empirical grounds. Researchers have found that in many oligopolistic industries rivals do in fact match price increases. Thus, we cannot consider the kinked demand curve model a general model of oligopolistic behavior but, rather, a model we can use to explain certain specific situations.

THE PRICE LEADERSHIP
OR DOMINANT FIRM
MODEL

The **price leadership** model explains one way firms eliminate the uncertainty of rivals' reactions to changes in price by implicitly colluding. In this model one firm, the leader or dominant firm, sets a price to maximize its own profit (the leader is usually the largest firm in the industry, such as GM in the automobile industry) and then allows other firms in the industry to sell as much as they want at that price. The leader then sells the rest.

The price leadership model is developed in Figure 14–6. We begin by deriving the demand curve for the dominant firm. The market demand curve is labeled D in the diagram. S_s is the supply curve of all the other smaller firms in the industry taken together. Since the smaller firms are price takers, S_s is derived in the same way we derived the industry supply curve for a competitive industry. S_s represents the output response of the smaller firms to whatever price the dominant firm sets.

To derive the demand curve for the dominant firm, we need to subtract the amount the smaller firms supply from market demand

| FIGURE 14–6 | THE PRICE LEADERSHIP MODEL OF OLIGOPOLY |

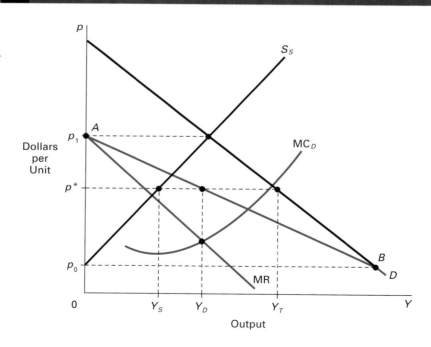

In the price leadership model, the dominant firm produces Y_D units of output and charges p^* per unit. At this price total demand is Y_T. The smaller firms in the industry make up the difference between Y_T and Y_D; thus, they supply Y_S units.

at each price. For prices above p_1, where S_s intersects the market demand curve, the smaller firms supply the entire market, and demand for the dominant firm is zero. For prices below p_1 but above p_0, we subtract S_s from D, which gives AB as the demand curve facing the dominant firm. For prices below p_0 the smaller firms supply nothing and the dominant firm supplies the entire market. Thus, the dominant firm's demand curve is ABD in Figure 14–6.

Given this demand curve, the dominant firm acts like a profit-maximizing monopolist. Profit is maximized when the dominant firm produces Y_D units of output (where MR = MC_D) and charges p^* dollars per unit. (The dominant firm's demand curve determines price.) At this price, total quantity demanded is Y_T; this means that the smaller firms in the industry supply Y_s units of output.

While this theory models price leadership, it does not explain its existence. Why would any firm *want* to play "follow the leader"? It is usually argued that in an oligopolistic industry price followers believe the leader has better information concerning the market demand curve prevailing in the present and in all future periods. It is also argued that firms follow a price leader because the leadership role rotates among a few of the largest firms in the industry. Essentially, it may provide a legal way for firms to collude.

Two industries characterized by price leadership are the banking and automobile industries. Small banks often view changes in the prime rates of large New York banks as an indication of future demand for loans. In the auto industry General Motors, Ford, and Chrysler seem to take turns being the leader. For example, if Ford is the designated leader, then the other two companies match any price increases, price-cuts, or discount financing packages proposed by Ford.

In the **entry-limit pricing** model firms in an industry agree implicitly to sacrifice short-run profits in order to obtain higher long-run profits by setting a price low enough to deter entry rather than charging the short-run profit-maximizing price. This model is similar to the price leadership model in that smaller firms usually follow a larger, dominant, firm in setting prices to deter entry.

In this model, we make three assumptions. First, firms currently in the business, as well as potential entrants into the business, want to maximize long-run profit. Second, existing firms believe that potential entrants expect them to maintain their current production

THE ENTRY-LIMIT PRICING MODEL

levels so that if entry occurs industry output will expand and price will fall. Third, we assume that potential entrants have higher costs than established firms.

In Figure 14–7, D represents the dominant firm's demand curve for good Y, LMC_D is the dominant firm's average and marginal cost curve, and LMC_e is the potential entrant's average and marginal cost curve. We assume that costs are higher for a potential entrant (otherwise, they would have been in the business to begin with) and, for simplicity, we assume that the marginal cost curves are horizontal. If there is no threat of entry, then the dominant firm maximizes profit, produces Y_1 units, and charges p_1 dollars per unit. Monopoly profit going to the dominant firm is given by area p_1AEp_0.

If the price is set at p_1, there is an incentive for potential entrants to enter; that is, since price exceeds a potential entrant's average cost, a newcomer entering the business can make a profit. But if entry occurs, price will fall, and profits of established firms will also fall (assuming that established firms do not change production levels); more specifically, if entry causes the price to fall to p_0, then profit earned by the dominant firm will fall to p_0GEF.

To prevent this from happening, the dominant firm can block entry by setting a price at or below the average cost of potential

---

| FIGURE 14–7 | THE ENTRY-LIMIT PRICING MODEL OF OLIGOPOLY |

In the entry-limit pricing model, the dominant firm deters entry by setting a price less than or equal to the price at which other firms could profitably enter the industry, p_0 for example. The dominant firm earns less profit than it would without the threat of entry but more than it would if entry did, in fact, occur.

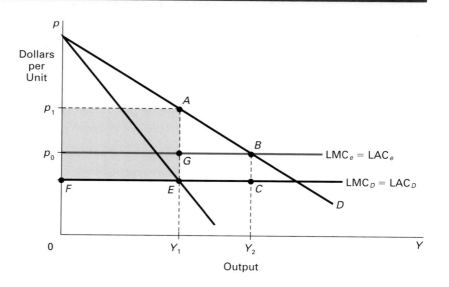

entrants. For example, if the dominant firm sets a price of p_0 dollars per unit, then price will fall below p_0 if entry occurs and the new entrant will incur a loss. Price p_0 is called the entry-limit price. Any higher price will lead to entry.

Note that if the dominant firm deters entry by setting a price less than or equal to the entry price, it earns less economic profit than it would if there were no threat of entry but more than it would if it did not deter entry. For example, if p_0 is the price that would prevail were potential entrants to enter the market and if p_0 is also the price set by the dominant firm, then the dominant firm earns a profit equal to area p_0BCF, which is larger than p_0GEF but smaller than p_1AEF.

The precise level of the limit price will depend on how difficult it is to enter the industry. In fact, oligopolistic firms may lower price to the entry-limit price when the threat of entry exists and raise price back up to the profit-maximizing price when the threat of entry subsides.

We can make one additional point concerning entry-limit pricing: if potential entrants have costs that are the same as or close to the costs of established firms, then the entry-limit price approaches the competitive price. In this instance, the only difference between oligopoly and competition is that there will be fewer firms supplying the competitive level of output.

■ When firms explicitly agree to cooperate in setting prices and output levels, a cartel is formed. A **cartel** is an agreement among independent firms to coordinate output and pricing decisions so that each firm in the cartel earns a monopoly profit. When a cartel is formed, rarely do all producers in a particular industry join; however, total participation is not needed for the cartel to succeed in driving price above the competitive level. If enough firms participate and if demand is relatively inelastic, then the cartel can have a significant impact on price.

In the United States, antitrust laws prohibit the formation of cartels; however, nothing prohibits firms owned by foreign producers from forming international cartels. The Organization of Petroleum Exporting Countries (OPEC) is probably the most visible international cartel in existence today. Since the mid-1970s OPEC has succeeded in keeping oil prices higher than they would have been without the cartel.

Suppose that a cartel is formed with the dual aims of restricting output and setting a uniform price for a particular good. What price should the cartel charge if its goal is to maximize profit? Figure 14–8 illustrates the answer to this question. Since the cartel is,

14.3 CARTELS

FIGURE 14–8	CARTELS

A cartel behaves just as a monopolist does in that it maximizes profit by producing at the level where marginal revenue is equal to marginal cost. Once the cartel determines its profit-maximizing output, Y_0, it must divide it between its members.

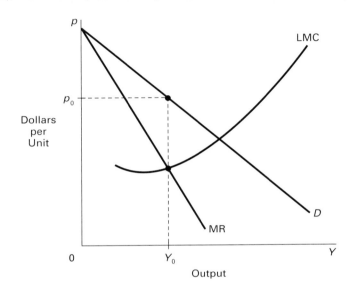

essentially, a monopolist, market demand curve *D* is the cartel's demand curve. Assuming that input prices do not change as industry output expands or contracts, then LMC represents the sum of the individual cartel members' cost curves. Profit is maximized when MR = LMC, or when Y_0 units of output are produced and sold for p_0 dollars per unit. Thus, a cartel—like a monopoly—leads to less output and higher prices than a competitive industry.

In addition to setting price, the cartel must also agree how to allocate production between its members. If its goal is to maximize total profit, then it should allocate output to firms in such a way that the marginal cost of production is equal across firms; any other allocation will result in lower profit (as you should be able to demonstrate using a marginal revenue–marginal cost argument). In reality, profit maximization is rarely the sole criterion used to allocate production. Usually, political considerations dictate distribution to a substantial degree.

CAN CARTELS SURVIVE?

We have shown that in a market where there are a few large firms supplying a product, each firm can increase profit by colluding and forming an industrywide cartel. We have also demonstrated that any collusive agreement can be very unstable because each party to the agreement has an incentive to cheat. A cartel gains monopoly profit by having each of its members agree to restrict output below the levels that each would choose if the cartel did not exist. The resulting reduction in industry output causes the price to rise. However, once the price rises each member of the cartel can increase its own profit further by producing more than its allotted share. This is especially true if the cheating goes undetected or if it proves difficult to enforce the collusive agreements between cartel members.

In the next example we use the prisoners' dilemma to illustrate the problems facing the OPEC cartel. As you work through this example, keep in mind that the OPEC cartel is still in existence today!

EXAMPLE 14–3

THE OPEC CARTEL

The Organization of Petroleum Exporting Countries, OPEC, is made up of 13 countries that together control about 75% of the world's known oil reserves. Saudi Arabia and Venezuela are two countries belonging to the OPEC cartel. Saudi Arabia's oil reserves are enormous. Thus, the Saudis have a strong interest in seeing the cartel survive in the long run. Venezuela, like many of the other OPEC members, has relatively small reserves and is more interested in the short-run monopoly profit that it earns because of the cartel.

OPEC's goal is to raise the price of oil by restricting supply. Each member of the OPEC cartel is assigned a quota for oil production. If Saudi Arabia were to cheat on the cartel and increase its oil production substantially above its quota, the price of oil would fall dramatically, possibly to competitive levels, and the cartel would collapse. In this instance, Saudi Arabian profits would fall substantially. If Venezuela or any other single producer were to cheat, however, neither total production of oil by the cartel nor the price of oil would be appreciably affected.

Suppose the U.S. government hires us to analyze the OPEC cartel. In particular, our task is to investigate the long-run stability of the cartel.

■ **SOLUTION** We can use the prisoners' dilemma model to discuss the stability of the OPEC cartel. First we must construct the appropriate payoff matrix. Since any action Saudi Arabia takes has a much more profound impact on the cartel's profits than any action Venezuela takes, the payoff matrix is not symmetric (as it was in our previous discussions). In order to capture this asymmetry, we distinguish between four different (economic) profit levels: zero, low, high, and very high.

Each country has two possible strategies: cheat or do not cheat. If neither the Saudis nor the Venezuelans cheat on the cartel, then both producers earn a high profit in both the short and long runs. If the Venezuelans cheat and the Saudis do not, then, in both the short and long runs, Venezuela earns a very high profit and Saudi Arabia earns a high profit. Cheating by Venezuela does not affect OPEC output to any large degree, which means that Saudi Arabia can maintain its production level and, hence, its profit level, even when cheating occurs. If Saudi Arabia cheats, the cartel collapses and all producers earn zero economic profit.

The payoff matrix in Table 14–4 illustrates these relations. Given this situation, what would we expect the Saudis to do? Comparing the right-hand column to the left-hand column, we see that the Saudis are always better off not cheating. Thus, we would expect Saudi Arabia to maintain the cartel price regardless of what the Venezuelans do.

What would we expect the Venezuelans to do? Comparing the top half of the payoff matrix to the bottom half, we see that no matter what the Saudis do, Venezuela is better off cheating. Thus, we would expect Venezuela to produce more oil than their agreement with the cartel permits.

So far, it appears that there will be no tendency for the cartel to dissolve. For the Saudis there is no prisoner's dilemma. It is always in their best interests to keep price high by restricting output. But up to this point we have assumed that only *one* producer other than Saudi Arabia has the chance to cheat. Will our conclusion be any different if *several* other OPEC firms cheat?

TABLE 14–4

THE PAYOFF MATRIX FOR SAUDI ARABIA AND VENEZUELA

		Saudi Arabia			
		Cheat		Do Not Cheat	
Venezuela	Cheat	S.A.:	zero	S.A.:	high
		Ven.:	zero	Ven.:	very high
	Do Not Cheat	S.A.:	zero	S.A.:	high
		Ven.:	zero	Ven.:	high

TABLE 14–5

THE PAYOFF
MATRIX FOR SAUDI
ARABIA AND
OTHERS

		Saudi Arabia			
		Cheat		*Do Not Cheat*	
Others	*Cheat*	S.A.: Others:	zero zero	S.A.: Others:	low very high
	Do Not Cheat	S.A.: Others:	zero zero	S.A.: Others:	high high

Table 14–5 gives the payoff matrix for the situation where several producers besides Saudi Arabia may opt to cheat. The left-hand column is the same as before. If Saudi Arabia cheats, all firms earn zero economic profit. However, the top half of the right-hand column is different now. If several members of OPEC increase production beyond their allotted amounts, they will earn very high profits. In order to keep price high, Saudi Arabia will now have to cut its production substantially, which will bring its profit down to a much lower level.

Given this situation, we once again would expect smaller OPEC producers to cheat. In the short run, they earn greater profits by cheating than by not cheating, whatever Saudi Arabia does. However, this gives the Saudis an incentive to discipline cheaters. In the long run, if several firms cheat on the cartel the Saudis must reduce production to maintain the cartel price, and this reduces profit to low levels. Rather than accept this long-run outcome, the Saudis can take short-run disciplinary action: they can increase their own output substantially, causing the price of oil to fall dramatically. Other OPEC members will then face deteriorating profits. Thus, their best strategy is once again to produce at their cartel levels and earn high, but not very high, profits.

What implication does this discussion have for the stability of the cartel? In the short run, there is always an incentive for smaller OPEC members to cheat. However, as more and more producers cheat, there is an incentive for Saudi Arabia to discipline cheaters by driving the price of oil to competitive levels. Thus, there is an inherent instability in the cartel. ■

Is our answer to Example 14–3 in accord with OPEC's historical record? When the cartel formed in 1973, the price of crude oil was $4 per barrel. As a result of OPEC, the price jumped to over $10 per barrel in 1974 and over $30 per barrel in 1979. However, by the mid-1980s cheating was so widespread that Saudi Arabia had to cut its oil production drastically to maintain the cartel. Rather than continue this policy indefinitely, the Saudis decided to punish cheaters by doubling their own production. This sent the price of oil tumbling to $15 by the end of 1986.

In order to succeed for a long period of time, a cartel must be able to impose strict penalties on cheaters. In countries where cartels are legal, the agreements drawn up between members are binding legal contracts. In these instances, cartels have a better chance of surviving because it is illegal for one member of the cartel to cheat on other members. However, even though cartels are very popular in countries where they are legal, policing these collusive agreements is still difficult—as is evidenced by the large number of breach-of-contract cases in the courts.

14.4 NONPRICE COMPETITION

■ As we noted earlier in this chapter, firms in oligopolistic industries may view price competition as a perilous means of attracting customers since it can start a price war. Thus, in such industries competition between firms tends to take the form of *nonprice competition*. Firms use nonprice competition to attract customers by convincing consumers that their products differ from those of their rivals; that is, they use nonprice competition to shift their demand curves to the right. Nonprice competition takes many forms. Firms may compete by offering "free" service contracts (banks offer "free" checking with certain types of accounts, while retail appliance stores and automobile dealers offer "free" maintenance contracts for a limited duration of time), by varying product quality, by varying packaging (manufacturers of aspirin and other headache remedies offer new improved "tamper-proof" bottles), or by advertising. In the U.S. the most important form of nonprice competition is advertising. According to the *Advertising Age* (May 12, 1986), U.S. companies spent over $94 billion on advertising in 1985.

Firms are willing to incur the costs associated with nonprice competition because they believe that in the short run the additional revenues generated by offering "free" service contracts or "tamper-proof" bottles outweigh the additional costs, so profits are higher. However, as we saw in Example 14–2, nonprice competition may result in *higher* costs to all firms in the industry because of the prisoners' dilemma. If one firm in an oligopolistic industry decides to advertise or to vary the style or quality of its product, then it is most likely that all other firms will follow suit. The cost of nonprice competition can be substantial.

■ In this chapter we have investigated some of the oligopoly models economists have developed. As we stated at the beginning of this chapter, there is no one model that can explain the behavior of oligopolistic firms in general. Most models are designed to address certain specific situations, so it is difficult to determine precisely how oligopoly affects output, price, and profits. Nonetheless, there are three general points that we can make about oligopoly.

First, price under oligopoly is greater than the competitive price and less than or equal to the monopoly price. The difference between the oligopoly price and the competitive price depends primarily on how many firms are in the industry, the ease of entry, and the degree to which firms collude implicitly or explicitly. The greater the number of firms, the easier it is to enter, and the less collusion there is, the closer the oligopoly price will be to the competitive price.

Second, if firms in an oligopolistic industry produce a homogeneous product, then output under oligopoly will be less than under competition but greater than under monopoly. However, if there is product differentiation, then we cannot be sure that output will be lower. Product differentiation may lead to an increase in demand, which could result in a higher price and output.

Finally, oligopolistic firms earn positive economic profit. Oligopoly profit approaches pure monopoly profit as oligopoly price and output approach monopoly price and output.

14.5 WHAT HAVE WE LEARNED FROM OLIGOPOLY THEORY?

SUMMARY

1. In a monopolistically competitive market, firms compete by producing and selling differentiated products that are close substitutes. Each firm assumes that its actions do not affect the actions of its rivals and that new firms can enter and exit easily. Even though they earn zero economic profit in the long run, monopolistically competitive firms produce less and charge more for their output than perfect competitors do.

2. An oligopolistic market consists of a few large firms producing one product. Modeling oligopoly is difficult as each firm must operate strategically; that is, each firm must consider the actions of its rivals. In oligopoly models, equilibrium prices and quantities depend crucially on how firms expect their rivals to act.

3. In the quantity-setting version of the Cournot model of oligopoly, firms produce a homogeneous product and each firm makes its output decisions taking the other firm's output as fixed. In equilibrium, each firm maximizes profit and has no incentive to change its output. Each firm's profit is higher than under perfect competition but lower than it could be if the firms colluded.

4. In the price-setting version of the Cournot model, firms produce a differentiated product and each firm makes its pricing decisions taking the other firm's price as fixed. In equilibrium, each firm maximizes profit and has no incentive to change price.

5. Firms could earn greater profits by collectively agreeing to raise prices; however, in the United States, explicit collusion is illegal. Each firm could, without colluding explicitly, raise price, reduce output, and increase profit, but the prisoners' dilemma makes this unlikely. Any one firm has an incentive to lower price, thereby increasing its market share.

6. In oligopolistic markets, the prisoners' dilemma leads to price rigidity. Firms are reluctant to lower price for fear of a price war. The kinked demand curve model illustrates price rigidity.

7. The prisoners' dilemma also leads to implicit collusion. The price leadership model explains one way firms can eliminate the uncertainty of rivals' reactions to changes in price. One firm sets price and the others follow suit by setting the same price. In the entry-limit pricing model, firms implicitly agree to give up short-run profit by setting a price low enough to deter entry.

8. Oligopoly models have different implications for specific equilibrium prices and quantities; however, we can conclude that, in general, equilibrium prices and outputs under oligopoly lie somewhere between competitive and monopoly levels.

9. A cartel is an agreement among independent firms to coordinate output and pricing decisions so that each firm earns a monopoly profit. The firms still face a prisoners' dilemma. For a cartel to succeed, there must be a way to discipline cheaters.

QUESTIONS AND PROBLEMS

1. Compare the assumptions of the theory of monopolistic competition to those of the competitive model. Explain the process by which an industry will attain a new long-run equilibrium if
   a) costs increase;
   b) one firm introduces a new brand.
2. "The greater the price elasticity of demand, the greater is the excess capacity for a monopolistic competitor." Evaluate this statement. Be sure to distinguish between market demand and the firm's demand.
3. In many real-world markets products are differentiated and firms have some degree of market power. Explain how you would decide which type of economic model—perfect competition, oligopoly, or monopoly—to use to analyze such markets.
4. a) Can there be too many brands of a product on the market? Explain.
   b) Can there be too few? Explain.
5. Explain carefully the difference between long-run equilibrium under oligopoly and long-run equilibrium under perfect competition.
6. Suppose that the market for breakfast cereal is oligopolistic.
   a) Explain, using the Cournot model, how the long-run equilibrium price and quantity of breakfast cereals are determined.
   b) If one firm in the industry implements a new cost-saving production process, explain the effect on long-run equilibrium prices.
7. a) What is nonprice competition?
   b) Is this an important consideration in most real-world markets?
8. Phillips Pit Stop and Call's Convenience Store are two retail stores supplying gasoline to a small city in Utah. Each firm can supply gasoline for fixed overhead costs of $3,000 per year. The marginal cost per gallon of gasoline is fixed at $1. The market demand curve for gasoline is estimated to be

$$Y = 22,000 - 2,000p$$

where Y is the number of gallons of gasoline sold per year and p is the market price.

a) Using the Cournot model of duopoly, determine the equilibrium output for each firm and the market price of gasoline.

b) If Phillips Pit Stop were the sole supplier of gasoline, what would be the equilibrium price and quantity?

c) If the market for gasoline were perfectly competitive, what would be the equilibrium price and quantity?

9. In oligopoly models, firms earn positive economic profits. Since this means firms are doing better than in the next best alternative, why do new firms not enter the market?

10. a) Using the kinked demand curve model, explain why a decrease in costs might not lead to a change in price or output. What happens to profits?

b) Repeat this exercise for a change in demand.

11. Suppose that the price of steel is $800 per ton. Jackson Steel faces a kinked demand curve given by

$$p = \begin{cases} 1,200 - Y & \text{if } p \geq \$800 \\ 1,400 - 1.5Y & \text{if } p < \$800 \end{cases}.$$

The firm's marginal cost curve is given by

$$LMC = Y.$$

a) Graph the demand, marginal revenue, and marginal cost curves.

b) Determine the profit-maximizing quantity for Jackson Steel.

c) If the government imposes an excise tax of $100 per ton of steel on steel producers, determine the new profit-maximizing quantity for Jackson Steel.

12. In 1983 one major U.S. airline proposed that all U.S. airlines adopt a uniform fare schedule based on mileage. Their proposal would eliminate the many different fares that were available at that time. Most major airlines applauded the suggestion and began to adopt the plan. Soon afterwards, however, various airlines began cutting fares to increase or maintain their market shares. Explain this type of phenomenon using the prisoners' dilemma.

13. Usually in the summer or early fall, one of the major U.S. automobile producers announces special incentive programs, such as rebates and special financing, designed to increase sales. Suppose GM announces 2.9% financing on all cars and trucks. Why doesn't Ford offer a substantially better deal?

14. In August 1989, TWA announced a substantial reduction in domestic airfares. Within a week, United Airlines announced similar price-cuts. The other major airlines were expected to follow suit soon after. Would you expect fares to continue to fall to competitive levels? Explain.

15. "As long as firms in an oligopolistic industry earn positive economic profits, there will be a threat of entry. If firms set price to deter entry, then they must set price equal to the competitive price." Is this reasoning true or false? Explain. (Remember, when you use an oligopoly model to explain something, you must take care to specify how firms expect their rivals to behave.)

16. Large expenditures on advertising or on research and development can deter entry into an oligopolistic industry. Using the entry-limit pricing model, explain the effects of such entry barriers on equilibrium price, quantity, and profit.

17. Carefully explain which model you would use—competitive industry, monopoly, or oligopoly—to analyze the behavior of firms that manufacture and sell personal computers. (What factors will influence your choice of theories? Suppose you were to use an oligopoly model. Which model would you pick? Why?)

18. a) Why do producers agree to form a cartel?
    b) Demonstrate the unstable nature of any cartel.
    c) Explain why the OPEC cartel has remained intact for over 15 years.

REFERENCES

Baumol, W., J. Panzar, and R. Willig. 1988. *Contestable Markets and the Theory of Industry Structure*. Rev. ed. San Diego: Harcourt Brace Jovanovich.

Friedman, J. 1986. *Game Theory with Applications to Economics*. New York: Oxford University Press.

Griffen, J., and H. Steele. 1986. *Energy Economics and Policy*. 2d ed. San Diego: Academic Press.

Kreps, D. 1990. *A Course in Microeconomic Theory*. Princeton: Princeton University Press.

Tirole, J. 1988. *The Theory of Industrial Organization*. Cambridge, Mass.: MIT Press.

ECONOMIC EFFICIENCY AND MARKET FAILURE

■ **CHAPTER 15** Economic Efficiency, Market Failure,

and the Role of Government

■ **CHAPTER 16** General Equilibrium and Economic Efficiency

■ *Most of the analyses in the first four parts of this book have*

focused on positive issues—how consumers and producers be-

have, how markets allocate resources, and how changes in the

economic environment affect individual decisions and market

outcomes. Only on a few occasions (for example, in the discussion

comparing monopoly to competition) has anything been said about

normative issues—that is, about the desirability of any particular

market result. Part 5 introduces normative analysis by describing the goal of economic efficiency and by discussing when markets do and do not allocate resources efficiently. The material in this part will help us understand one important role for government—intervening in markets when they fail to allocate resources efficiently.

■ Chapter 15 develops the notion of economic efficiency in the context of a single market and shows why a perfectly competitive market is efficient. It then goes on to investigate four of the most common sources of market failure: government intervention in competitive markets, monopoly power, externalities, and public goods. It shows that, in each instance, market prices do not accurately reflect the social costs and benefits of production and consumption when these result in an inefficient allocation of resources. Chapter 15 also shows how some market failures can be remedied through the assignment of property rights and private bargaining and some through government intervention. The material presented in this chapter shows, once again, how microeconomics can help us understand major issues facing most modern societies.

■ The analysis in Chapter 15 examines only a single market at a time. Chapter 16, on the other hand, gives a more complete picture of the circular flow of economic activity by extending the competitive model to take account of the interrelation between markets. The goals of this chapter are to characterize a general equilibrium involving many competitive markets, to develop more fully the notion of economic efficiency, and to show how competitive markets lead to an efficient allocation of resources in this general setting. While the material in this chapter is somewhat more complex than in previous chapters, it demonstrates how microeconomics can successfully model entire economies and why, for example, two nations might find it beneficial to engage in trade.

ECONOMIC EFFICIENCY, MARKET FAILURE, AND THE ROLE OF GOVERNMENT

15

LEARNING OBJECTIVES

After completing Chapter 15 you should be able to do the following:

■ Define economic efficiency and market failure.

■ Describe the marginal efficiency condition and the relation between a competitive equilibrium and efficiency.

■ Discuss the trade-off between equity and efficiency.

■ Compare corrective taxes and the assignment of property rights as methods of internalizing externalities.

■ Analyze the role of government in generating the efficient level of public goods.

EXAMPLES

In this chapter we define the notion of *economic efficiency* and describe the condition markets must satisfy if goods are to be distributed efficiently. We also discuss why perfectly competitive markets satisfy the efficiency condition. In the remainder of the chapter we investigate why markets may not work efficiently and what the government can do to correct this.

15.1 SOME INTRODUCTORY REMARKS ON METHODOLOGY

■ It will help us to put this chapter in perspective if we begin by discussing two issues: positive versus normative economics, and partial versus general equilibrium.

POSITIVE VERSUS NORMATIVE ECONOMICS

In Chapter 1, we distinguished between *positive* and *normative* economics. Recall that positive economics is concerned with evaluating the economic implications of a particular action or policy using a model based on assumptions that are independent of ethical considerations. Positive economics deals with hypotheses that can be evaluated with respect to their logical underpinnings as well as the empirical data at hand. Up to this point, we have dealt almost exclusively with positive economics.

Normative economics, on the other hand, deals with what is desirable or undesirable. Normative economics is based on assumptions that are not empirically verifiable but that reflect the beliefs of the person or persons evaluating resource use in an economy.

Both normative and positive economics are used in this chapter. We use normative analysis to identify desirable outcomes and positive analysis to determine whether or not a particular action or policy will achieve the desired outcome. Remember that in Chapter 11 we used positive economics to determine the economic effects of an excise tax on consumers, producers, and resource owners but did not address the issue of whether or not an excise tax was desirable in the first place. In this chapter, normative economics will help us make this latter determination.

PARTIAL VERSUS GENERAL EQUILIBRIUM ANALYSIS

When we evaluate a particular allocation of resources, it is important to distinguish between *partial equilibrium analysis* and *general equilibrium analysis*. Partial equilibrium analysis focuses on how an action or policy affects the equilibrium price and quantity associated with a *single* market. The analyses in Chapter 11 were all examples of partial equilibrium analysis. For example, when we investigated an excise tax on cigarettes, we did not consider the impact of the tax on the equilibrium price and quantity of cigars.

Partial equilibrium analysis is an extremely useful method of analyzing many economic problems; however, it does not provide us with a complete picture of the operation of the entire economy. *General equilibrium analysis* focuses on the economy as a whole; that is, it is the study of how buyers and sellers interact in *several* markets to determine the equilibrium prices and quantities of *many* goods and services. A general equilibrium analysis of an excise tax on cigarettes would consider not only how the tax affects the cigarette market but also how it affects all other markets.

In this chapter we will continue to use partial equilibrium analysis. We do this because, for the actions and policies examined here, a partial equilibrium analysis provides us with the same basic results as would a general equilibrium analysis. In the next chapter we will introduce general equilibrium analysis and discuss when we should use this approach to analyze economic problems.

■ **Economic efficiency** is a normative criterion for evaluating any allocation of resources. An allocation of resources is said to be *efficient* (or *Pareto efficient*, after the Italian economist Vilfredo Pareto who lived from 1848 to 1923) if production and distribution cannot be reorganized to make one person better off without making some other person or persons worse off. In other words, if an economy is operating efficiently, then the only way the welfare of one individual can be improved is at the expense of someone else.

Conversely, an allocation of resources is inefficient if production and distribution can be reorganized in such a way that someone becomes better off without making someone else worse off. If an allocation of resources is inefficient, then resources are being wasted in the sense that society's total welfare could be increased were those resources redistributed appropriately.

For most practical applications of the efficiency criterion, the definition of economic efficiency given above is difficult to use directly. Fortunately, in a partial equilibrium setting it is quite simple to derive a condition that is required for efficiency and that is extremely useful for addressing a wide range of economic problems. As we shall see, this condition is based on marginal benefits and costs and, hence, is called the **marginal efficiency condition.**

Any given quantity of a good or service that is available for consumption will provide a certain amount of satisfaction to those who consume it. This is called the total social benefit (TSB) of the given quantity. *Total social benefit* measures how well off society

15.2 ECONOMIC EFFICIENCY

THE MARGINAL EFFICIENCY CONDITION

FIGURE 15-1   THE MARGINAL EFFICIENCY CONDITION

(a) Economic efficiency is attained when the difference between TSC and TSB is as large as possible. (b) The marginal condition for economic efficiency is that MSB = MSC.

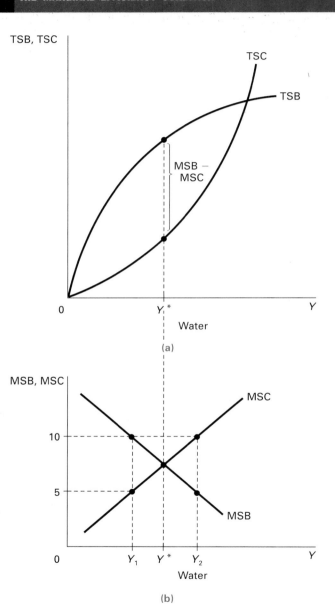

is because its citizens consume a certain amount of a particular good or service. In Figure 15–1(a) we have drawn the total social benefit curve for water. Each point on the curve reflects the value to society of consuming a particular quantity of water.

The **marginal social benefit** (MSB) of a good or service is the additional benefit society obtains by making one more unit of that good or service available for consumption. Typically, we measure marginal social benefit in dollars; that is, marginal social benefit is measured as the maximum amount of money that individuals would give up to obtain an additional unit of the good. For example, if the marginal social benefit of water is $10 per gallon, then some consumers would be willing to give up $10 worth of other goods in order to obtain an additional gallon of water since they would be neither better nor worse off by doing so. If they had to give up less than $10 worth of other goods they would be better off than before and if they had to give up more than $10 worth of other goods they would be worse off than before.

The MSB curve associated with the TSB curve drawn in Figure 15–1(a) is shown in Figure 15–1(b). Any point on this curve reflects the additional benefit society gains when another gallon of water is made available for consumption.

Society also incurs a cost when a particular quantity of a good or service is made available for consumption. This is called the total social cost (TSC) of a good or service. Total social cost measures the value of all resources needed to make a given amount of a good or service available for consumption. In Figure 15–1(a) we have drawn the total social cost curve for water. Each point on the curve reflects the value of the resources society must sacrifice to consume a particular quantity of water.

The **marginal social cost** (MSC) of a good or service is the additional cost society incurs by making one more unit of that good or service available for consumption. We usually measure marginal social cost in dollars; that is, marginal social cost is measured as the minimum amount of money that would need to be paid to owners of resources used in producing an additional unit of the good. For example, if the marginal social cost of water is $5 per gallon, then the minimum payment needed to compensate resource owners for the use of their resources without making them worse off than before would be $5 per gallon. If they received more than $5 they would be better off, and if they received less than $5 would be worse off.

The MSC curve associated with the TSC curve drawn in Figure 15–1(a) is shown in Figure 15–1(b). Any point on this curve reflects the additional cost society incurs when another gallon of water is made available for consumption.

We can find the efficient output of good Y by comparing the marginal social benefit and marginal social cost curves at different levels of output. First, suppose that, currently, Y_1 gallons of water are being produced and consumed. Using Figure 15–1(b), we can show that Y_1 is an inefficient level of output. Let us consider what happens if one more gallon of water is produced and consumed. At Y_1, marginal social benefit is $10 per gallon and marginal social cost is $5 per gallon. This means that consumers would be willing to give up a maximum of $10 to be able to consume one more gallon of water, since they would be no worse off by doing so, and resource owners whose resources are used to produce water would be willing to receive as compensation $5 to produce one more gallon of water, since this would leave them no worse off than before. Clearly, then, if resource owners were to receive from consumers $10 for producing an additional gallon of water, they would be better off, since $10 is greater than $5; and consumers would be no worse off either. This demonstrates that Y_1 is inefficient since, by making more water available, it is possible to make producers better off without making consumers worse off. (See if you can think of a way to make consumers better off without making resource owners worse off.)

It follows from this discussion that whenever MSB is greater than MSC, it will be possible, by producing more of the good, to make at least one person better off without making anyone else worse off. Allocating resources to produce more of the good results in a net gain to society up to the point where the marginal social benefit of the good equals the marginal social cost, or up to Y^* in Figure 15–1.

Next, suppose Y_2 units of output are being produced and consumed. Using Figure 15–1(b), we can show that Y_2 is also an inefficient level of output. Beginning at Y_2, let us consider what happens if one *less* gallon of water is produced and consumed. At Y_2, marginal social benefit is $5 per gallon and marginal social cost is $10 per gallon. This means that consumers would be willing to receive a minimum of $5 to consume one less gallon of water, since they would be no worse off than they were before, and resource owners whose resources are used to produce water would be willing to pay at most $10 to cut production of water by one gallon, since they would be no worse off than before, either. Clearly, then, if consumers were to receive from resource owners $5 for reducing consumption of water by one gallon, they would be no worse off and resource owners would be better off since $5 is less than $10.

This demonstrates that Y_2 is inefficient since, by making less water available, it would be possible to make producers better off without making consumers worse off. (See if you can think of a way to make consumers better off without making resource owners worse off.)

It follows that whenever MSB is less than MSC, it will be possible, by producing less of the good, to make at least one person better off without making anyone else worse off. Cutting back production and consumption results in a net gain to society up to the point where the marginal social benefit of a good equals its marginal social cost, or up to Y^* in Figure 15−1.

We can now state the *marginal efficiency condition*:

An efficient allocation of resources requires that resources be allocated in such a way that

$$MSB = MSC. \qquad (15.1)$$

In Figure 15−1, Y^* is the efficient output of water. If MSB > MSC, it is possible, by producing more, to make one person better off without making someone else worse off. The net gain to society of increasing output from Y_1 to Y^* is represented by area *ABC*. If MSC > MSB, it is possible, by producing less, to make one individual better off without making someone else worse off. The net gain to society of reducing output from Y_2 to Y^* is represented by area *CEF*.

Notice further that at the efficient level of output the difference between total social benefit and total social cost, which is called the *net total social benefit*, is as large as possible. Thus, the efficiency criterion for evaluating resource use weighs total social benefit against total social cost and recommends the output that maximizes net total social benefit.

The efficiency condition is valid for any type of economy.

■ We now want to examine the relation between economic efficiency and perfect competition.

15.3   PERFECT COMPETITION AND EFFICIENCY

THE FIRST OPTIMALITY THEOREM

The **First Optimality Theorem**, also called the First Fundamental Theorem of Welfare Economics, states that *every competitive equilibrium satisfies the efficiency criterion*. The First Optimality Theorem guarantees that a competitive equilibrium gives rise to an efficient allocation of resources; that is, under perfect competition all gains from trade are realized and no one can be made better off without making someone else worse off.

It is quite easy to demonstrate the validity of the First Optimality Theorem. We simply must determine whether or not a perfectly competitive market generates an allocation of resources satisfying the marginal efficiency condition.

Competitive equilibrium requires that consumers maximize satisfaction and producers maximize profit. We know from our earlier work that, given market prices, consumers maximize satisfaction by trading up to the point where the marginal private benefit (MPB) of consuming a good is just equal to the market price of the good. From the consumer's perspective, all gains from trade are realized when the amount of each good consumed is such that marginal benefit is equal to the market price.

In addition, the marginal private benefit received by those consumers purchasing the good or service is the marginal social benefit, provided that no other than the buyer receives any satisfaction when the good or service is consumed. On the one hand, therefore, when consumers maximize satisfaction,

$$p = \text{MPB} = \text{MSB}. \qquad (15.2)$$

Profit-maximizing firms, on the other hand, produce where price is equal to marginal private cost (MPC). From the producer's perspective, all gains from trade are realized when production is such that the marginal cost of producing an additional unit of output is equal to the market price of the product.

In addition, the marginal private cost of producing the good or service is the marginal social cost, provided that all economic (opportunity) costs are included in the producer's total costs. Thus, when producers maximize profit,

$$p = \text{MPC} = \text{MSC}. \qquad (15.3)$$

Under perfect competition, buyers and sellers face the same market prices, so these two equations together imply that under perfect competition all gains from trade are realized when

$$\text{MSB} = \text{MSC}.$$

At the level of output satisfying this equation, all consumers have adjusted the amount they consume until their marginal benefit is equal to the market price and all producers have adjusted the amount they produce until their marginal cost is equal to the market price.

If, when a particular good or service is sold, buyers are the only ones benefiting from the good's consumption and sellers are the only ones bearing the costs of supplying the good, then MSB = MSC for the good. Hence, the First Optimality Theorem guarantees that a competitive equilibrium satisfies the efficiency criterion.

Total economic surplus is defined as *the sum of consumer surplus and economic rent.* It is a dollar measure of the economic well-being of all market participants. The First Optimality Theorem implies that the efficient output is given by the intersection of the supply, or marginal private cost, curve and the demand, or marginal private benefit, curve. As Figure 15–2 shows, this means that the efficient level of production of a good or service corresponds to the output rate that maximizes total economic surplus.

At the efficient level of production, Y^*, the marginal benefit of the good is just equal to the marginal cost. If the market price is p^*, then market participants will buy and sell the efficient output. In this instance, consumer surplus is given by area p^*AB, economic rent by area p^*B0, and total economic surplus by area $0AB$. In Figure 15–2, the shaded area represents total economic surplus.

IMPLICATIONS OF THE FIRST OPTIMALITY THEOREM FOR TOTAL ECONOMIC SURPLUS

COMPETITION AND ECONOMIC EFFICIENCY   **FIGURE 15–2**

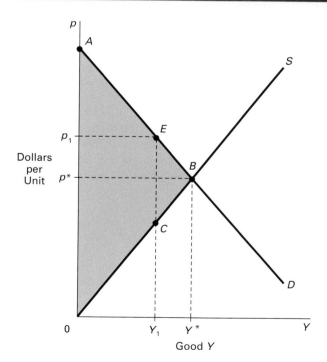

Competitive markets yield the efficient level of production, Y^*. At Y^* total economic surplus is maximized.

Now we must show that at any other price and quantity, total economic surplus is smaller than $0AB$. Suppose that only Y_1 units of output are traded, and at p_1 dollars per unit. In this instance, consumer surplus falls to p_1AE, economic rent becomes $0p_1EC$ (which may be either larger or smaller than before), and total economic surplus falls to $0AEC$.

15.4 EQUITY VERSUS EFFICIENCY

■ The efficiency criterion is not the only yardstick used to measure economic performance. Many economists argue that fairness, or **equity**, is (or should be) another. Of course, whether or not a particular allocation of resources is equitable depends on one's point of view. Two individuals may have quite different ideas of fairness.

When economists address questions of equity, they usually determine how different actions or policies affect the economic well-being of buyers, sellers, and resource owners. Recall that in Chapter 11 we always investigated who benefited and who was harmed by the particular policy under consideration. Policy makers have the task of choosing which distribution of economic welfare is appropriate.

THE TRADE-OFF BETWEEN EQUITY AND EFFICIENCY

Is an efficient allocation better than an inefficient allocation of resources? The answer to this question depends on the trade-off between improving efficiency and altering the distribution of economic well-being. To see what this involves, consider the *utility possibility frontier* in Figure 15−3. The utility possibility frontier shows the maximum attainable level of well-being for any one individual, given the level of well-being of all other individuals, their tastes, the quantity of resources available, and the technology. Each point on the utility possibility frontier in Figure 15−3 represents an efficient allocation of resources between individuals A and B. For example, suppose resources are allocated in such a way that point E represents the distribution of economic well-being. E is efficient because it is impossible to move away from E and make someone better off without making someone else worse off.

Points inside the frontier, however, represent inefficient allocations because resources *can* be reallocated in such a way as to make someone better off without harming anyone else. Beginning at point G, for example, both individuals would be in favor of changing the allocation of resources so that they would end up at some point on the line segment EF. Moving from G to any point on EF would make at least one individual better off without making the other worse off.

EQUITY VERSUS EFFICIENCY   **FIGURE 15–3**

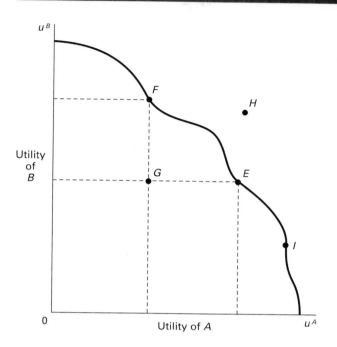

All points on the utility possibility frontier represent efficient allocations of resources. Points inside the frontier are inefficient. However, the efficiency criterion alone cannot rank all resource allocations. An inefficient point such as G may be preferred to an efficient point such as I because G is deemed more equitable.

Finally, points outside the frontier, such as *H*, are unattainable. Given the available resources and technology, the economy cannot produce enough output to achieve the levels of well-being associated with points outside the frontier.

Now, are efficient allocations better than inefficient allocations? Clearly, both individuals think that any efficient allocation giving rise to a point on line *EF* is better than the inefficient allocation giving rise to *G*. However, what if we compare *G* to *I*? If the economy begins at *G*, individual *A* thinks *I* is better since he or she is better off at *I* than at *G*; however, individual *B* thinks *I* is worse than *G* since at *I* he or she is worse off than at *G*. Even though *I* represents an efficient allocation of resources, at least one individual will oppose any move from *G* to *I*.

Being able to distinguish between efficient and inefficient resource allocations does not enable us automatically to decide which is preferable. There are many efficient allocations and we cannot choose which is the best using only the efficiency criterion; further, some inefficient allocations may be preferred to some efficient allocations based on equity considerations. Efficiency is desirable but we must always remember that equity considerations also play an important role.

15.5 MARKET FAILURE AND THE ROLE OF GOVERNMENT

■ Up to this point we have shown that in the absence of government intervention, a perfectly competitive market yields an efficient allocation of resources. Under the assumptions of the competitive model, the interaction of buyers and sellers leads to equality between marginal social benefit and cost.

In many instances, however, markets may fail; that is, they may not yield an efficient allocation of resources. Four of the most common sources of **market failure** are *government intervention in competitive markets, monopolistic power, externalities,* and *public goods.* Each of these types of market failure have one thing in common: prices do not accurately reflect the marginal social benefits and marginal social costs of production and consumption. The remainder of this chapter is concerned with each of these types of market failure and, in the latter three cases, with the role that government can play in correcting the failure.

GOVERNMENT INTERVENTION IN COMPETITIVE MARKETS

Governments often intervene in competitive markets in order to redistribute income, or economic welfare, from one group of individuals to another. In Chapter 11 we examined a variety of government policies that redistributed income in this way and, in so doing, gave rise to quite substantial inefficiencies. These illustrate the trade-off between equity and efficiency discussed above. They show how sometimes the government is willing to give up economic efficiency in return for a more equitable distribution of economic well-being.

Why does government intervention in competitive markets cause a loss in efficiency? The answer is that government intervention does not allow markets to operate where marginal social benefit is equal to marginal social cost. To see this, let us review the effects of an excise tax.

In Figure 15–4, D is the market demand curve for good Y and LS is the long-run market supply curve. In the absence of government intervention, long-run equilibrium is characterized by the point where demand is equal to supply or, in other words, where marginal private benefit is equal to marginal private cost. In this instance, the long-run equilibrium price and quantity are p_1 and Y_1 respectively.

Since we are assuming that this market is perfectly competitive, the market demand curve is the marginal social benefit curve as well as the marginal private benefit curve, and the supply curve is

MARKET FAILURE: EXCISE TAXES   **FIGURE 15–4**

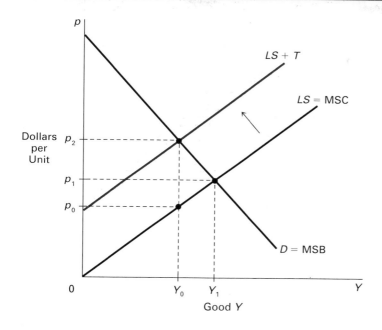

Government intervention in competitive markets can cause inefficiencies. An excise tax is one such example. After imposition of an excise tax, output falls to Y_0 units. This is an inefficient level of output since, at Y_0 MSB > MSC.

the marginal social cost curve as well as the marginal private cost curve. Thus, in the absence of government intervention, the interaction of buyers and sellers yields an efficient allocation of resources.

Now suppose the government levies an excise tax of T dollars per unit of good Y produced. From a firm's perspective, for every unit of good Y produced, cost has increased by T dollars. This means that the marginal private cost of producing good Y is no longer equal to the marginal social cost of producing good Y. In Figure 15–4, $LS + T$ is the marginal private cost curve after the tax is imposed and the new equilibrium price and quantity are p_2 and Y_0 respectively.

After the tax is imposed, the interaction of buyers and sellers yields less than the efficient output rate: $Y_0 < Y_1$. This is because the tax has caused a divergence between the marginal private cost of producing good Y and the marginal social cost of producing good Y. Thus, the price of good Y no longer reflects the marginal social cost of producing good Y. Prior to the tax the equilibrium price, p_1, reflected both the marginal social cost and the marginal social benefit of good Y. After the tax, the equilibrium price, p_2, reflects the marginal social benefit of good Y but not the marginal social cost, p_0, of good Y. The tax drives a wedge between what consumers pay and what producers actually receive for the product—between marginal social benefit and marginal social cost. Consequently, an efficient allocation of resources is no longer possible.

If excise taxes generate inefficiency, why do governments use them? The reason is, of course, that while they reduce efficiency they also generate redistribution of economic welfare. As we saw in Chapter 11, an excise tax on good Y harms consumers of good Y and owners of resources used to produce good Y. However, it increases the economic well-being of those individuals benefiting from the revenues generated by the tax. Economic welfare is redistributed from those participating in the market for good Y to other members of society.

When the government's goal is to redistribute economic welfare, government intervention usually leads to inefficiencies, and this trade-off between efficiency and equity policy makers must constantly weigh the arguments for and against. However, even in the absence of government intervention, markets do not always operate efficiently, and in some cases government intervention can improve the situation. In the remainder of this chapter, we look at three situations where markets, if left alone, do not allocate resources efficiently but where government intervention can help remedy this problem.

MONOPOLISTIC POWER

Another cause of market failure is market power. As we saw in Chapters 12 and 13, markets will fail to generate an efficient output when individuals have some degree of monopoly power. For example, consider the case of pure monopoly. Recall that a monopoly maximizes profit at the output rate for which marginal revenue is equal to marginal cost. This is shown in Figure 15–5.

The market demand curve, D, facing the monopoly is the marginal social benefit curve and, assuming that the monopoly's marginal cost curve reflects the value of all resources used to produce additional output, LMC is the marginal social cost curve. The monopoly produces where MR = MSC. Thus, it produces Y_m units of output and charges p_m dollars per unit. The monopoly price, p_m, reflects the marginal social benefit of Y_m units of output. But recall that, for a monopoly, price is always greater than marginal revenue; thus, at Y_m marginal social benefit is greater than marginal social cost and efficiency is not attained.

In this instance, can efficiency be attained through government intervention? As we saw in Chapter 12, the answer is yes. If the

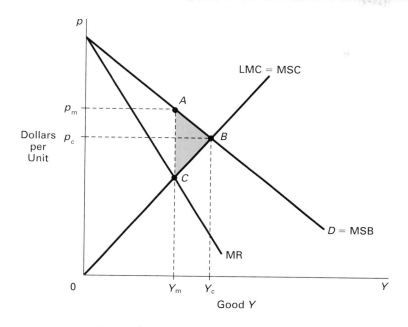

Monopolistic power also leads to market failure. At the profit-maximizing level of output, Y_m, MSB > MSC. The inefficiency of the monopoly is represented by area ABC.

government forces the monopoly to sell its output for p_c dollars per unit, then the firm will produce the efficient level of output, Y_c. The net gain to society of increasing output from Y_m to Y_c is area ABC in Figure 15−5. Government intervention, in this instance, leads to economic efficiency.

We have shown that government intervention can both cause and eliminate inefficiency. The next example illustrates how government provision of a good or service can be either efficient or inefficient depending on whether or not price accurately reflects marginal social benefits and costs.

EXAMPLE 15−1

EFFICIENCY AND THE PRICE OF POSTAGE STAMPS

In the U.S. the federal government provides mail services. The price of sending a first-class letter is currently $.29 per letter. If the market clearing price of first-class mail is $.50, illustrate the inefficiency that results from setting price below the market clearing level.

■ **SOLUTION** Figure 15–6 shows the marginal social benefit and marginal social cost curves associated with providing first-class mail service. These are also the demand and supply curves respectively. At a price of $.29 per letter, consumers will use the service until the marginal social benefit of doing so equals $.29. This implies that Y_2 first-class letters will be processed per year.

At Y_2 letters per year, the marginal social cost is p_2 dollars per letter, which is greater than the marginal social benefit. Thus, the government is providing more than the efficient level of mail services, $Y_2 > Y_1$. If it raised the price of first-class letters to the market clearing price, output would fall to the efficient level and net gains in well-being equal to area *ABC* will be possible. That is, area *ABC* represents the loss in efficiency arising from the government's pricing policy. ■

FIGURE 15–6   **GOVERNMENT-SUBSIDIZED SERVICES AND MARKET FAILURE**

If the price of mail services is kept artificially low at $.28 per letter, Y_2 letters will be processed each year. This level of production is inefficient since MSB < MSC.

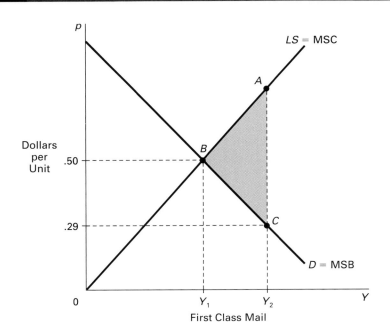

Market power gives rise to inefficiencies; however, in some situations even competitive markets do not yield an efficient allocation of resources. We now turn our attention to two of the more important reasons why competitive markets fail: externalities and public goods.

At times the production or consumption of a good or service generates side effects that affect the economic welfare of individuals not directly involved in the market transactions. These side effects are called **externalities** (because they are "external" by-products of the market transactions that actually generate the effects). When they are beneficial they are called *external benefits* (or *positive externalities*), and when they are harmful they are called *external costs* (or *negative externalities*).

Some examples will help to clarify what economists mean by externalities. One example of an external benefit is immunization against a contagious disease. If Clarence decides to be inoculated for measles, then he benefits directly because the chance of his getting measles is greatly reduced. In addition, however, other individuals benefit from Clarence's decision, because now they are less likely to get the disease from him. This beneficial side effect is an externality because it does not affect (is external to) Clarence's decision. Clarence's decision concerning whether or not he should get a measles shot is not affected by how his inoculation will benefit others. He is concerned primarily with the benefit he receives from the shot.

The most common example of an external cost is pollution. Driving an automobile, smoking tobacco products, and operating a factory that emits smoke into the air or sewage into the water are all activities that have external costs. Each of these imposes external costs on people not directly involved in the market transactions giving rise to the side effects, and in general these external costs are not considered when individuals drive to work or smoke a cigarette or when owners of firms decide how much output to supply.

Unless some type of government intervention occurs, competitive markets will lead to an inefficient allocation of resources when externalities are present. The reason for this should be quite clear. The market demand and supply curves reflect only the benefits and costs of those participating in the market; that is, they reflect only the marginal private benefits and costs of a particular good. They do not reflect the benefits and costs that fall on others. Thus, market participants will not take external effects into account when allocating resources.

EXTERNALITIES

For example, an individual may decide to purchase and consume an additional cigarette because the private benefits exceed the private costs of the transaction; however, it may be that if the external costs imposed on others is included, then the social cost of consuming one additional cigarette may outweigh the social benefits. If this is the case, then the consumer's decision to smoke will lead to an inefficient allocation of resources.

In the remainder of this section we will discuss various government policies designed to restore efficiency when externalities are present. We will focus on external costs because these are the types of externalities that, in recent years, have been of the greatest concern.

EFFICIENCY AND
EXTERNAL COSTS

Let us begin our analysis of external costs by determining the efficient level of production and consumption when there are harmful external effects. Suppose that, as the result of the production process, firms in a perfectly competitive, constant cost industry emit a variety of pollutants into a river. The pollution harms people living nearby because the river is no longer safe for recreational activities. Thus, firms in this industry impose external costs on the nearby residents and, because the owners of the firms do not take these external costs into account when they make their production decisions, the allocation of resources will be inefficient.

We can illustrate this situation with a supply and demand diagram that also includes the external costs generated by the production process. In Figure 15–7 the market demand and supply curves are D and LS respectively. In the absence of any government intervention, the equilibrium price and quantity are Y_c and p_c respectively.

Firms in this industry dump pollutants into the river for each unit of output they produce. The harm done by the pollution is represented by the **marginal external cost** curve, MEC in the diagram. The MEC curve is upward-sloping and reflects the assumption that each additional unit of production leads to increasing external costs imposed on those individuals living in the area. We obtain the MEC curve by summing the marginal external costs of each individual affected by the externality. For example, when production is Y_c units of good Y, then the MEC associated with this level of production is p_0, which means that the residents being harmed would be p_0 dollars better off if firms reduced their output by one unit.

Now, is Y_c the efficient level of production? Efficiency in any market requires that the marginal social benefit is equal to the marginal social cost. The market demand curve reflects the

EXTERNAL COSTS AND ECONOMIC EFFICIENCY

FIGURE 15–7

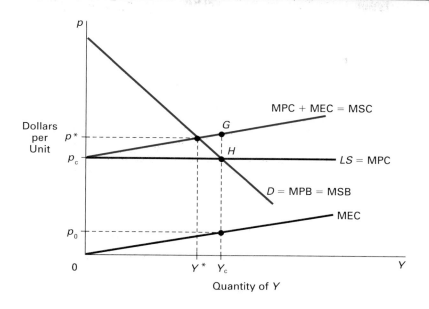

In the absence of government intervention, the equilibrium price and quantity are p_c and Y_c respectively. This is not the efficient level of production since at this point MSB < MSC. To achieve efficiency, production should be reduced to Y^*. At this level of production, MSB = MSC.

marginal private benefits of those consuming good Y. It also reflects the marginal social benefit of good Y. The long-run market supply curve reflects the marginal private cost of producing good Y instead of other goods in the economy. However, the long-run market supply curve does not represent the marginal social cost of production since it does not include the external costs. Instead, the MSC curve is the sum of marginal private costs and marginal external costs. In Figure 15–7, MSC is the marginal social cost curve. Notice that, for any level of production, we can measure MEC as the distance between the MSC curve and the LS curve. For example, when production is at Y_c, MEC is equal to p_0 which, in turn, is equivalent to GH.

Since efficiency requires that MSB = MSC, the efficient level of production is Y^* units of good Y. Notice that Y^* is less than Y_c; that is, when there are external costs, the competitive output is too large for efficiency. Producers expand production up to the point where the marginal private cost of producing good Y is just equal to the amount consumers are willing to pay to purchase good Y. However, the output at this point is too large for efficiency since firms have ignored the external costs imposed on those individuals living nearby. At Y_c, firms incur a marginal private cost of H dollars per unit of output, but nearby residents also incur a marginal external cost of GH dollars per unit of good Y produced. At the competitive level MSB < MSC, and society can gain if firms reduce output.

When harmful externalities exist, government intervention is needed to achieve an efficient allocation of resources. The government can do several things to correct for, or *internalize*, the externality. Internalization of an externality occurs when the marginal private benefit or cost associated with some good or service is adjusted so that producers or consumers of the good consider the actual marginal social benefit or cost of their actions. Essentially, internalization of an externality means that a "price" is attached to the externality and this "price" is taken into account by those producing and consuming the good or service giving rise to the side effect. Below, we will discuss two policy alternatives for achieving efficiency through government intervention: corrective taxes and assignment of property rights.

CORRECTIVE TAXES

One way for a government to internalize an externality is to induce producers to reduce output by imposing **corrective taxes** on production. An excise tax is a corrective tax. From the producer's perspective, an excise tax increases the marginal private cost of production and causes the long-run industry supply curve to shift upward. This particular policy is illustrated in Figure 15−8 (which is identical to Figure 15−7 except that the MEC curve is omitted). If the government levies an excise tax equal to the MEC at Y^*, EF, then the the marginal private cost curve becomes LS + EF, firms now produce only Y^* units of good Y, and consumers pay p^* dollars per unit. Hence, an excise tax equal to EF internalizes the externality and leads to the efficient level of production.

One important point to note is that the tax does not reduce air pollution to zero. Why is this? It reduces pollution only to the point where the benefit of decreasing output by an additional unit, and therefore of reducing pollution by the associated amount, is just equal to the cost. Any further reduction would not be worth it from society's point of view. Economic efficiency is attained by weighing benefit to residents (reduced pollution) against cost to consumers (reduced output).

WINNERS AND LOSERS

While we know that in moving the economy from Y_c, (the competitive level of output) to Y^* (the efficient level of production) society as a whole is better off, in microeconomics we are usually interested in who wins and who loses as a result of the government's action. We saw in Chapter 11 that when we have a constant cost industry the excise tax is borne entirely by consumers. The

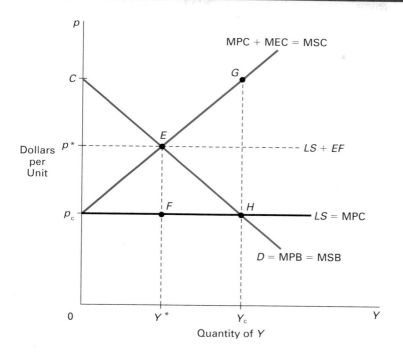

A tax equal to the marginal external cost associated with the efficient level of production, EF, shifts the long-run supply curve up to LS + T; production is lowered to the efficient level, Y*, and the price increases to p*. Consumers are worse off, the well-being of resource owners is unchanged, the government gains tax revenues, and those being affected by the externality are better off.

price consumers pay increases from p_c to p^*. Producers receive p^* from consumers but must deduct the tax payment from this. Producers pocket $p^* - EF = p_c$ dollars per unit of good Y, just as they did before the tax was levied.

Now we can determine who wins and who loses. Returning to Figure 15–8, let us begin by considering consumers of good Y. Prior to the tax, consumer surplus is represented by area p_cCH. After the tax, consumer surplus falls to p^*CE and consumers are worse off as a result of the tax.

Next consider owners of resources employed in this industry. Economic rent before and after the tax is zero so resource owners are neither better nor worse off after the tax is imposed.

Does anyone gain as a result of the tax? Clearly, among those who gain are those who benefit from the tax revenues collected by the government (area p_cp^*EF). In addition, those being harmed by the pollution gain. To see why, note that total external costs prior to the tax are given by area p_cGH. This area is simply all the MEC added together as output increases from zero to Y_c. After the tax, firms produce only Y^* units of good Y and total external costs decrease to p_cEF. Thus, those being harmed gain $FEGH$ as a result of the excise tax.

EMISSIONS FEES

In the discussion above, we implicitly assumed each unit of output was associated with a particular amount of pollution. This meant firms could reduce pollution only by reducing output. In this instance, a tax levied on output led to an efficient allocation of resources. However, in most cases the amount of pollution per unit of output is variable. Firms can reduce pollution not only by reducing output but also by substituting between inputs. Steel-producing firms, for example, can reduce air pollution by producing less steel or by equipping their smoke stacks with a device that reduces emissions. When this situation occurs, a tax levied on output will not allow firms to reduce pollution efficiently. Instead, the tax must be levied on pollution itself so that firms will have an incentive to reduce pollution in the least costly way. This type of tax is called an *emissions fee.*

To illustrate the use of an emissions fee to internalize an externality, consider Figure 15–9. The horizontal axis measures the amount of pollutants emitted by firms, while the vertical axis measures marginal cost and benefit. The marginal social benefit of emissions, MSB in the diagram, represents the maximum amount

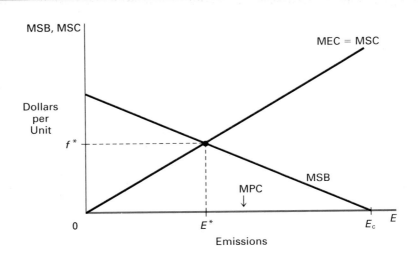

FIGURE 15–9	EMISSIONS FEES

In the absence of government intervention, E_c is the profit-maximizing level of emissions. This level of emissions is inefficient since MSB < MSC at that point. An emissions fee of f* dollars per unit of emissions internalizes the externality and causes firms to reduce emissions to the efficient level, E*.

firms are willing to pay for the right to emit pollutants. It is the firms' demand curve for emissions and it reflects the value of the reduction in output of goods and services necessary to reduce pollution. (Think of emissions as an "input" and MSB as a derived demand curve.) In the diagram, MEC represents the marginal external cost of emissions. This also is the marginal social cost of emissions.

In the absence of government intervention, the marginal private cost of emitting pollutants is zero, and firms will emit pollutants up to the point where marginal social benefit is zero. Thus, E_c is the level of emissions corresponding to the firm's profit-maximizing output rate in the absence of government intervention. That is, E_c corresponds to output Y_c in Figure 15–8. This level of emissions, and hence output, would be efficient only if the marginal external cost associated with emissions were zero.

The efficient level of pollution, E^*, is determined by the intersection of the MSB and MSC curves. If pollution were eliminated, then marginal social cost would be greater than marginal social benefit. If nothing were done about pollution, then emissions would be E_c and marginal social benefit would be greater than marginal social cost.

Now suppose the government levies an emissions fee of f^* dollars per unit of pollutant. This essentially raises the marginal private cost of polluting to f^*, so firms now have an incentive to reduce emissions to E^*.

What effect does the fee have on the price and quantity of the good that is being produced? When the fee is imposed, the marginal cost of producing good Y increases. This causes the long-run supply curve to shift up. Thus, after the fee is levied, the long-run equilibrium price increases while quantity falls. (Notice that an emissions fee has the same impact as the income tax discussed in Chapter 11.)

The distributional effects of an emissions fee are essentially the same as we found for a corrective tax levied on output. Consumer surplus falls so that consumers of the good being produced are worse off than before. Resource owners are neither better nor worse off since economic rent is zero. Those benefiting from the revenues collected by the government gain as do those being harmed by the externality.

In the United States, corrective taxes and fees are seldom used to internalize externalities. Instead, the primary method of controlling externalities such as pollution is through government regulations that establish *emissions standards*. Emissions standards are limits

EMISSIONS STANDARDS

on the amounts and types of pollutants that firms may emit into the environment. The emissions standards that U.S. citizens are most familiar with are the restrictions placed on automobile emissions. If producers do not meet these emission standards, then they must pay substantial fines.

Once again, the distributional impact of emissions standards is essentially the same as it is for corrective taxes. However, there are two basic problems with using standards instead of fees. First, standards allow firms to pollute up to the regulated level without incurring any penalty at all. This means that firms have an incentive just to meet the restrictions and not to do any better. Second, a uniform standard across firms does not take into account differences in the costs of eliminating pollution among firms. Those that are most efficient at reducing emissions should be given an incentive to do so to a greater extent than those firms that are inefficient at this task.

In the next example, we illustrate how to determine an emissions fee that will internalize an externality affecting many people across the United States—noise pollution.

EXAMPLE 15-2

NOISE POLLUTION

Individuals who live and work near airports often suffer from noise pollution. Aircraft noise can interfere with sleep and various outdoor activities; it can even damage hearing. Suppose the government has hired us to resolve the conflict between property owners living near an airport and the airlines (or airport authority). In particular, our task is to determine an emissions fee that will internalize the externality. We have the following information:

1. The noise pollution is harming 100 property owners.
2. $MEC = 1.5 \cdot E$ per property owner
3. $MSB = 10,000 - 100E$

where E is a measure of the average noise in the vicinity of the airport.

■ **SOLUTION** Currently there is no government intervention and airlines operate up to the point where the marginal social benefit of emitting noise is equal to zero. In this instance, the competitive level of noise pollution is $E_c = 100$ units.

We can find the efficient level of aircraft noise by equating marginal social benefit and marginal social cost. The latter is the sum of the marginal external costs of each property owner; that is, $MSC = 100 \cdot MEC = 150 \cdot E$. Setting MSC equal to MSB we have

$$MSB = 10,000 - 100E = 150E = MSC.$$

Solving this equation for E gives the efficient level of aircraft noise; that is, $E^* = 40$ units.

Now we must find the emissions fee that will lower aircraft noise from 100 to 40 units. Substituting the efficient level of noise into the MSC equation gives the desired fee: $f^* = 150E = \$6,000$ per unit of noise. Thus, an emissions fee levied on airlines (or the airport authority) of \$6,000 per unit of aircraft noise would yield an efficient allocation of resources. ∎

An emissions fee gives airlines an incentive to reduce noise pollution. They can accomplish this by reducing the frequency of flights or changing takeoff and landing patterns. The airlines could also react by eliminating the externality altogether. They could do this by moving the airport to an isolated area so that no one would be harmed by the aircraft noise, by buying up all the surrounding property so that no one else would bear the cost of aircraft noise, or by installing soundproofing devices on residents' homes.

In the United States, the government does not use emissions fees to internalize the externality associated with aircraft noise. Instead, various regulations, such as altering takeoff and landing patterns to reduce noise and restricting the maximum allowable noise level of new airplanes, are used to internalize the externality. As we mentioned above, these types of regulations do not always lead to the least costly way of reducing emission.

The most important features distinguishing external costs from other types of economic costs is that emitters of harmful side effects are not required to compensate those being harmed and individuals who are made better off as the result of beneficial side effects are not required to compensate those emitting these external benefits. If, on the one hand, a firm uses a resource to produce a good or service, then a cost is imposed on the owner of that resource since he or she cannot use the resource in another way. In return for bearing this cost, the resource owner receives payment from the firm. If, on the other hand, the firm pollutes a local stretch of water, then it imposes a cost on residents since they can no longer use the water to swim or fish in. However, in this instance the firm does not compensate individuals who can no longer use the water.

ASSIGNING
PROPERTY RIGHTS

Why is this difference between external cost and other economic costs so important? In order to employ resources, a firm must pay the owner of the resource at least his or her opportunity cost, which means that the firm must take this cost into account when making its production decision. However, if the firm can pollute the water without paying those who are harmed by the damage to the environment, then there is no incentive for the firm to take this cost into account when making its production decision. From the firm's perspective the water is a free, or zero-priced, input.

But why must the firm pay for the use of inputs such as capital and labor but not for the use of the water? The answer is that for inputs such as capital and labor there are well-defined and enforceable **property rights** indicating who owns these resources. For example, if the owners of a firm want to use our labor services in their production process, then they must pay us for the use of these services. Because we have the exclusive property rights to our labor services and these rights are enforceable—that is, no one can use them without our consent (slavery being illegal)—owners must compensate us for the use of these resources. For clean water, however, there are no well-defined and enforceable property rights, which means that firms are free to pollute the water. If residents who are harmed by the polluted water had the property rights to clean water, then the firm might still pollute but it would have to pay the residents for the right to do so. In that case, water would be like any other input and the firm would take into account the cost of using the water when making its production decision. That is, the externality would be internalized by market forces.

Once we realize that most, if not all, externality problems arise because of the nonexistence or inappropriate assignment of property rights, then we might think that the government, through the assignment and enforcement of property rights, should be able to internalize any externality without resorting to taxes or other means of regulating market transactions. However, to whom does the government assign the right to use a particular resource? Should firms or nearby residents have the right to use clean water?

In a now famous article, Ronald Coase addressed this issue and demonstrated that, under certain conditions, the particular assignment of property rights is irrelevant as far as economic efficiency is concerned. We can illustrate the essence of Coase's argument using Figure 15–8. First, suppose that the government gives the property rights to the homeowners being harmed by the dirty water and that these property rights are enforced. This means that firms cannot pollute the water without the consent of homeowners. What must the owners of firms do to get the consent of the homeowners?

Naturally, they must compensate them for the harm done by the externality. Now, what is the minimum amount that homeowners will take in return for allowing firms to produce an additional unit of good Y? Since MEC measures the costs imposed on residents when output increases by one unit, it is precisely the minimum amount of compensation that must be paid to homeowners. If firms must pay those being harmed the MEC for each additional unit produced, then, from the firms' perspective, the marginal cost of producing good Y is the MPC + MEC, which is precisely MSC. Thus, this particular assignment of property rights internalizes the externality by making the MSC the marginal cost curve facing firms and the equilibrium price and quantity will be p^* and Y^* respectively.

Next, suppose that the government gives the property rights to clean water to the firms producing good Y. Coase argued that the outcome, as far as efficiency is concerned, would be the same. If firms have the rights to clean water, then those being harmed by pollution can band together and offer firms a bribe not to produce good Y. Since the MEC measures the harm being done, it will also be the maximum bribe nearby residents will pay to have output reduced by an additional unit. From the firms' perspective, this means that the cost of producing an additional unit of good Y is MPC + MEC = MSC since for every unit produced the firm foregoes the bribe. Once again, the externality is internalized and the equilibrium price and quantity are p^* and Y^* respectively.

WINNERS AND LOSERS

As far as efficient resource allocation is concerned, it makes no difference who obtains the property rights; however, the distribution of income, who wins and who loses, is affected.

Consumers of good Y are worse off regardless of who has the rights to clean water. In either case, output falls to Y^* and the price increases to p^*, so consumer surplus falls from p_cCH to p^*CE.

If, on the one hand, the people being harmed are given the property rights, then owners of resources employed in this industry and those affected by the externality are better off. After the assignment of property rights, firms receive from consumers p_cp^*EF in excess of production costs. However, owners of firms must pay nearby residents an amount equal to the total external costs associated with a production level of Y^* units of good Y. In Figure 15–8, this is equal to area P_cEF. After the assignment of property rights, there is a transfer of income from consumers to producers, area P_cBEF, and from producers to those being affected by the externality, area P_cEF. Thus, economic rent increases from zero to p_cp^*E and resource owners are better off. In addition to the payment made by producers, the nearby homeowners also benefit because there is less pollution. This reduction in external costs is given by area $FEGH$.

If, on the other hand, property rights are given to owners of firms, only resource owners gain. Those affected by the externality must now pay firms not to produce. If they pay the maximum amount they are willing to pay to have output reduced from Y_c to Y^*, then the payment to firms will be equal to the reduction in total external costs, or area $FEGH$. Since this is a gain and a loss, homeowners are neither better off nor worse off. Resource owners receive $p_c p^* EF$ from consumers as well as the payment from homeowners, $EGHF$, so they are definitely better off.

PROBLEMS ASSOCIATED WITH THE PROPERTY RIGHTS SOLUTION TO THE EXTERNALITY PROBLEM

Coase's solution to the externality problem is quite elegant: regulation is not needed; rather, we only need the government to assign and enforce property rights. However, this solution does not always resolve externality problems. To see why, let us ask ourselves exactly what the Coasian solution involves. This solution requires bargaining between two groups of individuals: producers and those being harmed by the externality. But what if the pollution is affecting thousands of individuals? If property rights were given to these individuals, then firms would have to negotiate a deal with all of them simultaneously. In this instance, the transactions costs associated with the bargaining process would be so great that it would not be worth the time or money. Firms simply would not negotiate and, thus, pollution would be zero, which is no better than the initial situation in which firms polluted freely, because production ceases altogether. If property rights are given to firms, then the thousands of homeowners must get together and agree on how much to pay the firms. Typically, the transactions costs involved in this instance would also be high enough to make bargaining impossible.

In addition, even if the numbers involved are small, another obstacle to Coasian bargaining arises: strategic behavior. As we noted in Chapter 13, if a small number of economic agents face each other, then, even though all parties may be better off by making an agreement, this is no guarantee that an agreement can be reached.

We must conclude, then, that it will be difficult for competitive markets to yield an efficient allocation of resources when externalities are present, even if property rights are assigned and enforced.

PUBLIC GOODS

Another situation which leads to market failure is the existence of public goods. **Public goods** differ from the private goods and services we have considered up till now in two important respects: they are characterized by *nonrival consumption* and *nonexclusion*.

If a good is nonrival in consumption, then, once the good is produced, its consumption by one individual does not reduce the quantity of it available for consumption by other individuals. If a good is nonrival in consumption, then the additional cost of serving another consumer is zero because all individuals can simultaneously consume the good.

If a good is nonexcludable in consumption, then, once the good is produced, it is impossible, or extremely costly, to exclude any person or persons from consuming the good. This means that it is possible for an individual to consume the good or service without having to pay for it.

Goods or services that exhibit both of these characteristics are called *pure public goods*. National defense, police and fire protection, eradication of insects that are harmful to crops or people, and public radio and television are all examples of pure public goods. If one person is protected by the services of national defense, for example, then everyone else is simultaneously protected by the same quantity of defense and it is impossible, or would be extremely costly, to exclude certain individuals from the benefits of national defense. National defense is nonrival and nonexcludable in consumption.

Another example of a pure public good is the eradication of insects that are harmful to crops or people. In some midwestern states, state and local governments routinely spray entire cities in order to eliminate mosquitoes. It would be virtually impossible to exclude a particular citizen from the benefits of the spraying and everyone benefits from the same quantity of spraying.

Certain goods have some, but not all, of the characteristics of pure public goods and are called *quasi-public goods*. Goods such as public parks and museums, bridges and roads, and public golf courses are quasi-public goods. Each of these goods is nonrival up to a certain point but then, as additional consumers are added, crowding or congestion begins to reduce the benefits to existing consumers. Each of these goods, however, is excludable. For example, public parks and museums can exclude individuals by charging admissions fees.

We have shown how markets fail to produce the efficient amounts of goods when externalities exist. The same argument can be made for public goods. Suppose that national defense could actually be made available to individual consumers in markets.

DETERMINING THE
EFFICIENT QUANTITY
OF PUBLIC GOOD

Since national defense is nonrival, the purchase of national defense by one individual would generate beneficial side effects for all citizens; that is, the consumption of a public good by one individual would generate externalities for others. Thus, market provision of goods whose benefits are shared by individuals other than those who purchase them for their own use will not lead to an efficient output of the good. Once again, government intervention will be needed if efficiency is to be attained.

Efficiency requires that the quantity of a public good being produced and consumed is such that the marginal social cost of production is equal to the marginal social benefit of consumption. If there are no production externalities, then the marginal social cost of production is simply the marginal private cost of production; that is, it is the opportunity cost of using resources to produce the public good rather than some other good. The costs of producing public goods are no different than the costs of producing other goods.

The marginal social benefit of consuming a public good is the sum of the marginal private benefits of all potential users of that good. Since a public good is nonrival, all individuals consume the good simultaneously, which means that they all benefit simultaneously. Thus, for a given quantity of public good we calculate marginal social benefit by adding together all the marginal private benefits. Notice that this is just the same result that would arise for a positive externality.

In order to demonstrate how to determine the efficient quantity of a public good, suppose that the city council of the community of Fisherville has decided to provide public television for the citizens of the community. There are two types of citizens residing in Fisherville: type A and type B individuals. The marginal benefit curves associated with each type are shown in Figure 15–10(a). If the marginal cost of broadcasting is constant, how do we determine the efficient number of hours of public television?

Since there are no externalities associated with producing a public television show, marginal social cost is equal to marginal private cost. In Figure 15–10(b), LS is the marginal social cost of producing public television. However, since public television is a public good, marginal social benefit is equal to the sum of the marginal private benefits of all residents. In Figure 15–10(b), MSB is the marginal social benefit curve for the community of Fisherville and is obtained by adding together the marginal benefits of all individual for each quantity of the public good. (This is called summing "vertically".)

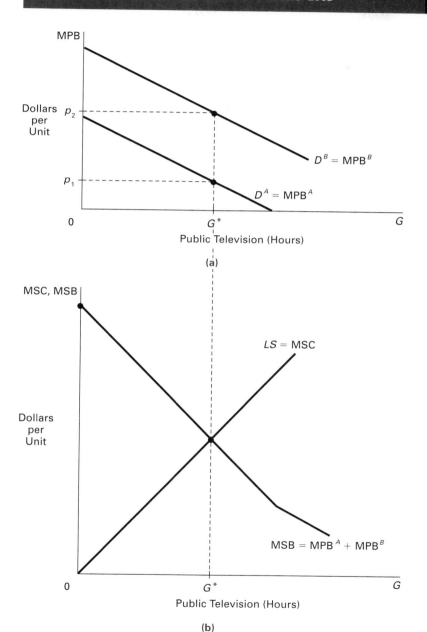

DETERMINING THE EFFICIENT QUANTITY OF A PUBLIC GOOD   **FIGURE 15–10**

Efficiency requires that MSB = MSC. In this instance, G* hours of public television is the efficient quantity.

The efficient number of hours corresponds to the intersection of the MSB and MSC curves. In this instance, the city should produce G^* hours of public television per day.

Private provision of goods that are nonrival and nonexcludable results in an inefficient allocation of resources—for the same reason that externalities cause economic inefficiencies. Once a public good is provided, everyone benefits regardless of whether or not they pay for it; that is, a given quantity of a public good generates benefits not only to those who pay for the good but also to those who do not pay. Economists call this the **free rider problem**. When a good or service is nonrival and nonexcludable, each individual has an incentive to free ride by letting others pay for the public good. Notice that, in this respect, public goods are just like positive externalities. When a positive externality exists, some individuals benefit without paying for those benefits.

When free rider behavior exists, competitive markets will not provide the efficient quantity of a public good and government intervention is warranted. To see why this is the case, consider the provision of public television for the citizens of the community of Fisherville discussed above. Public television is a public good for the residents of Fisherville in that everyone benefits and no one can be excluded at a reasonable cost. The question we want to address is, Will public television be provided without government intervention?

Private firms will be willing to provide public television if someone will pay them to do so. But who will pay? Just as with other types of goods, the individuals who benefit from consumption of the public good must pay. To finance public television the residents of Fisherville must all agree to pay their shares of the production costs.

One measure of an individual's appropriate share of the production costs is his or her marginal benefit. As shown in Figure 15–10(a), the marginal benefit to a type A individual if G^* hours of public television are provided is p_1 dollars per hour and the marginal benefit to a type B individual is p_2 per hour. Now, if each individual living in Fisherville would agree to contribute to a public television fund an amount equal to his or her marginal benefit, then the city council would have just enough money to pay for the public good.

However, getting individuals to contribute voluntarily to a public television fund is problematic. Since this is a public good, once shows are broadcasted all citizens of Fisherville will benefit whether they have paid their share of the production costs or not.

This means that each person has an incentive to understate the amount he or she is willing to pay to consume the public good. Even though public television generates positive benefits for each resident, each person has an incentive to free ride—that is, to state that the marginal private benefit of public television is zero so that he or she will not have to contribute to the public television fund. If there are enough individuals who free ride, then voluntary contributions will not be great enough to finance the broadcasts. In this instance, less than the efficient amount of the public good will be provided.

The government can overcome one aspect of the free rider problem by financing production of public goods with taxes or, in the case of quasi-public goods, with a combination of taxes and user charges. Individuals can be taxed according to their marginal benefits of consumption (called *marginal benefit taxation*) or they can be taxed according to their incomes (called *ability-to-pay taxation*). However, regardless of how the government raises tax revenues, one aspect of the free rider problem still remains: individuals still have no incentive to reveal their true preferences for public goods. In order to find the efficient amount of a public good to provide, we must know each individual's marginal benefit curve, and obtaining this information in practice is a difficult task. Resolving this difficulty is beyond the scope of this discussion; however, it is studied in detail in courses in Public Finance or Public Sector Economics.

Now let us use what we have learned about public goods to determine the efficient quantity of public television for Fisherville when we do, in fact, know the marginal benefit curves of the citizens.

EXAMPLE 15–3

PUBLIC TELEVISION

Suppose Fisherville city council has hired us as economic consultants to recommend an efficient quantity of public television and a way to finance these services. The council has given us the following information to aid us in doing our analysis:

1. The marginal benefit curves for public television are $MB^A = 1 - .06G$ and $MB^B = 5 - .14G$ where G is broadcast hours.
2. There are 100 citizens of each type.

3. The marginal cost of producing public television is constant at $400 per hour.

■ **SOLUTION** In order to determine the efficient quantity of the public good, we must find the level of services for which MSB = MSC. Since there are no externalities in production, MSC = MPC = $400. Since we are dealing with public good,

$$MSB = MSB^A + MSB^B = 100 \cdot MB^A + 100 \cdot MB^B$$

$$= 100(1 - .06G) + 100(5 - .14G) = 600 - 20G.$$

Setting MSB equal to MSC, $600 - 20G = 400$, and solving for G gives: $G^* = 10$ hours per day.

Next, we must find a way to finance the provision of 10 hours of public television per day. Since we have the marginal benefit curves, we can use marginal benefit taxation to finance provision of the public good. Substituting the efficient level of production into each marginal benefit curve gives: $MB^A(10) = 1 - .06 \cdot 10 = \$.40$ per hour and $MB^B(10) = 5 - .14 \cdot 10 = \$3.60$ per hour. Thus, each type A individual will pay $10 \cdot .40 = \$4$ per day in taxes, while each type B individual will pay $10 \cdot 3.60 = \$36$ per day in taxes. Note that total revenue collected will be exactly $400 per day, just enough to cover production costs. ■

1. Economic efficiency is a normative criterion for evaluating any allocation of resources. Economic efficiency is attained when no one can be made better off without making someone else worse off.

2. An allocation of resources is efficient if marginal social benefit is equal to marginal social cost. This is called the marginal efficiency condition and is used in most practical applications. Further, in the absence of government intervention, perfect competition yields an efficient allocation of resources.

3. While the efficiency criterion is very useful, it is not the only way to judge economic performance. In particular, many people argue that equity considerations are just as important, or even more important, than efficiency considerations. In many instances, policy makers must confront a trade-off between equity and efficiency.

4. There are four instances where competitive markets do not generate an efficient allocation of resources: government intervention, monopolistic power, externalities, and public goods. Each of these types of market failure occurs because prices do not accurately reflect the marginal social benefits and costs of production and consumption.

5. Externalities are side effects of market transactions. They affect individuals not participating in these market activities. Externalities are either costs or benefits not accounted for when individuals make their consumption and production choices. As a result, externalities lead to an inefficient allocation of resources. In the case of a positive externality, too little of a good is produced; in the case of a negative externality, too much is produced. In order to internalize, or correct for, the externality, the government intervenes. Levying corrective taxes and assigning property rights are two ways of internalizing externalities.

6. Public goods are goods that are nonrival and nonexcludable in consumption. For public goods, marginal social benefit is equal to the sum of all marginal private benefits of potential users of the public good. Just as is the case with externalities, competitive markets will not yield efficient quantities of public goods. The free rider problem arises making it unlikely that private arrangements will yield the efficient amount of the public good. Once again, the government must intervene if efficiency is to be attained.

SUMMARY

TERMS

Economic Efficiency	Marginal Social Benefit and
Marginal Efficiency Condition	Marginal Social Cost

First Optimality Theorem   Corrective Taxes
Equity   Property Rights
Market Failure   Public Goods
Externalities   Free Rider Problem
Marginal External Cost

QUESTIONS AND PROBLEMS

1. a) Define economic efficiency.
   b) Why might economic efficiency be a goal of policy makers?
   c) Should economic efficiency alone be used to evaluate a particular allocation of resources?

2. a) State and explain the marginal efficiency condition.
   b) Why does perfect competition lead to economic efficiency?
   c) Using the marginal efficiency condition, explain why import restrictions such as quotas lead to an inefficient allocation of resources.

3. Suppose that marginal cost is zero for a monopolist.
   a) Illustrate the profit-maximizing level of production.
   b) Is this the efficient level of production? Explain.

4. a) Define what economists mean by an externality.
   b) Why will private markets produce an inefficient allocation of resources when there are externalities?

5. a) If there is a positive externality associated with the production or consumption of some good, will a private competitive market result in overproduction or underproduction of the good?
   b) Illustrate your answer with a graph.

6. Environmentalists often argue for the elimination of such things as air and water pollution. Evaluate their argument on efficiency grounds.

7. a) What do economists mean when they talk of internalizing an externality?
   b) Is government intervention always necessary to internalize an externality?

8. Recently there has been a major controversy concerning oil exploration off the coasts of the United States. Suppose the government hires you to resolve the conflict between environmentalists and oil companies. Explain how you would determine the efficient quantity of shoreline to be set aside for conservation. (Discuss a tax on oil producers that would internalize the externality. Be sure to point out who wins and who loses as a result of the tax.)

9. In the past, conservation groups have been successful in having

laws passed prohibiting the killing of eagles. Western ranchers have ignored these laws and killed eagles to protect their livestock. The government has been unable to enforce these laws and the eagle is in danger of becoming extinct. Discuss an alternative to the assignment of property rights as a solution to this externality problem.

10. In the mid 1980s, the residents of Bryan, Texas, convinced the Texas Railroad Commission to order several oil companies with producing wells within the city limits to shut down their operations because of excessive flaring. (Flaring occurs when the natural gas, a by-product of drilling and pumping oil, is burned continuously in an open pit.)

a) Is this an efficient solution to the externality problem? Explain.

b) Carefully explain how to determine an emissions fee that would internalize this externality.

c) Compare this to an assignment of property rights that would, if feasible, lead to an efficient level of oil production.

11. a) What characteristics define a public good?

b) Will private markets produce an efficient quantity of a public good? Explain.

12. Suppose the city of Greenridge has hired you as an economic consultant to recommend an efficient amount of police protection services for the city per year. You have the following information:

(1) $MB^A = 100 - 10G$, $MB^B = -20G$.

(2) There are 20 citizens of each type in the community.

(3) The marginal private cost of providing police protection is given by $LMC = 220 + 290G$, where G is the number of police officers hired per year.

a) What is the efficient number of officers to hire per year?

b) If citizens are taxed according to their marginal benefits, how much will each citizen pay in taxes?

c) Will the revenue generated from such taxes cover the cost of providing the efficient quantity of police protection? Explain. (A diagram may help.)

13. a) Why does the free rider problem make the financing of public goods by voluntary contributions unlikely?

b) Describe a situation where free riding may not be a problem.

14. Suppose that a city is planning additional swimming facilities. The city council has hired you to recommend

a) an efficient number of pools, and

b) a way to finance their construction.

You have the following information:

(1) The marginal benefit curve for any family in the community is MPB = $50C - S$, where S is the number of swimming pools and C is the number of children in the family.

(2) The community consists of 10 families with no children, 10 with 1 child, and 10 with 2 children.

(3) The marginal cost of providing pools is a constant $1,350 per pool.

REFERENCES   Atkinson, A., and J. Stiglitz. 1980. *Lectures on Public Economics.* New York: McGraw-Hill.

Browning, E., and J. Browning. 1987. *Public Finance and the Price System.* 3d ed. New York: Macmillan.

GENERAL EQUILIBRIUM AND ECONOMIC EFFICIENCY

LEARNING OBJECTIVES

After completing Chapter 16 you should be able to do the following:

■ Define a general equilibrium and explain when general equilibrium analysis should be used.

■ Describe the marginal efficiency conditions.

■ Discuss how competitive markets lead to economic efficiency.

■ Compare the exchange contract curve, the production contract curve, and the product transformation curve.

■ Analyze the economic effects of a change in demand and monopoly using general equilibrium analysis.

EXAMPLES

■ **16-1** Finding Multi-Market Prices and Quantities

■ **16-2** Relative Prices in a Pure Exchange Economy

■ **16-3** The Gains from International Trade

In previous chapters we have focused on the way in which the interaction of supply and demand determines the equilibrium price and quantity in a single market. The supply and demand curves we used in our analyses were drawn assuming that prices of other goods and inputs were given. In this *partial equilibrium* framework, we viewed each market as independent; that is, a change in one market did not significantly affect other markets.

In reality, however, markets are very much interrelated. (Recall the discussion of the circular flow of economic activity in Chapter 1.) In many instances, one market's adjustment to a change in the economic environment will have a substantial impact on other markets. For example, if the demand for televisions increases, then the equilibrium price and quantity of televisions both increase. Previously we assumed that this adjustment in the television market did not affect prices and quantities in other markets. However, this assumption may be wrong. The market for televisions is not independent of the markets for other electronic products such as videocassette recorders, stereos, or video games. Thus, any change in the market for televisions will affect the equilibrium of other markets, and the changes that occur in these other markets will, in turn, have an effect on the television market.

Partial equilibrium analysis is appropriate when the effects of a change in the economic environment in one market have little repercussion on prices and quantities in other markets. For example, when we studied the effects of an excise tax on cigarettes in Chapter 11, the assumption that prices of other goods and services were fixed seemed to be an adequate representation of reality. However, if, in fact, the tax on cigarettes causes a substantial number of consumers to switch to cigars, we would need to modify our analysis in Chapter 11 to account for this. When changes in one market have substantial repercussions in other markets we must turn to *general equilibrium analysis*.

In this chapter we first discuss general equilibrium analysis and point out how one market can affect other markets. We will be concerned only with a perfectly competitive economy; that is, an economy in which all producers and consumers are price takers. Next we discuss economic efficiency in a general equilibrium setting, beginning with the exchange of goods between individuals. We then go on to describe the conditions that an economy must satisfy if goods and services are to be produced and distributed efficiently and to show how perfectly competitive markets satisfy the efficiency conditions. Finally, we use general equilibrium analysis to analyze the economic effects of a change in demand and monopoly.

■ In Chapter 9 we stated that in a competitive equilibrium for a single market resources are allocated in such a way that consumers maximize satisfaction, producers maximize profit, supply is equal to demand, and firms earn zero economic profit in the long run. A *general equilibrium* is defined analogously, only now we must take into account all markets simultaneously.

In **general equilibrium** resources are allocated in such a way that each consumer maximizes satisfaction subject to his or her budget constraint; each firm maximizes profit subject to the available technology; supply is equal to demand in every market (input and output markets), and each firm earns zero economic profit in the long run.

Given this definition, we may well ask whether such an equilibrium even exists. This is an important question and one that economic theorists have studied extensively. While a detailed discussion of the existence of a general equilibrium is beyond the scope of this text, we can show that such an equilibrium can be achieved under a broad set of conditions in a perfectly competitive economy. Now let us turn our attention to the task of finding the conditions that characterize a general equilibrium and the associated allocation of resources.

In most practical applications, we cannot do a complete general equilibrium analysis. It is simply too difficult to evaluate the effects of a change in one market on all other input and output markets in the economy. Instead, we usually confine our analyses to those markets that are closely related. For example, when looking at an excise tax on cigarettes, we might also consider the markets for cigars and pipe tobacco.

To illustrate how markets are interrelated and how they adjust to equilibrium, let us consider two perfectly competitive output markets: the markets for audiocassettes and compact discs. These two markets are closely related because most albums are available on both cassette and compact disc.

Figure 16–1 shows the supply and demand curves for cassettes and compact discs. In Figure 16–1(a), the initial equilibrium price and quantity in the cassette, good X, market are p_x^1 and X_1 respectively. In Figure 16–1(b), the initial equilibrium price and quantity in the compact disc, good Y, market are p_y^1 and Y_1 respectively.

Now suppose the government levies an excise tax on producers of cassettes. We can use a partial equilibrium analysis to determine how the tax affects the cassette market, just as we did in Chapter 11. The tax shifts the long-run supply curve up by the amount of the

16.1 THE DEFINITION OF GENERAL EQUILIBRIUM

AN EXAMPLE OF TWO CLOSELY RELATED MARKETS

FIGURE 16–1   **TWO INTERRELATED MARKETS**

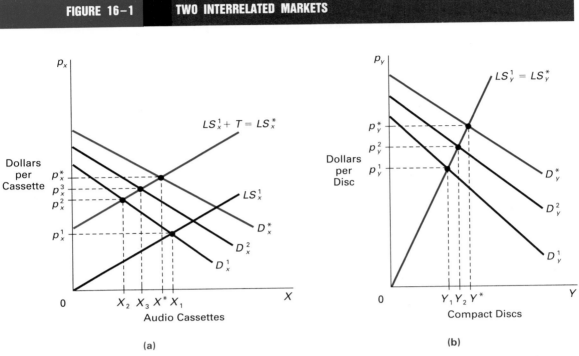

(a)

(b)

When two markets are closely related, we must consider the general equilibrium effects of a policy change. (a) A tax on audiocassette producers causes the supply curve to shift up from LS_x^1 to $LS_x^1 + T$, which in turn causes the price of cassettes to rise. The higher price of cassettes initially causes the demand for compact discs to increase from D_y^1 to D_y^2 which in turn causes the price of compact discs to rise. Similarly, the higher price of compact discs causes the demand for cassettes to increase from D_x^1 to D_x^2, which in turn causes the price of cassettes to rise even further. This process continues until general equilibrium is attained once again. This is shown as the intersection of D_x^* and LS_x^* in (a) and D_y^* and LS_y^* in (b).

tax, LS_x^1 to $LS_x^1 + T$ in Figure 16–1(a). Initially, this causes the price of cassettes to rise from p_x^1 to p_x^2 and quantity to fall from X_1 to X_2. In Chapter 11, this is where we stopped. However, since these two markets are closely related we can go further and look at how changes in the cassette market affect the compact disc market and how changes in the compact disc market affect the cassette market.

The initial demand curve for compact discs was drawn assuming that the price of cassettes was p_x^1 dollars per cassette. Because cassettes and compact discs are substitute goods, Figure 16–1(b) shows that the increase in the price of cassettes will cause an increase in the demand for compact discs. This is represented by the shift in the demand curve for compact discs from D_y^1 to D_y^2. This, in turn, causes the price of compact discs to increase from p_y^1 to p_y^2. That is, the tax on one good also has an impact on the prices of closely related goods.

Now, what about the cassette market? Remember, demand curve D_x^1 was drawn assuming that the price of compact discs was p_y^1; however, this is no longer true. The price of compact discs has increased to p_y^2 dollars per compact disc so the demand curve for cassettes will shift to the right from D_x^1 to D_x^2. The new equilibrium price is now p_x^3 dollars per cassette and the new equilibrium quantity is X_3. Notice that a partial equilibrium analysis of the effects of the tax would have underestimated the price increase and overestimated the reduction in quantity. This is why we should use a general equilibrium analysis when markets are closely related.

This process continues until the markets once again reach equilibrium. The equilibrium prices and quantities associated with a new equilibrium are found by equating demand and supply in both markets simultaneously. In Figure 16–1, the intersections of demand and supply curves D_x^* and LS_x^* and demand and supply curves D_y^* and LS_y^* give the new equilibrium prices and quantities. These are the equilibrium demand curves because D_x^* is drawn assuming the price of compact discs is p_y^* and D_y^* is drawn assuming the price of cassettes is p_x^*.

The next example demonstrates how we can find multi-market prices and quantities when explicit supply and demand functions are known.

EXAMPLE 16–1

FINDING MULTI-MARKET PRICES AND QUANTITIES

Suppose the demand and supply curves for audiocassette tapes and compact discs per month are given by

$$X^D = 5 - p_x + .5p_y \quad \text{and} \quad X^S = p_x$$

$$Y^D = 15 - p_y + p_x \quad \text{and} \quad Y^S = p_y$$

where X and Y are thousands of audiocassette tapes and compact discs per month respectively. Find the equilibrium prices and quantities.

■ **SOLUTION** In order to find the equilibrium price and quantities we must solve these equations simultaneously. Setting supply equal to demand in each market we have

$$2p_x - .5p_y - 5 = 0 \qquad \text{and}$$

$$2p_y - p_x - 15 = 0.$$

Solving the second equation for p_y and substituting into the first equation gives

$$p_x = 2.5 + .25(7.5 + .5p_x),$$

or $p_x^* = \$5$ and $p_y^* = 7.5 + .5p_x^* = \$10$. Thus, when both markets are in equilibrium, 5,000 (X^*) audiocassettes will be bought and sold per month for \$5 per cassette, and 10,000 (Y^*) compact discs will be bought and sold per month for \$10 per disc. ■

Example 16–1 illustrates the basic technique used to solve for equilibrium prices and quantities when two markets are interrelated. Now we turn to another issue that general equilibrium analysis can help us understand more fully—economic efficiency.

16.2 ECONOMIC EFFICIENCY IN EXCHANGE

■ In Chapter 15 we saw that economic efficiency in a partial equilibrium framework meant an allocation of resources such that marginal social benefit equals marginal social cost. We also saw that, in the absence of government intervention, a competitive market (with no externalities or public goods) yields an efficient allocation of resources. In the remainder of this chapter, we will investigate the notion of economic efficiency in more detail. In particular, we will discuss economic efficiency as it relates to the allocation of products among consumers, the allocation of inputs among producers, and the allocation of resources across the economy as a whole.

THE MARGINAL EFFICIENCY CONDITION FOR THE ALLOCATION OF PRODUCTS AMONG CONSUMERS

The marginal efficiency condition for the allocation of products among consumers, also referred to as the marginal efficiency condition for exchange, can be determined by focusing on a very simple economy. Suppose there are only two individuals, Smith and McCoy, and two goods, X and Y. There is no production in this economy, so the only economic problem is the allocation of a given amount of X and Y between the two consumers.

Prior to trading, Smith and McCoy have an *endowment* of each of the two goods. Since there is no production, endowments cannot be expanded. At the beginning of each trading session, individuals receive their endowments. During the session, individuals bring the goods and services making up their endowments to the market with the hope of exchanging some of their goods for a preferred bundle of goods. After all trades are consummated, individuals consume the commodities they possess. The question we want to answer is, What is the equilibrium allocation of goods between Smith and McCoy if they are free to trade with each other?

The device we use to examine the allocation of fixed total quantities of two goods between two consumers is the **Edgeworth exchange box diagram** (named for F. Y. Edgeworth, a nineteenth-century political economist, who suggested its use in 1881 in his "Mathematical Psychics: An Essay on the Application of Mathematics to the Moral Sciences," New York: August Kelly, 1953). Figure 16–2 shows the box diagram for Smith and McCoy. Mr. Smith's endowment consists of X_0^S units of good X and Y_0^S units of good Y, while Ms. McCoy's endowment consists of X_0^M units of

THE TRADING SET   **FIGURE 16–2**

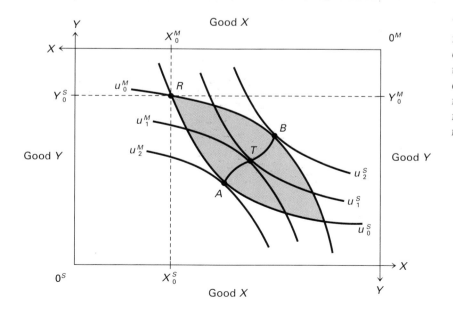

The shaded area represents the trading set associated with R. It is the collection of commodity bundles that make one or both individuals better off and neither worse off.

good S and Y_0^M units of good Y. In Figure 16–2, the endowment commodity bundles for Smith and McCoy are represented by point R. The dimensions of the box correspond to the total stocks of goods in the economy: $\overline{X} = X_0^S + X_0^M$ and $\overline{Y} = Y_0^S + Y_0^M$.

Each point in the box diagram represents an allocation of goods between Smith and McCoy. Given their endowments, Smith and McCoy begin the trading session at point R in the Edgeworth box diagram. At this point, their indifference curves intersect. The indifference curve labeled u_0^S represents Smith's level of satisfaction when he has his endowment. Indifference curve u_0^M represents McCoy's level of satisfaction when she has her endowment.

The only trades possible are those resulting in a mutually beneficial exchange of commodities. Given his endowment, Smith will trade if he can obtain a commodity bundle on an indifference curve to the northeast of u_0^S and McCoy will trade if she can obtain a commodity bundle on an indifference curve to the southwest of u_0^M. This means that the *trading set* associated with R—the collection of commodity bundles that make either individual better off and neither worse off—is the shaded area in Figure 16–2. It is all the points between u_0^S and u_0^M.

If Smith and McCoy exchange commodities, we know that the resulting distribution of goods will be represented by some point in the trading set. Smith and McCoy will trade commodities until all gains from trade are realized or, in other words, until no one can be made better off without making someone else worse off. This occurs when Smith's and McCoy's indifference curves are tangent; that is, when $MRS_{xy}^S = MRS_{xy}^M$, no one can be made better off without making someone else worse off. Thus, the marginal efficiency condition for the allocation of products among consumers is

$$MRS_{xy}^S = MRS_{xy}^M \qquad (16.1)$$

Equation (16.1) indicates that all gains from trade are realized when the marginal rate of substitution between any pair of products is the same for all individuals who consume both goods. If this condition does not hold, one or more consumers can benefit from further exchange of goods without harming anyone. In Figure 16–2, the allocation of goods represented by point T is such an allocation. At this point, no one can be made better off without making someone else worse off, which means that T is an efficient allocation of goods.

Within the trading set there are many points that satisfy the efficiency criterion. To find all possible efficient allocations of goods between Smith and McCoy, we would look for all points of tangency between their indifference curves within the trading set. Figure 16–2 shows the curve drawn through all such efficient allocations; it is called the *core* of the economy.

The core of the economy encompasses all efficient allocations that are possible given a particular endowment of goods. However, we can also find all the efficient allocations within the entire Edgeworth box. Figure 16–3 shows the curve drawn through all such efficient allocations; it is called the **exchange contract curve**. The contract curve shows all allocations of goods that satisfy the marginal efficiency condition for the allocation of products among consumers.

Since every point on the contract curve represents an efficient allocation of goods between Smith and McCoy, we cannot determine which point on the contract curve is "better" using only the efficiency criterion. There is no way we can move from point C, for example, to point D without making one person worse off.

While each point on the contract curve represents an efficient allocation of goods, each point also represents a different distribution of economic well-being between the two consumers. Thus, one

THE EXCHANGE CONTRACT CURVE   **FIGURE 16–3**

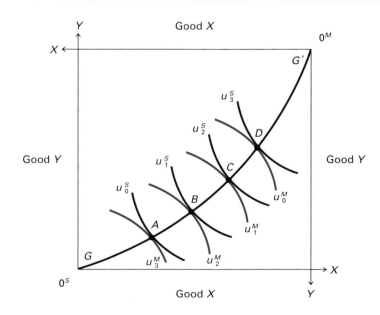

GG' is the exchange contract curve. It represents all efficient allocations of goods between consumers.

way to choose between points on the contract curve would be choose the distribution of economic well-being deemed *equitable*. For example, suppose Smith controls this economy. He may consider allocation *D* better than allocation *C* because he is better off with *D* and, according to his subjective evaluation, *D* is a more equitable allocation of goods. Efficiency implies that we should make all mutually beneficial trades, but it does not tell us which trades are best. We must use another criterion to choose between efficient allocations.

EXCHANGE EFFICIENCY WHEN MARKETS ARE COMPETITIVE

In a two person exchange economy, the outcome can depend on the bargaining strengths of the individuals. However, in competitive markets there are many buyers and sellers, so individuals may trade with those offering the best terms of trade. As a result, buyers and sellers take prices as given and determine how much to buy and sell at those prices. We can show how competitive markets lead to efficiency by using the Edgeworth box diagram to simulate a competitive market. To do this, suppose that Smith and McCoy are the representative or average consumers from a large group of consumers. This means that we can think of Smith and McCoy as price takers even though we are using a two person Edgeworth box diagram.

In a partial equilibrium framework, we found the equilibrium price and quantity by equating demand and supply. We must do the same thing here only we have to be sure that all markets clear simultaneously. But, in this pure exchange model, just what are supply and demand?

In order to demonstrate what we mean by supply and demand and to determine which point in the trading set is the equilibrium point, let us consider each individual's budget constraint. The budget constraints for Smith and McCoy are determined by each individual's income and the prevailing market prices. Let p_x be the price of good X, p_y the price of good Y, I^S Smith's income, and I^M McCoy's income. In a pure exchange model, income is simply the value of one's endowment. Thus, Smith's income is

$$I^S = p_x X_0^S + p_y Y_0^S.$$

I^S is the amount of purchasing power that Smith would have if he sold his entire endowment.

In order to relate what we are doing here to the consumer's optimization problem discussed in Chapter 3, suppose for the moment that Smith does sell his entire endowment and then uses the proceeds to buy goods. In this instance, Smith's budget constraint is

$$I^S = p_x X^S + p_y Y^S.$$

This budget constraint represents the requirement that the value of the goods Smith purchases and consumes must be equal to his income.

Now we can write Smith's budget constraint in terms of his endowment by substituting for I^S:

$$p_x X_0^S + p_y Y_0^S = p_x X^S + p_y Y^S$$

or, rearranging:

$$p_x(X^S - X_0^S) + p_y(Y^S - Y_0^S) = 0. \qquad (16.2)$$

Written in this fashion, Smith's budget constraint guarantees that the value of the goods that Smith buys is equal to the value of the goods that he sells.

Economists call the difference between the quantity of a good an individual consumes and his or her endowment the consumer's *excess demand* for that good. For example, Smith's excess demand for good X, denoted by E_x^S, is equal to $(X^S - X_0^S)$ and his excess demand for good Y, denoted by E_y^S, is equal to $(Y^S - Y_0^S)$. If Smith is a net demander of a particular good, then his excess demand for that good is positive; that is, the quantity he consumes is greater than his endowment. If Smith is a net supplier of a particular good, then his excess demand for that good is negative; that is, the quantity he consumes is less than his endowment.

Equation (16.1), Smith's budget constraint, can be written in terms of his excess demand for each commodity:

$$p_x E_x^S + p_y E_y^S = 0. \qquad (16.3)$$

This equation shows that the net value of Smith's excess demands must be zero. If this were not true, he would be violating his budget constraint.

Figure 16–4 graphs Smith's budget constraint, BC_1. The X-intercept of this budget constraint is I^S/p_x, the Y-intercept is I^S/p_y and the slope is minus the price ratio, $-p_x/p_y$. Budget constraint BC_1 must pass through point R, the endowment bundle, since Smith's income is equal to the value of his endowment.

FIGURE 16-4 **BUDGET CONSTRAINTS AND THE EDGEWORTH BOX DIAGRAM**

Budget constraint BC$_1$ divides the Edgeworth box into two parts—Smith's and McCoy's attainable sets. The price ratio is the slope of BC$_1$.

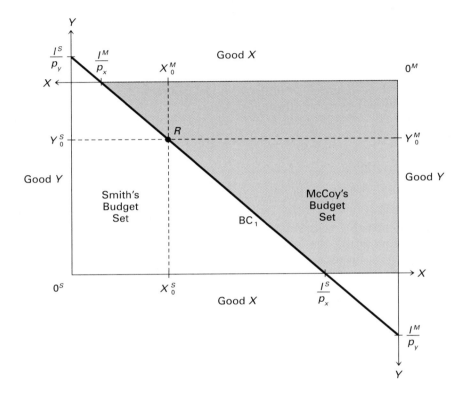

Similarly, we can depict McCoy's budget constraint in Figure 16–4. It too must pass through the endowment point, R. McCoy's budget constraint is given by

$$p_x X_0^M + p_y Y_0^M = I^M = p_x X^M + p_y Y^M \qquad \text{or}$$

$$p_x(X^M - X_0^M) + p_y(Y^M - Y_0^M) = p_x E_x^M + p_y E_y^M = 0.$$

The X-intercept of this budget constraint is I^M/p_x, the Y-intercept is I^M/p_y, and the slope is minus the price ratio, $-p_x/p_y$. Thus, McCoy's budget constraint, viewed from 0^M, is also the line labeled BC$_1$ in Figure 16–4.

Now let us put the individuals' indifference curves and the budget constraint together in one diagram. This is shown in Figure 16–5. Notice that if this economy moves from point R to any point in the trading set, Smith will be a net demander of good X and a net supplier of good Y, while McCoy will be a net supplier of good X and a net demander of good Y. This is precisely what we mean by supply and demand in a pure exchange economy. Smith demands good X and supplies good Y, while McCoy demands good Y and supplies good X.

Now suppose that, given BC_1, Smith maximizes satisfaction by moving from point R to point B, which involves exchanging good X for good Y. At point B Smith is maximizing satisfaction since his indifference curve is tangent to his budget constraint; that is, for Smith the marginal rate of substitution between X and Y is equal to the price ratio; that is, $MRS^S_{xy} = p_x/p_y$. Thus, given his endowment (income) and these particular prices, Smith would like to purchase $(X^S_1 - X^S_0)$ units of good X and he would like to sell $(Y^S_0 - Y^S_1)$ units of good Y.

McCoy, on the other hand, maximizes satisfaction by moving from point R to A which involves exchanging good Y for good X. At point A McCoy is maximizing satisfaction since her indifference

EXCESS SUPPLY AND DEMAND   FIGURE 16−5

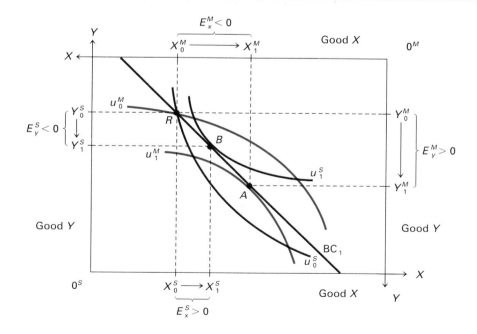

At points A and B the marginal rates of substitution are the same for Smith and McCoy. However, markets do not clear. There is excess demand for good X and excess supply of good Y.

curve is tangent to her budget constraint; that is, for McCoy MRS_{xy}^M = p_x/p_y. Thus, given her endowment (income) and these particular prices, McCoy would like to purchase $(Y_1^M - Y_0^M)$ units of good Y and she would like to sell $(X_0^M - X_1^M)$ units of good X.

Do the prevailing market prices, as reflected by the slope of BC_1, provide us with a general equilibrium? While it is true that both Smith and McCoy are maximizing satisfaction, Smith wants to buy less of good X than McCoy wants to sell, while Smith wants to sell less of good Y than McCoy wants to buy. Thus, supply is greater than demand in the X market, while demand is greater than supply in the Y market, and neither market clears. These prices and quantities are not the equilibrium prices and quantities.

In order to find the prices that generate a general equilibrium, the price ratio must change until we find the market clearing prices. If we can find a price ratio for which all markets clear, then we will have determined the general equilibrium prices and quantities.

Since the supply of good X is greater than demand, competition will cause the price of X to fall. Likewise, since the demand for Y is greater than supply, competition will force the price of Y higher. The end result is that competitive pressure will force the price ratio, p_x/p_y, to fall.

As the price ratio falls, the budget constraint rotates about the endowment point and the optimal commodity bundle for each individual changes. Smith's demand for good Y falls in response to the increase in the price of Y, and McCoy's demand for X rises in response to the decrease in the price of X. This process continues until supply is equal to demand in each market.

A general equilibrium for the pure exchange economy is shown in Figure 16–6. The equilibrium allocation of commodities is represented by point T in the trading set. At T each individual maximizes satisfaction given endowments and prices, and supply is equal to demand for both goods. At any other point in the trading set, markets will not clear. The equilibrium price ratio is given by the slope of the budget constraint passing through points R and T. Given this budget constraint, all markets clear. The supply of good X is equal to the demand, $(X_1^S - X_0^S) = (X_0^M - X_1^M)$, and the supply of good Y is equal to the demand, $(Y_1^M - Y_0^M) = (Y_0^S - Y_1^S)$. Further, since individuals are faced with the same prices, the marginal rate of substitution between X and Y is the same for both individuals; that is, $\text{MRS}_{xy}^S = \text{MRS}_{xy}^M = p_x/p_y$.

We can see from point T in Figure 16–6 that the allocation of goods in a competitive equilibrium is efficient. Point T must occur at a point of tangency between Smith's and McCoy's indifference curves. This result holds in both an exchange framework and in a

GENERAL EQUILIBRIUM IN A PURE EXCHANGE ECONOMY   **FIGURE 16–6**

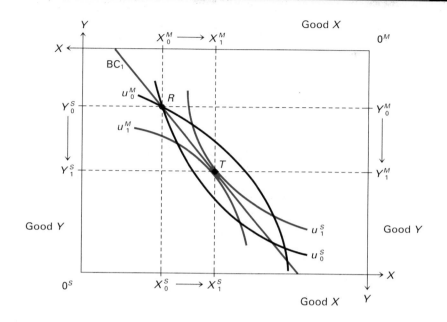

All conditions for equilibrium are met at point T. At T each individual maximizes satisfaction given endowments and prices, and all markets clear. The equilibrium exchange rate is given by the slope of BC_1.

general equilibrium framework in which all markets are competitive. The "invisible hand" works!

Summarizing, from the consumer's perspective resources in a general equilibrium are allocated in such a way that:

$$MRS_{xy}^S = MRS_{xy}^M = p_x/p_y, \qquad (16.4)$$

$$X^S + X^M = \overline{X}, \qquad (16.5)$$

and $$Y^S + Y^M = \overline{Y}. \qquad (16.6)$$

Equation (16.4) guarantees that individuals maximize satisfaction, while (16.5) and (16.6) guarantee that both markets clear simultaneously.

If all markets are perfectly competitive, an efficient allocation of resources will emerge; however, this is not the only means of achieving efficiency. For example, in a command economy, where the central government allocates goods and services, efficiency can also be achieved. One reason the competitive mechanism is often preferred to others is that it requires the least amount of information. Consumers need to know only their own preferences and the prices they face. They do not need to know who produces each good or service or the preferences of other consumers. Other mechanisms, such as the command economy, need much more information to achieve efficiency and, as a result, are more difficult and costly to manage.

In the next example, we are asked to find the general equilibrium prices and quantities in a pure exchange economy. As we work through this problem, we will discover a very interesting result: the equilibrium conditions above allow us to solve for relative prices but they do not allow us to determine absolute prices; that is, they do not allow us to determine the level of prices in the economy.

EXAMPLE 16–2

RELATIVE PRICES IN A PURE EXCHANGE ECONOMY

Robinson Crusoe, consumer A, and Man Friday, consumer B, are stranded on a deserted island. Crusoe has in his possession all the island's coconuts, good X, and Man Friday has in his possession all the island's bananas, good Y. There are a total of 100 coconuts and 100 bananas on the island.

Both Crusoe and Man Friday have the same tastes for coconuts and bananas and these preferences are such that the marginal rate of substitution between coconuts and bananas is equal to the ratio of bananas to coconuts; that is,

$$\text{MRS}_{xy}^{A} = Y^{A}/X^{A} \quad \text{and} \quad \text{MRS}_{xy}^{B} = Y^{B}/X^{B}.$$

(a) Draw the Edgeworth box diagram that represents the possibilities for exchange in this situation. (b) Determine equilibrium prices and quantities.

■ **SOLUTION** (a) The appropriate Edgeworth box diagram is shown in Figure 16–7. The reference point for Crusoe, individual A, is the southwest corner of the box while the reference point for Man Friday, individual B, is the northeast corner. The box is a square since there are 100 of both goods. The endowment commodity bundles are represented by point R which is the southeast corner of the box.

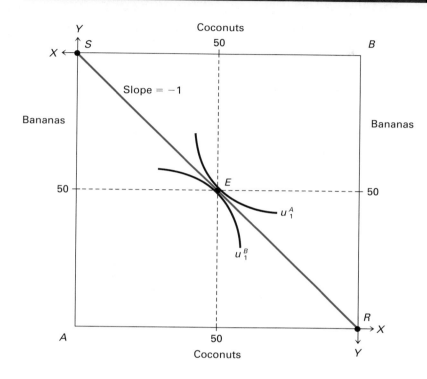

GENERAL EQUILIBRIUM FOR CRUSOE AND MAN FRIDAY

FIGURE 16–7

Given the initial allocation of bananas and coconuts, point E represents the competitive allocation of goods, and the slope of RS gives the equilibrium exchange rate.

(b) Equilibrium requires that each consumer maximizes satisfaction and that all markets clear. In order to find the market clearing price ratio we must derive each individual's excess demands for both goods. Consider first Robinson Crusoe. We assume that he maximizes satisfaction subject to his budget constraint. Since Crusoe is endowed with 100 coconuts and no bananas, his budget constraint is given by

$$P_x X^A + p_y Y^A = p_x X_0^A = p_x 100,$$

where p_x and p_y denote the prices of coconuts and bananas respectively.

Crusoe maximizes satisfaction by choosing a commodity bundle satisfying his budget constraint and for which the $MRS_{xy}^A = p_x/p_y$; that is, Crusoe chooses a commodity bundle for which $p_x(X^A - 100) + p_y Y^A = 0$ and $Y^A/X^A = p_x/p_y$.

Now we can derive Robinson's excess demand curves. Rewriting the two optimization conditions in terms of Crusoe's excess demand functions we have

$$E_Y^A/(E_X^A + 100) = p_x/p_y \qquad \text{and}$$

$$p_x E_x^A + p_y E_Y^A = 0.$$

Solving the second equation (the budget constraint) for E_Y^A and substituting into the first equation gives

$$(-p_x/p_y)[E_X^A/(E_X^A + 100)] = p_x/p_y.$$

Solving this last equation for E_X^A gives Crusoe's excess demand for coconuts: $E_X^A = -100/2 = -50$.

Crusoe's excess demand for coconuts is negative which means that he is a supplier of coconuts. Obviously, this had to be the case

---

FIGURE 16–8   **CRUSOE'S OPTIMIZATION PROBLEM**

Given the price ratio and his endowment, Crusoe maximizes satisfaction by choosing commodity bundle A on indifference curve u_1^A.

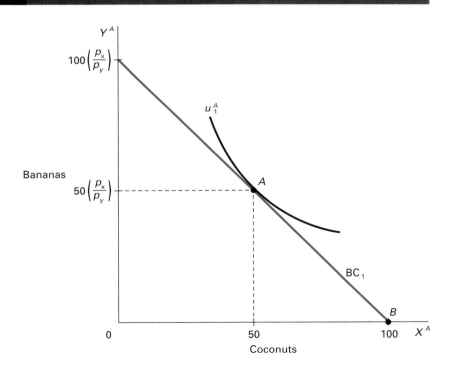

since Crusoe is endowed with all the coconuts and none of the bananas. Also, note that his excess demand for coconuts is independent of prices. Crusoe is willing to trade half his coconuts for bananas at any positive rate of exchange.

Robinson's excess demand for bananas follows immediately. From his budget constraint we know that $E_Y^A = -E_x^A(p_x/p_y)$. Substituting for E_x^A, we have $E_Y^A = 50(p_x/p_y)$. Crusoe's excess demand for bananas is positive, which means that he is a demander of bananas. Also, his excess demand for bananas is positively related to the price ratio. The more expensive coconuts are relative to bananas, the more bananas Crusoe demands in exchange for his 50 coconuts.

In Figure 16–8 we have illustrated the solution to Crusoe's optimization problem for an arbitrary exchange rate. Initially Crusoe possesses commodity bundle B which contains $X_0^A = 100$ coconuts. Given BC_1, Crusoe maximizes satisfaction by choosing commodity bundle A on indifference curve u_1^A. This commodity bundle consists of 50 coconuts and $50(p_x/p_y)$ bananas.

We can solve for Man Friday's excess demand curves in a similar fashion, and we find that $E_x^B = 50(p_x/p_y)$ and $E_Y^B = -50$. Thus, Friday is a demander of coconuts and a supplier of bananas. Again, this makes sense since Friday is endowed with 100 bananas and no coconuts.

Having obtained each individual's excess demand curve, we can solve for the equilibrium price ratio. Equilibrium requires that all markets clear. Consider the market for coconuts. Equilibrium requires that

$$E_X = E_X^A + E_Y^B = -50 + 50(p_x/p_y) = 0.$$

Solving the equilibrium condition for the exchange rate gives $p_x/p_y = 50/50 = 1$. That is, the equilibrium exchange rate is one. This, in turn, allows us to find the equilibrium quantities consumed by each individual. For Crusoe $X^A = E_x^A + X_0^A = -50 + 100 = 50$ coconuts, and $Y^A = E_y^A = 50(p_x/p_y) = 50$ bananas. For Man Friday $X^B = 100 - 50 = 50$ coconuts, and $Y^B = 100 - 50 = 50$ bananas. The general equilibrium for this economy is shown in Figure 16–7. Point E represents the competitive allocation of resources and the slope of RS represents the competitive exchange rate.

What if we had used the market clearing condition for the banana market instead of the coconut market to determine the equilibrium exchange rate? As we might expect, we would find exactly the same equilibrium exchange rate and quantities. This is because, in a two good world, if one of the markets clears, then the other must also clear. That is, of the six equilibrium conditions (two optimization conditions for each consumer and two market clearing conditions) only five are independent equations. Thus, we can determine only five unknowns—the quantities of each of the goods consumed by each of the individuals and the price ratio. We cannot determine the absolute level of prices. This means that the equilibrium conditions determine relative prices only. Intuitively this makes sense since it is only relative prices that influence the decisions of consumers. ■

16.3 ECONOMIC EFFICIENCY WITH CONSUMPTION AND PRODUCTION

■ In the last section we described the marginal efficiency condition for the allocation of goods between consumers. Now we must account for the possibility of production; that is, we must extend the general equilibrium analysis to an economy in which goods are both consumed and produced.

Again, we will use the simplest economy that still captures the important interactions among markets. We assume that there are only two commodities produced by firms, good X and good Y. In this economy consumers are endowed with the only two resources used in the production of goods and services: capital and labor. The total quantities of capital and labor available to the economy are fixed, but the quantities employed in each industry are not. The consumers own these inputs and they earn their incomes by selling the services of these factors of production to firms. Consumers use the proceeds from the sale of the services of their resources, their incomes, to purchase goods. Consumers are assumed to spend their entire incomes. All markets are competitive. (This is just a description of the circular flow of economic activity discussed in Chapter 1.)

While this is the simplest type of economy, there are still four markets to consider: the markets for labor, capital, good X, and good Y. Thus, to find a general equilibrium is a formidable task. We must find a set of prices, both input and output prices, and the corresponding quantities representing a general equilibrium; that is, we must find the prices and quantities for which consumers maximize satisfaction, producers maximize profit, supply is equal to demand in all markets simultaneously, and economic profit is zero for all firms. We will begin by deriving the condition that guarantees production efficiency.

THE MARGINAL EFFICIENCY CONDITION FOR THE ALLOCATION OF INPUTS AMONG PRODUCERS

Let $\bar{L}$ and $\bar{K}$ denote the total amounts of labor and capital available to the economy as a whole, L^X and K^X the quantities of labor and capital employed in industry X; and L^Y and K^Y the quantities of labor and capital employed in industry Y. If the total supplies of capital and labor are fixed, then $\overline{L} = L^X + L^Y$ and $\overline{K} = K^X + K^Y$. The amounts of capital and labor used to produce X and Y must sum to the total amounts available. If they do not, some resources will be left idle; that is, some markets will not clear.

In Figure 16–9, we use an Edgeworth box diagram to analyze the production opportunities available to the economy for the given amounts of capital and labor. The dimensions of the Edgeworth box represent the total amounts of capital and labor available to firms. Using the southwest corner of the box as a reference point, the horizontal axis measures the amount of labor allocated to the production of good X and the vertical axis measures the amount of capital allocated to the production of good X. Using the northeast corner as a reference point, the horizontal axis measures the amount of labor used to produce good Y and the vertical axis measures the amount of capital used to produce good Y. Each point in the box corresponds to an allocation of labor and capital, that is, an input bundle, that can be used to produce X and Y.

Now suppose that initially the firms in industry X employ L_0^X units of labor and K_0^X units of capital. Similarly, the firms in industry Y employ L_0^Y units of labor and K_0^Y units of capital. In the Edgeworth box diagram shown in Figure 16–9, point R represents the initial input bundles used in the two industries.

PRODUCTION EFFICIENCY   **FIGURE 16–9**

Production efficiency occurs when the MRTS between inputs is the same for all firms using the inputs. Line AB is the production contract curve and represents all efficient allocations of inputs among firms.

Given these amounts of capital and labor, how much output does each industry produce? To answer this question we must add each industry's production isoquants to the Edgeworth box diagram. In Figure 16−9, industry output of good X is indicated by the isoquant labeled X_0 (note that isoquant X_0 passes through point R) and industry output of good Y is indicated by the isoquant labeled Y_0. That is, firms in industry X initially use L_0^X units of labor and K_0^X units of capital to produce X_0 units of output while firms in industry Y initially use L_0^Y unit of labor and K_0^Y units of capital to produce Y_0 units of output. Note that here we are using isoquants to represent the output of an entire industry rather than the output of just one firm. The industry isoquants have the same characteristics as the isoquants of the firms making up the industry.

Production efficiency occurs when a fixed quantity of inputs are allocated in such a way that the production of one good cannot be increased without decreasing the production of some other goods. It should be clear from Figure 16−9 that point R is not an efficient allocation of inputs between the two industries. At point R the two isoquants intersect. This means that every allocation of inputs inside the shaded area shown in the diagram results in a larger output of both goods than the output occurring at point R. If firms were operating at point R, then, simply by trading inputs they already employ, output of both goods would increase at no additional cost to firms.

Production efficiency occurs when an isoquant representing production of one good is tangent to an isoquant representing the production of the other good. Production efficiency is attained when the marginal rate of technical substitution between capital and labor used to produce good X, MRTS_{LK}^X, is equal to the marginal rate of technical substitution between capital and labor used to produce good Y, MRTS_{LK}^Y. Thus, the marginal efficiency condition for the allocation of inputs among producers is

$$\text{MRTS}_{LK}^x = \text{MRTS}_{LK}^y. \tag{16.7}$$

Equation (16.7) indicates that production efficiency is obtained when the marginal rate of substitution between any pair of inputs is the same for all producers who use both inputs. If this condition does not hold, then an appropriate reallocation of inputs could produce a greater quantity of one or both goods without reducing the production of any other good.

In Figure 16−9, the allocation of inputs represented by point R' is an efficient allocation: all firms in industry X are outputting X_1 units while all firms in industry Y are outputting Y_1 units. At this point, both isoquants are tangent; thus, it is impossible to produce more of one good without producing less of the other.

We have drawn a curve, AB, between the X and Y origins through the tangencies of the X and Y isoquants. Points on this curve represent the allocations of capital and labor to industries X and Y that result in production efficiency. This curve is called the **production contract curve.** As we will see later on in this chapter, the production contract curve is used to determine the resource cost to the economy of producing and consuming additional units of any one good.

From our discussion of input markets in Chapter 10, we know that in a perfectly competitive economy input prices are the same across firms and industries. Let w be the price of labor and r, the price of capital. Then, as we saw in Chapters 8 and 9, given these prices each profit-maximizing firm in the economy will employ the input bundle that minimizes costs. That is, each firm will employ the input bundle for which the marginal rate of technical substitution between capital and labor is equal to the input price ratio: $MRTS_{LK} = w/r$.

Since all firms face the same input prices if markets are perfectly competitive, a competitive equilibrium in the input markets occurs when supply is equal to demand and each firm's use of labor and capital is such that the slopes of the isoquants are equal across firms and equal to the input price ratio; that is, $MRTS^X = MRTS^Y = w/r$.

Where the economy ends up on the production contract curve depends on consumers' demands for the two goods. For example, if consumers demand a lot of good X relative to good Y then the economy will end up at a point like C in Figure 16–10. Here, X_1 units of good X are produced and sold using L_1^x and K_1^x units of labor and capital respectively; Y_1 units of good Y are produced and sold using L_1^y and K_1^y units of labor and capital respectively; and the slope of isocost line IC_1 represents the equilibrium input price ratio.

Summarizing, in a competitive equilibrium in the input markets resources are allocated in such a way that

PRODUCTION EFFICIENCY WHEN MARKETS ARE COMPETITIVE

$$MRTS_{LK}^x = MRTS_{LK}^y = w/r \qquad\qquad (16.8)$$

$$L^X + L^Y = \bar{L} \qquad\qquad (16.9)$$

and

$$K^X + K^Y = \bar{K} \qquad\qquad (16.10)$$

FIGURE 16–10   GENERAL EQUILIBRIUM IN THE INPUT MARKETS

All conditions for a general equilibrium are met at point T. Firms are minimizing costs, and market excess demands for capital and labor are zero.

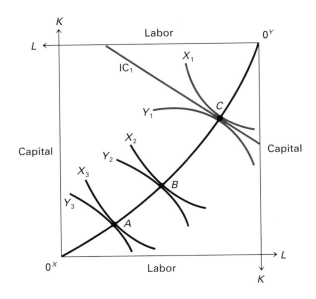

Equation (16.8) guarantees that firms in both industries are operating efficiently while (16.9) and (16.10) guarantee that both input markets clear.

We have determined the marginal efficiency conditions for the allocation of goods among consumers and inputs among producers and we have shown that perfectly competitive markets yield these efficiency conditions. Our final task is to determine the efficiency condition for the allocation of resources among goods. We begin by deriving what is called the *product transformation curve* for the economy.

THE PRODUCT TRANSFORMATION CURVE

The **product transformation curve** shows the different output combinations that can be obtained from the given quantities of capital and labor if firms operate efficiently. It describes the efficiently produced levels of both goods.

The production contract curve in Figure 16–9 can be used to derive the product transformation curve (also called the *production possibility frontier*) shown in Figure 16–11. The points that are labeled on the product transformation curve correspond to those points on the production contract curve. For example, R″ in Figure

16–11 represents the production of X_2 units of good X and Y_0 units of good Y using the available quantities of capital and labor efficiently. This information corresponds to R'' in Figure 16–9.

The negative of the slope of the product transformation curve is called the **marginal rate of transformation** of X for Y and is denoted MRT_{xy} for short. The marginal rate of transformation indicates the production trade-off between goods when inputs are in fixed supply. It measures the rate at which production of one good must be sacrificed to obtain more of the other good, holding total supplies of inputs fixed.

The product transformation curve is negatively sloped because to produce more of good X efficiently, labor and capital must be switched from the good Y industry to the good X industry—which, in turn, lowers the production of good Y.

The product transformation curve is concave, which reflects an increasing opportunity cost of producing either of the goods. As we move down along the product transformation curve, the MRT_{xy} increases; that is, as we move down along the product transformation curve an increasing number of units of good Y must be sacrificed to obtain an additional unit of good X. The reason for this is that initially, as production of good X increases, those workers

THE PRODUCT TRANSFORMATION CURVE

FIGURE 16–11

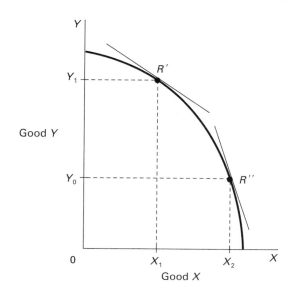

The product transformation curve indicates the quantities of the two goods that can be produced with a fixed total supply of inputs if firms operate efficiently. The slope of the product transformation curve, called the marginal rate of transformation, reflects the opportunity cost of producing one good in terms of the other.

and machines least suited for use in industry Y are reallocated to firms in industry X. As even more units of good X are produced, however, inputs better suited for the production of good Y must also be reallocated to industry X. Thus, the cost of producing additional units of good X, in terms of foregone units of good Y, increases.

We can also describe the shape of the product transformation curve in terms of the marginal costs of production. At point 0^y in Figure 16–9, only a small amount of good Y is sacrificed if one additional unit of good X is produced (the MRT_{xy} is small). Also at this point the marginal cost of producing good X is small since it takes only a little bit of labor and capital to produce that first unit and the marginal cost of producing good Y is very high since it takes a lot of labor and capital to produce another unit of good Y. This means that when the MRT_{xy} is low, so too is the ratio of the marginal production costs. Indeed, along the product transformation curve the marginal rate of transformation is precisely equal to the ratio of the marginal costs of production; that is, $\text{MRT}_{xy} = \text{MC}_x/\text{MC}_y$. Thus, just as the marginal rate of substitution measures the rate at which a consumer is willing to exchange one good for another, and the marginal rate of technical substitution measures the rate at which firms are technically capable of substituting one input for another, the marginal rate of transformation measures the rate at which the economy is able to substitute one good for another and yet maintain production efficiency.

THE MARGINAL EFFICIENCY CONDITION FOR PRODUCT SUBSTITUTION

For an economy to be efficient, it must be producing the combination of goods that consumers are willing to buy. Thus, the marginal efficiency condition for product substitution is

$$\text{MRS}_{xy} = \text{MRT}_{xy}. \qquad (16.11)$$

Equation (16.11) indicates that efficient product substitution is obtained when the output mix is such that the marginal rate of substitution in consumption equals the marginal rate of transformation in production. (This is just another example of marginal benefit equaling marginal cost.)

To understand this marginal efficiency condition, consider the following example. Suppose that the MRS_{xy} is equal to two; that is, consumers are willing to exchange two units of good Y for one unit of good X. Next, suppose that the MRT_{xy} is equal to one; that is, the cost of producing an additional unit of good X in terms of producing less of good Y is one. Clearly, this cannot be an efficient allocation of resources. By reducing the output of Y, the output of

X can be increased more than enough to keep each consumer on his or her original indifference curve. Thus, with an appropriate reallocation of resources at least one individual can be made better off without making someone else worse off. For example, reducing output of Y four units increases production of X four units. Since consumers are willing to exchange two units of Y for one unit of X, two additional units of X can be given to each consumer and both will be better off.

The marginal efficiency condition for product substitution is the efficiency condition that economists find most useful in analyzing real-world situations. In fact, it is equivalent to the marginal efficiency condition in a partial equilibrium setting (discussed in Chapter 15). To see why, simply note that the marginal rate of substitution measures the marginal benefit to consumers of consuming an additional unit of one good in terms of the other. This is exactly what we described in Chapter 15 as the marginal social benefit of consumption. The marginal rate of transformation, on the other hand, measures the marginal cost of producing an additional unit of one good in terms of the other. This is the marginal social cost of production. Economic efficiency, then, requires the equality between marginal social benefit and marginal social cost.

If we were the economic planners in charge of managing a *planned* economy, we would face a difficult task if our goal was to achieve an efficient allocation of resources. We would have to find the output mix for which the marginal rate of transformation is equal to the marginal rate of substitution for every consumer in the economy. But if consumers have different tastes for goods and services, determining the levels of goods and services to produce and determining the appropriate amounts to distribute to each consumer will be very costly. The resource cost of gathering information and coordinating economic activity will be enormous. However, as this section will show, if markets are *perfectly competitive* an efficient allocation of resources is obtained at a relatively low cost.

OVERALL EFFICIENCY WHEN MARKETS ARE COMPETITIVE

If output markets are perfectly competitive, profit-maximizing firms produce output up to the point where the marginal cost of production is equal to price; that is, $MC_y = p_y$ and $MC_x = p_x$. Since the marginal rate of transformation is equal to the ratio of the marginal costs of production, when firms are maximizing profit it must be the case that the marginal rate of transformation is equal to the output price ratio. Also, we know that consumers maximize satisfaction by consuming the commodity bundle for which the marginal rate of substitution is equal to the output price ratio. Since under perfect competition, buyers and sellers face the same market prices, it follows that

$$MRT_{xy} = p_x/p_y = MRS_{xy}.$$

Thus, under competition the production and distribution of goods will be efficient.

Figure 16–12 illustrates the efficiency of perfectly competitive output markets. If firms are operating efficiently, then some point on the product transformation curve will determine the equilibrium output mix; precisely which point will depend on endowments, tastes, and the technologies. Suppose the economy is currently operating at point A in Figure 16–12(a). At this point, X_0 units of good X and Y_0 units of good Y are being bought and sold.

FIGURE 16–12   **GENERAL EQUILIBRIUM IN THE OUTPUT MARKETS**

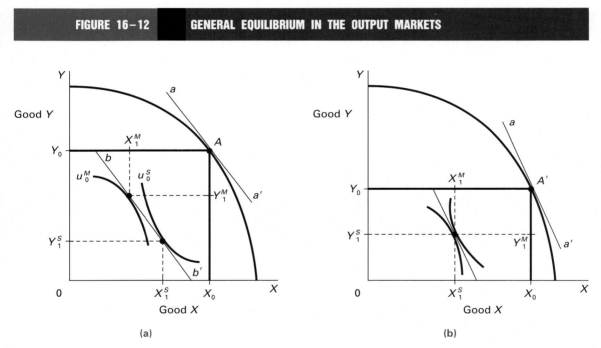

(a)

(b)

(a) In this instance, producers maximize profit and consumers maximize satisfaction but markets do not clear. There is excess demand for good X and an excess supply of good Y. (b) In this instance, all conditions for general equilibrium are fulfilled. Producers maximize profit, consumers maximize satisfaction, and all markets clear.

Earlier in this chapter, in the pure exchange economy, the dimensions of Smith's and McCoy's Edgeworth box were determined by their endowments of goods. Now this is not the case. Now the dimensions of their Edgeworth box are determined by how much of each good is *produced;* that is, if the economy is operating at point A on the product transformation curve, then the dimensions of the Edgeworth box are the output rates associated with A: X_0 and Y_0. In order to illustrate this point, as shown in Figure 16–12, we can construct an Edgeworth box diagram inside the product transformation curve.

In Figure 16–12(a), the price ratio that is consistent with profit maximization at point A is represented by the slope of line aa', which is tangent to the product transformation curve at point A. In addition, since the slope of any consumer's budget constraint is minus the price ratio, each consumer's budget constraint must have the same slope as aa'.

The precise location of the budget constraint in the Edgeworth box diagram will depend on each consumer's endowment of capital and labor. Suppose it is given by line bb'. Given this budget constraint, Smith (whose consumption bundle is still measured from the southwest corner of the box, while McCoy's is measured from the northeast) maximizes satisfaction by consuming commodity bundle B consisting of X_1^S units of good X and Y_1^S units of good Y. McCoy maximizes satisfaction by consuming commodity bundle C consisting of X_1^M units of X and Y_1^M units of Y. Since both Smith and McCoy face the same prices, $MRS^S = MRS^M = MRT$. Does this allocation of resources represent a competitive equilibrium?

For a competitive equilibrium all markets must clear. In this instance, neither one of the output markets clears. There is excess market demand for good X, $E_x = X_1^S + X_1^M - \overline{X} > 0$, and an excess supply of good Y, $E_y = Y_1^S + Y_1^M - \overline{Y} < 0$. This being so, competitive pressures will cause the price of X to rise and the price of Y to fall. Thus, the price ratio will rise, both aa' and bb' will become steeper, and the economy will move down along the transformation curve until excess demand in all markets is zero. In Figure 16–12(b), when the economy is operating at point A' all the conditions for general equilibrium are met. At this point all markets clear and the economy is operating efficiently.

Given the initial endowments of capital and labor, we have shown that a system of perfectly competitive input and output markets will achieve an efficient allocation of resources. Below we summarize our results.

A SUMMARY OF THE MARGINAL EFFICIENCY CONDITIONS

Efficiency and the allocation of goods

The distribution of goods must be such that the marginal rates of substitution between any pair of goods are the same for all consumers:

$$\text{MRS}^S_{xy} = \text{MRS}^M_{xy}.$$

A competitive market achieves this efficient outcome because consumers maximize satisfaction by finding the commodity bundle for which

$$\text{MRS}^S_{xy} = p_x/p_y = \text{MRS}^M_{xy}.$$

Efficiency and the allocation of inputs

The allocation of inputs must be such that the marginal rate of technical substitution between inputs is the same for all firms:

$$\text{MRTS}^x_{LK} = \text{MRTS}^y_{LK}.$$

A competitive market achieves this efficient outcome because producers maximize profit by using the input bundle for which

$$\text{MRTS}^x_{LK} = w/r = \text{MRS}^y_{LK}.$$

Efficiency and the output mix

The allocation of resources is such that the marginal rate of transformation is equal to the marginal rate of substitution:

$$\text{MRT}_{xy} = \text{MRS}_{xy} \text{ (for every consumer).}$$

A competitive market achieves this efficient outcome because producers maximize profit by producing up to the point where marginal cost is equal to price and consumers maximize satisfaction by consuming the commodity bundle for which the marginal rate of substitution is equal to the price ratio:

$$\text{MRT} = \text{MC}_x/\text{MC}_y = p_x/p_y = \text{MRS}_{xy} \text{ (for every consumer).}$$

16.4 USING THE GENERAL EQUILIBRIUM MODEL

■ We can use general equilibrium analysis to investigate how an economy responds to changes in the economic environment. Because markets are interrelated, even a simple change in demand for one good or service has quite complex repercussions in other markets. We will conclude our discussion of general equilibrium by looking at two applications: the effects of a change in demand and the welfare cost of monopoly.

Let us begin with an economy initially in equilibrium. In Figure 16–13, this initial equilibrium is represented by point A on the product transformation curve. At this point, X_1 units of good X and Y_2 units of good Y are being produced. For this output combination, the equilibrium price ratio is given by minus the slope of aa' and is equal to p_x^1/p_y. Now suppose consumer preferences change so that at current prices consumers want to consume more than X_1 units of good X. That is, demand for X increases while demand for Y decreases.

In order to trace out the effects of this shift in demand, we must remember that both the output and input markets are interrelated. In the short run, an increase in demand for good X will raise the price of X, which creates short-run profits for firms in the X industry. The decrease in demand for good Y has just the reverse effect on firms in the Y industry. In the long run the X industry will expand by increasing employment of labor and capital, while the Y industry will contract by reducing employment of inputs. In Figure 16–13, the economy moves down along the product transformation

AN INCREASE IN DEMAND FIGURE 16–13

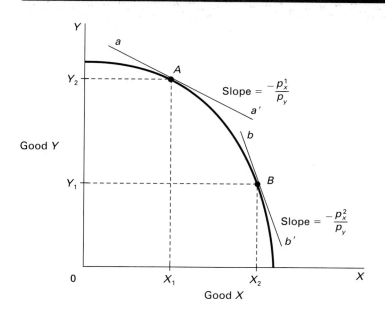

When the demand for good X increases, the economy moves down along the product trans- formation curve from A to B. More of good X and less of good Y are bought and sold. The equilib- rium price ratio increases as good X becomes more expensive relative to good Y. In addition, the change in output mix affects input prices. If the X industry is labor- intensive relative to the Y industry, the price of labor rises relative to the price of capital.

curve from A toward B, indicating that firms are producing more of good X and less of good Y.

Let us suppose that the final equilibrium can be represented by point B. This being the case, X production increases from X_1 to X_2 and Y production falls from Y_2 to Y_1. As a result, the relative price of good X increases. The new equilibrium price ratio is given by minus the slope of bb' and is equal to $p_x^2/p_y > p_x^1/p_y$.

The change in the output mix also has repercussions for the prices of inputs. For example, suppose that the good X industry is more labor-intensive than the good Y industry. Then the move from A to B in Figure 16–13 causes the wage rate to rise relative to the price of capital. The reason for this is that even though firms in industry X demand more of all inputs when they are producing more of good X, the increase in demand for labor is greater since industry X is labor-intensive. Thus, the price of labor increases relative to capital. (If industry X were capital-intensive and industry Y were labor-intensive, the price of capital relative to labor would increase.)

The change in input prices also means that incomes of consumers change. (Remember, consumers are the owners of the resources used to produce goods and services.) Individuals supplying labor services realize an increase in income, while those supplying capital services suffer a loss in income. Furthermore, this change in the distribution of income will also affect the final output mix—that is, the final equilibrium point on the product transformation curve.

A simple change in demand affects not only output prices and quantities but also input prices and the distribution of income. When a general equilibrium is once again attained, all markets will clear and the marginal efficiency conditions will hold once again.

MONOPOLY

In the discussion above, we assumed that both industries were perfectly competitive. Suppose, instead, that industry X is characterized by monopoly, while industry Y is competitive. In Chapter 15 we used a partial equilibrium analysis to show the inefficiency of monopoly. Now we can investigate this inefficiency further with a general equilibrium analysis.

We know from Chapter 12 that a profit-maximizing monopoly produces an output where marginal revenue equals marginal cost. Since price is greater than marginal revenue, this means that the monopoly charges a price greater than marginal cost; that is,

$$p_x > MC_x.$$

Firms in industry Y, the competitive industry, produce at the level where price is equal to marginal cost:

$$p_y = MC_y.$$

Dividing these two equations, we have a relation between relative prices and the ratio of the marginal costs:

$$p_x/p_y > MC_x/MC_y.$$

Graphically, this inequality is shown in Figure 16–14. Suppose A represents the output mix being produced and sold. Minus the slope of aa' is the marginal rate of transformation at A and is equal to the ratio of marginal costs. At A, however, the price ratio facing consumers is not equal to the ratio of marginal costs; in fact, it is greater. Minus the slope of bb' reflects this artificially high price ratio which is equal to p_x/p_y. Consumers maximize satisfaction subject to their budget constraints. The Edgeworth box diagram drawn inside the product transformation curve illustrates con-

MONOPOLY   **FIGURE 16–14**

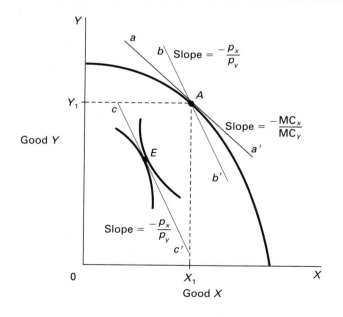

A monopolist charges a price greater than marginal cost which means that the $MRS_{XY} > MRT_{XY}$; or, in other words, the marginal social benefit of consuming good X in terms of good Y is greater than the marginal social cost of producing X in terms of good Y. Thus, the third marginal efficiency condition is violated. Too little of good X and too much of good Y are being produced.

sumer equilibrium which occurs at point E where the indifference curves are tangent to budget constraint cc'. That is, in equilibrium $MRS_{xy} = p_x/p_y$.

Now, are the three marginal efficiency conditions satisfied? Since consumers face the same prices, their marginal rates of substitution are equal at point E so the marginal efficiency condition for the allocation of products among consumers is satisfied. Also, since the economy is operating at point A on the product transformation curve the marginal efficiency condition for the allocation of inputs among producers is satisfied. However, the third condition is violated when a monopoly exists. At point E the MRS_{xy} is greater than the marginal rate of transformation, which means that the output mix is inefficient. The monopoly should produce more of good X since the marginal social benefit of producing more of good X in terms of good Y exceeds the marginal social cost. As a result of the monopoly, too little of the monopolized good is produced.

In the next example, we are asked to use general equilibrium analysis to illustrate how an economy gains when trade is allowed with other countries.

EXAMPLE 16–3

THE GAINS FROM INTERNATIONAL TRADE

In Figure 16–15, suppose the home country is initially isolated from world trade and is in equilibrium at point A on its product transformation curve. The equilibrium price ratio is represented by minus the slope of aa', which is two; that is, at A $p_x/p_y = 2$. Now assume that it becomes possible for the home country to engage in international trade. Assume the following: the terms on which other countries are willing to trade are established by world prices; the terms of trade are given by minus the slope of cc', which is one (that is, other countries are willing to supply the home country with one unit of clothing, good Y, for one unit of food); and exports are used to pay for imports. Determine the effects of opening this economy up to international trade.

■ **SOLUTION** If the home country can trade with other countries at a price ratio of one and the domestic price ratio is two, the domestic economy must adjust to a new equilibrium position. With the world price of food in terms of clothing less than the domestic

THE GAINS FROM INTERNATIONAL TRADE   FIGURE 16–15

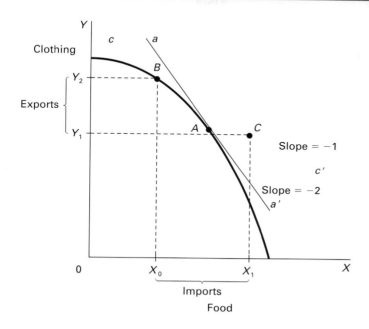

The world price of food relative to clothing is less than the domestic price of food relative to clothing, and the domestic economy adjusts by moving from A to B on the product transformation curve. In addition, international trade allows the home country to consume more than it produces as is shown by point C.

price, consumers of food will switch from domestic to imported foreign food and increase their consumption of food. As a result, some firms in the domestic food industry will suffer losses and exit the industry. Domestic output of food will fall.

At the same time, the clothing industry will expand. With the world price of clothing in terms of food greater than the domestic price, domestic producers can earn a profit by exporting clothing to foreign consumers. As a result, domestic firms are attracted to the clothing industry and output rises.

Domestic food production falls and clothing production rises. This continues until the domestic price ratio is equal to the world price ratio. In Figure 16–15, point B on the product transformation curve represents the new output mix produced by the home country. However, point B does not represent the quantities *consumed* by domestic consumers. By engaging in international trade, the home country can consume more than it produces. Point C on cc' represents one possible allocation. At this point, domestic consumption of food and clothing are X_1 and Y_1 respectively; domestic production of food and clothing are X_0 and Y_2

respectively; and $(Y_2 - Y_1)$ units of clothing are exported while $(X_1 - X_0)$ units of food are imported. (Actually, any point on cc' is feasible. Precisely where the economy ends up will depend on consumers' preferences for the two goods.) ∎

Notice that this analysis also demonstrates why some industries oppose free trade with foreign countries. While the domestic economy is operating efficiently before and after trade is opened up, not everyone benefits when the economy moves from A to B. Since domestic output in the food industry contracts, the owners of resources employed in that industry will lose, while those employed in the clothing industry will gain; that is, the opportunity for international trade alters the distribution of income in the home country. Thus, those resource owners supplying inputs that are specialized for food production will, most likely, oppose free trade with foreign countries (or, put another way, they will oppose removal of trade restrictions).

1. In a general equilibrium resources are allocated in such a way that each consumer maximizes satisfaction, each firm maximizes profit, supply is equal to demand in every market, and economic profit is zero in the long run. General equilibrium analysis should be used when changes in one market have substantial repercussions in other markets.

2. There are three conditions characterizing economic efficiency: the marginal rate of substitution between any pair of products must be the same for all individuals who consume both products; the marginal rate of technical substitution between any pair of inputs must be the same for all producers who use both inputs; and the marginal rate of transformation must be equal to the marginal rate of substitution.

3. If all markets are competitive, then each of the efficiency conditions will be met. The "invisible hand" works when markets are perfectly competitive.

SUMMARY

General Equilibrium
Edgewood Exchange Box Diagram
Exchange Contract Curve

Production Contract Curve
Product Transformation Curve
Marginal Rate of Transformation

KEY TERMS

QUESTIONS AND PROBLEMS

1. a) Explain the difference between partial and general equilibrium analysis.
   b) If we were interested in determining the effects of a reduction in the capital gains tax, would you recommend using partial or general equilibrium analysis? Explain.
   c) If we were interested in determining the effects of eliminating import restrictions on automobiles, would you recommend using partial or general equilibrium analysis?

2. Suppose coffee, good X, and tea, good Y, are substitutes for each other. Further, suppose that the supplies of both are fixed in the short run—that is, $X^S = 200$ and $Y^S = 400$, and that the demand functions for the two goods are given by

$$X^D = 208.4 - p_x + .2p_y \quad \text{and} \quad Y^D = 407 - p_y + .1p_x.$$

   a) Determine the equilibrium prices and quantities.
   b) If a new government trade restriction reduces the supply of coffee to 150, then how will the equilibrium prices change?

3. One condition for a general equilibrium is that all markets clear simultaneously. Why then, do we find goods on the shelves of stores when we go shopping?

4. a) Write down the conditions characterizing a general equilibrium in a pure exchange economy.

   b) Explain what each of these equations represents.

   c) If the government were to impose an excise tax on one of the goods traded in the pure exchange economy, would the economy still achieve efficiency? Explain.

5. a) Explain how the equilibrium price ratio is determined in a pure exchange economy.

   b) Why can't we determine the level of prices?

6. Sally and Linus are health food fanatics and consume sunflower seeds, good X, and raisins, good Y. Sally's preferences are such that her MRS between X and Y is $2X/Y$ and Linus' MRS is $2X/Y$. Sally is endowed with 20 pounds of raisins and 10 pounds of sunflower seeds. Linus is endowed with 10 pounds of raisins and 20 pounds of sunflower seeds.

   a) Find the exchange contract curve.

   b) Using an Edgeworth box diagram, illustrate the trading set.

   c) Find the equilibrium price ratio assuming Linus and Sally act like price takers.

7. a) Explain how the product transformation curve is derived from the production contract curve.

   b) Carefully explain what the slope of the product transformation curve represents.

8. Begin with an economy in general equilibrium. Now suppose demand for good X decreases. Using general equilibrium analysis, explain how the economy responds to this change.

9. How would an increase in the supply of labor affect the production transformation curve?

10. Historically, the U.S. footwear industry has argued against removing import restrictions because such a policy would cause thousands of workers to lose their jobs. Explain how general equilibrium analysis can be used to address this issue.

11 Labor unions artificially increase wage rates.

   a) Assuming a two good world with only one industry unionized, use general equilibrium analysis to show the inefficiency associated with labor unions.

   b) If labor unions create inefficiencies, why are they so popular in the U.S.?

12. a) Would the elimination of monopoly profit through government regulation lead to an efficient allocation of resources?

b) Discuss, using a general equilibrium model, who benefits and who is harmed by such a regulation.

13. "If supply is equal to demand in every market, economic efficiency will be attained." Comment on this statement.

14. Suppose the government passes a law that limits consumption of some good (cigarettes, alcoholic beverages, etc.) to an amount less than would be consumed under perfect competition. Discuss the effects of such a law using general equilibrium analysis and explaining which efficiency conditions, if any, are violated.

Kreps, D. 1990. *A Course in Microeconomic Theory.* Princeton: Princeton University Press.

Quirk, J., and R. Saposnik. 1968. *Introduction to General Equilibrium Theory and Welfare Economics.* New York: McGraw-Hill.

REFERENCES

INVESTMENT DECISIONS AND RISK

■ *Throughout most of this book we have ignored the elements of time and risk. Both these factors play an important role in real-world decision making; they are the subject matter for Part 6.*

■ *Chapter 17 shows how firms compare different profit streams and how they make their investment decisions. Since the interest rate is one of the most important factors affecting investment decisions, the chapter concludes by discussing how the equilibrium interest can be determined by applying the supply and demand model to the market for loanable funds.*

■ *Chapter 18, the last chapter in this book, investigates how individuals behave in risk situations. In a sense, the analysis in this chapter is an application of utility maximization. This chapter shows why some decisions—for example, determining where to locate a new franchise, choosing between risky investments, and buying insurance—cannot be understood without considering the risk associated with them and the risk-taking characteristics of the decision maker. Chapter 18 also investigates one more source of market failure, called asymmetric information. It shows that, when some economic agents have better information than others, competitive markets may not yield an efficient allocation of resources. This type of market failure is particularly important when either private firms or the government provide insurance, since, once again, prices might not reflect social costs and benefits.*

INVESTMENT DECISIONS AND CAPITAL MARKETS

17

LEARNING OBJECTIVES

After completing Chapter 17 you should be able to do the following:

■ Discuss the difference between a firm's capital stock and the flow of capital services it uses.

■ Compare the present values of different payment streams over time.

■ Explain the net present value rule for evaluating investment projects and compare it to the profit-maximizing rule for the employment of inputs.

■ Discuss the various factors that affect the discount rate used in making investment decisions.

■ Explain how to determine the optimal extraction rate of an exhaustible resource.

■ Use the supply and demand model to show how the interest rate is determined in a competitive market for loanable funds.

EXAMPLES

■ **17-1** Valuing Alternative Income Streams

■ **17-2** Investment Decisions

■ **17-3** Technological Innovations and the Interest Rate

In Chapter 8 we found that a profit-maximizing firm determines the quantity of an input to use per unit of time by comparing the marginal revenue product of that input to its marginal factor cost. Further, in Chapter 10 we saw how in competitive markets the decisions of all firms determine market demand for each input. Implicit in these discussions was the assumption that the cost of employing inputs and the revenue generated by selling output both accrue in the current single period. In other words, we assumed that the element of time was not important.

For inputs such as labor this assumption is reasonably accurate, but for capital it is not. Capital is a *durable* input—it contributes to the production process for several years after it is purchased. Once we realize this, the element of time becomes very important. When a firm decides whether to replace worn out or obsolete equipment with new equipment, or to expand production facilities by building another factory, it must compare the expenditures that it would have to make now to the additional profit the new capital would generate in the future. For example, in Chapter 1 we noted that General Motors invested over $3 billion dollars in its Saturn project. The firm used much of this expenditure to build a new plant and purchase new equipment that it would use for many years to produce the Saturn line of automobiles. In order to decide whether or not to make this investment, GM had to compare its *initial* outlays with the *future* profits the new capital would generate, and to make this comparison GM had to have a way of determining the value of future profits today. This kind of problem does not arise when firms use inputs such as labor that are not durable. To choose how many workers to employ, a firm need only consider the *current* marginal factor cost of the input and the *current* marginal revenue product it generates.

In this chapter, we will examine the investment decisions of firms. We will learn how to compare different profit streams and how to decide whether or not to undertake a particular investment. Since future profits resulting from a capital investment are often uncertain, we will also discuss how firms can take risk into account in making their decisions.

We also address one other intertemporal question that is particularly important today: How much of a depletable resource should be extracted today and how much should be extracted in the future?

Finally, since the *interest rate* one pays on borrowed funds or receives on loaned funds plays such an important role in both investment and intertemporal production decisions, the last part of the chapter discusses how interest rates are determined in competitive markets and what factors affect them.

■ In order to understand a firm's investment decisions, we must be clear about the difference between a firm's *capital stock* and the *capital services* it uses in the production process. A firm's **capital stock**, on the one hand, is the value of the quantity of tools, machinery, and buildings that a firm owns at a given point in time. For example, if a firm owns a factory and equipment worth $100 million, then we say the firm has a *capital stock* worth $100 million. *Capital services*, on the other hand, refer to the *flow* of services generated by the firm's capital stock as well as what it rents from other capital stock owners. When we discussed how a profit-maximizing firm decides on the quantity of capital to use in Chapter 8, we were talking about the quantity of *capital services*. We measure capital services just as any other input—in terms of a flow of services per unit of time. For example, a firm might use (or employ) 5,000 person-hours of labor services per month and 2,000 machine-hours of capital services per month to produce 10,000 units of output per month.

Firms can vary the rate of usage of their capital stock, but the actual quantity of capital they purchase—their capital stock—is fixed at any point in time. Our goal in analyzing capital in this chapter is to understand how firms make the decision to augment their existing capital stock; to do this we must investigate the costs and benefits of purchasing new capital goods.

17.1 CAPITAL STOCK AND CAPITAL SERVICES

■ Investment decisions involve choosing a quantity, or stock, of capital. For example, owners of firms must make decisions concerning how to allocate their resources efficiently among a variety of capital projects such as new or expanded production facilities, machines, computers, transportation equipment, research and development expenditures, and advertising.

But why would firms be willing to incur costs to finance investments in new capital? The reason is that the capital that is purchased may generate a flow of returns sufficient to cover the costs. Adding to a firm's capital stock increases production and future profit.

In order to determine which investment projects a firm should undertake, we must first determine how to compare costs that are incurred today with profits that will be received in the future. Simply comparing the total costs to the sum of future profits from each investment is not appropriate since, even if there is no risk associated with the investment, a dollar today is worth more than a dollar tomorrow. This being the case, we begin our study of investment decisions by discussing how to calculate the *present value* of an investment.

17.2 PRESENT VALUE

CALCULATING PRESENT VALUES

Consider choosing between $500 today and $500 five years from now. Which would you rather have? Surely you would choose the $500 today because you could always take the $500, put it in a bank account where it could earn interest, and collect more than $500 in five years. Now suppose you are offered $250 today or $500 five years from now. Which would you choose? In this instance, the decision is not as clear-cut. The $250 today may be worth more or less than the $500 five years from now, depending upon the interest that the money can earn if it is put into a bank account. The point is that if we are going to make economic decisions concerning opportunities for which the associated costs and returns occur at different points in time, then we must have a way to make the dollar values of these costs and returns comparable.

In order to demonstrate how to compare a dollar today to a dollar tomorrow, let us suppose that you invest an amount I in a bank account at an interest rate of $i \cdot 100\%$ per year. Let R_t be the return on the investment at the end of t years. At the end of one year, the account would have increased to $I + iI$ dollars; that is,

$$R_1 = I + iI = I(1 + i).$$

After two years, the account would have increased to

$$R_2 = R_1 + iR_1 = (1 + i)I + i(1 + i)I$$

$$= (1 + i)(I + iI) = (1 + i)(1 + i)I = (1 + i)^2 I.$$

Continuing this process for t years, we can calculate that the total return to an investment of I dollars for t years at $i \cdot 100\%$ per year is given by

$$R_t = (1 + i)^t I \qquad (17.1)$$

Equation (17.1) is the *future value* of an amount I for t periods at an interest rate i.

The future value calculation converts dollars today into dollars tomorrow. In order to examine investment decisions, however, it is convenient to convert future dollars into today's dollars. To accomplish this, we can calculate the present value of an investment project. The term **present value** refers to the current value of an amount of money that will be received at some time in the future. Essentially the future value calculation is reversed to arrive at present value. Future values are *discounted* to determine their worth in today's dollars.

TABLE 17–1

PRESENT VALUE OF
$1 PAID IN THE
FUTURE

Interest Rate	1 Year	5 Years	15 Years	30 Years
0.01	$0.990	$0.952	$0.861	$0.742
0.10	0.909	0.621	0.239	0.057
0.20	0.833	0.402	0.065	0.004

The formula for the present value of R_t dollars paid at the end of period t is

$$PV = R_t[1 / (1 + i)^t]. \qquad (17.2)$$

For example, the present value of $1 to be paid in at the end of five years if the interest rate is 10% is

$$PV = 1 / (1.1)^5 = 1 / 1.6 = \$.62.$$

If the interest rate is 10% per year, then $1 five years hence is worth $.62. Or, in other words, if we invested $.62 today in a bank account paying 10% per year, then in five years we would have $1 in our account. An amount to be received in the future is worth less today.

Table 17–1 shows the present value of $1 paid after one, five, fifteen, and thirty years for three different interest rates. The entries in this table illustrate two important points. First, for a given interest rate, the further off the payment, the less it is worth today. For example, if the interest rate is 10%, then a $1 payment that is expected 30 years from now is worth only $.057, while a $1 payment that is expected next year is worth $.909. Second, the higher the interest rate, the lower the present value of a given payment. For example, if the interest rate is 1%, then the present value of $1 paid 30 years in the future is $.742, but if the interest rate is 20%, the present value falls to less than a penny.

EXAMPLE 17–1

VALUING ALTERNATIVE INCOME STREAMS
Present value calculations can be used to help us understand why some people decide to get a college degree and why some do not.

Suppose that Jim must decide whether or not to go to college upon graduating from high school. If Jim does not go, he expects to get a job at a local factory that pays $15,000 per year. If Jim goes to college, he expects to earn a Bachelor's degree in economics and get a job with a local bank that pays $25,000 per year. Jim estimates that college will cost $10,000 per year and that it will take him four years to earn his degree. (a) If the interest rate is 5%, and if Jim plans to work until age 60 no matter what job he has, should he go to college? (b) If the interest rate is 20%, should he go to college?

■ **SOLUTION** (a) To choose between the two income streams we must calculate the present value of each. The present value associated with the factory job is

$$PV^F = 15,000 + 15,000 / (1 + i) + \ \ldots + 15,000 / (1 + i)^{41}$$

$$= 15,000 \sum_{t=0}^{41} [1 / (1 + i)^t],$$

where $\sum_{t=1}^{41}$ stands for the summation from the first period, $t = 1$, to to the last, $t = 41$. (We are assuming that Jim begins work at age 19 and retires at age 60.) Similarly, the present value associated with the bank job is

$$PV^B = -10,000 - 10,000 / (1 + i) - 10,000 / (1 + i)^2 -$$
$$10,000 / (1 + i)^3 + 25,000 / (1 + i)^4 + \ldots$$
$$+ 25,000 / (1 + i)^{41}$$

$$= -10,000 \sum_{t=0}^{3} [1 / (1 + i)^t] + 25,000 \sum_{t=4}^{41} [1 / (1 + i)^t].$$

Substituting $i = .05$ into these equations we have

$$PV^F = \$274,500 \quad \text{and} \quad PV^B = \$327,300.$$

(These calculations can be done using a present value table, by remembering the formula for a geometric sum:

$$R \sum_{t=1}^{T} [1 / (1 + i)^t] = (k / i)[1 - (1 + i)^{-T}]$$

or by cranking it out on a calculator.) Thus, with an interest rate of 5%, the present value of the bank job is greater than the present value of the factory job and Jim should choose college.

(b) If $i = .20$ we have

$$PV^F = \$58,403 \quad \text{and} \quad PV^B = 41,254.$$

Thus, with an interest rate of 20%, the present value of the bank job is less that that of the factory job and Jim should not choose college. ∎

This example shows the important role the interest rate plays when we compare alternative payment streams. A relatively high interest rate means that payments received in the future are discounted heavily and, as a result, carry less weight in the present value calculation. This is the reason Jim's decision changes. At an interest rate of 20%, the higher future income generated by the college degree does not offset enough the costs of college, while at 5% they do. This provides us with a glimpse of things to come—choosing between alternative future payment streams depends crucially on the rate at which those future payments are discounted. Thus, individuals with relatively high discount rates will tend to forego college because they put a relatively high weight on current payments.

An **annuity** is a financial agreement promising a series of equal payments made at the end of each time period for a fixed number of periods. There are many examples of annuities. Retirement pension payments, mortgage payments, or any promise to pay a fixed amount annually for a fixed number of years are all annuities. If, in fact, the annuity is paid forever, then it is called a *perpetuity*. Note that the primary characteristic distinguishing an annuity from any other financial agreement stipulates equal payments. A contract to make 5 annual payments each of which increases 5% per year is not an annuity.

The present value of an annuity payment of R dollars per period over T periods is simply the sum of the present values of each payment; that is,

THE PRESENT VALUE OF AN ANNUITY

$$PV = R / (1 + i) + R / (1 + i)^2 + R / (1 + i)^3 + \ldots + R / (1 + i)^T$$

$$= R \sum_{t=1}^{T} [1 / (1 + i)^t] \qquad (17.3)$$

As it happens, the formula for calculating the present value of an annuity can be simplified substantially. Multiplying both sides of the present value formula by $(1 + i)$ and subtracting the result from the original formula gives

$$PV - (1 + i)PV = -R + R / (1 + i)^T.$$

Now if we solve this equation for PV we find that

$$PV = (R / i) - (R / i) / (1 + i)^T = (R / i)[1 - 1 / (1 + i)^T].$$

This formula is simplified even further if the annuity is a perpetuity. As T goes to infinity, $1 / (1 + i)^T$ goes to zero and the perpetuity has a present value given by

$$PV = R / i. \tag{17.4}$$

From equation (17.4) it is clear that the present value of an annuity paying R dollars per year indefinitely is inversely related to the market rate of interest.

THE PRICE OF A BOND   A **bond** is a contract specifying that the issuer (borrower) agrees to pay the bondholder (lender) a stream of money. Corporations or governments issue bonds in order to generate funds to finance investment.

We can determine the price of a bond by applying what we have learned about the present value of a payment stream. Suppose that Melanie is considering buying a corporate bond issued by Solar Power, Inc., a large firm specializing in developing alternative energy sources. The face value of the bond is $5,000, which will be paid to Melanie when the bond matures in three years. In addition, the bond promises to pay $500 at the end of each year; that is, the bond promises to pay a "coupon" of $500 at the end of each year (three coupons in all). Given the market rate of interest, what price would Melanie be willing to pay for such a bond?

To determine how much the bond is worth, we simply calculate the present value of the bond. We have

$$PV = 500 / (1 + i) + 500 / (1 + i)^2 + 5,500 / (1 + i)^3.$$

Notice once again that the present value depends on the interest rate. If the interest rate is 5%, the present value of the bond is $5,681; that is, Melanie would be willing to pay $5,681 for the bond. If the interest rate is 10%, then the present value of the bond would fall to $5,006. As the interest rate rises, the present value of the bond falls, which means the bond's price also falls. As the

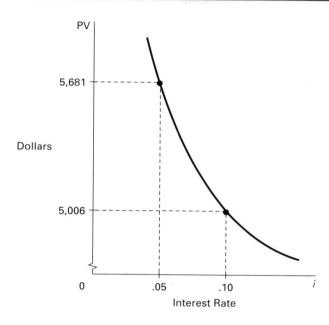

PRESENT VALUE AND THE INTEREST RATE

FIGURE 17-1

The present value, or price, of a bond is negatively related to the interest rate.

interest rate rises, it requires fewer of today's dollars to generate the same return in the future, so there is a negative relation between the price of the bond and the market rate of interest.

Figure 17-1 shows the negative relation between the present value, or price, of this bond and the market rate of interest. As the interest rate increases, the price of the bond falls steadily toward zero.

■ Throughout this book we have assumed that firms operate to maximize profit; however, we have not discussed what this means when time is an important element in the firms' operation. When time is important, we can generalize the notion of profit maximization in a straightforward manner by assuming that firms operate to maximize the present value of all expected future profits. That is, firms make decisions so as to maximize

17.3 PROFIT MAXIMIZATION OVER TIME

$$\Pi = \sum_{t=1}^{n} \frac{\pi_t}{(1 + r)^t},$$

where Π is the present value of all expected future profits of the firm, π_t is profit at time t, and r is the discount rate. (The appropriate discount rate is discussed in detail below.) Since profits at any point in time are equal to total revenue minus total cost, this equation can also be written as

$$\Pi = \sum_{t=1}^{n} \frac{TR_t - TC_t}{(1+r)^t}.$$

Maximizing the present value of expected future profits is a much more difficult task for owners and managers than is maximizing profit at each point in time, because now firms have the option of sacrificing current profits for the sake of increasing future profits. Firms must decide not only how much capital and labor to use each period, but also how much capital to purchase. The decision to sacrifice current profit in order to invest in new capital is of crucial importance to their survival in the long run. When time is an important factor, firms can incur costs today by purchasing capital goods that will yield a flow of benefits in future periods. They may spend huge sums of money on new factories and machines that will last for many years. The impact of these investments on future revenues and profits is often uncertain, and once such investments are made, they are usually irreversible. After a factory has been built or specialized machinery has been installed, their secondhand value is very small.

The remainder of this chapter will be concerned primarily with answering two questions: (i) How should a firm make its investment decision so as to maximize profit? (ii) How does the interest rate affect the profit-maximizing level of investment?

17.4 CHOOSING BETWEEN INVESTMENTS: THE NET PRESENT VALUE RULE

■ How should a firm decide when to add to its capital stock—that is, when to undertake a particular investment in new capital? One method of deciding whether or not to accept a particular investment project is to determine the net present value (NPV) of the project. The **net present value** of a project is equal to the present value of the expected stream of future cash flows minus the initial cost of the investment. If the net present value is positive, which means that the present value of expected future cash flows exceeds the cost of the project, then the investment project should be accepted.

Suppose an investment in new capital requires an outlay of C_0 dollars and is expected to generate a flow of profits over the next n years. The net present value of the project is given by

$$NPV = -C_0 + \sum_{t=1}^{n} \frac{\pi_t}{(1 + k)^t},$$ (17.5)

where π_t is expected profit in year t and k is the **discount rate** (sometimes called the *cost of capital*) we use to discount the future stream of profits. (Precisely what we should use for the discount rate is discussed shortly.) The value of the firm will increase if the NPV is positive and decline if the net present value is negative. Thus, a profit-maximizing firm should undertake the project if the NPV is positive and should not undertake the project if it is negative.

For example, if the discount rate associated with an investment project is 12%, the initial cost is $600,000, and expected profits from the investment are $200,000 per year for five years, then the net present value of the project is

$$NPV = -600,000 + \sum_{t=1}^{5} \frac{200,000}{(1.12)^t}$$

$$= -600,000 + 720,960 = \$120,960.$$

This project would add $120,960 to the value of the firm and therefore should be undertaken.

A firm should undertake an investment if the net present value of the investment is positive, but what is the profit-maximizing amount of investment to undertake? In Chapter 8, we found that a profit-maximizing firm should employ an input up to the point where the marginal benefit of hiring an additional unit—the value of the marginal product of the input—is equal to the marginal factor cost. We can put the present value rule for deciding on investments in this same light.

Suppose the firm has many investment opportunities available and that they are ranked in descending order according to their respective present values. The marginal benefit of undertaking one additional investment is simply the present value of future returns generated by the investment. The marginal cost of undertaking one additional investment is simply the additional money that must be spent to finance the investment. Profit maximization implies that investments be undertaken up to the point where marginal benefit equals marginal cost—that is, up to the point where the present value of the last investment is just equal to the cost of financing the investment. In terms of the net present value rule, a profit-maximizing firm should accept investments up to the point where the net present value of the last investment is just equal to zero. Thus, the net present value rule is another example of marginal decision making.

THE DISCOUNT RATE

The net present value rule provides a criterion for deciding whether or not to accept an investment project. However, the net present value of any project depends crucially on the discount rate used to calculate the present value. Figure 17–2 shows the NPV of the investment project discussed above as a function of the discount rate k. Note that if the discount rate is less than 20% the NPV of the project is positive; if it is greater than 20% the NPV is negative; and if it is exactly 20% the NPV is zero. Thus, for discount rates below 20% the project should be undertaken and for discount rates above 20% it should not be undertaken.

What discount should we use to calculate the present value of an investment project? If the firm is to maximize profit, then the discount rate must reflect the firm's opportunity cost of investing its funds in a particular project. If a firm invests its funds in one particular project, then it foregoes the opportunity to invest these funds in any other project. For example, instead of undertaking the investment discussed above, the firm could invest in an alternative project that would generate a different stream of profits, or it might invest in a bond that would yield a different stream of income. Had the firm not invested in one particular project, it could have earned a return by investing in a different project. Thus, the correct value

---

FIGURE 17–2   **NET PRESENT VALUE AND THE DISCOUNT RATE**

The net present value of an investment project is negatively related to the discount rate. An investment project should be accepted if the net present value is positive and rejected otherwise.

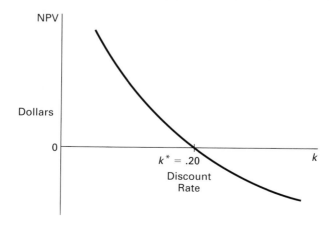

of k to use is the rate of return a firm could earn on an investment with similar risks. (Risk and risk-adjusted discount rates are discussed in Chapter 18.)

Suppose that a firm is considering investing in a project that has no risk; that is, the firm is certain of the future flow of profits that the project will generate. The opportunity cost of this investment is the risk-free rate of return, which is usually taken to be the return one could earn by purchasing a government bond. For example, if the investment was expected to last for 20 years, then the firm could use the interest rate on 20-year government bonds to calculate the net present value of the project.

Even if the appropriate discount rate is the risk-free rate of return, we must be careful to distinguish between real and nominal discount rates and real and nominal profit flows. Estimates of the future profits associated with an investment can be reported in *nominal* or *real* terms. The difference between nominal profits and real profits is inflation. That is, real profits are net of inflation while nominal profits include inflation. If future profits flows are reported in nominal terms, then the discount rate must also be in nominal terms. The reason for this is that the discount rate is the opportunity cost of the investment. If the expected future stream of profits includes inflation, then so too should the opportunity cost. Similarly, if future profits flows are reported in real terms, then the discount rate must also be in real terms. If the expected future stream of profits does not include inflation, then neither should the opportunity cost.

For example, if expected profits from a riskless investment are reported in real terms, then the discount rate used to calculate net present value should be the real interest rate on government bonds. The real interest rate is the nominal rate, the rate listed in the Wall Street Journal, minus the expected rate of inflation. If the nominal rate is 10% and the decision maker expects inflation to be 5% per year, then the real interest rate is $10 - 5 = 5\%$. This is the discount rate that should be used to calculate net present value.

WHY THERE ARE DIFFERENT INTEREST RATES

Interest rates may vary for a variety of reasons. At any point in time there is a *term structure* of interest rates; that is, different interest rates for bonds that mature at different points in time. For example, U.S. Treasury bills are short-term government bonds that mature in 1 year or less; U.S. Treasury notes are intermediate-term bonds that mature in 1 to 10 years; and U.S. Treasury Bonds are long-term government bonds that mature in 10 to 30 years. Associated with each of these bonds is a different interest rate. Typically, the rates increase as the length of time to maturity increases.

The primary reason for different interest rates at any one point in time is *risk*. Even if the maturity of different bonds is the same, bonds of foreign governments or corporations are usually considered riskier than U.S. Treasury bonds. This means that these bonds can be sold only at prices that generate a higher interest yield that includes a *risk premium*. A risk premium compensates buyers of bonds for the uncertainty associated with their purchase.

ADJUSTING THE DISCOUNT RATE FOR RISK

We saw that if future profits are certain, then the risk-free interest rate should be used to calculate the net present value of an investment project. However, for most projects future profits are not known with certainty. Such variables as future output prices, factor costs, and the state of the economy are all uncertain at the time when the investment decision must be made.

If future profit is uncertain, then how should the firm take this into account when making its investment decisions? The most common practice is to increase the discount rate by adding a *risk premium* to the risk-free interest rate. The reason for doing this is that future profits that are risky are worth less today than those that are certain, and if a risky investment is undertaken, then the firm must be compensated for the risk it is taking. Increasing the discount rate by adding a risk premium takes this into account by reducing the net present value of the investment.

There are several ways of determining the size of the risk premium. One common method is to use the *capital asset pricing model*. Essentially, this measures the risk premium by comparing the expected return on an investment project with the expected return on the entire stock market. If the expected return on the investment is high relative to the expected return on the stock market, then the risk premium is relatively large, while the reverse is true if the expected return on the investment is low relative to the stock market. (If you take a course in managerial finance you will investigate the capital asset pricing model in detail.)

In the next example we are asked to determine whether or not a firm should undertake a particular investment. As we work through this example, we should pay close attention to how sensitive our decision is to the size of the discount rate.

EXAMPLE 17–2

INVESTMENT DECISIONS
The owner of the Print-It Company is considering introducing a new, high-speed printer for IBM-compatible personal computers.

She has received the following estimates of costs and sales from the various departments of the firm. The cost of purchasing, delivering, and installing the new machinery that is required to manufacture the printer is estimated to be $1 million. The machinery is expected to be obsolete after five years, with a salvage value of $250,000. (That is, after five years the owner will be able to sell the machinery as scrap for $250,000.) Sales revenues are estimated to be $1 million in the first year of operation, rising by $100,000 per year. The variable cost of producing the printer is estimated to be 50% of sales revenues, and it is estimated that the firm will incur additional fixed costs equal to $350,000 per year. (a) If the risk-free rate of return is 8% and the firm is quite certain about future costs and revenues, should the firm undertake this project? (b) If the firm believes the investment is risky and attaches an additional risk premium of 7% to the project, should the firm undertake this project?

■ **SOLUTION** In order to answer questions (a) and (b), we must calculate the net present value of the project. Table 17−2 gives the estimated profit stream over the lifetime of the project.
 The NPV of the project is given by

$$\text{NPV} = -1,000,000 + \frac{150,000}{(1 + r)^1} + \frac{200,000}{(1 + r)^2} +$$

$$\frac{250,000}{(1 + r)^3} + \frac{285,000}{(1 + r)^4} + \frac{600,000}{(1 + r)^5}.$$

TABLE 17−2

ESTIMATED PROFIT STREAM FOR PRINT-IT (MILLIONS OF DOLLARS)

	Year				
	1	2	3	4	5
Sales Revenue	$1.000	$1.100	$1.200	$1.300	$1.400
Less:					
Variable Costs	.500	.550	.600	.665	.700
Fixed Costs	.350	.350	.350	.350	.350
Profit	.150	.200	.250	.285	.350
Plus Salvage Value of Equipment					.250
					.600

Substituting for the appropriate discount rate we have

$$\text{NPV}_{.08} = \$12{,}964 \quad \text{and} \quad \text{NPV}_{.15} = \$-92{,}212.$$

Thus, if the discount rate is 8%, then the net present value of the project is positive and the firm should undertake the investment. If the discount rate is 15%, then the net present value of the project is negative and the firm should not undertake the investment. ■

Business firms must make these types of investment decisions every day. In fact, deciding whether or not to invest in new capital in order to bring a new product to market is many times the most important decision a manager must make. A good example of this type of decision making was General Motor's decision to undertake the Saturn project. As we noted in Chapter 1, the Saturn project required an investment of over $3 billion. In order to determine whether or not such an investment would pay, GM had to undertake the same type of analysis shown in Example 17−2.

17.5 INTERTEMPORAL PRODUCTION DECISIONS

■ In general, firms' production decisions have important intertemporal aspects. Production decisions made today often have an impact on revenues and costs in the future. When time is an important consideration, the net present value rule is used to determine whether or not particular investments should be undertaken. In this section we will investigate one type of production decision for which time is an important consideration: when to extract an exhaustible resource.

An **exhaustible resource**, like oil, coal, or natural gas, exists within the earth in a limited quantity. Once it is used up, there is no more. We can use the notion of present value to develop a simple model for a firm's production decision regarding the extraction of an exhaustible resource.

Suppose there are only two time periods, year 1 (the present) and year 2 (the future). At the beginning of year 1 there are Y_1 barrels of oil available for extraction by firms making up a perfectly competitive oil industry. All the oil will be sold in years 1 or 2, and the greater the quantity sold in year 1, the less will be available in year 2. To simplify the analysis, we assume that the cost of extracting oil is zero; that is, oil gushes from the ground just waiting to be sold. (If we drop this assumption, the analysis becomes complicated but the results do not change substantially.)

Suppose further that there is no OPEC cartel and that the oil industry can be treated as perfectly competitive. Now, what should a profit-maximizing perfect competitor do? Should all the oil be sold in the first year, leaving consumers with no oil in the second year, or should a little be sold each year? If a firm sells oil in year 1, it receives p_1 dollars per barrel. If the firm sells oil in year 2 it receives p_2 dollars per barrel. We must remember that each barrel sold in the first year reduces by one barrel the amount that can be sold in the second year. This is what makes it an exhaustible resource. Thus, the marginal cost of selling a barrel of oil in year 1 is the foregone revenue, p_2, that could have been earned in year 2. Even though there is no production cost, there is an implicit cost of selling oil in year 1.

If the firm is a profit maximizer, whether or not oil will be sold in year 1 will depend on the current price relative to the future price. In addition, as we noted above, another important factor is the fact that a dollar received in the future is not worth the same as a dollar received today. That is, the firm must consider the present value of future revenues when making its extraction decision.

This being the case, the firm's profit-maximizing strategy is to sell oil now if $p_1 > p_2 / (1 + i)$ and to keep the oil in the ground if $p_1 < p_2 / (1 + i)$. Given the firm's expectations about future prices, this rule can be used to determine production.

But what can firms expect prices to do? As long as the current price is greater than the present value of the future price, profit-maximizing firms will sell oil in year 1. However, each barrel sold in year 1 reduces the supply of oil in year 2, which causes the price in year 2 to rise. This means that present sales will expand to the point where $p_1 = p_2 / (1 + i)$; that is, the price of oil should steadily increase over time at a rate equal to the rate of interest.

17.6 THE EQUILIBRIUM INTEREST RATE

■ We have shown that market interest rates are very important for making investment and intertemporal production decisions, but we have not yet discussed how market interest rates are, in fact, determined.

We can think of the market rate of interest as the price that borrowers pay lenders for the use of their funds. Just like any other market price, the equilibrium level is determined by the interaction of supply and demand. In particular, the equilibrium interest rate is determined by the supply and demand for **loanable funds**.

The *supply* of loanable funds comes from consumers who want to postpone current consumption and save in order to increase future consumption. For example, those consumers with current incomes that are large relative to their future incomes may want to save some of their current income in order to increase future consumption. Further, since consumers receive interest on the money they lend, higher interest rates will provide a greater incentive to save. Thus, the supply of loanable funds is positively related to the interest rate.

The *demand* for loanable funds has two components. First, consumers with low current incomes relative to future incomes may want to borrow against future incomes in order to finance additional current consumption. These consumers are willing to pay interest so that they will not have to wait to consume goods and services. However, as the interest rate increases, the cost of obtaining funds to finance additional current consumption increases, the cost of not waiting increases, and individuals will be less willing to borrow. Thus, consumer demand for loanable funds is negatively related to the interest rate.

Second, firms demand loanable funds to finance capital investments. As we demonstrated above, profit-maximizing firms will undertake investments as long as the net present value of an additional investment is positive. Since we also found that the net present value falls and the interest rate rises, we know that the demand for loanable funds to finance capital investments is also negatively related to the interest rate.

We can now discuss the determinants of the market rate of interest. Lenders (savers) supply funds that borrowers use to finance consumption and capital investments. In Figure 17–3, S represents the market supply of loanable funds, D_C represents the

| FIGURE 17–3 | THE EQUILIBRIUM INTEREST RATE |

The equilibrium market rate of interest is determined by equating the supply of and demand for loanable funds.

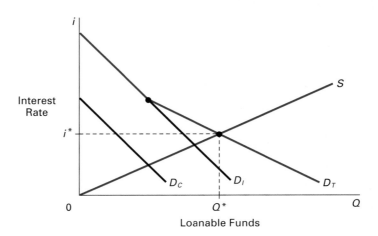

demand for consumer loans, and D_I represents the demand for capital investment funds. The market demand curve for loanable funds, D_T in Figure 17–3, is the sum of these two components. (We could also include the government's demand for loanable funds.)

The equilibrium interest rate depends on both the supply of and demand for loanable funds. In Figure 17–3, the equilibrium interest rate and quantity of loanable funds are i^* and Q^* respectively. In equilibrium, the demand for loanable funds from all sources must equal the supply.

In Example 17–4 below, we demonstrate how to use the supply and demand model discussed above to determine how a reduction in the marginal cost of producing new capital affects the interest rate and aggregate savings.

EXAMPLE 17–3

TECHNOLOGICAL INNOVATIONS AND THE INTEREST RATE

Suppose that the marginal cost of producing new capital falls due to a technological innovation. (a) Demonstrate that this will cause the equilibrium interest rate to rise. (b) What would happen if, at the first sign of rising interest rates, the government imposes an upper limit on the interest rate lenders can charge?

■ **SOLUTION** (a) Figure 17–4 illustrates the effect of a reduction in the marginal cost of producing new capital. Initially, i^* is the equilibrium rate of interest and Q^* is the equilibrium level of saving and investment. If the marginal cost of producing capital goods falls, the demand curve for loanable funds will shift to the right. At every interest rate the demand for funds to produce new capital goods will be greater. In Figure 17–4 this is represented by demand curve D shifting to D_1.

When the demand curve shifts, the equilibrium interest rate rises to i_1 and the equilibrium level of saving increases to Q_1. The cost-saving innovation results in an increase in the interest rate, saving, and investment.

(b) Now suppose that at the first sign of rising interest rates, the government imposes an upper limit of $i^*\%$ on the rate lenders can charge. (We can pick any upper limit and i^* seems to be the most convenient.) What happens? At this interest rate, demanders of loanable funds would like to borrow Q_2 dollars to finance new investment and consumption. However, suppliers of loanable

FIGURE 17-4	COST-SAVING INNOVATIONS AND THE INTEREST RATE

If the marginal cost of producing new capital goods falls, the demand for loanable funds increases as is shown by the shift in the demand curve from D to D_1. This results in an increase in the interest rate, saving, and investment. An interest rate ceiling imposed by the government at i* leads to a shortage of loanable funds.

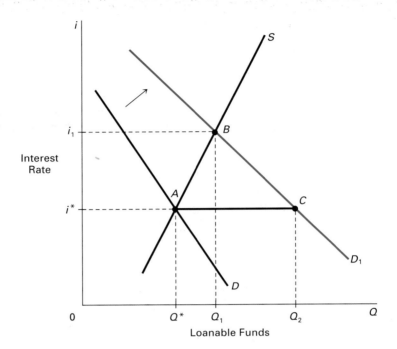

funds are willing to supply only Q* dollars. Thus, the interest rate ceiling results in a shortage of loanable funds. ■

The fact that an interest rate ceiling below the equilibrium interest rate results in a shortage of loanable funds has very serious implications for the economy. The upper limit on interest rates chokes off investment, $Q^* < Q_1 < Q_2$, which, in turn, means that economic growth will be stymied.

SUMMARY

1. In this chapter we investigated firms' investment decisions. We learned how to compare the current cost associated with a particular investment project to the expected future benefits by calculating the present value of the investment. The term *present value* refers to the current value of an amount of money that will be received at some time in the future.

2. In previous chapters we assumed that firms operate to maximize profit. When time is an important consideration, the notion of profit maximization means that firms operate to maximize the present value of all expected future profits. This assumption gives rise to the net present value rule: a profit-maximizing firm will choose to undertake an investment so long as the net present value of the project is positive.

3. In this chapter we also saw how the notion of present value can be used to model the extraction of an exhaustible resource. Once again we found that profit-maximizing firms make decisions by equating marginal revenue and marginal cost. In particular, we found that current sales will expand up to the point where the current price of the exhaustible resource is just equal to the present value of the future price.

4. Finally, we discussed how the equilibrium interest rate is determined by the supply and demand for loanable funds. The supply of loanable funds comes from consumers who want to save. The demand for loanable funds comes from consumers who want to borrow and firms that want to invest. The market rate of interest is the rate that equates supply and demand.

KEY TERMS

Capital Stock
Present Value
Annuities and Bonds
Net Present Value

Discount Rate
Exhaustible Resource
Loanable Funds

QUESTIONS AND PROBLEMS

1. Human capital is defined as the skills or abilities embodied in an individual.
   a) How might we measure human capital? (Be sure to distinguish between stocks and flows.)
   b) How does human capital differ from the physical capital discussed in this chapter?
2. Gerald Smith has a job as a software designer earning $50,000 per year, and he is deciding whether to take another job as the manager of the software division of another firm for $75,000 per year or to purchase a software company that generates a

revenue of $500,000 per year. In order to purchase the company, Gerald would have to use his $100,000 savings and borrow an additional $100,000 at an interest rate of 10% per year. The software company that Gerald is considering purchasing has additional yearly expenses of $200,000 for materials and supplies, $100,000 for hired help, $20,000 for rent, and $10,000 for utilities. Assume that income and business taxes are zero and that the repayment of the principal of the loan does not start before three years.

a) Should Gerald purchase the company?

b) Suppose Gerald expects to sell the company for $150,000 at the end of three years and that he requires a 20% return on his investment. Should he still purchase the company?

3. Suppose you are offered the choice of two payment streams. One is a bond that pays $100 per year for the next three years and then makes a principal repayment of $1,000 in the third year; the other is a bond that pays $250 per year for the next three years and then makes a principal repayment of $500 in the third year.

a) If the interest rate is 5%, which payment stream will you choose?

b) What will you choose if the interest rate is 15%?

c) If the interest rate is 10%, how much will you be willing to pay for each bond?

4. In wrongful death lawsuits, heirs sue to recover damages. One component of these damages is the future income the deceased person would have earned had the accident not occurred. Suppose Sandy Jones dies in an automobile accident at the age of 40. At the time of her death, Sandy was earning $25,000 per year and would have retired at age 65.

a) Assuming Sandy's salary would have increased an average of 5% per year, write down an expression illustrating how to calculate the present value of her lost earnings stream.

b) What discount rate would you choose to make these calculations? Explain.

5. Suppose a bond has two years to mature. It makes a coupon payment of $500 per year and a principal repayment of $1,000 after two years. The bond is currently selling for $950. If you were to purchase this bond, what would be your rate of return? (Hint: The rate of return is simply the interest rate that equates the price of the bond to the present value of the bond.)

6. Suppose you have 15 years left until you retire. Your employer makes available to you one of two supplemental pension

programs, each of which guarantees you a lump sum payment of $500,000 when you retire.

   a) If Program *A* requires you to contribute $20,000 per year for the next 5 years, while Program *B* requires you to contribute $5,000 until you retire, which program should you choose if the market rate of interest is 5%?

   b) What if the market rate of interest is 10%? What if the market rate of interest is 15%?

7. Calculate the net present value of the following:

   a) a duplex yielding $1,000 in rent, net of all expenses, forever

   b) a 30-year government bond that has a face value of $10,000 and promises to pay $100 per year until maturity

   c) a share of preferred stock that is expected to earn $5 per year indefinitely

8. Explain why the net present value rule is simply another example of marginal decision making.

9. a) What factors affect the discount rate used to calculate net present values?

   b) If the risk-free interest rate is 8% and the expected rate of inflation is 5%, what is the real-rate interest rate?

10. The Stereophonics Company is considering whether or not to introduce compact disc player *A* or *B* on the market. The initial cost of introducing either player is $500,000, and the net cash flows generated by each are indicated in the table below. Using a discount rate of 10%, determine which compact disc player the firm should introduce.

	Project A	*Project B*
Initial Cost	$500,000	$ 500,000
Profit		
Year 1	150,000	−50,000
Year 2	150,000	5,000
Year 3	150,000	150,000
Year 4	150,000	150,000
Year 5	150,000	700,000

11. Use the intertemporal production model to explain how an expected increase in future demand for an exhaustible resource will lead to greater conservation of the resource.

12. A third component of the demand for loanable funds is government borrowing to finance deficit spending. Analyze

how government borrowing affects the equilibrium interest rate.

13. "If people suddenly decide to save less, then the demand for bonds will fall; this, in turn, will lower interest rates." Evaluate this statement.

14. Explain how a law limiting the interest rate that lenders could charge would affect the equilibrium interest rate and level of investment.

REFERENCES   Solow, R. 1964. *Capital Theory and the Rate of Return.* Amsterdam: North Holland.

DECISION MAKING AND RISK

18

LEARNING OBJECTIVES

After completing Chapter 18 you should be able to do the following:

- Explain the difference between objective and subjective probability.

- Explain how risk and risk aversion are measured.

- Compare decisions based on maximizing expected value to those based on maximizing expected utility.

- Use the expected utility model to explain why people buy insurance.

- Discuss how asymmetric information can lead to market failure because of the adverse selection and moral hazard problems.

EXAMPLES

- **18-1** Choosing Where to Locate a Franchise

- **18-2** Choosing among Risky Investments

- **18-3** The Optimal Amount of Fire Insurance

Up to this point we have simplified our discussions of decision making by assuming that individuals know all relevant economic variables with certainty. For example, we have assumed that consumers know prices and incomes with certainty before making their consumption choices and that firms know revenues and costs (and, hence, profits) before making their input and output choices. Like most simplifying assumptions, this is not very realistic but, as we have seen in previous chapters, economic models that ignore uncertainty do a good job of explaining and predicting much real-world behavior.

For some purposes, however, we must abandon this assumption because *risk* is an important factor influencing choices. For example, deciding whether or not to obtain a college education, to buy a house, or to invest in the stock market are choices consumers must make that involve a lot of risk. Tuition may be higher or lower next year. Future incomes may or may not be enough to make mortgage payments or to repay student loans. An unexpected increase in oil prices may cause a dramatic fall in stock prices. Similarly, deciding whether or not to introduce a new product, to plant another field of wheat, or to invest in more capital are choices producers must make that involve a lot of risk. Estimated demand for a new product may be quite uncertain. It may or may not rain enough to yield a good harvest. Future profits may or may not be high enough to cover the cost of new capital purchases.

In this chapter we investigate the theory of decision making when risk is important. **Risk** refers to a situation where outcomes are uncertain, but where we can estimate the probability of each outcome. We begin by discussing what we mean by probability, after which we discuss expected value and the implications for behavior of maximizing expected value. Next we discuss one way to measure risk, what we mean by risk aversion, and the implications for behavior of maximizing expected utility. We then illustrate how we can use the expected utility model to explain the demand for insurance. Finally, the chapter concludes with a discussion of one more source of market failure—*asymmetric information*.

18.1 DESCRIBING RISK

■ The best way to introduce the notation and terminology we use to describe risk is to consider a simple example. Suppose Homer Brown, a typical midwestern farmer, must decide whether or not to fertilize his crops. He knows his crop yield, and hence his profit, depends on the weather. If he doesn't fertilize, Homer estimates his profit will be $6,000 if it rains and $4,000 if it doesn't rain; if he does fertilize, Homer estimates his profit will be $10,000 if it rains and $2,000 if it doesn't rain. (Homer does not have an extensive irrigation system. If it doesn't rain, applying fertilizer actually destroys some of the crop, resulting in a reduced profit.) In this instance, risk is important and cannot be ignored, because Homer must choose whether or not to fertilize *before* he knows if it will rain. In general, risk becomes important for consumption, production, and investment decisions when individuals must make their choices *before* they know what outcome will occur.

When we have a situation where there is uncertainty, we denote the various *states of nature* that can occur by θ_j. Each state of nature corresponds to one possible outcome. Homer faces two states of nature—it rains, θ_1, and it does not rain, θ_2. We denote the various *actions* available to the decision maker by a_i. Homer can take one of two possible actions—fertilize, a_1, or do not fertilize, a_2. The *payoff* associated with action a_i when event θ_j occurs is denoted by π_{ij}. Homer's payoffs correspond to the profit that he will realize in each state of nature for each outcome. For example, $\pi_{11} = \$10,000$ represents Homer's profit if he chooses to fertilize (action 1) and it rains (state of nature 1), and $\pi_{22} = \$4,000$ represents his profit if he chooses not to fertilize (action 2) and it does not rain (state of nature 2).

Even though Homer does not know which state of nature will occur prior to choosing an action, we assume that he does know, or can estimate, the *probability* with which each state of nature will occur. By **probability**, we refer to the likelihood that a state of nature will occur. We denote the probability associated with each state of nature by P_j. Probabilities are always nonnegative numbers between zero and one, and if the occurrence of one state of nature precludes the occurrence of any other, probabilities must sum to one. In Homer's case, the probability that it will rain might be, for example, $P_1 = .75$, and the probability that it doesn't might be $P_2 = .25$.

PROBABILITY

There are two interpretations given to the concept of probability. *Objective* probability, on the one hand, is based on the frequency with which a certain outcome occurs and can be determined by observing the outcomes of similar experiments. In the example above, Homer can determine objective probabilities if he has the Farmer's Almanac, which reports historical weather patterns. For example, the Farmer's Almanac may report that, of the last 100 planting seasons, 75 have been rainy and 25 have been drought. In this instance, $P_1 = .75$ and $P_2 = .25$ can be interpreted as *objective* probabilities because they are based on the frequency of similar events.

Subjective probability, on the other hand, is based on the decision maker's belief or perception that a certain outcome will occur and may or may not reflect the corresponding objective probability. When probabilities are subjectively determined, each decision maker may attach different probabilities to the same outcomes and thus make different choices. For example, if Homer did not have access to the Farmer's Almanac, then he would formulate a *subjective* probability of rain based on *his* evaluation of present and past weather conditions. Another farmer might attach a higher subjective probability than Homer does to the chance of rain because he or she has more information (he or she might have the Farmer's Almanac or might know a meteorologist) or because he or she is a better weather forecaster. Either different information or different abilities can explain why subjective probabilities may differ between individuals.

Whether we interpret probability as objective or subjective, it is an important factor that affects choices involving risk. In order to choose between different actions involving risk, the decision maker must consider not only the payoffs associated with each possible outcome but also the probabilities assigned to each. Having evaluated each plan of action, the decision maker must then choose the best strategy to follow. Our next task, then, is to investigate how a decision maker chooses the best plan of action.

18.2 MAXIMIZING EXPECTED VALUE

■ The first objective we will consider is one of choosing the action that maximizes expected value. The **expected value** (or mean) associated with a particular action is a weighted average of the possible outcomes, with the probabilities of the outcomes being the weights. Once again, consider Homer Brown. Suppose that he believes there is a fifty-fifty chance of rain; that is, as far as Homer is concerned, the probability that it will rain is .5, and the probability that it will not rain is .5. These are the subjective probabilities that Homer assigns to each state of nature. Since he is not a meteorologist, these probabilities may or may not reflect the objective probabilities.

Given this information, we can calculate the expected profit associated with each plan of action (fertilize, or do not fertilize). Expected profit is the probability of each state of nature times the resulting profit, summed over all states of nature. In Homer's case, the expected profit associated with the first plan of action, fertilize, is the profit expected to occur on average if he uses fertilizer:

$$E(\pi \mid a_1) = P_1\pi_{11} + P_2\pi_{12} = .5(10,000) + .5(2,000) = \$6,000,$$

where $E(\pi \mid a_1)$ denotes the expected profit of undertaking action one. If Homer chooses to fertilize, then the expected profit resulting from this decision is $6,000. Similarly, the expected profit associated with the second plan of action is given by

$$E(\pi \mid a_2) = P_1\pi_{21} + P_2\pi_{22} = .5(6,000) + .5(4,000) = \$5,000.$$

If Mr. Brown does not fertilize, then expected profit is $5,000.

Now which plan of action should Homer choose? If his objective is to maximize expected profit, then he should choose the strategy that yields the highest expected profit. In this case, he should choose to fertilize since, on average, he expects to earn $1,000 more by fertilizing than by not fertilizing.

EXAMPLE 18-1

CHOOSING WHERE TO LOCATE A FRANCHISE

After the Saturn went into production, General Motors had to decide which of its dealerships would receive a Saturn franchise. Suppose GM is considering two locations: Phoenix, Arizona or Albany, New York. Costs will be the same no matter where the franchises are located; however, revenues will depend on economic conditions. GM believes that in the event of a nationwide recession, Phoenix will be hit harder and estimates that profits will be $100,000 for a Phoenix franchise and $200,000 for an Albany franchise. If there is no recession, however, profit will be only $500,000 for the Phoenix franchise and $300,000 for the Albany franchise. GM's economists estimate that there is a .4 chance of a recession. If GM's goal is to maximize expected profit, which site should it choose?

■ **SOLUTION** Let action a_1 denote locating a franchise in Phoenix and action a_2 denote locating a franchise in Albany. The expected values of each of these alternative actions are

$$E(\pi \mid a_1) = .6(500,000) + .4(100,000) = \$340,000 \qquad \text{and}$$

$$E(\pi \mid a_2) = .6(300,000) + .4(200,000) = \$260,000.$$

Since action a_1 has the higher expected value, GM should locate the franchise in Phoenix. ■

One problem with assuming that individuals choose the plan of action that maximizes expected value is that the dispersion in payoffs is not considered. In Example 18–1, action a_1 has the highest expected value; however, it also has the lowest possible payoff, $100,000. Rather than risk earning a profit of only $100,000, GM might want to guarantee a profit of at least $200,000 by locating the Saturn franchise in Albany. Using only expected value to evaluate alternative strategies does not take into account the *risk* associated with each strategy.

18.3 MEASURING RISK

■ The risk associated with some plan of action is a measure of the dispersion in payoffs. If we are comparing two actions both of which have the same mean, then economists say that the action that has the greater dispersion in payoffs is *riskier* than the other. For example, suppose that an individual is considering two jobs. The first job, a_1, yields an income of $2,000 per month with certainty, while the second job, a_2, yields two equally likely incomes of $3,000 and $1,000 respectively. (Perhaps income from job 2 is based on commissions.) Since the income associated with job 1 is known with certainty, the expected income of a_1 is $2,000 per month. Note also that the expected income associated with a_2 is also $2,000 per month:

$$E(\pi \mid a_2) = .5(3,000) + .5(1,000) = \$2,000.$$

Both jobs have the same expected values; however, action a_2 is *riskier* than action a_1 since the dispersion in payoffs is greater.

One natural measure of risk is the *variance* in payoffs. The variance associated with an action is a measure of the spread or dispersion of the payoffs around its expected value. The variance of the payoffs associated with action a_i, denoted by $\sigma^2(\pi \mid a_i)$, is defined as the expected value of the squared difference between the payoff and the expected payoff:

$$\sigma^2(\pi \mid a_i) = \sum_{j=1}^{n} [\pi_{ij} - E(\pi \mid a_i)]^2 \cdot P_j.$$

For example, in this instance the variance in income of job 1 is zero, and the variance in income of job 2 is

$$\sigma^2(\pi \mid a_2) = .5(3,000 - 2,000)^2 + .5(1,000 - 2,000)^2$$

$$= .5(1,000,000) + .5(1,000,000)$$

$$= 1,000,000.$$

Both of these jobs have the same expected income, but job 2 is substantially riskier than job 1.

■ Suppose we must choose between the two jobs described above. Which would we choose? Clearly, if our objective were to maximize expected income, we would be indifferent between the two jobs; that is, if risk were not a consideration, then the jobs would be equally desirable. But what if risk is important? How will we evaluate these two jobs if risk considerations play a role in our decision-making process?

People differ in their willingness to bear risk. Some are *risk-averse*, some are *risk-loving*, and some are *risk-neutral*. An individual is **risk-averse** if he or she prefers to receive a certain given income equal to the expected value of a gamble rather than take the gamble itself. Given the two jobs described above, a risk-averse individual would choose the sure $2,000 rather than take the fifty-fifty chance of earning $3,000 or $1,000. An individual is **risk-loving** if he or she prefers the gamble to a certain given income equal to the expected value of the gamble. An individual is **risk-neutral** if he or she is indifferent between all gambles with the same mean. That is, for a risk-neutral decision maker only expected values matter.

In order to describe a decision maker's attitude toward risk, we use what is called a *Neumann–Morgenstern* utility function. The Neumann–Morgenstern utility function is named after John von Neumann and Oskar Morgenstern (John von Neumann and Oskar Morgenstern, *Theory of Games and Economic Behavior*, Princeton: Princeton University Press, 1944) who first developed and used this type of utility function. Do not confuse the Neumann-Morgenstern utility function with the utility functions we discussed in earlier chapters. It is a different type of utility function based on different axioms and is used to describe attitudes toward risk.

To simplify matters, we will assume that the utility individuals obtain from choosing between risky alternatives depends only on the monetary payoff associated with each outcome. For example, if we are considering consumers, then we assume utility is a function of income (or a market basket that the income can purchase); if we are considering firms, then we assume utility is a function of profit.

Now let us consider once again our midwestern farmer. Figure 18–1 shows how we can describe Homer's attitude toward risk with a Neumann–Morgenstern utility function. The horizontal axis measures profit and the vertical axis measures utility. The curve $u(\pi)$ represents the relation between utility and profit. It tells us the

FIGURE 18-1   **RISK AVERSION**

Homer is risk-averse because he prefers $6,000 with certainty, point R, to a fifty-fifty chance of $10,000 or $2,000 respectively, point T.

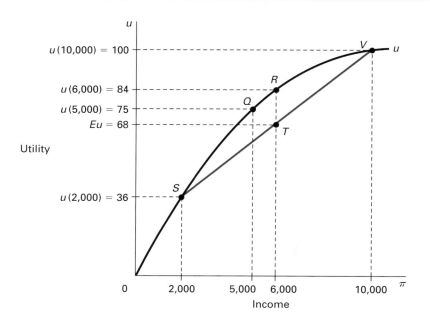

level of utility that Homer can attain for each level of profit. For example, if Homer's profit is $6,000, then his utility is 84. In this instance, utility increases as profit increases, but at a decreasing rate; that is, the utility function is concave. This means that marginal utility (the slope of the utility curve) diminishes as profit increases.

If Homer is risk-averse, then the utility function representing his preferences must reflect the fact that he prefers the expected value of any gamble to the gamble itself. The utility function shown in Figure 18-1 reflects risk aversion. To see this, recall the uncertainty faced by Homer. In Figure 18-1, point S represents the payoff and utility realized if Homer fertilizes (action a_1) and it does not rain, while point V represents the payoff and utility if he fertilizes and it does rain. Recall that the expected value of this plan of action is $6,000. In the diagram, point R represents the payoff and utility realized if Homer were to receive $6,000 with certainty.

But where in the diagram can we see expected utility? Suppose we connect points S and V with a straight line. The slope of this line is

Slope = [u(10,000) − u(2,000)] / [10,000 − 2,000]

= [u(10,000) − u(2,000)] / 8,000.

Given the slope, the equation of the line is given by

[u − u(2,000)] / [π − 2,000] = [u(10,000) − u(2,000)] / 8,000,

or, solving this expression for u:

u = [(π − 2,000) / 8,000]u(10,000) − [(π − 10,000) / 8,000]u(2,000).

If π = 6,000, then u = .5u(10,000) + .5u(2,000) = $Eu(\pi \mid a_1)$. Thus, point T in Figure 18−1 represents the expected utility of undertaking action a_1.

Since Homer's utility function is concave, u(6,000) > .5u(10,000) + .5u(2,000) = $Eu(\pi \mid a_1)$, which implies that Homer would prefer $6,000 for certain to a gamble with a fifty-fifty chance of $10,000 or $2,000. Thus, a concave utility function means that Homer is risk-averse.

Similarly, we can represent risk-loving behavior by a convex utility function and risk-neutral behavior by a linear utility function. These types of utility functions are shown in Figures 18−2(a) and (b) respectively.

RISK-LOVING AND RISK-NEUTRAL PREFERENCES   **FIGURE 18−2**

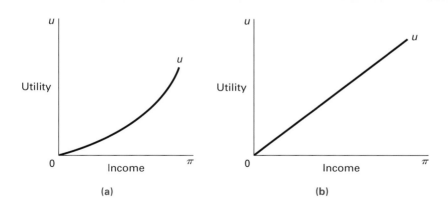

(a)

(b)

(a) Risk-loving preferences are represented by a convex utility function. (b) Risk-neutral preferences are represented by a linear utility function.

■ Now we can develop a systematic way to describe how decision makers choose between different actions when risk matters. The model we will use is based on the notion of *expected utility*. **Expected utility** is equal to the probability of each state of nature times the utility resulting from the realization of the payoff arising in that state, summed over all states of nature. If we let $u(\pi)$ denote the utility that arises when the payoff is π, then if there are only two possible outcomes, the expected utility of some action a_i is given by

$$Eu(\pi \mid a_i) = P_1 u(\pi_{i1}) + P_2 u(\pi_{i2}).$$

The *expected utility hypothesis* asserts that a decision maker chooses the plan of action with the greatest expected utility; that is, the decision maker's objective is to maximize expected utility.

To illustrate, let's suppose that, instead of maximizing expected value, Homer Brown maximizes expected utility. Which plan of action will he choose now? If he takes action a_1, denoted $E(u \mid a_1)$, Homer's expected utility is

$$Eu(\pi \mid a_1) = P_1 u(\pi_{11}) + P_2 u(\pi_{12})$$

$$= .5u(10{,}000) + .5u(2{,}000) = .5 \cdot 100 + .5 \cdot 36 = 68.$$

His expected utility if he takes action a_2 is

$$Eu(\pi \mid a_2) = .5u(6{,}000) + .5u(4{,}000) = 74.$$

Thus, if Homer maximizes expected utility, he will choose action a_2 rather than action a_1; that is, he will choose not to fertilize. The risk of losing much of his crop if he fertilizes and it does not rain outweighs the higher expected income associated with fertilizing.

EXAMPLE 18–2

CHOOSING AMONG RISKY INVESTMENTS

Suppose that the owner of Intercom, a firm that manufactures and sells communications equipment, must choose between two investment projects denoted by a_1 and a_2. The probability distributions for the payoffs for each investment are shown below in the table. Each payoff represents the present value of all future net profits.

	a_1		a_2
Probability	Payoff	Probability	Payoff
.5	$240	.2	$1,000
.5	0	.8	− 100

The owner's utility function is $u = 100\pi - \pi^2$ where π is the payoff. (a) Is this decision maker risk-averse? (b) If the decision maker's objective is to maximize expected net present value, which investment should be undertaken? (c) Which investment project is riskier? (d) If the decision maker's objective is to maximize expected utility, which investment should be undertaken?

■ **SOLUTION** (a) If the decision maker is risk-averse, then he or she should prefer the expected value of a gamble to the gamble itself. To see whether or not this is the case, we can select any two dollar payoffs, say $10 and $50, and assign to each payoff an arbitrary probability, say .6 and .4 respectively. The expected value of this gamble is

$$E\pi = .6(10) + .4(50) = 6 + 20 = \$26.$$

Using the decision maker's utility function, the utilities associated with $10 and $50 are $u(10) = 100 \cdot 10 - 10^2 = 900$ and $u(50) = 100 \cdot 50 - 50^2 = 5,000 - 2,500 = 2,500$ respectively. Therefore, the expected utility of the gamble is

$$Eu = .6u(10) + .4u(50) = .6(900) + .4(2,500)$$

$$= 540 + 1,000 = 1,540.$$

However, if this same individual were offered with certainty $26, the expected value of the gamble, his or her utility would be $u(26) = 100 \cdot 26 - 26^2 = 2,600 - 676 = 1,924$. Because utility is higher for the certain prospect, the individual is risk-averse.

(b) The expected net profits for each investment are

$$E(\pi \mid a_1) = .5 \cdot 240 + .5 \cdot 0 = \$120 \qquad \text{and}$$

$$E(\pi \mid a_2) = .2 \cdot 1,000 + .8(-100) = \$120.$$

Thus, if the decision maker's goal is to maximize expected profit, then he or she is indifferent between the two investments.

(c) Investment project a_2 is riskier than a_1 since it has a greater dispersion in payoffs. For example, if we use the variance to measure risk, then the riskiness of each investment is given by

$$\sigma^2(\pi \mid a_1) = .5(240 - 120)^2 + .5(0 - 120)^2 = 14,400 \qquad \text{and}$$

$$\sigma^2(\pi \mid a_2) = .2(1,000 - 120)^2 + .8(-100 - 120)^2 = 193,600.$$

(d) If the goal of Intercom's owner is to maximize expected utility, then we must calculate the expected utility associated with each investment. This gives

$$Eu(\pi \mid a_1) = .5u(240) + .5u(0)$$

$$= .5(100 \cdot 240 - .01 \cdot 240^2) + .5 \cdot 0 = 23,424$$

and

$$Eu(\pi \mid a_2) = .2u(1,000) + .8u(-100)$$

$$= .2(100 \cdot 1,000 - .01 \cdot 1,000^2)$$

$$+ .8[100 \cdot (-100) - .01(-100)^2]$$

$$= 18,000 - 8,080 = 9,920.$$

The expected utility of investment project a_1 is higher; thus, for an expected utility maximizer project a_1 is the preferred investment. ■

This example confirms our discussion in Chapter 17 concerning the net present value rule when future returns are uncertain. A risk-averse decision maker will consider the riskiness of the investment as well as its expected value.

18.6 AN APPLICATION USING THE EXPECTED UTILITY MODEL: INSURANCE

■ The expected utility model can be used to explain many interesting economic problems concerning individual decision makers. In this section we will examine one of the most important: choosing the optimal amount of insurance coverage. (The appendix to this chapter considers another application—how firms reduce risk through hedging.)

Suppose that John Treadlightly is considering purchasing fire insurance for his home. Currently, he owns a house worth $90,000.

John estimates that the probability of a fire in his home is .5, and that if a fire does occur, the house would be a total loss and he would be left with a piece of land worth $10,000. (John lives out in the country where access to his home by fire-fighting personnel would be difficult.) Thus, if John does not insure against fire (call this action a_1), then he faces a .5 chance of a $90,000 payoff and a .5 chance of a $10,000 payoff. As Figure 18–3 shows, the expected utility of this action is given by the height of C; that is, $Eu(\pi \mid a_1) = .5u(90,000) + .5u(10,000)$.

Insurance offers John a way to reduce risk by changing the payoffs associated with each possible state of nature. Suppose an insurance company offers John a contract that will pay him $80,000, in the event that his house burns down, in exchange for some premium payment. How much is John willing to pay to have this insurance contract?

Assume that John is an expected utility maximizer. In order to determine the amount John is willing to pay for insurance, we must compare the expected utilities of the two actions (insure, and do not insure). If John purchases insurance (action a_2), then he must pay the premium, denoted by PR, whether his house burns down or not. This means that if he purchases insurance, then he has a .5

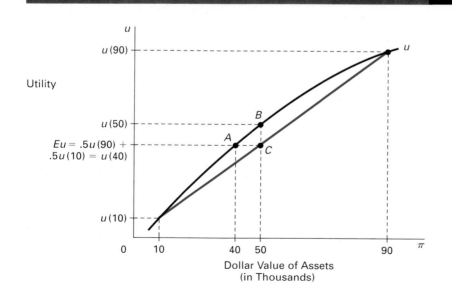

RISK AVERSION AND INSURANCE   **FIGURE 18–3**

An insurance contract guaranteeing John $40,000 has the same expected utility as a fifty-fifty chance of $90,000 or $10,000 respectively. Thus, John is willing to pay up to $50,000 to insure his home.

chance of a payoff of $(90,000 - PR)$ dollars and a .5 chance of a payoff of $(90,000 - 80,000 + 80,000 - PR) = (90,000 - PR)$ dollars. Thus, by purchasing the insurance, John will in effect have a guaranteed payoff of $(90,000 - PR)$ dollars.

Now recall that John's expected utility if he does not purchase insurance is given by the height of C in Figure 18–3. Notice that this is equal to the height of A, which corresponds to John's utility if he were to receive \$40,000 with certainty; that is, from Figure 18–3 we conclude that $Eu(\pi \mid a_1) = u(40,000)$. If John is an expected utility maximizer, then he is equally happy with a guaranteed income of $(50,000 - AC) = (50,000 - 10,000) = \$40,000$ as with the gamble. Thus, John would be willing to pay a premium of $[90,000 - (50,000 - AC)] = \$50,000$ to avoid the risk of his house burning down. By purchasing the insurance for \$50,000, John has transformed the uncertain gamble of a fifty-fifty chance of \$90,000 or \$10,000 into a certain payoff of \$40,000, which has the same expected utility.

EXAMPLE 18–3

THE OPTIMAL AMOUNT OF FIRE INSURANCE

The owner of a small manufacturing firm, Carol Lee Jenkins, has been paying an annual premium of \$5,000 per year for \$100,000 of fire insurance on her plant. The firm is expected to earn a profit of \$100,000 in the coming year. A consultant hired by the firm to determine if the insurance policy should be renewed estimates that the probability of a fire during any year is only .004. Assuming that if a fire breaks out, the warehouse would be a total loss, the consultant recommends that the insurance be renewed. Evaluate this recommendation if (a) Carol's objective is to maximize expected profit, or (b) her objective is to maximize expected utility, where utility is given by $u = 150\pi - .001\pi^2$.

■ **SOLUTION** (a) The decision maker has available two possible actions. Action a_1 is to renew the insurance policy. If this action is undertaken, and there is no fire during the year, then Carol earns a profit of \$100,000 less the \$5,000 insurance premium, or \$95,000. If she renews the policy, and there is a fire, then Carol earns a profit of \$100,000 less \$100,000 in fire loss, plus the \$100,000 the insurance company pays less the \$5,000 insurance premium, or \$95,000. Thus, if she renews the insurance, Carol earns a profit of \$95,000 with certainty.

Action a_2 is to cancel the insurance policy. If Carol undertakes this action, and there is no fire during the year, then her profit is $100,000. If she cancels the policy and there is a fire, then the firm earns a profit of $100,000 less $100,000 in fire loss, or $0. Given that the probability of a fire is .004, the expected value of a_2 is

$$E(\pi \mid a_2) = .996(100,000) + .004 \cdot 0 = \$99,600.$$

Since $E(\pi \mid a_2) > E(\pi \mid a_1)$, if the owner of the firm aims to maximize expected profit, then she should not follow the consultant's recommendation and should cancel the insurance policy.

(b) Now let us see if Carol's decision is different if she is an expected utility maximizer. The expected utility associated with action a_1, (renew) is simply the utility of the certain profit of $95,000 per year:

$$Eu(\pi \mid a_1) = u(95,000) = 150(95,000) + .001(95,000)^2$$

$$= 150(95,000) + 95(95,000) = 5,225,000.$$

The expected utility associated with action a_2 (cancel) is

$$Eu(\pi \mid a_2) = .996u(100,000) + .004u(0) = .996u(100,000)$$

$$= .996[150(100,000) + .001(100,000)^2]$$

$$= .996[150(100,000) + 100(100,000)] = 4,980,000.$$

Since $Eu(\pi \mid a_1) > Eu(\pi \mid a_2)$, Carol should follow the consultant's recommendations and renew the insurance. ■

■ So far we have discussed how risk affects an *individual's* choices. In the remainder of the chapter we will address the issue of how risk affects market results—that is, how uncertainty affects the interaction of buyers and sellers and, hence, equilibrium prices and quantities. We will see that when some individuals know more than others, that is, when there is *incomplete information*, competitive markets fail.

In Chapter 8 we noted that there are four essential requirements for perfect competition: buyers and sellers are price takers; the product or resource being traded is homogeneous; resources are perfectly mobile; and buyers and sellers have complete information concerning all relevant variables. When there is uncertainty, these requirements need to be modified somewhat. In particular, in the presence of uncertainty the four requirements for perfect

18.7 MARKETS WITH INCOMPLETE INFORMATION

competition are as follows: buyers and sellers cannot affect the probability distributions describing the economic environment (this is equivalent to the price taker requirement); the product or resource being traded is homogeneous; resources are perfectly mobile; and buyers and sellers have complete information concerning the probability distributions of all relevant variables.

If these requirements are met, then competitive markets will yield an efficient allocation of resources just as they do when there is no uncertainty. Demand curves will reflect marginal private and social benefits of consumption, and supply curves will reflect marginal private and social costs of production.

However, in many instances competitive markets fail when there is uncertainty. There are two primary reasons for this. First, competitive markets will fail if either buyers and sellers do not have complete information about market prices, product quality, or other relevant variables; second, they will fail if either buyers or sellers can affect the probabilities or the magnitudes of the payoffs associated with the various states of nature that can arise. In the next two sections we will discuss these two reasons for market failure. We will focus on the market for insurance, although the analysis is relevant for any market in which buyers and sellers face uncertainty.

THE ADVERSE SELECTION PROBLEM

Earlier in this chapter, we discussed insurance from the buyer's side of the market. In particular, we determined how much an individual buyer would be willing to pay to purchase insurance. Now let us extend this discussion to include both buyers and sellers of insurance and illustrate one problem that can arise when buyers and sellers do not have access to the same information.

Suppose that there are two kinds of people willing to buy medical insurance: high-risk people and low-risk people. Also, suppose that both buyers and sellers *can identify* high- and low-risk individuals; that is, buyers and sellers have complete information. In this instance, there will be two markets for medical insurance, as illustrated in Figures 18−4(a) and 18−4(b). In the first diagram, S_L is the supply curve for insurance for low-risk individuals, and D_L is the demand curve for the same group. The supply curve reflects the marginal private and social cost of producing health insurance. The demand curve reflects the marginal private and social benefit of purchasing insurance. Similarly, in the second diagram S_H and D_H are the supply and demand curves for insurance for high-risk individuals. These curves also reflect private and social benefits and costs. Note that S_H is higher than S_L because it is more costly to insure high-risk individuals, and sellers must

THE ADVERSE SELECTION PROBLEM   **FIGURE 18–4**

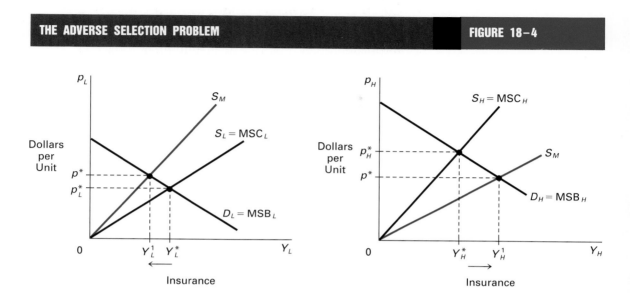

If firms cannot distinguish between high- and low-risk individuals, then adverse selection results in an inefficient allocation of resources. Too few low-risk individuals will be insured, $Y_L^1 < Y_L^*$, and too many high-risk individuals will be insured, $Y_H^1 > Y_H^*$.

receive a higher price to do so. Also, D_H is higher than D_L because high-risk individuals are willing to pay more for insurance. As the diagrams show, the market price for insurance is p_H^* for high-risk individuals and p_L^* for low-risk individuals, Y^* individuals of each type are insured, and perfect competition yields an efficient allocation of resources.

So far we have assumed that buyers and sellers have complete information in that they can tell which individuals are high-risk and which are low-risk. In reality this is usually not the case. People buying insurance know much more about their general health than does any insurance company or, at least, it is very costly for insurance companies to find out the same information. As a result, this competitive market will fail.

If buyers have information concerning their health that insurance companies do not, then initially insurance companies might operate under the assumption that it is equally likely that any one individual is high- or low-risk. When selling insurance, then, sellers would view all individuals as being of medium-risk. The supply curve for insurance for medium-risk individuals is S_M in

Figure 18–4. It lies below S_H but above S_L. This curve reflects the marginal private cost of insuring medium-risk individuals.

Unfortunately, since there are no medium-risk individuals in the market, supply curve S_M does not reflect the marginal social cost of insuring high- and low-risk individuals. As shown in Figure 18–4, the equilibrium price of insurance will rise to p^*. At this price, the number of low-risk individuals falls from the efficient level, Y_L^*, to the competitive level, Y_L^1, while the number of high-risk individuals increases from the efficient level, Y_H^*, to the competitive level, Y_H^1. Because suppliers cannot distinguish between buyers, the competitive equilibrium does not yield an efficient allocation of resources.

Incomplete information, therefore, leads to too many high-risk individuals being insured relative to the number of low-risk individuals. This phenomenon is known as the adverse selection problem. **Adverse selection** arises when buyers and sellers have different information, and it leads to inefficiencies.

This kind of market failure creates another role for government. In the case of health insurance, adverse selection provides an argument in favor of some type of government-financed health insurance program. By providing insurance for all individuals, the government can eliminate the adverse selection problem.

THE MORAL HAZARD PROBLEM

Even if the adverse selection problem can be solved, another problem arises, called the moral hazard problem. In general, **moral hazard** arises when individuals who want insurance can affect the probability or magnitude of the payoff associated with a certain outcome. This, in turn, creates a divergence between marginal private and marginal social costs and prohibits competitive markets from allocating resources efficiently.

Both governments and private insurance companies must deal with the moral hazard problem. For example, in the United States the government provides health insurance for the poor under the age of 65 through Medicaid and health insurance for the elderly through Medicare. Figure 18–5 illustrates the moral hazard problem. Let us assume that medical services consumed can be measured by office visits and that the medical services industry is a perfectly competitive constant cost industry. In Figure 18–5, LS is the long-run supply curve for the industry, and it represents both the marginal private and marginal social costs of supplying medical services. The demand for medical services, D, represents both the marginal private and marginal social benefits of consuming medical services. The equilibrium price and quantity in the absence of any moral hazard problem are p^* and Y^* respectively.

THE MORAL HAZARD PROBLEM

FIGURE 18-5

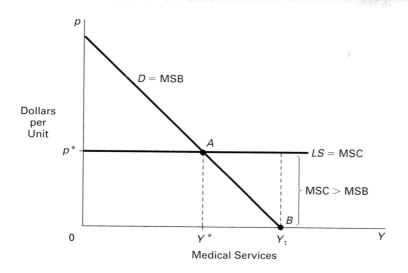

When private firms or the government attempt to remedy the adverse selection problem by providing complete insurance coverage for everyone, individuals tend to consume more than the efficient quantity of services, $Y_1 > Y^*$.

After medical insurance is purchased, however, the price of health care falls essentially to zero. Thus, individuals have an incentive to be more lax in maintaining their health. At a zero price, quantity demanded increases to the point where marginal private benefit is zero, point B in Figure 18-5. At this level of consumption the marginal social cost of providing medical services exceeds the marginal social benefit of consuming those services; that is, the program results in an inefficient allocation of resources.

Whenever governments finance the provision of certain goods or services, there is a tendency for those persons who are eligible for the program to consume more than the efficient amount. Private insurance companies also must face this problem. Insurance policies that offer unlimited (or full) coverage create an incentive for beneficiaries to consume more than they would if they had to pay the price of the service themselves.

Concern about the moral hazard problem has resulted in various schemes to make consumers pay part of the cost of the services they consume. If the insurance companies can monitor each individual buyer, then they can charge higher fees for those who submit more claims. If they cannot effectively monitor behavior (or cannot do so at a reasonable cost), then one common scheme to reduce the magnitude of the moral hazard problem is to require buyers to meet a deductible amount before their benefits will be paid. Another scheme is called coinsurance. Coinsurance requires the insured person to pay a certain percentage of the cost of the services while the insurance company pays the rest. Coinsurance has become particularly popular with insurance companies that provide group health insurance programs. Finally, insurance companies can reduce the moral hazard problem by agreeing to pay only a fixed amount (reasonable and customary) for certain services. In the U.S. the federal government uses this scheme with the Medicaid and Medicare programs.

1. In this chapter we have investigated choices involving risk. Risk is important when individuals must make their choices before they know what outcome will occur.
2. Probability refers to the likelihood that a state of nature will occur. Probabilities are used to describe risk and allow the decision maker to compare alternative actions.
3. One viable decision rule is to choose the plan of action that maximizes expected value. While this decision rule is useful as a first approximation, it is not completely satisfactory because it does not consider the dispersion in payoffs or the riskiness of different actions.
4. One alternative to expected value maximization is expected utility maximization. If a decision maker chooses the plan of action that maximizes expected utility, then both the expected value of an action and the risk associated with the action are important.
5. The expected utility model can be used to explain why risk-averse individuals purchase insurance. Basically, insurance is a way to reduce risk—something risk averters will pay to be able to do.
6. Problems lead to market failure when buyers and sellers have incomplete information. The adverse selection problem arises when buyers and sellers have different information concerning the probabilities of different events' occurring. The moral hazard problem arises when one economic agent can affect the probabilities or payoffs of an event by altering his or her behavior. Both problems lead to an inefficient allocation of resources.

Risk

Probability

Expected value

Risk-averse

Risk-loving

Risk-neutral

Expected Utility

Insurance

Adverse Selection

Moral Hazard

1. a) Explain the difference between certainty and uncertainty.
   b) Explain the difference between objective and subjective probabilities.
2. Harvey Brunner, a salesperson for an encyclopedia publisher, estimates that in his new territory he will sell an encyclopedia in 2 of every 20 homes that he visits. In a typical week, Harvey will visit 60 homes. If it costs Harvey $20, which includes all

implicit as well as explicit costs, to visit one home, and if his commission is $100 for each encyclopedia sold, determine Harvey's expected profit per week.

3. Janice is considering purchasing a lottery ticket that costs $300 and that offers a .5 chance of winning $1,000 and a .5 chance of not winning anything.

   a) If Janice is an expected value maximizer, will she purchase a lottery ticket?

   b) What is the most Janice would pay for a ticket?

   c) If her preferences can be represented by a utility function, $u(\pi)$, for which $u(0) = 0$, $u(250) = 50$, $u(500) = 75$, and $u(1,000) = 1$, is Janice risk-averse, risk-neutral, or risk-loving?

   d) Will Janice purchase a ticket if she is an expected utility maximizer?

4. a) Explain the difference between risk-averse and risk-loving.

   b) Would an expected utility maximizer ever play gambling games in which dollar returns are expected to be negative?

5. Will an expected value maximizer behave the same way as an expected utility maximizer who is risk-neutral? Explain.

6. Suppose Tanya Take-a-Chance must choose one of two gambles:

   Gamble 1: Win $500 with probability 1/2; loose $500 with probability 1/2.
   Gamble 2: Win $1,000 with probability 1/3; loose $500 with probability 2/3.

   a) Calculate the expected values of both gambles.

   b) Which gamble will Tanya take? Explain.

7. Otis O'Keefer is an independent trucker. He has contracted to haul oranges from San Antonio, Texas, to Detroit, Michigan. The contract gives Otis one week to transport 10,000 pounds of oranges. Otis' truck is large enough to hold all 10,000 pounds of oranges; however the truck is not refrigerated, and Otis knows that there is a 50% chance that all the oranges hauled in any one trip will rot. Otis is considering two possible actions— making one trip and hauling all 10,000 pounds of oranges, or making two trips and hauling 5,000 pounds each trip.

   a) If each trip to Detroit costs $500 and Otis is paid one dollar for each pound of oranges delivered in good condition, how many trips will Otis make if he maximizes expected profit?

   b) How many will he make if he maximizes expected utility?

8. The owner of Tristar, a firm that manufactures and sells satellite dishes for televisions, is considering two alternative strategies for marketing a new type of dish. The probability distributions

for the payoffs associated with each strategy are shown below, where a_1 and a_2 denote strategies 1 and 2 respectively. Each payoff represents the present value of all future net profits in millions of dollars.

	a_1		a_2	
Probability	Payoff	Probability	Payoff
.5	$10	.1	$20
.5	4	.9	0

a) If the owner's objective is to maximize expected profit, which strategy should he choose?

b) If the owner's utility function is $u = \sqrt{.000001\pi}$ and his objective is to maximize expected utility, which strategy should he choose?

c) Compare your answers to parts (a) and (b), and explain why they differ.

9. Suppose the owner of Genestar, a perfectly competitive firm that manufactures and sells stereos, must decide between two production strategies. The first strategy, plan a_1, results in an output rate of 15,000 stereos, while the second, plan a_2, results in 35,000 stereos. The owner must make the production decision before the price of stereos is known with certainty. She estimates that there is a fifty-fifty chance that the price of a stereo will be $1,000 and a fifty-fifty chance that it will be $400. The long-run cost curves are given by

$$LTC = .01x^2 \quad \text{and} \quad LMC = .02x,$$

where x is the number of stereos produced.

a) If the owner of the firm is risk-neutral, which production strategy will she choose?

b) If the owner of the firm is risk-averse with $u = \sqrt{.000001\pi}$, which production strategy will she choose?

10. Jean Treadlightly, John's sister, also owns a house worth $90,000. Jean lives in the city not far from the fire station, and she estimates that there is only a .01 chance of a fire in her home, and that if there were a fire, the damage would be approximately $10,000.

a) How much is Jean willing to pay for an insurance contract that pays her $10,000 in the event of a fire?

b) Illustrate with a graph.

11. The owner of a firm has been paying \$2,500 per year for \$50,000 of fire insurance. The firm is expected to earn \$200,000 in the coming year. The probability of a fire during any year is estimated to be .1.
    a) If the owner's objective is to maximize expected profit, should the firm continue its insurance policy?
    b) If the owner's objective is to maximize expected utility, where utility is given by $u = \sqrt{.001\pi}$, should the firm continue its policy?
12. Can the adverse selection problem be used to explain why people over 65 have difficulty buying medical insurance?
13. a) Credit card companies must charge the same interest rate to all borrowers. Explain how this leads to an adverse selection problem.
    b) Lenders often use computerized credit histories to distinguish between high- and low-risk borrowers. Does this reduce the adverse selection problem? Explain.
14. Many automobile manufacturers offer extended warranties on their cars and trucks. Usually the warranties are for 5 years or 50,000 miles and cover parts and labor for mechanical problems. Will a program like this create a moral hazard problem? Explain.
15. Consider two types of health insurance: complete coverage beyond a \$2,000 deductible; 80% coverage on all medical bills. Compare these types of policies in terms of the moral hazard problem.

REFERENCES   Kreps, D. 1990. *A Course in Microeconomic Theory*. Princeton: Princeton University Press.

Laffont, J. 1990. *The Economics of Uncertainty and Information*. Cambridge: The MIT Press.

HEDGING AND THE PRICE-TAKING FIRM

A *forward contract* is an agreement between buyer and seller that fixes the future price of the good being traded. One of the most common methods owners of firms use to deal with price uncertainty is to use forward contracts to sell all or part of their output. This is called *hedging*. Hedging allows price-taking firms to eliminate the risk associated with an uncertain output price.

When a price-taking firm is confronted with uncertainty, in general the profit-maximizing level of production depends on the probability distribution of the price and on the risk-taking characteristics of the owner of the firm. However, when forward contracts are possible, we can use the expected utility model to show that a risk-averse price-taking firm will produce a level of output that is independent of both the firm's risk-taking characteristics and the probability distribution of output price.

Let us begin by assuming that a price-taking firm faces an uncertain market price, p, for its product, good y. For simplicity, suppose that there are only two possible states of nature that can occur: high price, p_H, and low price, p_L. The probability that the high-price state will occur is P_1, and the probability that the low-price state will occur is P_2, where $P_1 + P_2 = 1$. Output can be produced at cost of $C(y)$ and can be sold in the future at the uncertain market price or sold forward for a certain price of $\hat{p}$. The amount of output that the owner of the firm hedges is denoted by $\hat{y}$.

If the owner of the firm is an expected utility maximizer, then his or her choices about how much output to produce and how much to hedge must be determined by what will make the expected utility of profit as large as possible. That is, the owner of the firm must choose y and $\hat{y}$ to maximize

$$Eu(\pi) = P_1 u(\pi_H) + P_2 u(\pi_L), \qquad (A18.1)$$

where $\pi_H = [p_H(y - \hat{y}) + \hat{p}\hat{y} - C(y)]$ and $\pi_L = [p_L(y - \hat{y}) + \hat{p}\hat{y} - C(y)]$ are profit in the high-price and low-price states respectively. In equation (A18.1), the terms $p_H(y - \hat{y})$ and $p_L(y - \hat{y})$ represent the uncertain portions of total revenue and $\hat{p}\hat{y}$ represents the certain portion. Note that if all output is hedged—if $y = \hat{y}$—then profit does not depend on the uncertain price and the problem reduces to the standard profit maximization problem we studied in Chapter 8.

In this problem there are two choice variables, y and $\hat{y}$, so there are two conditions describing the situation where expected utility is maximized. The first condition concerns the choice of y. If expected utility is maximized with respect to y, the change in expected utility per unit change in y must be equal to zero:

$$dEu(\pi) / dy = P_1MU(\pi_H)(p_H - MC) + P_2MU(\pi_L)(p_L - MC) = 0,$$

(A18.2)

where $MU(\pi) = du / d\pi$ is the marginal utility of profit, and MC is marginal production costs. The second condition concerns the choice of $\hat{y}$. If expected utility is maximized with respect to $\hat{y}$, then the change in expected utility per unit change in $\hat{y}$ must be equal to zero:

$$dEu(\pi) / d\hat{y} = P_1MU(\pi_H)(\hat{p} - p_H) + P_2MU(\pi_L)(\hat{p} - p_L) = 0.$$

(A18.3)

Next, since both of the expressions in equations (A18.2) and (A18.3) are equal to zero, we can add them together, which gives

$$P_1MU(\pi_H)(\hat{p} - MC) + P_2MU(\pi_L)(\hat{p} - MC) = 0,$$

or, factoring out $(\hat{p} - MC)$, the optimal level of production must satisfy

$$(\hat{p} - MC)[P_1MU(\pi_H) + P_2MU(\pi_L)] = 0.$$

(A18.4)

For any risk-averse decision maker the marginal utility of profit is positive, which means that the equation given above can only hold if $(\hat{p} - MC) = 0$. Thus, the owner of a price-taking firm will choose the level of output corresponding to the point where marginal production costs are equal to the forward price of the good.

This is a very interesting result. If firms hedge, then the optimal level of production is affected neither by the risk associated with the uncertain future price of the product nor by the risk-taking characteristics of the decision maker. Hedging allows the optimal level of production to be chosen just as if output price were certain.

EXAMPLE A18-1

Yadanei, Inc., manufactures and sells compact camcorders. Firms in the compact camcorder industry are price takers. Total and marginal costs of producing camcorders, good y, are $C = 5y^2$ and $MC = 10y$ respectively. At the time the owner is making the production decision, the market price for camcorders is not known with certainty. Yadanei's economists estimate that in the coming year it is equally likely that camcorders will sell for $600 or $400. Camcorders can be sold in the future at the prevailing market price or can be sold forward for a certain price of $500 per camcorder. (a) If the owners of Yadanei, Inc., want to maximize the expected utility of profit, and if the relevant utility function is $u = (60,000\pi - \pi^2) / 100,000$, then how many camcorders should the firm produce and how many should it hedge in the forward market? (b) How does your answer change if Yadanei's economists estimate that in the coming year there is a fifty-fifty chance that the price of camcorders will be either $800 or $400?

■ **SOLUTION** (a) As we demonstrated above, in order to determine the output level that maximizes expected utility, we must find the level of output corresponding to the point where marginal cost equals the forward price of camcorders. Setting marginal cost equal to the forward price and solving for y, we have: $y^* = 500 / 10 = 50$ camcorders per year.

Next, we must find the optimal number of units to hedge when there is a fifty-fifty chance that the price of camcorders will be either $600 or $400. Again, as we demonstrated above, the condition giving the optimal amount of hedging is

$$.5MU(\pi_H)(\hat{p} - p_H) + .5MU(\pi_L)(\hat{p} - p_L) = 0,$$

where $\pi_H = p_H(y - \hat{y}) + \hat{p}\hat{y} - 5y^2$, $\pi_L = p_L(y - \hat{y}) + \hat{p}\hat{y} - 5y^2$, and $MU(\pi) = (60,000 - 2\pi) / 100,000$. Since we want to solve this equation for $\hat{y}$, it will be helpful to rewrite the profit functions by isolating this variable; that is, $\pi_H = (\hat{p} - p_H)\hat{y} + p_H y - 5y^2$ and $\pi_L = (\hat{p} - p_L)\hat{y} + p_L y - 5y^2$. Substituting for the parameter values given in the problem and the optimal level of production, we have

$$\pi_H = -100\hat{y} + 600 \cdot 50 - 5 \cdot 50^2 = -100\hat{y} + 27,500;$$

$$\pi_L = 100\hat{y} + 400 \cdot 50 - 5 \cdot 50^2 = 100\hat{y} + 18,500;$$

$$MU(\pi_H) = [60,000 - 2(-100\hat{y} + 27,500)] / 100,000$$

$$= (200\hat{y} + 5,000) / 100,000; \qquad \text{and}$$

$$MU(\pi_L) = [60,000 - 2(100\hat{y} + 18,500)] / 100,000$$

$$= (-200\hat{y} + 2,500) / 100,000.$$

Substituting these results into the condition given above, we have

$$.5[(500 - 600)MU(\pi_H) + (500 - 400)MU(\pi_L)]$$

$$= (50 / 100,000)[(-200\hat{y} - 5,000) + (25,000 - 200\hat{y})]$$

$$= (50 / 100,000)(20,000 - 400\hat{y}) = 0.$$

Solving this last equality gives the desired result: $\hat{y} = 20,000 / 400 = 50$ camcorders. Thus, the expected utility maximizing strategy is to sell all 50 camcorders produced at the certain forward price of $500 per camcorder—that is, to hedge all units produced.

(b) Our last task is to redo our calculations when there is a fifty-fifty chance that the price of camcorders will be either $800 or $400 dollars. Since the optimal level of production is independent of the probability distribution of prices, the firm should still produce 50 camcorders. However, it should hedge a different number of units.

Substituting the new high price into the appropriate equations, we have:

$$\pi_H = -300\hat{y} + 37,500;$$

$$MU(\pi_H) = [60,000 - 2(-300\hat{y} + 37,500)] / 100,000$$

$$= (600\hat{y} - 15,000) / 100,000;$$

and $.5[(500 - 800)MU(\pi_H) + (500 - 400)MU(\pi_L)]$

$$= [150(15,000 - 600\hat{y}) + 100(25,000 - 200\hat{y})] / 100,000$$

$$= (4,750,000 - 110,000\hat{y}) / 100,000 = 0.$$

Solving the last equation for $\hat{y}$, we find that $\hat{y} = 4,750 / 110 \simeq 43$ camcorders. Thus, when the estimated high price increases to $800, the optimal hedge falls to 43 camcorders. ■

The last result, showing that the optimal hedge falls when the high price estimate rises, is actually a general principle of this model. Notice that when the estimated high and low prices are $600 and $400 respectively, the expected market price for camcorders is $(.5 \cdot 600 + .5 \cdot 400) = \$500$, which is precisely the certain forward price. When this occurs—that is, when the forward price is equal to the expected market price—the firm should always hedge all of its output.

When the estimated high price increases to $800, the expected market price becomes $600, which is greater than the certain forward price. In this instance, the firm should hedge less than the total amount produced. Thus, as the expected market price increases relative to the certain forward price, the amount of output hedged falls as the firm trades off higher expected profit for greater risk. The precise amount of output hedged will depend on the risk-taking characteristics of the owners of the firm.

ANSWERS TO ODD-NUMBERED QUESTIONS AND PROBLEMS

CHAPTER 1

1. In a market economy, only those consumers willing and able to pay market prices can obtain goods and services. As a result, prices "ration" goods and services among those consumers who value them most.

3. Theoretical models should be judged according to how well they explain and predict what they were designed to explain and predict, and not solely on the basis of their assumptions.

5.

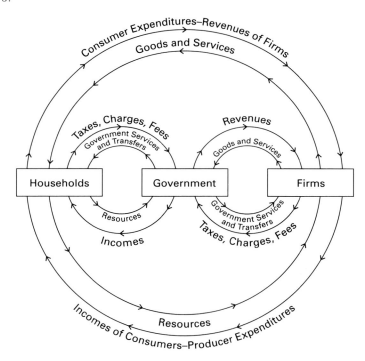

CHAPTER 2

1. a) Since the cost of manufacturing software is independent of the number of packages produced, $c = \$150$, and the relation between profit—total revenue minus total cost—and the number of packages produced is given by $\pi = pn - cn = 300n - 150n = 150n$.

b)

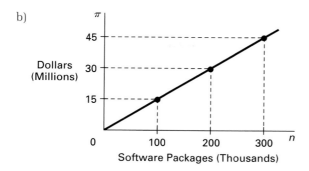

c) Now cost per package varies with the number of packages produced:

$$c = \begin{cases} \$150 & \text{if } 0 < n \le 100{,}000 \\ \$200 & \text{if } \quad\;\; n > 100{,}000 \end{cases}.$$

The relation between profit and the number of packages produced also has two parts:

$$\pi = \begin{cases} (p - c)n & \text{if } 0 < n \le 100{,}000 \\ \$5{,}000{,}000 + (p - c)(n - 100{,}000) & \text{if } n > 100{,}000 \end{cases}$$

d)

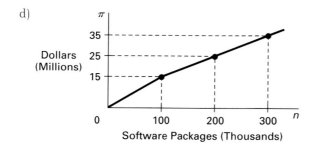

3. a) Let L denote the number of workers, w the wage rate, c labor costs, and Y the number of suspenders produced each day. Labor costs are the wage times the number of workers employed ($C = wL$), and the number of suspenders produced is 100 times the number of workers employed ($Y = 100L$). Thus, the function relating the number of workers employed to suspender production is $L = Y/100$. The relation between labor costs and suspender production follows directly: $C = wL = w(Y/100) = 1.5Y$.

b)
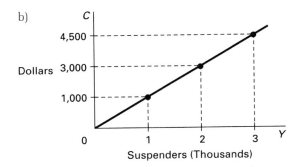

5. The equilibrium price and quantity of cigarettes fall.

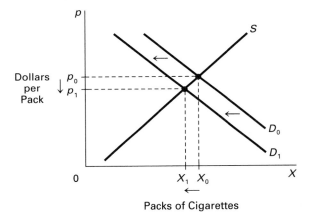

Packs of Cigarettes

7. When a university provides student health care at a price below the equilibrium price, quantity demanded exceeds quantity supplied. As a result, students must wait in line to receive treatment.

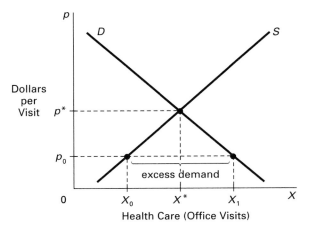

Health Care (Office Visits)

9. You should study until the marginal value of time is equal to the marginal cost of studying. Thus, if the marginal cost of studying is zero, then you should follow your friend's suggestion.

11. **a)** Setting marginal revenue equal to zero and solving for Y gives the revenue-maximizing quantity: $Y^* = 50,000$. If this quantity is sold, revenue will be $500,000.

   b)

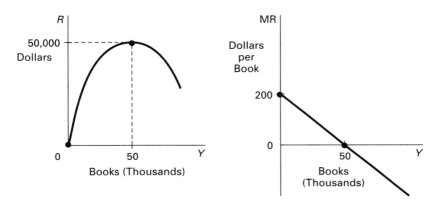

13. Andy should allocate his time so that the marginal value of time is equal for each subject, provided that he spends no more than 12 hours studying. As the table below shows, Andy should study 1 hour for marketing, 5 hours for accounting, and 6 hours for economics.

Andy's Marginal Value of Study Time			
Study Time (Hours)	MV_t^a	MV_t^m	MV_t^e
0	—	—	—
1	0	**10**	5
2	4	3	18
3	6	2	20
4	12	0	15
5	**10**	0	12
6	2	0	**10**
7	2	0	5
8	2	0	3
9	2	0	2
10	2	0	1
11	1	0	1
12	1	0	1

15. No. To maximize his expected returns, he should allocate his funds so that the marginal return is the same across stocks, provided he spends only $1,000. Since the total returns are the same, the marginal returns are the same, which means that Ivan should invest equal amounts ($500) in each stock. You can check this by substituting into the return function.

CHAPTER 3

1. The budget constraint indicates all the combinations of goods that an individual can purchase with his or her limited income. The price ratio determines the slope of the budget constraint and reflects the opportunity cost of purchasing an additional unit of one good in terms of the other.

3. The budget constraint becomes AB, and the budget set is reduced to the shaded area.

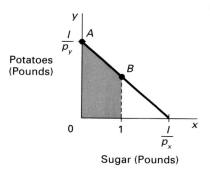

5. The lump-sum fee shifts the budget constraint from AB to ACD and shrinks the budget set from $0AB$ to $0CD + AC$.

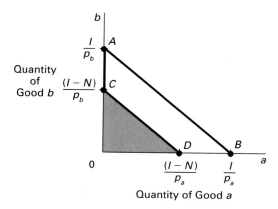

7. Winning the lottery shifts the budget constraint out parallel to the original budget constraint, which in turn expands the budget set. This means there are more market baskets that are affordable.

9. Let C denote expenditures on all other goods, G expenditures on charity, and t the income tax rate. For any arbitrary tax rate, Ms. Willis' budget constraint is $I - t(I - G) = G + C$, where $(I - G)$ is her taxable income. Combining like terms and sustituting for t gives the following:
   a) BC_1: $.95I = .95G + C$.
   b) BC_2: $.9I = 9G + C$. Her budget set shrinks from $0AD$ to $0BD$.

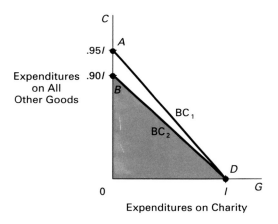

11. The budget set consists of market baskets A, B, D, E and all those vertically below A, B, D, and E.

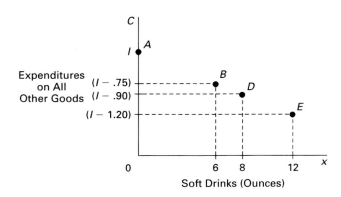

13. The pretax budget constraint, BC_1, is $I = p_x x + C$ and the after-tax budget constraint, BC_2, is $I = (p_x + .10)x + C$. The tax shrinks the budget set from $0AB$ to $0AD$.

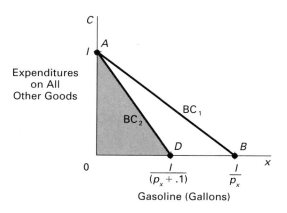

15. a)

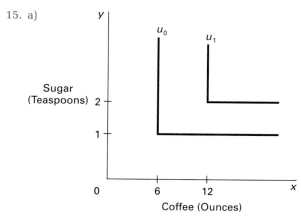

b) Roy's preferences violate Axiom 3 (more is preferred to less). These types of goods are called perfect complements because they are consumed in fixed proportions.

17. a) It depends on the order of the voting process. For example, if they vote on French and Italian, French wins. Then if they vote on French and German, German wins, and they will go to a German restaurant. However, if they begin by voting on French and German, German wins. Then if they vote on German and Italian, Italian wins, and they will go to an Italian restaurant.

b) Whether or not a group's preferences are transitive depends not only on the preferences of the individuals in the group but also on the mechanism by which a choice is made (majority rule, for example). Thus, it is not a natural assumption.

19. a) When $x = 3$ and $y = 3$, $u = 27$. When $x = 2$ and $y = 4$, $u = 16$. Thus, Joe prefers the market basket with three glasses of milk and three cookies to the one with two glasses of milk and four cookies.

   b) Joe will trade if he is better off. When $x = 2$ and $y = 2$, $u = 8$. When $x = 1$ and $y = 3$, $u = 3$. Thus, he will not trade.

21. Since $MRS_{xy} = 10/28 = 5/14 < 5/7 = p_x/p_y$, the consumer should purchase more of good y and less of good x, because this will make him or her better off.

23. Let x denote hard rock and y denote punk. Then $MRS_{xy} = MU_x/MU_y = 5/2$, which is greater than the price ratio ($p_x/p_y = 5/8$). Thus, he should increase his purchases of hard rock LPs and reduce his purchases of punk LPs, because this will make him better off.

CHAPTER 4

1. Figure 4–4 (a) illustrates the case we are interested in. When the price of good x falls from p_x^0 to p_x^1, the quantity of good x purchased increases from x_0 to x_2. Plotting these price–quantity pairs gives the demand curve. Note that even though x is an inferior good, the Law of Demand still holds.

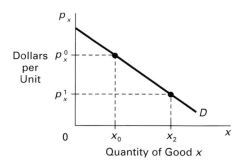

3. a)

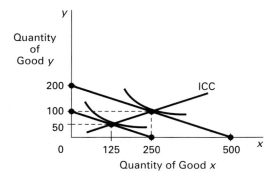

   b) There are two price–consumption curves we could illustrate. One corresponds to varying p_y, holding p_x and I constant, while the other (shown below) corresponds to varying p_x, holding p_y and I constant.

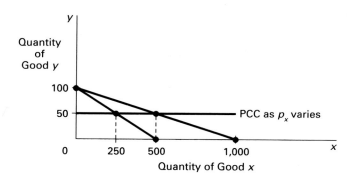

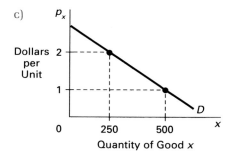

5. a) The demand curve shifts to the left for a normal good and to the right for an inferior good.
   b) Assuming coffee and tea are substitute goods, an increase in the price of tea causes the demand curve for coffee to shift to the right.
   c) Assuming tea and sugar are complementary goods, an increase in the price of sugar causes the demand curve for tea to shift to the left.
7. An increase in the price of margarine causes real income to fall. The substitution effect implies a decrease—x_0 to x_1—in the quantity of margarine purchased (because margarine is relatively more expensive. The income effect implies an increase—x_1 to x_2—in the quantity of margarine purchased (because margarine is an inferior good). Since the demand curve is assumed to be downward-sloping, the income effect must be less than the substitution effect.

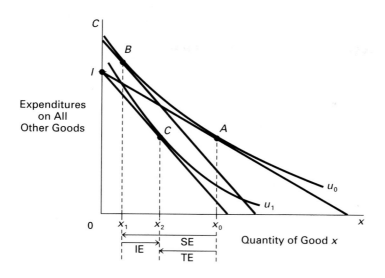

9. a)
$$D_M: X = \begin{cases} 115{,}000 - 26{,}500p & \text{if } 0 < p \le 4 \\ 15{,}000 - 1{,}500p & \text{if } 4 < p \le 10 \\ 0 & \text{if } p > 10 \end{cases}$$

  b) $X = 10{,}000$ when $p = 3.33$.

11. a) Consumer surplus increases from $p_x^0 AB$ to $p_x^1 AC$ because price falls and quantity increases.

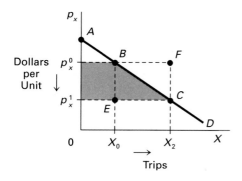

  b) The cost of the program to the government is $(p_x^0 - p_x^1) \cdot x_1$, or area $p_x^1 p_x^0 FC$, which is greater than the increase in consumer surplus, $(p_x^1 p_x^0 BC)$.

13. a) $X = 8,900$.
    b) $X = 8,600$.
    c) $X = 6,400$.

15. a) If $p_x = 300$, $x = 70$, and $\epsilon_{xx} = 3/7$.
    b) Since demand is inelastic, a price increase would lead to an increase in expenditures.

17. a) If $\epsilon_{xx} = 0$, then the demand curve is vertical and the equation for the associated demand function is $X = k$, where k is a constant.
    b) If $\epsilon_{xx} = \infty$, then the demand curve is horizontal and the equation for the associated demand function is $p = k$, where k is a constant.

19. a) No. The income elasticity is positive, which means that an increase in income would lead to an increase in demand.
    b) Necessities are goods for which there are few substitute goods; hence, demand for them tends to be inelastic. Luxuries are goods which usually have many substitute goods; hence, demand for them tends to be elastic. Restaurant meals would be classified as a luxury good.

21. If demand is price inelastic, this strategy will work; however, if demand is price elastic, then a price increase will lead to lower revenues for farmers.

CHAPTER 5   1. a) A $500 gift shifts the budget constraint out from BC_1 to BC_2, and real income rises.

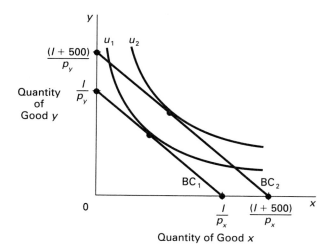

b) The tax on cigarettes shifts the budget constraint in from BC_1 to BC_2 and real income falls.

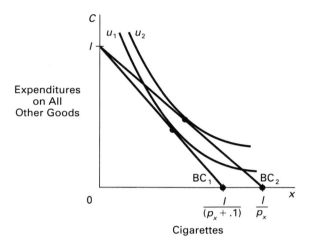

c) Nonlabor income is income that is independent of hours of work. Let I denote nonlabor income. The budget constraint becomes $C = wL + I$. A tax on nonlabor income shifts the budget constraint in from BC_1 to BC_2, and real income falls.

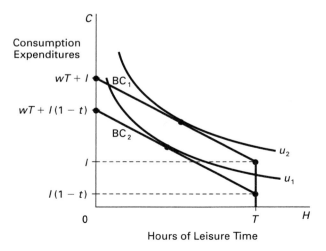

d) A fall in the interest rate shifts the budget constraint from BC_1 to BC_2. Real income rises for a borrower and falls for a lender.

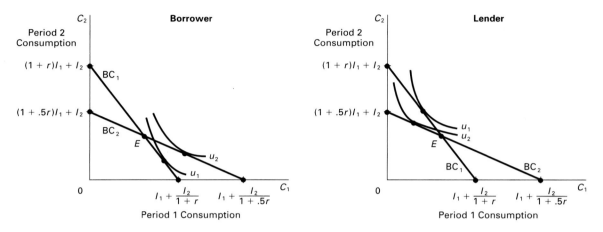

3. AC is the pre-rationing budget constraint and AB is the post-rationing budget constraint. Real income and sugar purchases both fall. (We are implicitly assuming that the individual under consideration would purchase more than one pound of sugar in the absence of rationing. If this were not the case, rationing would have no impact on the consumer.)

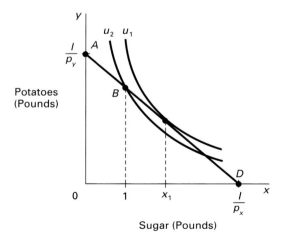

5. There are two types of individuals to consider: those who initially purchase at least 10 units of x and those who initially purchase less than 10 units of x. In the diagrams below, AD is the initial budget constraint and ABE is the new budget constraint. In each instance, real income increases or remains the same.

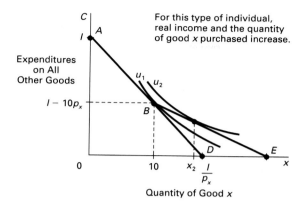

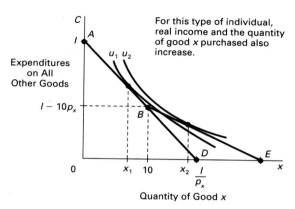

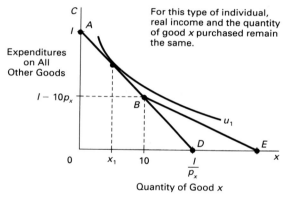

7. As a result of the raise, the price of leisure time and real income both rise. The substitution effect indicates a reduction in leisure time (an increase in work effort). The income effect indicates an increase in leisure time (a reduction in work effort). Thus, the total effect is ambiguous. If the substitution effect dominates, the raise will lead to an increase in work effort. If the income effect dominates, the raise will lead to a reduction in work effort.

9. If all goods are subject to the sales tax, then it shifts the budget constraint in parallel because it reduces all prices by the same proportion. As a result, real income falls as does consumption of all normal goods. If some goods, such as food, are exempt from the sales tax, then it acts just like an excise tax in that it distorts relative prices. Real income falls, and if the Law of Demand holds, consumption also falls.

11. Providing free food shifts the budget constraint out from BC_1 to BC_2 (see page 656). Real income and food consumption increase (assuming that food is a normal good).

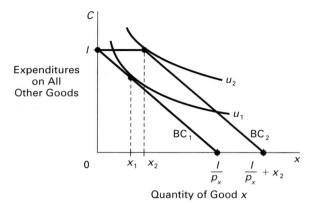

13. Phil will play more than four rounds of golf per month. In fact, he will play until golf becomes a bad or until he exhausts his time constraint.

15. As a result of the tax rate increase, real income and the price of charity fall. (It is now cheaper to give since she gets a larger tax break.) The substitution effect indicates that Ms. Willis should increase the amount she gives to charity, but the income effect indicates that she should give less (assuming charity is a normal good). Thus, the total effect depends on preferences. If the substitution effect dominates, then the tax rate increase will cause her to give more. If the income effect dominates, it will cause her to give less.

17. The wage rate subsidy increases the price of leisure time (the cost of not working has risen) and increases real income. The substitution effect indicates that participants should purchase less leisure or work more. The income effect indicates that participants should purchase more leisure time or work less. Thus, the total effect depends on preferences. If the substitution effect dominates, the wage rate subsidy increases work effort. If the income effect dominates, it reduces work effort.

19. She will be better off and become a lender.

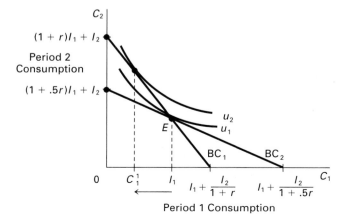

1. a) The primary reason firms exist is that they can reduce transaction costs.

   b) If you make French pastries yourself, you incur the explicit cost of the ingredients as well as the implicit cost equal to the value of your time. If the cost of buying French pastries from a bakery is lower than the cost of making them yourself (explicit plus implicit), then you will buy from the bakery.

3. a) Explicit costs are those costs that involve an actual monetary payment to another party. Implicit costs are those costs associated with using resources in one activity instead of the next best alternative activity.

   b) Economists worry about implicit costs because they are interested in explaining how costs influence output decisions.

5. She must earn at least enough to cover her explicit costs and her implicit costs. If the interest rate is zero, Carrie's explicit costs are $16,000 and her implicit costs are $300,000. Upon graduation, she must earn at least $11,539 per year to cover these costs. (If the interest rate were not zero, then she would also have to include foregone interest as an implicit cost.)

7. a) Accounting profit = revenue − explicit costs = $150,000 − $130,000 − $13,000 = $7,000. Economic profit = accounting profit − implicit costs = $7,000 − $40,000 = −$33,000.

   b) If the interest rate is 10% on money borrowed or saved, accounting profit would be $150,000 − $130,000 = $20,000 and economic profit would be $20,000 − $13,000 − $40,000 = −$33,000.

9. a) A production table is a menu indicating the maximum amount of output that can be obtained from given amounts of inputs per unit of time. A production function is an equation showing the maximum amount of output that can be produced from any specified amounts of inputs.

   b) These are different ways to represent a firm's technology.

   c) If inputs are being used in a technologically efficient way, then the maximum amount of output is being produced given any combination of inputs.

   d) No. We also need information on revenues and costs.

11. a) The Law of Diminishing Marginal Productivity asserts that as the use of one input increases, holding all other inputs constant, a point is reached beyond which the marginal product of that input falls.

    b) All other inputs.

13. a) The short run is the period of production during which some inputs cannot be varied. The long run is the period of production during which all inputs can be varied.

    b) It is important because economic behavior can be very different in the short and long runs.

    c) Service firms typically have relatively short short runs, while manufacturing firms typically have relatively long short runs.

15. a) If one more bus is purchased, MTA can lay off seven workers and still maintain the required output of bus services. Yes. The MRTS measures the rate at which buses can be substituted for maintenance

personnel while maintaining the same level of passenger services per year.

b)

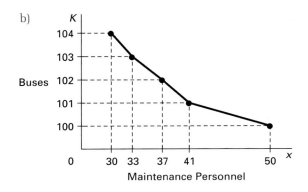

17. Mary is correct. If the production function exhibits variable proportions, then output can be increased even if one input is held constant.

CHAPTER 7

1. The Law of Diminishing Marginal Productivity implies that a point is reached beyond which short-run total cost increases at an increasing rate. This, in turn, implies that the short-run marginal cost curve is U-shaped.

3. a) The SMC and AVC curves will be positively sloped everywhere. The SATC curve will be U-shaped.
   b) The SMC and AVC curves will be horizontal initially and then become positively sloped. The SATC curve will be U-shaped.

5.

Output	TFC	TVC	STC	AFC	AVC	SATC	SMC
1	$100	$10.00	$110.00	$100.00	$10.00	$110.00	$—
2	100	16.00	116.00	50.00	8.00	58.00	6.00
3	100	21.00	121.00	33.33	7.00	40.33	5.00
4	100	26.00	126.00	25.00	6.50	31.50	5.00
5	100	30.00	130.00	20.00	6.00	26.00	4.00

7. Mandatory health insurance increases the firm's cost per worker, which results in steeper isocost curves. As a result, for a given level of output, the firm must substitute capital for labor to minimize costs.

9. The input price ratio does not change but now a higher level of expenditure is associated with each isocost curve. This means that the long-run cost curves shift up.

11. Capacity is the output rate which is optimal for a given plant size. If the LAC curve is U-shaped, then the SATC curve shifts down as capacity increases, up to the minimum point of the LAC curve.

13. If the number of hospital beds is restricted to K_1, the hospital must operate along EP_2 and the cost of producing each level of output will be higher. Thus, the long-run cost curves shift up and the restriction actually leads to higher health care costs.

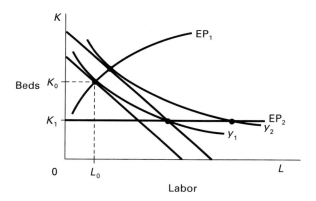

15. $\text{LTC} = wL = y^2/100$, $\text{LAC} = \text{LTC}/y = y/100$, $\text{LMC} = y/50$.

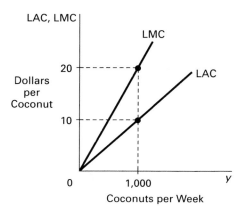

17. a)

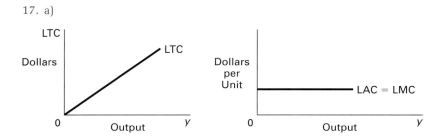

b) If labor costs fell, the long-run cost curves would shift down.

CHAPTER 8

1. Marginal revenue is the change in total revenue per unit change in output. Since a competitive firm is a price taker, each unit of output can be sold at the market price. Thus, marginal revenue is equal to price.

3. Since the systems boards currently sell for $100, the firm should follow this plan of action since it would earn an economic profit of $100 per PC. (Notice that if the historical cost of the systems boards was used to calculate profit, the firm would wrongly decide not to produce the PCs.)

5. a) TFC = 200.
   b) Setting SMC equal to AVC and solving for y gives y = 10.
   c) Setting p equal to SMC and solving for y gives $y^* = (.4 + \sqrt{.16 + .12\,[p - 5]})\,/\,.06$.
   d) Profit is maximized at the output rate corresponding to minimum average total cost if price is equal to minimum average total cost; otherwise profit can be increased either by increasing production (p > SMC) or by decreasing production (p < SMC).

7. a) Setting SMC = AVC and solving for y gives the output level corresponding to the minimum point of the AVC curve: y = .9/.008 = 112.5. Substituting this level of output into the AVC function gives the shutdown point: p = $238 per unit.
   b) Setting p = SMC gives the profit-maximizing output: y^* = 150.

9. a) In this instance, variable costs per unit are constant, so SMC = AVC = $15 per unit. Since p = 450 > 15, the profit-maximizing output rate is the maximum: y^* = 5,000. At this level of production, π = (450 − 15) · 5,000 − 545,000 − 112,000 = $1,518,000.
   b) The firm should shut down if the price falls below $124 per unit since at this price, revenue is just enough to cover variable and quasi-fixed costs.

11. A tax on economic profit has no effect on the profit-maximizing output rate in the short or long run. However, it will increase the shutdown point.

13. a) Setting MRP_L = w and solving for L gives the profit-maximizing level of employment: $L^* = (250p/w)^2$ = 625 workers.

b) If the wage rate doubles, the profit-maximizing level of employment falls to 625/4 workers.

15. a) The per-unit cost curves shift up by the amount of the tax.
   b) Since the SMC curve shifts up, the profit-maximizing level of output falls, and the long-run supply curve shifts to the left.
   c) The tax reduces input demand (just like a reduction in output price) and thus causes the input demand curves to shift to the left.

17. When the relative price of labor rises, the substitution effect implies a reduction in the amount of labor used. In addition, an increase in the wage rate causes the entire marginal cost curve to shift up, and the firm reduces output. Thus, the output effect also implies a reduction in the amount of labor used.

1. Short-run competitive equilibrium: an allocation of resources such that consumers maximize satisfaction, producers maximize profit, and supply is equal to demand. Long-run competitive equilibrium: an allocation of resources such that consumers maximize satisfaction, producers maximize profit, supply is equal to demand, and producers earn zero economic profit. In the short run firms may make profits or losses. In the long run, entry and exit guarantee that profit is zero.

CHAPTER 9

3. From problem 2, the equilibrium price is $400 per bed. Setting p = SMC and solving for y gives the profit-maximizing output for an individual price-taking firm: $y^* = 75$. Profit is $\pi = py^* - [100 + 100y^* + 2(y^*)^2] = \$11,150$.

5. a) Let SS_r and SS_f denote domestic and foreign supply to U.S. retailers respectively, and let D_r denote U.S. retailers' demand for children's clothing. (We have assumed that foreign supply is perfectly elastic only to simplify the diagram.) Initially, the equilibrium wholesale price is p_w^1. At this price, U.S. retailers demand Y_r^1 units, domestic producers supply Y_r^0 units, and imports are $(Y_r^1 - Y_r^0)$. A quota reduces imports to, for example, $(Y_r^3 - Y_r^2)$. This causes an increase in the wholesale price from p_w^1 to p_w^2. Retail demand falls to Y_r^3 while domestic production increases to Y_r^2.

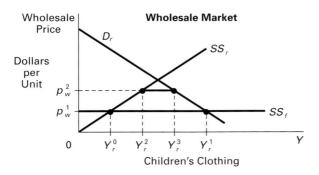

b) SS denotes U.S. retailers supply and D denotes U. S. consumer demand for children's clothing. Initially, the equilibrium retail price and quantity are p_r^* and Y_r^* respectively. Since the quota increases the wholesale price, retail production costs are higher, which causes the short-run supply curve to shift from SS_1 to SS_2. The equilibrium retail price rises to p_r^1 and the equilibrium quantity falls to Y_r^1.

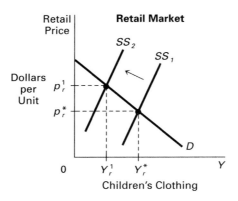

7. a) The positive economic profit will encourage other firms to enter the industry. As a result, the short-run supply curve shifts to the right, and the prices of gymnasium services falls until each firm earns zero economic profit.
   b) In equilibrium, price must be equal to the minimum of the LAC curve. Setting LMC = LAC and solving for y gives equilibrium output per firm: $y^* = 500$. Substituting this into the LMC or LAC function gives the equilibrium price: $p^e = \$487.5$ per hour.
9. a) Demand shifts to the right. Price and quantity both increase.
   b) Supply shifts to the left. Price rises and quantity falls.

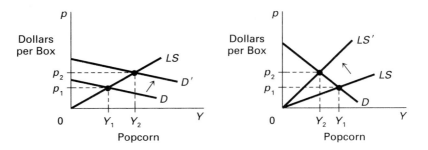

c) Production costs increase, causing the supply curve to shift to the left. Price rises while quantity falls (see part [b]).

11. Accounting profit is total revenue minus all explicit costs (and possibly some implicit costs). Economic profit equals accounting profit minus all implicit costs not included in calculating accounting profit. Economic rent measures the gains to resource owners from being able to sell the output produced with their input services at the market price. Resource owners can earn economic rents even if firms earn zero economic profit.

1. a, b) Setting $MRP_L = w$ and solving for L gives the short-run demand for labor: $L = 10 - w/500$. Given a wage of $3,000, this firm will employ four workers per month.

 CHAPTER 10

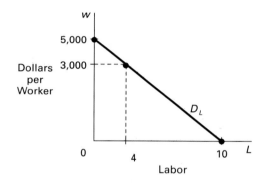

3. a) If the price elasticity of demand is 2, then a 10% increase in the wage rate will cause employment to fall 20%.
   b) If the price elasticity of demand is .2, then a 10% increase in the wage rate will cause employment to fall only 2%.
5. This statement is false. In the short run, the supply curve of neurosurgeons is probably vertical; however, in the long run, a higher wage rate for neurosurgeons would attract to the profession other individuals with the required ability, and a lower wage rate would discourage individuals from entering the profession.
7. a) Setting demand equal to supply and solving for w gives the equilibrium wage rate: $w^* = 40$. Substituting w^* into the demand or supply function gives the equilibrium level of employment: $L^* = 16$.
   b) The demand function becomes $L = 20 - .1(w + 1)$. Setting this equal to supply and solving for w gives the new after-tax wage: $w^1 = 35$; that is, firms pay $45 per hour, with $35 going to workers and $10 going to the government. The equilibrium level of employment falls to 15.5.
9. a) Assume that the apple and orange industries are constant cost industries. (This seems to be a reasonable assumption since firms in these industries employ inputs that can be used generally in other industries.) Given this assumption, the increase in demand for

apples causes the price of apples to rise in the short run from p_1 to p_2. In the long run, price falls back to p_1 and quantity increases to Y_2. The increase in apple production increases the demand for labor, as shown by the shift in the labor demand curve from D_L^1 to D_L^2. Since this is a constant costs industry, the labor supply curve is horizontal. Thus, the increase in demand causes employment to increase from L_1 to L_2, but the wage rate remains at w_1.

b) Apple consumers benefit because more apples are available at the same market price.

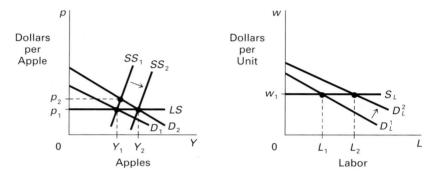

11. a) Doctors will be paid more than janitors if demand is greater and/or supply is lower for health care than for janitorial services. Since becoming a doctor requires a lot of costly investment in formal education and training as well as a lot of innate ability, the supply of physicians is much lower than the supply of janitors. It is unclear whether the demand for doctors is significantly greater than the demand for janitors.

b) A higher wage rate does not necessarily imply a higher value to society. In order to make this determination we would have to compare the value to society of the total output produced by doctors and janitors; that is, we would have to compare the consumer surplus generated by each profession.

13. a) Economic rent is the difference between payments actually made to resource owners and the minimum amount necessary to keep them in their current employment. In terms of the supply and demand apparatus, the area above the supply curve and below the input price represents the economic rent earned by a particular input.

b) This is true if the supply of land is fixed or, at least, extremely inelastic. This is why economists often recommend property taxes as a means of financing government expenditures.

15. No. It depends on the elasticities of the labor demand and supply curves. For example, as shown below, if the labor supply curve is vertical, then workers bear the cost of national health insurance in the form of reduced wages. Firms pay w_1 but workers receive w_2. The difference is the per-worker cost of the health insurance.

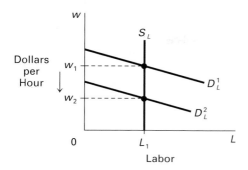

1. a) If a product has few good substitutes, then demand tends to be inelastic (see Chapter 4). When demand is inelastic, consumers pay most of the tax. For example, if demand is perfectly inelastic, then a tax levied on producers causes the price consumers pay to rise from p_1 to p_2. Consumers pay the entire tax even though it is levied on producers.

CHAPTER 11

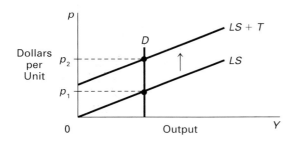

   b) Since cigarettes and liquor have relatively few substitutes, demand tends to be inelastic and excise taxes levied on producers are ultimately paid almost entirely by those individuals who buy these products. Most policy makers view this as a desirable result. In addition, economists often recommend taxing these types of goods because when demand is very inelastic the inefficiency associated with an excise tax tends to be small.

3. First we show that the economic effects of the tax are the same no matter how it is initially divided between employers and employees. Let's compare the two extreme cases, one where the employer pays the entire tax and one where the employee pays the entire tax. As shown in the diagram below, if a tax of T dollars per worker is levied on employers, then the labor demand curve shifts down by the amount of the tax. As a result, employment falls from L_1 to L_2, firms pay w_2 per hour, and workers receive w_1 per hour. If a tax of T dollars per worker is levied on employees, then the labor supply curve shifts up by the

amount of the tax and the economic effects are the same. (This means that the government really cannot control who ultimately pays the tax by the way it is collected.)

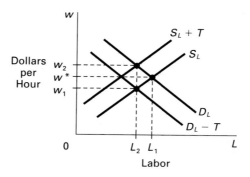

Since it doesn't matter how the tax is divided, to answer this question let's suppose the tax is levied entirely on employees. Then the analysis of income taxes in the text is applicable and we conclude that firms pay more per hour, workers receive less per hour, employment falls, producers earn zero economic profit, consumers are worse off because output falls and price rises, workers are worse off, and other resource owners are most likely worse off.

5. a) Initially, the equilibrium price and quantity of medical services are p^* and Y^* respectively. After Medicaid goes into effect, the price consumers pay for medical services falls to zero and, as a result, demand increases to Y_2. Those enrolled in the program benefit. Consumer surplus increases from p^*p_2A to $0p_2E$. In order to get producers to supply Y_2 units of medical services, the government must pay p_2 per unit. Thus, taxpayers are worse off by $0p_2CE$, which is the total subsidy, and resource owners are better off because economic rent increases from $0p^*A$ to $0p_2C$.

   b) The inefficiency of the program is area ACE.

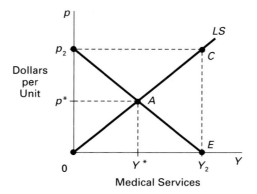

7. a) When a price ceiling of p_1 per unit is imposed, quantity falls to Y_1. Given this quantity, some consumers would be willing to pay p_2 per unit and a black market might arise. If producers are liable for their black market activities, then the supply curve shifts from SS_1 to SS_2 (because production costs are greater). The equilibrium black market price is p_3, which is greater than the pre-price-ceiling price, p^*.

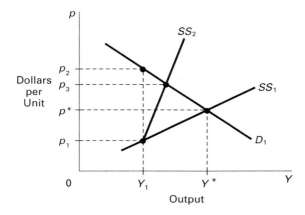

b) If consumers are liable for their black market activities, then the demand curve shifts from D_1 to D_2 (because marginal benefit is lower). The black market price is p_4, which is lower than the pre-price-ceiling price, p^*.

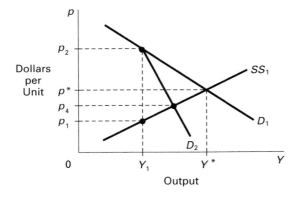

9. a) See Examples 11–3 and 11–4.
   b) Price controls redistribute income in a way deemed desirable by policy makers.

11. Initially, milk sells for p_2 dollars per unit and $(Y_2 - Y_1)$ is the surplus quantity of milk being purchased by the government. If dairy farmers slaughter some of their cows for beef, the long-run supply curve will

shift to the left. In order to eliminate the surplus completely, the government would have to offer a payment large enough to compensate resource owners for the economic rents that are lost when the long-run supply curve shifts from LS_1 to LS_2. This is area $0CB$. After the surplus is eliminated, consumers still pay p_2 per unit of milk and consume Y_1 units of milk.

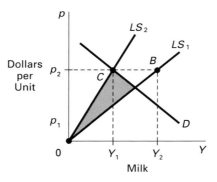

This program increases the supply of beef and has the following consequences: the price of beef falls, quantity rises, consumers are better off, and resource owners may be better off or worse off depending on the elasticities of the supply and demand curves.

13. In the short run there are profits to be made by the firm or firms that are first with the innovation. Thus, there is always an incentive to be the first firm with a new idea.

15. A sales tax (also called an ad valorem excise tax) levied on consumers shifts the demand curve from D_1 to D_2. Notice that this is not a parallel shift as it was for an excise because the per-unit amount of the tax increases as quantity increases. The economic effects of a sales tax are the same as those of a per-unit excise tax: price increases, quantity decreases, consumers are worse off, resource owners are worse off, and those who benefit from government spending are better off. (See Example 11−1).

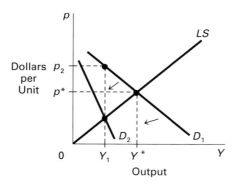

17. A tariff generates government revenues while a quota does not. Otherwise, they have the same economic effects. As shown in Example 11−7, trade restrictions make consumers worse off, producers better off, and resource owners better off. Thus, consumers would be in favor of eliminating trade restrictions, while owners of firms that would exit the industry and workers would be against eliminating trade restrictions.

19. a) Setting demand equal to supply gives $p^* = 80$ and $Y^* = 2.6$ million.

b) Domestic production falls to 2.0 million, quantity demanded increases to 2.75 million, and imports are .75 million.

c) Price increases from $50 to $70, domestic production increases to 2.4 million, quantity demanded falls to 2.65 million, and imports fall to .25 million.

CHAPTER 12

1. Local markets, because oftentimes geographical distance is a barrier to entry.

3. False. A profit-maximizing monopoly is constrained by market demand.

5. It will lower the price of sod.

7. a) In a perfectly competitive market, entry and exit guarantee that firms earn zero economic profit and, hence, operate at the minimum points of their LAC curves. A monopoly is not constrained to operate at zero profit.

b) No. The cost curves under perfect competition may be higher than those of a monopoly.

9. In the absence of any production agreement, the equilibrium price and quantity are p^* and Y^* respectively. If the firms in this industry agree to cut back production to Y_1 units and to charge p_1 dollars per unit, each firm will earn monopoly profit since p_1 is greater than LAC.

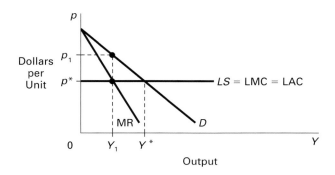

11. a) In effect, the licenses give taxi owners monopoly power, which leads to higher taxi fares and fewer taxi cabs.

b) You would be willing to pay an amount equal to monopoly profit.

c) They can charge an amount equal to monopoly profit.

13. The patent gave Go Video monopoly power; thus, you would want to

calculate foregone monopoly profit per year, area p_1ABp^*, over the effective life of the patent.

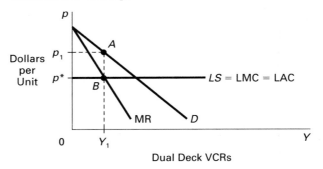

Dual Deck VCRs

15. A monopoly hires fewer workers, $L_1 < L^c$, and pays a lower wage, $w_1 < w^c$.

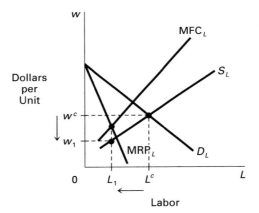

Labor

CHAPTER 13   1. a) If the regulated price is greater than average cost, then the monopoly will make a loss. If it is less than average cost, the monopoly will continue to make a profit.

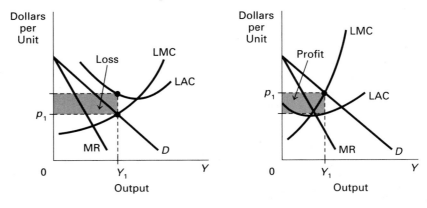

b) For a public utility, marginal cost pricing yields a regulated price greater than average cost, and if used it will cause the firm to incur a loss. The government would then have to subsidize the firm to keep it in business (see Example 13–1).

3. a) Price discrimination is the practice of charging different groups of buyers different prices for the same product when the different prices are not associated with differences in costs. Price discrimination is a profit-maximizing strategy by which buyers can be separated into distinct groups with different demand elasticities.

   b) Peak-load pricing is like price discrimination in that different groups of buyers are charged different prices; however, it is not a true form of price discrimination because the different prices arise because of different cost conditions.

5. Disney was practicing third degree price discrimination. The rebate program separates buyers into two groups, those that take the time and effort to fill out and mail a rebate form along with the necessary documentation, and those that do not. If Disney had lowered the price by $3, everyone would have paid a lower price and Disney's profit would have been lower.

7. This is an example of price discrimination. The weekday rule sorts individuals into two groups—those that can travel during the week and those that cannot—and airlines prohibit the resale of tickets.

9. a) Since the goal of the monopoly is to capture as much consumer surplus as possible, the firm should set the usage fee equal to marginal cost, and the entry fee equal to consumer surplus for each consumer. Thus, as the figure below shows, consumers pay T^* to enter the park and $p^* = \text{LMC}$ per ride, and the firm captures all the consumer surplus.

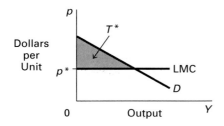

   b) Only if LMC = 0.

11. This is a feasible pricing strategy when all of the conditions for price discrimination are met: The firm has some market power, buyers can be separated at a reasonable cost (domestic and foreign buyers), and there is no resale market. The good is sold more cheaply abroad when the price elasticity of demand is larger for foreign consumers than for domestic consumers.

13. Because notebook paper can be stored at a very low cost to the bookstore.

15. a) This is not an example of peak-load pricing, since marginal cost does not vary over the day. It is an example of price discrimination.

Individuals are sorted into two groups—those for whom the opportunity cost of seeing a movie early in the day is low and those for whom it is high—and theaters prohibit the resale of movie tickets.

b) Typically, special engagements are movies that are expected to be extremely popular for one reason or another. If the price elasticity of demand for special engagements is the same for both types of consumers, then charging a uniform price is the profit-maximizing strategy.

17. In this instance, a monopoly (the UAW) is selling to a monopsony (management). Let S_L denote the supply curve for union auto workers and D_L denote the demand curve. If this labor market were competitive, L^c workers would be employed at w^c dollars per worker.

a) If management dictates the terms of the contract, it will choose the point where $MFC_L = D_L$, and L_1 workers will be employed at w_1 dollars per worker.

b) If the UAW dictates the terms of the contract, it will choose the point where $MR_L = S_L$, and L_2 workers will be employed at w_2 dollars per worker.

c) How about the competitive wage?

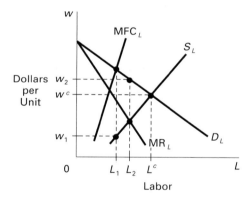

CHAPTER 14

1. a) In both the competitive and monopolistically competitive models, firms ignore the effects of their actions on the decisions made by other firms in the industry, and firms earn zero economic profit. However, monopolistically competitive firms have some degree of market power and, hence, do not produce at minimum average cost.

b) Referring to Figure 14–1(b), an increase in costs would cause the LAC curve to shift up. Firms would now make economic losses and some would exit the industry. As firms exit, the demand curves facing existing firms shift to the right. This process continues until firms earn a zero economic profit again. If one firm introduces a new brand, then the demand curve facing each existing firm shifts to the left. Firms would now make economic losses causing exit from the industry. As firms exit, the demand curves facing existing firms shift to the right until firms once again earn zero economic profit.

3. If we asked 100 economists this question, we might get 100 different answers. However, I believe the choice of which economic model to use depends largely on the question being addressed. Generally speaking, if the question deals with the impact of the public policy on prices and quantities, the competitive model is usually the most useful, and if the question deals with pricing strategies, the monopoly model can be used as a first approximation and then if further study is needed, an oligopoly model can be investigated. For example, a competitive analysis of the economic effects of a tariff on computer imports would provide an accurate assessment; however, if we want to study the pricing of personal computers, then it would be best to model IBM as a monopoly or the personal computer industry as some type of oligopoly.

5. Long-run equilibrium in the competitive model means firms maximize profit assuming that their actions have no impact on the decisions of their rivals, consumers maximize utility, markets clear, and profit is zero. Long-run equilibrium under oligopoly means that firms maximize profit given some conjecture concerning the behavior of its rivals, consumers maximize utility, and markets clear.

7. a) Nonprice competition occurs when firms try to attract customers by varying such things as product quality, the location at which it is sold, servicing, packaging, and advertising.

   b) Nonprice competition can occur in both competitive and oligopolistic markets but it is far more likely in the latter. This is because oligopolistic firms try very hard to avoid direct price competition with rivals so that price wars can be averted.

9. Barriers to entry, such as economies of scale and large costs associated with nonprice competition (advertising costs, for example), inhibit firms from entering oligopolistic industries.

11. a)

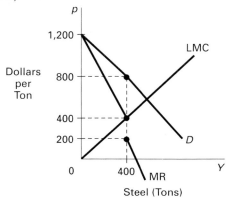

   b) Since LMC(400) = 400, $Y^* = 400$.

c) Marginal cost is now given by LMC = $Y + 100$. Setting MR = LMC and solving for Y gives $Y_1 = 1{,}100/3$.

13. If Ford were to offer a substantially lower financing rate, a price war might ensue which, in the end, would reduce profits of both firms. Ford is better off competing with GM via nonprice competition.

15. We can use entry limit pricing to show that if established firms have lower costs than potential entrants, then this statement is false. In the diagram below, LMC_0 and LMC_D are the marginal cost curves of potential entrants and established firms respectively, and p^c is the competitive price ($D = LMC$). If established firms set a price of p^c dollars per unit, then entry will be deterred and established firms will earn zero profit. However, entry can also be deterred by setting a price of p_0, and at this price established firms earn a profit equal to p_0GEp^c.

17. a) The PC industry is characterized by a few large firms producing a differentiated product and earning positive economic profits. To address questions dealing with how foreign competition, trade restrictions, excise taxes, or technological innovations affect price and quantity, the competitive model would provide a reasonably accurate assessment. To address questions dealing with Apple's pricing of particular products, the monopoly model could be used. To address questions dealing with overall pricing strategies within the industry, an oligopoly model should be used.

   b) Since firms in the PC industry engage primarily in nonprice competition, the price leadership model could be used to analyze pricing decisions, while the prisoners' dilemma could be used to explain, for example, advertising budgets (see Example 14–2).

CHAPTER 15

1. a) Economic efficiency means that production and distribution cannot be reorganized to make someone better off without making someone else worse off.

   b) Economic efficiency would be a goal of policy makers if they wanted to attain the largest aggregate surplus possible.

   c) This question itself is a normative question. I would say no because I believe that equity, or income distribution, questions should also be given some consideration.

3. a)

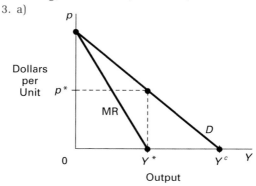

b) No. Y^c is the efficient level of production since at this point MSB = MSC = 0.

5. a) When there is a positive externality, a private competitive market will provide too little of the good or service because MPB < MSB.

b) In the figure below, MSB = MSC at Y^* units of output. At the competitive level of production, Y^c, MSB > MSC and hence, output should be increased.

7. a) An externality is internalized when market participants are confronted with a system of incentives that cause the competitive mechanism to provide the efficient level of output.

b) Some type of government intervention is needed either directly in the particular market itself (this might mean corrective taxes) or in the assigning and enforcing of property rights.

9. One alternative would be to impose a tax on ranchers equal to marginal external cost at the efficient level of production. Such a tax would lead to a reduction in livestock production and hence a reduction in the number of eagles killed by ranchers.

11. a) A good is a public good if, once it is produced, consumption by one person does not diminish the quantity consumed by anyone else, and no one individual can be excluded from consuming the good.

b) Private markets will not produce the efficient quantity of a public good because MPB < MSB.

13. a) Once a public good is produced, everyone benefits from it regardless of whether or not they pay for it. This means that individuals have an incentive to let others pay for the good—they have an incentive to free ride—which makes voluntary contributions unlikely.

b) Free riding is less of a problem when a public good provides benefits to a small group of individuals. For example, small communities usually can raise funds for community parks via voluntary contributions.

CHAPTER 16

1. a) Partial equilibrium analysis focuses on one market at a time and does not consider explicitly the interdependence of markets. General equilibrium analysis considers all relevant interrelations between markets.

b) Since capital is used in nearly every industry, a general equilibrium analysis would be appropriate here; however, as a first approximation I would begin with a partial equilibrium analysis of the capital and labor markets.

c) Since the main concern here would be with the automobile industry, a partial equilibrium analysis would be appropriate.

3. Our competitive model cannot account for inventories because we have not considered the time aspects of production and consumption. However, remember that a theory abstracts from the real world, so we can explain and predict certain behavior but not necessarily all behavior. (The competitive model can be generalized to address the issue inventories.)

5. a) As in the partial equilibrium framework, the forces of supply and demand determine the equilibrium price ratio in a pure exchange economy. Relative prices rise in markets where there is excess demand and fall where there is excess supply.

   b) When individuals maximize satisfaction subject to their budget constraints, only relative prices affect quantity demanded. If absolute prices all change in the same proportion, quantity demanded remains the same. Thus, in the pure exchange economy, only relative prices emerge from the equilibrium conditions. This may seem odd to you since in our earlier partial equilibrium discussions we always talked about the level of prices; however, in these analyses we took the prices of other goods as given. In the pure exchange economy, if we are given one price then we can also determine the level of other prices.

7. a) The product transformation curve shows the different output combinations that can be obtained from the given quantities of inputs if firms operate efficiently. It is derived by plotting the output combinations associated with each point on the production contract curve.

   b) The slope of the product transformation curve measures how much of one good society must give up in order to obtain more of another good; in other words, it measures the marginal cost to society of increasing production of one good in terms of the other good.

9. An increase in the supply of labor causes the product transformation curve to shift out.

11. a) A labor union in one industry leads to a higher wage rate for workers in that industry than for workers in other industries. This results in an input allocation that is off the production contract curve, point A for example, because the MRTS_{KL} is different for the union and nonunion industries. As a result, the economy operates at a point inside the product transformation curve. This does not mean inputs are unemployed; rather, it means inputs are inefficiently allocated between industries.

   b) They redistribute income to union workers.

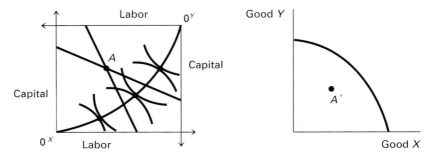

13. This statement is true if (i) all markets are perfectly competitive; (ii) there are no externalities or public goods; (iii) there is no government intervention.

1. One's stock of human capital can be measured by years of education or formal training, experience, and innate ability (usually proxied by some IQ measure). The flow of human capital services is more difficult to measure. Typically economists use person-hours per unit of time adjusted for the stock of human capital.

CHAPTER 17

3. $NPV_1 = \sum_{t=1}^{3} 100/(1 + r)^t + 1,000/(1 + r)^3$

$NPV_2 = \sum_{t=1}^{3} 300/(1 + r)^t + 100/(1 + r)^3$

a) If $r = .05$, then $NPV_1 = 1,136$ and $NPV_2 = 1,113$, so you should choose the first bond.

b) If $r = .15$, then $NPV_1 = 888$ and $NPV_2 = 899$, so you should choose the second bond.

c) You would be willing to pay their net present values (1,000 and 997 respectively).

5. The rate of return is the interest rate that solves the following equation: $500/(1 + r) + 1,500/(1 + r)^2 = 950$. The implied interest rate is $r = .547$.

7. a) $NPV = 1,000/r$

b) $NPV = \sum_{t=1}^{30} 100/(1 + r)^t + 10,000/(1 + r)^{30}$

c) $NPV = 5/r$.

9. a) The discount rate must reflect the decision maker's opportunity cost of investing funds. The most important factors affecting the discount rate are inflation and risk.

b) The real interest rate is equal to the nominal rate minus the expected rate of inflation or, in this instance, 3%.

11. Profit maximization implies that current production expands to the point where $p_1 = p_2(1 + i)$. If expected future demand increases, p_2 rises, which means that less will be produced in the current period, causing p_1 to rise until the equality given above holds.

13. This statement is false. Referring to Figure 17–3, if people suddenly decide to save less, the loanable funds supply curve shifts to the left, which leads to a higher interest rate. Put differently, when the demand for bonds falls, the price of bonds falls, meaning that the interest rate rises.

1. a) In microeconomics, certainty refers to the situation where decision makers know all relevant economic variables prior to making their choices. Under certainty, there is no risk. Uncertainty refers to the situation where decision makers do not know all the relevant economic variables prior to making their choices; hence, risk is an important consideration.

CHAPTER 18

b) Objective probability is based on the frequency with which a given outcome occurs and can be determined by observing the outcomes of similar experiments. Subjective probability is based on the decision maker's perception of the frequency with which a given outcome occurs.

3. a) The expected value of the ticket is $500. Since this is greater than the costs of the ticket she will buy it. The most she would be willing to pay is $500.

   b) The expected utility of the ticket is 50, point C in the diagram. Since $u(500) = 75 > 50$, she is risk-averse. Since $u(300) > Eu(\pi)$, she will not purchase the ticket.

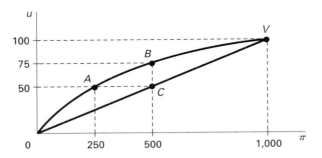

5. Yes. A risk-neutral decision maker does not care about risk and thus is an expected value maximizer.

7. a) Let π_1 and π_2 denote the profit earned if Ottis makes one or two trips respectively. If Ottis is an expected profit maximizer, he will make one trip because $E\pi_1 = \$4,500 > E\pi_2 = \$4,000$.

   b) It will depend on his risk-taking characteristics because each strategy has a different expected value. If Ottis is sufficiently risk-averse, he will make two trips.

9. a) If the owner is risk-neutral, plan a_2 would be chosen because $E(\pi|a_1) = 12$ million $< E(\pi|a_2) = 12.25$ million.

   b) If the owner is risk-averse, plan a_1 would be chosen because $Eu(\pi|a_1) = 3.655 > Eu(\pi|a_2) = 3.045$.

11. a) The insurance policy should be canceled because expected profit is $199,000 if it is canceled and $197,500 if it is continued.

    b) The policy should be continued because expected utility is 13.95 if the policy is canceled and 14.05 if it is not.

13. a) Charging the same interest rate to high- and low-risk individuals attracts more high-risk borrowers, which causes the interest rate on credit card purchases to rise, which attracts more high-risk borrowers, and so on.

    b) Credit histories allow credit card companies to distinguish between high-risk and low-risk individuals, which substantially reduces the adverse selection problem.

15. Both of these types of policies tend to reduce the moral hazard problem because they require the insured individual to pay part of the health care costs. The first type is probably more effective because nothing is covered by the insurance company until the deductible is met, while the second type requires payment from the insurance company even for small claims.

A B C D E F G H I J
1 2 3 4 5 6 7 8 9 0